Praise for *The Hanged Man*

'Thirty-five years after the event, Richards has brought us the definitive account; cool, thoroughly researched and fair, meticulously fair.'
—Les Carlyon, *The Bulletin*

'This book has been the work of half a lifetime. It shows in the extraordinary depth of research and detail of the narrative. Although we know how the story will end, the second half of the book is especially tense and dramatic, an effect heightened by Richards' clean, detached prose ... Richards' account of Ryan's life and death is a parable of the futility and moral squalor of mere retribution.'
—Hugh Dillon, *The Sydney Morning Herald*

'Richards' detailed examination of all that happened between Ryan's escape on December 19, 1965, and his hanging on February 3, 1967 is compelling.'
—Chris Brice, *The Adelaide Advertiser*

'Using previously unpublished documents and personal accounts drawn from interviews over many years, Richards constructs a historical account of the last man hanged in Australia that at times reads like a crime thriller ... In this superbly crafted book Richards provides us with an intricate portrayal of a doomed man and the social and historical period that sealed his fate.'
—Paul Wilson, *The Courier-Mail*

'A book that has stayed with me, Mike Richards' *The Hanged Man*, challenges the idea of the criminal as a romantic figure. A failure as a husband, thief and armed robber, Ronald Ryan was obsessive and unattractive. Richards has done an impressive job in bringing Ryan to life and making the reader feel some sympathy for the last man hanged in Australia.'
—John Dale, *The Sydney Morning Herald*

'Mike Richards' book is the definitive account of the case.'
—Julian Burnside, *The Age*

'The importance of Richards' biography is that he asks us to reconsider a small-time criminal who, inadvertently, challenged a generation to question its beliefs about more than punishment. At the end of this accomplished book, we know Ryan.'
—Christopher Bantick, *Australian Book Review*

'A moving and compellingly readable life of Ronald Ryan.'
—Peter Craven, *The Age*

'This is a sensational read, full of fascinating detail and as gripping a plot as anything you will find in fiction … One of the best books I have read for a long time.'
—Liz Gaynor, *Crime Factory*

'The story of Ryan's life, his crimes, his escape from Pentridge Prison in Melbourne, the manhunt to recapture him, his trial and subsequent efforts to avoid the noose are well told in this highly readable story. It is a tale as much about Australian society in the 1960s as about Ryan, his brush with fame, his late reconversion to the Catholic Church and the extraordinary efforts to save his life.'
—Justice Michael Kirby, *Criminal Law Journal*

Scribe Publications

THE HANGED MAN

Mike Richards started his working life as a journalist with *The Age*, and his later career has involved him as an academic, government adviser, management consultant, and media executive. In the early 1980s he left the Melbourne University politics department to become a senior adviser to the Victorian premier, John Cain; later, he became director of policy and research in the Department of Premier and Cabinet.

In the late 1990s he was assistant publisher and deputy CEO of *The Age*, after a period as associate editor and columnist. He has also been a director and partner of an international management consultancy. He now runs his own management consultancy specialising in strategy and organisation effectiveness.

Mike Richards holds a PhD in political science from the University of Melbourne, and is a fellow of the Australian Institute of Company Directors. He lives in Melbourne with his wife and three children.

The Hanged Man was runner-up in the 2003 National Biography Award, and a joint winner of the 2002 Ned Kelly Award for true crime.

The Hanged Man

the life and death of Ronald Ryan

MIKE RICHARDS

Scribe Publications
Melbourne

Scribe Publications
18–20 Edward St, Brunswick, Victoria 3056, Australia
2 John St, Clerkenwell, London, WC1N 2ES, United Kingdom
3754 Pleasant Ave, Suite 223w, Minneapolis, Minnesota 55409 USA

First published by Scribe Publications 2002
Reprinted with minor corrections in this format 2003
Reprinted 2017, 2026

Typeset in Minion by the publisher
Cover design by Pauline McLenahan, Captured Concepts
Printed and bound in Australia by Griffin Press

Scribe is committed to the sustainable use of natural resources and the use of paper products made responsibly from those resources.

Scribe acknowledges Australia's First Nations peoples as the traditional owners and custodians of this country, and we pay our respects to their elders, past and present.

978 0 908011 94 0 (Australian edition)
978 1 922072 07 8 (ebook)

Catalogue records for this book are available from the National Library of Australia.

scribepublications.com.au
scribepublications.co.uk
scribepublications.com

In memory of

Jack Galbally
1910–1990

and

Graham Little
1939–2000

Nothing is easier than to denounce the evildoer;
nothing is more difficult than to understand him.

Fyodor Dostoevsky

With regard to my guilt I say only that I am innocent of intent and have a clear conscience in the matter. I was not content to have my loved ones committed to a life of drudgery and sought the means to establish the chance for [my wife] and … children. For this odd thinking I must, for excuse, point to my childhood and history.

Ronald Ryan

If I'd run into [Pentridge prison governor Ian Grindlay] during the escape, I would've dropped the gun and given up immediately.

Ronald Ryan

Contents

Photographs appear between pages 106 and 107, and 330 and 331

Conversions

Pre-decimal currency values and imperial weights and measures have been retained in this book as they were in existence for most of the period from 1925 to 1967, and are enshrined in virtually all of the official documents quoted. The table below indicates *approximate* conversion values for length, distance, currency, temperature and weight:

1 inch = 2.5 centimetres
1 foot = 30 centimetres
1 yard = 0.9 metres
1 mile = 1.6 kilometres
12 pence = 10 cents
10 shillings = $1
£1 (pound) = $2
100 degrees Fahrenheit = 38 degrees Celsius
2 pounds (weight) = 1 kilogram
10 stone = 64 kilograms

Acknowledgments

A study of this kind cannot be completed without the help of a great many people who have contributed either through assistance with sources, or by reading parts of the manuscript, or by agreeing to be interviewed about the story of Ronald Ryan.

A number of people kindly provided documents or information, or guided me through libraries, archives, and other sources. Many of them have moved on from their positions at the time in which they were helpful to me, but I have listed their contemporary positions below. Among them are Ms Amanda Baker, Old Melbourne Gaol; Mr Harry Barbon, Crema Group (Pentridge prison redevelopment); Ms Tamara Bell, Herald & Weekly Times; Mr Adrian Bellis, Melbourne Magistrates Court; Mr Colin Benjamin, Students Anti-Hanging Committee, Melbourne University; Mr Brian Bourke, barrister; the Rev Father John Brosnan, Chaplain, HM Prison Pentridge; Mr John Buckley, Criminal Law branch, Office of the Crown Solicitor, Victoria; Mr James Butler, Supreme Court of Victoria Library; Hon Justice John Coldrey, Supreme Court of Victoria; Mr Stan Cox, Community Services Victoria; Ms Susie Cram, researcher, Hector Crawford Productions; Mr Charles Curwen, official secretary to the governor of Victoria; Mr Ray Davie, *The Age*; Hon Brian Dixon, MP, Minister for Social Welfare, Victoria; Ms Marita Dunbar, Justice Department, Victoria; Rev Father Michael Elligate, Chaplain, University of Melbourne; Mr Kevin Fenton, Ryan's former classmate, St John's, Mitcham; Mr Geoff Flatman, QC, Director of Public Prosecutions, Victoria; Associate Professor Anne Freadman, University of Queensland; Mr Bob Galbally, Galbally Rolfe; Ms Diane Gardiner, National Trust at the Old Melbourne Gaol; Mr Michael Gawenda, *The Age*; Mr Tim Goodman, auctioneer; Mr Bruce Guthrie, *The Age*; Brother Reg Hamilton, Rupertswood Old Boys Association; Ms Bronwyn Hammond, Office of the Director of Public Prosecutions,

Victoria; Major DRH Harris, Central Army Records Office, Melbourne; Mr Steve Harris, *The Age*; Mr Frank Hart, Privy Council Office, London; Mr Darren Hobbs, Justice Department, Victoria; Mr Thos Hodgson, barrister; Mr Tony Howard, QC, barrister; Mr Sek Hulme, QC, barrister; Hon Barry Jones, MP; Mr John Jost, *The Age*; Mr Ian Killey, Department of the Premier & Cabinet, Victoria; Dr Paul Knapman, Westminster Coroner's Court, London; Mrs Joyce Kotze, Ryan's former classmate, St John's, Mitcham; Mr Luch Kremmer, Crema Group; Mr Sacha Kumara, *The Age*; Mr James McKinnon, Public Records Office of Victoria; Ms Rachel Mcleod, *The Age*; Mr Allen McRobb, St Pancras Coroner's Court, London; Sister Madonna, Little Sisters of the Poor, Abbotsford; Hon Race Mathews, MP, Minister for Police and Emergency Services, Victoria; Mr Ian Morrison, Baillieu Library, University of Melbourne; Ms Shirley Mulligan, Victorian Government Reporting Service; Dr Philip Opas, QC, barrister; Mr Paul Ormonde, journalist; Ms Ann Piggott, Public Records Office of Victoria; Miss Ruth Potter, Correspondence School, Department of Education, Victoria; Mr Martin Powell, Victoria Police Historical Unit; Mr Frank Prain, *The Age* library; Mr Tom Prior, journalist; Mr Len Radic, *The Age*; Mrs Joan Roczniok, local historian, Nunawading; Mr Peter Ryan, Melbourne University Press; Ms Barbara Ryszkowska, Westminster Coroner's Court, London; Ms Monica Simpson, *The Age* library; Mr Greg Spithill, Department of the Treasury, Victoria; Ms Laraine Tate, NSW Police Service; Mr Michael Thompson, Victorian Government Reporting Service; Ms Olga Tsara, State Library of Victoria; Mr Lon Vasiutas, Criminal Law branch, Office of the Crown Solicitor, Victoria; Mr John Watherston, Registrar, Judicial Committee of the Privy Council, London; Mr Norman Wearne, Department of Social Welfare, Victoria; Mr Iain West, deputy state coroner, Victoria; Mr Evan Whitton, journalist; and Ms Beverley Williams, Balnarring Picnic Racing Club.

Others kindly agreed to read parts of the manuscript in its differing forms and at various stages of its gestation. Among them are Professor Don Aitken, Mr Greg Armstrong, Ms Carole Barns, Mr George Brouwer, Hon John Cain, Mr Charles Curwen, Rev Father Michael Elligate, Mr John Feltham, Mr Ralph Freadman, Sir Robert Gatehouse, Hon Justice Paul Guest, Mr Bryan Harding, Mr Tony Howard, QC, Mr Sek Hulme, QC, Mr Anthony Fitzwilliams-Hyde, Professor Ken Inglis, the late Father Terry Jennings, SDB, Hon Dr Barry Jones, Dr Douglas

Kirsner, the late Mr Leon Peres, Mr Peter O'Brien, Ms Margot Rosenbloom, Mr Richard Searby, QC, the late Hon Sir John Starke, QC, the late Mr Ron Syme, Professor James Walter, and Mr John Watherston. Dr Elizabeth Wood-Ellem produced the index against an impossible deadline. Miriam Rosenbloom skilfully produced the pictorial sections. I owe a special personal debt to Dr Roger Buckle.

Friends and family have been generous with their time and support in seeing this book to publication. John Carroll kindly agreed to read the whole manuscript; it has benefited enormously from his astute comments, and I thank him for his wise counsel. Rob Southey was similarly generous in reading the entire manuscript and saving me from numerous infelicities of expression and worse. As well, Rob went beyond the call of friendship in doggedly tracking down an old portrait of Jack Starke that had seemed lost to history; his support throughout this project has been tireless. My daughters, Regan and Vanessa Richards, diligently read the completed manuscript, and offered many valuable comments and suggestions. David Broadbent, Creighton Burns, John Cain, Ian Collens, Bill Gurry, Meg Gurry, John Guy, Ian Haig, Gail Hambly, Nigel Henham, Brad Hooper, John Ridley and Don Watson have been supportive and encouraging over many years.

I have enjoyed the confidence of a number of people intimately involved in the life related here. I am greatly indebted to Ronald Ryan's family and especially to his three daughters, Janice, Wendy, and Pip. Ryan's late half-brother, George Thompson, and his three sisters, Violet, Irma, and Gloria, all gave unstintingly of their time in interviews, often in recalling incidents and events that were clearly painful to them, and made available private correspondence. So, too, did Dorothy, Ryan's wife of fifteen years, who responded generously to the many demands I made on her time and privacy even though the discussion was frequently distressing. (Dorothy Ryan was twice re-married after her divorce from Ronald Ryan. For simplicity I have retained her name 'Dorothy Ryan' throughout endnote citations.)

Particularly, I wish to thank the many people who gave so freely of their time in interviews. Since the program of interviews started in 1968, some are now deceased; others interviewed have wished not to be identified. It is appropriate that the contribution of those interviewed is gratefully acknowledged here: Mr Allan Ashbolt, Mr Jack Ayling, Mrs Carole Barns, Mr Neil Beggs, Mr Colin Benjamin, Mr David Biles, Rev

Father John Brosnan, Rt Hon Arthur Calwell, MHR, Dame Kate Campbell, DBE, Mr Geoff Clancy, Mr Mike Crewdson, Inspector Bill Crowley, Mr Bill Davey, Mr John Dawes, Mr Brian Dixon, MLA, Mr Neville Drummond, Mr Lionel Dunk, Mr Kevin Fenton, Mr John Finemore, QC, Hon John Galbally, MLC, Mr Keith George, Mr Ian Grindlay, Hon Justice Paul Guest, Hon Rupert Hamer, MLC, Mr Bryan Harding, Sister Hildegarde, Mr Tony Hill, Mr Clyde Holding, MLA, Mr Tony Howard, QC, Mr David Hundley, Mr Anthony Fitzwilliams Hyde, Rev Father Terry Jennings, SDB, Mr Keith Johanson, Mr Barry Jones, MLA, Sister Madonna (Margaret Kingston), Mr Brian Kitching, Mrs Joyce Kotze, Mr Ranald Macdonald, Mr Richard McGarvie, QC, Mr Brian Morley, Mr Barry Muir, Mr Frank O'Brien, Mr Peter O'Brien, Ms Janet Paterson, Mr John Penlington, Mr Graham Perkin, Mr Alex Poynton, Mr Tom Prior, Mr Lionel Pugh, Mr Leonard Radic, Mr Darren Room, Mrs Irma Russ, Miss Gloria Ryan, Ms Janice Ryan, Mr John Ryan, Ms Rhonda 'Pip' Ryan, Ms Wendy Ryan, Mr Peter Samuel, Mr Kevin Sanders, Mr David Scott, Mr Richard Searby, QC, Mr Corbett Shaw, Mrs Violet Smith, Hon Sir John Starke, Mr Frank Sylvester, Mr Les Tanner, Mr Patrick Tennison, Mr George Thompson, Mr Peter Walker, Mr Norman Wearne, Rev John Westerman, Mr Roy Wolfe, and Mr Eddie Wong.

I am grateful to the Attorney-General of Victoria for permission to quote from transcripts of proceedings in the Supreme Court of Victoria, General Sessions, Magistrates, and Coroners courts, and to reproduce photographic exhibits tendered at the trial of Ryan and Walker in March 1966; to The Age Co Limited for permission to reproduce photographs; to Mark, Judy, and Michael Tanner for permission to reproduce the cartoon of Sir Henry Bolte by Les Tanner; to the Herald & Weekly Times for permission to reproduce photographs; to Mrs Dorothy Pirois, Mrs Violet Smith, Miss Gloria Ryan, and Mrs Irma Russ for kind permission to reproduce photographs; to Mr Thos Hodgson for kind permission to reproduce the portrait of John Starke by John Bloomfield; and to the Keeper of Public Records for permission to reproduce documents held in the Public Records Office, Victoria.

Foremost among the many people who have provided support and encouragement to me was Dr Graham Little, my close friend of more than 30 years, who died suddenly at the age of 60 in February 2000. Graham was tremendously supportive and helpful in the early stages of writing this book. My great intellectual and personal debt to him is expressed in the dedication.

This book is primarily dedicated to the late Hon John Galbally, MLC, Labor opposition leader in the Victorian Legislative Council from 1955 to 1979. Annually for 21 years from 1955, Jack Galbally moved his private member's bill to abolish capital punishment in Victoria. Each year it was defeated on party lines but with every debate on the bill the forces for abolition in the parliament grew such that by April 1975, in a vote on a private member's bill introduced by Liberal premier Dick Hamer, a majority of members carried the day and hanging was abolished. This was a historic achievement for Hamer and those members in the parliament who supported it. The dedication of this book to the memory of Jack Galbally acknowledges the singular contribution he made to the abolition of the death penalty in Victoria.

My publisher, Henry Rosenbloom, has been patient beyond reckoning in waiting for the manuscript of this book. Henry was an early believer in the project, and his boundless enthusiasm and support—and his fine editing expertise—has been crucial in bringing the manuscript to publication.

Finally, my wife, Wendy, and our children, Regan, Vanessa, and James, have lived with my enduring preoccupation with this project—my 'grand obsession', Wendy has called it—and the boxes of books and mountains of documents in the house, for longer than any of us cares to remember. To them go my heartfelt thanks. Now they can get the house back.

It seems unnecessary to add that none of the many people who helped me in this project is to be held accountable for whatever shortcomings the book may possess. Despite their best efforts, the judgments are mine alone.

Mike Richards
28 December 2001

Prologue

THE DATE IS 2 FEBRUARY 1967. The place is Coburg, a light-industrial and residential suburb north of Melbourne on the great highway connecting that city with Sydney. Set back from the road behind high stone walls is a forbidding grey-granite building, Her Majesty's Prison, Pentridge, the 116-year-old penal institution that serves as Victoria's maximum-security prison. It is early evening, around 7:30PM on this Thursday, and the air outside is still warm after a hot summer's day. In cell 15 of the top-security section of the gaol, H Division (known to inmates as Hell Division), a prisoner takes a long roll of thin, prison-issue toilet paper. Using a blue ballpoint pen, he clandestinely begins to write in a taut, mannered script, carefully avoiding the perforations in the paper as he does so. He sets the name 'Dorothy Janet Ryan (née George)' at the top, underlines these words, addresses the letter to 'My Darling Wife & Daughters', and begins to write:

> It has been of the utmost concern to me that I have lost contact with you through what—to use a dramatic phrase—has been my darkest hour. It is my considered opinion that during crisis a family should be closer together in spirit and loyalty presenting a closed and united front to hostile elements and affording each other—as only a family can—comfort and support. This despite the nature and rights and wrongs of the situation.[1]

The prisoner continues writing, tortuously reviewing his life and reflecting on 'the situation', the momentous events as well as the personal failings that have brought him here. This will be the last letter he will ever write. When he has finished, the toilet paper will form a narrow, unbroken scroll more than ten feet in length.

As the prisoner writes, a man with whom his destiny is inextricably linked has already entered the prison. The man had announced himself to the guards, requesting entry, at around 7.30PM at the visitors' gate on the south side of Pentridge. Identifying himself as Mr Jones, the fictitious name arranged in advance between the sheriff of the Supreme Court of Victoria and Pentridge's governor, Ian Grindlay, he has been admitted and awaits Grindlay's arrival.[2] Aged in his sixties, the man is around six feet two inches tall, with a thin build and ruddy complexion. He is wearing a sports coat and trousers, sunglasses, and a peaked tweed cap. He is affable, if not jovial, with prison officers before Grindlay arrives and escorts him to the office of the prison's chief of security in D Division.

Upon entering the office, Mr Jones immediately approaches a padlocked, black wooden box, unlocks it, and inspects the several pieces of apparatus inside. Before him are three sets of leather body-harness, six leg and arm shackles, two sets of leg straps, a single white calico cap, heavy lead weights, and three stout manila ropes each of twenty-eight feet eight inches in length, with the last thirty inches covered with soft, sewn leather. The one-inch diameter ropes have been fashioned into nooses by the addition of a two-and-a-half inch brass eyelet sewn into the end of the rope through which the rope is run.[3] From the way in which this man handles the accoutrements of his great art, Grindlay is in no doubt that he is no stranger to the box or its contents. Nor should he be. This man is the public executioner, and these are his tools of trade.

Years before, this same man had had recourse to the contents of the hangman's box in the chief's office. On a warm Melbourne day in February 1951 he had come to Pentridge to execute three prisoners convicted of the murder of Carlton SP bookmaker William 'Pop' Kent. On that day, Norman Andrews, 39, Robert Clayton, 34, and a woman, Jean Lee, were hanged by the neck until they were dead. It was a day the hangman would rather have forgotten. Clayton's hanging had been botched, and Lee had collapsed under terror and sedation and had to be seated in a chair on the drop. She died on the gallows, although many people wrongly believed that she was dead before she went through the trap. She was just 31 years old.[4]

Now the state strangler, the representative of the public will, is on a new commission. Paid a retainer all these years, his name having been kept on a list of approved executioners by the sheriff's office, he is to conduct the first execution in Victoria for more than fifteen years. Mr Jones had prepared for this execution three days before on the night of 30 January, but it had been postponed because of a last-minute reprieve. Now the shackles and harness are once more checked. The rope is stretched on the scaffold, using sandbags filled to equal 12 stone, the condemned man's weight in his clothes. The trap crashes loudly as Mr Hangman Jones sends the sandbags plunging through the drop at the end of the rope.

Preparations for the execution are now under way elsewhere in the prison. Since the scaffold is in D Division, all the prisoners in the division—almost 200 in all—are cleared from their cells the next morning at 6:00AM and taken to the dormitories in F Division. The condemned man, Ronald Joseph Ryan, who has been kept under maximum security in the prison's H Division for thirteen months, is then moved at 6.45AM to D Division, where he is put in a first-floor cell, number 67, on the north side of the drop. Mr Jones is put in a cell on the opposite side. Just before 7:00AM the first of eleven journalists from the press, radio, and television is admitted to the gaol through the south gate.

At two minutes to eight, the sheriff of the Supreme Court, Gerry O'Brien, an archetypical ruddy-faced Irishman, reads the death warrant to the prisoner. In a strained and halting voice, O'Brien begins reading. But, with the warrant only halfway through, and with his voice trailing away with emotion, O'Brien cannot complete his recital, and the formality is dispensed with.

Ryan is then made ready by the hangman, as the Roman Catholic chaplain of Pentridge, Father John Brosnan, intones a prayer below the scaffold. The hangman works quickly. He straps the leather waist-harness on Ryan to pin his arms behind him, then secures the ankle shackles. Finally, he puts the white calico cap on Ryan's head, although with the flap not yet lowered to cover his face. At twenty seconds to the appointed hour, eight o'clock, the condemned man is taken from his cell and walks the five steps to the scaffold. Just three weeks away from his 42nd birthday, Ryan stands silently on the edge of doom.

THIRTY-FIVE YEARS ON, there are stories to tell and a life to recount in this book about the life and death of Ronald Ryan—the man in cell 15, whose fate became, for many Australians, the central moral drama of the last 50 years. I never met Ryan. In 1967, as acting secretary of the students anti-hanging campaign, I was involved in efforts to secure a reprieve for Ryan; but in that summer of 1966-67 I did not know much about him at all. What motivated me and my student colleagues, and many others in the anti-hanging campaign, was revulsion for the death penalty. Most of us did not believe Ryan was innocent—only that the punishment was inappropriate in a civilised community. While we felt deeply for the innocent victims and their families, how could a society, we reasoned, assert the sanctity of human life in response to a homicide by itself sanctioning legalised killing through judicial execution? While my views have been sorely tested at times by more recent mass killings in Australia, it is a philosophical position from which I have never departed.

This, then, is the story of Ryan's life as I never knew it in 1967, and an account of the case that became a *cause célèbre* in Australian political history. In 1968 I began research in which I sought to analyse and understand the decision of the Victorian cabinet that confirmed Ryan's sentence of death, and the media and protest campaign in opposition to the hanging. In the course of trying to turn that research into a book, I realised that I still did not know anything about Ryan himself. He had been described in newspaper articles at the time as a small-time crook who specialised in cheque forging, and shop-breaking and stealing. He was a devoted father—'a homing pigeon', police who knew him had said—and passionate about his family. Other articles referred to his good prison record. How, I wondered, did such an unlikely minor criminal find himself at the end of a rope after shooting a prison officer during the course of a daring and ambitious escape from Victoria's highest-security prison?

Answering that question to my own satisfaction led to still further research, in which I sought to understand why Ryan turned to crime and became a professional criminal. The question became more insistent in 1978 after I interviewed the former governor of Pentridge prison, Ian Grindlay, the man who stood next to Ryan as he dropped through the trap on that fateful day on 3 February 1967, and who was deeply affected by the hanging. Grindlay had also known Ryan in the early 1960s when Ryan was first imprisoned at Bendigo Training Prison where Grindlay was governor of the gaol. After Grindlay described Ryan in detail, particularly his impressive record of educational achievement in prison, his exemplary conduct, and his strong commitment to rehabilitation, I asked him whether he would regard Ryan as a model prisoner. 'No, no, not *a* model prisoner,' Grindlay answered in measured tones. 'In my 30 years of prison service, Ryan was *the* model prisoner.'[5]

Answering the question posed by the paradox of Ryan as 'model prisoner' versus 'ambitious criminal executed for murder' has occupied me on and off for more than 30 years. This book distils the essence of what became extensive archival research, and more than one hundred interviews with Ryan's family and other people, like Grindlay, who were involved in the case. Although there have been numerous media stories about Ryan over the years, there has been no comprehensive biographical treatment of his life. In biography, of course, one is usually writing of a distinguished or notable life where, as often as not, laurels are being laid on. Ronald Ryan, however, is distinguished not by his achievements in life but by the circumstances of his death. While many people were opposed to the death penalty being imposed in his case, and saw commutation of his sentence as the desirable course, Ryan's was *a life* few people at the time saw as especially warranting attention. In so far as the public knew much of his life, he seemed not at all distinctive from other convicted criminals in capital cases. He did not even seem especially adept as a criminal: he was repeatedly caught and convicted.

While there has been periodic and inconclusive public debate since 1965 about whether Ryan was guilty of the murder charge that brought about his execution, establishing his guilt or proving his innocence was not my primary reason for writing this biography, although the book does come to a definitive conclusion on that issue. The fact that Ryan was put to death in the name of the people allows us—perhaps even obliges us—to ask questions about him. What kind of an upbringing did he have? How did he live his life? Was he a good father to his children? What sort of a man was he? Did he have redeeming qualities? Did he deserve to die on the gallows?

Ryan was intelligent and impressive to many who came into contact with him, but he was deeply flawed. Born into poverty and neglect, he exhibited evidence from an early age of obsessive behaviour: he was a compulsive gambler, he was slave to an elaborate hand-washing ritual, and he always (in one way or another) confessed to his crimes. When he was first imprisoned, he behaved impeccably and showed an outstanding potential to reform. However, when freed of the constraints of prison discipline upon release, he quickly re-offended and developed grandiose ideas of becoming Australia's leading criminal.

The dominant theme running through the Ryan story is his reckless, self-destructive approach to life. Whether wagering large amounts of money, committing a crime, or escaping from prison, Ryan was inexorably drawn to the reckless gamble—the big plunge. His credo was, 'Who dares, wins'. Ryan took absurd risks, and always ended up losing: he lost at gambling, lost jobs, lost businesses, lost his wife and children through divorce and, ultimately, lost his life. It was as if, always conscious of his low birth and few life opportunities, he risked everything in a great gamble to come out on top. In some ways, his whole life can be seen as a headlong rush towards a dramatic and inevitable downfall.

This is the story of Ronald Ryan as it has never been told before. Much of it is shocking. The book narrates Ryan's life and crimes—frequently in great detail because his anti-social tendencies and criminal record are still the subject of dispute—and concludes with his execution. While in no way sanitising an infamous criminal career, the book relates the tragic life and notorious death of the man who became the last person hanged in Australia.

CHAPTER ONE
Childhood

[B]eing a child under the age of seventeen years [Ryan] was living under such conditions as indicated that he was lapsing or was likely to lapse into a career of crime, and is thereby deemed to be a neglected child.

—Police Magistrate Robert Dawes, JP

As Ronald Ryan stood on the Pentridge gallows and prepared to depart this world, the attention of the whole community was fixed on him in this hideous place. He was, for a moment, the most famous man in Australia. The circumstances of his birth 42 years before, however, could not have provided a greater contrast. For Ryan was born into the most abject poverty and obscurity. Although his name is now associated with Australia's best-known capital case, Ronald Joseph Ryan was not the name with which he entered the world. What is more, he was born illegitimate, and the family secret that gave rise to this circumstance was to have a significant effect on the young Ryan's life: Ronald's mother, Cecilia, having separated from her husband but still married to him, had conceived a child by another man.

Taking the surname of his mother's then husband, the child was born Ronald Edmond Thompson on 21 February 1925 in the Women's Hospital, Carlton.[1] The doctor who delivered the child, a 26-year-old woman who had just commenced residency at the hospital, was Dr Kate Campbell, MD (later Dame Kate Campbell, DBE), who was to become the most distinguished paediatrician of her generation.[2] Although the certificate registering the birth does not record the name of the father, the child was named Ronald after his natural father, John Ronald Ryan, then aged 42, the Sydney-born son of an Irishman with whom Cecilia Thompson had been cohabiting for some time.[3]

Ronald's parents, both of them Roman Catholic, were products of the urban working class. Ryan's mother, Eveline Cecilia Young, was born on 6 May 1890, the second daughter of George Bernard Young, carpenter, and his wife, Jane, in the family's small terrace cottage at 87 Moor Street, in the inner-city Melbourne suburb of Fitzroy.[4] At the age of 24, after working at various jobs including domestic help and later as a waitress, Cecilia married George Harry Thompson, 30, a labourer from Brunswick, at the Melbourne Registry Office in March 1915.[5] At the time of the marriage she was already five months pregnant. Four months later, in July 1915, she gave birth to her first child, George William Rupert, in the small cottage where they were living at 47 Victoria Street, East Brunswick.[6]

The Great War then raging in Europe was to disrupt the marriage. Six months after the birth of the child, Harry Thompson enlisted in the Australian Armed Forces, and in July 1916 he embarked on the vessel HT *Themistocles, en route* to Plymouth, England. Thompson fell ill shortly after his arrival in England, and was admitted to hospital and finally shipped home in August 1917, where he was discharged as medically unfit in November 1917.[7] His marriage to Cecilia was never resumed. His illness persisted, and he seems still to have been in indifferent health when he was killed ten years later in a traffic accident on 15 August 1927. Thompson jumped from a fast-moving tram in Sydney Road, Brunswick, not very far from Pentridge prison, and was struck by a passing car. Admitted to hospital, he died later that day from a fractured skull that he had sustained in the accident. A passenger on the tram gave evidence at the subsequent coronial inquest that he had seemed preoccupied moments before he quickly got up, rushed out, and took a 'flying leap off' the tram, which had been travelling at full-speed.[8] It seems that Thompson had missed getting off at his stop at the Victoria Street intersection with Sydney Road, and had jumped off the speeding tram when he realised his mistake. The coroner's verdict was that he had died accidentally.[9]

Cecilia's marriage to Thompson seems to have foundered even before his enlistment for service, and she had been forced to seek domestic work away from Melbourne. In 1924 she was working at Woods Point, in the high country about 100 miles east of Melbourne, where she found casual employment as a waitress in one of the cafes serving the town's gold miners. John Ryan was one such miner.[10] Then aged 40, he had worked in the mines in New South Wales and at the scheelite mine in Zeehan, Tasmania, before coming to Victoria in 1911. Jack Ryan—as he was known—was born in the inner-city working-class area of Redfern in Sydney in 1884, the son of an Irish-born labourer, Henry Ryan, who seems also to have been known as John, and Alice Noble, a local Redfern girl.[11] In 1924 Jack Ryan was working in the Morning Star gold mine, having also worked in the A1 mine between Gaffneys Creek and Woods Point.

Jack Ryan was soon forced to leave the mines as his health deteriorated, suffering as he was from miners' phthisis, the disease that had killed many miners before him in Victoria. Variously known as black lung, pneumoconiosis, or silicosis, miners' phthisis is a lung disease. It is caused by constant inhalation of fine silica-dust particles produced by drilling rock, silicon being the abundant constituent of most rocks. The disease is the distinctive legacy of work down dusty, poorly ventilated mines; it brings about a change in the formation of the lungs, resulting in severe difficulty in breathing, accompanied by a recurring cough and, very likely, tuberculosis.[12] While there is no necessary connection between miners' phthisis and tuberculosis, miners suffering the disease very frequently contracted an infection of the bacillus, and hence became tubercular. A gold miner all his working life, Jack Ryan had silicosis in an advanced stage by the time he was 40 years old.

Reduced to a wheezing invalid and unable to continue in the mines, Jack moved with Cecilia late in 1924 to Melbourne, where they set up house in a small worker's terrace cottage at 70 O'Shanassy Street, North Melbourne, several hundred yards east of the North Melbourne football ground. Although they were not to stay there for very long, it was while Jack and Cecilia were living in this house that Ronald was born.[13] Jack Ryan was virtually illiterate and, apart from gold mining, he knew no trade.[14] Dependent upon odd jobs, and some work at the nearby Victoria Market selling seedlings and later on the wharves where he did casual labouring loading cargo on the vessel *Edina* at no. 1 wharf in the port of Melbourne, he was unable to keep up rent payments. As a result, he and Cecilia were frequently evicted.[15] Often they would pay the first week's rent, move in, and stay without paying rent until they were evicted.[16] A succession of addresses followed as the family tried to keep a jump ahead of landlords and their agents.

In 1927 they moved to a small brick cottage at 54 Stanley Street, West Melbourne; there, on 28 March 1927, Cecilia gave birth to their second child, Violet Esmee Estelle.[17] The following year they moved again to Peel Street, North Melbourne and then to 1 Byron Street, North Melbourne where, on 29 August 1929, their third child was born—a second girl, Irma Dawn.[18] Here a measure of stability entered their lives. They stayed at Byron Street, just a few blocks from the North Melbourne Town Hall, for three years. More importantly, with Cecilia now a widow, there was no longer an impediment to her marriage to Jack. On 31 October 1929 they were married in a ceremony conducted by Father Thomas O'Ryan at their local church, St Mary's Roman Catholic Church, West Melbourne.[19]

One effect of Jack and Cecilia's marriage was to diminish the illegitimate social status of Ron and the two girls born to them. Up till then, the children had had natural parents who were not married, even though Cecilia had assumed the name Mrs Ryan in their *de facto* relationship. Although such relationships were common enough in the working class for that not to be a problem, their marriage diminished the social stigma somewhat.

Not so easily dealt with, however, was the legal status of the children. The common law, then and now, presumes that a child born to a married woman is a child of that marriage. Since Cecilia's children were presumed in law to have been the product of her marriage to Harry Thompson, her subsequent marriage to Jack Ryan did not make them Ryan's children. Jack Ryan claimed paternity of Violet and Irma when their births were officially registered, giving his name as that of the children's father, and this fact would be important in law if the matter was ever tested.[20] But in Ronald's case paternity was not claimed, at least at registration; hence, legally, there would be a strong presumption in law that Ronald was Thompson's child.

Indeed, it has been held in law that the children born to a woman could not be legitimised by her subsequent marriage to the biological father unless at the dates of their respective births she was legally free to marry him. But, because Harry Thompson was still living, Cecilia Thompson was not free to marry Jack Ryan in February 1925 when

Ronald was born, nor in March 1927 when Violet was born. At Thompson's death in August 1927 she became legally free to marry Jack Ryan, but this would affect only the legal status of Irma. Ronald and Violet were the illegitimate children of Jack Ryan, and hence unable lawfully to share in his estate, such as it was, should he die intestate. Had it ever been tested, a court would have found that only Irma, born in August 1929, was legitimised by the subsequent marriage of Cecilia and Jack in October 1929.[21]

The Ryans seem to have recognised, and been troubled by, the legal status of their offspring for several years after the marriage. Indeed, on 13 July 1931, when a fourth child, Gloria May, was born, Jack Ryan, acting as the informant in the registration of birth formalities, gave the marriage date required for the birth certificate as 31 October 1919, exactly ten years earlier than in fact had been the case.[22] Several years later, in 1937, Cecilia disclosed to the Victorian Department of Children's Welfare the circumstances of Ronald's birth:

> I wish to inform you that my son Ronald was registered under the name of: Ronald Edmond Thompson. Mr. Ryan was not married to me at the time of his birth 21 February 1925. My first husband was then alive. Mr. Ryan is taking steps re his adoption to himself as the gentleman at the Statist Office advised him to. If he goes to a Clerk of Petty Sessions and goes through the Court he can have it done. If however you have any other advice I would be glad of it.[23]

This advice was certainly correct on the point of Jack Ryan needing to adopt Ronald as his legal son. However, adoption proceedings were never undertaken. In law, throughout his life, Ronald Joseph Ryan was the child of his mother's marriage to Harry Thompson. And, more importantly, there is some evidence that he was to bear the psychological scars of illegitimacy as he grew up in the knowledge that his natural parents were not married at the time of his birth.

Jack and Cecilia's marriage had other consequences as well. Two years after the marriage, Cecilia's son by her first marriage, George, indicated his wish to be more independent. By 1931 he was sixteen years old and, after frequent and sometimes severe beatings by his stepfather, he was intent on leaving home.[24] Now, he told himself, he would make his break. He jumped the rattler to Queensland in search of seasonal work, chip-cutting and banana-cutting, although he seems to have survived on susso, the sustenance allowance paid by the Queensland government. As an itinerant, unemployed male, George received coupons to the value of six shillings per week: three shillings for groceries, two shillings for meat, and one shilling for bread.[25] While he was later to play a very significant role in Ronald's life, for now he was out of the picture.

For the young Ronald, as the effects of the Great Depression deepened, these first years were spent in harsh and extremely poor circumstances. Unable to maintain regular work, Big Jack or Paddy Ryan, as he was variously known, was soon dependent on Cecilia's meagre income as a domestic. But that was not enough and, reportedly at Jack's instigation, she worked as a prostitute, primarily around the docks and in the North Melbourne and West Melbourne areas.[26] Jack did some odd jobs but, as the Depression worsened, the family's circumstances became still more desperate, and the children were often neglected. Frequently leaving quickly from houses when rent was in arrears (what was known as doing a midnight flit), and owing money to traders, their poverty forced them to keep moving to the newly developing semi-rural areas to the north-east and east of Melbourne: first to Greensborough and then, in quick succession, to Bayswater, Montmorency, Boronia, Ferntree Gully, and the orchard district of Mitcham.[27]

Although housing accommodation was cheaper in the outer areas of Melbourne, employment prospects were bleak. Early in 1934, the family went back to the inner city, this time to Brunswick, to a small two-bedroom cottage at 4 Prentice Street, just three blocks from Sydney Road, and not far from Pentridge prison. Jack Ryan's silicosis had worsened, and he was in extreme pain.[28] By now he was judged permanently incapacitated for work. He was granted a Commonwealth government invalid pension, for which he received £1-15-0 per fortnight—although it seems that this amount was later reduced when a means test was applied.[29] About half the value of the basic wage at the time, £1-15-0 was a meagre income, and scant compensation for the ruination of his health down the mines.[30] A common sight for his children was to see him bleeding from the mouth, ears, and nose; he would not uncommonly fill a dish with coughed-up blood. His already heavy drinking increased as he drank incessantly—red wine and methylated spirits, anything he could get his hands on—to blunt the pain.[31]

By then, too, Cecilia was a hopeless alcoholic, and she was commonly found drunk by the children when they returned home from school. During her frequent absences the children thought their mother was working as a waitress at the Bluebird Cafe; in fact, she was working as a prostitute. Frequently the children waited alone for hours for their mother to return home. Once when she returned home with coins, Jack was furious with her when he found that one was a dud. He sent her out again to buy fish and chips to pass the dud coin.

At this time Jack was friendly with a number of local criminals, and his domestic behaviour reflected that of the company he kept. A womaniser and a bully, Jack frequently terrorised his children when drunk. Ron was particularly subjected to regular beatings by his father, who was seized with the idea that the boy was not his own child. Jack just 'couldn't stand' Ron from the outset.[32] Jack had often beaten George, the stepson whom he resented, but he favoured the three daughters born to him and Cecilia after Ron.[33] Although there seems no reason for him to have doubted that he fathered the girls (Cecilia's prostitution notwithstanding), Jack, when drunk, would often taunt them with the names of their putative fathers.

In one incident at Prentice Street, Jack began destroying property with an axe as he sought out Cecilia, whom he suspected of philandering. Cecilia and the two younger children were being protected in a neighbour's house next door; the girls were cowering at the end of a bed in one room when the front door splintered under Jack's axe. Raving drunk, Jack came through the door, beating Cecilia and taunting the children: 'Any 'ow, yer not mine,' he cruelly shouted at them. 'You're Irma Dean, and you're Gloria West! Yer father's a man from the market!'[34]

The Ryans were not to stay at Prentice Street for very long, however. Years of rent arrears and midnight flits caught up with them yet again; this time the landlord's agents were in no mood to delay proceedings for rental recovery. To make matters worse, when the agents arrived late on the night of 28 March 1934 Cecilia was drunk and Jack was well on the way.[35] When the agents simply moved their furniture out of the house and dumped it in the gutter outside, Cecilia flew into a drunken rage at this unseemly exit, and cursed the agents profusely. The police were called and Cecilia, shouting obscenities, was arrested by Constable James Lowe for drunkenness, and was placed in the Brunswick Police

Station lock-up. Some time later, when Jack took Ron and Irma to the police station, Cecilia could be heard screaming in the cells.[36] Although he was himself far from sober, Jack was left to take Cecilia home and organise a friend's truck to take the belongings away. This time they had nowhere to go but back to Mitcham. Loaded onto the back of this flat-tray truck, they arrived early next morning, and Jack organised yet another place for them to live.

This time, home would be in a large timber house at 31 Casella Street, the last house on the city side, just a short way from a pond formed by the Mullum Mullum or Deep Creek. One of the rooms would have to be rented out (a woman and her twelve-year-old child would later take the room), but at least they were off the street.[37] That same morning, Thursday, 29 March, Cecilia's case was heard in her absence by Osmond Smith, JP, in the Brunswick Court of Petty Sessions, where she was charged with being 'drunk in a public place, to wit Prentice Street'. As was often the case in matters of drunkenness, Cecilia was discharged without further penalty.[38]

At Mitcham, Jack's drinking grew still worse. Unable to afford plonk, he took to drinking metho, which Ron was often sent to buy. On one such errand, Ron and Violet were unwittingly given turpentine instead of the methylated spirits they had asked for. Jack took a hard swig at it and went berserk.[39] His drunken bouts increasingly turned ugly, and his violence was especially directed at Cecilia and at Ron. One night, Jack again took an axe and, dragging Ron and Violet with him, launched off in search of Cecilia, whom this time he suspected of philandering with one of the roadworkers nearby. As Gloria and Irma slept, Jack, still clutching Ron and Violet scruffily, tore through the road workers' tents looking for Cecilia, who in fact was being protected by neighbours. Not finding her, and exhausting himself by his rage, Jack collapsed in a drunken stupor.

On this occasion Cecilia escaped Jack's drunken wrath. At other times she was not so fortunate. The children, especially Ron, did not escape either. Jack would explode with rage at Ron's misbehaviour, usually taking off his belt and administering a hiding, or sometimes giving his son a backhander to go on with.[40] He would beat Ron with a leather belt; sometimes, he would hit him on the top of his head with his fist. Jack Ryan stood six feet two inches tall with a huge frame, but the pride of this big man had been destroyed by a system that had exploited his labour, ruined his health, and cast him aside as an unemployable invalid. His silicosis had been complicated by infection, and he was marked for a slow and agonising death as tuberculosis gradually corroded his lungs. At times, when his health improved, his behaviour would also improve, and the family's circumstances would look a little brighter.[41] The times when he was on the wagon were ones of meagre pleasure and a little joy. Jack was a good cook, and when he was not drinking he would make his own yeast and bake bread. At such times he planted vegetables in the back yard, and produced good crops of potatoes, tomatoes, and runner beans. Conditions at Mitcham, a new suburb that up till recently had been mainly orchards, were relatively primitive.[42] There was no electricity, and lighting was provided by hurricane lamps. These privations would have mattered less had Jack kept off the grog. When he was sober he managed the children without violence, and the gentler side of his nature came through.[43]

Once at Christmas, Jack arrived home with a bag of toys for the children. At another time he bought Violet a piano for her sixth birthday, and heaved it into the house himself and began to teach her Irish songs. Several weeks after he bought it, however, he had to pawn it again to pay creditors. The pain would always return for Jack Ryan and gnaw at his insides and so, too, would his drinking return. At such times, his violence dominated the household. One night at Mitcham, Jack found a cat sleeping on baby Gloria's face as she slept in a cot. In a rage, Jack seized the cat and killed it by bashing it repeatedly against a wall. This brutal act was overheard by the horrified children; they found the remains of the cat the next morning.[44] Jack's drinking was at the base of this behaviour; several times at Mitcham he was locked up for being drunk and disorderly.[45]

One of the immediate prompts for Jack's violent treatment of Ron was his truancy. He frequently avoided school, perhaps because he found difficulty in settling, with home life as it was and after so many moves.[46] Prior to Mitcham, Ron had already been to several primary schools in Brunswick, Boronia, and Montmorency. After less than two years at Mitcham State School, Ron and his sisters transferred in 1936 to the local Roman Catholic primary school, St John's. Ron was now eleven years old, although he was small for his age. With thick, dark hair and thin lips, his face made him look severe if not tough, at least until he smiled. In 1936 there were about 60 pupils at St John's, a school run by the nuns of the Sisters of Mercy, who travelled from Lilydale by train.[47] A St John's school photo taken in 1936 shows Ron unsmiling, sitting cross-legged in the front row holding a small blackboard upon which are chalked the words: 'St John's Primary School, Grades V to VIII, 1936.'[48] Assigning the job of holding the blackboard was often a photographer's shrewd way of momentarily containing the restless instincts of the more troublesome small boys. One suspects that this photographer, grown expert with the experience of hundreds of such school photographs, was quite astute in identifying young Ryan as the tearaway in this group.

At Mitcham, the personality traits that were to present more forcefully in Ryan's later life became obvious to those around him. He was from a young age fastidious about his appearance and the cleanliness of his clothes. He would fussily brush his hair, spending inordinate periods preoccupied with brushing down the cowlick on his crown. He was similarly excessively fussy about the spotlessness of his clothes, and detested wearing shirts that were not scrupulously clean. He would often ask his sisters to wash his clothes again because, he said, his mother did not get them clean enough. Similarly, in the first reported instance of what would later become a dominant ritual, he would wash his hands repeatedly during the course of the day.[49]

Ron was also confirmed in the Roman Catholic Church at St John's in 1936, and he exhibited considerable religious faith, even at an early age.[50] This became evident once when, while returning from the pictures at Mitcham with Violet and Irma, a storm broke and lightning struck. Huddled under a tree, Ron urged them to hold onto their rosary beads and pray. His confirmation photograph, taken on 15 August 1936, shows him tight-lipped, but smiling this time. His cowlick has caused his hair to fall untidily over his forehead; he seems distinctly less well turned-out for this special occasion than the other boys and girls. Unlike most of the boys who have jackets, and all who have ties, he has neither.[51] This was the day, too, that he took on the confirmation name Joseph. His parents had chosen this saint's name, the patron saint of workers.[52] Now he was Ronald Edmond Joseph Ryan. However, since he did not like the name 'Edmond', he very rarely used it after this time, except very much later when it was used as a special code.[53]

In 1936, Ron's parents had no regular work and no prospects, and there seemed little hope of better. However, in October 1936 the

Victorian Treasury began payment to Jack Ryan of a miners' phthisis allowance under a special scheme set up to give compassionate assistance to miners made invalids by their contraction of silicosis.[54] He was one of some 800 recipients of this benefit in that year.

Although the amount was meagre indeed. Ryan received £6 every three months, less than ten shillings per week at a time when the basic wage was £3-9-0 per week. Jack Ryan had no work and less than one-seventh of that to support a wife and four children. Jack's allowance was increased to £7 per quarter from October 1938; to £8 from October 1941; and to £10-10-0 from October 1942. In all, over ten years, Jack Ryan was to receive just over £300 by way of miners' phthisis allowance.[55] This amounted to less than the value of 35 ounces of the gold which Jack Ryan had broken his health to mine.

Life in Mitcham for the Ryans was literally a battle to find the next meal. Students at St John's were generally poor, but the Ryans were well known to nuns and students alike to be destitute.[56] Cecilia and the children used to unpick flour bags to make sheets for their beds, and Ron used to go ferreting for rabbits. At other times he would steal food, especially when his father had kept him away from the house for truancy or some such misdemeanour. Sometimes the neighbours would feed the children but, mostly, they would go hungry.[57]

By 1936, too, Ron was showing anti-social traits. He had already been brought before the Children's Court, charged with breaking and entering, and had been placed on a bond to be of good behaviour for a period of twelve months.[58] In November 1936 came a second offence, for which he would pay dearly. On the morning of 9 November, Ron left home for school. At about 9:30AM, at a short distance from his home, he stood and watched a neighbour, Mrs Mary Noase, leave her house in Casella Street; Mrs Noase lived there with another elderly woman. Wishing to be sure the owner would not return, he first waited at the side of the house and then went to the back door, where he saw a notice on a slate asking the baker for a quarter-loaf of bread. Sure now that Mrs Noase would not return, he opened the back door, which was closed but not locked, and entered the house. Moving through three rooms of the house, he turned out the drawers searching for money, but found none. Then he came upon a gold men's watch resting on a piece of leather on the front-room table. He pocketed the watch and its suede pouch and, taking some string from the pantry, left by the back door.[59]

Outside again, he went straight to the house of a young friend, Frank Warway, in Carween Avenue, Mitcham. A little later, on the way to the tile works at Mitcham, Ron showed Warway the watch, and told him he had broken into a house and stolen it.[60] He then asked Warway how much he would give him for the watch. 'Two ducks', was Warway's reply. Ron agreed, but he cautioned Warway: 'You want to plant the watch or you'll get found out.' Although a wish by Ryan to boast is understandable, his confession to Warway meant that 'getting found out' was now much more likely for him than for his friend.

Heeding Ron's warning, Warway then got a red tobacco tin and, as Ron had suggested, planted the watch in it and hid it in a drain at the back of his house. But the deception proved futile and, before the end of the day, investigations by the local police officer, First Constable Stanley Browne of the Mitcham Police Station, had led directly to young Ryan. Constable Browne confronted Ron, searched his pockets, and found the suede pouch and the piece of string. Ron then confessed to taking the watch. At about 6:00PM that day, Ryan went with Browne to Warway's house, where Warway recovered the watch from its hiding place in the drain. A short time later, Ron signed a statement, produced by police, in which he set out the detailed circumstances of the theft. The statement concluded:

> I knew that I was doing wrong when I opened the door and took the watch. The suede pouch and the string which I had in my pockets when searched by 1st Constable Browne are those which I took from the house when I got the watch.

And, in his own handwriting, Ron added, as he was evidently directed to do:

> I have read this statement, it is true, I knew what it means and it is made of my own free will. Ronald Ryan.[61]

Ron was subsequently committed to the Children's Court sitting at Ringwood on 23 November 1936, where he faced two charges. The first was, in the legalese of the official record, 'that he did break and enter the dwelling house of Mary Anna Noase (of Casella Street, Mitcham) and steal therein a gold filled Elgin gents watch ... the property of Mary

Anna Noase.' The second charge had more serious consequences than the first although, as a status offence, it depended on the first for its force. It was that, in the terms of the *Children's Welfare Act 1928*, 'being a child under the age of seventeen years he was living under such conditions as indicated that he was lapsing or was likely to lapse into a career of crime, and is thereby deemed to be a neglected child.'[62]

The hearing was held before Police Magistrate Robert Dawes, JP. The police informant, Constable Browne, listed the cause of committal as 'house-breaking and neglected child', and gave Ron's school as 'Mitcham Roman Catholic School, 5th Grade'. He described the Ryan family's circumstances as 'poor', and added: 'father is a drunkard and mother little better.' Jack was further described as an invalid pensioner; later he and Cecilia were both described as 'not employed'.[63]

After hearing the evidence relating to the theft of the watch and the circumstances of the boy's family, Dawes ruled that Ron was to be made a ward of the state committed to the care of the Children's Welfare Department under the provisions of the *Children's Welfare Act 1928* and the *Children's Court Act 1928*. What this meant, in effect, was that Ron was being taken away from his parents and given over to the custody of the Victorian Children's Welfare Department, where he would be placed in an institutional home, notionally until he reached his eighteenth birthday.[64]

While most neglected children were voluntarily committed to the Department of Children's Welfare by parents who could either no longer cope with or care for them, there were 81 such cases of neglected children which found their way into Victoria's children's courts in 1936. In all, 348 young offenders were committed by the court to the care of the Children's Welfare Department in that year; 118 others were committed to reformatories.[65] Ron was not being sent to a reformatory, but he took his removal from his parents and sisters as a severe punishment—as indeed it was, when looked at even by nineteenth-century standards. In England, exactly one hundred years before Ron's offence, similar law-breaking by juvenile offenders would merit a gaol sentence, to be sure, but one of relatively brief duration. In 1836, at the Staffordshire Quarter Sessions and Assizes, for example, one William McDonals, aged fifteen, was sentenced to three months' imprisonment on a charge of stealing a watch, while a contemporary received a six months' gaol sentence on a similar charge.[66]

Allowing for the very harsh conditions of nineteenth-century English gaols, Ron was being committed to what was essentially custodial care for a period of up to six years for the theft of a watch valued in court evidence at £4-10-0.[67] He was just eleven years and nine months old.

CHAPTER TWO

Wardship

I beg to report that Master Ron Ryan ... [has] absconded this morning. It is very doubtful whether Ryan is going to settle down.
Father Bortolo Fedrigotti, SC

IMMEDIATELY FOLLOWING the court hearing, Ronald was taken that day in November 1936 to the Boys' Depot, much later renamed the Melbourne Juvenile Justice Centre, run by the Children's Welfare Department in Royal Park, on the northern fringe of inner-city Melbourne. Established in 1876, this was a reception and assessment centre where institutional placement for new wards was considered by case officers of the department.[1] Young offenders between eleven and fourteen years of age were sometimes placed in so-called industrial schools where they could receive training. Industrial schools had been established in Victoria by the *Neglected and Criminal Children's Act 1864*.[2] This act declared that children committed to such schools could be taught to be useful members of society by training in 'habits of decency and order'.[3]

The era had seen some extraordinary developments in the accommodation of state wards in Victoria. In the latter part of the nineteenth century, state wards were housed in hulks, much like convicts in Dickensian England. Between 1866 and 1870, for example, the hulk *Nelson* and three other hulks were acquired by the Victorian government to accommodate some of the 1,560 wards then under the care of the government. They joined the fleet of five convict hulks then moored in Hobson's Bay, off Williamstown.[4]

By the 1930s, offenders aged between fifteen and eighteen might be placed in a reformatory school (what would later be called a youth training centre). At that time in Victoria there were two industrial and four reformatory schools, but the Department of Children's Welfare had no institutional homes of its own for neglected children who had been made state wards. In 1936, in the midst of the Great Depression, there were 5,409 neglected children as state wards, and a further 198 children in reformatories.[5]

Given those large numbers, state wardship took several forms: a child might be put in an institutional home, given probation to the care of friends if the child had come from a reformatory school, placed at service or in an apprenticeship, or boarded out to a foster home—placed in what later became known as foster care. The most common practice was for a child to be placed with a foster mother, who received payments for the maintenance of the child while the child remained formally under the responsibility of the department. The payment was twelve shillings and sixpence per week for each child under the age of eighteen months, and seven shillings per week for older children.[6]

This was scarcely adequate, even judged by the standards of the time. In 1936, child welfare payments in Victoria to neglected children boarded out were the lowest in Australia. Contemporary medical evidence estimated 'that the average cost for a normal diet for a child of twelve to fourteen should be 8s 9d, or with the meat ration halved, around 7s 8d. The average child welfare payment in 1936 was 7s 1d, yet this comprised the entire income for many fatherless families.'[7] Deprivation such as this was by no means confined to children dependent upon welfare. In 1935, malnutrition affected up to 25 per cent of children within the boundaries of Melbourne City Council. Of the population of five-year-olds, the figure was 43 per cent.[8]

Through the 1930s about half the state wards were boarded out to foster homes in this way, although the trend was for more and more of them to be cared for in government-approved institutions.[9] In 1936, the Central Mission Training Farm, Tally-Ho; the Methodist Babies Home, South Yarra; and the Salvation Army Girls' Home, East Camberwell, were just three of some 27 institutions in Victoria, most of them run by the churches, that had been approved by the government for the care of some 1,636 state wards.[10] As well as the approved institutions, there were a number of other registered schools and orphanages receiving per capita grants from the government for the care of state wards.

When the case officers of the Children's Welfare Department came to consider Ronald Ryan, their recommendation was that he be placed at St Augustine's orphanage in Geelong, a boys' home registered with the department and run by the Roman Catholic Christian Brothers.[11] But Ron was destined never to go to the orphanage. It was the practice of the then rector of the Salesian Fathers' Home at Sunbury, Father Joseph Dunne, to frequently go to the Boys' Depot and ask if there were 'any Roman Catholic boys needing a home?'[12] Father Dunne was concerned to select boys with some possibility of advancement. It seems that, in early December 1936, Father Dunne made just such a visit, and Ron was the lad he picked out. Ryan was now Children's Welfare Department ward no. 63819, placed at Rupertswood, the Salesian Fathers' Home in Sunbury, from 8 December 1936. His file recorded that he was to be released from institutional care on 21 February 1943, his eighteenth birthday.

Living conditions at Rupertswood in the 1930s were somewhat spartan, which reflected the school's origins. Rupertswood was begun as a school in 1927 by the Salesian Fathers of Don Bosco, a Roman Catholic clerical order founded in Turin in 1874 by Father John Melchior Bosco.[13] Originally the pastoral land of the prominent landowner William John 'Big' Clarke, Rupertswood was the name given to the grand 50-room mansion that was built on the Sunbury property in 1874 by his son, the first Baronet of Rupertswood, Sir William Clarke. The mansion was named for Sir William's nine-year old son Rupert, and became home for him and later members of the Clarke family.[14] In 1927, a subsequent owner negotiated the sale to the Salesians of the mansion, along with 840 acres excised from the total landholding, for the vast sum of £40,000.[15]

Rupertswood was now to become the Salesian Fathers' Home, later Salesian College, the first permanent foundation of the Salesian Order in Australia. However grand the building and its surroundings, the large mortgage debt that buying it had required ensured that the school had extremely difficult beginnings. The Salesians were a very new order in the church, and the small group of Salesians who had arrived in Australia in 1923, most of them Italian and other Europeans, faced severe hardship as they worked to establish the school and pay off the debt for the property. Indeed, in the early years conditions were so harsh that the Salesians were sometimes left with no money in the house, and depended upon catching rabbits for their meals.[16] This is significant for the way in which the home was run in those early years. Taking state wards as pupils, and thereby obtaining from the Department of Children's Welfare the per capita grant (seven shillings per week for each child in 1936), was one way of helping to pay off this debt.[17]

Despite these early hardships, the order managed to consolidate its house at Rupertswood, taking its first pupils in February 1929. Through the 1930s, especially under the legendary Father Joseph Ciantar as rector, the school steadily progressed in furthering the special educative mission of Father Bosco—preparing poor and abandoned youths to take their place in society.[18] As the Sunbury *News* in 1928 put it, referring to the mission of the Rupertswood Salesians: 'Boys who were in danger from perilous surroundings would be taken in hand and placed in the way of an honoured Christian and civic life.' [19] At the time that Ronald Ryan was there, Rupertswood—'Ruppo', as it was known to the boys—is best understood as a school primarily for poor and neglected boys and also, as in Ryan's case, for boys who had shown some anti-social traits but who showed promise of better. Although the Roman Catholic Church was elsewhere involved in running reform schools or reformatories, Rupertswood was not a reformatory, nor was it ever intended to be. Indeed, the Salesians in Victoria had elsewhere resisted church approaches to run a reformatory.[20]

From 1928 to 1957, Rupertswood was a registered charitable institution, and it was an educational institution registered with the Department of Children's Welfare as one appropriate for boys like Ron.[21] A feature of the school that further distinguished it from others was that, as well as a strong scholastic element, it had from the beginning a farming component based on the school's farming land.[22] It did not have agricultural tuition, as such, until the 1950s, but from the early 1930s working boys in the care of lay-Brothers of the order ran a mixed farm running sheep and poultry, and comprising a dairy, piggery, and market garden.

Soon after Ron's arrival at Rupertswood on 8 December 1936, his mother applied to the Children's Welfare Department to have him allowed home for Christmas, as was usually the case with state wards in such institutional care. Responding to the approach, an administrative clerk in the department, Basil Rush, considered the matter. Rush phoned Mitcham Police and spoke to First Constable Matthew Donoghue, who said it would be most unwise to approve such a request 'as in addition to the fact that the boy's offence was so recent, both parents are drunkards and home conditions are bad.' Accepting Constable Donoghue's advice, Rush informed Cecilia that the department could not approve her request.[23]

Whether it was as a result of such a denied request that a further offence was provoked is unknown; in any event, ten days after this joyless Christmas, Ron and another boy, Roy Wolfe, aged twelve, absconded from Rupertswood in the early morning of Sunday, 3 January 1937.[24] From unlocked dormitories where they slept, Ryan and 'Wolfie', as he was known, slipped away from the school before the Brothers were awake. Ron had suggested to Wolfie that he was going to 'nick off', and he had asked him if he wanted to come, too. Wolfe, who had absconded several months before, readily agreed. He wanted to visit his mother in Melbourne. Ryan, on the other hand, told Wolfe he planned never to return to Rupertswood.

Absconding from Rupertswood was a common-enough occurrence, as indeed it was at many of the other homes for neglected children in Victoria. Boys committed to the custody of the Children's Welfare Department periodically ran away, and the police took it seriously. The *Victoria Police Gazette* (the confidential weekly record of criminal offences, police apprehensions, missing persons, and convicted persons released from prison) regularly listed absconding custody boys under the heading 'Escapees'. In 1937, the number of boys absconding from Rupertswood averaged one a fortnight. After Ryan and Wolfe escaped, the *Police Gazette* would list them as escapees and issue descriptions of them. Wolfe was described as a 'Ward of the State, 11 years, 4 ft. 6 in., fair hair and complexion, slight build, blue eyes, wore dark clothes.' Ryan was described as 'Ward of the State, 11 years, 4 ft. 5 in., dark hair and complexion, dark eyes, medium build, wore dark clothes.'[25] This would be the first of many descriptions issued by police describing Ryan as 'Escapee'.

Once clear of the school buildings, Ryan and Wolfe made their way to the railway line just 300 yards from the dormitory. Special trains had stopped on various occasions in the past at Rupertswood, where a railway siding and private wooden platform had been built some time after the mansion was completed in 1876. Ryan and Wolfe waited for a freight train bound for Melbourne and the freight yards at Spencer Street railway station at the western end of the city. Sunbury, about a mile down the line from Rupertswood towards Melbourne, was a water stop. Trains took on coal from the red gum bunkers beside the line, and so the trains commonly slowed as they passed the school. On this Sunday morning, as no trains approached, the boys walked to Sunbury where they found a freight train preparing to depart for Melbourne.

They clambered into an empty grain car and roughly secured the tarpaulin above them. The 25-mile journey to Melbourne was uncomfortable, but passed without incident. When the train arrived at the goods yards at North Melbourne, one stop before their destination, they decided to get off rather than face the railway inspectors they expected to find at Spencer Street. Railway inspectors were an ever-present hazard to errant wayfarers like themselves; the Depression had caused many people to use the railways without paying, and railway detectives were on hand to police the system. Ryan counselled Wolfie that, once out of the freight car, they would have to 'run like hell' to avoid the detectives. Having succeeded, the boys set off to walk the seven miles to Wolfe's narrow two-storey terrace house at 159 Camberwell Road, East Hawthorn. They accomplished this task before midday.

Pleased as she was to see Roy, Mrs Wolfe insisted that he would have to return to Rupertswood. A short, attractive woman with greying hair, Henrietta Wolfe had endured personal hardship in her 42 years: Roy's father was an alcoholic, and he frequently beat Henrietta. A bully of a man, he took to Roy as well.[26] Mrs Wolfe gave the boys some bread and dripping to eat. After they had spent the afternoon at her house, she sent them on their way in the early evening, expecting—incredibly—that they somehow would make their way back to Rupertswood. The boys had other ideas.

Heading back towards the city from the Wolfes' house opposite the Camberwell tram depot, they walked a mile and a half along Camberwell Road to Farey Brothers' Bakery in Liddiard Street, Hawthorn. Farey's was an establishment well known to small boys for making the best cakes in the district.[27] It was by now Sunday evening around 8:30, and the bakery was, of course, closed. With high brick walls and no windows on the street, the bakery offered little opportunity for them to sample the wares. Undaunted, they hurried back to another well-known cake shop, The Buttercup, at 825 Burke Road,

Hawthorn, near the Camberwell junction, owned by a man known to all around simply as Devvey. Here they found many cakes in evidence, baked ready for Monday morning. Ron found a short iron bar in the backyard of the shop, and jemmied open the back door. When the pair emerged, Ryan had two large seven-penny jam tarts; Wolfie had four smaller ones.

Later, as they sauntered up Burke Road eating the tarts, the boys were approached by three plain-clothed policemen on bicycles, Detective Constables Frank Jordan, George Lamont, and Doug Trainor, all of whom were stationed at the Criminal Investigation Branch at Camberwell. As a local lad of errant ways, Wolfe was well known to these policemen and they to him. As the detectives drew close, Lamont called out: 'Hang on, you fellas, we want to see you!' Ryan tried to make a break for it, but Lamont was too quick; grabbing Ryan by the scruff of the neck, he gathered him up while the other two detectives cornered Wolfe. Aware, of course, that Wolfe was a state ward, the detectives were suspicious. 'What are you fellas doing here?', Lamont enquired. Noticing the cakes, he answered his own question. 'Don't tell me! Either be Farey's or the Buttercup that you'd get 'em.' After a few moments thought, he added: 'Well, you might as well finish them off, then.'

The boys did some fast talking. They had been to Wolfe's house, they said. Mrs. Wolfe had given them the cakes. They had done nothing wrong, and now they were on their way home. Highly suspicious, but distracted by more pressing duties than interrogating twelve-year-old boys about jam tarts, the detectives reluctantly let them go.[28] By now Ryan and Wolfe were exhausted by their adventure, and wanted only to rest. Mrs Wolfe would not have them back, so they looked around for somewhere to hide out till morning. A nearby motor garage proved the best prospect, and the pair broke in and were soon fast asleep. Their sleep was short-lived, however, when they were disturbed by Detective First Constable Ernest James of Camberwell CIB, who promptly arrested them.[29]

Before long, the boys found themselves in the lock-up at the Camberwell Police Station, where it was learned from Ryan, who confessed, that both offenders were escapees from the Salesian Fathers Home at Sunbury.[30] So their escapade had failed. Now they were to be returned to Ruppo, where punishment doubtless awaited them for having absconded. There was an unexpected pleasure, however, as they waited in the cells behind the sergeant's house adjoining the station at 58 Riversdale Road, Camberwell as the sergeant arranged their return. Thomas 'Tommy' Gunn was the station sergeant, a 50-year-old decorated returned serviceman from World War I, who had been in the police force since he was twenty years old, and was an old hand.[31]

Sergeant Gunn's wife Elizabeth brought the boys a roast dinner—meat and potatoes, and all the trimmings. 'Don't do anything foolish,' Mrs Gunn counselled as she sat them down to eat. 'I'm going back inside and I'll bring you some scones shortly.'[32] She was as good as her word, and so were the boys. It was after midnight by the time they had finished eating and were taken by police car to the Boys' Depot at Royal Park.[33]

It took a week for authorities to act but, finally, on 12 January 1937, Ryan and Wolfe were returned to Rupertswood to face their punishment.[34] At Rupertswood punishment was taken seriously by the Brothers, although it was less severe than the disciplinary regimes at schools and institutions run by other orders. Minor misbehaviour might bring kitchen duty, commonly peeling bags of potatoes. Unruly behaviour or swearing might bring a caning, usually six strokes of the cane on the backside, with perhaps an additional penalty for frequent offences of a prohibition on visitors for a month or two. In such cases, the monthly Visitors' Sunday would be banned.[35] What lay in store for the boys, however, was a more dreaded punishment, known to them as knee drill. This was meted out by the Brothers for more serious misdemeanours. A boy who had absconded, or who was otherwise recalcitrant, would be made to kneel upright on both knees in a corner for half an hour or more. The pressure on the knees so caused was excruciatingly painful. When Ryan and Wolfe were returned to Rupertswood, they were made to do knee drill.[36]

At this stage, too, it seems that court proceedings arising out of the break-in at Camberwell during the escape were being contemplated. The Department of Children's Welfare wrote to Ron's mother, seeking further information about his background and family.[37] Cecilia responded several days later in a letter in which she recalled the theft of the watch at Mitcham, and rather astutely commented upon the Camberwell break-in:

> The charges against Ronald should in the first case have been larceny from ... [Mrs. Noase's] dwelling, as he did not break into

> the house, as the door was not locked only closed, and in the second case, he says he was only sleeping in a motor garage at Camberwell. So it should have been illegally on the premises.[38]

In the event, no charges were laid against Ryan and Wolfe arising out of their escape and the break-in at Camberwell.

With the commencement of the school year 1937, Ronald was placed in a grade-six class under the watchful tutelage of Brother John Brennan, a caring young Brother and a gifted teacher.[39] There were, perhaps, 70 or 80 boys at Rupertswood at that time, and Ron was placed in a class of nine other boys. Although he had taken his first communion at St John's in Mitcham in 1936, he was also baptised again.[40] His progress in class was not promising, and the Rupertswood Fathers were soon fearful of Ron's prospects.[41] On 21 April, Father Bortolo Fedrigotti, SC, prefect at Rupertswood, sent a letter to the Children's Welfare Department.[42] This was the first of several plaintive letters to the department concerning Ron. It read:

> I beg to report that Master Ron Ryan and Peter Cortina, of your Department have absconded this morning. It is very doubtful whether Ryan is going to settle down.[43]

The *Police Gazette* duly recorded the absconding of these twelve-year-old boys. According to the entry for Ryan, he had grown more than twelve inches in three months (he was now described as being five foot six inches in height), and his hair and complexion were now described as 'fair'.[44] Despite the obvious inaccuracy of this description, Ron was quickly identified, apprehended, and returned to Rupertswood, this time on the day of his escape.[45] His escape this second time brought a harsher penalty than the first, a punishment that was not uncommon for custody boys who frequently absconded: his hair was cut off and his head clean-shaved. While head shaving was sometimes a last-resort treatment for head-lice, the reason in Ron's case could not be mistaken. The purpose of this punishment was that a boy who repeatedly absconded could be more easily recognised and apprehended if he repeated the offence. As Ron was the Rupertswood boy who at this time seemed most likely to escape again, he alone had his head shaved.[46] The other boys dubbed him 'Baldy' Ryan, and the nickname stuck: he was called Baldy for the remainder of his term at Rupertswood.[47]

Meanwhile, Ron's academic work was soon so improved under Brother Brennan that he rose from ninth out of ten in his class in first term 1937 to first out of nine in second term. In first term, his weakest subjects were written arithmetic, for which he scored 4 out of twenty, and mental arithmetic, for which he scored 5 out of twenty. His best subjects in term two showed a pattern of interest that he maintained throughout his life: religious knowledge, for which his mark was 19 out of twenty; reading and recitation, 18 out of twenty; and dictation and spelling, 18 out of twenty. He finished term two with an 80 per cent average result over sixteen subjects. By the end of the year, Ron had consolidated his scholastic work, although his marks for conduct and diligence—both 9 out of twenty—betrayed a restless and oppositional attitude. He finished second in his class at the Christmas exams with a 59 per cent average, and Brother Brennan recommended his promotion to grade seven.[48]

The year had been productive in many ways, although separation from his family wounded him deeply. Boys at Rupertswood seldom had visitors, and Ryan was no exception. His mother visited him only once during 1937 and, apart from one or two more visits, she would not do so again during his period at Rupertswood. Ron's father never visited him at all during the whole of his stay. On the other hand, George, Violet, Irma, and Gloria visited several times in those first few months until the winter of 1937. Once, having mistakenly boarded an express train for Bendigo, almost 80 miles beyond Sunbury, George and the girls had to plead with a conductor to stop the train at Sunbury so they could see Ron at Rupertswood. Their pleas and their tears succeeded, and there was a joyful reunion when they made it to the school.[49]

The winter of 1937 was to bring the last of the family visits to Ron for more than a year. By now, Cecilia's alcoholism had grown worse, largely in response to the increased level of violence from Jack, who had become very seriously ill and was drinking still more heavily. Each fortnightly pension day, Jack would go on a binge, arrive home drunk, and beat Cecilia. On Saturdays, the pair would usually be dead drunk.[50] For several years as a child, Irma had headaches on Saturdays, fearing the situation she would have to endure.

Irma responded by a retreat into fantasy. In her imaginative world, she was Linda Jane Morgan, a rich girl who had all the things that she longed for: a bountiful mother, a kindly distinguished father, fine clothes, and lots to eat. Never going without anything, that is how life was for Linda Jane. Irma was to return again and again to this fantasy when the harshness of life made her feel miserable. Once when she chided her father about his drinking, Jack cruelly tagged her with an epithet for the police he despised. 'Copper-girl', he called her. It was a wound she nursed as Linda Jane Morgan, who had nice parents who never said hurtful things like that.[51] Eventually, Jack became so violent that he began threatening even the girls, and in June 1937 George finally contacted the local Mitcham police, who in turn called the Children's Welfare Department.[52]

Their response was swift. At the Children's Court sitting at Ringwood on 28 June 1937, Violet, Irma, and Gloria were themselves made wards of state. The care-and-protection application made to the court charged that they were 'neglected children with unfit guardianship.'[53] On that same day, the girls were taken from their parents to the Girls' Depot in Royal Park before decisions were made about their wardship placements. Violet was then ten years old, Irma was almost seven, and Gloria was just two weeks short of her sixth birthday. Several weeks after their committal from Ringwood, all three girls were placed at St Catherine's Orphanage in Geelong.[54] Although for the younger girls the committal to an institutional home meant forcibly being taken away from their mother, for Violet the move was not altogether an unwelcome one. She was pleased to be away from the domestic violence and the drunkenness, and she looked forward to the new opportunities St Catherine's might bring. 'Will I be able to learn to play the piano in the orphanage?', she asked George.[55]

The girls could no longer visit Ron, but at least with Christmas approaching the prospect of spending the holidays at home was rekindled. In fact, after losing all of her children to wardships, Cecilia made a brave attempt to improve her situation. She had left Jack at Mitcham and taken a position as housekeeper with Douglas and Theadora Blackwell and their family at Garfield in Gippsland, on the Princes Highway, some 80 miles south-east of Melbourne.[56] From Garfield, Cecilia moved back to Melbourne, where she took a further position as housekeeper for a man named Croaker living at 29 Park Street, Abbotsford. With her living conditions thus improved, Cecilia sought to have her children returned to her, as she had first done whilst at

Garfield. In a plaintive letter to the secretary of the Children's Welfare Department, John Henry, Cecilia pointed out that Croaker was willing for her to have all her children with her, as she had been 'caring for his four little children so well':

> Mr. Croaker here has plenty of furniture and accommodation and as it is better for me to be earning my keep here and having the use of everything I thought I would write and ask if you would please let me have my children now. If not all of them at once surely you will give me little Gloria as she has such a terrible time with abscesses and I know it is only through fretting over me and she will never be well until you let her come to me.[57]
>
> I am away from my husband and got a good position and home and can give you good references from both the people I worked for at Gippsland and this man here to say how well I looked after both homes and children during the mother's absence.
>
> I worry so much over the children and especially Gloria that I will be ill if you do not let me have just one of them and Ron is anxious to come home for Xmas. We are all going to Bendigo to Mr. Croaker's relations. If you let me have Gloria and Ron I will take them with me and if the other two could just come for the Xmas holidays, Mr. Croaker will go responsible for them.
>
> Please let me know as soon as possible … Hoping you will let me have Gloria soon.[58]

Cecilia's entreaties fell on deaf bureaucratic ears. Henry replied that the answer to her request was 'No'. The department did not consider it advisable at present to return her children to her care, although there would be some consideration of Ron being able to spend the Christmas holidays at home.[59] Somewhat encouraged about having Ron for the holidays, Cecilia then applied to the department for approval for that to happen, and the views of the Rupertswood authorities were sought.[60] The prefect at Rupertswood, Father Fedrigotti, subsequently reported that Ron had 'improved and [there are] no objections to him having proposed holiday at home.'[61]

The department was not yet ready to agree, however. June 1937 had brought an outbreak in Melbourne of an epidemic of poliomyelitis—infantile paralysis as it was then called, because it struck at children in particular. State health authorities were alarmed at its high mortality and the permanent crippling of survivors. In the words of a later official history of Victorian education, the epidemic 'struck terror in the schools [as] the number of cases increased with frightening rapidity.'[62] When school holidays started in December 1937, more than four hundred Victorian schools were wholly or partially closed. In what was the worst poliomyelitis outbreak in the state's history, 2,096 cases of polio among children were reported in 1937-38, of whom some 113 died.[63]

In those circumstances, the Department of Children's Welfare took measures to ensure that living conditions for wards spending the holidays in Melbourne were such as not to put them at risk of the disease. Following an urgent request from the administrative clerk responsible for such matters as holiday visits, just two weeks before Christmas a departmental inspector visited Mrs Ryan regarding the 'suitability of accommodation and conditions in her home' for Ron's holiday.[64] The inspector, Mary Lavelle, subsequently made a report on Mrs Ryan, who was now renting a single room at 388 Queens Street, Melbourne, having moved from Abbotsford and resumed living with Jack. Of Cecilia's room, Lavelle said in her report:

> It was clean and tidy at the time of my visit. Mrs. Ryan informed me that her husband's pension has been restored; he is also engaged selling seedlings at Victoria Market. He works four days a week; his average earnings are 15 shillings per day. [Mrs. Ryan] also earns 12 shillings per day. I saw Mrs. Flynn from whom [Mrs. Ryan] is renting the room. She will provide a room for Ronald, the person who has it now will be away for the holidays.
>
> | | |
> |---|---|
> | Husband earn | £3. 0. 0 |
> | Hus. pen. M[iners Pthisis]. - Fund | 10. 0 |
> | [Mrs. Ryan] earns | £2. 8. 0 |
> | | £5.18. 0 |
>
> Rent 10/-
>
> [Mrs. Ryan] rather surprised me regarding her income. I questioned her closely. She said that the amount was correct.[65]

After noting on the file that Ron's holiday could be approved if his mother and father were to be home each day during the holiday to supervise him, an official requested Cecilia to call into the department's offices in the Railways Building in Flinders Street to sign an apparently obligatory indemnity form. Dated 20 December 1937, this grotesque departmental document read:

> In consideration of my son Ronald Ryan being permitted to spend the Xmas vacation from 23-12-37 until 10-1-38 in my care, I hereby indemnify the Secretary of the Children's Welfare Department against all responsibility in the event of his contracting Infantile Paralysis .
>
> (Signed) Eveline C. Ryan, 388 Queen Street, Melbourne.[66]

When he had witnessed her signature, the official explained to Mrs Ryan the times for her to meet Ron and return him to Rupertswood. Adding a further indignity, she was instructed, according to policy, to send a shilling to Rupertswood for his fare.[67] And so, two days before Christmas, Ron was included among those boys to be brought by train to Melbourne, where his mother met him.[68] Happily for the peace of mind of the Children's Welfare Department, this twelve-year-old's two-and-a-half weeks' holiday was spent uneventfully—and he did not contract polio.

At the end of the holidays, Ron returned to Rupertswood to be placed in the seventh grade. By now he seemed to have adapted to the school; he was well liked by some boys, although feared by others. Some of those who liked him seem to have hero-worshipped him to some extent. Separated from their families as they were, many of the boys wanted to abscond, and so Ron's escapes only added to his stature with some of them. Athletic, aggressively assertive and adventurous, Ryan was looked upon as a tough kid and something of a natural leader, although he was sometimes a bully to younger boys.[69] Ryan at the age of eleven or twelve was frequently combative: he fought with everybody at Rupertswood including, at times, younger boys aged nine or ten, who were known as the bubbas.[70]

Nonetheless, in 1938 he was made captain of the Rupertswood football team and won the trophy for best and fairest for the season. A contemporary of Ryan's at Rupertswood, John King, confirms Ryan's achievement as captain of both the football and cricket teams, further describing him as an all-round athlete.[71] And, like all the other boys, he sang in the school choir and was an altar boy.[72] Many years later, Ryan would write that, in this period, under the influence of Father John

Cerutti, whom he considered 'a saintly person', he had thought about becoming a priest.[73] This was a common response among the boys. This new-found focus by Ryan had a good academic outcome. By the May exams in that year his marks for diligence and conduct reflected his new stability and progress: 100 per cent and 90 per cent respectively. His class average was now 84 per cent.[74]

Ron's parents' life conditions were a little better, too. They had moved from Queen Street, Melbourne to a larger freestanding timber house at 66 Hickford Street, East Brunswick.[75] After a number of appeals to the department, Cecilia convinced it to allow the girls to be returned to her care, and on 2 July 1938 they were given home release, pending permanent discharge if things went well.[76] Violet, Irma, and Gloria were pleased to be home. Their mother and father had visited them only once during their eleven months at St Catherine's. Cecilia had several times sent small gifts, but it was not the same as a family visit. On the solitary visit to St Catherine's, Jack had mortified the girls by cursing the nuns for—as he believed—breaking Gloria's Shirley Temple doll. However miserable home life was, there they could be close to their mother once more.

The pleasure of being home again soon turned sour, however. Jack and Cecilia's drinking began again, and before long the old patterns of life emerged: both parents getting drunk, Jack beating Cecilia, and the children being left hungry. Food had never been plentiful, but at Hickford Street the children were often starving. Gloria, then aged seven, was so hungry that she braved the taunts of a neighbour's child as she picked her way through insect-infested bread that the neighbour kept for the chooks.[77]

Sometimes Cecilia would have fits of alcoholic remorse, and frantically scrub the house from top to bottom. But as the beatings and misery persisted, so did her drinking return. Within four months it was obvious that she could not cope with the three girls and, at the direction of the Children's Welfare Department, their wardships were resumed. Hence, on 24 November 1938, all three were taken back to the Girls' Depot at Royal Park, where they were to spend the next six months before long-term arrangements could be made for them.[78]

As this took place, Ron had continued to make scholastic progress at Rupertswood. His average over eighteen subjects at the term-two exams had risen to 88 per cent. However, he failed the externally conducted

Merit exam at the end of the year because of fails in Maths and Arithmetic, which were always his worst subjects.[79] As he contemplated having to repeat seventh grade in 1939, Ron learned that the worsened home conditions, which had brought about the removal of Violet, Irma, and Gloria to institutional care once more, would prevent him spending Christmas holidays at home.

On 13 December 1938, Cecilia received a letter from Edward Pittard, the successor to the recently retired John Henry as secretary of the Children's Welfare Department, indicating that Ron would not be allowed home for the holidays. This letter was based upon advice from his department which said that 'in view of Police reports, etc, ... concerning this mother and her home and recent removal of other children, this proposed holiday cannot be approved.'[80] Cecilia, who was now living at 34 Capel Street, West Melbourne, immediately appealed against this decision, pointing out that 'last Xmas the circumstances [of his holiday] were exactly the same …' and requesting that, in the event of his not coming, Ron spend the holidays with George.[81] Responding to this appeal, a departmental official telephoned First Constable Henry McGuinness of Brunswick East Police Station who, it was believed, knew the family well. Constable McGuinness reported that George had 'been concerned in brawls and drunken parties at his mother's home (when she was living in East Brunswick),' and he informed the official that he did 'not consider [George] a fit person to have charge of this boy for a holiday.' The official's advice was 'Refuse still.'[82] On the basis of this advice, Cecilia's appeal was not approved.[83] Ron would have to spend the summer at Rupertswood.

This denial proved a decisive spur to Ron's long-held wish to escape from his wardship. He had mixed feelings about Ruppo; he had made many friends, and he was looked up to by some of the other boys. In some ways a natural leader—perhaps through fear that he aroused in younger lads—he had more sway with the boys than some of the Brothers.[84] But his attitude was that, however cruel and tormenting life had been with his mother and father, home and family were preferable to this institutional existence, and he longed to be able to provide a family home for himself and his sisters. John King has written of Ryan's 'all-possessing thought [of] how he could get his sisters out of the convent where they were placed and give them the same opportunities as other girls of their age.'[85] Escaping to provide a home for his mother and his sisters would become a significant refrain. 'The worst home is always better than the best institution' expressed Ryan's attitude. Like most of the boys, he lived for the time when he could be reunited with his family.

While it was certainly not a loveless environment, conditions were harsh at Rupertswood even by the Depression standards of 1938.[86] Meals were usually thin gruel, with little or no cereal or porridge, dry bread and honey, stew and potatoes, and *blancmange* custard. Despite the mixed farm at the school, eggs and fruit and milk were rarely, if ever, to be had by either Salesians or boys, as almost all of the farm produce had to be sold to pay the mortgage debt of the school. There were wood-slat beds for the bed-wetters, and the dormitories were cold and dank.[87] The deprived conditions experienced by the boys were on occasions brought home to them in unwelcome ways. Among such occasions were the visits of the Roman Catholic social club, the Knights of the Southern Cross, who—in a group perhaps a thousand strong—had held their annual picnic at Rupertswood since 1929, and who were generous contributors to Salesian funds.[88] Some of the Knights used to throw lollies and sometimes pennies into the air for the boys to scramble and fight over. Although well meant, this demeaning enterprise was bitterly resented by some of the boys.[89]

In 1939 Ryan became one of what were known as the working boys at Rupertswood. When boys turned fourteen, and hence had reached the legal age at which they could leave school, they were sent to work in the fields, learning farming by doing the agricultural work on the farm that sustained the school. It was the practice of the Salesian Fathers throughout the year to give the boys a good-conduct star, essentially an asterisk on a slip of paper. These good-conduct slips, worth sixpence per asterisk, were redeemable at the so-called mission store, essentially a school tuck shop in a large cupboard, run by the Fathers and open once a week. By the time of the Royal Agricultural Show in September 1939—less than a month after the outbreak of war in Europe—the working boys had all cashed their conduct slips ready for their visit to Melbourne and the Show, and they had put the money in their lockers ready for the big trip.[90]

Early on Monday, 26 September, Ryan adopted a course that would effectively put him outside the law for a long time, and would bring about a decisive break from his peers. In company with another ward of state, James Sullivan, aged thirteen, Ron rifled the working boys' lockers and stole the money in them—some ten shillings in silver coins—as well as a pair of trousers and a coat.[91] Ron then took a bicycle and, with Sullivan, rode to the railway station at Diggers Rest, several miles to the south. When he reached the station, Ron hit Sullivan over the head with a soft-drink bottle and made off with all the money, leaving Sullivan and the bicycle on the side of the road.[92] From Diggers Rest, Ron took the train to Melbourne and made his way to South Melbourne, where George was living in a rented room in Cecil Street.[93] Sullivan rode on towards Melbourne before abandoning the bicycle in the outer-northern suburb of Broadmeadows, where it was later found by local police.[94] Sullivan was traced by police some two weeks after the escape.[95]

Ron was pleased to see George. Now 24 years old, George was again working for sustenance payments undertaking manual work on projects such as the sports grounds around South Melbourne, for which, as an itinerant unemployed male, he received seventeen shillings and sixpence per week. At this time there were more than 14,000 Victorians working for susso.[96] When Ron arrived at his room that night, he told George that he had run away from Rupertswood and was never going back.[97] He also said so in a letter to the rector, Father Ciantar, which he sent within a few days. With extreme bitterness, Ron set out a litany of injustices he felt he had suffered at Rupertswood. Spiced with obscene language, Ron said that Rupertswood was a prison, that he had been harshly treated, and he swore retribution against the Fathers. He concluded with a message to the Fathers to 'get stuffed'.[98]

When he received the letter, Father Ciantar rang the school bell summoning the boys, and read it out to them. When he had finished, Father Ciantar cannily pinned the letter on the school notice-board, adding: 'If any boy wants to go and follow Ryan, you're welcome to go, but you'll never come back to this place!'[99] None did. Neither would Ron ever return to Rupertswood. His theft of the Show Week money had set the boys against him, the vitriolic and crude language of his denunciations did not impress them, and there were no volunteers to follow him.[100]

Now aged fourteen-and-a-half, Ron had become a tortured and unhappy soul at Rupertswood. He had not had much of a life, he was listed in a police bulletin as an escapee, and worse was still to come. But by his escape Ryan had forced an end to his wardship.

CHAPTER THREE

Manhood

[Ron] was like a husband and father to us.
—Cecilia Ryan

After absconding from Rupertswood, Ron stayed with George for more than two months in South Melbourne, from late September to early December 1939, sleeping on the floor in his room. In that time they talked about and planned how they might find work, and especially how they might help Ron avoid police and the children's welfare authorities.[1] The idea was conceived that they go to Balranald in New South Wales, 540 miles west of Sydney on the Murrumbidgee River near where it joins the Murray.

George had been to Balranald several years before, doing seasonal work picking peas, beans, and tomatoes. George's room-mate in Cecil Street had recently been to Balranald, and it was at his suggestion that George and Ron decided to seek seasonal work there. An additional reason commending it was that the township was in New South Wales and, hence, outside the jurisdiction of the Victorian Children's Welfare Department. To make the trip they would have to ride bicycles, as any other way was too expensive. So George bought Ron a second-hand bike for ten shillings. Soon after, early in December 1939, they set off on the journey to Balranald.[2]

What should have been a direct distance of a little over 300 miles became one-third as much again as they took a route through the less-populous mountain country to the east and north-east of Melbourne to avoid the notice of police or others who might have barred their progress. The ride would have been an arduous one under any conditions, but rural Victoria and southern New South Wales were then still in severe drought; 1938 had seen only two to four inches of rainfall in northern Victoria.[3] Earlier in 1939 disastrous bushfires had raged in various parts of the state. On Friday, 13 January 1939, the so-called Black Friday bushfires had devastated almost five million acres of Victorian bush, such that practically the entire mountain country of Victoria was ablaze with bushfires. Judge Leonard Stretton, appointed a royal commissioner to conduct an inquiry into the Black Friday devastation, was later to write that 'on that day it appeared that the whole State was alight … [it was] the most disastrous forest calamity the State of Victoria has known.'[4]

In the north-east of Melbourne, George and Ron rode through still-blackened forests, mute symbols of fires which twelve months before had claimed 71 lives and destroyed more than one thousand houses.[5] They covered the journey from Melbourne to Balranald in five days, riding 60 to 80 miles a day, living off handouts from people in return for work. They usually camped on riverbanks, or slept under a tree or a bridge.[6] Despite the outbreak of war and the large-scale enlistment of soldiers, the effects of the Depression were still being felt, especially in rural areas. George and Ron were sleeping rough, as were scores of other people. The road made many friends.

In Balranald, which was situated on a flat saltbush and mallee plain, they found that the drought affecting New South Wales was also very severe. The Murrumbidgee River ran dry in 1939 for the only time since records had been kept. At the time Balranald was a town of around one thousand inhabitants, with a local economy historically based on wool growing and the river trade.[7] At first, George and Ron found casual work picking tomatoes, but the season soon ended and they were forced to re-assess their prospects.[8]

Now almost fifteen years old, Ron was an appealing lad. Before long he was taken on by Harry Sylvester on his dairy farm Riverlea, not far out of Balranald. Ron was to be a general farmhand. He was to be paid ten shillings a week plus board, which meant he shared a room with young Frankie Sylvester, Harry's five-year-old son. Harry and his wife Nance had three other children: Mavis, thirteen; Kathleen, eleven; and a toddler, Ann, aged three. Ron and the Sylvesters, honest, hard-working bush battlers, quickly struck up a close relationship, and before long Ron was regarded as one of the family.[9]

With Ron now well looked after, George felt able to leave him for a time when he went to Mildura picking grapes in February 1940. After being with the Sylvesters for a few months, Ron began to look around for more profitable work. He talked with 'Old Jack' Grey, a local steam-engine hand, and decided that he would stay with the Sylvesters but would try wood-cutting. Harry Sylvester arranged with a neighbour, Les Purtill, for Ron to cut wood for their joint irrigation steam pump. This involved cutting three-feet lengths of Murray red gum, for which he was paid three shillings and sixpence per ton. Working ten hours a day, Ron could cut and stack up to eight tons; his earnings were thus raised from ten shillings a week to almost thirty shillings a day. However, it was while he was cutting timber that Ron sustained an injury that substantially limited his vision. He was cutting red gum with George one day when sap spurted into his left eye as he struck the tree. Although he wiped it out, some sap remained and caused the eye to ulcerate. When he sought medical treatment some time later, it was too late; the damage had been done, and he had substantially impaired the sight of his eye. The injury also caused the lid permanently to droop a little, giving him something of a furtive appearance.[10]

This period—doing physically demanding work outdoors, and earning reasonably good money—was the happiest of Ron's life. He had a family who took care of him and, in George, he had a benign father-figure from whom he could draw strength and stability. During this time he also formed an attachment to Mavis Sylvester. Their relationship was to last several years; indeed, everyone expected that one day they would be married. Mavis was an attractive young girl of fourteen when Ron first took up with her. They would go on outings together, often to the Royal Picture Theatre in Balranald.[11]

Apart from the demands of work and the pleasures of courtship, in a small town like Balranald there was not much to do for a lad like Ron. By the time he was fourteen or fifteen he had fallen into gambling on the weekends at Condos' cafe next door to the Royal, playing poker or euchre with the locals. At first his gambling was social and small scale, but later he turned to punting on horses by placing bets with the local SP bookmaker in the Shamrock Hotel. He usually lost his money.[12]

In 1942 Ron took up bike riding as a sport. He dispensed with his old bike, bought himself a decent racing-machine, and began regular practice on long rides around the district, almost always alone. Soon he was good enough to race competitively, and entered track and road events at towns along the Murray: Euston, Mildura, Swan Hill, and Kerang, and especially at Nyah, which held an annual New Year's Day road race. Ron developed into a strong rider, and he won quite a few races. The highlight of his bike riding came in January 1944 when, for the first time, he won the feature New Year's Day race. Years later he admitted that he had not ridden to his potential in the lead-up races in order to improve his gambling odds later on. Years later he wrote:

> [I] recall smiling at myself after a bike race when Irma expressed her amazement that I hadn't won after her prayers. I was running dead, but on New Year's Day I won every race on the program.[13]

On that night Ron was the toast of Balranald.[14]

If Ron's unsporting inclinations passed unnoticed, his athletic and cycling skills, and organising enthusiasm were recognised when, in June 1944, he was elected the foundation secretary of the newly created Balranald Amateur Cycle and Athletic Club. There were 25 members present at the inaugural meeting of the club, and it is testimony to the regard in which he was held locally that this nineteen-year-old was elected secretary. This was to be the start of a very productive and successful period of office for Ron as he and his committee set about organising a fixture of cycling and athletic events.[15]

For the remainder of 1944, at least, the local paper was seldom without a notice over Ron's name of coming events organised by the club and staged at the Balranald Recreation Reserve: Australian Rules football matches, cycle road races, foot races and field events for junior and senior athletes, boxing matches, as well as novelty events for young and old. Ron frequently figured prominently in these events as a competitor, excelling at cycling on track and road, but also winning a number of foot races and playing football. He was one of those who chose the teams to play in a charity football match for the Red Cross.

The innovation of a five-mile road cycling event saw Ron placed fourth at its first staging, and in a very short time he was regularly winning road races. At one meeting in July 1944 he won both the four-lap senior bicycle race and the senior fifteen-lap race, while Mavis Sylvester won the Slow Cycle race for girls. Ron was soon the scratch marker in these events, but he continued to win them anyway. He was such a keen competitor that on one afternoon in September 1944 Ron won the Open Cycle race and the 100-yard dash, and was second in the eight-lap Open Cycle race.[16]

During this period Ron's sisters' situation had changed as well. After spending six months in 1938 at the Girls' Depot in Royal Park, Violet, Irma, and Gloria had been finally placed in May 1939 at the Convent of the Good Shepherd in Abbotsford. This institution was run by the Little Sisters of the Poor, an order devoted to the care of poor and orphaned girls.[17] Here Ron's sisters were placed in classes with other state wards. To the Ryan girls the convent was a rigid and repressive environment; although the nuns were capable of great charity and love, the convent regimen was harsh and authoritarian. Certainly the Ryan girls experienced it as a guilt-inducing religious institution. From the windows of the convent, Irma, now ten years old, could see the working girls as they arrived for work in the woollen mill down the street. She was told not to look at them because factory girls were said to be wicked. These repressive attitudes took other forms. Violet was told during the war that looking at a black man would result in a terrible disease. Irma was also led to believe that kissing a man would bring horrific consequences.

Even though the girls had their favourites among the nuns, the convent was pervaded by an atmosphere of fear and shame. Living conditions at the convent were spartan. Breakfast was thin gruel, often with weevils; lunch was stew or cottage pie; and tea would be pumpkin. Usually seconds could be had by the girls as a reward for shelling peas, and the chore of scrubbing the wooden verandah would bring a biscuit. Saturday nights brought a small treat when the girls were given two pieces of bread and honey. At Christmas, roast and jelly was the order of the day. Cecilia would visit the girls at the convent, and sometimes Jack came, too, although the girls had mixed feelings about visits from their parents. Pleased as she was to see them, Irma worried that her mother 'wouldn't be dressed nice' and that her father would be 'full'.[18]

Violet was to spend almost three years at Abbotsford until March 1942 when, still under the responsibility of the department, she 'entered service' as the maid of Mary Nunan, the wife of a manager, Vincent Nunan, at 67 Park Street, Moonee Ponds, in Melbourne's north-western suburbs.[19] Placing girls in service was a departmental policy at this time in order to prepare state wards for the workforce.[20] Violet's earnings were paid into a special account and were made available to her when she ended her wardship. When Mary Nunan took holidays with her friend, Miss Hanna, in the countryside at Kangaroo Flat, Violet went with her. Altogether she spent eighteen months in service until June 1943 when she was discharged on probation to her mother, who was then living at 13 Byron Street, North Melbourne. Her discharge was to become permanent on 28 July 1944. Irma and Gloria were to spend longer periods at Abbotsford. For them it would be five-and-a-half years before they were discharged from their wardships. Irma would be fifteen years old when she was given probationary discharge to her mother in December 1944. Gloria would be thirteen years old. Through no fault of her own, she would spend over seven years, more than half her young life, in institutional care.

The situation that brought about the early discharge from wardship of Violet, Irma, and Gloria was that by 1945 Ron had earned enough money to bring his sisters and mother to Balranald to a home that he had established. At that time, of course, Violet was on probationary discharge from her wardship, but Irma and Gloria still had several years to their notional discharge. It was, in fact, a request by Ron—a rather audacious one, given his own history with the department—which brought about the girls' early discharge from their wardships. Now beyond the notional expiration of his own wardship, which had been reached in February 1943, Ron wrote to the Department of Children's Welfare and convinced them that the home he had created in Balranald for his family was such as to allow their wardships to be terminated. His plea to the department dwelt on the theme of preserving family unity and safeguarding the family. In Irma's case, her notional discharge was almost three years away; Gloria was still four-and-a-half years away.[21]

In order for that move to be effected, Ron sought to persuade Cecilia to leave the marriage with Jack—this time for good. According to his siblings, the ultimatum was delivered after an incident in which Jack pawned furniture and cutlery that Ron had bought for her. Ron insisted that he get it out of pawn, and forced the issue with his mother. Although Ron defended his father to his sisters (and anyone else for that matter), Cecilia would have to choose between Jack and Ron. She chose to go with Ron, to a small house Ron had set up in Church Street,

Balranald, where she would be sober for more than a year.[22] Cecilia would much later describe this period as one where Ron had made a home for her and his sisters: 'He was like a husband and father to us.'[23] Before they left Melbourne, Ron insisted that the girls go to see their seriously ill father in the upstairs room he rented in a terrace house at 137 Peel Street, North Melbourne. It was the last time they would see him.[24]

By now Ron had accomplished much of what he had set out to achieve. He was a successful sportsman in the local competitions, and he was respected as an effective organiser of the Athletic Club. More importantly, he had earned enough money to set up a new home for his mother and sisters, and he had realised his 'all possessing' dream of re-uniting them in Balranald. His life prospects looked bright, indeed. But, just as he seemed to be flying in this period of his life, his gambling led him into wrongdoing.

It was evidently to pay gambling debts to the local SP bookmaker that, in 1945, Ryan set out to commit his first major crime, a break-in and failed attempted robbery of the Bank of New South Wales on the corner of Court and Myall Streets, Balranald.[25] During the course of the attempted robbery Ryan was discovered upon leaving the premises by the bank manager, whom he hit over the head with a piece of wood from a wood pile. Undaunted, the manager grappled with Ryan and fired a shot at him as he sought to escape over the back fence, but the shot missed. Ryan escaped, but was subsequently interviewed by police and seems to have been the prime suspect. Ron claimed to police that he was in the bush cutting timber when the attempted robbery took place, and George corroborated his story. Perhaps for lack of hard evidence that would stand up in court or perhaps because of George's alibi, Ryan was never prosecuted for this offence. It was a significant escape.[26]

Later, this bank-robbery attempt was an important factor in losing Mavis, his long-standing girlfriend. This occurred when Ron briefly came to Melbourne. On his return he found that Mavis had taken up with another local boy. There is some evidence to suggest that Mavis's mother, Nance, had influenced Mavis because of her suspicions about Ron's involvement in the attempted bank robbery. Another critical reason, it seems, was that Ron was seeing another girl in Footscray on his visits to Melbourne, and that Mavis discovered the liaison.[27]

Throughout this period Jack Ryan had stayed on at Peel Street,

North Melbourne. But he was already seriously ill, and late in October 1945 he was admitted to St Joseph's Nursing Home in St Georges Road, Northcote, an inner-northern suburb of Melbourne.[28] The home was run by the Little Sisters of the Poor, the same Roman Catholic Order of nuns that administered the Abbotsford convent where the girls had spent their wardships. Here, on 8 June 1946, some eight months after his admission, Jack Ryan, aged 62, finally succumbed to the illness that had affected him for more than twenty years. The official cause of death was 'chronic pulmonary tuberculosis' of an indeterminate number of years' duration.[29]

Certainly he had turned bad, and had brought abject misery and violence to his wife, and emotional and physical pain to his children. But for all that, here was a life blighted not merely by wrong choices or by the bad things that he had done, but by life circumstances that were not all of his making. Since taking up with Cecilia in 1924 Jack had lived in dozens of different places, and had always been on the run from landlords or agents. When he was carried to his final resting place there was no family to bid farewell to Jack Ryan, nor even someone to pay for his funeral. After a Roman Catholic service he was buried in a pauper's grave at the Springvale Cemetery on 12 June 1946.[30] Ron and his mother and sisters were in Balranald when they heard the news. Irma and Gloria came home from school to be told by Cecilia that their father had died. Now he could not suddenly arrive one day and spoil things for them, they thought. There were few tears—there was too much remembered pain for that—but the small house to which they had moved on Ballandalla Street was quiet for a time. And giving way to her grief, Cecilia began drinking again.[31]

Notwithstanding the bank-robbery attempt, the Balranald years of late 1945 and 1946 were highly successful ones for Ron. He had reunited his family after the deprivation of their wardship years, his mother was happy and devoted to him and the girls and, with George as his friend and mentor, he took on a more disciplined approach to life. His timber-cutting for the Sylvesters continued; indeed, he still stayed with them from time to time, and he became physically very fit. Photographs of him aged 21 in Balranald show a muscular, athletic young man, grown strong by his long hours of daily labour with George in the bush. George was a gentle, non-judgmental father figure who could provide the support and stability he had never had at home. These years were not without further setbacks, however. There had been a fire at the house at Church Street, and all their possessions, furniture, bedding, and effects were destroyed. There was no insurance.[32]

The immediate post-war period brought further changes. In 1946 George left Balranald, and in April 1947 he was married in Morwell to a local girl. Ron was still cutting redgum in Balranald and, with his mother and sisters established, he felt able to try his hand at other things. Later in 1947, when job opportunities in Balranald became limited, he took up George's offer to share-crop a patch of land near Tatura, growing tomatoes. It was a small plot of some 30 acres at Harston, between Tatura and Rushworth in northern Victoria.[33] The venture proved successful at first, and Gloria, now sixteen years old, joined them for a season to help with the picking. Through that year and the next, Ron used to go to Melbourne at weekends. It was here on a Sunday afternoon in May 1948 that he met Dorothy Janet George at a dance held aboard a Yarra River ferry, the *Fairyland*. However, this was to be anything but a fairytale romance.[34]

Dorothy George was a strikingly vivacious brunette with sparkling eyes and an engaging smile that hinted at a keen sense of fun. Dorothy was the only daughter of a Hawthorn City councillor, Harold William George, JP, a prominent local businessman, and (Janet) Ethel Bleach. Harold George was a man made wealthy by the success of his business, a workshop building tray-bodies for trucks, in Brighton Street, Richmond. He was from an established church-going family, well known locally for several generations. George was later to serve four terms as mayor of Hawthorn, and he was an influential force in local politics. As was commonly the practice for conservatives in local politics, Harold George always stood as a non-Party candidate, but was, in fact, a staunch Liberal although not a member of the Liberal Party.[35]

At this time Dorothy was a nineteen-year-old girl who had not long before left the middle-class private girls' school Methodist Ladies College, and she was in rebellion from her affluent background when she met Ron. Feeling herself emotionally distant from her mother Ethel, Dorothy seems to have been initially attracted to Ron, perhaps unconsciously, because his working-class background and anti-social inclinations were precisely the personal features most likely to provoke her parents, especially her strict father.[36] And, in Dorothy, Ron found someone who stood for the very things he lacked and evidently craved: a patriarchal family of solid status, affluence, and social connections. As well, of course, he believed these attributes in a wife were no more than what he deserved: he had, after all, been the 'father to his own family'. Marriage into the George family would well satisfy his sense of himself.

At this first meeting in May 1948 these considerations were pushed very much to the background. They met at the ferry dance several more times in the next few weeks before arranging to go out together. Before long the relationship was steady and serious enough for the Georges to express their disapproval. That attitude was steadily worn away over time, although the Georges felt they could not get close to Ron and hence had reservations about him. If the Georges did not encourage the relationship they were nevertheless hospitable; for the next twelve months or so, Ron travelled to Melbourne from Tatura each weekend to see Dorothy, and would stay with the Georges at their large house at 64 Urquhart Street, Hawthorn.[37]

During this courtship period Dorothy came to see some of Ron's fussy qualities. As a child Ron had frequently asked Violet or Irma to rewash his clothes and iron the creases in his trousers as, he said, his mother did not get them clean and sharp enough. Now this concern became more evident as Ron ironed his trousers himself by using up to six layers of damp tea-towels and brown paper. Once, he even insisted that Dorothy iron the pleats in the casual shorts he was to wear on a solo fishing trip. His detestation of dirt manifested itself in several ways: one was his fussiness about clean clothes. Always a natty dresser, Ron would have a complete change of clothes several times a day. More importantly, from an early age Ron had been prisoner to a hand-washing ritual that would see him washing his hands 40 or more times a day. While there were a variety of prompts for the ritual, it would often take place while he was reading a newspaper: he would put the paper down, complaining that he had newsprint on his fingers, leave the room, and wash his hands. This ritual would be repeated numerous times during the course of a sitting.

His concern about cleanliness became more evident to Dorothy during one particular incident. She and Ron would sometimes spend the weekend at her parents' cottage in the timber country at Yarra Junction, 40 miles by rail east of Melbourne, where they would go for bush-walks. A photograph she took of Ron around February 1949 at Britannia Falls near Powelltown shows him in his sharply creased Fletcher Jones trousers, grey fedora, starched shirt, and tie, sitting on a huge fallen gum tree. Not only is his attire inappropriately formal for bush-walking, but a close look at the photograph shows that Ron has very carefully unfolded a clean white handkerchief and placed it beneath him on the log to prevent the possibility of his trousers getting dirty.[38]

Dorothy scarcely gave these behavioural traits a second thought as she contended with her parents' disapproval of her relationship with Ron. As before, their attitude was perhaps an additional spur to its continuance. Dorothy's conflict with her parents grew when, on 21 May 1949, against their wishes, she announced that she was engaged to be married to Ron. Her father was adamant in his opposition, but couched it in terms of securing from them both an undertaking that they would wait twelve months before marrying. Determined not to have to wait, Ron and Dorothy eloped to Sydney in November 1949 intending to marry there; or, if not to marry, at least to demonstrate to Harold and Ethel that they were serious about their relationship and determined to marry before the twelve months had passed. Ron left a note for the Georges when they left Urquhart Street telling them that he and Dorothy had eloped. Harold George responded by sending Dorothy's brother Keith to Sydney to find them and bring them back. Locating them in a Sydney hotel where they were staying, Keith persuaded Dorothy that they had to return to Melbourne. It seemed for a moment as if the couple's plan had failed, and that all they had succeeded in doing was alienating Dorothy's parents even further.[39]

But with Dorothy threatening a repeat of that kind of behaviour, the Georges acquiesced. With Ron and Dorothy now living with the Georges, an engagement party was subsequently arranged, and Dorothy and Ron were married several weeks later, on Saturday, 4 February 1950, Dorothy's 21st birthday and, hence, the earliest day upon which her father's permission to marry was no longer legally required. The wedding ceremony was held at 4:30PM at St Stephen's Church of England in Richmond, where Dorothy had been confirmed and had taught Sunday school. Dorothy's family had long-standing connections with St Stephen's. Her great-great-grandparents had attended the first service in the church, and both her parents had been brought up in Richmond and had continued the family association with the church. Although Dorothy had not wished it, Ron decided to renounce his Roman Catholicism and accept the Anglicanism of his bride. Without telling her, he had spoken to the minister at St Stephen's, Rev RM Hudson, and formally undertaken the necessary procedures. It seems, though, that this change was a nominal one—Dorothy never regarded it as anything other than token by Ron—and was, perhaps, more for social reasons or to appease the Georges.[40]

If the wedding was traditional in its middle-class style so, too, was the guest list. The wedding was a notable social occasion locally, and the 100-or-so guests, largely chosen by the Georges, included local Hawthorn and Richmond councillors, businessmen, and civic leaders generally. There were very few young people invited. Ron's family attended, of course, but were in a distinct minority and felt themselves outnumbered, if not out of place. Ron's mate 'Bluey' Turner, who had a musical group called 'Bluey Turner and his Yodelling Pals', was best man. Bluey was a friend of Violet, and she had sung in his band for a time. Keith George was Ron's groomsman and, reflecting their friendship and affection for each other, Dorothy had asked Irma to be matron-of-honour.

The reception at the Masonic Hall in Launder Street, Hawthorn, was a rather formal occasion. Violet felt distinctly out of place (too la di da, she thought) and could not wait to be out of it. The Georges for their part were starchily correct, especially toward Cecilia. She went, too, of course but, having promised to stay sober, a promise she had kept at the engagement party, drinking only lemonade, she proceeded to get drunk.

Cecilia's *faux-pas* notwithstanding, Ron revelled in this company. Dorothy would have preferred something more relaxed, but Ron enjoyed the traditional formality of it all. He had long felt himself socially excluded, and hence saw the wedding offering an opportunity to be accepted by the respectable middle class. He overruled Dorothy's wish for the men in the wedding party to be dressed in dinner suits, and insisted on the still more formal white-tie-and-tails. Ron was not to be denied his opportunity to dress up. Feeling himself matched with the wedding party, Ron displayed the most correct social manners, and was thoroughly charming. He had made sure, too, that his family were suitably attired, buying an expensive bridesmaid's dress for Irma and stylish new dresses and bouquets for Violet and Gloria. Ron's going-away outfit, too, was stylish, if a little over-stated: a well-cut dark suit and silk tie. He had purchased his wardrobe at Henry Bucks, a well-known Melbourne men's store.[41]

The wedding, generally, showed a glimpse of Ryan's preoccupation with social status and position. Ron was striving for acceptance by a class to which he aspired, but he was deeply ambivalent about his aspirations. While he could be perfectly comfortable with the battling working-class position of his family and was always solicitous of his mother and his sisters, he had a defensive attitude about his class origins. His political beliefs were similarly ambivalent. Although he only seldom talked about politics with Dorothy, he was deeply engaged by the ideas and struggles of the labour movement—as statements much later in his life were to make clear.[42] Yet he bitterly rejected the Australian Labor Party as lower class and beneath him, and always voted for the Liberal Party as representing the middle class of his aspirations. Once, outside an election polling booth in full view of people voting, he tore up an ALP how-to-vote card proffered by a Labor Party worker and tossed it at his feet. He told Dorothy never to vote Labor.[43]

The social disparities of the wedding aside, Ron and Dorothy had had a successful wedding. The honeymoon, however, was to reveal another, more devastating, behavioural trait of Ron with which Dorothy would have to contend for the remainder of their married life: his gambling, which had been prolific for several years, right back to the poker games in Condos' cafe in Balranald. Dorothy was to spend almost her entire two-week honeymoon in Swan Hill staying indoors at a hotel, while Ron was across the river gambling on the races with the local SP bookmaker. Since at Swan Hill the Murray River forms the border between Victoria and New South Wales, Dorothy joked that she and Ron had honeymooned in separate states. Behind the jokes, her disappointment was profound.[44]

Having married well, as he thought, Ron clearly expected that he would be taken into the firm as the boss's son-in-law.[45] Her father's tray-body company employed some 50 workers, and the idea of working as a trainee executive with a rapid rise to the top appealed to Ron's sense of himself. He was taken into the firm, but it was not even in a junior-management role. He was made a trainee mechanic, essentially an assembler, which position evidently did not meet his expectations at all. Years later Ryan would describe his position at George's as 'a sort of executive', but it was not. It involved working in overalls in an oil-stained factory-well, fitting hoists into tip-trucks. This role was not exalted, he thought, and his career was destined not to move quickly enough to meet his expectations.[46]

The disparity between expectations and reality were well expressed in the way Ryan invariably dressed for work. Beneath his workman's factory overalls, carefully opened at the collar, could be seen a starched white business shirt and tie. If this was evidence of the management role Ryan saw for himself, it was a view not shared by Harold George. Bitter and resentful at his rejection, Ryan soon sought an opportunity for more rapid advancement elsewhere.[47] There was, too, an additional reason for his yearning to succeed. Three months after their wedding, Dorothy was pregnant with their first child.

CHAPTER FOUR

Decline

I ask you to remember that my decline started with Noojee.
—Ronald Ryan

SOME FOUR OR FIVE MONTHS after his wedding, in mid-1950 Ryan moved from Melbourne, leaving his father-in-law's firm to once more take up timber cutting in the high country in eastern Victoria. From their rented house in Kooyong Koot Road, Hawthorn, Ron and Dorothy moved to a caravan at Healesville and later Marysville, in the foothills of the Great Dividing Range north-east of Melbourne. Here they lived in a two-room hut while Ron and George, who had now joined them for a time, cut timber under contract for the Saxon timber mills at Licola.[1] Christmas 1950 found them living in a big tent near the Macalister River at Licola, in the high country, not far from where Jack Ryan had mined gold at Woods Point and Gaffney's Creek 25 years before.

After George left, for the next three years Ron and Dorothy were periodically on the move through the timber country. While they were living at Newborough, a small town between Moe and Yallourn, east of Melbourne, Dorothy gave birth to their first child, a girl, Janice Elizabeth, on 19 February 1951.[2] On that morning, 80 miles away in Melbourne, the convicted murderer Jean Lee was being hanged for murder at Pentridge prison, the last woman to be executed in Australia.

At the end of April 1951, with winter approaching, Ryan managed to get a job with the State Electricity Commission of Victoria (SEC) as a painter. Working in the municipal section of the SEC's construction division, he was engaged painting houses in Yallourn as part of the commission's house-maintenance program. He was to earn reasonably good money with the SEC, and he and Dorothy and the child lived in a commission house at Moe until 15 August 1952 when he left the job.[3] Then he was on the move again, cutting timber at Licola, then further north to Mansfield and, finally, in October 1952, with his family, south again, to Noojee, 90 miles by rail east of Melbourne.[4]

During this time Ryan earned between £20 and £25 a week, as he was an accomplished axeman and a hard worker. He now worked for the Noojee Logging Company, and he and Dorothy lived in a four-room, weatherboard company house in Powelltown Road, Noojee, paying £4 a week rent. Although he earned good money as a pulpwood cutter, Ryan's gambling yet again brought the prospects of financial ruin. Three months after he moved into the house, and with his situation made desperate by gambling debts that he could not pay, Ryan embarked upon a course that was effectively to put him outside the law for the rest of his life. He decided to set fire to his house and to claim the contents insurance, £300.[5] He may have had another reason for wanting to burn down the house he rented from the manager of the Noojee Logging Company, Jack Van Damme. At the time Ryan harboured suspicions about Van Damme's attentions to Dorothy, and he may have seen the arson as retribution for Van Damme's part in a perceived marital infidelity. Fourteen years later, just before his execution, in a letter to Dorothy—the last letter he ever wrote—Ryan said pointedly, in reference to his adult turn to crime: 'I ask you to remember that my decline started with Noojee.'[6]

With Ryan in this criminal enterprise was Frederick Simpson Allan, a 24-year-old Englishman who was also employed as a timber worker by the company. Allan had lived with the Ryans in their house for a short time, but when these incidents took place he was living in Van Damme's house. Late in January 1953, while working together in the bush, Ryan broached with Allan the subject of setting fire to his house. Ryan told Allan that he was leaving the place and did not want to take the furniture or anything away with him.

'Will you be in it?,' Ryan asked.

Although Allan gave no decision then, several days later Ryan took up the plan with him again.

'You could burn it down; there would be no risk, only the inside would go,' Ryan said.

Allan finally agreed. Ryan told him: 'I've fixed everything up. The keys are in the spout; do it on Saturday.'[7]

With these arrangements made, Ryan and Dorothy returned to Melbourne on Saturday morning, 31 January 1953, where they were to stay with the Georges for the weekend at Urquhart Street, Hawthorn. Anticipating the fire, but not letting on to Dorothy, Ryan packed into the car the family's two most treasured possessions, his racing bike and Janice's tricycle.[8] Later that Saturday, at about midnight, Allan started out to burn the house, but about halfway there he got 'cold feet'. At lunchtime on Sunday, 1 February, he phoned Ryan at the George's house in Hawthorn and told him that he had not, after all, gone through with it.

Ryan's response was to chastise Allan: 'What's wrong with you? Are you getting soft?'

Reacting to the rebuke, Allan told Ryan that he would do it that night.

'If you don't do it, I will have to do it myself,' Ryan replied.[9]

In the early hours of the next morning, Monday, 2 February, at around 1:30AM, Allan went to Ryan's house, took the keys from the spout where, by arrangement, Ryan had left them, and unlocked and entered the house. In the kitchen he found an iron that had been left on the top of the ice chest. After switching on the iron he found some paper, stuffed it in a hole in the wall near the iron, and lit it with a match. Sure now that the fire was well alight, Allan left the house and went home. With a tar and malthoid roof, the house was ablaze from end to end within minutes.[10] The damage to the house and garage, which contained a tractor and logging gear, was later valued at £2,500.[11]

Later that day Ryan returned from Melbourne to find the house and its contents completely destroyed; there was also substantial damage done to the nearby garage. Ryan saw Allan, and told him that he would give him the money for doing the job as soon as his claim had been paid by the insurance company. In the meantime Ryan gave him five quid, which he owed him anyway.[12] What Ryan did not know, however, was that there was a third person who knew about the arson. When Allan had returned to his room at Van Damme's after setting fire to Ryan's house, he was surprised to find that a new employee of Van Damme,

Stanley William Frost, who had been with him at a meal at Van Damme's earlier that night, was staying over at the house and was now asleep in another bed in his room. Breathing heavily and in a great hurry to get undressed in the dark, Allan disturbed the sleeping Frost, who woke up and asked Allan what he was doing out of bed.

Allan blurted out: 'Shut your guts. I haven't been out of bed, it's worth twenty quid to you. I have just set fire to Ryan's house.'

'Righto, you can trust me,' Frost replied.[13]

Several minutes later Van Damme called out that Ryan's house, only three hundred yards away, was on fire. Allan and Frost quickly got out of bed: the house was by then almost burnt down, and the garage nearby was burning fiercely. Allan and Frost helped to put out the fire and, under instructions from Van Damme, remained on the scene for the rest of the night to ensure that no further outbreaks occurred.

Later that week Frost and Allan were drinking in the Noojee Hotel. During the afternoon Allan booked in at the hotel, and paid for his room with a £5 note.

'Where are you getting your money from?', Frost asked Allan.

'Ryan gave it to me,' Allan replied, 'and in about a week or a fortnight I am going to town to get more.'

'What a bastard of a thing,' Frost retorted.[14]

Frost consumed a good deal of liquor that afternoon, and his conscience kept bothering him about the fire and what he had heard and seen. Later that night he approached Van Damme and told him his story. Together they went to the Warragul Police Station. Within 24 hours police had interviewed Allan, who confessed to the offence, implicating Ryan.[15] On Saturday, 7 February 1953, Detective Bryan Traynor and Senior Constable Donald Withan of the Warragul Criminal Investigation Bureau called at Urquhart Street and told Ryan they wished to ask him some questions regarding the fire. They then went to the Richmond police station where Ryan was told of Fred Allan's admissions, and that Allan had said Ryan had offered him £50 to do the job.

'It looks bad for me,' Ryan said, 'but it is not true. Allan and I have been mates for a long time.'

Senior Constable Withan then asked: 'Why would Allan make a statement like that?'

Ryan replied that he could not say. Seeing Allan's statement on the table, Ryan asked if he might read it, and was told he could. Having read it, he was asked by Withan if it was true. Ryan told him that he preferred to consult his solicitor before discussing the matter. Withan then informed Ryan that he would be charged with conspiracy and with setting fire to a building.[16]

Allan was subsequently brought before the Petty Sessions Court at Neerim South on 12 February 1953, and committed for trial at the Supreme Court at Melbourne. Following a request from Detective Withan on 21 February 1953, Allan's case was brought on quickly by the crown solicitor so that he could be used as a witness against Ryan. As Withan correctly observed in comments he made in that request, there was 'insufficient evidence to convict Ryan without the evidence of Allan.'[17] Hence, on 16 March 1953 before Mr. Justice John Barry, Allan pleaded guilty to the charge of arson and was sentenced to a bond of £10 to be of good behaviour for three years.[18]

Ryan's path was not to be so smooth. As if imminent prosecution for the offence were not enough, Ryan now discovered that the household contents insurance policy, which had been the keystone of this criminal scheme, was out of time and the company, Gresham Insurance, was indicating that it would not pay the claim. Ryan had gambled and lost the money set aside for the renewal of the policy, but had not realised that it was out of time.[19] Faced with financial disaster, Ryan appealed to Harold George to intercede on his behalf to Gresham, with whom George Tray Bodies had extensive insurance policies. Harold George, not aware of the truth of the arson charge, used his influence, or the implicit threat of a loss of his firm's insurance business, or both, to have Gresham settle the contents claim. They did so, and Ryan received £300 payment. It was not the last time that Harold George, perhaps strongly against his better judgement, would bail out his son-in-law.[20]

If the question of the insurance was now settled, it remained to deal with the criminal charges. The case came to trial late in June 1953 before Judge Dethridge and a jury in the Warragul General Sessions Court. Leo Dethridge was a very experienced and compassionate judge, having been appointed to the County Court in 1946 after a wide general practice at the bar from 1929.[21] This was Ryan's first court appearance since the stolen-watch case before the Ringwood Children's Court in 1936. He was charged with having 'unlawfully set fire to a house with intent to injure and defraud', and pleaded 'Not guilty'.[22] The conspiracy charge, in all likelihood a fallback charge anyway, had been withdrawn. Harold

George had paid for Ryan to be defended by prominent Melbourne barrister John Bourke.[23] The Crown called several witnesses, including Fred Allan and Jack Van Damme and, of course, the police informants. Since Ryan had made no admissions, the prosecution's case rested heavily on the testimony of Fred Allan.

Allan's evidence was damning as he recounted the conversations between Ryan and himself prior to the fire. His evidence was, however, uncorroborated. In a bold move, given that he was opening himself to cross-examination by the prosecution, Ryan entered the witness box to give his defence. Led by his counsel, Ryan denied the charge and said he had made no arrangements with anybody to burn down the house at Noojee. When he had been asked by Warragul Police if he knew how the fire started, he said, he had told them that he did not know. He further told the court that he had no insurance in his own name, but that he knew Dorothy had some insurance on her glory box to the value of some £500. He said all the contents in the house when it burned down were his and his wife's; they were insured for about £300, although he had given consideration to doubling the amount to £600.[24]

With Ryan's testimony concluded, it was obvious that there were two quite conflicting accounts of the fire. It would be up to the jury to make up its mind on the evidence of Allan, on the one hand, and Ryan, on the other, as to which of them was telling the truth. But the defence had another witness whose evidence may well have been crucial. Called by Bourke, Dorothy Ryan entered the witness box. The jury could not have been unaware of her condition as she took her place to give evidence: she was seven months pregnant. Dorothy truthfully gave evidence about Ron's whereabouts at material times, believing him to be innocent of the offence.[25] With Dorothy's testimony completed, Judge Dethridge gave his summing up and the jury retired to consider its verdict. After being out an hour and twenty-five minutes, the jury returned its verdict: Ryan was not guilty. He had been given another chance.[26]

For the next ten months Ryan worked, if somewhat erratically, to take advantage of that narrow escape. Living at 102 Brighton Street, Richmond, a five-room timber house owned by Harold George, he again began work at his father-in-law's tray body works as Dorothy prepared for the birth of their second child. On 13 September 1953, Wendy Dorothy was born at Bethesda Private Hospital in Erin Street, Richmond.[27] It was at this time that negative features of Ryan's behaviour became more obvious: his womanising, which had been suspected by Dorothy but now became more open, and his bad temper, which would see him flare and sometimes hit Dorothy. After such domestic violence Ryan would leave the house and not return until the next day, usually full of remorse and promises to reform.[28] The Georges learned of his womanising, too, when Ryan was discovered with another woman in the house during Dorothy's confinement.[29] Not long after that, the woman came to see Dorothy at her parents' house, saying she wanted to marry Ryan. In response, Dorothy commenced divorce proceedings but, after talking through the issue with Ron, she withdrew the petition that had been drawn up by her solicitors.[30]

Thus reconciled, within a month of the birth of his second child Ryan took the family to the country. As if wishing to return to the stability he had once known with George at Balranald, he went timber cutting once more. By now it had become a familiar pattern; he would try other things, but always he would seek to recreate the security and contentment he had known in Balranald. The family moved back to Moe, in the familiar timber country of eastern Victoria, where he tried contract sawmilling for a time. When that did not work, Ryan was taken on by Keith Johanson, a logging contractor based in Warburton. Johanson had a pulpwood business employing log-fellers and billet splitters at various locations in the high country around Matlock, very close to Woods Point where Ryan's mother and father had first met.[31]

Ryan worked in the bush from two to four weeks at a time, then took a long weekend off. There were 20 to 30 men in several groups living in portable bungalows in the bush and logging the Alpine Ash as pulpwood to fill contracts Johanson had with Australian Paper Mills. Ryan worked at Matlock next to Springs Paddocks near the Thomson River. He worked hard and well, and earned up to £50 per week on piecework rates. In all, Johanson employed about one hundred men. Although Ryan was clearly a much better woodcutter than his workmates, he had Johanson divide the group earnings equally.[32] As he had done before, Ryan would turn to other jobs in winter when tree-felling was closed down, but he stayed with Keith Johanson for two summers until 1955. In that year he and Dorothy returned to Melbourne, this time to a flat at 183 High Street, St Kilda, about a mile from St Kilda beach. For a time, he took up contract painting, sometimes alone and at times with other men.[33] As well, through advertisements in *The Sporting Globe* newspaper, the bible of working-class Melbourne punters and footy-goers, he sold a betting system which netted him some £80 per week.[34]

The past two-and-a-half years had been good ones for Dorothy, although Ryan's gambling had persisted. But there were new worries for her. For months after the trial, possessions that she had believed destroyed in the Noojee fire began reappearing in the house: her sewing machine, crystal, and silverware, among a number of items. Ryan's explanation was that he had retrieved them from a pawnbroker. It seems, however, that these were household items that he had secreted somewhere to avoid the fire.[35]

Soon they were on the move again, this time back to Moe, where Ryan tried his hand as a sawmiller and logging contractor. The worries of the Noojee fire temporarily were put aside with the arrival of their third child, another girl, Rhonda Gloria, born at the Latrobe Valley Community Hospital in Yallourn on 1 September 1955.[36] As a residue of their hope that this third child might be a boy, the name Rhonda was chosen, the closest to Ron. The infant Rhonda was to be called Ronnie.

While Dorothy looked after the children in their small house in Elizabeth Street, Moe, Ryan worked at developing his sawmilling business. Soon it was apparent that his efforts as a logging contractor were not succeeding. He was not a businessman, and the enterprise soon faltered. As with so many of his ventures, the big money did not come quickly enough and, without a disciplined long-term approach to financial management, the business inevitably failed. The compulsion to gamble soon got him into deep financial trouble, as he turned again to unlawful means to recoup his losses. At the beginning of 1956 Ryan had very substantial gambling debts to SP bookmakers and gambling associates.[37]

Then in April Ryan discussed with a friend, Norman Heard, of Armadale, how they might make some quick money. Heard, 31, had worked for Ryan as an employee sawyer at the sawmill at Moe. The plan was to open a cheque account in an assumed name and then pass off forged cheques as payment for goods obtained from shopkeepers. Putting the scheme into effect, Heard went to the branch of the ANZ Bank in suburban East Malvern on 5 April 1956, opened an account, and obtained a cheque book. Later that day Ryan went to several stores in Dandenong, east of Melbourne, and began cashing the cheques. He first went to Pigdon & Lardner's store at 157 Lonsdale Street,

Dandenong, purchased goods to the value of £1-16-2, tendered a cheque for £27-17-4 as payment, and received change. The cheque bore the signature C Truscott, the name of a well-known Pakenham sawmiller. Ryan next went to the store in McCrae Street, Dandenong, of the South-Eastern Timber Company, purchased paint and a brush to the value of £5-9-6, gave a cheque for payment, and received change.

Later the same day he purchased a tyre from the General Tyre and Rubber Co, giving a cheque in payment, and again receiving change. The next day, 6 April, Ryan added to these offences by further cashing cheques. This time he went to Blanchard's garage in Springvale and purchased a fog lamp, tendered a cheque, and received £10-13-9 in change. In each of these cases the cheque presented bore the signature C Truscott. Ryan and Heard split up the money in the train coming back to Melbourne, and Ryan received about £30 as his share.[38] In Melbourne, Ryan committed a still further offence when, on that day, he presented a worthless cheque for £22-10-0 at the Myer department store, and received goods and change. It all seemed like easy money.[39]

With the apparent success of this forging and uttering, Ryan and Heard resolved that they would wait a while and try it again, this time more systematically. Two weeks later, on Sunday, 22 April, they met to consider a plan to forge more cheques, this time in Warrnambool, 150 miles south-west of Melbourne.[40] In discussions about their new scheme, Heard said that he had a letter from a man named Len Anders, a contractor from Woolsthorpe about twenty miles from Warrnambool, and that the letter had Anders' signature on it. 'That could be handy', Ryan said.[41] Anders banked at the National Bank of Australasia at Koroit, Heard said, which was about midway between Woolsthorpe and Warrnambool. They agreed that Ryan would open an account at the National Bank at Koroit, as Heard had cashed cheques there before and was well known in the district. They agreed to go to Warrnambool together. They also agreed to register a business name to lend authenticity to their cheque-cashing scam.

Later Ryan went to the Registrar General's office in Melbourne and registered the name Bee Line Fencing and Timber Company in the name of John Charles Groves. The idea of registering a name was that if Ryan were questioned about the cheques he would produce the certificate of registration as evidence of his bona fides.[42] Ryan landed on the name 'J Groves' by looking up the Swan Hill telephone directory at the

GPO in Elizabeth Street, Melbourne and finding the name there. It appeared in the directory as 'J Groves, Nyah Road, Swan Hill, Fencing Contractor'. They had specifically wanted a country contractor's name to further establish a credible identity, but one that was not easily checked: Swan Hill was more than 200 miles north of Koroit, on the Murray River border with New South Wales.

On the afternoon of 23 April 1956 Ryan and Heard went to Warrnambool by train and stayed that night at Eckers Hotel. They spent the evening practising the signature of L Anders, as it appeared on the letter that Heard had obtained. Ryan found that he could not copy Anders' signature well enough: his own handwriting was too distinctive, he said. The next morning, Ryan and Heard took a taxi to Koroit, a distance of only ten miles from Warrnambool. Heard stopped off at one of the hotels while Ryan went to the National Bank and opened an account there by depositing £8, and obtained a cheque book. He also showed the manager the certificate of registration of the Bee Line Fencing and Timber Co, and the manager took a copy of it.

The pair then returned to Warrnambool and went to their hotel where Ryan again practised the signature L Anders. Completing all ten cheques in the book made out to J Groves for £25 each, Ryan signed them L Anders. Ryan waited outside while Heard went into different shops, obtained goods with the cheques, and collected change. Heard went into Youngers Pty Ltd and obtained sports trousers; Ezywalkin Pty Ltd, a pair of shoes; Gill the Jewellers, jewellery; Tattersall's Hotel, a bottle of whisky; Rome's shoe shop, another pair of shoes; the Grand Hotel, more whisky; Harry Taylor's Men's Shop, two shirts; Cramond and Dickson, clothing; and, finally, Batros Shoe Emporium, more shoes. By now the pair had perpetrated serious frauds on Warrnambool shopkeepers, had acquired a substantial quantity of goods, and had received as change a great wad of cash. Ryan hailed a cab, put all the parcels in it, and picked up Heard. Heard went to one more shop, C Stephens Stores, where he obtained further clothing, and they immediately left Warrnambool in the taxi heading for Melbourne.[43]

Their worthless paper trail had not gone unnoticed. Before the cab was even half way to Terang, some 30 miles away, police had been alerted and were on the lookout for them.[44] As they passed through Terang, their car was stopped by local police, and the pair taken to Terang police station for later questioning by Warrnambool detectives.

After investigations until late at night Heard was arrested, but Ryan somehow managed to escape.[45] All the goods and a substantial sum of money, believed to be all the proceeds of these offences, were recovered from Heard.[46] In custody, Heard quickly confessed to the offences and implicated Ryan.

At around 2:30PM that day, Tuesday, 24 April, acting on advice from Warrnambool police who had issued an alert for Ryan, Detective First Constable Bryan Harding of St Kilda Criminal Investigation Bureau went to Heard's house at 24 Grandview Grove, St Kilda, where he questioned Heard's wife about Ryan's whereabouts. Later that evening Harding went to Ryan's two-room flat at 183 High Street, St Kilda, where he knocked on the door and Dorothy answered. Dorothy told Harding that Ryan was not at home; but, on entering the flat, Harding could see that an external window to High Street was wide open. When Harding asked Dorothy if Ryan had fled through the window when he knocked, she admitted he had. This was a second-storey flat, and there was a big drop to the garden below. Harding was a fit man, 25 years of age, but he decided that he was not about to make the same jump after a criminal who most likely had effected his escape anyway. After he left, Harding set up surveillance of the premises from the street, hoping to intercept and arrest Ryan; but, with no appearance by his man, he gave up at 2:00AM the next morning and went home.[47]

On 30 April 1956, less than a week after his arrest, Heard pleaded guilty to each of the ten charges of false pretences in the Warrnambool Magistrates Court before stipendiary magistrate Kevin McDonald. Heard had three prior convictions for larceny, and was sentenced to two months' gaol on each of the ten charges, the last two sentences being made concurrent, making a total of eighteen months' gaol in all. In the course of the hearing, Heard confirmed the identity of Groves.

'Groves is not his real name,' Heard told the court. 'It is Ronald Joseph Ryan. I used to work for him as a sawyer.'[48]

At this stage police still had not arrested Ryan, but it was only a matter of time before they traced his whereabouts. A hunch about Ryan's gambling proclivities led Detective Harding to Ryan just two days later. Ryan had placed a regular ad for his betting system in *The Sporting Globe*. The ad invited would-be purchasers of the system, which Ryan had called The Insurance Betting System, to respond to a post box number at the Albert Park Post Office, not far from High

Street, St Kilda. Anxious to have the Warrnambool matter with police cleared up, Dorothy had told Harding about the ads in *The Sporting Globe* and Ryan's post office box. Harding calculated that, by mid-week, replies to the ad in the previous Saturday's *Globe* might be delivered to Ryan's post box. So from 8:45AM on Wednesday, 2 May, Harding kept watch at the post office hoping that Ryan would come to collect the mail. At around 10:00AM, almost on cue, Ryan appeared, and was promptly arrested by Harding and taken to the St Kilda CIB for questioning.[49] The interrogation by Harding and Senior Detective Jack Wright went on until 1:00PM. Ryan at first denied the charges, maintaining that he had gone to Warrnambool with Heard to do some contract fencing.

'The day after we arrived,' Ryan told them, 'Norman decided to return to the Anzac Day march in Melbourne. I decided to return with him and see my wife and family. We hired a taxi and left for Melbourne, on the way back, we were stopped by the police at Terang.'[50]

Police did not believe this story and, after a meal-break, the interrogation went on until 7:00PM. Finally, Wright and Harding confronted Ryan with the evidence of Heard's admissions about the Warrnambool forgeries, and the evidence of the business name registration and a more detailed account of the commission of the offences. Faced with the evidence, Ryan confessed, but persisted in his claim that it was Heard who had actually forged the cheques. Ryan then signed a statement setting out these admissions.[51]

Several days after this police interview, the job Ryan had been waiting for with the SEC was finally approved, when work became available, and on 9 May 1956 he started work as a painter in the SEC's civil construction section at its metropolitan services branch at Footscray.[52] This job was to be short-lived. His services were terminated on Friday, 18 May, when on that day he was again interviewed by Detectives Wright and Harding, following which he was taken into custody.

The next day, Ryan was brought before the Melbourne Court of Petty Sessions where police laid three charges against him for the Warrnambool offences. In addition, in relation to cheque-forging in Springvale, he was remanded to appear at the Court of Petty Sessions at Dandenong on the following Monday morning. Bail was fixed at £150. The second charge related to one of the Dandenong cheques, and was similarly adjourned to the Dandenong Court for Monday. A third charge of unlawful possession was withdrawn.[53]

Unable to raise bail, Ryan was taken to Pentridge Gaol, to D Division for prisoners on remand. It was to be his first day in Pentridge. Two days later, on 21 May, the offences at Dandenong came before the Dandenong Magistrates Court, where Ryan pleaded guilty to each of four charges of obtaining money by fraud. Two charges against him of uttering cheques were withdrawn.[54] Ryan was not represented by counsel because of the cost involved. In an appeal to the stipendiary magistrate, Allan Pfeifer, Ryan took a line that he later frequently adopted with magistrates and judges when he was being sentenced: he was the injured party, and hence he had committed offences for which he now sought leniency from the Bench:

> I realise what a fool I've been. I wasn't very happy about it but I was out of work and couldn't get a job. I'm willing to repay the money if I can.[55]

Ryan said that when he committed the offences he did not realise the seriousness of his position. He did now. He had disgraced his wife and family who had suffered by his acts, and he asked to be treated leniently as he had, he said, never been before a court till now.[56]

Magistrate Pfeifer was unimpressed:

> Almost every defendant who comes before the Court says he did not realise how serious the position was until he was caught ...[57]
>
> You should have thought of your wife and family before you committed these offences. This is a very serious offence: you systematically endeavoured to defraud these business people. You will be sentenced to one month on each charge, the fourth to be concurrent.[58]

Ryan had, in effect, been sentenced to three months' gaol. Still in custody, he was next day brought before the Melbourne Court of Petty Sessions to be charged with the cheque fraud against the Myer store.[59] He was again remanded to the same court until Friday of that week when, having consented to the charge being tried summarily and determined, Ryan pleaded guilty and was convicted and fined £25, in default to be imprisoned for two months. But he was unable to pay the full amount of this fine—all he had in the world was £13-2-4.[60] Although he handed that money over, in the absence of the fine being entirely paid Ryan was imprisoned again at Pentridge.[61]

While Dorothy tried to raise the balance of the fine, Ryan lodged an appeal against the severity of his sentences so far and, most importantly, he prepared himself for the remaining charges, the ten more serious offences at Warrnambool.[62] The case came up five days later in Warrnambool Petty Sessions Court. On Monday, 28 April, Detective Harding drove Ryan from Melbourne to Warrnambool to face these charges; the next day Ryan pleaded not guilty and reserved his defence. The result of that hearing was that he was remanded in custody in Melbourne and committed for trial at Warrnambool to be held late in July 1956. Two days after this committal hearing, however, Ryan changed his plea to 'Guilty', and requested a change of venue from Warrnambool to Melbourne. That request was acceded to, and the case was newly set down for early in July 1956 at the Melbourne Court of General Sessions.[63]

While these legal manoeuvrings were going on, Dorothy still was having great difficulty raising the balance of the £25 fine. Finally she appealed to her father for help and, late in June, Harold George provided the £200 bail that was required to have Ryan released.[64] Several days later, on 26 June 1956, Ryan and Dorothy paid the balance of his fine, £11-17-8.[65] He was released that day, having served five weeks in Pentridge.[66] What is more, within days his appeal against the sentence at Dandenong was heard before Judge Leo Dethridge in Melbourne General Sessions, sitting as an Appeals Court. At this hearing his three months' gaol term was varied to one of a bond of £10 to be of good behaviour for three years. It was a condition of the bond that Ryan not associate with Norman Heard during that three-year period.[67]

The remaining charges of forgery at Warrnambool finally were heard on 13 July 1956 in Melbourne General Sessions before Judge Ben Dunn. Peter McGavin appeared for the prosecution. The well-known criminal barrister Tom Doyle represented Ryan. With Ryan having pleaded guilty, the trial simply took the form of the presentment of evidence and a plea from the defence on sentence. Doyle was a skilful criminal barrister, whose courtroom wit and pleas to the Bench on sentencing had been legion among his peers. On one courtroom occasion, Doyle was making a plea for an accused burglar, and asked the crown prosecutor for the full record, whereupon he learned that his client had pleaded guilty to no less than twelve counts of burglary. Undeterred, Doyle addressed the bench:

'If Your Honor please, my client has burgled twelve houses, a situation which may lead Your Honor to adopt a stern attitude towards him. But I suggest Your Honor should raise your eyes, and look round this vast metropolis and consider all the houses that he hasn't burgled.'[68]

Doyle's expansive approach put him in good stead for his appearance for Ryan. In making his plea, Doyle put to the bench that the ten counts of forgery at Warrnambool now before the court, and the two other matters at Dandenong and at Myer (which were not before the court except insofar as they would be taken account of in sentencing), ought to be seen as forming one criminal episode. Doyle invited the judge to treat these matters as merely one lapse:

> *Doyle*: May it please Your Honor, despite the formidable number of counts in this presentment it is felt that there are a number of matters connected with this case that will incline Your Honor to leniency in deciding what is the best thing to do with this man. As Your Honor will see, all of these ten counts arise out of matters on the same day and it is put that these particular forgeries and two other matters which are not before Your Honor yet and strictly should not come before you except that I have to use them, have all formed one criminal episode, and Your Honor would be justified in treating this as merely one lapse. This man is now aged 31. I take it Your Honor has read the depositions.
>
> *His Honor:* Yes.
>
> *Doyle*: A lot of what I have to say is in there. He is now 31. When his father died at the age of 16 he became the main support of his family which then consisted of his mother and two sisters, and for eight years he worked in the Balranald district and maintained the family until they were independent of his support. In 1950 he became married and he now has a wife and three children aged five, two and a half, and nine months.
>
> Last year he had been working as a timber worker and he went into business for himself as a logging contractor. It was not successful because the timber in the site which he had obtained would not return saleable timber, the good stuff cut out, and eventually his

business had practically failed. He then had to return his plant to the hirers and left in debt at the time and came to Melbourne, and since then he has been working more or less casually as a painter. He is an expert painter, had done some work for the State Electricity Commission, but for the last seven or eight months work has been of a casual nature more or less. He had this young family and was compelled to pay £4-15-0 for the one room in which the family lived with rather disastrous results as far as the health of the children was concerned, and he then shifted with his wife and children and took two furnished rooms for £9 a week. At this time he was not in regular employment. He applied for permanent employment on the railways, was classed as unfit and applied to the S.E.C. who had employed him before and was informed he would be taken on but there was no work available for a few weeks. His youngest child had become very ill with kidney trouble that necessitated her treatment in the Children's Hospital for a month, and it was at this time when he was desperately hard up, only getting casual work and finding it very hard to get anything, that he met this man named Heard who appears so much in the depositions. He had known him before in the timber industry and it was Heard who made the suggestion in every case in which an offence was committed. Detective Harding informs me that he knows Heard as a man with a long criminal record and he has been dealt with for these particular matters. The first thing Heard suggested to the prisoner was that he should assist him to utter some cheques, and that was done, each of them cashing two cheques. The next day the prisoner cashed a cheque himself at Myers for the sum of £22-10-0, and those were the only monies that he got out of it. It was then that Heard put to him this scheme whereby the prisoner was to open a bank account and get the bank book which was given to Heard who wrote out all the cheques and uttered the cheques which have brought the prisoner before the Court. Of course, as far as the legal aspect is concerned, he is equally guilty because they acted in concert. Practically all I have told Your Honor can be verified by the detectives, but the subsequent events are of great importance in this case. Just before the episode at Warrnambool, Heard and the prisoner had each cashed two cheques and he was prosecuted for those two offences and sentenced to a month's imprisonment on each.

That was, if I remember rightly, on the 21st May, after this trouble. He appealed against this sentence and came before Judge Dethridge—and here it becomes all important—and Judge Dethridge quashed those sentences and released this man on a bond of £10 to be of good behaviour for three years. A good indication of the way the Judge thought is that it was a condition of the bond that he must not associate with the man Heard. That bond is still in existence and has not been broken.

His Honor: That is May this year?

Doyle: That is May this year. Then on the 25th May he came up in the City Court in respect of this cheque that was cashed at Myers and he was then fined £25 in default two months' imprisonment. After he had served about a month or five weeks of it his wife managed to raise the balance of this fine and he was then released, so he has had a taste of gaol. It is suggested that in the circumstances of this case Your Honor might feel those five weeks were sufficient to give him an idea of what it is like, as useful a preventative as we could get in the circumstances without doing some damage to the man himself. His wife is here: I do not want to call her unless Your Honor feels it's necessary. She would tell Your Honor he is a good husband and a good father as far as his means have permitted. His being out of regular employment has meant hardship for all of them, of course, but the State Electricity Commission have told him employment is available. I got my Solicitor to verify that, and they said his work has always been satisfactory and as soon as a suitable vacancy occurs he will be taken on. That does not mean he will be taken on immediately; it is entirely in their hands. The thing that is urged on Your Honor here is that all the material I have put to you has been considered by His Honor Judge Dethridge and he has given this man a chance.

His Honor: With a knowledge of this, I take it?

Doyle: I have taken that for granted. Perhaps I had better call Detective Harding on that.

His Honor: You need not call him; just enquire from him and tell me.

Doyle: I wish to call him anyhow, Sir.[69]

Doyle then called to the box Bryan Harding, the detective who had interviewed and later arrested Ryan for the Warrnambool offences now before the court. Harding's evidence appears to have been crucially important to the outcome of this plea on sentence. Harding had spent several hours with Ryan on their long car trip from Melbourne to Warrnambool and back on 27 and 28 April, and during their overnight stay in Warrnambool, and they had talked at length.[70] Harding told the court that he had got to know Ryan well during and since the time of the offence:

> I have come to know him and his family rather well through this matter. I have visited their lodgings at 183 High Street, St Kilda and I know Ryan has a deep attachment for his wife and family which is reciprocated.
>
> As I said I have seen the conditions they are living in; there are three young kiddies in a single room and the mother and father. The kiddies are all suffering from colds and sniffles and I think what may have motivated Ryan's action in this case is the fact that he wished to get money hurriedly and seek better lodgings for his family. I believe he has learnt a lesson from the time he has been in gaol and I think it has made a very deep impression on him and I think he has a desire to keep away from the place in future. Heard is a convicted criminal, has been convicted of a number of criminal offences. I have no doubt that Heard is responsible for this trouble.[71]

It is not all that unusual to find police giving evidence of this kind in a plea. However, Detective Harding's submission to the court was particularly positive and well made. Judge Dunn had come to the bench after more than 25 years as a barrister, with an extensive practice in practically all jurisdictions, specialising in the common law; but he had been appointed to the County Court only eight months before this case.[72] What he had before him was an unusually presentable, well-dressed defendant about whom the arresting police officer had made a positive plea. When Harding had finished, it became obvious that Judge Dunn had been greatly influenced by his submission. Dunn asked Doyle if Ryan had any war service. Told that there was none that Doyle was aware of, Dunn said: 'I only asked that question because I thought I might be able to put him in touch with an organisation that would help them over the difficulty.'[73] The organisation was 'Carry On', a well-known and highly successful welfare organisation that helped ex-servicemen and their dependants. Dunn was the president of 'Carry On'.[74]

Coming to his sentence of Ryan, Judge Dunn began:

> Ryan, you have pleaded guilty to ten counts of forgery which, as you probably realise now, is a very serious offence. I must say that when I saw you walk in I was surprised to find a man of your appearance in circumstances such as these, and I am very gratified to hear the evidence that Mr. Harding has given about you and about your family association. In the circumstances I feel justified in yielding to the plea that has been made on your behalf and placing the same confidence in you that Judge Dethridge has already placed. In respect of each count you will be released on a bond in your own recognisance of Fifty pounds to be of good behaviour for five years. That is a longer bond than the one you have already.
>
> *Ryan*: I wouldn't care if it was fifty years, Your Honor.
>
> *His Honor*: You understand the nature of it and the consequences of your being led into further difficulties. I wish you luck, Ryan. I hope you keep out of any bother.
>
> *Ryan*: Thank you, Your Honor.[75]

Although it was Friday the thirteenth, Ryan's luck had held. He had been given yet another chance.

CHAPTER FIVE

Crime

Ryan has during the past few months become obsessed with the idea that he is a 'big time' criminal with enough intelligence to outwit the forces of law and order. I have no doubt that this man has finally made up his mind to live outside the law and there is nothing I can say in his favour.

–Senior Detective Ray Tobin

THE YEAR 1956 was a historic one for Victoria, and particularly for the city of Melbourne; it marked both the beginning of regular television broadcasts and the staging of the XVI Olympiad. For several weeks in November, as 'the friendly games' provided some respite from international political tensions, world attention was focused on the city. For the Ryans life might have begun to take on a more settled routine: Janice was now five years old and had started school, Wendy was three, and Rhonda had had her first birthday. The stability and security of home life was affected, however, by Ryan's criminal activities, which soon became entrenched as a way of life. Even in the period immediately after his court appearance before Judge Dunn in July 1956, he was involved in increasingly extensive illegal activities.

As far as his criminal record shows, Ryan was not charged with any offence in the three-year period between July 1956 and September 1959.[1] But the lure of quick money and easy gains, and Ryan's need to finance his gambling overcame any sense that he would not re-offend.

Before long he was committing, on average, about one robbery a week.[2] Usually involving shop-breaking and entering, his robbery targets were predominantly electrical-goods stores and shops selling household consumer goods. Sometimes he would break into butchers' shops to steal meat and poultry.[3] As a point of pride, and according to a code among some criminals, he said that he would never steal from working men, but would target established businesses. Alcohol does not seem to have been a factor in these criminal activities, as Ryan was only a light-to-moderate beer drinker.[4]

Through 1957 he tried a number of different business ventures, but all failed. In May 1957 he and Dorothy moved from St Kilda to Cranbourne, 25 miles south-east of Melbourne, where they were to stay for two years. One venture, begun while they were living in Cranbourne, involved a fruit-shop business in Highfield Road, Camberwell. Travelling from Cranbourne each day, Dorothy ran the shop for about six months and Ryan worked, but not diligently, on Saturday mornings. Even though it exceeded break even within a short space of time, the business was only marginally profitable and, after some months, Ryan decided it was not a success and closed it.[5]

His attitude to the fruit shop, in any event, was not commercially realistic, but purely opportunistic. For Ryan, the business was a cash stream for his gambling, predominantly on horse-racing, trotting, and greyhound racing, but also in illegal casinos. While at Cranbourne he owned a greyhound for a time but, again, he operated as a gambler rather than an owner.[6] Once, he left a race meeting where he had lost heavily to go back to the fruit shop for the last £1 in the cash register to bet on a horse in a later race.[7]

This erratic and self-destructive course had another expression. While Dorothy was running the shop, Ryan worked at a parcel-delivery business that he had started when they were living in St Kilda, using a 30cwt Commer van operating under contract to Thomas Nationwide Transport (TNT). Although he had averaged about £45 per week from these jobs, he became frustrated with the venture when TNT did not give him as much work as he wanted and his van was often idle.[8] In November 1957, on the road between Cranbourne and Dandenong, he set fire to the van and drove it over a culvert—jumping clear as he did so, but not without singeing his clothes. He later successfully claimed insurance on the written-off vehicle.[9]

In the early part of 1957 Dorothy became pregnant again, but during the winter months of 1957 she contracted German measles and influenza. These illnesses, combined with her arduous work in the fruit shop, weakened her physically. Two weeks before the baby was due in December, Ryan told her he had to go away hurriedly for a time. In an evident move to avoid questioning by police about criminal offences in which he had been involved, he went back to Balranald where he shot kangaroos and rabbits for several weeks. While he was still away, on 20 December 1957, his fourth child, a boy, was stillborn. Named Rodney George Ryan, the baby is thought to have been affected by Dorothy's illness with German measles. When Ryan learned of the stillbirth, he took the news badly. He had desperately hoped for a son and, with three sisters and his own three daughters, he was also concerned that the Ryan name would not be carried on.[10]

Ryan saw his child's stillbirth as yet another of the injustices of life to which he had been subjected. And there were many injustices to which he would point: his impoverished childhood, his brutal father and neglectful mother, the somewhat loveless environment of his wardship at Rupertswood, and the house fire at Balranald that destroyed his uninsured belongings. These were among many of the raw deals to which Ryan believed he had been unfairly subjected in his life. Now he had lost the only son who might have carried on the Ryan name. 'I [am] the last of the Ryans', he would later defiantly declare, in an angry and threatening letter that would recite a litany of injustices that he believed he had suffered at the hands of police, judges, and prison officers.[11]

Notwithstanding this blow to Ryan, home life at this time was reasonably happy. He was a devoted father to his girls—Janice, now seven, Wendy, five, and Rhonda, two—and was concerned to ensure they had a sound upbringing. In what may be taken as a revealing expression of his own inner feelings, Ryan used to counsel the girls when they were naughty: 'You have a naughty man on your shoulders, brush him off!'[12]

At this time, Ryan became a close friend of Ronald Joseph Gallagher, a fellow drinker at his local hotel, the Doutta Galla, in Racecourse Road, Flemington. Ryan and Gallagher shared first and second Christian names, religion, and criminal ambitions. Gallagher was a driver by occupation, employed by a firm of carriers at the Railways and, at 32, was the same age as Ryan.[13] Like Ryan, Gallagher was a Roman Catholic, having been educated at St Joseph's Christian Brothers' School in North Melbourne.[14] Six feet one inches tall (and of larger build than Ryan, who was five feet, seven-and-a-half inches tall, weighing ten stone, six pounds), Ron Gallagher was to become a familiar figure in the Ryan household.[15] To the Ryan children, he was 'Big' Ron to their father's 'Little' Ron. Janice and Wendy understood that the two Ronnies were close friends, and there were many days spent together with their father and Big Ron, usually at the races. The routine was for the children to be taken to the Doutta Galla Hotel, where they would spend the afternoon while their father, Gallagher, and other men went to the racecourse nearby, returning from time to time to bet with the hotel's SP bookmaker. During such times the children would be seated on bar stools and given what seemed like endless glasses of raspberry cordial and lemonade.[16]

Sometimes their father would have a good day punting, and several times he did exceedingly well. He once told police that he would bet £200 on a horse or dog about which he had received reliable information.[17] One day he returned from the races and tossed at Dorothy, as she sat at the kitchen table, what seemed to the children like hundreds of £10 notes.[18] From every pocket he pulled money, and still there seemed more to come. But however large the win, it was usually lost again very quickly. He never knew when to stop. He would bet in amounts of hundreds of pounds, frequently winning as much as two or three thousand pounds, but he would lose it all again and leave the track empty handed, often without even the fare home. He once won £2,000 on a horse at Flemington, but lost it again. To a social gambler, winning and then losing amounts of £2,000 would be devastating, but the losses seemed never to bother Ryan. He was never despondent when he lost, even when his losses were very substantial. He was, instead, perfectly calm. It was the same with crime. Ryan said that the adrenalin flowed before he committed a crime, and afterward he had a feeling of indescribable calm.[19]

In 1958 Ryan engaged in a new venture, professional fishing. But, like so many of the enterprises he had embarked upon in the past, a long-term commitment to the business, a determination to overcome the setbacks inevitably besetting ventures of this kind, seemed beyond him. Adversity became a still further justification for the notion that he had injustices heaped upon him. His 40-foot shark-boat, which he named *Little Lady*, his affectionate name for Dorothy, was anchored at the fishing village of San Remo on Victoria's Westernport Bay, but it developed engine trouble and the season had been poor.[20]

In early 1959, the Ryans moved from Cranbourne to the city, to a house at 43 Broomfield Road, Hawthorn where, ostensibly to raise money for a new engine for his boat, he embarked upon what his own legal counsel would later describe as a 'systematic criminal career' involving an extensive series of factory break-ins and thefts.[21] Ryan was the leading figure in an organised criminal gang whose crimes in that period involved the theft of property valued in court evidence at £38,483 (and that sum only related to offences for which he was prosecuted).[22] There were numerous robberies in this period, but it was not until September 1959 that he was arrested for any of these offences. In the period from 1956 to 1960 Ryan's criminality developed and deepened, but he was charged with only perhaps one-eighth of the crimes for which he was responsible.[23]

Ryan's gambling—which was compulsive—had a lot to do with it. The dynamic of gambling and crime began to gather pace toward what seemed like an inevitable downfall. His obsessive behaviour also persisted, and along with his compulsive hair-brushing and ritual hand-washing could now be added a new phenomenon, his obsessive shaving: Ryan never believed he could shave his face close enough, and he would risk injury to achieve the closest shave possible. And now he began to display further irrational behaviour: rage at slights he imagined against himself. After Ryan had committed a crime he would read the newspaper looking for a report of his criminal triumph. If there were none, he would be miffed. Once, when there was only a very small item on an inside page, he flew into a rage.[24]

The first of the offences for which Ryan was subsequently charged had its genesis on the afternoon of 22 July 1959, when Ryan and Ron Gallagher conceived the idea of breaking into a knitwear factory at 91 Glenferrie Road, Hawthorn, the premises of Knitrex Knitting Mills. Having decided to reconnoitre the premises first, Ryan and Gallagher drove in Gallagher's Volkswagen van to the factory, and spent a little time establishing the layout of the premises and the likely point at which they could break in.

Two nights later, on 24 July, the pair met at the Doutta Galla Hotel in Flemington before setting off in the van to commit the robbery. They arrived at about 11:00PM, but sat in the van for a while to make sure the operation would go undisturbed. Gallagher parked the van up a side street, and the pair walked back to the lane behind the factory. At the back of the factory there were a couple of pickets off the fence through which they gained entry. Then, using a pinch bar, also known as a jemmy, they forced the steel grille protecting the back window, broke the window, and climbed through. Working quickly, they removed an estimated 1,620 women's cardigans and jumpers from the shelves, and piled them near the window. Ryan climbed back out again, and Gallagher passed them through while Ryan stacked them against the back gate. Gallagher retrieved the van, and after loading it with the knitwear they drove off. In the following week they sold the goods at various hotels, fetching £1 for some items and less for others. On average they sold the knitwear for about fifteen shillings each. The goods were valued at £3,320, and netted Ryan and Gallagher about £600 each.[25] Profitable as it seemed, this was merely the first of a series of breaking offences, which would go on with monotonous regularity for many months.

Two weeks after this robbery, with Gallagher in Sydney for a short time, Ryan decided to continue alone, and he undertook another break-in just like the first. This time his target was Senga Knitting Mills Pty Ltd in Hoddle Street, Abbotsford. On the afternoon of 7 August, after drinking for some time at the Nelson Hotel in South Melbourne, Ryan drove Gallagher's van to Abbotsford to survey the scene. Finding the Senga factory a good prospect, he returned to his home in Broomfield Street, Hawthorn and had a meal. At about 10:00PM that night he left home and returned to the factory. With no back fence to negotiate, Ryan proceeded to the back door and, with the aid of a jemmy, managed to force the door after about half an hour.

Most of the goods Ryan found inside were women's and men's wear, mainly cardigans and pullovers. Conveniently packed in cartons ready for consignment, some ten large boxes of knitwear were loaded by Ryan into the van in the space of about an hour. In the following week Ryan again sold the goods in hotels in the Flemington and South Melbourne area, and also kept some for his own use. The value of the stolen goods was about £1,250.[26]

Two weeks after the Senga break-in, on 22 August 1959, Gallagher and Ryan broke into the shoe factory of Rampling and Hall Pty Ltd at

396 Hoddle Street, Clifton Hill by breaking a hole in the tin-walled side of the factory. After gaining entry they stole 743 pairs of shoes valued at £2,218.[27] The operation took a familiar course: Gallagher and Ryan loaded the shoes into Gallagher's van and then drove home. During the next week they got rid of all the shoes, taking them to pubs in the North Melbourne and Flemington areas. They averaged about £1 each for the shoes.[28]

Less than a fortnight later Ryan, again with Gallagher, broke into yet another knitwear factory, this time a firm in Sydney Road, Coburg. Employing the same methods as they had found successful in the past, the pair first drove around Brunswick and Coburg in Gallagher's van seeking an appropriate target for break-in. On the afternoon of Wednesday, 2 September 1959, they decided upon the Gotex Knitwear factory at 11 Sydney Road, Coburg, near the corner of Sydney Road and Moreland Road. Having agreed upon their target, Ryan and Gallagher separated to meet again several hours later at the Doutta Galla Hotel. At dusk the pair drove to the Gotex factory and, using a pick-head, forced the steel grille on a back window to the factory and gained entry.

When they had finished loading the van with knitwear—some 2,800 men's and women's pullovers and cardigans, together with 364 school pullovers that were valued at cost at £4,600, together with some tools valued at £100—Ryan and Gallagher took the goods to 31 Woolsley Avenue, Kensington, where Gallagher had rented a bungalow as a secure store for stolen property.[29] Their plan for the sale of the stolen knitwear was one that they had adopted many times before. They would sell the goods outside the Port Melbourne football ground at a Sunday Victorian Football Association match.[30]

That plan was thwarted, however, when several days after the robbery Ryan was arrested by police in the bayside suburb of Mordialloc driving the VW van to meet up with Gallagher at the nearby Chelsea Hotel. It was about 2:00PM on Monday, 7 September when detectives intercepted Ryan following their search of the bungalow in Kensington from which a quantity of stolen goods had been recovered. Interviewed by detectives from the breaking squad attached to Russell Street police headquarters, Ryan was questioned at the Mordialloc police station about the recent robberies. The van, he said, belonged to a friend, 'Ron Scott', whom, he told police, he was driving to meet at the Chelsea Hotel. Confronted by Detective Allan Williams with the evidence of some eight or nine hundred Gotex garments recovered from the van, Ryan confessed, taking the blame:

> Just let's say that I did it ... I did a job the other night and this is the result of it ... If you have had a look at it you will soon work that out.[31]

Ryan could not for long maintain the fiction that he had committed the robbery alone. The van's registration pointed to Gallagher, and police were quick to point that out to Ryan. 'Well, I suppose you will find out sooner or later; we did it together', he said.[32] From the Mordialloc police station, police went with Ryan to Gallagher's house in Elsie Grove, Chelsea, where they were let in by Gallagher's wife. A search of the house disclosed a small quantity of Gotex knitwear and some hand tools. Later that day Gallagher was arrested at the Doutta Galla Hotel while attending a football club social meeting. Taken to the offices of the Russell Street CIB, where Ryan had now also been taken, Gallagher at first denied any involvement: 'No, not me. I bought some of that stuff,' he protested. When police put it to him that Ryan had been caught in his van loaded with the stolen goods, and that Ryan was making a statement about the whole thing, Gallagher stood firm: 'No, he wouldn't say that ... I don't want to be unreasonable about this, but I would like to know what Ron says before I say anything.'[33]

Of course, Ryan had already seen the futility of further denials, and after a time he was brought from an adjoining room and asked by detectives to identify Gallagher as his accomplice in the robberies at Gotex and Knitrex. Ryan confessed, and written statements were then taken from both men in relation to two robberies in Gallagher's case, and all three in Ryan's. In his statement in relation to Gotex, Ryan set out his relationship with 'Scott' and the circumstances of the break-in, and concluded:

> I am a professional fisherman by trade. The engine of my boat broke down. Owing to a poor season and no savings, all my money was invested in the boat. I decided to take a chance on getting a few pounds to finance the purchase of a new engine by breaking into a factory.[34]

In the following two weeks Ryan and Gallagher appeared at a succession of Petty Sessions court committal hearings: at Brunswick on 14 September regarding the Gotex offences; at Hawthorn on 16 September in relation to Knitrex; and at Collingwood on 21 September for the Senga offences. Represented by counsel and pleading 'Not guilty' in each case, they were committed for trial to the Melbourne General Sessions Court set down for its October sittings on charges of shop-breaking and stealing.[35] Released on bail to await that trial, the pair seems not to have been deterred from committing still further offences. Within a week of their appearance at the Collingwood Court of Petty Sessions they were in trouble again, this time involving allegations of factory breaking and stealing 103 motor mowers. The allegations against Ryan and Gallagher were that on the night of 28 September 1959 they broke into the factory of Victa Consolidated Industries at 156 Burwood Road, Hawthorn, and stole a truck and its load of 90 Victa motor mowers, as well as a further thirteen mowers found in the factory. The mowers were valued at £5,000.[36]

Police were alerted to the whereabouts of the stolen mowers when Ryan and Gallagher were reported to be offering motor mowers for sale in hotels around Flemington and Preston. They were interviewed by detectives following the arrest of a man charged with receiving stolen goods. The arrested man, who was subsequently convicted of the offence and placed on probation, identified Ryan as the person who had delivered 37 mowers to his house at South Seaholme. While Ryan and Gallagher made no admissions in relation to these offences, they were subsequently charged with factory breaking and stealing—to which they entered pleas of 'Not guilty'.[37]

Still further offences were committed in November 1959, this time involving a warehouse break-in and theft of cigarettes, tobacco, and other goods to the value of £3,728. As with the break-in at Victa, the offence involved a break-in at the warehouse premises of tobacco wholesaler Leo Hemingway & Son Pty Ltd, at Notting Hill, and the theft of a fully loaded delivery van, as well as the theft of other goods found in the warehouse. The break-in took place on the night of 14 November 1959, following which the stolen goods were delivered to several people with previous histories of receiving.[38]

Ryan was to escape detection for this crime for several months, until interviews with those receiving the stolen goods identified Ryan and

Gallagher as having been responsible. During this period, although robberies by Ryan became a matter of regular routine, he was charged with only a fraction of the criminal offences he actually committed.[39]

A further robbery that did subsequently come to the notice of police occurred on 9 February 1960, when Ryan and Gallagher broke into the factory of Vacu-Lug Pty Ltd in Market Road, Brooklyn and stole 147 tyres and office equipment to the value of £2,200.[40] The method of entry was by forcing a door, but this time there was a serious new element to the break-in: the safe on the premises was blown open using explosives.[41] Later interviewed by police, Ryan said that there had been another man with him when he and Gallagher had committed the robbery, 'another chap I only know as Old Charlie …', he said. Asked by police to identify the person who blew the safe, Ryan replied: 'That's what Old Charlie came along for. He did that while we took the rest of the stuff out.'[42]

In the course of the police interview, Ryan admitted to the robbery when it became evident that two men who had received the stolen goods were likely to be charged with the break-in as well. He told police:

> Look, they shouldn't be in strife. I only gave them a tenner to do me a favour and they finish up being locked up. I can't leave them in that … I'll tell you everything.[43]

Ryan was subsequently charged with the robbery, as was Gallagher. Ryan was given bail in relation to this offence, a condition of which was that he report daily to the officer-in-charge of the CIB at Hawthorn.[44] As later events demonstrated, if he did so report it was when he was not otherwise involved in further offences. Certainly, the person who had put up the surety for his release from prison when he was on remand at this time had cause to believe he was not a good risk. The person providing the surety, Ron Gallagher's father, Henry Gallagher, had paid the £500 surety to secure Ryan's release, but had caused a warrant to be issued against Ryan when he believed he was about to abscond. Ryan was re-imprisoned on 24 February 1960, but was later released when a new surety was put up.[45]

As was evident in the Gotex case, this was not the first time that Ryan had confessed and, more particularly, accepted the blame on behalf of others. As his crimes, and his arrests for those crimes, grew in number over the next few years, he would confess many times to police, without duress, and frequently to avoid blame being directed at his accomplices. At other times he would implicate others. In the course of one particular interrogation of Ron Gallagher, after Ryan had told the whole story of a break-in to police, an exasperated Gallagher said to his police interrogators: 'That bloody Ryan has lived up to his reputation again and spilt the beans.'[46] Less than a month later, Gallagher, in a similar interrogation by police, again vented his frustration about Ryan's propensity to confess and tell all:

> That's just his form, he makes out he's a little tough guy and when he's questioned he dobs everyone in, the little bastard.[47]

It was not until 15 March 1960, four months after the Hemingway robbery, that Ryan and Gallagher were finally identified by police as suspects in relation to that crime.[48] During the course of interrogation Ryan again confessed, and he was subsequently charged with the breaking offences. The record of interview with Ryan taken by police on that day gives some illustration of the criminal culture in which Ryan had by now immersed himself. Speaking about the Hemingway offences, Ryan gives the impression of someone for whom criminal activity of this kind was matter-of-fact, that he was a 'professional' criminal. Confronted by police with the statement of someone who already had been charged with receiving the stolen goods and who had outlined details of the offences, Ryan responded:

> Fred's told you the right story, except he didn't say he helped us carry the stuff in, and he says he only got the £100, everything else is right, but old Nick has covered up a bit, you cannot blame him a bit I suppose.
>
> *Detective*: How did you get into the factory?
>
> *Ryan*: Through a window.
>
> *Detective*: You were a bit greedy weren't you, Hemingway's say that you were apparently not satisfied with the load that was on the truck as you also took property from two other trucks in the place.
>
> *Ryan*: That's right, but it's not greed, that's good business.
>
> *Detective*: How did you pick on Hemingway's to break into?
>
> *Ryan*: You've got to have the inside information before you can

pull a job like this. We had it so we weren't taking much of a risk.

Detective: Where did you get the information from?

Ryan: I can't tell you that, it was not given to me, Ron [Gallagher] told me all about the set-up but didn't tell me who told him.

Detective: What happened to all the £2000 you received for the goods?

Ryan: I had some solicitor's fees to pay and I lost a lot on the horses, I gave the wife three or four hundred pounds to bank for me from the last lot that Nick paid me. Of course, Ron got his share, I didn't get the lot.

Detective: You are going to be charged with this matter ... Do you wish to make any statement?

Ryan: No, but I will probably nod the nut to this one.

Detective: Well why not make a written statement then?

Ryan: I have got my reasons.

Read by police a record of the questions he was asked, and the replies that he gave, Ryan was asked if it was a true record.

Ryan: Yes it seems OK to me.[49]

The notes of the police interview record that he was 'frank and cooperative. There was no hesitancy on his part.' He was later charged with factory-breaking and stealing.[50] Undeterred, Ryan planned and executed another theft of large quantities of cigarettes less than a fortnight after this interview with police and his charging on the Hemingway offences. The robbery, on 28 March 1960, involved a break-in at the premises of a subsidiary of the North American Vending Machine Company at 157 Alexandra Parade, North Fitzroy, during which a very large quantity of cigarettes, valued at cost at £2,167, was stolen.[51] Later police evidence showed that Ryan and an accomplice, Robert Brian Banks, broke into the warehouse by cutting a hole in an iron wall with a pair of tinsnips and, following the method adopted at Hemingways, drove off with a fully loaded cigarette delivery van. The cigarettes were then stored in St Kilda by Ryan and later sold by him around hotels and coffee bars.[52] In a subsequent police interview about the matter, Ryan said that the sale of the cigarettes had netted him £1,130, but he had lost it gambling on horses: 'I blew most of it on the Neddies,' he said.[53]

The spate of offences continued when, on the night of 12 April 1960, Ryan and Gallagher broke into the premises of clothing manufacturer Dunne Bros. Pty Ltd at 106 Franklin Street, Melbourne, and stole men's clothing to the value of £14,000. Ryan and Gallagher had gained entry to the factory by Ryan kicking in the rear door. In two separate visits to the factory that night, once in company with Gallagher, and later with Robert Banks, the accomplice who figured in the American Vending Machine offences, Ryan stole 350 men's suits, 97 jackets, and 53 rolls of cloth. The stolen goods were taken in several trips in Ryan's Bedford panel van to a wood yard, rented for the purpose by Ryan using the name John Scott, at 168 Albion Street, Brunswick, where they were stored. The next day the stolen property was distributed to others who would sell some of it in hotels around Melbourne.[54]

The next night, 13 April 1960, police interviewed Ryan at his home in Hawthorn, and put to him evidence that had been taken from Banks about the commission of the break-in at Dunne Bros. Ryan at first denied involvement, but when he took police to his van and a search of the van was undertaken, a label marked 'Dunne Bros. 104 Franklin St., Melbourne' was found.

Faced with evidence and the admissions made by Banks, Ryan confessed his role in the break-in and told police: 'This lot certainly finishes me.' Asked who was in the break-in with him, Ryan replied: 'Why don't you ask the other bloke—the one that dropped me? I'm not going to bag anyone.' Ryan and Gallagher were subsequently charged with factory-breaking and stealing. They indicated their intention to plead 'Not guilty', and were remanded in custody until their cases were later set down for hearing. Some £8,500 of the stolen property was later recovered when police searched the premises of suspects and seized a quantity of suits and cloth.[55] During the course of the interview on 13 April with Ryan about the Dunne Bros. break-in, he was also questioned by detectives about the North American Vending Machine robbery. Although, as usual, he would not sign a statement relating to the offences, the police record of interview records him making admissions. Ryan and Banks were charged with breaking and entering, and indicated they would plead 'Not guilty'.[56]

The series of offences with which they were now charged had occurred in the nine-month period from July 1959 to April 1960.

Notwithstanding the likelihood that there were many more offences for which they were not arrested and charged, this had been a very extensive period of criminal activity. Arising out of the offences at Knitrex, Senga, Gotex, Victa, Vacu-Lug, Hemingway, and Dunne Bros., Ryan and Gallagher were subsequently charged on multiple counts of breaking and entering and theft, and receiving goods knowing them to be stolen.[57] Ryan and Banks were also charged with the American Vending Machine robberies.

Still greater substance was to be added to the already lengthy presentment of charges. Remanded to Pentridge Gaol, Ryan, Gallagher, and Banks were brought before the Court of Petty Sessions at Melbourne on 21 April 1960, for a committal hearing on charges arising out of the break-in at Dunne Bros. Evidence was led from a director of the company about the break-in and the goods stolen; but, with the hearing incomplete, the case was adjourned, and they were again remanded in custody to appear at the Court of Petty Sessions (now the old Magistrates' Courts in Russell Street), on 29 April. Since the case was not finished by 2:00PM, as was the court practice at the time, the accused men were not returned by prison van to Pentridge prison as expected. Instead, at 4:30PM they were taken to the police cells next door in the City Watch-house, where they were to be held in custody overnight. Placed six to a cell, the prisoners were given a meal and a blanket, and the cells were inspected by a police officer on duty periodically until 11:00PM, when an officer in charge of the watch-house commenced duty.

Some time between 11:40PM that night and 12:30AM the next morning, five prisoners in cell 8 broke through the roof of their cell and escaped from the watch-house. The escape was led by Ryan, who stood on the taller prisoners' shoulders and, using a hinge he had prised off a wall in the watch-house prisoners' washroom, forced off a length of timber ridging and broke a small hole in the thirteen-feet-high zinc ceiling of the cell. This operation had taken some two hours, interrupted by periodic police inspections of the cells. Once through the ceiling Ryan had peeled back a section of the iron roof and helped the others climb through, using a length of blankets knotted together.

From the roof of the watch-house the prisoners moved to the roof of the court and, using the cell blankets to muffle the noise of their movements on the roof, climbed down into a courtyard. They reached the street outside by entering the court building and leaving through the main front entrance of the court at the corner of LaTrobe and Russell Streets. The five prisoners who took part in the escape were Ryan, Gallagher, Banks, Neville Raymond Burgess (another prisoner on remand accused of minor larceny offences unrelated to the other accused), and Saaed Hassan, an Egyptian accused of stowing away aboard the vessel *Castel Felice*, then in Melbourne, who was awaiting deportation by Commonwealth immigration authorities. The sixth prisoner in cell 8, a young German, chose not to join in the escape. Once clear of the court building the escapees mostly separated and went in different directions.[58]

This was the first escape from the watch-house in one hundred years, and the break-out was a big story for the Melbourne press.[59] Next morning a report of the escape led page one of late editions of both *The Age* and *The Sun* newspapers.[60] The papers also reported the fact that one of the five escapees, Burgess, had already been recaptured. And, in what was the first of a number of later stories to lead the Melbourne newspapers involving Ryan escaping from legal custody, police were reported as describing Ryan, Gallagher, and Banks as 'dangerous prisoners' who were 'likely to fight if cornered'. The source of this police characterisation was identified as a detective chief inspector, but this was perhaps a routine response by police when prisoners escape custody. The police logic may have been that prisoners desperate enough to escape from legal custody might well be dangerous to anyone inhibiting their attempt to abscond.

At that time, however, none of the three escapees had convictions for crimes of violence. Police reports on the antecedents of Ryan and Gallagher did not identify a disposition toward violence. In Gallagher's case, a CIB report on his antecedents written just four days before the escape for use at the committal hearing, observed that he 'comes from a good family, and so far as is known, none of the other members of his family have come under suspicion to the slightest degree. His associates, other than in one or two instances, are good ...' The report also recorded that Gallagher 'has some convictions, though for minor offences and larcenies only.'[61]

A police report on Ryan's antecedents, again written for the same purpose just four days before the escape, similarly recorded that he has 'convictions for minor offences only'. The report also observed that '[h]is wife is the daughter of the ex-Mayor of Richmond [sic], Vic. and appears to come from a respectable family.' The remainder of the report concentrated on Ryan's 'prolific' punting and sought subtly to establish his criminal proclivities by linking the large amounts of money he would commonly bet on a horse and the fact that 'he has not been known to be employed now for the last six months at least.' As in Gallagher's case, there was no mention of Ryan having a disposition toward violence.[62]

However, there was another CIB report written at this time that offered a quite different assessment of the character of Ryan and Gallagher. Two days after the CIB antecedents, a character report on Ryan and Gallagher was forwarded to the crown solicitor by Senior Detective Ray Tobin of Russell Street CIB. Dated 19 April 1960, the report recorded Ryan's birth date and married status, and continued:

> Ryan usually gives his occupation as a fisherman or painter and docker, but in actual fact has not worked for the last nine months at least. Ryan has during the past few months become obsessed with the idea that he is a 'big time' criminal with enough intelligence to outwit the forces of law and order. I have no doubt that this man has finally made up his mind to live outside the law and there is nothing I can say in his favour.
>
> Ryan during his early criminal career did not associate with other known criminals, but of late has been associating with notorious criminals such as, Robert Banks, John Elliott, and Charlie Robinson, and others.[63] Among the criminal element Ryan is said to be a dangerous man, and has, in fact, been carrying an automatic rifle and shot gun when he has been arrested by Police.[64]

The reference to the firearms is at odds with other statements by police when Ryan was arrested during this period. In all the depositions of police there are no references to weapons of any kind, although there is some other evidence that Ryan kept firearms.

Tobin went on to assess Ron Gallagher, in the course of which he made further observations about Ryan:

> Gallagher has at various times during the past nine months made some attempt to work honestly, but invariably drifts back into

> company with Ryan and again turns to crime ...
>
> Gallagher has not the brains or ability of Ryan, but by the same token, he is a criminal of no mean ability. Whilst he continues his friendship with Ryan, I can see little hope of him staying out of trouble with the Police.
>
> Gallagher does not associate with any known criminals except Charles Robinson, and, of course, Ryan.
>
> There is little doubt that in these criminal enterprises Ronald Ryan was the ringleader, and if allowed his freedom will continue to prey on unsuspecting business people in the community.[65]

Apart from Tobin's reference to Robert Banks being a 'notorious criminal', convictions for violence seem unlikely. Banks, aged 23, was on remand charged with the factory-breaking offence with Ryan and Gallagher at Dunne Bros. Burgess, aged nineteen, was on remand charged with the larceny of a car radio.[66] Having been already recaptured, he was not included in the police characterisation of the escapees as 'dangerous'.

In the event, all five escapees, including the three 'dangerous' prisoners, were re-captured within 72 hours and, although there were reports to the contrary, there was no real resistance by any of them. Two of the escapees, Hassan and Burgess, were recaptured within hours of their escape. Burgess was apprehended at around 3:30AM on 22 April, at Kilmore, 40 miles north of Melbourne, when a car he had stolen from Carlton overturned several times and crashed into a tree. Only slightly injured, he was arrested by police and taken to Kilmore Hospital for treatment. Hassan was arrested at 5:00AM just several city blocks from the watch-house. Later that day he was returned by immigration officers to the *Castel Felice*, which sailed from Melbourne that afternoon.[67]

As police set up road-blocks and raided houses of known associates, Ryan, Gallagher, and Banks remained at large during the course of the following three days. Gallagher was arrested after a police raid of a house in Burnley. Later evidence related how police entered the house, and found Gallagher and several other people sitting around drinking beer. Gallagher gave no resistance and was arrested.[68] Again, in what was a precursor of later events involving Ryan, the Melbourne newspapers gave a great deal of news prominence to the escape and police efforts to recapture the escapees.[69] At the time of the escape Ryan and Banks had proceeded from the court building to Elizabeth Street in the city and taken a taxi to Maidstone, where they slept under a school for two days.[70] They later walked to the bayside suburb of Elwood, where they moved to a rented upstairs flat Ryan had arranged at 24 Tennyson Street. They were there when, acting on a tip-off from one of the other escapees, six armed detectives and thirteen other police raided the flat on the night of Sunday, 24 April, just three days after the escape.[71] Police knocked on the door and called out: 'Police here—open up.' A voice behind the door said: 'If you want us, you'll have to come and get us.' The door was forced open and police found Ryan and Banks alone. As one detective took hold of Ryan's arm, another sought to take his other arm. After a short struggle he was subdued, as was Banks in the same way. The police informant, Detective Duggan, later stated that 'the struggle with Ryan and Banks was brief. I have had greater resistance.'[72] One newspaper account of the recapture the next day said that the arrest in the flat had taken just seven minutes.[73] Another newspaper characterised the recapture quite differently, quoting Senior Detective Tobin (the author of the character report on Ryan and Gallagher quoted above) as saying that 'the escapees violently resisted arrest, but were subdued after a ten-minute struggle in which furniture in two rooms was wrecked.'[74]

Later interviewed at police headquarters, Ryan offered the following in explanation of his escape from the watch-house:

> Look, I was going to try and get away for 12 months and get a job and do the right thing. I would've come back then, and given myself up, after I had some money for the wife and kids ... I wanted some money for the wife and kids before I went in—I know I've been a bloody fool, though.[75]

This was not the last time that Ryan would escape from legal custody.

All four escapees (the Egyptian, Hassan, having already been deported) were subsequently charged with escaping from legal custody and remanded to Pentridge prison. Crown prosecutors then combined the breaking and theft offences with the escape from legal custody, and the case was set down for hearing at the June sittings of the Court of General Sessions, Melbourne. When the case was heard on 17 June 1960, Ryan pleaded 'Guilty' before Judge Buller Murphy to seven counts of factory-breaking and stealing, one count of store-breaking and stealing, and one count of escaping from legal custody. Gallagher pleaded 'Guilty' to seven counts of factory-breaking and stealing, and one count of escaping from legal custody. Banks pleaded 'Guilty' to one count of factory-breaking and stealing, one count of store-breaking and stealing, one count of office-breaking, and one count of escaping from legal custody.[76]

After the presentment of the charges, Ryan's defence counsel Bill Lennon began the plea on sentence. Ryan did not blame anyone but himself, Lennon said:

> It is just a waste of time for me to say there are any mitigating circumstances. Between last July and last March, he embarked on a systematic criminal career which allegedly netted him property worth more than £40,000.[77]

However, Lennon continued, Ryan's only other brush with the law was five years before at Dandenong for frauds for which he was eventually given a bond. Until he was 31 years old, he said, Ryan was honest, hard-working, and a decent citizen, despite hardships imposed on him by invalid parents. Now he had an honest desire to reform.[78]

Called to give character evidence under oath, Dorothy Ryan told the court that Ron was an admirable husband and a wonderful father to his children, aged nine, six, and four. His concern about his financial position at the time of the offences was due to his consideration of the family, she said. To the crown prosecutor, Roland Leckie, Dorothy said she thought her husband was working at the time his crimes were committed. But she was not sure now. 'I did not know anything about his criminal activities,' she said. 'He used to go out as usual in the morning and I got my usual house-keeping money. At one time he deposited about £500 in my bank account,' she said.[79]

Following pleas on behalf of Robert Banks, and a statement from Ron Gallagher, who was unrepresented, the hearing was adjourned for sentence on 9 August. In the plea on that day, Ryan's counsel introduced a novel assertion about responsibility for the series of offences when, according to newspaper reports of the hearing, he put it to the court that the mastermind behind the thefts had never been apprehended.[80] Lennon said that reports of the men being involved in robberies amounting to £40,000 were overstated. He put the figure in the vicinity of £8,000 to £10,000.[81] Lennon said that the last of the money was being used by Ryan's wife to maintain herself and her children while her husband was in gaol.[82] Judge Buller Murphy responded that almost £29,000 in stolen property was unaccounted for from the robberies, and he would have to take this into account.[83]

In an unsworn statement to the court, Ryan said that he had made up his mind he had finished with crime, big or small, and offered to make restitution on his release from gaol. He told the court he had not made crime pay, and his example might deter other potential criminals. 'I have proved it the hard way,' he said.[84] This was a persistent refrain from Ryan in pleas to the bench. Even as he got deeper and deeper into crime, he persisted with the statement that he had seen the error of his ways and was abandoning his life of crime.

In an unusual statement to the court, given that he was one of the arresting officers in Ryan's recapture at Elwood, Detective Sergeant Arthur Slater, who was head of the breaking squad, gave evidence about Ryan. Slater was a figure revered by Ryan, whom he knew by his nickname, 'Wogsie'. An old-fashioned police officer, Slater went out of his way to help criminals who showed an inclination to reform or the promise of better. Ryan would not uncommonly visit Slater on his way home after being released from prison.[85] Giving his evidence, Slater said he believed that Ryan would not engage in crime again.[86]

Judge Basil Buller Murphy was a new judge to the County Court, having accepted a temporary appointment only several months before.[87] When he pronounced sentence it was clear he viewed the offences before him very seriously. Gallagher was convicted and sentenced to a total of seven-and-a-half years' imprisonment, with a minimum of three-and-a-half years to serve in relation to the seven charges he faced of factory-breaking and stealing, and the charge of escaping from legal custody. In relation to the charges against Robert Banks of one count of factory-breaking, one of store-breaking, one of house-breaking, and the charge of escaping from legal custody, he was convicted and sentenced to a maximum of four-and-a-half years' imprisonment, with a minimum of eighteen months to serve.[88]

In relation to Ryan, Judge Buller Murphy evidently did not agree with Detective Sergeant Slater's optimistic assessment of his potential to reform. He convicted Ryan on all charges, and sentenced him to three years' imprisonment on each of five counts of factory-breaking and stealing; two years' imprisonment on one count of store-breaking and stealing; and twelve months' imprisonment on a sixth count of factory-breaking and stealing. He directed that these sentences be served concurrently.

In effect, for the offences at Knitrex, Senga, Gotex, Victa, Vacu-Lug, and Hemingway, Ryan was sentenced to three years' imprisonment for the break-ins. On the charge of escaping from legal custody, Ryan was convicted and sentenced to six months' imprisonment. On a seventh count of factory-breaking and stealing, the break-in and theft of suits and cloth at Dunne Bros., he was convicted and sentenced to five years' imprisonment.[89] In all, Ryan was sentenced to a maximum of eight-and-a-half years' imprisonment to be kept to hard labour. But, with a minimum of three-and-a-half years to serve, there was, at least, some hope for Ryan that he might be released after the lesser period—if his behaviour in prison warranted it.[90] The notional date for his release, were he to serve the full term of the sentence, was 30 November 1968.[91] After a period in which he had systematically flouted the law and engaged in criminal activities on a large scale, it was now clear that Ryan would be going to prison for a long time.

CHAPTER SIX

Prison

[Ryan] has been an excellent prisoner and his future prospects are very good.

–Ian Grindlay

FOLLOWING HIS CONVICTION on 9 August 1960, Ryan was taken to Her Majesty's Prison, Pentridge, in Sydney Road, Coburg, where he began his eight-and-a-half-year sentence of imprisonment. Following his recapture after the escape from the City Watch-house in April, bail had been refused for Ryan, and he had been on remand in Pentridge since 24 April 1960.[1] A multi-purpose, bluestone-walled institution, Pentridge was the state's maximum-security prison. It housed some 1,100 prisoners and, dating from 1851, was Victoria's oldest gaol still in use.[2]

At least as he began his sentence Ryan had a glimmer of hope that he would serve only the minimum of three-and-a-half years. His sentence from the Court of General Sessions was regarded as having commenced from 1 June 1960, the notional first day of sittings—in which case he could expect to be eligible for parole on 30 November 1963.[3] Prison policy at that time was that the effective term of sentences could be reduced incrementally by prisoners earning remissions for good conduct. The purpose of the remission system was to provide an incentive for prisoners to accept prison discipline and behave well, and thus assist prison authorities in the secure management of the prison population. Given good conduct, Ryan might have his sentence reduced, perhaps by as much as four months in a term of three-and-a-half years.[4]

Within days of his arrival at Pentridge, Ryan underwent the classification processing that was a routine requirement for new prisoners, whereby he was assessed for the most appropriate regime of work, accommodation and, where suitable, training. After an initial assessment and assignment was made of a prisoner, supervision and periodic review and adjustment was undertaken to ensure that the regime was still appropriate. Ryan was classified following examination in respect of a comprehensive range of issues. These involved his physical and mental health, inclination to attempt escape, suitability for open prisons, aptitude and interest in trade training, educational needs and interests, employment history and skills, domestic situation, potential for recidivism, amenability to discipline, and the length of his sentence.[5] For all the information that might be collected about a prisoner such as Ryan, the purpose of classification was less to assist authorities in his rehabilitation than to ensure his effective management and secure incarceration. As the prisons division section of an annual report of the Social Welfare Department at this time bluntly observed, since 85 per cent of the 9,000 or so prisoners received into the system each year were serving sentences of less than six weeks, the imperative was to ensure that every prisoner 'was assigned to the correct niche ... These prisoners have to be fed, clothed, housed and employed. The question of reform simply does not arise.'[6]

It was in the context of this bleak and limiting process that a classification file was raised for Ryan, in which particulars about him that were largely accurate were entered.[7] His previous occupation was described as 'labourer'. He gave his religion as 'Church of England', the church to which he had converted from Roman Catholicism at the time of his wedding. His criminal record was listed and a social history was taken, which noted birth details, parents and sibling data, marital status, and education record. A summary of his work experience and criminal history was also taken.

A medical officer made a medical and psychological assessment of Ryan. The note entered on the file by Dr Levick was brief and to the point:

> Physically fit—ex-sleeper cutter—has no particular interest in employment or occupation.[8]

After individual interviews with each member of the classifications committee, and then an interview by the committee as a whole, Ryan's classification was completed. He was now Pentridge prisoner registered number 60/540, assessed as a medium-security risk, and assigned to B5 gang, meaning B Division, gang 5. A notation on his file recorded that he should be considered in six months' time for transfer to the Bendigo Training Prison, where he would be trained in sheet-metal work.[9] However, he was first assigned to work as a mill hand in the Pentridge woollen mill, primarily working as a bobbin-head spinner, for which he was paid three shillings per day. After only a month he was given work as a mule spinner in the mill, a job he was to continue to do for the next twelve months; his conduct assessment rose from 'satisfactory' to 'good', and his industry assessment rose from 'satisfactory' to 'very good'. In the November monthly progress report, three months after he started his term, a prison officer commented on Ryan: 'Doing very well. Interested in his job.'[10] He had made a rather better start than the one foreshadowed by Dr Levick in his medical assessment.

Like all prisoners, especially new ones, Ryan's classification was periodically reviewed. The procedure was a routine one for officers of the prisons division of the Social Welfare Department in Melbourne. At the regular weekly Classifications Committee review, chaired by the director of prisons, Eric Shade, on 4 December 1960, Ryan's classification was discussed with particular reference to advice that had come from the governor of Pentridge several days before. Telephoned to the secretary of the classifications committee, Edwin McMillan, on 28 November 1960, the advice was to the effect that the governor, Charles McGann, opposed Ryan's transfer from Pentridge. In particular, the message said that the governor was 'strongly opposed to the transfer of prisoners Robert Burns, C2 Gang, and Ronald J. Ryan, B5 gang, to any country Institution.'[11]

The reason for this advice is not recorded. No breaches of conduct were cited, nor were suspicions expressed about a disposition to escape legal custody. The advice seems to have been considered in a context of some serious concern about Ryan's secure imprisonment, however, because at its meeting on 4 December 1960 the committee resolved that Ryan would be assigned to the maximum-security division at Pentridge, H Division, for three months.[12] H Division, much later described by Ryan as Hell Division, was a very much harsher environment than B

Division.[13] H Division was reserved for hardened criminals held to hard labour, and prisoners being punished. In the event, Ryan did not complete the three months in H Division, but was returned to B Division after spending less than a month there. Nonetheless there seems to have been a residual concern about Ryan's security, or at least continuing support for the earlier advice from the governor of Pentridge. Ryan's request for a transfer to the Prison Training Farm at Beechworth in northern Victoria, a country institution, in the term used by the governor, was denied by the classifications committee at its meeting on 6 February 1961.[14]

With his progress reports all reporting 'very good conduct' and 'very good industry' from March to June 1961, Ryan again applied to the committee at its meetings on 26 June 1961 and again on 7 August for transfer, this time to the training prison at Bendigo, 100 miles northwest of Melbourne in central Victoria. Each time the decision was deferred to await advice. Finally, on 14 August 1961, Ryan's transfer to the Bendigo Training Prison was approved by the committee with the notation that he be assigned to training in the sheet-metal workshop. He was transferred to Bendigo ten weeks later on 21 October 1961.[15]

Bendigo was an old, walled prison dating back more than a century to the gold-rush era in Victoria. Like the country prisons, generally, it had a much less repressive atmosphere than Pentridge and, with a little over 100 inmates, was only one-tenth its size.[16] More importantly for Ryan, Bendigo had a progressive reputation and an innovative training program under its governor, Ian Grindlay. Whether Ryan ever received training in sheet-metal work is unclear, but the question is of some interest given Ryan's later safe-breaking activities involving oxy-acetylene cutting equipment, the standard tool of sheet-metal work. On his arrival Ryan was assigned duties as a billet, a prisoner allotted to specific but varied odd jobs such as coffee-making, cleaning, or delivering messages. He was to remain a billet for twelve months after he was transferred to Bendigo.[17]

The period of almost two years, from October 1961 to August 1963, that Ryan spent at Bendigo Training Prison were among the most settled and productive of his life. He was a focused and disciplined prisoner in Bendigo, and he made the most of his opportunities to better himself and, perhaps, to expedite his release from prison. He was recognised as having above-average intelligence, and his highly disciplined application to the tasks assigned to him marked him out among his peers.[18] Before his transfer to Bendigo, Ryan had begun studies in Pentridge for his Intermediate Certificate (year ten) by correspondence.[19] He had not been involved in formal study for more than twenty years, since his eighth-grade schooling at Rupertswood, although he had been a keen if irregular reader since that time, and exhibited a fondness for Shakespeare.[20]

The course he undertook was run by the Victorian Education Department's Correspondence School in Melbourne, and his progress was recorded as 'very good' and his attitude as 'excellent'.[21] At the end of 1961, after his transfer to Bendigo, he sat the external school Intermediate examination in English Expression and Arithmetic, and gained a pass in both subjects.[22]

At the start of the school year in 1962 Ryan enrolled for further Intermediate subjects, Maths A and Maths B. He submitted work set for these subjects, and the Bendigo Prison education officer, Neville Gray, noted that Ryan was a 'very keen and capable student' who was achieving 'excellent' results. Ryan, he concluded in his monthly report, was an 'outstanding student'.[23] With Intermediate level work obviously not challenging him, after first term had started in 1962 Ryan enrolled for four Leaving Certificate subjects by correspondence, English, Commercial Principles, Commercial Practice, and Economics.[24] Outside of formal study, it was noted that Ryan was interested in art, an interest he was to sustain for the remainder of his term at Bendigo.[25] He also excelled at woodwork and carpentry.[26]

Critical to Ryan's more settled period at Bendigo was the governor of the prison. Ian Grindlay was a progressive and reforming prison administrator, and Ryan was to find some stability in the security and opportunity that the prison offered. In the period after his time at Bendigo, Ryan spoke and wrote about it as a formative time in which he developed with Grindlay a close relationship of mutual trust and respect.[27] Ryan revered Grindlay, whom he described as a man of initiative, one who was dedicated, considerate, and humane.[28]

If prison life for Ryan was now taking on a more settled character, his family was enduring his prolonged absence as well as a loss of financial support. With his transfer to Bendigo, too, visits were more difficult as he was now further away. At this time, Dorothy and the children were living at 15 Cotter Street, Richmond, in a small four-bedroom timber house owned by her father, to whom she paid rent. Her parents and her brothers had assisted in comfortably furnishing the house. As the spouse of an imprisoned man, Dorothy was entitled to, and received, the Widow's Pension of £7 per week, together with small payments for child endowment. But that was not enough to live on, and so she took a part-time job as a secretary, for which she received £5 per week. The children, Janice, now aged eleven, Wendy, eight, and Rhonda, nicknamed Pip, six, were all attending Brighton Street State School, where they were in grades six, three, and two, respectively. Dorothy endeavoured to make home life as normal as possible for the children. They went to Sunday school and gymnasium club at St Stephen's Church of England in Richmond (where she and Ron had been married), and Jan and Wendy were in the Girl Guides and Brownies.[29]

Prison visits were important, for the children especially. Getting to Bendigo once a month was difficult, but at least Dorothy and the children could now visit him for two hours every month, double the time permissible at Pentridge. Travelling to Bendigo by train (or, sometimes, in her small Morris car), Dorothy would take the children for the visit at 2:00PM and they would catch the 4:00PM train back to Melbourne. It was a family day they all looked forward to.[30] Dorothy had not missed a monthly visit since his imprisonment. The impact on the children of Ryan's incarceration was considerable, and they all fretted for their father. Janice had had rheumatic fever and appendicitis, and fretted so much that, when Ryan was initially in Pentridge, Dorothy obtained her doctor's permission to take her there, provided she was carried at all times. Wendy always asked when her father was coming home; Pip thought her father was in hospital, and prayed to God to make him better.[31]

In April 1962, having spent two years in custody, including his time in Pentridge on remand, Ryan sought to expedite his release from prison. He took the initiative to enlist the assistance of his father-in-law in making representations to the Victorian government on his behalf for his early release. Eventually, the initiative would see Harold George writing to his friend, Sir Ewen Cameron, a Liberal member of parliament in the Victorian Legislative Council, who in turn made representations to the attorney-general, Arthur Rylah. Ryan's initiative took the form of a long, rather mawkish plea to George, some 1,500 words in all, in which he addressed his father-in-law as 'Sir', and set out his case for early release based upon the impact of his imprisonment on his family and his assurances that he had learned his lesson in prison. In setting out his case, Ryan clearly understood the unusual administrative process by which his sentence might be reduced.[32] He was now keen, he wrote, to take a new direction if he could just be reunited with his wife and family.

Dating the letter 17 April 1962, Ryan wrote:

> Sir,
>
> I would appreciate seeing you at your convenience, to discuss the possibility of your interceding, on my behalf, to the proper authorities for an early release.
>
> It is with mixed feelings that I pen this letter to you. There is the knowledge that I am leaving myself open to censure and, just possibly, ridicule through what might be considered my effrontery. Not so much for this letter on its own account, but viewed in conjunction with my past disappointments to you. However, I assure you that there is not the slightest vestige of selfish motivation in my asking you to intercede for us. If there was I could not bring myself to write this letter.
>
> I have keen perception and this leads me to deduce that you are thinking of making some effort to hasten my reunion with Dorothy and the children. This means so much to us. It is necessary to know the depth of Dorothy's love, the strength of her emotions and her urgent need of love and comfort to appreciate the worth of what you can do. Even if your efforts are of no avail, they will have an immediate effect, and a very important one in view of Dorothy's nervous strain and mental health. It will give her some hope, something to cling to and brighten her horizon. Without prospects life can be very uninteresting. As Dorothy is your daughter you must be aware, as I am, of her quality and right to happiness.
>
> Already, you have done much for which I am very grateful. A little help at the right time is more useful than a lot as attempted remedy, that is why I ask this now. I am aware of the reasons for your obvious reluctance in the past, and I am hoping you will realise you are dealing with a person of changed perspective. Unless you could be sure of that, and of my absolute sincerity and unselfish motives, I know you would hesitate to do anything. I am very aware

that, by my past, I have forsaken any right to hope for consideration on my own account. My acute awareness of this makes the writing of this request hard and embarrassing. I do not lack finer feelings and this heightens my reluctance. It is purely because of the existing effect, and possible irreparable influences on Dorothy and the children, and my absolute faith in the future, that I make this effort.

That I must benefit from your helping Dorothy and the children is obvious. This I know and do appreciate, but I am most emphatic and sincere in saying this is not part of my incentive. I am very deeply and, I can <u>now</u> say, unselfishly in love with Dorothy and our children. Their welfare and our family life is of inestimable value to me. I am aware that these are considerations I should have borne in mind earlier, but due to my warped perspective and false sense of values, I jeopardised all I treasure. That is done and I will always regret it. Yet, in view of my new awareness, I must admit that it is an experience from which I have benefited. I am thankful, very, very thankful, for being jolted back to sanity, and for this new awareness of that which I was treating so casually and carelessly, and which I would have lost. The past events have highlighted one important fact, that is Dorothy's whole-hearted, unselfish love and devotion. I am very aware of this great love and treasure it beyond all else, knowing what a rare treasure I possess. My future efforts and devotion to my family will reflect my deep gratitude.

I could ramble on and say what I will do and what I won't but say only this: I am very, very sincere. My motives stem from my great love of Dorothy and the children and my desire to foster and protect our family ties, and my awareness of their great love for me and what an early reunion means to them, both for the present and in the future, from benefits which would have their roots in the immediate effects and influence. Dorothy and the children need me. I can fill a need which otherwise must remain vacant. In the meantime, faulty foundations could be laid which could not be remedied. I am positive that my being home is essential to my family. I am sure they will all benefit from my proper perspective and new sense of values, and they need my love, protection and guidance. It is essential that any avoidable mental stress and strain be averted.

For my reference I offer the only one I can; but it is an infallible one: my wife's love and devotion, after twelve intimate and soul-revealing years. If there were any real faults then Dorothy would know them. Not even the most blindly devoted person, or even one lacking any other prospects, would endure the trials of my gambling as she has, if she wasn't sure of the fundamental worth of her partner. My place in the affections of my daughters supports this.

In my misguided efforts to get for my family what I thought they deserved, I developed a passion for gambling. It was along this supposedly short course that all my hopes went. My drive and ambition only hastened and enlarged my ultimate disillusionment and made my crash the heavier. Yes! crash I did, and hard, disillusioned almost to the point of being broken spirited. However, my vision cleared and, on finding my bearings, I was amazed at how far off-course I had floundered; how close to being wrecked and lost I had steered all which means so much to me. In the isolation of my gambling mania I had lost my perspective and sense of values. It was only due to my initial good judgment in picking such a wonderful wife that I owe my survival and future prospects. Yes! We have prospects and, as a family, second to none, having the bond of true and tested love and devotion. I have faith in my ability and still have ample drive which, now, will be put to proper use.

Time is opportune for various reasons: I have made every possible effort I can from here and I wish to repay my debt to society in a more useful manner. My proper perspective and true sense of values must be evident and it is [in] the mind that the change must take place. Judge Buller Murphy's words reflected his hope for my future, and regret that he must maintain a uniformity of sentence in my case, and regret for his task. The severity of sentence is relative to the individual, and the effects of worry, heartache and mental stress over my family, heightened by my awareness of the incalculable heartache and suffering of Dorothy and the children, how my deeds affect and reflect on others, together with the dread of losing all that matters to us; and my inability to foster and protect my family has been a sentence of the greatest possible stress and torture. My suffering has been heightened by my sincere love and need of my family and my awareness of their need for me. Our need to be as a family should be. I have served over two years, which could be considered adequate in view of certain facts.

> It is with conviction, and after careful consideration, that I say: any further time spent here is unnecessary, having learnt my lesson thoroughly. Lack of incentive and inability demonstrate my good faith is harmful [sic]. The utter futility of needless waste of time, so precious at this stage and age is frustrating. It is precious because of the guidance and influence the children need; the loving protection and moral support which only I can give, and which a family needs.
>
> If you have enquired, you will know that all the Parole Board can do is release me on my minimum date, less remission earned. For an earlier release it is necessary to get the approval of the Victorian Government, through the Crown Law Department, and Attorney-General, who must be approached through your local member of Parliament. This is a lengthy and involved process calling for prestige and a reasonable case on which to base your plea. It can be done, and has been done on at least three occasions recently. You have the prestige and proper approach; but the final decision is yours.
>
> I like to think it was not necessary to write this letter, but I do so to express my concern and give you some tangible evidence of my good faith and sincerity.
>
> I realise you have other worries and your time is in demand, but I rely on your innate sense of values and precedence to deal with this matter. I repeat that I am very sincere and, on that note, leave the matter to your judgment.
>
> —Ron[33]

As well as his own letter, Ryan enlisted Dorothy in writing a supporting statement that would accompany his own. Written on 16 May 1962, Dorothy set out a 'Statement re myself and husband, Ronald J. Ryan, at present in H.M. Training Prison, Bendigo.' The statement outlined some of the family's financial and social circumstances, and the children's schooling and their recent illnesses. Dorothy wrote, inter alia:

> I am very dependent on Ron for both financial and moral support and although I have managed so far I honestly feel that I am at the end of my tether. I worry should I fall sick and at the thought of my inability to do at least as much as I have been doing. This would, I feel, reflect very unfavourably on our children. Their future is so

> very important to both Ron and I and their welfare is the main consideration to us. Ron is a wonderful husband and father and his absence is having its effect on the children despite my efforts to maintain the previous high standard of guidance and control in their upbringing. As you may imagine their schooling and general behaviour has suffered.
>
> I too feel the strain in my efforts to provide for my children while at the same time maintaining the proper care which a family needs. My health has been affected by the sickness of the children …
>
> I have made every effort in Ron's absence and was not content to rely solely on the Widow's Pension and Children's Welfare and when our youngest daughter started school I took a part-time job as Secretary to help us financially from 9:30AM to 3PM daily and in that way I am only absent from home while the children are at school. I make a point of being home when they arrive as I do not want them to feel neglected in any way that I can help and I try to make up to them to the best of my ability for the loving attention their father has always given them … I long for the time when we can be together always as a family should be …
>
> It is very hard for me to manage financially and the worry of bringing the children up properly on my own is very hard and I hope you can understand my feelings in this matter and that this information will assist in my hopes.
>
> —Dorothy J Ryan[34]

As these documents were going forward to Harold George to assist any submission he might make, Ryan was engaged in a prison activity that, less than five years later, would elicit some notable resonances. Early in 1962 Ryan had become involved in the Bendigo Training Prison Drama Group as it prepared for a performance at the local eisteddfod, the well known Bendigo Competitions. Under the direction of a local drama teacher, Celia Douglas, the prison drama group had performed publicly for charity outside the gaol in the past, which was thought to be the first time a penal authority anywhere had taken a prison drama group outside to perform.[35] Now they were to perform in a public eisteddfod.[36] Douglas had chosen *The Valiant*, an American one-act play first performed in 1921.[37] Since that time and for many years it was, perhaps, the most popular one-act play in America. Rehearsals for the play started in the prison in March 1962 in preparation for the competition performance in Bendigo on 18 May. The small cast of six, including Ryan in a non-speaking role, was made up of Bendigo prisoners, and the sole female part was played by an outsider, a local actress.[38]

The play, written by Holworthy Hall and Robert Middlemass, relates the story of a condemned prisoner, James Dyke, awaiting execution. But Dyke is not his real name, and the prisoner has not revealed to anyone his true identity and the reason he killed a man, although the audience later suspects that the murder may have been either in self-defence or a matter of honour. The timeframe and focus of the play is the last few hours that the condemned man spends with the warden of the gaol and the Roman Catholic prison chaplain as they seek to persuade him finally to reveal his identity, which he will not do in order to protect his mother who is unaware of his imprisonment and imminent execution. A visit from a young woman who believes she may be his sister and who has not seen him for ten years is the dramatic centrepiece of the play. Despite the condemned man, Dyke, persuading her that he is not her brother, it becomes obvious to the audience that he is, and that his disavowal of the relationship is in order to protect her and his mother from the ignominy of association with a condemned man. Hence, the notion of 'the valiant'. The audience learns, too, that Dyke is a bookish young man of some sensitivity who recites Shakespeare and exhibits a finely honed moral sensibility. Neither the prison warden nor the priest nor the young woman succeed in discovering his identity and the young man is executed.

Ryan was cast as Dan, the jailer, who escorts the condemned man to his execution by hanging.[39] The dramatic finale of the play is the quotation by the condemned man, as he is led to the gallows, of Caesar in Shakespeare's *Julius Caesar*:

> Cowards die many times before their deaths;
> The valiant never taste of death but once.[40]

Significantly, given the group's lack of competitive experience, *The Valiant* won the one-act play section of the competitions, defeating five other entrants and just edging out an experienced Melbourne drama group, the Kew Repertory Players, by half a point, 84 points to 83 and one-half.[41] The prison group's appearance and its winning performance were the highlights of the competitions.

Two weeks after the eisteddfod win, Ryan's appeal to Harold George was advanced when, on 2 June 1962, Sir Ewen Cameron passed Ron and Dorothy's letters to the attorney-general. In his covering letter, Cameron wrote that Dorothy's parents were 'Councillor and Mrs Harold George, of Hawthorn, who have been intimately known to me for many years.'[42] Councillor George had asked him, he wrote to Rylah, to approach him 'with a view to seeking Ryan's release on parole in view of his conduct record and his outlook as expressed in letter to his father in law ...' Cameron added: 'It is unnecessary to mention the fact that the parents have not neglected their daughter nor her family during the husband's prison term and that they will do their best should Ryan be released. I commend same to your consideration which would be appreciated.'[43]

Upon receiving Cameron's letter, Rylah referred it to the director-general of the Social Welfare Department, Alec Whatmore, for advice.[44] In turn, Whatmore sought a report on Ryan's convictions from the director of the prisons division, Eric Shade. So advised, Whatmore (who was also a member of the Parole Board) wrote to the under-secretary of Rylah's department, John Dillon, on 28 June 1962, listing Ryan's convictions and making his recommendation:

> I am not at all impressed by the expressions of changed outlook as written to his father-in-law. In view of the nature of his offences and the length of sentence imposed, I do not feel that this is a case for release by special authority, but is one that should be left in the discretion of the Parole Board when he becomes eligible for parole.[45]

Essentially, the procedure by which it was submitted Ryan should be released was one termed special authority. This involved an order by the governor in council, made on the advice of the chief secretary, that a prisoner be released prior to the expiration of a fixed term taking into account any remissions. At this time, there were in Victoria usually fewer than six prisoners released each year on special authority.[46] In 1962, however, Ryan was not one of them. Whatmore's advice was evidently accepted, and nothing further was done about Ryan's early release on special authority. There, it seems, the matter was to rest.[47]

Through 1962 Ryan continued his prison studies for his Leaving

Certificate by correspondence; although, having taken up Leaving subjects, he did not sit the Intermediate examination.[48] His progress was so good that it was described as 'outstanding' by the head teacher at the prison, Neville Gray.[49] In November he was assigned to the Education Centre of the prison where he could study full-time.[50] In December 1962 he sat the external Leaving Certificate examination, and had 'no trouble in passing' all four subjects, completing an 'outstanding year's work', according to the training report written by his teacher.[51]

In February 1963 Ryan enrolled for Matriculation Economics, and within a month his good progress was recognised again when he was recommended for a Special Merit Remission. Neville Gray, who had written 'Outstanding!!' in Ryan's March training report, wrote to the director of prisons forwarding the recommendation for three days' remission of sentence:

> This trainee has completed two years outstanding study to pass Intermediate and Leaving Certificate Examinations conducted by the University of Melbourne.[52] In addition, he has also completed Correspondence Courses in Accounting and Auditing and Commercial Law A.[53]
>
> His attitude is at all times above reproach; his co-operation excellent; his courtesy faultless.[54]

The recommendation was supported by prison governor Ian Grindlay, and approved by the director of prisons, Eric Shade. Two months later, Gray had cause to write again to the director of prisons to commend Ryan's work and to propose a further three days' remission. The recommendation was approved: 'Ryan's work, co-operation and attitude in the Education Block is outstanding.'[55]

Given this progress, it is not surprising that governor Ian Grindlay shared his head teacher's high regard for Ryan. Prisoners were notoriously lacking in direction, and only a few maximised their prospects of advancement by adopting a disciplined approach to prison work or study. In 1963 only 22 Bendigo prisoners were engaged in full-time study in the prison's education centre.[56] Ryan stood out as the prisoner who was focused, courteous, disciplined, and determined to succeed. In terms of an assessment about a prisoner's prospects of rehabilitation, he excelled.[57] His correspondence teacher in Leaving English in 1962,

Neville Drummond, later described Ryan as the best student in this subject he ever taught.[58]

Governor Grindlay, too, had a high regard for Ryan. Born in the Melbourne inner-city suburb of Richmond, Grindlay was a child of the Depression, and shared with Ryan some formative early experiences of deprivation and hardship—among which was the fact that, to support himself, Grindlay had gone timber-cutting in his youth.[59] Grindlay was a prison officer for almost 30 years. In that time, he was exposed to several thousand convicted men in prisons at Pentridge, Ballarat, and Bendigo. Of all those prison inmates over his entire career, Grindlay regarded Ryan as not merely *a* model prisoner; he thought of him as *the* model prisoner.[60]

With the evidence of Ryan's outstanding educational work and his positive attitude, in May 1963 prison authorities at Bendigo began preparations for his possible release on parole. Ryan had done the best part of two terms' work for his Matriculation Economics. However, with such excellent progress noted by his prison supervisors, his prospects for parole were such that he did not see out the year at Bendigo, and he never did enter for the final examination in Economics.[61]

As he approached parole, a 'Summary of his Institutional Record' was prepared, noting that his conduct, industry, and response to training were all 'Excellent'.[62] Ian Grindlay wrote an assessment:

> Ryan's progress has been consistently outstanding. A mature man with ability and he has made full use of the opportunities at this prison. He has been an excellent prisoner and his future prospects are very good.[63]

The parole officer to whom Ryan had been assigned was Neil Beggs. Asked to assess Ryan and prepare a parole plan, Beggs reported on 30 May 1963 as follows:

> This man has had an exemplary record since coming to Bendigo Training Prison. He is also most impressive in interview. He claims to have matured a good deal, admitting that it has been a belated development. While in prison, he has gained his Intermediate Certificate, and is now studying for his Matriculation. Although his

> prior convictions for false pretences suggest some caution is needed, his self-awareness seems sincere, complete and likely to keep him on the right side of the law. In fact, he speaks of crime like a social worker.
>
> His wife comes from a good family, and has remained loyal to him despite pressure from her parents.[64]

In his parole plan, Beggs wrote that Ryan would be living with his wife at 15 Cotter Street, Richmond, in the house rented from his father-in-law. In relation to possible employment upon release, Beggs recorded that the prison's education officer, Neville Gray, 'is hoping to arrange employment with National Cash Registers', adding the reassurance in parenthesis, 'in a job without financial responsibilities.'[65] All of these reports were forwarded to the Adult Parole Board in Melbourne.

The Parole Board at the time comprised Supreme Court justice Sir John Barry as chairman, and eight other members, including the director-general of social welfare, Alec Whatmore.[66] The role of the board was to implement the parole provisions of the *Crimes Act 1958*, which set out the basis and conditions under which prisoners might be released at the expiration of the minimum term fixed at sentencing. Victoria's parole system had been for some years Barry's special project, and he had been chairman of the board since its inception. A radical penal reformer, strong abolitionist, and passionate believer in the goal of the rehabilitation of prisoners rather than simply their secure incarceration, Barry had pioneered the establishment of the Victorian parole system in 1957 and had chaired the weekly meetings of the Parole Board since then.[67]

At its meeting on 26 July 1963 the board considered the reports on Ryan, and noted that he had earned 114 days' remission of sentence for 'Good Conduct' and a further remission, related to his educational achievements, of nine days for Merit. Noting that Ryan's expected eligibility date for parole was 30 July 1963, the board decided that he would be paroled after review at the next Parole Board meeting one week later. Thus, on 2 August 1963, Ryan appeared before the board sitting in Melbourne and was released on parole on that day. He had served three years of his three-and-a-half years' minimum sentence; although, including the period on remand from April 1960, he had been in prison for a little over three years and three months. With his clothing returned to him, and his prison earnings of £72, he was released into the community on the basis that he report regularly to his parole officer and that, if he re-offended within the remainder of his eight-and-a-half year sentence, he would be returned to prison to serve the unexpired portion of it—five years, three months and 29 days.[68] In 1963, Ryan was one of 809 prisoners in Victoria released on parole from a prison population in the state of a little over two thousand.[69]

Following his release, Ryan immediately began work at Mobil Oil Australia Limited at its office building at 2 City Road, Melbourne, working in the general ledger section of the accounting department. This was a responsible clerical job, concerned with the accounting aspects of Mobil service-station leases.[70] Harold George had been instrumental in utilising his motor industry contacts to secure this employment for his son-in-law.[71] For a time, Ryan seemed to be progressing well, and his superiors reported his work as satisfactory.[72] To his fellow clerical workers at Mobil, Ryan was a softly spoken, nattily dressed man who always wore a fedora hat and was fond of horse racing. He was seen as rather private, and did not have many friends in the firm. He did not, for example, join with those groups of staff who sometimes went to the local hotel for a drink after work.[73] Still, he was engaged enough by the company to join his colleagues at a Mobil social evening. A photograph of a group of employees and their spouses and partners shows Ryan and Dorothy smiling and obviously enjoying the occasion.[74]

Ryan was to work at Mobil for less than ten weeks. On 9 October 1963 he told his immediate superior that he had a dental appointment at Port Melbourne after lunch. He left the office at lunchtime, but never returned.[75] For some time he kept up for his family the appearance of going to work at Mobil each day.[76] However, while he may have worked as a contract painter for a time, Ryan was already involved in criminal activities.[77] Ryan was later to tell police that he left Mobil because his mother had been victimised in the aftermath of a car accident at Balranald, and that he was required to take Cecilia to hospital for additional treatment and to attempt to gain for her some form of compensation.[78]

No doubt all parolees carry with them the hopes and expectations of the Parole Board and their parole officers that their conditional return to the community will be successful. There can have been few prisoners released on parole with higher expectations of success than the hopes held for Ryan by those who had supervised his imprisonment at Bendigo Training Prison. Even though at Mobil he had secured the sort of position he had hoped for—white collar, responsible, in an established, well-known corporate firm—he could not sustain it.[79] He returned to crime within a very short space of time. Precisely how soon after his release on parole he did so is not known, but he was first charged with an offence that was committed on 30 October 1963, just three months after his release from prison, and three weeks after his disappearance from Mobil.[80] It seemed that Ryan's self-destructive streak had returned.

St John's Roman Catholic primary school, Mitcham, 1936. Ron Ryan aged 11, is sitting cross-legged in the centre of the front row holding the chalk board. Ryan was in grade five in 1936.

Ryan's confirmation day, St John's, Mitcham, 15 August 1936. Ryan is in the back row, extreme right. He appears distinctly less well turned out than the other boys, having neither jacket nor tie.

Rupertswood, Sunbury in the 1930s. Built in 1874, this was the 50-room mansion of Sir William Clarke, the first baronet. The mansion and 840 acres were bought by the Salesian order in 1927 for £40,000, and turned into a school. Ryan was made a ward of state and sent to Rupertswood in December 1936.

Some early Salesians at Rupertswood. The Salesians were a new Roman Catholic order, and their early years at Sunbury were extremely difficult, owing to the huge mortgage debt over the property.

Ron's sisters, (left to right) Irma, Violet, and Gloria, at the Convent of the Good Shepherd, Abbotsford, circa 1941, where they had been placed in wardship since May 1939. In 1941, Violet was aged fourteen; Irma, twelve; and Gloria, ten.

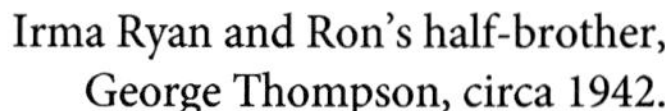

Irma Ryan and Ron's half-brother, George Thompson, circa 1942.

Ron's mother Cecilia at Balranald, circa 1945, with the family dog, Slipdrew. The picture was taken in the garden of the house in Church Street to which Ron brought his mother and sisters in early 1945.

Ron on his racing bike in Balranald, circa 1943. Aged almost nineteen, he won the feature race at Nyah on New Year's Day 1944.

Ron in the garden at Balranald, circa 1946. Aged 21, he had grown fit through arduous work in the bush, cutting timber.

Ron and Dorothy in 1948, not long after they had first met at a dance in Melbourne on the Yarra River ferry, the *Fairyland*.

Ron during a bushwalk at Britannia Falls, Yarra Junction, Victoria in 1948. Note the handkerchief he has carefully placed on the fallen log to prevent his trousers getting dirty.

Dorothy and Ron in 1949. The picture was taken at St Stephen's Church of England, Richmond, after Ron had converted to Anglicanism.

Ron and Dorothy on their wedding day, 4 February 1950, St Stephen's Church of England, Richmond.

Ron (second from right, at back) and Dorothy (second from right, front) with some of Ron's work colleagues and their wives from Mobil Oil Australia at a Mobil Centre dance, September 1963.

From left: Janice, Wendy, Dorothy, and Pip, early 1960.

Pentridge Prison, Coburg, where Ryan was taken in November 1964 to begin what he thought was a thirteen-years sentence of imprisonment. Established in 1851, Pentridge was Victoria's maximum-security prison. *(F. S. Feeley)*

This picture shows the timber and metal grappling hook, with two knotted bed-spreads, used by Ryan and Walker to scale the wall below the no.1 guard post in B Division during their escape on 19 December 1965.
(Constable David Richardson, Victoria Police)

The no-man's land between the B Division exercise yards, on the left, and the wall below the no. 1 post. The many pipes and service cables running along these walls, which Ryan and Walker used to scale the wall at right, can be clearly seen.
(Constable David Richardson, Victoria Police)

The Pentridge no. 1 post turret at the point at which Ryan and Walker scaled the wall using the grappling hook during the escape. The cables to which they attached the hook and pulled themselves up can be seen curving around the tower just below the top of the wall. *(Constable David Richardson, Victoria Police)*

The Pentridge car-park looking down from no. 2 post. The external gate through which the escapees exited the prison can be seen at the end of the path. Salvation Army chaplain Brigadier James Hewitt was taken hostage and marched through the gate and into the car park. Prison officer William Bennett trained his rifle on the escapees from this post. *(Constable David Richardson, Victoria Police)*

An aerial picture of Pentridge prison showing, in the right foreground, B Division, the car park through which the escapees ran, and St Paul's Roman Catholic Church where Walker took cover behind a low brick fence.
(The Herald & Weekly Times)

This picture shows the no. 1 post, no. 2 post, and the external gate through which Ryan and Walker escaped. The picture also shows the intersection of Champ Street and Sydney Road, where Hodson was fatally shot.
(The Herald & Weekly Times)

Police photograph showing the intersection of Sydney Road and Champ Street, outside Pentridge prison. The prison officer in the foreground was asked to stand on the spot where prison officer George Hodson fell. The officer further away in the centre of the picture is standing where Ryan stood when he aimed his rifle at Hodson. *(Constable David Richardson, Victoria Police)*

This picture, looking west from below no. 2 post, shows the intersection of Champ Street and Sydney Road with the BP Service Station on the corner of O'Hea Street opposite.. *(Constable David Richardson, Victoria Police)*

Prison officer George Henry Hodson who, unarmed, bravely gave chase to the escapees after they had exited into the prison car-park. Hodson was shot in Sydney Road as he closed in on Walker; he died where he fell.
(The Age)

The scene in Sydney Road moments after Hodson was shot and fell mortally wounded on the tram tracks. He died within minutes.
(The Herald & Weekly Times)

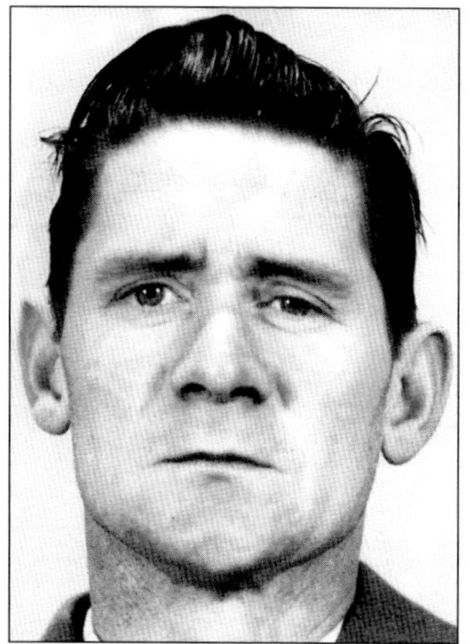

The photographs of Ronald Ryan (left) and Peter Walker (right) released by police after their escape from Pentridge. *(The Age)*

The Vanguard sedan that Ryan and Walker commandeered to make their getaway from Pentridge was later found by police abandoned in Bruce Street, Kensington. *(The Age)*

Arthur Henderson, a 24-year-old tow-truck driver who was shot and killed by Peter Walker in Middle Park on 24 December 1965, while the escapees were on the run. *(The Age)*

Christina Aitken, a 23-year-old prostitute who had been Henderson's girl-friend not long before he was killed. She was later charged with harbouring the escapees, but was eventually acquitted. *(The Age)*

The toilet block in Beaconsfield Parade, Middle Park, where Henderson was killed by Walker. *(The Age)*

CHAPTER SEVEN

Relapse

[Ryan], you ask me not to impose a crushing sentence. You have already got a good long sentence to serve, but my word, this sort of thing has got to be stopped somehow.

—Judge Len Read

BY COMMITTING OFFENCES and breaking his parole in October 1963, Ryan was risking a return to gaol. This was not merely for whatever sentence he might ultimately receive for these offences (and other crimes for which he might subsequently be charged), but for the unexpired portion of his earlier prison sentence—five years, three months and 29 days—that he would then be required to serve. Hence, in an offence of some consequence, on 30 October 1963 Ryan broke into and entered the butcher's shop owned by BJ Clarke Pty Ltd (trading as James Meats) in Hamilton Place, in the Melbourne outer suburb of Mount Waverley.[1] Ryan had never before been charged with safe-blowing although, as indicated earlier, safe-blowing did feature in at least one earlier robbery undertaken by an accomplice in the Vacu-Lug factory-breaking and stealing offence of February 1960.[2]

On that day, Ryan drove his car to Mount Waverley, taking with him a breaking implement, some gelignite, fuses, and detonators. After forcing the back door of James Meats by levering it open with a jemmy, he searched for and found the safe. He then charged the safe up by setting the explosive charge on top of it and blowing off the top, and then set another charge inside it in the combination shaft hole. But, as he later told police:

> [the safe] ... failed to blow, and I could see that it was futile and I could see that it was impossible to retrieve the explosive. I then decided to abandon the attempt on this safe. I was worried about the explosive left in the safe as somebody might get hurt poking around. I left a warning note saying: 'Danger beware explosives'.[3]

Ryan's account of events was subsequently confirmed by the manager of James Meats. He told investigating police that, on the evening of 30 October, he had placed £178 in the shop's floor safe before securing it, and locking and leaving the premises. Returning the following morning, he had found a bag of sawdust and a bag of salt lying across the top of the safe, upon which was a handwritten note reading, 'Safe loaded with high explosives', and containing a warning to be careful.[4] An explosives expert later found traces of explosive inside the safe.[5]

Ryan's failure to blow the safe at James Meats was not the end of this particular criminal episode. Undeterred, he simply chose another butcher's shop in the same shopping centre in Mount Waverley. He went to Dewhurst Butchery, a butcher's shop owned by William Angliss & Co Australia Pty Ltd, where he broke into and entered the shop by forcing a grille off the back window. He found the safe against a wall, proceeded to fill the keyhole with gelignite and a fuse, covered the safe with bags, lit the fuse, and blew it. He then stole £180 in cash that he found in the safe.[6]

Butchers' shops were to become a regular robbery target in the weeks ahead. On one such occasion Ryan took his daughter, Wendy, aged ten, in his car to a location in Richmond where he planned a robbery of a butcher's shop in Swan Street, Richmond, just down from Dimmey's store. This was the first time her father had taken Wendy anywhere with him by herself, and she was excited. As she sat in the back of her father's Morris car with another man also in the front, Ryan drew a map of the layout of the premises with particular emphasis on the location of the safe at the back of the shop. After they returned home, and she was put to bed, she could hear her father and the other man planning the robbery through the wall in the next room.[7]

The incident involving the warning note about explosives suggests an usual degree of sensitivity by a criminal to the prospects of injury to an unwitting party. When Ryan's behaviour later became known to others, this incident gave rise to the sobriquet that journalists used about him: 'the gentleman safe-cracker'. This was not the last time in this period that Ryan became anxious about his own aggressive acts. His note and his warning hint at an internal conflict: he seems aware of his own aggression and yet recoils from it. It is as if he cannot easily establish the boundaries of his aggression which, once unleashed, assumes lethal proportions. It was not the only time Ryan exhibited this kind of behaviour, although another criminal incident during this period was far from gentlemanly.

This incident, involving robbery with violence, began at 10:00AM on 18 November 1963, when Ryan rang the manager of the Mutual Finance Company Pty Ltd on the fourth floor of Champion House, 57 Swanston Street, Melbourne. Using the alias 'John Myers from the Victorian Market', Ryan arranged an appointment for 10:45AM to discuss a loan. Arriving at the appointed time, Ryan spoke to the manager, Ernest Jansen, 75, of Manning Road, East Malvern. Jansen was alone in the office; his secretary, Patricia Oman, had left for a short time to deliver a message. Ryan told Jansen, who had never seen Ryan before, that he wanted £200, and gave the impression that he wanted the money as a loan. Jansen told him that this amount was out of the question, but said that if Ryan liked he could probably arrange a much smaller loan, about £25 to £30. Ryan thanked Jansen and moved to the door as if he was going to leave, but then came back and bashed Jansen several times on the head with a cosh, a short rubber truncheon. Jansen fell to the floor, dazed and bleeding. As Jansen lay slumped near the safe, Ryan went through his pockets and found his keys, and demanded to know which key opened the safe. By chance, Ryan was holding it. Jansen nodded confirmation of the right key after Ryan hit him again.

Ryan opened the safe, rummaged inside, grabbed £700 cash and then, after wrenching the office telephone from its wall socket to prevent any quick alarm being given, quietly walked out. After a few minutes Jansen, apparently badly injured, was able to stagger to a next-door jeweller's office to tell the jeweller, Maurice Cochaud, of the attack. Cochaud rang police and an ambulance, which took Jansen to the Royal Melbourne Hospital. What neither Jansen nor Cochaud knew was that Ryan, too, had called an ambulance. When he left the office, Ryan was seized with anxiety that his blows to Jansen had been fatal. After ringing the ambulance, Ryan waited around a corner for it to arrive and, reassured that it had, went home, where he told a horrified Dorothy what he had done. That night he had a terrible nightmare that he had killed the old man.[8]

Despite Ryan's anxious belief, Jansen was not as badly injured as appeared, and he recovered quickly. After treatment for his head and neck wounds he was well enough to be discharged from the Royal Melbourne hospital the next morning. Jansen later told police that the offender was about 35, with fair hair, and was well dressed. Although this closely matched Ryan's description (he was 38, with fair hair, and always well dressed), he was never questioned about this offence by police, for whom the description was probably too general to be of much use.[9] Since it was also outside Ryan's usual pattern of criminal activity, he would not have been an obvious suspect.

Whether Ryan went to the finance company office on the pretext of inquiring about a loan in order to learn of the whereabouts of the safe, intending to return later and blow it, or whether his intention from the outset was to stage a robbery in the manner that in fact occurred is unknown. Perhaps the opportunity presented by an elderly manager being temporarily alone offered an irresistible temptation to Ryan. Notwithstanding that Ryan was struck with anxiety and remorse for his actions, it was a brutal and cowardly attack on a defenceless old man. Until now, Ryan has never been linked with this assault and robbery; it is disclosed for the first time in this book. The revelation of the assault casts serious doubt on the common belief that Ryan had never committed a crime involving violence prior to his escape from Pentridge in 1965.

As far as further discovered offences were concerned, whatever remorse Ryan felt over the attack only deterred him for a short time. Less than four weeks later, on the night of 13 December 1963, he broke into JC Huttons Limited, a large meat and smallgoods factory at 50 Oakover Road, East Preston. The robbery involved Ryan jemmying open an upstairs factory door and proceeding to the office, where he found a small safe which he dragged out to the middle of the floor. He rammed gelignite into the keyhole and inserted a detonator and fuse, but the subsequent explosion failed to open the safe door. Ryan then slid the safe down the back stairs, rolled it out through a back gate, and put it in the boot of his car. He took the safe to a secluded location among the Tea-tree foreshore in the Melbourne bayside suburb of Seaford. Here, using an oxy-acetylene kit he had picked up on the way, Ryan cut the safe open and removed the contents: £875 in cash, some cheques, which he tore up, and a .25 calibre Colt.

The very next night Ryan and an accomplice drove to Colac, 90 miles south-west of Melbourne, in Ryan's Morris car. After midnight on that night, 14 December 1963, they broke into Foy Bilsons store in Murray Street, Colac, intending to blow the safe. But upon inspecting the safe they changed their minds, and instead stole food, liquor, cigarettes, clothing, and electrical goods by loading them onto one of the firm's trucks and driving off with it. The value of the goods stolen was £2,100. Setting off for Melbourne, Ryan's accomplice drove the truck while Ryan drove ahead of it in the Morris. However, when the truck was intercepted by police at Mount Moriac, and the driver arrested, Ryan escaped by quickly driving the car into bushes and waiting for police to leave. Later he drove the car to Werribee and left it there before hitching a ride home.

Three weeks after the Colac break-in Ryan attempted another robbery of a butcher's shop, this time at Pre Pack Meats at 343 Victoria, Street, Abbotsford. Ryan had passed the shop and noticed the safe under the counter, and planned to come back to steal it. Returning on the night of 4 January 1964 with his breaking implements and two accomplices, Terrence Greig and Alfred Marsden, Ryan broke into the shop through an old brick wall at the rear of the premises. Finding the safe, he dragged it from the front to the side door, and then loaded it into a Holden utility which was parked at the side door of the shop. With Marsden driving the utility, Ryan and Greig drove off in Ryan's own car, intending to travel in convoy to another location where they would cut open the safe.

As Ryan and his accomplices were driving south along Church Street, Richmond, not far from the Pre Pack premises in Victoria Street, his car and the utility driven by Marsden were stopped by police. Ryan fled from the car but was chased by police, apprehended, and returned to the car. Searching the vehicle, police found house-breaking tools on the floor and a .25 calibre automatic pistol, loaded with five rounds in the magazine but none in the chamber, in the parcel tray under the glove box. All three men were then arrested and taken to Russell Street CIB for questioning. Police then went to 115 Alma Road, St Kilda, part of which had been rented by Ryan for a period of four weeks. In two rooms of Flat 4, a bungalow at the rear of the premises, police found two sticks and two half-sticks of gelignite, a number of safety-fuse detonators, and an electric detonator with wire attached. They also found a quantity of .45 calibre ammunition and .25 calibre ammunition. In a wardrobe, they found oxy-acetylene equipment and a cutting torch that had been purchased by Ryan from Commonwealth Industrial Gases (CIG) using the name of Thompson, his birth name.[10] Later police investigations showed that the car Ryan had been driving was registered in the name of Ronald Victor Eddy (another variation of his birth name Ronald Edmond), who was believed by police to be Ryan.

Interviewed by police at Russell Street police headquarters, Ryan at first denied the offences. But following the search and discovery of the gelignite and cutting equipment at his St Kilda flat, police again put to him questions relating to the offences at James Meats, Dewhurst Butchery, JC Huttons, and Pre Pack Meats, and also relating to the Colac break in. This time he confessed. Asked by police for the names of those who had assisted him in the commission of the offences at Pre Pack Meats the night before, Ryan replied: 'You've got me. I won't put anybody else in. I did it alone. I'll take all the blame.' Asked what he did with the money from the Dewhurst offence, Ryan replied: 'I've got a wife and three daughters and I spent it on food and clothes for the family.' Further asked by police why he had committed the Huttons robbery, Ryan said he was short of money, and that he had used the proceeds from the robbery to pay some bills and buy some more oxy-acetylene equipment.

Ryan was charged with these break-and-enter and theft offences; the day after his arrest, on 6 January 1964, he appeared at the Melbourne Court of Petty Sessions and was remanded in custody. Further court appearances at Melbourne Petty Sessions followed through January until 3 February 1964, when he was released on bail of £600.[11] When Ryan failed to appear for a preliminary hearing at the Richmond Court of Petty Sessions four days later on 7 February, police believed he had fled to New South Wales.[12]

It is uncertain when Ryan first began committing offences in New South Wales, but it is clear that, from early April to mid-July 1964, he committed a lengthy string of offences about which he later made confessions to NSW police.[13] The first offence about which he later made admissions took place on 4 April 1964, when he broke into and entered the Cootamundra Country Club, and stole £5 and some cigarettes. Later the same day he broke into and entered the Guildford Returned Servicemen's League and Ex-Serviceman's Club, and stole £350 from the strongroom. On 23 May he broke into and entered a chemist shop in Enfield, and stole property valued at £300. On 3 June he broke into the Club Hotel at Campbelltown, and stole the safe containing £124-13-0. On 24 June he forced a window at the Chatswood Bowling Centre and, using butter instead of the usual plastic clay to attach gelignite to the strongroom door, blew off the door and stole £300.[14] On 3 July he broke into GJ Coles store in Enfield and stole groceries valued at £382. More break-ins at Coles stores were to follow; three days after the Enfield robbery, on 6 July, he broke into the GJ Coles store at Merrylands, and stole groceries to the value of £340. Another theft followed on 11 July when he stole groceries from another Coles store, this time at Greenacre, valued at £656.[15]

The most serious of the NSW offences involved an attempted armed robbery by Ryan and others of the Rosehill Bowling Club on 28 June 1964. On that night, Ryan, wearing a hood over his head and armed with a .32-20 calibre rifle, and in company with three other men, entered the Rosehill Bowling Club by a side door and ordered the club officials present to put up their hands, saying, 'This is a stick-up!' Ryan then fired a shot—through being tense, he later said.[16] The subsequent police charge was that Ryan 'then being armed with an offensive weapon, to wit, a rifle, did assault Lionel Livermore [the club assistant manager] with intent to rob him.' Further police evidence related that Ryan had bought ammunition for this weapon the day before at Mick Simmons Store in Sydney. The offenders then demanded that the officials open the strongroom, which had a combination lock. When the officials told Ryan that they did not have the combination, they were locked in a room and the offenders left the premises. However, as they left in a car, they were pursued by a young motor cyclist who had witnessed the offenders leaving the premises and had given chase. According to police, 'Ryan, who was driving, then crashed the following motor cyclist.'[17]

Newspaper reports of this crime, and the court hearing that followed, related a somewhat different account of the incident, and key features of the crime did not conclusively bear the meanings police attributed to them. According to *The Daily Telegraph*'s report of the crime the next day, 'the man with the rifle fired a warning shot through a glass door, a few feet from the [drink] stewards. They hit a club official twice over the head with the rifle butt when he said he could not open the strongroom.' *The Telegraph*'s account also reported: 'Police said they were satisfied the shot was not meant to hit any of the stewards but only to frighten them.'[18] A further newspaper report the next day related that 'police yesterday charged three young men with attempted robbery at the Rosehill Bowling Club on Sunday night. They will appear in Parramatta Court this morning.'[19]

Newspaper reports of that court hearing make it clear that Ryan was not one of those charged and, more importantly, the court evidence indicated that he was not the offender in possession of the rifle who had committed the assault. The police prosecutor told the court that one of the three men charged, Ronald Vincent McGarrity, 29, a labourer, of Mountford Street, Guildford, had struck the assistant manager of the bowling club over the head with a rifle butt. It was McGarrity who was charged with having assaulted Livermore while armed with a .22 calibre rifle with intent to rob him.[20] All newspaper reports of the court hearing made it clear that only one rifle was used in the robbery.[21] One local newspaper report related that 'police were maintaining a State-wide search, 24 hours a day, for a fourth man, believed to be armed with a rifle.'[22] This fourth man was evidently Ryan.

The final point is that the police account that Ryan had 'crashed the following motor cyclist' is open to dispute, as well. In a page-one story, *The Daily Telegraph* related an interview with the young motor cyclist who had pursued the offenders' car for some distance from the scene of the crime. As he related it, he was pursuing the car when its brake lights showed suddenly and the car went into a skid, blocking his machine. His motor cycle struck the rear of the car and he was flung off, suffering a broken collarbone and lacerations. While the motor-cyclist was quoted as saying that he believed the offenders had deliberately caused his machine to crash into the rear of their fleeing car, even these circumstances are significantly different from the perception created by the police report that Ryan had deliberately *driven into* the following motor cyclist.[23] According to a signed hand-written confession made by Ryan when he was in custody at Melbourne CIB, the cyclist had crashed into the car when the driver braked to turn a corner.[24] This statement by Ryan also suggests that he was not himself the driver, which would be consistent with his previous criminal activities.

Following the last offence at Greenacre on 11 July 1964, and with a warrant for his arrest having been issued for him after he had absconded whilst on bail early in February 1964, Ryan travelled to Melbourne. He arrived unannounced at his home at 15 Cotter Street, Richmond on the night of 14 July. His appearance was different, too; to avoid detection by police he had grown a moustache, and had coloured it black using boot-polish applied with a toothbrush.[25] By now he had been in New South Wales for more than five months, although he had secretly returned home several times during that period, usually leaving home before daybreak to return north.[26] It was dark when Ryan arrived at Cotter Street. Jan, aged thirteen, was standing in the kitchen when she heard a tapping on the back window. It was her father, wearing a black and white hat, which somehow irritated her as it seemed too young for him. She had missed her father terribly during his absences, but now his arrival prompted resentment at his neglect. After she let him in, there was time for some talk before she went to bed. But this particular return was to be an unwelcome homecoming, as Janice soon became aware. Ryan threatened Dorothy and physically assaulted her. This was not the first time that he had physically assaulted Dorothy, but it was the worst assault in their fifteen years together. Physical violence had been a periodic feature of their marriage virtually from the beginning. Alcohol was not involved. Ryan had an explosive temper and, perhaps once or twice a month, he would fly into a rage and hit Dorothy. The pattern of these assaults was that he would blow up when he was shown to be wrong about some point of dispute between Dorothy and him. At such times he would go out and not return till the next day. After such violence Ryan was usually stricken with remorse. He recognised that he had a temper, and sought to contain it.[27]

On the night of 14 July 1964 Ryan's surprise return and the suddenness of the assault had shocked Dorothy and the girls, who became aware of it. The girls were fearful of further assaults by their father against their mother.[28] Very early the next morning, Dorothy told Jan to 'go next door and ring Uncle Frank', which she dutifully did. Frank George promptly rang the police.[29] A short time later, police telephoned the house to speak to Dorothy and have her confirm what they had been told by a relative.[30] Dorothy managed to convey the fact that Ryan was, indeed, present in the house, saying, 'Yes, yes, he's here,' but telling Ryan when he inquired that she was speaking to an aunt.[31]

Within minutes, at around 6:30AM, police raided the house, coming through the front door while Ryan hid behind the bedroom door where, ignominiously, he was discovered by nine-year-old Pip. 'Why are you hiding behind the door, Daddy?', she innocently asked.[32] Ryan was arrested, and appeared later that day at the Court of Petty Sessions at Melbourne where he was remanded in custody to appear at St Kilda Court of Petty Sessions on a charge of shop-breaking and stealing. On 22 July his case was heard before a stipendiary magistrate; he was found guilty, convicted, and sentenced to six months' imprisonment.[33] On the same day he was interviewed by NSW police from the safe squad, CIB, about the attempted robbery at the Rosehill Bowling Club. Interviewed by safe squad Detective Sergeant Noel Morey, Ryan admitted the offence and made a handwritten confession.[34] New South Wales police subsequently issued extradition warrants for Ryan in relation to the Rosehill offence and the other offences discussed above. Given his imprisonment and the later charges he faced in Victoria, however, the warrants were never executed.[35] On 23 July, at St Kilda Court of Petty Sessions, Ryan's breach of parole was reported, and he was directed to serve the unexpired portion of his sentence. On 4 August 1964 he was sent to Pentridge to begin his sentence.[36] It had been just twelve months and two days since his release from Bendigo Prison.

Further court appearances by Ryan were to follow. On 18 August a committal hearing was held at Richmond Court of Petty Sessions on charges of breaking and entering. A police report forwarded for the information of the crown solicitor and forming part of the prosecutor's Brief of Evidence at that hearing related that 'Ryan appears to associate with criminals and it would appear that he is an organiser of crime.' The police informant also noted that 'Mrs Ryan appears to be a decent respectable woman and has a clean well-kept home and family. I am of the opinion that she was aware of her husband's activities.' The informant added in the report:

> I am unable to find any special circumstances which could explain his commission of these offences, other than his desire to gain large amounts of money quickly. It is known that Ryan was a heavy gambler. He also applied himself to learning the latest oxy-acetylene cutting techniques, and was found to possess a very comprehensive kit.[37]

At this hearing Ryan, still in custody, was committed for trial at the Melbourne General Sessions Court at its October sittings.[38] On 28 August Ryan again appeared in the Richmond Court of Petty Sessions and, in relation to the charge of having absconded whilst on bail, forfeited his recognisance and was sentenced to a fine of £500 or three months' imprisonment.[39] Unable to pay the fine, he was returned to Pentridge where he was imprisoned while he awaited the court hearing on the breaking and entering charges of October and December 1963, and January 1964. Assigned to D Division, Ryan was set to work as a spinner in the prison's woollen mill.[40]

With the Colac offences listed for 27 October at Colac, Ryan wrote to the prothonotary on 12 September seeking to have all cases heard in the Melbourne Court of Petty Sessions instead.[41] In the event, the venue was shifted to the Melbourne Court of General Sessions, and on 14 October Ryan made an application for an adjournment, indicating his intention to change his earlier plea of 'Not guilty' to that of 'Guilty'.[42]

Thus, on another Friday the thirteenth, 13 November 1964, Ryan faced a criminal trial before a judge; but this time luck would be against him. Ryan pleaded 'Guilty' before Judge Len Read in the Melbourne General Sessions court to one charge of shop breaking with intent; shop breaking and stealing (three counts); and possessing explosives in suspicious circumstances and receiving stolen goods (two counts). Unrepresented by counsel, Ryan addressed a very long, handwritten plea to the judge prior to sentencing. This was a characteristic approach by Ryan; he had used it before with Harold George in 1963. In his plea for leniency to Judge Read, Ryan set out his remorseful attitude and his changed perspective, and related it in the context of the narrative of his family history, particularly dwelling on his claim always to be the wronged party, and on the injustices and misfortunes which had beset him at various points through his life.

The letter, highly articulate in its own way, was written over five foolscap pages, each of which Ryan had meticulously ruled top, bottom, and side in red ballpoint. It was as if he was trying to put a boundary around the long criminal history he was about to relate:

> Your Honour,
>
> I realise I cannot—when viewed in retrospect—justify my actions, nor can I reasonably expect you to accept the following

points as extenuating circumstances. However, I set them down and you may choose to see them as a backdrop against which to view my crimes, determine motivation and assess my degree of culpability. I hope for your understanding and empathy while reading what may unavoidably and at times, seem maudlin and self piteous.

First, a brief résumé of childhood and youth: In 1935 when I was ten, my three sisters and I were sent to Catholic institutions as a result of my father's ill-health (Miner's Phthisis). After four years I ran away, got a job as contract wood cutter and, subsequently, as a sleeper-cutter. I saved my money and set up a home. As I was comparatively young and of small stature, this required great physical effort and mental discipline. My Mother and I—my father at this time was at point of death in a sanatorium—went to the Welfare Department and sought permission—on the basis of my bank balance, home and potential—to take my sisters from the convent. After asking me was I aware that they could cast me back, but conceding that they'd hold this in abeyance pending enquiries, they ultimately released my sisters. Thus, allowing us to become a family again. I then put them through school, had them taught typing, music, etc, and, today, they are happily married with families. As a result, my own schooling was neglected, and I was unable to marry the girl with whom I'd been lovingly associated for seven years. When, finally, I was able to it was too late.

Later, I went share-farming. The first year was profitable. Then my mother and sisters were burnt out, losing everything. I had recently bought new furniture, but was naive enough to be uninsured. The second year I was ruined by torrential rain and floods. Then I came to the city to seek easier work as I was in poor health, and unable to continue the exacting bush work. I eventually met and, in 1950, married my present wife. We have been extremely happy; but tragically, that is seemingly finished. Ironically, I stand to lose the family life and ties I have sought after, fostered and cherished all my life. To appreciate the extent of this tragedy it is necessary to know the degree of our love and happiness as a family. My Daughters are now 13, 11 and 9 years respectively. They are doing extremely well at school—all being in the top group in their classes. The eldest is a senior prefect. The effect of my actions on their lives increases the tragedy.

In 1956, as a result of helping a previous work-mate, I first fell foul of the Law. I was then naive, certainly foolish. In 1959, in desperation after the ill-health of myself and the children, I sought to bolster my family's welfare by stealing. I was caught and that one unlawful venture became a sequence as I tried to cover the legal expenses and get money to leave with my family during my expected imprisonment. I was ultimately sentenced to 8 1/2 years with a 3 1/2 yr minimum. This was a fatal blow to myself and my family. However, I resolved to set about securing my family's future by resuming the studies I had been forced to neglect as a youth. Despite adverse conditions I obtained my Intermediate and Leaving Certificates, completed Stage I of Accounting and Auditing and was half-way through Matriculation upon release in August 1963.

After a humiliating round of interviews and rejections, I eventually secured a good position in the main Accounting Dept. of Mobil Oil. But, in life the good things usually come too little or too late.

Our separation had a devastating effect upon my wife's health. She was on the point of a complete physical and mental breakdown when I returned home; but the children reflected the effort it had cost her. My wife's health had deteriorated to an alarming degree. Once robust and healthy, she had lost about three stone in weight. She had worked—leaving home after getting the children off to school and returning just before them so as not to leave them alone or have them come home to an empty house—even continuing when she was on crutches after a foot operation. During all this time she was under severe emotional stress, should have had an operation for gall-stones which caused her excruciating pain and had to sustain the added shock of the serious illness of the children—scarlet fever, peritonitis, crushed hand.[43] She bore this alone while suffering extreme loneliness and heartache because of our separation. I repeat, that it is necessary to know of our deep attachment as a family to properly conceive of her extreme suffering. Furthermore, my Mother who is 76 and a pensioner had a near fatal road accident and, because of lack of witnesses and her own infirmity was unable to properly press her claim. Unjustly, she had to accept a nominal settlement.

Therefore, upon release, I was frantic at my family's plight. My income was inadequate to sustain us and make provision for school clothes and books, etc, and my wife not only could not work, but needed an operation. I was subjected to all this pressure while settling into an important job during what statistics show is the crucial period for parolees. Consequently, my ability to see things in their true perspective was impaired and my sense of values warped. I contend that my being here today is a sequel to, and direct result of my previous escapades, the resultant sentence and its insidious effects. The punishment for my initial waywardness was, and is having a cumulative and lasting effect—Ruinous, pathetically wasteful, and tragic for my family. Hence, I ponder on the policy of maintaining uniformity of sentence and its relation to single and married men.

Having been through such experiences, I cannot be expected to be quite the same man again. I have been, in my own mind, almost to the end of everything and know its worth. I seek to free myself from the whirlpool of crime. Previously, necessity was the ultimate justification, goaded on by the fact that, as a youth, I'd not had a chance in the melon patch. The conception I now have of my role is that of doing my bit to the best of my ability, within my own special capacity, to the furtherance of conditions, generally; rather than the narrower, selfish thoughtless and shortsighted policy of immediate material personal gain. This can best be done in my own family circle where my presence and influence are all important. But now, ironically and wastefully, when, through my tempering experiences, I am mature enough, aware of my obligations and eager to put it all to practical effect, I am unable to do so. In fact, the original tragedy is to be compounded.

I maintain that, basically, I am honest and have the necessary qualities and potential and, despite what else may be said of me, I am a good father and husband. It is my absolute conviction of this, and the faith in my ability to justify any faith you may see fit to place in me that prompts me to ask you not to make this sentence a crushing one: do not deny me hope!

I realise that you must feel what any humane man must feel when finding yourself the reluctant instrument of a disaster that I have invited upon myself. For this I apologise, and I hope that you may see fit to range yourself on the side of mercy which, in my case, will prove both an added incentive to reform and a deterrent through the moral obligation I'd bear when through your actions you say in effect; 'I understand, I believe & trust.'

Finally, in support of my plea for leniency I point out that most of the money and goods involved was recovered. I bring to your notice the redeeming feature that I left a warning note when explosives were involved. The men involved with me have been dealt with and received 9 months and 12 months respectively for two of the offences. I am at present serving six years one month, i.e., 5 years 4 months broken parole plus 6 months and 3 months. Furthermore, I have two more charges pending (possession of the pistol from the safe you sentence me on and burglar tools). Then £100 or 3 months for absconding bail. I will not be re-paroled. Therefore, I ask that you consider making my sentence a straight one. Thus I may gain some remission. Or, alternatively, that the sentence you give me be made concurrent with the one I'm already doing.

As you see, I have in my stupidity, placed myself and my family in a tragic situation. I am forty years of age and, seemingly, what is left is jeopardised. My greatest punishment lies in the imminent loss of my family and my awareness of the effect my actions have on the lives and property of others. I again assure you of my absolute sincerity.

Yours sincerely,

Ronald J Ryan[44]

Of course, Ryan's plea that the judge might provide an empathic response to his plight was a forlorn hope. When the court resumed after the presentment of evidence by the prosecutor, Mr Roberts, it was clear that Judge Read was unmoved by Ryan's letter. Len Read was an experienced judge of almost twenty years' standing, and at the time was the chairman of the County Court judges. He could not at this moment have realised that he was about to sentence a man whose notoriety would, in time, approach that of the man whom his grandfather had defended—Ned Kelly. Judge Read's grandfather, Albert Read, a barrister who signed the bar roll in 1841, defended Kelly on two occasions at Beechworth Court in the 1870s.

Judge Read had come to the bench from the bar where, over 25 years, he had built up a large common law practice with particular emphasis on traffic accident cases.'[45] He was a judge perceived by members of the bar to be a tough on sentencing. In response to Ryan's plea, Judge Read made it clear that, if Ryan's was a con man's story, he was not taken in by it. His Honor said that he had heard it all before.

Brought to the bar of the court, and unsworn, Ryan was asked by Judge Read if there was anything else he wanted to say before sentence was pronounced:

> *Ryan*: There is very little I can add to my plea, sir. If there is any question arising out of it, I would be only too happy ...
>
> *His Honor*: It is just a normal plea that all men like you make, 'How my wife and children will suffer.' You ought to think of that before you commit these offences. Only in 1960, when you were up on a number of charges, you were sentenced to eight and a half years' imprisonment, and given a great chance then by having a minimum term of three and a half years fixed, and you were released at that time, weren't you?
>
> *Ryan*: That's true, sir.
>
> *His Honor*: Which would be, when, were you released about the middle of 1963?
>
> *Ryan*: August 1963.
>
> *His Honor*: August 1963. Then you start off again straight away. The first safe you blew after that was October, the one at Mt. Waverley, 30th October. You are going on doing it systematically, 13th December, January. Anything else you want to say to me? You ask me not to impose a crushing sentence. You have already got a good long sentence to serve, but my word, this sort of thing has got to be stopped somehow.
>
> *Ryan*: I realise I am completely on the wrong side of things, and there is very little I can do to justify myself.[46]

Judge Read then delivered his sentence:

> Prisoner at the bar, you have pleaded guilty on one presentment to one count of shopbreaking with intent to commit a felony therein [the James Meats offence], three counts of shopbreaking and stealing [the Dewhurst Butchery; J.C. Hutton; and Pre Pack Meats offences], one count of possession of explosives in suspicious

circumstances, and on another presentment you have pleaded guilty to one count of shopbreaking and stealing [the Bilsons, Colac, offence].

You are 39 years of age, and you have got a bad record. Starting back in 1956 you had a number of convictions, leading up to the only one that really concerns me at the moment. You were convicted in the Court of General Sessions at Melbourne on 1st June, 1960, on five counts of factory breaking and stealing, one count of storebreaking and stealing, and one other count of factory breaking and stealing, escaping from legal custody, and another count of factory breaking and stealing, and you had imposed on you various sentences which totalled eight and a half years' imprisonment. The learned Judge who passed that sentence upon you gave you a chance by fixing a comparatively small minimum term so as to give you a chance to get back to your wife and children, and to lead a decent, honest life again, and he fixed a minimum term of three and a half years. You came out of gaol, you tell me, that time, in about August of 1963.

It is interesting to look at the present charges. I see the first of these charges relates to a shopbreaking at Mt. Waverley on the 30th October 1963, only quite a short time after you were released from custody. Since your release from custody in that short period, you had apparently accumulated quite a good stock of explosives and other necessary tools to carry on your trade of shopbreaking and safe-blowing. The first place you went into you did not succeed in blowing the safe, so you just calmly went close by to another store and broke in there, blew the safe successfully and got away with quite a sum of money, about £180, out of that safe.

Not very long afterwards, on the 13th December, you go out to Preston armed with all your tools of trade. You tried to blow a safe there, failed, but you were not going to be deterred from your purpose. You put the safe then in the back of your car, and took it down to Seaford, and succeeded in opening it down there and getting a little over £800 out of that safe. Two days later, at Colac, you and a companion broke into a shop down there. You stole from that shop goods to the value of £2,100, all of which you calmly stacked in the motor truck belonging to the owner of the shop that you had broken into, and unfortunately for you, that truck was intercepted on the way back to Melbourne, but of course you were not driving it at that time.

Then ... after that, the 4th January, 1964, you carry on your trade again by going and doing another shopbreaking and stealing, but this time you were caught. You had in fact removed the safe from that shop after breaking into the shop, but you were caught, and then apparently you absconded from your bail. You have handed to me a long, long statement and I have read every word of it carefully. There is nothing unusual, may I say, in the statement you have handed to me. I have read many statements like that, where prisoners set out the unfortunate childhood they had and how they gradually drifted into crime, and then they always seem to be, people like yourself, always seem to be the most devoted husbands and loving fathers of all. I do not believe it. You could not have had the affection and love for your wife and children that you set out so fully in this note if you are now prepared to go on doing this sort of thing.

In passing sentence upon you I would have passed a heavier sentence upon you than I am about to pass on you only for the fact that I realise you owe the parole board nearly five and a half years already, and you are undergoing other sentences as well. But these sorts of crimes systematically carried on as a trade or business by a person like yourself, who has done it before and is obviously going to go on doing it while he has his freedom, must be stopped.

First of all, you have got to be punished for the very serious crimes you have committed. Secondly, the community have got to be protected against a man like you for a very long time. Having regard to your age, having regard to your prior convictions, having regard to the very serious nature of the facts disclosed in the depositions, the sentence of the Court is on the first presentment that you be imprisoned and kept to hard labour for two years on each count, and on the second presentment that you be imprisoned and kept to hard labour for two years on the one count there. But I direct that the sentences on the first and seventh counts on the first presentment be served concurrently with all other sentences, which is a total term of imprisonment of eight years. Exercising the powers which I have under the section of the *Crimes Act* relating to minimum terms, I do not propose to fix any minimum term. It is

> quite inappropriate, in my opinion, having regard to the nature of these offences, having regard to the fact that you have already been given a chance to be on parole and it did you no good. I fix no minimum term whatever. The total term of imprisonment is eight years.[47]

Of course, with his breach of parole to be taken into account, Ryan was now required to serve the unexpired portion of his 1960 sentence: five years, three months, and twenty-nine days. Hence, Ryan's effective sentence was thirteen years, three months, and twenty-nine days. As he began his sentence, with all his sentences taken into account, he believed that his maximum expected date of release was 3 March 1977.[48]

Ryan saw this sentence as precisely the severe one he had urged Judge Read not to impose. He later referred to 'ill-considered, harsh sentences by the judiciary,' and elsewhere said he was 'shocked by the severity of the ... sentences,' as if he could not quite accept that a judge might not see him in the same light as he saw himself.[49] While he took the sentence as a crushing blow, Ryan seems not have been aware, as no doubt Judge Read was, that the sentence he would actually serve was likely to be about half the sentence he now contemplated.

The reason is that, while Judge Read had imposed a sentence without fixing a minimum (for which, he had indicated, he had discretionary powers under the *Crimes Act*), the Parole Board could determine an effective minimum given a prisoner's good behaviour in prison. While there was no minimum term fixed by the court for the eight-year sentence, prison authorities could grant remissions for good behaviour, and the Parole Board also might consider a minimum term for the unexpired portion of the sentence. In fact, as Ryan's classification file states, the notional minimum term recorded for him, assuming good behaviour, was not 3 March 1977, as he thought, but 6 March 1971. His likely sentence, in other words, was not thirteen years but six.[50]

It was a weakness of the system that prisoners were not adequately advised about the intricacies of prison sentences.[51] Although it was common for prisoners to have etched in their minds the day on which they believed they would be released, Ryan seems never to have been aware (or refused to accept) that he might serve only a little over six years before he was again eligible for parole. For the remainder of his time in prison he referred to his thirteen-year sentence—a sentence, he was later to say, that was 'too long, unfair and guaranteed to "break me".'[52]

Still further court appearances were to come. Two weeks after this sentence, on 27 November 1964, Ryan appeared in the Richmond Court of Petty Sessions to answer a charge of being a felon in possession of a pistol. Of all the charges Ryan had faced up to this point, this was the only one where, he said, police had framed him. Ryan had been arrested outside a boxing match at the West Melbourne Stadium one night after police had searched his car and found a pistol in the glove box. Certainly, Ryan had owned guns—including pistols—in the past, and guns had been a feature of the Ryan household for years.[53] This time, however, he believed police had planted a weapon in his car and falsely charged him with possession.[54] Nevertheless, his 'Not guilty' plea was unsuccessful, and he was convicted and sentenced to twelve months' imprisonment with a minimum fixed at three months.[55]

It was on the grounds of the severity of his sentence on the breaking and theft charges that Ryan lodged an appeal to the Full Court of the Supreme Court. The case was heard on 1 December 1964 before Chief Justice Sir Henry Winneke, and Justices Hudson and Gowans sitting as a Court of Criminal Appeal. The chief crown prosecutor, Bill Irvine, appeared for the Crown. Ryan was unrepresented, but appeared in person. His application was refused.[56]

WITH THE PROSPECT that Ryan would be imprisoned for several years, Dorothy finally took the step to end their marriage. Ryan had come to believe that Dorothy's parents had urged this course on her for several years. Indeed, he told his parole officer, Neil Beggs, that his wife's family 'had spared no pains in its efforts to persuade her to leave [him].'[57] Later, Beggs reported Ryan's belief that 'his wife's parents have promised her every advantage if she breaks off with him, and he expects that she will now do this.'[58] But this had not, in fact, been the case. Certainly the Georges had indicated their willingness to assist Dorothy should she file for divorce; but to describe the situation as one in which she felt under pressure from her parents to end the marriage was not well based.

The reason she finally took the step of instituting proceedings was that the children had a growing recognition of their father's criminal activities, and she was concerned to protect them. As well, Ryan's assault against her on 14 July had crystallised her view that, despite her feelings for him, the marriage should end.[59] Hence, on 18 December 1964 solicitors acting for Dorothy served Ryan in Pentridge with notice of a petition for divorce on the ground of frequent convictions, a provision under the *Matrimonial Causes Act 1959.* Before the matrimonial case was heard, Ryan made a further appeal to the General Sessions Appeal Court sitting at Hawthorn, this time against his conviction on the charge of being a felon in possession of a pistol. That appeal was heard on 3 February 1965 and, like his earlier appeal, was dismissed.[60]

A greater setback was to follow. Dorothy's divorce petition was heard before Mr Justice Esler Barber in the Supreme Court sitting in Melbourne on 2 June 1965.[61] Justice Barber was a recognised authority on divorce when he was appointed to the Supreme Court from the County Court earlier in 1965, and he sat mainly in the divorce jurisdiction of the court.[62] Dorothy's parents had assisted in engaging experienced, senior counsel. Representing her was Joan Rosanove, regarded as the leading figure at the Victorian bar in matrimonial law and related matters, who was later that year to be appointed Queen's Counsel.[63] Rosanove was instructed by a firm of city solicitors, Vail & McBain, of Bourke Street, Melbourne. Ryan had no money and was, therefore, unrepresented.

In making an application for a *decree nisi*, Dorothy's petition set out the formal shape of a turbulent marriage of almost fifteen years: the children, houses, property, and the separation (Ryan's absconding from bail on 3 February 1964, and subsequent return to the matrimonial home on 14 July 1964, and arrest the next day).[64] The evidence on the issue of property was that Dorothy owned no real estate, but owned a motor car valued at £185. Her income was given as £5 per week earned from part-time employment and child endowment. Ryan's financial position was described as 'no property; no income; and financial commitments unknown.'[65]

The most important particulars in Dorothy's application related to the facts that were the basis of her petition: Ryan's frequent convictions. The ground Dorothy was relying upon to have her petition succeed was that, under the terms of section 28 (g) of the *Matrimonial Causes Act 1959*, Ryan had, within a period not exceeding five years since the marriage, suffered frequent convictions for crime in respect of which he had been sentenced in the aggregate to imprisonment for not less than three years, and had habitually left her without reasonable means of support.[66]

To prove those facts Dorothy subpoenaed Ryan's old 'mate', Detective Sergeant Arthur Slater of Brunswick CIB, the man he knew as Wogsie, who had given evidence on his behalf in August 1960 following his arrest and prosecution for breakings and escaping from lawful custody.[67] Also subpoenaed was another Ryan 'mate', Detective Sergeant Jack Wright of Frankston CIB, who had been involved in Ryan's arrest in relation to the cheque forgeries at Warrnambool in 1956.[68] Essentially, Slater and Wright were subpoenaed to give evidence on Dorothy's behalf and bring with them the police records that related to Ryan's convictions during the previous fifteen years and six years respectively. Seven sets of sentences were set out to the court involving Ryan's convictions of 21 May, 23 May, and 13 July 1956; 17 June 1960; and 23 July, 13 November, and 27 November 1964.[69]

At the end of the hearing, Justice Barber indicated that he was satisfied that Ryan, as respondent, had suffered frequent convictions in the meaning of the act, and that Dorothy, as petitioner, had been left without reasonable means of support. Barber therefore 'decreed that, upon and subject to the decree of the Court becoming absolute, the marriage solemnised on the 4th day of February 1950, at Richmond in the State of Victoria between Dorothy Janet Ryan, then Dorothy Janet George, spinster, the petitioner, and Ronald Joseph Ryan, bachelor, the respondent, be dissolved.' Having had a submission put to him that Dorothy proposed to continue to support her three children with the assistance of her parents and brothers, Barber also ordered that she be granted custody of the children. Further, under the terms of the act, the *decree nisi* granted by Barber was to become absolute after three months, on 3 September 1965.[70]

Ryan's situation was that, after a period of sustained criminal activities lasting some ten years or more, he was broke. Although his offences had involved thefts of property having a face value of around £200,000 (the value only for those offences for which he was prosecuted but, it should be said, having a realisable street value of perhaps only one-tenth that amount), now he had no assets and no money. At this moment, the depths to which Ryan had sunk could hardly have been more stark. The all-or-nothing approach, the big plunge that Ryan had gambled on all his adult life, had brought him to a point where he was imprisoned for what he thought was thirteen years, his wife had divorced him, and he had lost his children to the custody of his ex-wife. Within months of the divorce, Dorothy would re-marry. His fall seemed now complete: he had no freedom, no family, no money and, perhaps worst of all, no prospects.

Sitting in his cell in Pentridge, Ryan resolved to do something about these desolate and constraining circumstances. Escape was what occupied him now. As he had done so many times before in his life, he turned his mind to the thought of breaking free.

CHAPTER EIGHT

Break-out

So you go through the tower where they don't expect to see you. The last thing they'd reckon on was you being in there with them—in their own territory.

—Ronald Ryan

RYAN SIMPLY COULD NOT ACCEPT the turn of events that saw him as a long-term prisoner in Pentridge. He could not accept that Dorothy had re-married, and he firmly believed that he could win back her affections and re-establish himself with her and the children. If he could just escape from gaol, and get enough money to leave the country and establish himself abroad, he thought he could eventually reunite his family—much as he had done with his mother and sisters in Balranald twenty years before. The idea of an English-speaking country appealed to him but, through his reading of books in the prison library, he had discovered that Australia had no extradition treaty with Brazil.[1] Perhaps that was where he would go—to Brazil, beyond the reaches of the law, much as Balranald had been beyond the jurisdiction of the Victorian Children's Welfare Department in 1939.

The steps Ryan took were to gather methodically information about security weaknesses at the prison, observe and scrutinise the behaviour of prison officers to determine who might constitute a weak link, and prepare physically for the demanding task of scaling the prison walls. Unlike most inmates, who were content to relax and stand around talking during periods of recreation in the exercise yards, Ryan began an extensive program of physical activity designed to increase his fitness and flexibility. His unusual exertions initially attracted the watchful attention of suspicious prison officers supervising the exercise yards; but, as these activities went on for weeks and then months, official interest waned.[2] Outwardly through all this, Ryan ensured that his behaviour at work in the gaol was faultless. Through 1965 he was a card hand in the B Division mill, and later a cloth finisher and presser. Official reports over the course of the year show that his conduct was regarded as 'very good' and consistently record that he was 'doing very well'.[3]

The next stage in the elaborate escape plan was to put in place the means by which he could quickly get away from the prison once he had cleared the walls. Through outside contacts established during gaol visits, he made arrangements for a safe house to go to in Heidelberg, east of the prison. There was also a house in Kensington, in the inner-western end of Melbourne, where a contact had been alerted to the possibility that Ryan might attempt an escape and head for that locality.[4] Ryan also organised a car, a Holden sedan, to get him there. Once the signal was given that a break-out was imminent, the car would be parked outside the walls of the gaol.[5] A critical decision for Ryan was who would accompany him on the escape bid. There seem to have been as many as nine prisoners intimately involved in the escape plan, although only one would go over the wall with him.[6] Ryan had begun an escape attempt once before but, as he later said, the prisoner with whom he had made the attempt had 'jibbed at the wall and we had to go back'.[7]

The prisoner whom Ryan now chose for his escape was Peter John Walker, 24, a young offender who had several serious criminal offences behind him, most recently attempted armed robbery and shooting with intent to do grievous bodily harm.[8] Walker's early unlawful activities were in the nature of juvenile stupidity. They had started in country Victoria when he was fifteen, and the wrongdoing involved—illegally using motor cars—was, and remains, common to young male offenders.

Like most serious criminal offenders, Walker's early life had been devastated by family trauma and neglect. He was born on 5 May 1941 in Amersham, a small town dating back to pre-Saxon times, 27 miles north-west of London in the county of Buckinghamshire. The place where he was born was Shardeloes, the ancestral home of the Tyrwhitt Drake family, the lords of the manor, which served as a maternity hospital for women coming from war-time London into the countryside to have their children. Peter Walker was the second of three children, all boys, born to Private Robert Arthur Walker, a driver in the Queen's Royal Regiment, and Alma Maud Walker, née Harvey, who were living in the Buckinghamshire village of Gerrards Cross.[9]

If the circumstances of his birth were auspicious, his early childhood was distinctly less so: his parents' marriage foundered under the devastation of Alma being battered by her husband. Bob Walker was a heavy drinker who was both mentally and physically abusive to Alma, and neglectful of his children. As an infant, Peter Walker was sent to an orphanage for a time, when his mother could not look after him. Later, when the family was living in a four-room rented flat at 11 Kensington Gardens Square, Paddington East, the young Walker was subjected to a horrific experience, the effects of which would dramatically affect his young life.

In the early morning of 10 January 1949, when Walker was seven years old, he was woken by his elder brother, Derek, eleven, to be told that there was a smell of gas in the house and that his mother could not be roused from where she slept on her bed. In the adjoining bed-sitting room Alma Walker lay dead. Beside her, stretching into the kitchen and connected to the gas oven, was the long rubber hose that on the previous day she had sent Derek down the street to buy. The night before, Alma had put three-year-old Brian at the other end of the flat, put the other boys to bed, and blocked up the spaces under the doors before turning on the gas.[10] The subsequent coroner's inquest found that Alma Walker, 33, had died from carbon monoxide (coal gas) poisoning administered by her own hand, and that she had killed herself 'while the balance of her mind was disturbed.'[11] Alma had suffered prolonged bouts of depression over several years because of her abusive situation, and had been particularly depressed in the period leading up to her death.[12]

In the immediate aftermath of their mother's death, the Walker boys were sent to an institution in Fulham before arrangements were made by their father for their passage to Australia under the Church of England Boys' Scheme. In late October 1949 Bob Walker farewelled his sons at Waterloo station bound for Southampton and passage aboard the *SS Asturias* to Australia. They arrived in Fremantle on 2 December 1949, subsequently continuing on to Melbourne.[13] Although Bob Walker would later travel to Australia and stay for some time, Peter Walker would never see his father again after he left England. He was eight years old.

The boys were institutionalised and sent to the St John's Boys' Home at Canterbury in suburban Melbourne. Walker attended the Balwyn State School and later Richmond Technical School to eighth-grade level before being sent at age fourteen to the Burton Hall Training Farm at Tatura in country Victoria, an institution linked to the St John's Home, where he spent the next eighteen months.[14] He later worked as a farm hand on a dairy property at Yarrawalla near Cobram in northern Victoria before falling foul of the law with the offences for illegal use of motor cars.[15]

On 9 July 1958, aged seventeen, he had been convicted in the Cobram Court of Petty Sessions and sentenced to one month's imprisonment and ordered to pay £39-5-0 damages for illegally using a car.[16] Walker served the sentence at Pentridge. At Kilmore Court of Petty Sessions on 12 April 1960 he had been similarly convicted over the illegal use of a motor car, as well as for possession of an unlicensed rifle. Sentenced to three years' imprisonment, his sentence had been suspended and he had been given probation on the condition that he underwent psychiatric treatment under the supervision of the court.[17]

Walker had then moved to New South Wales, where he was unable to find work. Less than three months later, on 27 June 1960, he had been convicted in the NSW Central Court of Petty Sessions on a charge of vagrancy. His sentence of three months' imprisonment had been suspended on him entering a recognisance of £30 to be of good behaviour for two years.[18] On 13 September 1960, at the Court of Quarter Sessions at Moruya on the NSW south coast, he appeared on charges of breaking and entering, and two charges of larceny of motor cars, for which he was sentenced to three years' imprisonment. With that conviction came another offence, the breach of the recognisance of 27 June, and he was sentenced to a further three months' imprisonment. He served two years' imprisonment at Long Bay gaol in NSW for those offences. Prior to his imprisonment, by his own admission Walker had been committing breaking offences at the rate of one or two a week.[19]

Released from prison in September 1962 at the age of 21, Walker moved back to Melbourne where he lived with his brother, Derek, who by now had a wife and two young boys. Working initially at Borthwick's meatworks and later at a carpet factory at Tottenham, Walker seems to have settled down well for a time until his brother re-located to East Doncaster. Walker remained near his work at Tottenham, later getting a job as a transport driver; but, with the break from Derek and his family, Walker entered a period of aimlessness and instability as he drifted around from place to place in St Kilda and Footscray. Soon gambling and losing at the harness races got him into financial debt. At the age of 23, he sought to overcome his situation by the attempted armed robbery of a bank on 12 April 1965, the offence for which he was now serving his term of imprisonment at Pentridge.[20]

The offence had involved an attempted hold-up with a pistol of the Brooklyn branch of the Bank of New South Wales in the western suburbs of Melbourne, and the robbery of £4,050. The robbery attempt had been thwarted by the bank's manager and accountant, who had detained Walker at pistol point after shots were exchanged between them.[21] Following his arrest and trial for this offence in the Supreme Court of Victoria, Walker had been sentenced on 6 July 1965 to a total of twelve years' imprisonment—with nine years to serve before being eligible for parole—for attempted armed robbery, shooting with intent to do grievous bodily harm, and illegally using a motor car.[22]

To Ryan, Walker seemed a likely lad. After his aborted escape attempt some months before, he had 'mated up' with Walker, who was also keen to escape because he resented what he saw as the severity of his twelve-year prison sentence.[23] Ryan believed that Walker was athletic and tough, and had the right temperament to carry out an escape. With Walker's armed-robbery experience, and his skills in hot-wiring cars, Ryan considered that he would be a useful accomplice in his hold-up plans after the escape.[24] With Walker's help, Ryan had sought to escape several months before. This had involved Ryan, Walker, and others constructing an elaborate hideaway inside a box of spinning bobbins used in the 5 Gang mill. The empty bobbins were packed in boxes in the mill before being picked up by a truck that would take them away to be refilled. The prisoners created a hiding space inside the box by packing the bobbins around a wire cage in which Ryan was hiding ready for the truck pick-up. But this attempt, too, was aborted when prison security learned of the plan and Ryan quickly had to be taken out of the box. The next time, Ryan resolved, they would go over the wall.[25]

After having carefully observed security arrangements at the prison, Ryan believed he had found a point of weakness near the sentry point on the no. 1 post—an elevated guard post on the prison's outer wall. He believed that if they went over the inner wall near the prison's boiler house, and then scaled the outer wall below the sentry post on the east side, the prison officer on the tower would not be expecting it. One day, as they sat in the B Division exercise yard opposite the wall, Ryan had said to Walker that he was thinking of breaking out and, pointing to the outer wall, said: 'What do you think about that wall there?' Ryan said that was the way he was thinking of going, 'straight up and through the tower'.

'Will you be in it?' he asked Walker, who looked at the wall and the tower with the guard in it.

'Ron, I think that's a bit rude. I mean, the bloke's up there, mate.'

Ryan asked him what he thought would happen if he tried to climb the wall a bit further down.

'I'd be shot!', Walker replied.

'Yeah, that's right', Ryan said. 'So you go through the tower where they don't expect to see you. The last thing they'd reckon on was you being in there with them—in their own territory.'[26]

Ryan's analysis of the security situation at this point and in the gaol generally was astute, although the last prisoner who tried to escape at this point in B Division had been shot dead during the attempt thirteen years before.[27] On 14 April 1952 Kevin Albert Joiner, 25, a prisoner serving a life sentence without remissions for murder, and a persistent escapee, was shot by a prison officer on no. 2 post after he had scaled the wall in B Division east exercise yard near no. 1 post and had made it over the wall into the street beyond the gaol. Joiner had used a carved wooden pistol to hold-up a prison officer and commandeer his rifle. He had clambered on the shoulders of his fellow escapee, Maxwell Carl Skinner, 23, and pulled Skinner up after him, but Skinner was captured before he made it to the top. After he was shot by the prison officer on the wall, Joiner staggered on for 40 yards before collapsing in the grounds of St Paul's Roman Catholic church next to the prison. He died in a bed of churchyard lilies, grown for church decorations.[28]

After Joiner was killed there were no attempted escapes from Pentridge in the intervening thirteen years, and a degree of complacency about security at the prison had set in. As it was later assessed by officials, by 1965 security was inadequate, and senior officers in the prisons department believed that 'in recent years, more relaxed conditions and changed procedures without any serious troubles [had] tended to lull all staff into a sense of false security'.[29] It seemed that newer officers joining the prison and working under these conditions had tended to be less security conscious than was essential in a maximum-security prison. At this time Pentridge was 30 officers below its authorised strength of 266; on Sundays, when staffing was particularly stretched, there was, for a few minutes, no guard in the east exercise yard.[30] As well, during a meal break, the guard on no. 1 post was relieved for an hour. Ryan resolved that when the prison officer on the post went on his lunch break and was replaced, he would make his move.

Further elements in the plan by Ryan and Walker involved methods for scaling the walls and a clever attempt to defeat security attention. Their plan to scale the wall centred on the use of one of the thick, timber bench seats that were fixed on either side of a table positioned under the rain shelter in the exercise yard. Surreptitiously, over several days, Ryan and Walker had cut around the nails that fixed the bench-top to its timber base, using a sharp instrument made for them in the prison boot-shop. The instrument had been fashioned from a sharpened rod taken from a heavy-duty prison sewing machine.

Seated strategically over the dozen or so nails on the timber bench, and with other prisoners milling around them to form a screen, Ryan and Walker had taken turns to painstakingly bore around each of the nails by twisting the concealed cutter, which they operated by hand through holes in their jacket pockets. The result was that the nails were eventually cut away from their anchor points in the timber. With that task completed, the last step was to remove the several timber cross-members reinforcing the benches and fixing them to the ground. Over several days, groups of prisoners had spirited these long timber stays out of the yard and smuggled them into the hobby room; there, using a circular saw, they were sawn into unrecognisable smaller lengths of timber. With the bench top essentially severed from its base, Ryan and Walker simply rested it in place until they were ready.

The second key element in the break-out preparations involved talking up plans for an escape. Ryan had concluded that the only way to keep their escape plan secret was to make it no secret at all. If everyone 'knew' that prisoners planned to go over the wall, nobody could be sure if it was real. So for two months they talked up the prospect that an escape was in readiness, and encouraged their supporters among the prisoners to do the same. The tactic worked. Prison authorities mounted frequent raids on gangs and divisions in the prison but, with no hard evidence, were led to conclude that the escape talk was just prisoner hot air.

With preparations complete, the right conjunction of events for an escape came to pass on Sunday, 19 December 1965. It was a pleasant sunny afternoon—a typical early-summer Melbourne day—and prison officers were enjoying their annual Christmas lunch in the officers' mess near no. 1 post. This was a vital factor for Ryan: there were relieving staff on security duty on the towers as the officers joined their colleagues in relay in the dining room. What followed next was the execution of an audacious plan that, in differing ways, involved most of the prisoners in the B Division exercise yard.[31]

At 1:05PM, prison officer Helmut Lange, known to his colleagues as Ben, relieved the officer on no. 1 post, Fred Brown, so that he could join the lunch. 'You'd better be back in time as I have to take some [prisoners working on the prison farm] out again,' Lange had told him.[32] A further vital element in Ryan's plans also fell into place at this time: he and Walker were momentarily left unguarded in the B Division exercise yard. The total muster of B Division on that day was 148 prisoners, most of whom were keeping to a weekend prison regimen of recreation and sports activity involving basketball, table-tennis, watching television, or pursuing hobbies.

At 2:00PM, Ryan and Walker were among 50 prisoners at recreation in the east yard. The chance that Ryan had waited for came when prison officer Patrick Quinlan, who was supervising the east yard alone, was seconded by the chief prison officer of B Division to escort five prisoners from the division to a Salvation Army church service in A Division. This had been a routine procedure at the prison for many years, and Ryan was aware of the security lapse that it represented. To make sure that the routine was followed, he and Walker had seen to it that enough prisoners went to the service.[33] When this happened, the officer supervising some 37 prisoners in the west yard, John Hewlett, was instructed to supervise the east yard in Quinlan's absence.[34] While

Hewlett was on duty in the west yard, leaving the east yard momentarily unsupervised because he was preoccupied with a pre-arranged commotion by prisoners, Ryan and Walker seized their opportunity. Walker was athletic, and Ryan had been exercising for weeks for the effort they would have to make to scale the two walls of thirteen feet six inches and sixteen feet six inches that lay between them and the outside of the gaol. Now they were fit and ready.[35]

The two high bluestone walls ran around the prison at this point in B Division, separated by a somewhat derelict twelve-feet-wide passageway—a virtual no-man's land—covered at points with unkempt grass and scattered with rubble. The first wall ran along the southern boundary of the B Division east exercise yard and joined a north-south wall on the eastern side of the yard. At the south-east corner the north-south wall ran beside the prison's boiler-house. This point represented a blind spot to the prison officer on tower 1 if—as was commonly the case in good weather—he was seated on a chair at the western end of the catwalk. It was easier from that position for the duty officer to observe and allow entry to those authorised personnel coming and going through the external gate below, which was opened by a lever on the catwalk, but he could not see anyone scaling the wall in the corner. There was a similar blind spot on the second, outer wall: a prisoner climbing up the wall on the eastern side of the tower could not be seen from that point.

Promising as these points of vulnerability were to Ryan and Walker, they knew that they needed assistance. There was no shortage of prisoner volunteers to help. In the view of the director of prisons, Eric Shade, B Division had for some time exhibited 'deep and widespread tension and unrest ... among long sentence prisoners and more specifically those denied parole or who considered their chances of parole remote'.[36] First, a diversion was created by a prisoner in the bake-house baking a cake and giving it to prison officers for afternoon tea in the B Division block, thus encouraging them to stay out of the yard. Next, several prisoners positioned themselves to delay entry by prison officers to the exercise yard and prevent the exit of any prisoners who had a mind to raise the alarm. With this cover in place, Ryan and Walker took their timber bench, turned it over, and placed it vertically against the north-south wall in the south-east corner so that, with its bottom up, the timber cleats on the underside could serve as steps.[37] With momentum from a short run, and while Walker held the bench steady, Ryan leapt on to the first cleat and scaled the ten-feet long bench, using its thick end against the wall as the final step. Next, Walker repeated the effort while a prison mate, Ronnie 'Shifty' O'Keefe, held the bench steady.[38]

When they had hauled themselves to the top of the wall, Ryan and Walker had to contend with the barbed wire that ran the length of the wall. This was a precarious exercise, and they had prepared for it by wearing socks over their hands to prevent cuts as they rolled over the barbed wire and broke their fall in a deep bed of ashes behind the boiler-house.[39] Now, in the passageway between the walls, Ryan retrieved a ten-feet long grappling apparatus from amid the ashes. It had been hidden there earlier by a prisoner who worked in the boiler-house and was permitted to move around the prison in this area.[40] The apparatus consisted of a rake or broom handle taped to another piece of timber by a white adhesive bandage, and with a metal hook fashioned from strong wire and driven into one end of the handle.[41] It had been made by a supportive prisoner working in the engineering department of the gaol.[42] Attached to the grappling hook were two knotted bedspreads which Ryan and Walker had taken from their beds and concealed by wrapping them around their bodies when they went to the exercise yard. While they were momentarily in the no-man's land, Ryan also picked up a piece of iron pipe, about nine inches long, which had been left there.[43]

Although, at sixteen feet six inches, the second wall confronting them was higher than the first, scaling it was easier because of a significant security weakness: the internal, prison side of the wall carried numerous service pipes and cables placed there by the public works department over many years.[44] These pipes ran about three feet below the top of the wall. With the grappling apparatus hooked around one of these water pipes at a point hidden from the sentry officer's view by the entrance tower, Ryan was able to climb part way up the wall by hauling himself, hand over hand commando-style, up the knotted bedspreads.

This was a manoeuvre for which Ryan and Walker had both trained assiduously. Daily for several months, they had practised hauling themselves up from the floor in 5 Gang mill using a strip of denim secured overhead. Now, when Ryan had reached a point on the wall where he could grip directly onto a pipe, Walker did the same, ending up beside him similarly suspended from a pipe. Ryan then swung around behind him and, clambering up Walker's back and using his shoulders as a platform, pulled himself the remaining few feet to the top of the iron railing that ran around the tower. He then pulled Walker up behind him, reaching the top of the wall at the eastern end of the catwalk of no. 1 post.[45]

At that moment, just after 2:00PM, further along the catwalk on the other side of the post, prison officer Lange's attention was attracted to the sound of empty milk bottles being rattled by two prisoners in the passageway below the wall. Milk was delivered to the prison in crates that were deposited and picked up at the side gate entrance by 'trustie' prisoners who were allowed to traverse the no-man's land to do so. Earlier in the passageway Ryan and Walker had asked the young prisoners to wait a minute and then give their crate a good rattle.[46]

Reacting to this attempt to distract him, Lange leaned out over the wall and looked down until the prisoners cleared the passage on the inside of the prison. When he turned around Lange was astounded to see, standing opposite him in the tower, a man wearing the distinctive prison garb of grey-blue jeans and grey-white shirt with his arm raised, holding a length of iron water pipe. Ryan's theory about the important element of surprise in climbing through to the sentry box had worked. As Lange reacted, Ryan turned and, pushing Lange aside, made a grab for the prison-issue rifle—a .30 calibre M1 American carbine—in the rifle-rack on his left-hand side, which was closer to him than to Lange. Ryan quickly pulled the cocking lever and released it, forcing one round into the chamber. (Ryan would later claim that, as he inexpertly pulled the lever, a live round was ejected from the chamber and spilled onto the floor of the tower, and that he had to repeat the action to load the rifle.[47]) This round was one of the regulation eight rounds kept in the fifteen-round magazine of the carbine, a light-automatic weapon, which had been the standard-issue rifle for US servicemen during World War II. With that action the rifle was ready to fire. It did not require further cocking to fire all cartridges in the magazine, as each shell case was ejected automatically by a gas-operated mechanism.

Holding Lange at bay, Ryan tried to operate one of the lever handles located in the tower. There were three levers in the tower that were operable by the prison officer on sentry duty. One lever opened the passage gate leading back into the prison grounds; a second opened the external gate to the car park in the street; and a third was permanently fixed and inoperable, as it had been installed to open a planned gate that had never eventuated.[48]

After he had tried unsuccessfully to move the dead lever, Ryan—in a state of rising tension and agitation—asked Lange which lever opened the external gate. In an attempt to forestall the escape, Lange deliberately pointed to the wrong lever, the one opening the passage gate, which Ryan operated before ordering Lange to move in front of him towards the eastern end of the tower leading to the staircase. As they moved along the catwalk, Walker came into view as he was beginning to descend down the spiral staircase in the tower. 'It's all right, the gate's open!' Ryan called to Walker, who came back up the steps. With Walker in front, Ryan herded Lange at gunpoint down the winding stone stairs, only to find their way from the tower barred by a locked door. Walker pushed the lever upwards with his hands and kicked the door open.[49]

From there they marched Lange to the night officers' lodge—an office-like cubicle below no. 1 post—through which they had to pass to exit to the street via a cyclone-wire gate within a gate, called a wicket gate. Standing at the lodge was prison officer Brown, who was returning from lunch to resume duty on the tower. As Ryan reached the door behind Walker and Lange he stopped, menaced Brown with the rifle and, pointing to Lange, said: 'If you make a move, I'll shoot this man.'[50]

Still brandishing the rifle, Ryan—with Walker in front—forced Lange and Brown towards the gate below no. 1 post. 'Open the gate!', he shouted to Brown, who could immediately see that the lugs on the gate's lock had not been lifted by the operation of the lever. Ryan, too, could see what had happened. Realising that he had been tricked by Lange, he turned on him:

'You bastard, you knew about this when you were up there. You turn around; we're going back,' he said.[51] 'Make sure you operate the right one, this time!', he added.[52]

With the iron piping that Ryan had handed him, Walker menaced Brown, saying 'Don't you move—you stay where you are!'[53]

Lange went up the tower stairs with Ryan following him, with the gun pressed into Lange's back. When he reached the levers, Lange pulled the correct lever for the wicket gate. Walker called out from below: 'Come on, the gate's open!' Still aiming the rifle at Lange, Ryan backed up towards the stairway before descending the stairs and running behind Walker to the wicket gate. As Ryan disappeared quickly down the stairs Lange phoned the prison's main gate to raise the alarm: 'One Post: two prisoners escaped!', he yelled. Lange also twice gave three short blows on his whistle, the prison-security procedure for signalling a break-out.[54]

As Walker ran ahead to the wicket gate leading to the car park outside in the street, he encountered the Pentridge Salvation Army chaplain, Brigadier James Hewitt, who was leaving the prison just as Tommy Toogood, a 'trustie' prisoner who had been working in the gardens outside, came in.

'Oh, shit!', Toogood exclaimed as he saw what was going on.[55]

Walker grabbed Hewitt by the collar and shouted: 'Right, we're going out!' as he marched him through the gate and into the car park outside.[56]

As he did so, the security siren at the prison began to blow loudly, signalling that an escape was in progress. Within seconds, Ryan had caught up to Walker and Hewitt. But the car that Ryan and Walker expected to find in the car park outside the prison was not there. There was a rising sense of panic when they realised that the arrangement for a get-away car to be left for them simply had not been carried out.[57] They realised they would have to commandeer another vehicle. Still holding the rifle in one hand, Ryan grabbed Hewitt by the lapels of his coat with the other, and demanded his car keys. Taken aback with surprise, Hewitt did not immediately answer.

'Come on, give me the keys of your car!', Ryan shouted insistently.

'My car's not here!', Hewitt blurted out.

'Come on, we're having you as a hostage,' Ryan said, becoming more agitated. 'Where are the keys of your car?'

Hewitt repeated his reply: 'My car's not here!'[58]

At that moment, the prison officer on no. 2 post, William Bennett, responding to Lange's whistle and the wailing siren, appeared at the top of the wall. From his position west of tower no. 1, closer to Sydney Road, he could see Ryan, Walker, and Hewitt approaching 50 yards away. Initially, Bennett did not have his rifle with him; crouching, he ran back to the post and got his rifle from the tower, and quickly returned. Bennett—who had been a prison officer on active duty for less than five months—tried to load the rifle, but the cartridge loaded crossways in the breech and it jammed.[59] When Ryan, Walker, and Hewitt were only about twenty feet below him on the south side of the wall, Bennett pointed his rifle at Ryan as if to fire at the escapees.

'Throw down your rifle or I'll fire!', he called out.

Looking back at him, Ryan yelled: 'Throw down your rifle or I'll shoot!'

Bennett called back: 'I can't! They'll crucify me!', whereupon Ryan repeated his threat.[60]

Although Bennett lowered his weapon to his side, Ryan demanded, 'Drop the gun or else I'll shoot the man!'[61]

Bennett dropped to his knees out of sight of the escapees before blowing his whistle to signal escape. With that, almost in one movement, Ryan raised his rifle, pushed Hewitt away, and struck him on the top of the head with the rifle butt. As Hewitt lay beside the footpath on the car park, conscious but dazed and bleeding severely from the cut to his head, Ryan and Walker raced towards Sydney Road. Hewitt was later treated by the prison doctor for the cut to his head, and later still was taken by ambulance to the Royal Melbourne Hospital where he was admitted and kept under observation for five hours. Severe as his wound appeared, it required no stitches and—contrary to later media reports and published accounts—he had not lost consciousness.[62]

While this had been happening, prison officer George Henry Hodson, 41, had been lunching in the prison officers' mess and had responded to Lange's whistle. Hodson was a heavily built man who stood six feet one inches tall and weighed sixteen stone. The English-born Hodson was a popular prison officer with his colleagues, and he was a regular and well-liked patron at the prison staff watering hole, the Coburg Hotel, opposite the prison—although now he was off the drink and sticking to lemon squash.

With his wife Enid, Hodson had emigrated several years before from England. He had worked as a plumber for the Board of Works in Ainsdale, a suburb of the seaside resort town of Southport in Lancashire, where he had been born and grown up. Hodson had seen service in the Royal Navy during World War II, and his service record had stood him in good stead when he applied for, and won, employment as a Pentridge prison officer soon after arriving in Melbourne. Hodson had a thirteen-year-old daughter, but his marriage to Enid had broken down four years after emigrating, and he was living apart from his wife in a self-contained flat at the rear of a house in Inkerman Street, East St Kilda. On this fateful day Hodson was not even meant to be working at Pentridge. He had been rostered off, but had swapped shifts with a fellow prison officer in order to spend Christmas Day with his daughter.[63]

Coming out of the officers' mess, Hodson called out to Lange as he ran towards no. 1 post, where Lange had returned to the tower: 'What's going on?'[64]

The siren was sounding as Lange yelled back that two prisoners had escaped. Hodson asked in which direction they had gone. From his vantage point in the tower, Lange gestured towards Sydney Road. As he pointed, Lange could see Ryan standing at the intersection of Sydney Road and Champ Street, attempting to stop a car at gunpoint. Although he was unarmed, Hodson did not hesitate to give chase. He ran off towards Sydney Road, not knowing who the escapees were.[65]

Initially, both Ryan and Walker had run in a zig-zag route towards the nearby St Paul's Roman Catholic church (where Kevin Joiner had died in 1952), but Walker had paused there as Ryan had sought to flag down a car with his gun. Moments before, Walker had discarded the iron water pipe tucked into his belt as he ran towards the church.[66] In Champ Street, which ran at an angle into Sydney Road in front of the prison, a Ford Falcon sedan, light blue with a white top, slowed and then stopped at the corner to allow cars to pass before it turned south into Sydney Road. The Falcon was driven by Franck Jeziorski, who was travelling with his pregnant wife Pauline in the passenger seat. Jeziorski was Polish and his wife was Ukrainian, and their command of English was limited. As the car stopped, Ryan ran up and stepped in front of it, brandishing the rifle which he carried at his hip, and pointing it at the windscreen while motioning for Jeziorski to get out.

'This is a hold-up!', Ryan yelled.[67] 'I want your car!'[68]

When Jeziorski did not move, Ryan yelled again: 'I mean it! If you don't, I'll shoot!'[69]

Jeziorski complied, telling his wife: 'You'd better get out of the car.'

Instinctively, Jeziorski switched off the engine and shifted the gears into the 'park' position. Ryan moved to the driver's side of the car, opened the door, grabbed Jeziorski with one hand around his neck, and yelled 'Come on!', and 'Get out, or I'll shoot your girl-friend!'[70] Ryan pulled him out, and got into the driver's seat as Pauline Jeziorski got out of the passenger seat.

Then Mrs Jeziorski remembered that she had left her handbag and cardigan on the back seat. So—incredibly—she opened the car door again and leaned over the back of the front seat to retrieve them, saying to Ryan in the driver's seat: 'Wait a minute, I want my bag!'[71] After Mrs Jeziorski had got out again with her belongings, Ryan started the ignition and hit the accelerator, but could not make the car move because Jeziorski had modified the Falcon's gear transmission to be a floor shift. Ryan had failed to quickly appreciate the change.[72]

As Ryan was desperately trying to get the car to move, two prison officers, William Mitchinson and Thomas Wallis, who had come out of the prison through the main gate in Champ Street in pursuit, came around the back of the car to intercept him.[73] They were unarmed. As they had left the prison to give chase to the escapees they had requested firearms but—in what was later described by the director of prisons as a 'grave error of judgment'—were initially denied them by the officer in charge of the main gate.[74] Mitchinson headed for the driver's side, while Wallis, somewhat further away, approached the passenger side.

When Mitchinson reached the car, Ryan was in the driver's seat holding the rifle with his left arm and resting it on his knee as he looked down at the instrument panel trying to figure out how to get the car going. Pushing his left hand through the open driver's side window, Mitchinson made a grab for Ryan's collar saying: 'Right you are, fellow, the game's up!' Ryan avoided the manoeuvre, and shifted quickly to the passenger side of the car, shouting: 'Stand back or you'll get this!' as he menaced Mitchinson with the rifle.[75] Mitchinson sought to calm him, but Ryan continued to point the rifle and repeated: 'Get back! ... Don't come close because I'll shoot!'[76] (Mitchinson and Wallis would later receive prison Valour Award medals for their bravery in this incident.)

As this was happening, Walker was still in the grounds of the church in Sydney Road. Prison officer Bennett, who by now had moved to a position further west on no. 2 post, called out to Walker to halt or he would fire. Walker, who was about four yards from the corner of the church fence adjoining Sydney Road, immediately dropped to his knees behind the fence. When Walker raised his head to look back towards the tower, Bennett called out to him: 'Move your head and I will blow it off!' When Walker again raised his head to look back at Bennett, the prison officer repeated his warning: 'Move your head and I will blow it off!'[77]

As Bennett kept watch on the pinned-down Walker, Hodson raced from the prison, running along the car park towards Sydney Road.

Hodson looked up to Bennett in the tower, and Bennett shouted to him that two prisoners had escaped, one had a rifle, and he had the other one pinned down behind the church fence.[78]

'I don't know where the fellow is with the rifle', Bennett called to Hodson, 'but there is one down behind the brick fence as I've got a line on him.'[79]

Hodson headed for Walker behind the fence, and hit him a glancing blow on the side of the head.[80] The weapon was the length of water pipe that Walker had discarded back in the car park area moments earlier.[81]

Bennett—seeing Hodson close on Walker and believing that he had been captured—turned his attention back to the prisoner carrying the rifle.[82] But he saw only confusion in the intersection of Sydney Road and O'Hea Street, with cars banking up and people running around the cars, and his view was further obstructed by electric light poles and overhead wires. In the event, Walker had eluded arrest by Hodson. Escaping from the clutches of his pursuer, Walker fled south along Sydney Road with Hodson, running hard, still giving chase. The prison siren was still sounding as Walker doubled back, and Hodson continued to chase after him.

Moments earlier, prison officer Robert Paterson, who had been present during Lange's telephone call of alarm to the main gate, ran from the front gate into Champ Street at the front of the gaol and saw the commotion with Ryan, beside the Jeziorskis' car, holding Mitchinson at bay with the rifle. Paterson ran back inside the prison, quickly asked for and was given a rifle, and ran back out again. Seconds later, Paterson was on the lawn near the main gate. He could see Ryan still holding Mitchinson and Wallis at bay as he stood at the end of Champ Street where it intersects with Sydney Road, directly opposite no. 2 post.[83]

About twenty yards away from Ryan, Walker and Hodson were running northwards along the tram-lines set in the centre of Sydney Road, almost at the beginning of the BP service station situated on the south-west corner of Sydney Road and O'Hea Street. Hodson closed in on Walker, who was shouting loudly as he headed towards Ryan, waving his arms around, and frantically pointing to tower 2 where Bennett had his rifle directed at the scene: 'Mate, the tower! The tower!'[84] Walker fell to his hands and knees as Hodson finally grabbed him by the arm.[85] As he did so, Ryan took three or four paces forward in front of the Jeziorskis' car, raised the rifle to his right shoulder, and—at a range of about twenty feet—aimed in Hodson's direction.[86]

Moments before, prison officer Paterson was running to the lawn in front of the gaol. From his position on the lawn he could still see Ryan. Paterson raised his gun and took aim at him, but found he had to fire between the two officers to get him, so he lowered the gun and jumped over a low brick wall to get a better shot. He would later tell police that he then took aim at Ryan, and took the first pressure on the rifle's trigger, but that as he took the second pressure a woman came into view, and he had to raise the gun and let the shot go into the air.[87]

While all this was going on, the loud, whip-like crack of a single shot was heard, and Hodson fell heavily to the ground. He had been struck by a bullet which wrought massive internal destruction and haemorrhage. Travelling from front to back and in a slightly downward trajectory, the bullet had entered his right shoulder, fractured—and possibly deflected off—the collar bone, fractured five ribs and his backbone, pierced his right lung, and severed the right innominate artery and vein. The bullet had exited through his back about an inch lower than the point of entry in his shoulder. There was also a wound at the back of Hodson's head, amounting to bruising of the posterior cerebellar lobes at the back of the brain with a small subdural haemorrhage. This wound had probably resulted from Hodson hitting the ground in his fall.[88]

Mortally wounded, Hodson lay on the tram-lines as passers-by and others gathered around to render assistance. The first to reach him was Margaret Murray, who had been travelling along Sydney Road in a car driven by her husband, with three of her children in the back seat. Murray opened the door to their car and ran towards the dying Hodson, who was lying face down on the road, bleeding badly from the nose and mouth. As she knelt over Hodson she heard him say the word 'father', and thought that he was trying to say the 'Our Father', so she recited the Lord's Prayer over him.[89] Moments later, Pentridge acting governor Ian Grindlay, who had been at his residence within the prison when the escape took place, arrived on the scene. By now Grindlay could see that Hodson was alive but unconscious. He would die within minutes.[90]

(Back in tower 1, prison officer Lange was soon to learn that his colleague George Hodson had been killed by the weapon taken from him in the tower. Although he had acted with courage in endeavouring to thwart the escape of the prisoners and would receive an official certificate of commendation, Lange would later be haunted by the tragic events that were unfolding before him, and blame himself for Hodson's death. A little over three years later, on 12 April 1969, he would commit suicide whilst on duty in J Division at Pentridge, shooting himself in the head. In a note he left, Lange wrote: 'I can't help thinking about George. All the time I kept asking myself if I couldn't have saved his life by jumping the gun.'[91])

In the preceding few confused moments, Ryan and Walker had run towards a blue Vanguard sedan that had stopped in Sydney Road amid the chaotic scenes. The driver of the Vanguard, Brian Mullins, had been driving north along Sydney Road when he had had been forced to stop. Ryan and Walker raced towards him in his car, and told him to get out: 'Are you going to give us a go, mate?', Ryan yelled to him.[92] The escapees jumped into the car and, cutting the corner of the driveway apron of the BP petrol station, scattering and brushing past pedestrians as they did so, sped away down O'Hea Street.[93] With Walker driving, the fugitives took the first left-hand turn after the railway line some 300 yards west of Sydney Road in O'Hea Street, and continued to do right-hand and left-hand turns to avoid long stretches of straight road and, hence, minimise the possibility of being spotted by pursuers.[94]

Mitchinson meanwhile had run back to below no. 2 post and called to Bennett to throw down his gun to him, which he did. Now armed, Mitchinson and Wallis commandeered a car driven by a passer-by. They quickly gave chase down O'Hea Street, but lost sight of the escapees' car near the railway crossing.[95] It had been less than five minutes from the moment when Lange had encountered Ryan in the tower to the point when the escapees had sped off in the Vanguard. In the estimation of some witnesses, it had seemed less than two minutes.[96]

Inside the prison, a hastily organised muster of prisoners in B Division finally disclosed the names of the escapees as that of Ryan and Walker. Until that point—except for Robert Paterson, who knew Ryan well, but did not recognise Walker—none of the prison officers had any idea who the escaped prisoners were.[97] Later, when the first radio news bulletins of the prison break-out were broadcast and heard by B Division inmates, there was some cheering at the report that the prisoners had successfully escaped. Prison authorities quickly substituted a program of music.[98]

Elsewhere, in the Melbourne southern suburb of Highett, the events at Pentridge were about to change a young life forever. In a double-fronted brick house at 20 Royal Terrace where she lived with her mother, thirteen-year-old Carole Hodson, the only child of George Hodson, returned home from Sunday school at the Moorabbin Methodist church in nearby Wickham Road. Something had seemed terribly wrong when she got there; but her mother, not wishing to spoil Carole's enjoyment of the Sunday school nativity play in which she was appearing later that afternoon, delayed telling her: 'Something's happened, but we'll talk about it when you come home,' she had said.[99]

Carole had seen her father at least once a week after her parents' separation, and she was close to him. They had shared a passion for the St Kilda football club, and during winter they would go to the football every week to follow the team. Now, when she returned from the play, her mother sat Carole on her bed to explain things. She told her, protectively, that her father had died after 'an accident' at work. News of her father's death profoundly shocked Carole Hodson, and she would not learn the awful truth of exactly how her father had died for several years. More than 30 years later, she would say that she had never fully come to terms with his death.[100]

By now, police car radios crackled with the bulletin that two prisoners had escaped from Pentridge, a prison officer had been shot, and the offenders had made their getaway in a commandeered car. Police would soon be mobilised all over Melbourne to be on the lookout for the fugitives. As Mitchinson and Wallis continued their search for the escapees' car—travelling as far north-west as Melbourne's airport at Essendon—the escapees were heading south-west. From O'Hea Street, Ryan and Walker drove the Vanguard as hard as they could in a circuitous route through the streets of Coburg, Pascoe Vale, North Melbourne, and Footscray before heading for the pre-arranged safe house—the house of someone Ryan knew—in the inner-north-west suburb of Kensington.[101]

Their destination was a narrow two-storey terrace house at number 107 McConnell Street, the home of Keith Desmond Hurley, labourer, 53, and his *de facto* wife Edna O'Reilly and their boarder, Walter 'Bobby' Bradford.[102] Just down the street and around the corner—a brisk five-minute walk away in nearby Racecourse Road, Flemington—was Ryan's old haunt, the Doutta Galla Hotel, the pub that had figured so prominently in his earlier criminal activities. In going to the Kensington/Flemington area, Ryan was not only seeking refuge in a neighbourhood he knew extremely well; he was going home.

Across Melbourne at this time, police were moving quickly to throw a protective cordon around Ryan's former wife and children. The girls had been picked up by police from the local Hawthorn swimming pool and then, with Dorothy, they were whisked away from the family home in Hunter Street, Hawthorn and taken to the house of Dorothy's brother, Keith George, at 2 Clarke Street, Blackburn, in the outer-eastern suburbs of Melbourne. Within a short time, Harold and Ethel George would also be taken to Blackburn, as police said they feared they might also be at risk. Three police officers would be assigned in shifts to watch over the household; they would stay there around the clock until Ryan and Walker were re-captured.[103]

Back at Pentridge the chief of the homicide squad of the Victoria Police, Detective Inspector Frank Holland, arrived at the prison not long after 2:30PM and was briefed on the escape. He was later joined at the gaol by homicide squad Detective Sergeant Kevin Carton and Senior Detective Harry Morrison. After ascertaining the facts, Holland and Carton checked the firearms in the prison armoury, which followed a numbering system enabling weapons to be identified as assigned to a particular post in the prison. They were further briefed on the prison regulation requiring eight rounds to be kept in the fifteen-round magazines of prison rifles. Holland found that the no. 1 post weapon (Brown/Lange's) was missing. He further noted that prison officer Paterson's rifle had been fired, and that there were only seven bullets in the magazine. Holland also found that none of the other rifles had been fired, including the rifle of prison officer Bennett on no. 2 post, whose weapon was checked by Carton and himself. They found that Bennett's rifle contained the requisite number of rounds—eight—in the magazine. Holland took Paterson's rifle with him when he returned to Russell Street police headquarters.[104]

While they were at the prison, Carton and Morrison began the arduous task over several hours of taking statements from fifteen prison officers who had been caught up in the escape. They included officers from the seniority level of the acting prison governor down to the newest prison officer member of staff. These were critically important investigations by Holland, Carton, and Morrison. While they may have seemed like routine inquiries at the time, the weapons inspections, in particular, would acquire major significance for the conduct of subsequent court proceedings and the legal campaign to save Ryan from the gallows.

When Ryan and Walker arrived at McConnell Street some time around 2:45PM, Edna O'Reilly, a short, plump woman aged 43, answered the door to Ryan, who asked for Keithy. Keith Hurley was a mate of Shifty O'Keefe, who several weeks before had passed a message to Hurley to 'expect a couple of blokes breaking out of Pentridge'.[105] O'Reilly told Ryan that Hurley had just left the house. Ryan said he had been sent by a friend of Keith's, and asked if they could come in. Walker then appeared from the lane beside the house carrying the carbine wrapped in paper. They told O'Reilly that they had broken out of Pentridge.[106]

Hurley was at a barrel party in nearby North Melbourne when the escapees turned up, but he was quickly fetched by O'Reilly in a cab.[107] After a short time the escapees decided they needed to dump the Vanguard; so, after exchanging his prison shirt for one of Hurley's T-shirts, Walker drove the Vanguard, while Hurley followed in his Prefect. They headed away from the house until Walker found a suitable location in Bruce Street, Kensington, a quiet street—deserted on this Sunday—in a light-industrial neighbourhood near a major railway line. 'Don't park near me', Walker had warned Hurley before setting off. 'I don't want anyone seeing me get out of one car and straight into another!'[108] Hurley was overly conscientious in response, and parked a considerable distance away in Bruce Street. Walker left his own and Ryan's prison shirt in the back of the Vanguard, and made his way to the Prefect unnoticed. Hurley drove him back to McConnell Street, a distance of about half a mile.[109]

When police later found the abandoned Vanguard they surmised that the escapees might have boarded an Adelaide-bound goods train that had earlier passed the Bruce Street railway siding. Police telegraphed Ballarat, and the train was boarded and searched by 30 heavily armed police when it arrived there some time later.[110] The police boarding was without success because Ryan and Walker were still at the Hurleys.

The way Hurley and O'Reilly later told their story to police, they had never met Ryan or Walker before they turned up at the door.[111]

According to Hurley, who had a prior conviction, Ryan told him that he and Walker had just 'busted out of Pentridge' and that Shifty O'Keefe, who was serving a sentence in Pentridge when Ryan was imprisoned there, had told them to lob at his friend Keith Hurley's place when they were out.[112] Hurley told police he was unimpressed when Ryan and Walker arrived:

'Bugger this, you can't stay here. The law is liable to lob at any minute. You can't stay here,' he told Ryan.

Hurley says he gave Ryan a £1 note and said: 'Take this and give me a go.'[113]

Ryan was insistent: 'You've got no risk. Tell them we busted in.'[114]

Although Walker would later give a different story to protect those assisting them, the fugitives would stay this crucial first night at the Hurleys, hoping that police would not come bursting through the door at any moment to capture them.[115] In fact, the possibility of discovery was much closer than they realised. Although none of them was aware of it, just yards away later that afternoon was the prison officer who, from no. 2 post, had aimed his rifle at the escapees as they bailed up the Salvation Army chaplain, and later had Walker pinned down behind the church fence. By an extraordinary coincidence, William Bennett lived opposite the Kensington railway station at 170 Bellair Street, Kensington, the next street running parallel to McConnell Street; the back fence of his house was in the same block, only sixty yards away from the back fence of the Hurley's house at 107 McConnell Street. When Bennett returned home after finishing his shift at 5.00PM, just as the two escapees were becoming the subject of the biggest man-hunt in the state's history, Ryan and Walker were hiding out only a stone's throw away from the very man who, less than four hours before, had come closest to preventing their escape.

By now, radio news bulletins were flashing the news that there had been an escape from Pentridge and that a prison officer had been killed. Details were sketchy and, in the first hurried reports, there was some confusion. On that first afternoon, one radio news broadcast described Ryan as 'Ronald James Ryan, aged 40, who is serving nine years for armed burglary.'[116] More serious media errors were to come.

At about 7:30PM that Sunday night, Alec Whatmore, the director-general of social welfare, and the most senior state public servant responsible for prisons, arrived at Pentridge to be informed of developments. Homicide squad detectives Holland, Carton, and Morrison were still at the gaol interviewing prison officers who had been caught up in the escape, fifteen of whom would make formal statements. Whatmore was briefed about the escape by the director of his department's prisons division, Eric Shade, but he did not interview any officers or peruse the documents being prepared, leaving before they were completed. Later that night, at his Caulfield home, Whatmore took numerous phone calls from journalists writing stories about the escape. In response to reporters' questions, he gave an account of the escape, which he believed was accurate, including the statement that a prison officer (whom, it later emerged, he mistakenly believed was Paterson) had fired a shot from a rifle thrown to him from no. 2 tower.[117] (The officer on the ground who was thrown the gun from no. 2 post was, in fact, Mitchinson, but he did not fire a shot.)

Back in Kensington later that same night, the escapees were preparing for the confrontation they expected would come. Walker rang around his underworld contacts trying to buy a handgun. He finally succeeded with Lennie Hunter, a fence who dealt in firearms.

'What have you got, Lennie?', Walker asked.

'Not a lot', was Hunter's cautious reply.

'Anything will do!', Walker insisted.[118]

At around 9:30PM Walker got O'Reilly to drive him in Hurley's Prefect car to Albert Park, where they drove around the lake and up to Alma Road, St Kilda. At the corner of Alma Road and another street, Hunter was waiting in the shadows under a canopy of trees. Walker got out of the car and went over to him, gave him £4, and returned with a .32 calibre Harrington and Richardson revolver. Walker was later to discover that his insistent plea to Hunter that 'anything will do' had been taken literally: the revolver could fire, but the chamber did not spin.[119]

The next morning, Monday, 20 December, Melbourne's daily newspapers carried extensive coverage of the dramatic break-out and the shooting of Hodson. One of the reports, in *The Sun News-Pictorial*, significantly varied from other newspaper reports. It quoted Whatmore directly as saying: '*The warder on No. 2 Post fired one shot* at the escapees, but was forced to hold his fire because one of the escapees shielded himself behind the woman who had been forced from the car'. This statement effectively confused William Bennett, the officer on no. 2 post, with Robert Paterson, who had run from the main gate to the front of the gaol. Paterson had never been at either no. 1 post or no. 2 post. Whatmore was further reported (again in direct quotes) as saying: 'Hodson was shot *three times* in the chest *and back*.'[120]

Whatmore would much later repudiate these statements in a confidential memo to the head of the chief secretary's office, writing that they were not what he had told the journalist from *The Sun*: 'I do not use the term "warder" nor do I recall ever making the statement or believing that the officer on the tower had fired a shot.' He would also add that he had no recollection of telling *The Sun* journalist that Hodson had been shot three times.[121] Whether Whatmore had been inadequately briefed or he had not fully absorbed the detail of the brief and had mis-stated events to the journalist—or whether the report itself was in error—is uncertain. Regardless of their source, these published statements were significant errors of fact and, in time, they would add to confusion about the number of shots fired, and would fuel claims that someone other than Ryan had fired the fatal shot. Other factors would later come into play but, with Whatmore's reported statements in *The Sun*, the first seeds of the notion that a warder on the wall might have fired the fatal shot were sown.

As Melburnians were reading their morning newspapers, the escapees were waking to their first day of freedom. For the moment, at least, they had succeeded in their daring break-out from Pentridge. A brave prison officer had been killed in the course of their getaway, and their escape had prompted the start of a massive police operation to find them. Police command cancelled all leave for CIB officers, and within a short time more than 120 heavily armed police in 40 cars would be mobilised to scour the state in pursuit of the escapees. Ryan and Walker were free, but now they were hunted and on the run.

CHAPTER NINE

Manhunt

You know, a screw's like a cop, mate. Do you realise if they blame us for this, it's a hanging offence?
—Ronald Ryan

As police began early-morning raids of houses all over Melbourne, turning over known and suspected criminal haunts, Ryan and Walker awoke to take in their first day out of gaol. After stealing a car in Kensington, they drove to St Kilda and went to the Prince of Wales Hotel in Fitzroy Street, where—incredibly—they drank beer with other patrons. As they left the hotel, an intoxicated patron recognised Ryan and called out to him: 'F—u—c—k! Ron!'[1] Ryan and Walker just kept walking, and managed to avoid further scrutiny. The fugitives spent much of that first day desperately trying to find a place to hide out. A number of the contacts they had visited or phoned in various places around the inner city simply shut the door or put down the phone when they rang.[2]

The escape story was already dominating newspaper front pages, but some radio news broadcasts were still having difficulty accurately identifying Ryan's criminal history and getting the escape story straight. Describing the Pentridge break-out the previous day, one newscast reported that '... Ronald Ryan, aged 41, serving nine years for armed burglary seized the warder and shot him dead ...'[3]

Ryan and Walker walked around St Kilda for much of that first day before going to the house of a woman Walker knew, looking for help. At about 4:30PM they went to the home of Patricia Puccini at 47 Thomas Street, Prahran, where Puccini, 29, lived with her husband Frank and their two children. They were looking for Christina Aitken, a 23-year-old prostitute, whose address they had been given by a fellow prisoner at Pentridge.[4] Walker and Ryan knew Chrissie Aitken, and they knew, too, that, like them, she had been on the wrong side of the law.[5] Aitken, also known as Christina Weston, had six convictions for prostitution going back to December 1962. Five of those convictions had been between April and July 1965 when she had been prosecuted for prostitution offences in the St Kilda/Prahran area.[6]

'We're just out of the college and Vic Allard said that Christina would put us up', Ryan told Puccini. 'Does Chris come here every day?'[7]

Unable to find Aitken, they had gone to Pat Puccini's, Ryan said, because Allard had told them Puccini was her friend and would know Aitken's whereabouts. Invited in by Puccini, the fugitives entered the narrow, two-storey 1920s terrace house, went up the stairs, and sat down on a sofa in the lounge. Ryan was carrying the carbine in a long parcel wrapped in Christmas paper, which Puccini later said she thought might have been a present for Aitken's two-year-old daughter Sharon. The wrapping paper was coming off the parcel, and Puccini offered to stick it down for him with a roll of tape from the mantlepiece. 'No, it's all right, I'll do it', Ryan said.[8] When he had stuck it down, he slid the parcel out of the way under the couch.

Puccini and the men were enjoying a cold drink when Aitken unexpectedly arrived. Aitken lived only about a half a mile away, not far from the St Kilda junction, at 18 Henry Street, Windsor, in one of the upstairs flats of a house divided into apartments.

Puccini said: 'Christina, there're two friends of Vic's in here want to see you.'

'Hullo,' she said to the men. 'What do you want to see me for?'

'Vic said you might be able to find us a place to stay.'

Aitken said that there were people at her flat and she could not help them, adding: 'How come you're hot?'[9]

Ryan asked if he could speak to Aitken for a minute outside, where he then told her that they had escaped from Pentridge. With Aitken unwilling to have the fugitives at her own flat, she said she would try to arrange for them to be put up for a couple of nights with her friend Veronica Vitko, who was minding Aitken's daughter Sharon. She said she would go and come back later in the evening.

In the meantime, Ryan was trying other possibilities for help. At about 6:30PM he went to a house at 12 Linton Street, St. Kilda, to be greeted by Gail Farn, who had known Ryan for about three years.

'Do you remember me?', he asked.

'I cannot think of your name straight away', Farn replied.

'I've been in the papers', Ryan added.

'Yes, I read it this morning—Ron.'[10]

Ryan asked Farn how she was, and whether her husband was at home (he was out), and related how the drunk had recognised him in St Kilda. Ryan went on to talk about the escape, telling her that it was planned, but that when he got out the warder had got in the way, and everything went wrong after that. He made no mention of anybody getting shot. After talking for a few minutes to Farn and her brother, who appeared but did not recognise him, Ryan quietly left the house.[11]

Meanwhile, Aitken had phoned Vitko from a phone box and—without letting on to Vitko who the men were—asked if two friends of hers, 'John' and 'Derek', could stay at her place for a night while they found a flat.[12] When she agreed, Aitken drove Ryan and Walker to Vitko's flat in Ormond Road, in the beachside suburb of Elwood, only three miles away. Number 93 Ormond Road was a brick, three-storey block of flats built in the 1960s, close to the middle of the Elwood village shopping centre. The flat was right next door to a branch of the National Bank and opposite a branch of the Commonwealth Bank. It was not far from the flat in Tennyson Street, Elwood to which Ryan had fled and in which he had hidden away when he broke out of the Melbourne city watch-house in April 1960. Vitko's flat, Number 8 on the middle level next to the stairs, was a cramped one-bedroom flat with a very small lounge room, a narrow kitchenette, and a tiny bathroom, with a small alcove between the kitchen and the bathroom.

After Vitko let them into the flat, Walker said to Aitken in the bedroom: 'You say anything to her and you're all gone and [pointing to Sharon] she gets it first!'[13]

Aitken stayed on at Vitko's with the fugitives as the pair took it in turns to keep guard. Later, Walker was driven to a vacant allotment in Albert Street, Windsor (not far from Aitken's flat) where, in order to make the carbine more manageable and less conspicuous, he shortened it by sawing off the butt end of its wooden stock. He discarded the butt in rubbish on the block.[14]

The next morning, Wednesday, 22 December, Vitko went to work leaving the others to stay in the flat. Aitken had already been shopping for newspapers, food, and liquor—beer, whisky, and brandy. Now she was sent on a new errand. During the course of the morning, Aitken drove to a chemist shop in Chapel Street, Prahran, where she bought some peroxide with the £1 Walker had given her. Walker used it to bleach his hair a yellow-blonde colour, and Aitken tinted his eyebrows for him.[15]

Ryan and Walker discussed the prospect of robbing a bank to fund their getaway plans. They needed £10,000, they reasoned, if their plans to buy false passports and fund sea passages to Brazil were to be realised. Using Aitken's car, an early-model green Falcon station wagon that was seriously mechanically faulty, they drove around the area looking for a suitable target.[16] To further their hold-up plans, Walker stole a cream-coloured Holden from near the Caulfield racecourse, which they would use as a getaway car for the robbery.[17] According to Walker, they went to a bank in Grey Street, St Kilda, intending to rob it; but, as they pulled up outside the bank, a police car parked in front of them and four plain-clothed policemen got out. The police did not give the fugitives a second look, but it was enough to cause them to abort the robbery attempt.[18] Walker later drove off alone in Aitken's car, and returned about an hour or so later, excitedly telling Ryan: 'Ronnie, I've got a beauty!'[19] Walker had found a bank in Brooklyn, in the western suburbs of Melbourne, that he said had only four tellers. He had also checked a number of other banks in the St Kilda area. The escapees decided, however, that the first job they would do would be the ANZ branch at 553 North Road, Ormond, only four miles away, almost due east from the flat in Elwood. The bank, on the corner of North Road and Ulupna Road and flanked by a strip of shops, seemed quiet enough. They spent some time talking and planning in low whispers how they would stage the hold-up at the bank the next day.

The next morning, Vitko went off to work as usual, but by now she was annoyed that Ryan and Walker were not looking for a flat as Aitken said they would. She told the men that they would have to go that day because she was going to Brisbane for a holiday. Later in the morning, at his usual 9:30AM press conference in the Old Treasury Building at the top of Collins Street, chief secretary and attorney-general Arthur Rylah sounded an ominous public warning to the escapees, and for the first time raised the spectre of the death penalty. Rylah was asked by a journalist from *The Age* about the escapees and what might await them. In a comment that was reported the next day, he said he thought that the killing of Hodson during the escape was 'the worst Victoria had known', adding that the killer had to be caught, presented for committal in the Court of Petty Sessions, and tried in the Supreme Court:

> If he is sentenced to death the matter will be placed before the State Executive Council. The Council will consider all aspects of the killing, and reports from the police department and the judge's comments. The 'Hanging Act' is still in force in Victoria.[20]

If Rylah's comment was a direct threat, Ryan had other ideas on his mind. As he was about to embark on what he thought was the beginning of a major new series of criminal activities, he sat down to write an extraordinary, open letter to the Melbourne public. During the time they had been at the flat, he and Walker had spent a lot of time watching television news bulletins, listening to radio news, and reading newspaper accounts of the massive police operation to catch them. They were disbelieving when TV news reported that prison officer Hodson had been killed. As with the newspaper reports, they thought this was just police propaganda designed to stir up public feeling against them.[21] Nevertheless they revelled in the attention.[22] Now Ryan would add his own spin to the whirl of publicity surrounding the escape. Directed to *Truth*, a popular tabloid Melbourne weekly paper, this was the first of two letters that the paper would publish from Ryan on behalf of the escapees.[23] The letter, which was published two days later, exhibited Ryan's preoccupation with seeing himself as a big shot, one whose ambition had been frustrated by people in authority. His letter also contained echoes of the literary denunciation and self-justification of another Irish Australian outlaw on the run, Ned Kelly.

The letter is similar in many ways to Kelly's defiant Jerilderie letter of February 1879, and not merely because of the sustained attack on the Victoria Police. In a vituperative letter of defence and defiance, Kelly had written of 'the brutal and cowardly conduct of a parcel of big ugly fat-necked wombat-headed big-bellied magpie-legged narrow-hipped splay-footed sons of Irish Bailiffs or English landlords which is better known as Officers of Justice or Victoria Police . . . '[24] Given its availability in a number of published works about Kelly, it is quite possible, of course, that Ryan had himself read the historic Kelly letter; nevertheless the common elements of passionate rage against perceived injustice are quite striking:

> To Whom It May Concern
>
> We, the Pentridge escapees, are the van of a new era in crime in Victoria—a role which we are loathe to adopt! The present state of affairs and its explosive potential have been forced upon us by a combination of factors. The partial corruptness of the Victorian Police Department, injustice at their hands, ill-considered, harsh sentences by the judiciary; the practice of brutality and mental torture by the Gestapo-like prison warders in 'HELL' Division at Pentridge.
>
> I, Ronald Ryan, in my plea to the bench respectively requested that they 'should not deny me Hope' by too harsh a sentence. My Associate—Peter Walker—(a fundamentally decent lad of potential) was also denied hope through his harsh sentence: $12^1/2$ years. Let me state, and most emphatically, that neither of us are at heart anti-social nor were we beyond rehabilitation. However, we refuse to accept the present social pattern and its inherent lack of fairness and chances of equality in the sense of just reward. The worker does not get a fair share of production and, consequently, is condemned, along with his family, to a life of glorified slavedom. I, as the last of the Ryans, on the male side, intend to put a stop to this.
>
> My children's children will have scope to develop their endowment, enjoy and contribute to life and infinitum. (That's assuming I survive our Police hatchet men.) Peter has like aspirations. So Beware those of you who have accumulated an unjust share of production. We are bent on redistribution. You, the public, can thank a Judge of foresight— Mr. Leckie—who could have placed another man in our desperate plight and endangered the lives and property of others. However, this chap really appreciated the chance extended to him and I am sure it will prove mutually beneficial. How we wish we could have been sentenced by such an enlightened man.
>
> It would indeed open your eyes to see the way the young

offenders are brutalised and embittered by their archaic treatment at the hand of their moronic Warders. In fairness I point out that there are some dedicated, considerate, humane men on the staff. Mr. Ian Grindlay—acting Governor—is conspicuous in this regard. The men are optimistic of a vast change for the better when this man of initiative and with the courage of his convictions becomes Governor. I was fortunate to benefit by his methods while he was in charge of Bendigo Training Prison. It's unfortunate that his good work was negated. We don't want any maximum security soul-destroying prisons; rather we need to attract a better type of man to the job of rehabilitation—hence higher salary. Men must not be denied hope and they must be given a chance to foster and protect their family ties—their best anchor-sheet and incentive.

It is a false economy to underpay. It is regrettable that our families must suffer mental anguish. We are hopeful that they may in years to come see our actions in true perspective and that others may consider our sacrifice worthwhile. There are many more men out there who have been 'denied hope'; they too may pluck up courage to remedy this. They will respond to kindness and consideration. Brutality and poor conditions will spark that imminent Riot. We have acted as a safety valve. Now what do you intend doing?

Ryan & Walker
per R.R.[25]

As with Ned Kelly, thoughts of mother figured strongly for Ryan during this period. The day before he sent the letter, he had sent a Christmas card to Cecilia, reassuring her that he could look after himself:

Mum,

Please try not to worry!! I'm a big boy now and will be O.K! Don't take notice of all you hear on news and in papers. Most of it is wrong. We will be O.K. Love and kisses.

(The last of the Ryans!) Ron
Keep your chin up, Mum!!!
x x x x x
Love and kisses to all the Gang.
x x x x x x x x x x x x *x*[26]

If Ryan's letter to *Truth* was meant to be a criminal call to arms, his own response was swift as he and Walker made ready to rob the ANZ Bank in Ormond. Walker drove Aitken to a hardware shop in Ormond Road, and got her to buy two small tins of enamel paint, one black and one white, and a small paintbrush.[27] Walker used the paint to alter the registration plates of the stolen two-tone Holden from GES 380 to GBS 880.[28] At around 11:00AM on this Thursday, Ryan and Walker left the flat in Elwood, and headed for the bank in North Road, driving separately in the stolen Holden and Aitken's Falcon station wagon. They left Aitken's car about two miles from the bank in Mimosa Street, Carnegie, intending to pick it up again after the robbery.[29]

As this was happening, just ten miles further south from Elwood, the funeral of the slain prison officer, George Hodson, was being held at a funeral parlour in Cheltenham. More than 150 uniformed prison officers and police marched behind a police band at slow time with drums muffled in a funeral procession, following the brief service conducted by the Anglican chaplain of Pentridge, the Reverend Bill Frawley. Hodson's widow Enid was the chief mourner, followed by John Dillon, the under secretary of the Chief Secretary's Office, representing the chief secretary, Arthur Rylah. Others present included the director-general of social welfare, Alec Whatmore; the director of prisons, Eric Shade; the acting governor of Pentridge, Ian Grindlay; and assistant police commissioner Jim Rosengren. The Prison Officer's Valour Medal, posthumously awarded to Hodson, was carried on a velvet cushion alongside his war medals.[30]

At 11:30AM, after waiting until they believed there were only a couple of customers in the bank, Ryan and Walker entered the building, bursting through the front door. Ryan was armed with the sawn-off carbine and Walker with the .32 Harrington & Richardson revolver he had recently bought.[31] To further disguise his appearance, Walker was wearing a floppy white tennis hat and sunglasses with dark green lenses. Ryan was dressed in an open neck white shirt and blue slacks, and was smoking a thin cigar. As Ryan approached the tellers, Walker went into the bank manager's office, looking for guns that he believed were kept there.[32] When Ryan was about six feet away from the counter of the no. 2 teller, Robert Sipthorpe, he pointed the rifle at him, saying 'This is a hold-up! We're the escapees!', and ordered all the staff and customers to the back of the bank.[33]

When Walker burst through the bank manager's door, the manager, John King, was sitting behind his desk having a discussion with a customer.

'Get up! Get out! You with him!', Walker demanded of them, as he pointed a pistol at King's head: 'All of you are going into the strongroom.'[34]

King responded, but the customer kept sitting there.

'You, too!', Walker shouted at him.[35]

As the manager and his customer hurried from the office, Ryan ordered them all into the strongroom in the office area at the back of the bank, saying: 'Don't try anything!' Looking at one of the bank staff, George Robertson, Ryan said: 'I can see you're not scared—watch it! This is an American rifle M1 and I've already killed someone with it!'[36] (The ANZ Bank branch accountant, Ken Munro, who was one of those put in the strongroom, remembered Ryan as saying: 'I killed someone with this rifle yesterday!'[37])

As he moved to close the strongroom door with the ten staff and customers inside, Ryan said reassuringly: 'I'll ring up and get someone to get you out', adding: 'Is there any money in here?'[38]

King replied that there was none, that the tellers had it all. In fact, there was a great deal more cash in the vault than there was in the tellers' drawers.

Walker was positioned in the tellers' area, crouching behind the caged counter and rifling through the tellers' boxes, when a customer, June Crawford, a local resident of North Road, entered the bank and approached the counter. As she did so, Walker bobbed up from his position behind the counter, pointed his gun at her, and said: 'Don't move or I'll shoot!' Just then Ryan emerged from the strongroom, and said: 'That's right, lady, we're the escapees, we're desperate and we'll shoot!'

As Walker continued going through the teller's drawer looking for another weapon and putting money into a bank coin sack, Ryan gave some notes to Crawford, saying: 'Here, take this!'

Crawford looked dumbfounded.

'Go on, put it in your bag!', Ryan repeated.

Not wanting to upset an armed bank robber, Crawford took the money, which was between £5 and £10 in single pound notes. Ryan resumed helping Walker empty the tellers' drawers of bank notes into a small gladstone bag, as Crawford, shocked and feeling sick, stood still and then quietly put the money on the counter to the side of the teller's window. As she stood there, Crawford could see two unspent rifle bullets—both .30 calibre for the carbine—lying on the floor to her right. They had spilled out of the gun earlier as Ryan had mistakenly pressed the magazine release instead of the safety catch and the magazine had fallen to the floor.[39]

Still carrying the carbine, Ryan came out from behind the counter, took Crawford by the arm, and told her: 'Go into the manager's office, we're desperate [and] we'll shoot, we're the escapees!'

Crawford remained in the manager's office for a minute or two before Ryan returned and repeated: 'We're the escapees, we're desperate!'

He put the rifle into the same large paper wrapping he had brought it in and, as he left the office, said to Crawford in a different tone of voice: 'Give us ten minutes to get away.'[40]

With that, the pair ran from the bank, Walker started up the stolen car without any problem and, with Ryan in the passenger seat, drove off.[41] From inside the bank Crawford heard a car revving up outside in North Road, and she crossed to the window to see the early-model light-coloured Holden drive off in an easterly direction at high speed.[42] From beginning to end, the robbery had taken a long time—perhaps, ten minutes—but their getaway was unimpeded. After dumping the stolen car in Carnegie, the escapees picked up Aitken's car and drove straight back to the flat.[43]

Several minutes after the escapees had run from the bank, one of the tellers inside the vault, Graham Townley, was able to open the door and release the staff by pushing back the bolts. Ryan had not spun the combination lock when he closed it. Police were called and arrived within minutes, cordoning off the surrounding area with roadblocks. It was too late, however; the escapees had made their getaway. As police looked on, the tellers checked their boxes to determine what had been stolen. The bank's accountant found that there was £4,423-18-0 missing from the tellers' drawers, together with two Browning .32 automatic pistols on issue to the tellers.[44]

Police began the process of interviewing and taking statements from staff and customers about the robbery. They initially formed the view, on the basis of staff being shown photographs of the escapees, that Ryan had certainly been involved; but the second man could not so easily be recognised. Walker's appearance had been so changed by his bleached blonde hair and glasses that staff did not conclusively identify him, and police were not entirely convinced that he had taken part in the robbery. There was also speculation by police that a third man may have been involved in driving the getaway car.[45]

Within fifteen minutes of the hold-up, Ryan and Walker were back in the flat in Ormond Road, drinking whisky and brandy and counting the cash.

When Aitken asked where they had been, Ryan said: 'It'll be on the news in a minute.'

He told Aitken: 'Pete was nervous. I had to fill him up with whisky.'

When they found that there was less than £5,000 in their haul, Ryan was furious. He began to think that the bank staff must have been on alert for their coming, and had hidden much of their cash in the vault. He said that it was just as well they got something, otherwise they would have shot the place to bits.

Ryan was adamant: 'This is only for expenses; we've got to do a big job yet.'

Walker agreed: 'The Brooklyn's a beauty, it should have forty thousand in it.'[46] Discussion turned to the prospect of acquiring further weaponry, including shotguns ('shotties') from a gun-collector's place in Beaumaris, and the more pressing job of getting ammunition because—apart from the four remaining shells in the carbine—they had none. They decided they would try a pawnbroker first.

Later in the afternoon, Ryan and Walker looked through the Houses to Let columns of *The Age* from the day before, and found a promising advertisement for a house to rent. Aitken subsequently rang the landlady, and later was driven by Walker to 83 Trevellyan Street in South Caulfield.[47] There she spoke to Mrs Paula Fordyce, the owner. The furnished house was in the bayside suburb of Frankston, some 30 miles south-east of the city, and it was available immediately:

> **Frankston—**Reas. rent, Furn.
> Holiday Home, near bch., 2
> bedr., avail. immed. 53 7541[48]

After discussing the house and rental terms, Aitken paid Fordyce £40 for two weeks' rent and took the key.[49]

Later that night, Ryan and Walker watched the Hodson funeral on television news. If they had had any doubts that the prison officer had died during the course of the escape, they were dispelled by the television images of the casket amid 150 uniformed prison officers and police in Hodson's funeral procession. Walker was later to write:

> We didn't believe until then that anyone was dead. We still were convinced that all the stuff in the papers was police propaganda put out to stir up a sort of mass hysteria against us. Now we knew there was a body. And Ronnie looked at me and said: 'You know, a screw's like a cop, mate. Do you realise if they blame us for this, it's a hanging offence?'[50]

The next day, Christmas Eve, the Victorian government announced a £5,000 reward for information leading to the capture of the escapees. Announcing the reward, the chief secretary, Arthur Rylah, said: 'The Government believes Ryan and Walker are extremely dangerous. In the interests of public safety, it is urgent they are caught as soon as possible.'[51] When the fugitives heard the news of the reward, they joked between themselves that they were worth more to a bounty hunter than they had taken in the bank robbery.[52]

With frequent news bulletins of the hunt for the escapees and daily publication of photographs of them on the front pages of the Melbourne newspapers, Ryan and Walker adopted a new sense of urgency about getting a car. They talked about trading in Aitken's car for something more suitable. Ryan wanted a panel van because he said that having one person driving, and the other in the back of the van, would be less conspicuous. He said he did not want to pay more than £100 above the trade-in price. Aitken and Walker went off to the strip of car-yards along the Nepean Highway at Brighton, not far from the flat, but they had no success because the prices were higher than they wanted to pay.

They then went to Kevin Dennis Motors in High Street, Preston, on the north side of the city. There was one panel van left in the yard, an off-white 1960 Holden. While the car salesman was working out a payout figure on Aitken's car, Aitken and Walker went to a pawnbroker, the Australian Mont de Piete Loan & Deposit Company, in nearby High Street, Northcote. Before going in, Walker told Aitken to 'play up to the bloke in there and act nice'.[53] After some discussion, Aitken—using the name Miss R Burke of Closeburne Avenue, Windsor—finally bought a double-barrelled shot-gun and a box of cartridges, and paid £39-10-0 for them.[54] At around 4:30PM Aitken and Walker returned to Kevin Dennis Motors to trade-in Aitken's station wagon on the panel van. The pay-out figure for her car had been calculated and, after some negotiation about the trade-in price, she signed the necessary papers and took the van.[55] From Preston, Walker and Aitken drove to Frankston, using all the back roads along the way to avoid police, to look at the house that Aitken had rented. After a walk-through of the empty two-bedroom house in Beach Street, Walker was pleased with what he found. 'This'll do for a hide-out,' he said. 'It'll be perfect!'[56]

Back at the flat, Ryan was nervous. It was now 9:15PM, Walker and Aitken had been away since early that morning, and he was fearing the worst. When they came through the door of the flat, Ryan, who had braced himself before realising who it was, said: 'You're lucky I didn't shoot you, you've been so long! I thought they must have got you!'[57]

Shortly after, Aitken left in a cab for the Christmas Eve party of her friend Jan Cannon, leaving Sharon with the escapees and telling them she would be back at 1:00AM. Ryan and Walker told Aitken they might be gone by then. Janice Daphne Cannon, who was described in later court evidence as having been a prostitute at some stage, and who was also known as Sandy Cannon and Jan Howarth, rented the upstairs flat opposite Aitken's at 18 Henry Street.[58] By the time Aitken got to the party a number of her friends were already there. Five minutes after she arrived, John Fisher, Arthur Henderson, and Lorraine Van Kruizen—who had all heard about her situation and were worried about her getting caught up with the escapees—arrived, saying they had been out looking for her. Henderson and Fisher, who were close friends, had been drinking beer together at the Star Hotel in Clarendon Street, South Melbourne, since late afternoon.[59]

As they stood outside in the street, Henderson, a tow-truck driver for Melbourne Towing, who previously had been Aitken's boyfriend and had lived with her for about three months, kept telling her: 'You haven't got a brain in your head!' Fisher grabbed Aitken and tried to put her in Henderson's tow truck, saying: 'You're going straight around to the police station—now!'[60] Aitken resisted, worried that Sharon was still in the flat with Ryan and Walker. Initially, Henderson wanted to get a shotgun and go to the flat and get the child.

Later Cannon came down from the party and, together, the four of them—Aitken, Cannon, Fisher, and Henderson—went in Cannon's red Volkswagen to the flat where Ryan and Walker were hiding out. They had decided on a bold but risky course of action: they would tell Ryan and Walker that Aitken's parents wanted to see Sharon, and that they needed to take her back to the party to see them. The risk was that Ryan and Walker would be alarmed by an influx of new people who knew who they were, and the prospects of their betrayal to police would be significantly increased. For the escapees, the circle of people 'in the know' would now be suddenly and threateningly widened.

Sometime around 10:00PM Fisher and Aitken went up to the flat first. The door was open and Ryan was inside. Just inside the door there was a large desk, upon which lay several weapons—a pistol, a revolver, and a rifle.[61] Ryan was sitting at a table with his gun drawn, pointing it at Fisher and Aitken as they came through the door.[62] After a moment, Aitken told Ryan that her parents were at the party and wanted to see Sharon. Ryan was initially suspicious, but relented.

'All right, get her dressed and take her', he said eventually.

When Aitken went into the bedroom, she could hear Fisher say to Ryan: 'Remember me, I was in can with you.'

As it happened, Fisher and Ryan had been in the Bendigo Training Prison at the same time. Ryan replied: 'Sit down, and I'll get you a drink.'

Despite his cordial invitation to Fisher, Ryan was worried. He went straight into the bedroom and confronted Aitken, who was dressing Sharon. He was holding one of the stolen Browning .32 automatic pistols from the bank hold-up.

'Right, the three of you are gone!' he said.

Alarmed, Aitken replied: 'What do you mean?'

Ryan repeated: 'You're gone!'

Aitken said: 'Arthur and Johnny were very concerned about Sharon and they got a bit rough with me. They're full and I had to bring them.'

Just as Ryan raced out to Fisher, Walker—who had been having a drink with two young women outside their flat downstairs—appeared at the door. The room suddenly tensed as Walker, seeing Ryan with his pistol drawn, pulled out his Browning.

Ryan said to Fisher: 'I think I'll take you for a walk around the block.'

Aitken tried to calm the situation: 'It's only the beer with them,' she said. Ryan asked Aitken who was downstairs. He was still jumpy as Walker went down to get Henderson and Cannon from the car and, asking them to come up for a Christmas drink, brought them back upstairs.

When they came in the door, Ryan was still tense. He said, unconvincingly: 'I think I'll make this into a party. Everybody sit down and we'll have a beer.' Despite the invitation, there was an undercurrent of terror among the group, as they sat and tried to look like they were enjoying this Christmas Eve drink, fearing that any moment might be their last. As Aitken nervously made sandwiches, Ryan joined her in the kitchen.

'The three of them are going to get it!', he said. 'We'll have to take them for a walk somewhere.'

'Turn it up!,' Aitken responded, 'They're all right now. They won't say a word.'

'Johnny Fisher's all right because I did can with him,' Ryan said. 'What about your mate, Jan?'

'I've known her for five years,' Aitken told him. 'She wouldn't say a word. She's got too much to lose.'

'Well, Arthur?' Ryan went on.

'No,' Aitken said firmly, 'He's a married man with two children. He won't talk.'

With that, Ryan's mood seemed to change.

'Everything's fine,' he said finally. 'It's turned out all right.'[63]

Ryan went back to join the group, and was soon laughing and joking again. He later played a guitar and sang.[64] In the course of the conversation that followed, according to Fisher, Ryan said that they had robbed the ANZ Bank, and also that he had shot Hodson.[65] Ryan said that the people he had ordered out of their car during the Pentridge escape (the Jeziorskis) 'had guts' for defying him.[66] At another point in the conversation, Ryan said—and Walker agreed—that they would not be taken alive, they would shoot it out with police, and kill anyone who would give them up.[67]

The next hour or so were passed amid some tension, as Walker dismantled one of the .32 Browning automatics in order to show it to people. The others looked on as he took it to pieces on the floor. Ryan was sitting on the desk playing the guitar between drinking beer and talking.[68] At one point he was talking to Fisher about the Bendigo

Training prison.[69] Later, according to Cannon (denied by Walker), Walker took his pistol and, holding a pillow at her head, asked her if she was frightened. He could shoot her now and no-one would hear, he said.[70]

Sometime before midnight, the dozen bottles of beer they had started with ran out, and Henderson said he knew a sly grog shop in Buckhurst Street, South Melbourne, where he could get more. Ryan agreed, but he and Walker went to the small adjoining alcove where Fisher and Aitken heard them whispering.[71] Walker later said that Ryan had told him to be careful, that they both had relatives in that area and that police might be watching. When they returned, Ryan gave Walker some money—a handful of £5 notes—and Walker said: 'Come on, Arthur, we'll get some more beer.' Before leaving together in the panel van, Walker picked up the Browning automatic and pushed it in to his pocket.[72]

What happened after Walker and Henderson left the flat to go to the sly grog in South Melbourne will never be known for certain, because there were no independent witnesses. Walker has said that he drove the panel van and, with Henderson giving directions, they navigated through back streets to a terrace house in Buckhurst Street near Ferrars Street, South Melbourne. There they bought a carton of beer from a woman in the house who got it from the boot of a car parked outside. Paying £5 and getting change, they took the beer and drove to a shop where they bought cigarettes.

Back in the car, according to Walker, Henderson suddenly said: 'I know this Ryan fellow back there. I recognised him from the papers and my mate [Fisher] knows him.' Henderson said that he was thinking of going to the police over the £5,000 reward. Walker has said he played him along for a moment and then said: 'I'm the other escapee.' Henderson looked at him, laughed and said: 'You're joking!' Walker said he told Henderson: 'Mind, I've dyed my hair, got glasses and that on.' Henderson said that Walker did look like the escapee a bit, but the photographs in the papers were not very good. Walker has said he had a fair idea that Henderson had realised who he was. During the conversation that followed, Walker said that he raised with Henderson the prospect of his helping the escapees. One way he could help would be to get car number plates off wrecked vehicles. He said he offered him £200 if he would give them some help and keep his mouth quiet about where the escapees were. For the next few minutes they drove around the streets and continued to talk things over, with Henderson saying that he could easily get the bodgie number plates.[73]

By now, according to Walker, he was lost and wanted Henderson to guide him back to the flat, which was less than four miles away. But Henderson said he wanted to 'have a leak' and asked Walker to 'pull up down the beach'. Walker turned into Beaconsfield Parade next to the beach and, after driving a short distance, stopped the car opposite the toilet block, which was in the centre of the roadway. The block was opposite Mills Street, which runs into Beaconsfield Parade at a T-intersection to the east. On the western side of the block was a bluestone sea wall and kiosks. On the eastern side there was a large convent building. Henderson ran over towards the beach and entered the toilet. A moment later Walker got out of the car and followed him in.[74]

When Walker reached the toilet, Henderson was standing facing away from the urinal with his arms folded. According to Walker, Henderson said: 'You don't scare me!' and accused him of having sex with his girlfriend, Aitken.[75] Henderson began to throw punches at Walker, landing blows to his jaw and forehead. Henderson was a fit and solid young man of 24 years of age, standing five feet nine inches tall and weighing just under thirteen stone. Later evidence would show that he had consumed a large amount of beer, and that at the time he had a blood alcohol reading of .128—two-and-a-half times the legal driving limit.[76] According to Walker, a fight ensued, with the pair trading blows and both being forced back against the walls of the toilet as they scuffled for what seemed a long time but was probably less than a minute. As they grappled, Henderson tried to grab Walker's gun from his pocket, but Walker resisted and hit him across the face with it. As Walker later recounted: 'He spun half around [in a half-circle] and was going down. I then brought [the gun] down to his head … There was a loud bang and I [had] shot him. … He dropped straight to the ground … I stood looking at him when he was lying on the floor … I noticed the spent shell near his boot … I picked it up and threw it over the wall … That was it … He was dead.'[77]

Later forensic examination by the senior government pathologist showed that Henderson had sustained a fatal bullet wound to the back of the head, just to the right of the midline of the scalp, with the bullet proceeding from back to front and upwards at an angle of about 45 degrees. According to evidence from a police firearms expert, the bullet had entered Henderson's head at virtually point-blank range, causing a multiple fracture of the skull and profuse haemorrhaging of the brain tissue. According to later medical opinion, death could have been instantaneous, or he could have lived for up to 40 minutes.[78]

Eventually taken by ambulance to Prince Henry's Hospital in St Kilda Road, at 2:00AM Henderson was found by a young doctor on duty in the casualty department, Dr David Middleton, to be dead on arrival.[79] Henderson's body also showed other facial injuries caused by his having sustained an impact to his nose and face. These injuries—bruises and abrasions and a possible broken nose—were consistent with his having fallen after being shot, and having hit his head and face on the concrete floor of the toilet. They were also consistent with his having sustained blows to his nose and face as the result of a fight.[80]

According to Walker, he, too, was bearing injuries from the scuffle—bruised ribs, a swollen jaw, and bruises to the head—but he was not advertising them.[81] Some 45 minutes after he had left with Henderson, Walker returned to the party at the flat, carrying beer. He told everyone that Henderson had gone to pick up his tow-truck and do some work.[82]

Taking Ryan aside, he told him what had happened.[83]

Ryan exploded: 'You're a fucking fool!', he yelled at Walker. 'Why did you do it?'[84]

Although this was said outside the hearing of the others, they picked up a sense of dread. The mood in the room, previously one of barely subdued terror, turned even more chilling. Cannon nervously suggested to Aitken, who had been lying on the floor sleeping, that it was getting late and time to go, and that she would take her and Sharon home. Ryan looked disapproving. Sensing his unease, Aitken said: 'No, I'll stay.'[85] Cannon and Fisher stayed another fifteen minutes or so before Ryan and Walker told them to get going. 'Keep your mouth shut! Don't say anything', Ryan added.[86]

Cannon and Fisher quickly left in Cannon's car before Aitken went to the bedroom, from where she could hear the escapees talking. There was a rising sense of panic between them.

'Are you sure he's dead?', Ryan asked.

'Of course, I'm sure!' Walker replied. 'He had no pulse and there was a big pool of blood.'[87]

Aitken joined them in the lounge. 'Did you kill Arthur?', she asked.

Ryan replied: 'Yes', and then added quickly, 'Right, you go your way and we'll go ours,' before heading down to the panel van parked below.[88]

After Cannon and Fisher had left the flat in Ormond Road, they drove very fast to Aitken's flat to see if Henderson's tow-truck was still there. Cannon collected from a wardrobe in Aitken's flat a parcel of Ryan's and Walker's prison clothes wrapped in newspaper, which Ryan had asked her to do.[89] They then went to the offices of the Melbourne Towing Service, where Fisher made inquiries about Henderson's whereabouts.

Aitken herself wasted no time after Ryan and Walker left the flat. At 1:30AM on what was now Christmas Day she went directly to the Elsternwick police station to tell them what had happened. Just minutes later, at about 1:40AM, Henderson's body was discovered by a motorist, Norman Haywood, a contractor, of George Street, South Melbourne, who had stopped in Beaconsfield Parade to use the toilets. He saw Henderson lying face down on the concrete floor with his head facing out of the entrance and his feet towards the urinal. In the darkened, badly lit toilet Haywood at first thought he might have been drunk. 'Hi mate', he said. 'Are you all right?'[90] Striking a match, Haywood saw that blood was coming from Henderson's mouth, and in the gloom he was able to read 'Melbourne Towing' in red lettering on the back of his overalls. Thinking that Henderson may have fallen and hit his head, Haywood quickly left the toilet block and drove to a telephone box in nearby Kerferd Road, rang Melbourne Towing, and was told that someone would be down in a couple of minutes. Haywood returned to the toilet block, and within five minutes Stephen Prince, a director of Melbourne Towing, arrived at the scene.[91] Entering the toilet with Haywood, Prince turned the body over and recognised it as that of Arthur Henderson. He saw blood running from his head. He felt for a heartbeat and pulse, but found none; the body was very cold.[92] Alerted by their management via the tow-truck company's radio network, work-mates of Henderson soon began arriving at the toilet block.

Shortly after this happened, Ryan and Walker took a big risk. With Walker driving, they headed for Beaconsfield Parade. As they approached the toilet block, there were tow-trucks, police cars, and people everywhere. An unwitting police officer diverting traffic around the crime scene yelled at their car: 'Move! Get the hell out of the way!' The pair needed no second warning, and drove straight back to the flat.[93] When they got there they found the lights were out and there was no-one there, so Walker lifted up the kitchen window and climbed in. They quickly gathered together their gear, especially the weapons that they had accumulated in the previous week, before hastily leaving.

By now Ryan and Walker had a substantial armoury of two pistols, a shotgun, and two rifles. It comprised the two Browning .32 calibre automatic pistols stolen from the ANZ Bank, the shotgun bought from the pawnbroker's, a .22 calibre rifle belonging to Veronica Vitko, and the .30 carbine taken from the no. 1 post at Pentridge. As well, there was a box of cartridges for the shotgun and three boxes of shells for the .22.[94] Within minutes of the import of Aitken's statement to police becoming evident, armed detectives raided her house in Windsor, and the flat in Ormond Road. In the flat police found two small tins of paint, cigar butts, and a bottle of peroxide hair bleach.[95] The escapees had been gone for less than an hour.

Meanwhile, as word of the discovery of Henderson's body filtered through to his friends, they gathered at the toilet block in Beaconsfield Parade. Jan Cannon was one of them. She still had the parcel of Ryan and Walker's prison clothes in her car as she joined others in witnessing the distressing scene of Henderson's death. After she had visited the toilet block she drove around for some time before hiding the escapee's clothes under a carton on a vacant block of land in Prahran.[96]

For several hours the escapees drove around aimlessly, trying to think where they could go. Finally, they headed for the place they had started at almost a week before, when they first broke out of Pentridge: Keith Hurley's house in McConnell Street, Kensington.[97] At around 4:00AM on Christmas Day, armed with guns, Ryan and Walker broke down the back gate on the lane and climbed through a rear window of Hurley's house. Laughing, they went into the Hurleys' bedroom, carrying cans of beer.

'Santa Claus has come!', Ryan announced.

Edna O'Reilly was unimpressed: 'You'll have to go, you can't stay here!', she insisted.

Ryan and Walker, who each had Browning pistols tucked into their belts, flashed their weapons with a hint of menace: 'Do you want us to leave?'

With that, they sat down and drank beer till daylight—interrupted only by Walker leaving to dump the panel van—and then began looking around the house for somewhere to sleep. Shown a small room upstairs by Hurley, they bedded down. For the next 36 hours one slept while the other warily held guard with the sawn-off carbine.[98]

As Henderson's murder became the subject of news reports later in the morning of Christmas Day, scores of armed detectives in a fleet of cars combed Melbourne streets. Telephone reports by people who thought they had sighted the escapees were hitting the police switchboard at the rate of one every ten minutes. Such was the widespread apprehension in the days that followed that one newspaper ran a report of the concern of Melbourne people at the escape under the headline: 'A City Gets the Jitters'. The report said that a 'peculiar uncomfortable atmosphere' had crept into Melbourne. Nothing like it had been experienced in the city since 1942, when the murderer of three Melbourne women had been on the loose.[99] People coming home from holidays, the report added, were frightened that they might find the escapees occupying their premises, and parents were keeping their teenage children home at night, not allowing them to go out to parties and dances.[100] The Victorian government, too, was alarmed. This period was later described by one minister as exhibiting a 'reign of terror' in which, he said, 'the veneer of law and order in our ... community is not very thick.'[101]

With this second murder, the community was now fully mobilised against the escapees, and police efforts were redoubled to recapture them.[102] Ryan and Walker, the desperate escapees at the centre of all this concern, had become the most notorious men in Australia.

CHAPTER TEN
Recapture

Congratulations! Congratulations! It was a bloody great pinch!
—Ronald Ryan

Christmas Day, 1965 dawned in Melbourne humid and mild with some early-morning drizzle, but as dawn was breaking Walker and Hurley were on an errand. At around 5:00AM, while most Melburnians had not yet begun this festive day, Walker took Hurley and drove the panel van to North Essendon, where they abandoned it in Gillies Street, a quiet street next to a primary school about five miles from Kensington. This was far enough from McConnell Street to lead police away from the escapees' hideaway and yet close enough to Essendon Airport, less than a mile away, to create an impression that they might have flown interstate. From Gillies Street they walked the short distance to Keilor Road, where they waited in the half-light for a passing cab. Having no luck, Walker decided to thumb a ride on the spur of the moment, and was surprised to be picked up by an obliging driver of a ute.

'You're up early', Walker said to him.

'Yeah, I'm a milkman', the driver said. 'I'm on my way to work.'

The milkie drove them to the Kensington railway station, dropping them off not far from Hurley's house.[1] It was not long before the abandoned van was located by police. Alerted to it by information from Aitken, police searched extensively, and found it the next day.[2]

Meanwhile, police were employing tactics of disinformation to gain an advantage against their adversaries wherever they could. Homicide squad detectives told journalists that police had raided houses in the mostly outer-Melbourne suburbs of Springvale, Moorabbin, Surrey Hills, and Chelsea. It seems likely, however, that police were foxing about exactly where they were focusing their search, in order not to disclose how close their raids were getting to the fugitives.

Now on the run for two murders, the escapees were concerned to go to ground for the next few days and not venture out unless they had to. They installed themselves in a hideaway room below Hurley's house. There was an access door below the floor level leading from the rear of the house to a small room. Another doorway from the small room led out to the southern side of the house, which ran beside a steep laneway leading down towards the Kensington railway station just 100 yards away. It was in this room that Ryan and Walker would stay for almost a week. Oblivious to the nearby presence of the most wanted men in Australia, prison officer William Bennett—the officer on no. 2 post—would come and go to his house in the next street every day while they were there.

Later on Christmas morning Ryan talked at length with Hurley about getting a high-powered car from a car-yard. With the police manhunt in Melbourne intensifying following the Henderson killing, Hurley was told he would have to go interstate to buy the car. Later, at around 11:00AM, Hurley went off to drink at the Doutta Galla Hotel around the corner, where he met up with a labourer friend, Norman Harold Murray, 49, and he told him of his need for a car: 'Look, I'm in awful bother,' he told Murray. 'Ryan and Walker are there, and I've got to get them a car to get away.' Murray, who was also known as Norman Harold Benson and had criminal convictions dating back to 1936, said he would help him out. Together they returned to the McConnell Street house, where Hurley introduced Normie Murray to the escapees as his mate 'Danny'.[3]

The escapees were initially unimpressed with Murray's arrival: 'Who's this mug you've brought in?,' one of them said to Hurley. But when Hurley explained that Murray could help them get a car, they said 'everything would be sweet'.[4] Ryan subsequently gave Hurley a big roll of money—£1,100, which was part of the proceeds of the ANZ Bank robbery—telling him that £1,000 was for the car, and that he could keep £100 for himself. Murray was also given money. Later that Sunday night,

Hurley and Murray set off for Sydney in Murray's small Austin car, which was more than ten years old and something of a bomb. With Hurley away, Ryan and Walker remained in the house, alternately sleeping or keeping watch at the front window, and sending O'Reilly out for groceries from time to time. On one occasion, O'Reilly was given £20 and told to buy food, and also more peroxide hair bleach for Walker, which she got from a chemist shop in Puckle Street, Moonee Ponds. For the next few days she would cook for the escapees as they waited for Hurley and Murray's return with a car from New South Wales. With the pair confined to their room for days on end, seldom leaving the house except occasionally to make phone calls, the tension in the house began to rise.[5]

Usually, Ryan and Walker spent each day watching television news broadcasts and listening to the radio for news bulletins of the police search. They were desperate for any news of their exploits. They were not disappointed. Daily reports of the police manhunt and reported sightings of the pair dominated newspaper front pages. Following raids on the flat in Elwood used by the fugitives, police said publicly that they believed they were less than 24 hours behind their quarry. With banks closed for the Christmas-New Year break, other businesses holding large amounts of cash were being given special police protection. TAB betting agencies, in particular, were being staked out by armed police in case another hold-up eventuated.[6] Police were also using the media to sow the seeds of distrust between the fugitives, suggesting to reporters at one point that Walker had phoned the homicide squad asking to speak to the squad chief, Detective Inspector Frank Holland, but that the line went dead before Holland could take the call. Later that day in *The Herald*, Holland got the headline he was evidently looking for: 'Is Walker trying to make a deal?'[7]

Hurley and Murray had taken 24 hours to reach Sydney because Murray's Austin was slow and it had broken down in the NSW country town of Holbrook, and Hurley had been forced to make running repairs. When they reached Sydney late on the night of Monday, 27 December, they had slept in the car before the next day going to the suburb of Waverley, where Murray had been told through one of his Sydney friends that they could get a large, powerful car, a Chrysler Plymouth. When they got there, they found that a serious motor car—a grey-blue 1960 Plymouth V8 with extravagant rear fins and

Queensland licence plates—was available. Using a false name, Murray put down £250 deposit, gave a further two months' advance payment of £90, and—leaving his own car in a garage—they drove the car away, setting off for Melbourne soon after.[8]

By this stage, the escapees had been at large for more than a week. They had staged a daring bank robbery, and Walker had killed Henderson, but efforts to track them down were not producing results. Police had arrested Aitken and Puccini, who were now under guard, but each time they thought they were closing in on the escapees, the leads seemed to go cold. Homicide squad detectives decided to appeal to Ryan's ex-wife, Dorothy, for help. On 28 December, a homicide squad detective, First Constable Ronald Jackson, with Dorothy's consent, placed an advertisement in the personal columns of *The Sun* newspaper, using Ryan's affectionate nickname for Dorothy, Little Lady. The ad, designed to flush Ryan out from wherever he was hiding in Melbourne and to lead the escapees into a trap, constructed a story of marital regret and concern about his children, and asked Ryan to go to the Melbourne GPO to pick up a letter addressed to George Norman Russ, an alias Ryan had used in Sydney.[9] Appearing in the Missing Persons columns the next day, the ad read:

> R.J.R., made mistake, children
> fretting, am very worried, contact
> GPO, letter for Russ. Little Lady.[10]

What police did not realise, however, was that the initials RJR were never used by Ryan in situations like this. Ryan and Dorothy had long ago agreed that they would use the Missing Persons columns of *The Sun* to communicate, but they would adopt the initials RER—for Ronald *Edmond* Ryan—as a code to establish authenticity when he was on the run and secrecy was required.[11] That middle initial in the advertisement (standing for his adopted confirmation name, Joseph) was a give-away. When Ryan saw the ad for RJR he believed it probable that police would be waiting for him at the Post Office.

Wary as he was, Ryan was not deterred from elaborating further on his criminal plans, and on the same day he wrote a second letter to *Truth*. Dated 29 December 1965, like the first it set out an ambitious criminal manifesto and outlined his grandiose plans:

To Whom It May Concern

We, Ryan and Walker, categorically state that the people charged for harbouring are blameless. They were under duress from us!! Seemingly, they have also been under duress from the 'Bully Boys' @ Russell Street. Hence the Statements. We shall spare no expense to retain the best legal aid to represent anyone similarly victimized. Mr. R. H. McMennemin has been retained to brief counsel on their behalf. Bail was also arranged by us; but others had already come to the young Ladies aid. Bail will also be readily available for anyone else whom the Police charge in their efforts to detract from their inability to achieve results.

Certainly, the police have spared no effort, and by now must have run out of poses for the T.V., and dramatic statements to the Press. It is regrettable that they do not apply themselves so wholeheartedly to the apprehension of the more despicable type of criminal. How about the Shirley Collins affair and this recent appalling murder of a beautiful young woman? I am sure we express public sentiment when I say 'I hope they are not neglecting that more serious investigation by hunting two men who will harm no one without cause.' There is an oft-used saying by the Crims—and please excuse the crude terms —'You can Fuck them, but you can't Rob them.'[12]

In support of this, we point out the concerted efforts to run down and annihilate us as against the feeble attempts in the case of the poor girl. Note the immediate offer of a large Reward in our case as against no offer in the girl's case. We feel that the offer of this immediate and large reward reflects their physical fear of courageous, unjustly treated men, and an acknowledgment of their fear of being shown as incompetent. This latter has been highlighted the past few days and not all the public are being duped by their 'Cops and Robbers' antics in front of T.V. cameras.

We, Ryan and Walker, are respected by our contemporaries and have been unanimously elected to highlight their case for a better deal; (a) at the hands of the Police; (b) In the courts and by the Judges; (c) by the public, after paying their debt to society; (d) the furtherance of the enlightened rehabilitation programme now in its infancy; (e) no 'Devil's Island' penal institutions where men are denied hope; (f) Banishment of Hell Division @ Pentridge and its sadistic moronic, staff; (g) Higher salaries for the men who are called upon to assist the prisoners prepare for a better life. It is essential that men of humanity, depth and delicacy of sensibilities, capable of empathy be attracted. At present—excepting those few dedicated men such as Mr Ian Grindlay – acting Governor—the fact that a person accepts such a job reflects most unfavourably on them. They are social misfits who even lack the final grace of trying to do something about it. It has been said that 'a Turnkey—Screw—is a man who has judged himself'.[13]

We advocate a greater share of production for all workers - a more even distribution of the country's wealth. Do we ever hear of unrest and dissatisfaction in such firms as 'Fletcher Jones and Staff'? And is their product not of the highest quality? This more reasonable income will allow families self-respect. Children are very sensitive to having less than the neighbour, being deprived of the necessities of life. My own Father—a man's man—contracted Silicosis through working in the Gold Mines in poor conditions. When his health was gone, hence his value as a 'slave', he was pensioned off on the princely sum of £10 a month. On this he must endeavour to support a wife and ~~three~~ four children. Can you imagine the mental anguish of a proud man as he saw his loved ones in sad plight. It is happening today! Are we going to sit mutely by and see it continue? We say No!!!

We implore you to support the dedicated men of the Trade Unions. We, ourselves, may not benefit materially; but our children, and their children, will have been bought from bondage and given their rightful chance to develop their endowment. Evolution will accelerate with the human being attaining his inherent God-like stature.

'Hatred of oppression makes ~~comrades~~ Friends of Criminals and Law-abiding Citizens'!!![14]

We thank the Press in general, and Truth in particular, for the fair coverage to date. We hope they do not succumb to the Police smear tactics. It seems that the first of the Bounty hunters has got his 'reward'. A very ill-considered move Messrs. Bolte, Rhylah.

P.S. Those Bank boys certainly deserve higher pay!! Let them remember that while we admire courage, we abhor stupidity.

Ryan-Walker

> & Associates,
>
> per R.J.R.
>
> WARNING: Ryan and Walker are both excellent marksman, having both earned their living as hunters, where the game had to be head-shot to protect the skin and carcase. Do not provoke us. We wish harm to no-one.[15]

That Wednesday night, at around 6:00PM, Hurley and Murray arrived back at McConnell Street with the Plymouth. They were hoping that, with their mission accomplished, Ryan and Walker would leave: 'We've got the car!', they announced triumphantly. Ryan and Walker were pleased with what they had bought. Later, Hurley handed over to Ryan £500 remaining from the car purchase and the Sydney trip. The rest, some £160, had been spent on 'petrol, eats, smokes, a couple of tyres and a battery', as well as 'giving it to mugs and [having] a few quid on the horses'. Though it did not make up for all the worries, nor for the fact that—with Murray—he later would be charged with harbouring the escapees and subsequently go to gaol, Hurley had made a tidy profit out of the exercise.[16]

The next day, Thursday, 30 December, the day after the Missing Persons ad in Dorothy's name appeared, Ryan expressed his suspicions about the ad in a letter he wrote to a good friend and the wife of a relative, Dianne Everett. The letter crudely threatened retribution against Dorothy if his suspicions about the ad proved correct. He also told Everett that he would be using her address in an ad as a contact point for Dorothy and warned her that, if Dorothy's ad was a police plant, Everett should expect some attention from the law:

> Dear Dianne,
>
> Hi Kids!! We'll bring a team that will whack them!! How about that now—, and I haven't got into stride yet.
>
> I do hope they have not been worrying you too much. It seems one's friends must always bear the brunt of things. Never mind sweetheart, I'll see you are properly rewarded. I always look after my friends, and my enemies get their just reward also. If you see any of those 'bounty hunters' tell them to beware. We have the strength behind us. This is a very well organised affair, a little of which I have disclosed in this week's Truth. I expect they will publish my most

recent letter today—Thurs. 30—.

Dorothy has tried to contact me through the Missing friends column. I am dubious, as it could be a decoy and a trap. However, fool that I am, I will take a chance and see what happens ... They say love is blind and I guess I'm a fool. She says 'I made a mistake—children are fretting—and a letter is waiting for you.'

I have made discreet arrangements to have the letter picked up so's I'll not be picked up. However, I must make other arrangements for the future, so I'm taking the liberty of giving Dorothy your address. She can write there c/o you.

I will then have a chap called 'BURNIE' collect it and I'll get it eventually. I do hope you'll not mind? I won't come near you and you just don't know anything about me.

Darling, please don't ever think of trying to collect that £5000. All Bounty hunters will be dead ones. If I can't then one of my many mates will 'Hit'. I relize you won't, but just caution anyone else. This is for real Kid! We are not playing 'Cops and Robbers' anymore.

Should you wish to contact me do so through The Sun or Sydney Morn Herald 'missing Persons'. The Sun any day, but Syd Morn H. only on Saturday, only START the message, 'Eric' and sign it 'Di'.

I don't know Dorothy's address, but will use your address. They know you are friends and won't think much of her calling. Tell her to destroy any letters on the spot. You watch her and no matter what she says see her burn them before you.

I won't enclose much money just yet, in case you are being too closely watched, but I'll not forget you 'BABS'.

Love Ron

P.S. I bet you (as well as the Jacks [police]) were surprised to know we were just around the corner!! The Phantom strikes again soon.[17]

Before sending it off, Ryan enclosed a £10 note with the letter for Everett, and inside the letter was another letter in an envelope addressed to Dorothy and marked Personal.

Suspicious though he was, Ryan made arrangements to have the Russ letter picked up by an associate, Burnie Davitt, 28, of Crimea

Street, St Kilda. In a note to Davitt, which was conveyed through a woman intermediary, Margaret Calleson, in a pub in St Kilda, Ryan sent him £100 and asked him to pick up the letter at the Melbourne GPO.[18] In his note to Davitt, Ryan wrote:

> Burnie, Enclosed £100. Use as you see fit. Don't let Chris [Aitken] or anyone else know you are doing any business with us. We just can't trust anyone. So beware of dogs, etc. Now, it is probable, that the Jacks have a shadow on Chris. Hence, she could bring everyone she comes in contact with undone. Be careful, and don't underestimate the shadow squad. Brother they are efficient!!
>
> There should be [a] letter there for me ... But I repeat, be very wary as it could be a decoy or a trap. I'll contact you sometime today [30th] about its contents. It is from my wife, but again, say nothing. Trust nobody. I'll phone you.
>
> R. & P.[19]

Although Ryan did not know it at the time, his fears about the Missing Persons ad were well based. When Davitt went to the GPO on 30 December to pick up the letter he was promptly arrested by waiting police.[20]

On the same day, Ryan told O'Reilly he wanted her to place an ad in *The Sun.* He gave her £10 to buy some frocks for herself, and sent her off with Walker in Hurley's car. O'Reilly took her silky terrier, Penny, with her. In order to prevent the escapees' whereabouts being flagged to police if the ad's lodgement was traced, O'Reilly was driven by Walker at around midday to find a newsagent in Footscray, some distance away in the western suburbs. Walker gave O'Reilly a further £3 for the advertisement. He waited in the car while she went into a dress shop, the New Jersey Fashion House, at 135 Nicholson Street, Footscray, where she bought two frocks for £2-19-11 each with the money Ryan had given her. O'Reilly then asked the saleswoman how many people worked in the shop. Told that there were three, O'Reilly gave her six shillings for them all to 'have a drink for the New Year'.[21] Carrying the silky terrier with her in a bag, which made her highly conspicuous, O'Reilly then went to Ward's newsagency at 105 Nicholson Street, where she lodged the ad for a cost of £2–5–0.[22] It took some time, as she had to write the ad out again because the shop assistant said that O'Reilly could not keep the original (Ryan, ever wary, had told her that he wanted it back.)[23]

Now that they had a 'cold' car—one difficult to trace to them—Ryan decided that he and Walker were almost ready to make their move. First they needed some new clothes. So Ryan sent Hurley and Murray to the city on Friday morning, New Year's Eve, to buy suits and shirts. Of course, Ryan had to have the best. He sent Hurley to the menswear department of the high-class Georges store in Collins Street. Paying cash and giving a false address, Hurley bought a well-cut, dark suit for £41-10–0.[24] He also went to Georges' hat department and bought two hats, one of which was a dark grey fedora.[25] Murray bought a dark-grey Michaels-Stern suit for Walker at Ottrey's menswear further down Collins Street, and shirts and ties as well.[26]

Later that night, Walker ventured out in the Plymouth to go to Burnie Davitt's house in Crimea Street, St Kilda. It was Walker's practice never to drive directly to a location, but to warily approach it by a more circuitous route in order to minimise the prospect of police ambush. As he drove down an adjacent street, he noticed an unmarked police Studebaker sedan positioned down a side street near Davitt's house, and a man standing alone next to a telephone box. Suspicious, Walker pulled up at the corner kerb in Wellington Street to observe events before moving closer to Davitt's. He quickly realised that this was a police stakeout of Davitt's house; but, before he could drive off, an unmarked police car pulled up on the other side of the road, and a police officer got out and walked back to Walker's car.

'What're you doing here?', the officer asked Walker through the driver's side window.

'I'm on holidays from Queensland,' Walker said, sure that the policeman had already seen the interstate registration plates.

'Where're you from?', the policeman asked.

'Ipswich', Walker quickly responded.

Evidently keen to get this illegally parked car out of the stakeout zone, the police officer had not recognised the heavily disguised Walker, who was himself a target of the police operation.

'Well, don't park here', he said finally.

'Yeah, all right', Walker replied, not needing a second invitation. He started the motor and drove off. As he passed the police car, Walker could see two large photographic prints of himself and Ryan fixed onto the dashboard.[27]

The following day, Friday, 31 December, Ryan's ad appeared in the Missing Persons columns of *The Sun*:

> **LITTLE LADY** Contact Dianne, 31 Kingsley Street, Elwood. Love you, Kisses, girls.—Dad.[28]

Ryan's suppositions about police involvement in Dorothy's original ad were well founded. When the ad appeared, police were alerted to it; in fact, Ryan's letter to Everett and a car-load of police arrived at her Kingsley Street door at the same time.[29] Police now had uncovered a link to the fugitives, and they began to formulate plans to close the net around them. As Ryan had alluded in his letter to being 'just around the corner', Everett's small timber house in Kingsley Street in Elwood ran off Ormond Road, only several hundred yards from where Ryan and Walker had been hiding in Vitko's flat at number 93 just five days before.

Later that day, Ryan and Walker took a drive east of Melbourne to Mansfield, and to the familiar hills and mountains of Ryan's days cutting timber in the Warburton ranges in the early 1950s.[30] This was also near the route that he had followed when he and George had ridden their bicycles to Balranald in the summer of 1939. The drive took them through the Strezlecki ranges, where the pair briefly panned for gold. Ryan later claimed to have found some. While in the hills, they were almost discovered by a camper in a Land Rover, but managed to avoid detection and returned to Melbourne to prepare for their departure interstate.[31]

The next day, New Year's Day 1966, Ryan repeated the ad in *The Sun*. On the day it appeared, it seemed that Ryan's instructions had been quickly followed by Everett. There, in the same columns, was an ad placed by Everett with a telephone number for Ryan to call:

> **ERIC**——Eric 91-4668. Di.[32]

In fact, the ad had been placed by homicide squad detectives, who were hoping to trace the call and get a fix on Ryan's whereabouts. But the escapees were no longer in Melbourne. At daybreak that day they had left Hurley's place and driven off in the Plymouth heading for New South Wales, telling Murray to travel by train to Sydney and join them there. Murray knew Sydney well, and his underworld contacts there could ease the way for the escapees.

Ryan and Walker were confident they could make it to Sydney in the Plymouth, as it had Queensland registration plates and they believed that police would be looking for them hiding in the backs of trucks or utilities.[33] So they headed up the Hume Highway in broad daylight. Although they encountered police road-blocks at several points, the Plymouth attracted little attention. They managed to push on to Sydney, even though they were hampered by the Plymouth's brakes, which were worn and subject to fade.[34] By now they were tired and jumpy. They had been on the run for two weeks, and the strain of keeping one step ahead of the massive police manhunt was beginning to show. Neither of them was getting much sleep, and when they hit Sydney the next day, Sunday, 2 January, they stayed for two days in a house organised for them by Murray with one of his mates.[35] Finding a secure flat took the next two days as they searched through advertised listings and contacted real estate agencies.

On their first day in Sydney the escapees went into Kings Cross, where Ryan tried to make contact with an underworld figure whose name he had been given. While Ryan went looking for his contact, Walker sat in the parked Plymouth in Victoria Street, but dozed off. He awoke to find a local parking officer telling him that his meter had expired. Having noted the car's Queensland licence plates, and obviously mindful of that state's well-known Gold Coast tourist promotion of young women putting coins in expired parking meters, the unwitting officer said to Walker: 'We've got no bikini-dressed meter maids here to look after you—*move*!'[36]

Ryan also began trying all of his Sydney contacts in an effort to arrange a passage on a freighter bound for South America, either as stowaways or crew. His long-standing objective of skipping the country to the sanctuary of Brazil seemed a little closer, as Murray used his contacts on the waterfront to get something going.[37] The first priority, however, was to set up a hideaway. On Tuesday morning, 4 January, Ryan sought to re-establish contact with a woman he had boarded with during the period of his spree of shop-breakings in Sydney in 1964. Going to her house, he found she was not at home, but struck up a conversation with her 20-year-old daughter. Ryan, who used the name George, then arranged to see the young woman, who had undertaken to contact her mother and set up a meeting. The rendezvous was arranged for 9:00PM on the following night outside the Concord Repatriation Hospital, where the young woman worked.[38]

However, what Ryan did not know was that the young woman had recognised him. After he left, she contacted Sydney police, who quickly put into place a massive undercover operation to recapture the escapees. Homicide squad detectives in Melbourne were also quickly advised by their NSW counterparts that Ryan and Walker were in Sydney. In order to create an impression that police were unaware of the escapees' actual whereabouts, homicide squad detectives, with the cooperation of the Melbourne press, put out a story that they believed they were still hiding out somewhere in Melbourne. The story first appeared in the Melbourne *Herald* as a page-one lead: 'Escapees in City—Police' and reported: 'Detectives said today they got a new lead last night which proved that Pentridge escapees Ronald Ryan and Peter Walker were still in Melbourne.'[39]

The operation to recapture Ryan and Walker was led by New South Wales' most famous and feared police officer. In the course of his long career, Detective Inspector Ray Kelly of Sydney CIB had killed three criminals and brought in more than a dozen others on the NSW most-wanted list. Kelly was renowned as the detective who always got his man.[40] Now Kelly led the team of some 50 detectives and five women police officers in a stakeout to capture the Pentridge escapees. Under Kelly's supervision, two officers from the safe squad, Detective Sergeant Maurie Wild and Detective Jack Whelan, prepared the operational plan in advance of the rendezvous arranged for 9:00PM on Wednesday, 5 January. At 2:30PM on Wednesday afternoon, wearing plain clothes, Wild and Whelan went to the Concord Hospital area on a reconnaissance mission and to work out the likely points of access and egress near the escapees' intended meeting point. They also drew upon aerial and council maps to provide the necessary level of detail. Walking all over the site, they identified the locations at which the police would be positioned to capture the fugitives and deal with any eventuality should they make a break. The operation was going to be difficult, they believed, because there was so much open ground.

As this was happening, Ryan and Walker were finally having some success with accommodation. Through a real estate agency in the beachside suburb of Coogee, they had managed to rent a flat in Mount

Street, Coogee, after Ryan, using a false name, posed as an oil executive to the landlord. Paying £18 for a week's rent, Ryan took the keys and, on Wednesday afternoon, with Walker and Murray, he went to the flat to move in. When the three appeared at the back door of what they thought was the flat, a young woman, Mrs Dianne Murray, appeared.

'Is this the vacant flat?', Ryan asked.

Told it was the adjoining one next door, Ryan smiled broadly and said: 'Oh, my mistake, thanks very much.'

They then proceeded to unload from the Plymouth boxes of food that they carried into the flat, grinning and nodding as they passed the young woman in the backyard. When Mrs Murray's husband, Robert, arrived home later in the afternoon, she voiced her anxiety about them.

'I don't like the look of those men who moved in this afternoon', she said. 'I think they're criminals or gangsters or something.'

'Don't be silly', Murray replied, 'Of course, they're nice people. You'll be sure to like them once you get to know them.'[41]

Later that night, police were finalising their operational plans to recapture the escapees if they showed at the Concord Hospital. Detectives drawn from the safe squad, consorting squad, general duties detectives and CIB ballistics experts were given a final briefing on the plan to recapture Ryan and Walker, with secrecy a prime consideration.[42] At 7:30PM the plan swung into operation, and police in casual clothes gathered in designated positions in and around the hospital. Kelly deployed six teams of detectives near the hospital gate, with each five-member team armed with Winchester and Remington repeating 12-gauge shotguns and Smith & Wesson .38 revolvers. Given detailed descriptions of the escapees, two of the police teams were assigned to Ryan and two teams to Walker.

Other detectives, armed with teargas and heavy weapons, took up positions in the trees and shrubs around the hospital entrance. Several detectives were positioned in a white Craven A cigarette van parked outside a small shop, Tom's Delicatessen, opposite the hospital gate. Women police officers were deployed to masquerade as hospital staff, and others took up positions in company with male detectives to pose as courting couples in cars. On the Parramatta River behind the hospital a motor launch was moored with two armed detectives aboard with the usual crew, in case Ryan and Walker sought to escape through the bush. Overseeing this massive operation, Kelly was positioned in the inquiry office at the hospital gate. A central command point had been set up there as a radio-communication centre to link the operational force. In all, 55 Sydney police were involved in the biggest arrest operation mounted by NSW police in its history.[43]

The key to the operation was the positioning of two women decoys at the gate. One was Del Fricker, a small, softly spoken police sergeant with 16 years' experience in the NSW force. Based at police headquarters, Fricker had been involved in dangerous operations in the past. The other decoy was the young woman Ryan had contacted at her home when he went there looking for her mother. The plan was for Fricker and the young woman to wait until the escapees' car had pulled up, and then for Fricker to drop her handbag as a signal to police. As they stood there, Fricker and the young woman anxiously studied every headlight as it approached down the street. As the minutes ticked by there was almost a disaster when a young couple in an L–plated vehicle stumbled upon the set-up where detectives were hiding in trees. The woman learner-driver got out of the car and walked under a tree, almost hitting her head on a policeman's leg.[44] When twenty minutes had passed after 9:00PM, the time that had been set for the rendezvous, police hopes that the escapees would show began to fade. Perhaps, police thought, they had been tipped off and fled. At 9:25PM the women decoys at the gate were instructed by Kelly via radio to leave the area and return shortly afterwards, in case they were being watched by the escapees to determine if it was a trap.

Four minutes after Fricker and her fellow decoy moved away from the front of the hospital, the Plymouth bearing the Queensland registration plates NWU-616 was seen by police observers to be proceeding east in Fremont Street, Concord, with two men in it. The car swung into Hospital Road and then pulled up in front of the hospital. The police officer in charge of the operation on the ground was Detective Sergeant Fred Krahe of the New South Wales CIB based at Surry Hills, who was positioned with other heavily armed police in the cigarette delivery-van outside the delicatessen.

From his vantage point in the van opposite the hospital gate, Krahe watched Ryan as he got out of the car. Ryan was wearing the stylish clothes bought for him in Melbourne by Keith Hurley—the dark, well-cut Georges suit, white shirt and tie, and dapper dark-grey hat from the Georges hat department. Walker, too, was smartly dressed in his dark-grey Michaels-Stern suit, neat tie, and highly polished shoes. With the two young women obviously not at the rendezvous point, Ryan walked to the entrance of the hospital and spoke to the man on the gate, asking him if there was any message for George. Told there was not, Ryan returned to the car, where Walker was worried that they might be driving into a trap. He did not like the look of the burly fellow on the front gate, who he felt might be a police officer. 'Let's go!', he yelled to Ryan as he got back in the car.[45] For a moment they debated the situation, driving 50 yards further along Hospital Road; but, deciding that it might be OK after all, they made a U-turn and went back almost to their original position opposite the gate.

Ryan got out and went to a telephone box. The phone was out of order, and he returned to the car to tell Walker he was going to make a call from the shop to make contact with the young woman. As Ryan walked across the road to the delicatessen, Walker got out, lifted the car bonnet, and inspected the troublesome brake cylinder before getting back into the driver's seat. Sitting in the Plymouth, he was struck by a rising sense of foreboding as he stared fixedly ahead of him at the cigarette van outside the shop.

Inside the delicatessen, the owner—known as Tom to hospital staff—was cleaning up and preparing to close as Ryan walked in and asked if he could use the phone. He handed Tom sixpence and began his call. Ryan's separation from Walker was the crucial moment the police operations team had planned for, and it gave them the edge they needed. As Ryan had entered the shop, a vehicle had turned into Hospital Road, moving erratically down the street and heading towards Walker in the Plymouth. It was an unmarked police vehicle, and Krahe had given the order for the driver to block the front of the escapees' car. As Walker watched this activity, the penny dropped in his brain: he had been a driver himself once, and he knew that a cigarette van would not be making deliveries at this time of night.[46] But it was too late. Before he could react—other than to curse his own stupidity—the approaching car had driven to the front of the Plymouth, blocking its path. From behind him another police car drove up quickly to pin the car from the rear.

At that moment the back door of the cigarette van swung open, and heavily armed police piled out. As Ryan emerged from the shop, six police officers—drawing upon the element of surprise—rushed at him from the shadows. He went for his gun, the Browning .32 pistol in his pocket, but it was too late, and he fell under a heavy wedge of police. The pistol spilled to the ground. Although he threw punches and struggled fiercely to break free, he was quickly pinned down and prevented from moving. Resistance was impossible and it was all over in a matter of seconds.[47] Handcuffed and put into the back of a police car, with the right sleeve of his Georges suit almost ripped away from the shoulder, all Ryan could say to his captors was, 'Congratulations! Congratulations! It was a bloody great pinch!'[48]

Walker had not fared any better. As the cigarette van disgorged its heavily armed police occupants, Krahe, moving quickly, poked a shotgun through the driver's-side window of the Plymouth, and pressed it at the side of his head: 'Police here! Put both your hands on top of the wheel, and quickly!'[49] Walker had the .32 Browning thrust down his belt with the butt end protruding, and the revolver in his pocket, but he made no move towards either.[50] In no position to argue with the next demand, he stuck both his arms out of the open window, and Krahe put the shotgun down and grasped both of his wrists. Walker was quickly handcuffed, removed from the car, and placed in the rear seat of a police car separate from Ryan. After two days of intensive planning and a final nerve-racking wait by police, the recapture of the most wanted men in Australia, who had eluded police in two states for seventeen days, had taken less than five minutes. And not a single shot had been fired.

This was a considerable achievement in the light of Ryan and Walker's reported statements that they would shoot it out with police to avoid recapture, and given the extent of the armoury carried by the fugitives or stored in the Plymouth. As well as the two .32 Browning pistols, the .32 Harrington & Richardson revolver, the 12-gauge shotgun, the .22 rifle and the .30 carbine they had brought from Melbourne, police recovered a .303 calibre rifle—known as a Jungle carbine—modified to .25 calibre. All of the weapons were fully loaded.[51] From the car, police also recovered boxes of ammunition for all the weapons, an axe, jemmy, two coils of rope, a hacksaw, and two pairs of boiler suits. Under the bag were four car number-plates.[52] The last item recovered from the car suggested how high the cost of freedom had been for the escapees: in the boot was an airline bag containing all that remained of the £4,423 they had stolen from the ANZ Bank just two weeks before—£200 in notes and a handful of silver. If the cost of freedom was high, the price of capture may have been high as well. Walker has claimed that, in fact, they had about £2,000 between them in their pockets when they were recaptured. What happened to the money after they were arrested by police is unknown.[53]

Within moments of the arrests, police officers came from their vantage points all over the hospital site to exchange congratulations and express pride and relief at a successful arrest. The size of the operation became more obvious when the full police contingent from around the hospital converged upon the arrest scene: eighteen police cars choked the street. It had been a massive operation, flawlessly executed. Still holding a shotgun, Detective Inspector Kelly was quick to praise his men: 'It was a great job by a fine bunch of policemen.'[54]

In the back of the police car, Ryan was subdued but full of praise for his police captors. In the other police car, Walker sounded relieved.

'I'm glad it's over', he said to Krahe. 'I had a feeling something was going to happen tonight. Do you know, this is the first place we've come to without having a good look around it first.'

'What caused that?' Krahe asked.

'We got lost,' Walker replied. 'That's why we were late!'[55]

Ryan and Walker were taken to CIB headquarters in Campbell Street, Sydney, where they were interviewed by detectives. Walker was interviewed by Krahe and two other CIB police, Detective Sergeant Fred Smith and Detective Ron Rudgeley. Another detective approached, holding a prison photograph of him.

'He doesn't look anything like Walker!', he exclaimed, momentarily put off by Walker's bleached blonde hair, eyebrows, and glasses.

Peering again, he corrected himself: 'Yeah, that's him,' he said. 'That's him!'[56]

Krahe began by asking him how long the pair had been in NSW. Walker said: 'We only arrived yesterday.' Asked where he and Ryan were staying, he said: 'We're not staying anywhere. We're sleeping in the car.'[57] Told that homicide squad detectives were flying from Melbourne to interview him, Walker said that he would tell the detectives anything about the bank hold-up, but he said he did not want to talk about Hodson or Henderson. Without a detailed knowledge of these matters, the NSW detectives could not take the interviews much further. That would await the arrival of the homicide squad detectives from Melbourne.

The next day, the escapees were taken to Sydney's Central Court, where police brought the holding charges against them of being illegally in possession of firearms. A crowd gathered in Liverpool Street opposite the entrance to the court, and spectators packed the public gallery in Court 2 as detectives led the men, handcuffed together, into the dock for the short hearing. Ryan said in court that he would not be making any statements. Later that afternoon, a contingent of detectives from the homicide squad, led by its chief, Inspector Frank Holland, flew to Sydney to interview Ryan and Walker and to arrange for their extradition back to Melbourne. Although Holland praised the efforts of NSW police in capturing the escapees, his team was smarting at the one-upmanship of its Sydney colleagues. Upon their arrival in Sydney, the homicide squad prepared for their interviews with Ryan and Walker at the Clarence Street detectives' office the next morning, Friday, 7 January.

It was decided by Holland that the formal interview with Ryan would be conducted by Detective Sergeant KP 'Bill' Walters and Senior Detective Noel Murphy. When they arrived to start the interview at 8:00AM, Ryan was seated in Room 10 in the presence of Detective Sergeant Frank Charlton of the Sydney CIB. After introductions, Ryan said he wished to make a statement. As Ryan dictated, Charlton took it down on a typewriter:

> I, Ronald Joseph Ryan, have nothing personal towards you three and the Police in general, in fact they are to be highly commended particularly the New South Wales Police, for their efficiency and their remarkable restraint.
>
> Violence was one of the furtherest things from our minds. We had no intention of firing at the Police, nor any member of the public, freedom was our main objective.
>
> I have no further statements to make at this stage, either verbal or written. I will act under instructions after seeing my Counsel, Mr. McMenniman on my return to Melbourne.[58]

After reading over the statement, which had taken less than five minutes to dictate and type, Ryan signed and dated it. Walters then said to Ryan:

I intend to ask you a number of questions putting certain allegations to you. I think it can be said that the public have heard one side only. You may, if you wish, give your own account.

Ryan: If it is off the record, I will tell you what happened.

As Murphy picked up his pen to write in his folder, Ryan said:

No, no, no writing. I have already told the Court I am making no statement so you fellows will not be able to use this. I have to leave myself some scope for later on.[59]

Walters proceeded to ask Ryan questions without himself or Murphy taking notes; but, 90 minutes later, Walters would go to a room in the detectives' office and write out from memory an account of what he and Ryan now said:

Walters: Mr Ryan, it is up to you what you want to tell us.

Ryan: In a way, I'm glad this is over. We had no intentions of firing at the police. I have no quarrel with you. All I wanted to do was to go to Brazil where they have no extradition treaty. Where do you want me to start?

Walters: From the beginning will do.

Ryan: The girls you charged with harbouring will not stick. We forced them to help us, they had no option.

Walters: You can always give evidence for them.

Ryan: Yes, I intend to.

Turning to the escape, Ryan said:

It was simply getting out, nothing planned. We got up on the wall before the screw realised we were there. He mucked us about a bit by operating the wrong lever. I think he thought I was going to shoot him when I marched him back up the tower to open the right lever. There were three other screws at another gate, one got down on his hands and knees and pleaded with us not to shoot him. The Brigadier [Hewitt] was game, he would not give me his car keys. I don't know whether he was stalling us or frightened.

Walters: What about the Brigadier's injuries?

> *Ryan*: In the heat of the moment you sometimes do an act without thinking. I think this is what happened to Hodson. I did not know him personally. I know his kind … He had no need to interfere, he was stupid. He was told to keep away. He grabbed Pete and hit him with an iron bar. He caused his own death. I didn't want to shoot him. I could have shot a lot more. There was the screw in the tower who operated the wrong gate or the wrong lever. There were the three at the gate and there was another screw in the tower who had the drop on us, and there were the fellows who drove the car at us.
>
> Finally we got a car and we drove to Kensington … I do not intend to tell you of the people who helped us or the places we went to. We did spend some time in the Strezlecki's. I found some gold. I intend to stake a claim when I get out. A land rover nearly copped us in the hills.[60]

After a short conversation between Walters and Ryan, Walters said that he was going to formally ask Ryan some questions. After he warned him about his rights to remain silent, it quickly became clear that—unlike his candour in what he thought was an off-the-record discussion—Ryan was going to be less than fully cooperative in any formal interview. However, as Walters asked the questions and Murphy typed Ryan's answers, several significant admissions slipped out. Asked about the escape, Ryan initially said he respectfully declined to answer, and wanted to speak to his counsel and would act under his instructions. Walters persisted through seven further questions; Ryan repetitively said 'The same answer.' Then Walters got to the nub of his questioning about the escape and the shooting of Hodson:

> *Walters:* Do you remember pointing the carbine at a warder at a post or tower and threatening to shoot him if he did not lower his carbine?
>
> *Ryan*: I will leave it at the same answer. It will give me more scope later …
>
> *Walters*: During your escape from the gaol an unarmed penal officer named Hodson was shot. What do you know about his death?
>
> *Ryan*: To the best of my recollection I did not shoot a penal

officer. I leave it at that.

Walters: Do you know who did shoot him?

Ryan: I was not aware that a penal officer had been shot until I read it in the papers and heard it over the radio. Even then I refused to believe this until I saw his funeral on TV. It is a regrettable instance.

Walters: Witnesses have said that they saw the deceased—the penal officer—grappling with Walker and that you levelled the carbine at him and fired a shot.

Ryan: I would not consciously shoot a fellow human being.

Walters: In the excitement of the moment do you think that you possibly shot him?

Ryan: I would say no. As that would be so out of character.

Walters: Did you see a penal officer grappling with Walker?

Ryan: The events moved too fast for a clear recollection of the details. Our only objective was freedom.

Walters: Did you know Warder Hodson?

Ryan: Not as an individual.

Walters: How many shots did you fire?

Ryan: To the best of my recollection I fired no shots.

Walters: Did you hear any shots fired?

Ryan: Again I am unsure but I thought I heard several detonations but this could have been backfiring from motor vehicles. I was very confused and excited at the time. I think that is covering it well it allows me a bit of scope.

Walters: Could you give me any reason that witnesses at the scene should say that you shot Hodson?

Ryan: None other than perhaps mob panic or auto suggestion. There have been many instances in the past of the well meaning public gaining false impressions.

Walters: Have you anything else that you want to say about the shooting of Hodson?

Ryan: I can think of no other way I can assist you at this stage.[61]

Told by Walters that he would be charged with Hodson's murder, Ryan was asked to read and sign the record of interview. After he read it, Ryan was asked by Walters if there were any alterations or additions he wanted to make:

> Yes. There are a couple of passages which I was not conscious of saying. I would like to have these deleted. On page 2 the words: 'It will give me more scope later'. I wish to have these deleted, and again further down on the same page the words: 'I think that is covering it well it allows me a bit of scope'. I would like these deleted. Other than that it is a true record of interview. I think that covers it.[62]

With the pace of the interview governed by the typing of the record as the questions and answers proceeded, it had taken an hour. At the end of the session, Ryan signed the record of interview, and initialled his amendments and deletions. Although the veracity of these statements by Ryan—whether in the off-the-record conversation with Walters, or in the formal record of interview—would later be seriously challenged by Ryan's legal counsel, they constituted significant admissions, the importance of which was not lost on his police interrogators. Although Ryan had sought to retrieve his comments about allowing himself 'a bit of scope later', the damage was done. These statements would come to play an important role in his subsequent prosecution for murder.

As Ryan's interview had proceeded, elsewhere in the building Walker was being interviewed by detectives Harry Morrison and Krahe, with Holland periodically coming into the room.[63] In the interview, which commenced at 8:50AM and concluded at 10:07AM, Morrison had concentrated on the escape and the killing of Hodson rather than the murder of Henderson. But Walker was not cooperative. Asked by Morrison if he became friendly with Ryan in gaol, Walker replied that he had:

> *Walker:* Yes. I met Ryan in the gaol. I did not know him before that.
>
> *Morrison*: When did you agree with Ryan to try and escape from the gaol?
>
> *Walker:* Well no agreement at all, just the opportunity came and we went.
>
> *Morrison*: Do you want to tell us what happened in your own words, what led up to your escape from gaol?
>
> *Walker*: No.
>
> *Morrison:* Did you and Ryan manage to get up into the sentry post with a wooden grappling iron?

Walker: Yes. We just got out.

Morrison: Did you see Ryan take the carbine rifle from the sentry post?

Walker: No.

Morrison: Did you see him armed with the carbine rifle when he got into Sydney Road?

Walker: No, I was in front of him.

Morrison: Did you, yourself, have a struggle with prison officer Hodson shortly after you got out of the gaol?

Walker: No, definitely not. He was behind me, the first thing I knew he was there was when he hit me on the head with an iron pipe.

Morrison: When you got into Sydney Road and were running across the road was the prison officer close behind you?

Walker: No, I don't know where he was at all.

Morrison: Did you see Ryan out in Sydney Road at that time?

Walker: No, I didn't see Ryan until I climbed into that Vanguard.

Morrison: Did you hear a shot fired?

Walker: No, I did not hear a shot.

Morrison: When you got in the car with Ryan, was he then armed with the carbine rifle that was shown you earlier this morning?

Walker: No comment.

Morrison: Where did you go when you left the gaol area in the Vanguard car?

Walker: We just drove as hard as we could.

Morrison: Do you know where you drove to?

Walker: I dumped the car in Kensington.

Morrison: Was it Bruce Street, Kensington?

Walker: It was just a quiet street, I don't know the name of it.

Morrison: Where did you go when you dumped the car?

Walker: No comment, I can't answer that.

Morrison: Where did you spend the first night, the Sunday night?

Walker: I can't remember.[64]

With their interviews concluded, Ryan and Walker were taken to the Sydney Central Court where, at 12:30PM, they faced extradition proceedings on charges of escaping from lawful custody. Appearing before stipendiary magistrate Norman Hawes, Ryan said he wished to make a statement:

> I wish to state that myself and Mr. Walker ... have made certain non-committal verbal statements mainly that we will act under the instructions of our counsel and I wish to state further that we will make no further statements on the trip back to Melbourne.[65]

During the course of the day, police raided the flat in Mount Street, Coogee, and found Norman Murray still there. When detectives arrived they found him shaking like a leaf.[66] Later in the afternoon, Victoria Police chartered a Fokker Friendship aircraft, in which they flew the escapees and Murray back to Melbourne. Apart from the aircrew, the aircraft was empty save for Ryan, Walker, Murray, and the four homicide squad detectives acting as escorts. All prisoners were manacled and under armed guard. In the course of the flight Ryan was handcuffed to Senior Detective Morrison, who was sitting in the window seat as Ryan sat next to him in the aisle seat. The seats immediately around them were empty as Ryan struck up a conversation with Morrison. Much of the conversation ranged over matters of current affairs, but then Ryan broached the subject of the escape:

> We were set to go last Christmas. When we got to the wall the fellow who was with me jibbed at the wall and we had to go back. Peter and I mated up. He wanted to go also so we planned it. We had to wait until we got the right man on the wall and Sunday was the day. The warder spoilt the whole show. If he had not poked his great head into it he would not have got shot. It was either him or Peter.[67]

Again Ryan had made damaging admissions, which would later be used against him during his trial for murder. Consistent with the pattern evident throughout his criminal career, Ryan had 'confessed' to his crime in interviews or in unprompted conversations with police.

Security for the return of the escapees continued as the Fokker approached Melbourne. As part of these extraordinary security arrangements, the plane did not land at Essendon Airport but proceeded to the Royal Australian Air Force base at Laverton, fifteen miles south-west of Melbourne. Once off the plane, Ryan, Walker, and Murray were taken in police convoy out the back road of the airfield heading towards the city, with police motorcycles and cars in front, behind, and beside the escapees. Ryan was in the second police car, seated in the back with two detectives. Walker was in the fourth car, and put a hat over his face to shield himself from photographers. This convoy of eight police vehicles moved as a phalanx up the Princes Highway, with police blocking traffic at every major intersection along the route into Melbourne. There had never been a police operation like it. NSW police had recaptured Ryan and Walker, but the Victoria police were putting on a show of their prized prisoners back in custody. Their destination was Russell Street police headquarters, where they arrived at 6:15PM, were taken into separate rooms, and interviewed for 30 minutes. At the end of the interviews, Ryan and Walker were taken across the street to the City Court, where they were formally charged with the murder of prison officer Hodson on 19 December 1965.

From Russell Street, the escapees were taken to Pentridge prison, which had also stepped up security for their arrival. Acting governor Ian Grindlay was there to supervise the special arrangements for their incarceration, and to make sure that nothing untoward happened to them before they had their day in court. There was a lot of animosity towards the escapees from prison officers, and there was also heightened tension among prisoners in the gaol. Grindlay personally attended their arrival at 8:00PM, and noted that neither prisoner bore a scratch; they were unmarked.[68] After they were strip-searched and processed, they were put in cells, where there was a bucket for a toilet, two rough canvas blankets and no bed, and the light was kept on all night. Nineteen days and six hours after they had scaled the walls and broken out of this maximum-security gaol, they were back behind bars in the prison from which they had infamously broken out. This time, however, they were in the feared H Division, and there would be no prospect of escape.

As the days passed, Ryan and Walker were kept strictly apart in the prison, and they were under a tough disciplinary regime. Sleep was difficult enough but, to add to their woes, every 30 minutes they were subjected to prison officers carrying out an inspection. This took the form of prison officers shining a torch or banging on the door to wake them.[69] While they were not in solitary confinement, as such, Ryan and Walker were kept in observation cells and not permitted to see or speak to each other or any other prisoners. At first, they were exercised only briefly in the exercise yard. Later they were exercised on their own each day from 8:30AM to 11:00AM, and from 12:40PM to 3:00PM. The rest of the time they were kept in their cells, and were subject to different disciplinarian conditions to other H Division inmates.[70]

As they endured the harsh conditions in H Division, the realisation dawned that they were both in deep trouble. Between them, they had killed two men and terrorised a community in a rampage of lawlessness that had frightened law-abiding citizens and deeply troubled political leaders and officials responsible for law and order. Their escape and recapture had excited the interest of the media, and speculation began about the fate that awaited them. Some of the speculation was pointed. Three days after the re-capture *Truth* blazoned a page-one story with the headline: 'SHOULD WE HANG GUNMEN?' Although the story made no specific reference to Ryan or Walker, it was prominently positioned beside a photograph of Ryan on his wedding day—headed 'The man of the moment'—in such a way that the association was obvious. *Truth* said that the recent spate of crime in Victoria, with several murders unrelated to Ryan and Walker, had roused this controversy to its highest pitch. The paper sounded an ominous warning:

> Decisions may soon have to be made ... If a jury were to find any person in Victoria now guilty of a capital offence, the question of sentence would immediately boil to the forefront. Nobody has been hanged in Victoria for 15 years. It has been generally felt that the time for executions has passed. But six violent deaths in three weeks can go far in influencing the public mind.[71]

During the seventeen days that Ryan and Walker were at large the Melbourne daily press had seized on the escape, and the story had seldom left the major news columns till the pair's re-capture. Many of the stories that appeared had the effect of arousing major public fear of the escapees. They were branded as desperate criminals who had taken a prison chaplain hostage before bashing him to the ground. During the escape a prison officer had been shot, and innocent motorists had been held at gunpoint as the prisoners made their getaway. A bank had been robbed at gunpoint, and staff and customers terrorised. A young man had been brutally shot in a public toilet and left to die in a pool of blood. Photographs of the escapees had been featured on the front pages of every newspaper in the country, and their descriptions had been broadcast continually on radio news services. The police manhunt to recapture them had dominated television news reports, and the government had offered a reward of £5,000 for information leading to their recapture.

Ryan and Walker had become the best-known men in Australia. But, as legal proceedings against them approached, doubts were raised about whether a fair trial was possible. To some journalistic observers, the nature and extent of the massive publicity had so conditioned the mind of the general public that, long before a jury was empanelled to try them, there were concerns that the Pentridge escapees had been already judged and convicted out of hand. As they awaited the start of the legal process that would see them jointly on trial for murder, the sentence that awaited Ryan and Walker seemed a foregone conclusion.[72]

CHAPTER ELEVEN

Trial

[At] no time did [I] fire a shot … Freedom was the only objective.The rifle was taken in the first instance so that it could not be used against [us].
—Ronald Ryan

IN THE IMMEDIATE AFTERMATH of his recapture, Ryan began to sense the enormity of what had occurred during the course of the escape with Walker and their period at large. He also understood the impact it was having on his family. As he wrote to his mother on 24 January 1966, less than three weeks after his return to Pentridge:

> Now Mum, I don't want you worrying too much about the way things turned out. Don't come to the court at any time as it would prove too much of a strain for you. Also, don't place too much reliance in what you read in the papers, etc, as most of it is mere sensationalism. The press and T.V. are playing the whole affair up too much. Don't let them annoy you too much. I was indignant at the way they pestered you. I saw you on T.V. and heard your broadcasts. I was very proud of you and the way you handled the whole affair. I couldn't contact you or any of the family as I did not want to involve you more than could be avoided. I understood what you meant to convey and knew I had your love and best wishes.

Ryan then went on to make an oblique but meaningful acknowledgment of what had occurred during the course of the escape:

> Bad luck! I had my go and it blew up. My only objective was freedom. It's deeply regrettable that others have been hurt.[1]

Ten days later, on 3 February 1966, the inquest into the death of George Hodson began in the Third Court of the Melbourne Magistrates Court in Russell Street. The two-fold purpose of the hearing before stipendiary magistrate and acting city coroner Jim Duggan was to establish the cause of Hodson's death, and to determine whether there was sufficient evidence to warrant criminal proceedings being brought against the person or persons the coroner found responsible for causing the prison officer's death.

Over two days in a courtroom crowded with journalists and onlookers, counsel assisting the coroner, Geoffrey Byrne, took 35 witnesses through their evidence relating to Ryan's and Walker's imprisonment, the escape from Pentridge on 19 December leading to the shot that killed Hodson in Sydney Road, and the autopsy that established the cause of his death. Prison officers recounted their evidence of the escape; and motorists and bystanders told how they saw Ryan raise and aim the carbine as Hodson chased Walker, how they heard and saw a shot being fired, and how they saw Hodson fall mortally wounded on the tram-tracks. As well, there was the evidence of John Fisher and the admissions he said Ryan had made at the party in Elwood. More damaging still were the admissions that homicide squad detectives Morrison and Walters swore that Ryan made to them after his recapture in Sydney.

Given the weight of the sworn testimony by witnesses, the outcome of the hearing seemed a mere formality. But for Ryan and Walker's barrister, Brian Bourke, it provided an opportunity to gauge the strength of the evidence that the prosecution would lead at a subsequent trial. At the end of the hearing, Duggan found, as expected, that Hodson had died from the effects of a gunshot wound that had been 'unlawfully, feloniously and maliciously' inflicted by Ryan during the course of the escape, and that Ryan had murdered Hodson 'in furtherance of their joint attempt to escape from legal custody in a gaol and to prevent their lawful apprehension'. Duggan directed that Ryan and Walker stand trial on a charge of murder in the Supreme Court at its March sittings.[2] Although he did not make a ruling to this effect, as such, Duggan was committing both Ryan and Walker to stand trial because of the law in relation to 'acting in concert'. Even though the evidence indicated that Ryan had fired the rifle, the fact that the pair had acted in common purpose in feloniously escaping from gaol meant that they were both criminally liable for Hodson's murder.

The case against Ryan and Walker was formidable but, as preparations for the trial proceeded, Ryan was not without hope that a successful defence could be mounted. He spent a great deal of time in his cell painstakingly analysing and making notes upon the evidence presented at the inquest. For days he pored over the transcript of evidence, marking passages, astutely pointing up conflicts in the testimony of prosecution witnesses, and writing detailed marginal comments to his solicitors drawing attention to matters for further investigation and follow-up. Beside the evidence of a police ballistics expert about the firing characteristics of an M1 carbine, Ryan pencilled a question: 'Have tests been made to ascertain whether or not a puff of smoke is emitted?' On another page, beside the testimony of a prison officer about what Ryan had done in Sydney Road, he wrote the comment 'NOT so!! Saves face!' At still another point, Ryan drew up a page-long list of some twenty significant discrepancies in the evidence of witnesses relating to the moments before and after the shooting. The list, which was meticulously cross-referenced by page numbers to the transcript, drew attention to the detail of witness evidence placing Ryan, Walker, and Hodson at widely differing points at key moments in Sydney Road.

At times, Ryan's comments seemed like the protestations of a defendant agitated about the mounting case against him. For the most part, however, they read like the clinical observations of a barrister to his instructing solicitor, providing an outline of a credible courtroom defence. On the back of the transcript of Lange's evidence, he pencilled an astute summary of the key elements of the evidence—all the while referring to himself as Ryan:

> Despite conflicts as to position of Ryan, distances from Hodson @ time of shot; as to whether there was a puff of smoke, sign of recoil or other visible signs that the gun in Ryan's hand was actually fired at Hodson, the general impression gained by a majority of

> witnesses was that Ryan definitely aimed the rifle, they heard a shot & Hodson was seen to fall almost simultaneously. There is difference of opinion as to whether Ryan was stationary or moving @ the time the shot was heard. Also, as to whether Hodson was stationary or moving.
>
> However, there is some evidence to support the fact that it was @ the same time that a Warder aimed his rifle @ Ryan, who was in line with Hodson, with Walker close by, and that he fired a shot. This shot he alleges was up into the air as, just when he pulled the trigger, a woman ran into view. It is important to note that throughout the evidence there has been only one shot heard. One only! And the warder alleges he fired a shot.
>
> Ryan does not deny that he aimed the rifle in that general direction; but he insists that he was aiming it at, 1st the driver of the green (Plymouth) car, then at the driver of the cream falcon (Dobson's); then @ the Vanguard which was ultimately used as the getaway-car. In support of this I refer you to evidence of Bailey, Page 77, also Dobson, Page 73, [par.] 1. Ryan's and Walker's object was to commandeer a car to effect their escape. Ryan insists that @ no time did he fire a shot. In fact, the Rifle had jammed in No. 1 Post and was still jammed during the escape & until they reached their first hideout. Then, the rifle was cleared. Further, the safety catch had been on the safe position throughout. Also Ryan realized that if anyone were injured during the escape it would create such a furore that their chances of remaining at large would be drastically reduced. Freedom was the only objective. The rifle was taken in the first instance so that it could not be used against them.[3]

These were remarkably acute observations for a prisoner to make on potential prosecution evidence and, in time, they would come to form the core of the submissions his counsel would make at his trial. As he contemplated the prospect that the case against him might see him sentenced to death for murder, Ryan himself had set about creating a coherent basis for his own defence.

Appearing for Ryan would be Philip Opas, QC, one of the leading figures at the Victorian bar, who had defended many murderers during the course of his career and had earned a wide reputation as a brilliant advocate and forceful cross-examiner. Opas was a small, muscular man, who had excelled at boxing in his time in the Air Force and retained the physique of a much younger man. He had been educated at the elite Melbourne Grammar School before studying law at the University of Melbourne, where he graduated in the same year as the Victorian solicitor-general who would be prosecuting Ryan and Walker.

In February 1966, Opas' name had been at the top of the roster of barristers prepared to accept briefs from the public solicitor in murder cases, and he regarded it as his bounden duty to take it. (His wife, Stella, was unimpressed, however. Like so many other people in Melbourne at the time, she had felt anxious during the escapees' 'reign of terror' when at large, and she was aghast when Opas told her he had taken the brief for Ryan's defence: 'If you get him off, don't come home!', she had said.[4])

Despite the fact that he thought it was a 'hopeless case', Opas began the task of carefully formulating a defence with his customary professionalism and attention to detail.[5] Opas was a supporter of capital punishment, and his involvement in the Ryan case would be a life-changing experience for him; in time, he would come to be convinced of his client's claim to innocence.[6] But this conclusion was some time away; first he had to fully immerse himself in the evidence in order to understand the points of weakness in the prosecution case. Given the prospect that the M1 carbine commandeered by Ryan would figure centrally in the evidence, Opas set about mastering the intricacies of the weapon to ensure that his cross-examination was well–informed. With the public solicitor, Allan Douglas, he went to the rifle range at the RAAF base at Laverton and received expert tuition from an armament instructor in the handling characteristics of the carbine. Opas was still an officer in the RAAF reserve; Douglas also had seen service in the AIF during World War II, later rising to the rank of lieutenant-colonel in the Army Reserve, and he was knowledgeable about automatic and semi-automatic weapons.

Together Opas and Douglas fired several hundred rounds to observe the action of the carbine in several crucial respects. Did the rifle emit any smoke when fired, as one prison officer, Wallis, had testified at the inquest, when he said he saw smoke coming from the rifle aimed by Ryan? Did it recoil when discharged, as another witness said had happened when he saw Ryan take aim and fire at Hodson? Did the trigger have a first pressure, as prison officer Paterson had testified, when he said he had fired his carbine outside the prison? These were all potential points of vulnerability in the prosecution's case. Opas hoped that this witness evidence might be weakened if not discredited if it could be shown that none of these phenomena was characteristic of the M1 carbine.[7]

Opas was also concerned to explore other aspects of the carbine's handling that were important for the defence case. Was it possible easily to jam the rifle when operating the bolt to load a bullet into the chamber? In clearing the jam, would a live round be ejected and fall out? These issues were relevant to Ryan's claim that, when he had grabbed Lange's rifle in tower 1, he had, through inexperience, jammed it, and a live round had been ejected and spilled out on the floor when he tried to load it. Opas hoped to show that, if Ryan had indeed ejected a live round onto the floor of the tower, he could not be guilty because all eight rounds in the magazine had been otherwise accounted for.

Opas also enlisted the assistance of an old friend, Dr Keith Bowden, a former government pathologist, to help him understand the physiological issues associated with the entry and exit of the bullet that killed Hodson. With Bowden's assistance, Opas went to the School of Medicine at the University of Melbourne, where he observed the dissection of several cadavers, and had staff trace on them the path that the fatal bullet had taken in entering Hodson's shoulder and exiting his back. With the help of other medical academics he studied human bone structure and, using medical skeletons, sought to establish the probability of a man of Ryan's height firing a shot at a taller man and the bullet following a downward trajectory after impact.[8] On the basis of what he learned, Opas consulted Terry Speed, a Monash University mathematician, and asked him to make some calculations plotting the course of the fatal bullet from various distances to the point in Sydney Road where Hodson was struck. Speed's calculations yielded some startling results relating to the likely height of the weapon that fired the fatal bullet. Opas would draw upon Speed's calculations at the trial.[9]

As he intensified his research, Opas believed—in line with Ryan's own analysis—that there was a solid basis upon which to construct a defence to murder. Despite the fact that the prosecution seemed to have an overwhelming case, the Crown was required not merely to prove Ryan's guilt but to prove it beyond reasonable doubt. Given that requirement, Opas believed that he could mount a credible defence case that just might persuade a jury that his client should be acquitted.

On the morning of Tuesday, 15 March, amid the glare of intense media publicity, the case of *The Queen v. Ryan and Walker* began in the magnificent Italianate Renaissance building of the Supreme Court of Victoria, in the court that had first held sittings in 1884. Court Four was one of the finest courtrooms in the country, and it had been the scene of many of the most famous murder trials in the state's history. The courtroom lacked the opulent splendour of the ceremonial Court One, but it was complete with ornate Victorian bench and canopy in dark polished cedar, soaring high ceilings with dentil cornices, and a balustraded cast-iron balcony in the public gallery. Crowds jammed the public galleries, and hundreds more were waiting outside the court building as barristers and solicitors took up their positions at the bar table at 10:30AM, and members of the jury panel crowded the aisles. At the small press table, there was scarcely room enough for half the large contingent of journalists present. Although this was to be a drama in which Ryan would play a secondary role, his presence in the dock with Walker ensured that he would share centre stage with the well-known legal figures who prepared to present themselves in court.

The barristers and solicitors seated at the bar table constituted an impressive line-up of legal talent and experience. Leading for the prosecution was Basil Lathrop Murray, QC, appearing as the state's solicitor-general, with Geoffrey Byrne as his junior. Murray and Byrne were instructed by Victoria's crown solicitor, Tom Mornane. Further along the bar table, Opas sat with his junior, criminal barrister Brian Bourke. Appearing for Walker was barrister Jack Lazarus, a steely advocate and experienced criminal defender. (Lazarus's sister, Joan Rosenove, had been Dorothy Ryan's counsel in her divorce case just nine months before.) The defence team was instructed by the public solicitor, Allan Douglas; since Ryan and Walker had no assets, their defence was being funded through the public purse.

As barristers shuffled through their papers and prepared for the courtroom drama about to unfold, everyone awaited the entry of the trial judge. The roster of judges sitting in the civil, criminal, and appellate divisions of the Supreme Court had been drawn up in the usual way by the chief justice at the beginning of the year; judges would go to a different list on a three-monthly rotation. Who among the judges in any of the divisions would hear a particular case depended upon which of them was not part heard when a new trial was set down. By this random stroke of administrative fate, the judge assigned to the criminal trial list for March was Justice John Erskine Starke. It was Starke, a tall, dominating figure clothed in the crimson robes and wig of a Supreme Court judge, who now entered the hushed court. He would come to play a significant—if not extraordinary—role in the events shaping Ryan's fate, not merely in the trial about to commence.

Those who did not know him well, and who saw him now take his seat on the elevated bench, may have taken John Starke for a WASPish Establishment man. Superficially, his background certainly suggested as much, for he had come from an illustrious legal and political family. Starke was born in Melbourne in December 1913, and—like Opas, who would follow him there—had been educated at Melbourne Grammar. Although of Irish origins, Starke had first attended a Catholic school; but he was 'too much for the nuns to handle', and he had been sent to Melbourne Grammar and later to Trinity College at the University of Melbourne.[10] His father, Sir Hayden Erskine Starke, was a justice of the High Court of Australia from 1920 to 1950, who had been before his appointment to the bench the leading figure at the Victorian bar. His mother, Margaret, was a member of the Gavan Duffy family that had produced, in a period of 60 years, a Victorian premier, a judge of the Supreme Court of Victoria, and a chief justice of the High Court of Australia.

But Jack Starke was a rebel. He had been in his youth a hell-raiser whose larrikin exploits were legendary among his fellow students, particularly during his time at Trinity, which had been both turbulent and short-lived. It was the period of his life in which, by his own account, he 'discovered drink, women and horse-racing', and he had been 'kicked out' of Trinity in 1932 for being seriously drunk.[11] Starke marked his departure from the college by leaving in a hansom cab after breaking a bottle of champagne over the door knob of the warden's lodge. This followed the gesture of Sir Stanley Argyle, the premier of Victoria at the time, who had left Trinity in a hansom cab after being sent down in 1890.[12]

Although he would not complete his studies at Trinity, in due course Starke acquired his law degree and was articled to Jim (much later Sir James) Forrest at the big city firm of Hedderwick, Fookes and Alston before signing the bar roll in 1939. Starke read with barrister Len Read, who—later, as a General Sessions judge—sentenced Ryan for the breaking offences for which he had been imprisoned at Pentridge at the time of the escape. After active service in the Second AIF as an artillery officer during World War II, attaining the rank of major, Starke resumed his practice at the Victorian bar in 1946, where his brilliance and courtroom flair quickly earned him a leading reputation. For two years he shared a room in Selborne Chambers with Phil Opas, and they formed a friendship based upon their common experience. Starke's rise to prominence was marked in 1951 when he was junior defence counsel to Don Campbell, KC, in the prosecution for criminal libel of Frank Hardy, the author of *Power Without Glory*. As the leading advocate at the bar, Starke acted in the big cases. Appointed Queen's Counsel in 1955, he appeared in a number of royal commissions and important boards of enquiry, including the King Street Bridge Enquiry, and the Victoria Market Enquiry. As Sek Hulme, QC, has written, 'Within Victoria it was never a real show until the big fellow arrived. Within Australia he had no peer.'[13]

Starke was an imposing presence in any company. Standing six feet three inches and with a massive frame, he was down to earth, without pretensions: in his barrister days, he could be seen in his chambers with his coat off, braces prominently on display, with his feet on the desk and eating a meat-pie. At the bar, Starke was also famous for his rough language and volcanic temperament, toweringly rude rather than aggressive. His candour and bluntness may have owed much to his father, who was notoriously difficult in his personal relationships with his brethren on the High Court.[14] It has been famously said of Starke (again by Hulme) that 'in society he was turbulently charming, and sometimes, but only intentionally, astronomically and apocalyptically rude and offensive. Never, let it be said, to the gentle or weak.'[15] Starke's kindness to young barristers was legendary. At the bar, the door to his chambers was always open, and his extensive library was freely available to all. It was typical of Starke that, when he once flew to London, the door remained open and the light was on.[16]

Appointed to the bench of the Supreme Court of Victoria in February 1964, Starke brought outstanding credentials in the criminal law to the trial of Ryan and Walker. He had made his mark as the foremost criminal barrister in the country when he acted for the defendants in two of the most famous capital cases in Australian history. In 1959, in South Australia, he appeared for Rupert Max Stuart in the Royal

Commission of Inquiry into his conviction for murder and sentence of death.[17] More notably still, he acted for Robert Peter Tait in his trial for murder in Victoria in 1961, and in the dramatic injunction application before the High Court that saw Tait escape the gallows in October 1962.[18]

Now, by a quirk of fate, Starke would preside at the trial of what would become a third, even more famous capital case. Like the great, late-eighteenth century British advocate Thomas Erskine, for whom, like his father, he had been named, Starke asserted the dignity, independence, and integrity of the bar in upholding the principle of impartial justice. Starke's proud credo, after Lord Erskine, was that the fearless defence of an accused man—however unpopular his cause—underpinned the civil liberties of all men. Starke was fond of quoting the liberal Erskine, particularly a passage from his address to the jury in the trial for seditious libel of Tom Paine in 1792:

> If the advocate refuses to defend, from what he may think of the charge or of the defence, he assumes the character of the judge. Nay, he assumes it before the hour of judgment and, in proportion to his rank and reputation, puts the heavy influence of perhaps a mistaken opinion into the scale against the accused in whose favour the benevolent principle of English law makes all presumptions, and which commands the very judge to be his counsel.[19]

Starke's chance assignment to the criminal list and thus to the Ryan and Walker murder trial carried with it another striking feature: Justice John Erskine Starke was a passionate and life-long opponent of capital punishment. Starke could not remember when or how he had become an abolitionist, but it was a visceral commitment to a philosophical position from which he was absolutely unshakeable. Starke simply believed that hanging was barbaric. He could not envisage any circumstances under which capital punishment could be justified.[20]

'All rise!', intoned the tipstaff as the judge entered the court, and counsel at the bar table led those assembled in the customary bow of respectful greeting. Starke's first duty was to proceed to the selection of a jury; a pool of 165 potential jurors had been summoned. The prosecution was allowed an unlimited number of peremptory challenges; the accused, twenty each. Before this could begin, however, Walker's counsel, Jack Lazarus, told Starke that he wished to make an application in the absence of the jury panel. With the jurors out of the court, Lazarus submitted to the judge that Walker was disadvantaged by being tried together with Ryan, and made an application for a separate trial. In his submission, Lazarus argued that it was inevitable that evidence led by the prosecution about Ryan's role in the murder would reflect, by extension, upon Walker's role. This evidence would be otherwise inadmissible, and hence constituted a prejudice to Walker's defence. After brief argument and some discussion, Starke refused the application: the trial of the two accused would be jointly held.[21]

At 11:40AM, Ryan and Walker were finally led into court. They had been waiting in an anteroom, handcuffed to prison officers. Now free of the cuffs, they were led to the dock under heavy security. Two prison officers sat on either side of them in the dock while another stood at the entrance. The doors to the court were guarded by two policemen. No-one in the court was left in any doubt that the authorities were taking no chances with the most notorious criminals in the country. Ryan and Walker looked grim in the dock, and occasionally whispered to each other as the charge of murder was read out and they both pleaded 'Not guilty'.[22]

Starke began by making an appeal to the assembled jury panel:

> Gentlemen of the jury, before the jury is empanelled, you have now heard the two accused, Ronald Joseph Ryan and Peter John Walker, each plead not guilty to murder. Now, we must look at the realities of the thing and I suppose every one of you has read something about this case in the newspapers. If any of you feels that, because of what you have read or heard, you would be unable to fairly try their case—and, by fairly, I mean fairly to the Crown and fairly to the accused—will you let me know, please.[23]

All jurors remained silent. Empanelling the jury continued, and it took the whole of the first morning. Ryan and Walker were assisted in the process of exercising their right to challenges by clerks from the Public Solicitor's Office. Each of the accused challenged their limit of twenty jurors, and the Crown stood aside a further three before a jury of twelve, all men, finally was struck.

In the proceedings about to commence, the Crown had to prove four things in order for a guilty verdict to be brought in, and it had to establish the proof according to law and the rules of evidence. The first was that Hodson was killed unlawfully. The second was that the accused, Ryan and Walker, caused his death whilst they were each of sound mind. Third, the Crown had to prove—not merely to assert—that the act by the accused that brought about Hodson's death was intentional, voluntary, conscious, and deliberate. And, finally, the Crown had to prove that, at the time it was done, the act was done by the accused either with the intention of killing Hodson or with the intention of doing him grievous bodily harm.

A number of legal tests had to be satisfied in association with each of these propositions. The case against Ryan and Walker seemed self-evidently strong; but, as in all murder cases, the trial had to be conducted according to law, the judge would establish the applicable law, and the jury would be required to reach its verdict according to the facts as proven in the trial. For its part, the defence could not plead guilty. Although this requirement in law was changed several years later, counsel for the accused in a murder trial were required to make out a defence case.

Opening the case for the prosecution, Murray carried the authority of the office of solicitor-general as he addressed the jury. A small, quiet man with a large patrician head, Murray had a courteous and correct manner lightened by an impish wit. He was renowned as a penetrating cross-examiner, particularly in criminal cases, where as often as not he appeared for the defence. He had enjoyed a brilliant career at the bar in a diverse practice at all jurisdictional levels. Called Tony since childhood—the gift of older sisters—he had been born in Perth, Western Australia in May 1917 and educated at Hale School, Perth, before moving to Melbourne where he studied law at Trinity College at the University of Melbourne. He had signed the bar roll in 1946 following service in the Royal Australian Navy during World War II, during which he rose to the rank of lieutenant. He built up an extensive practice at the junior bar, and took silk in 1960.

Although crime was not the principal focus of his practice at the bar, Murray had a deep knowledge of the criminal law. He had worked tirelessly as defence counsel in criminal trials, where he became known for his tolerant and compassionate nature. In one murder trial he appeared for the defence in what was described as a hopeless case, but his address for the defence was remembered for many years as one of the best defence addresses of its time. Nevertheless, the verdict was 'Guilty'. Next morning, a relative of his convicted client appeared at Murray's chambers and left a small girl, saying that, since Murray had got her father convicted, he could look after the child. Murray later chided his junior for his unreadiness to support the child from the fee that he had earned on the public solicitor's brief.[24]

In September 1964 Murray had been appointed Victoria's solicitor-general, making him the state's senior counsel advising and appearing for the Crown, frequently in constitutional cases before the High Court. It was a measure of the importance attaching to the trial of Ryan and Walker that Murray was now prosecuting the two most famous criminals in the country in the first prosecution he had led since his appointment as solicitor-general. Like Starke, Murray, too, would come to play a significant role in Ryan's fate some months after the conclusion of the courtroom case he was about to present.

Quietly and unemotionally, Murray began by outlining to the jury the prosecution's case against Ryan and Walker. The events that led to the charge of murder against the accused had occurred during what turned out to be a successful escape from Pentridge, he told the twelve jurymen. In graphic terms, and drawing upon aerial photographs of the prison and its environs, he described in detail the sequence of events that saw Ryan and Walker scale the wall, confront the prison officer in the tower, and break out of the prison gate—events that culminated with Ryan taking aim at Hodson as he pursued Walker along the tram-tracks in Sydney Road.

While Hodson was struggling with Walker, Murray said, Ryan had held up the car with the rifle at the Sydney Road intersection with Champ Street. By this time, the prison siren was sounding, and three prison officers had given chase after Ryan. He was in Jeziorski's car, trying to start it, when one of the officers rushed up. Ryan then threatened the officer with the rifle, and got out of the car. A number of cars had halted by this time. Walker was now running across the road with Hodson in pursuit close behind. Walker appeared to be bending over and almost stumbling, Murray said. It was at this stage, at a range of 18 to 30 feet, that Ryan raised the gun and fired.

'Warder Hodson pitched forward and fell face down on the road', Murray said. 'The two then drove away in a Vanguard car. Nobody can say how long this drama took, but it seems not improbable that the time taken from when they got out of gaol until they finally drove away in the car was less than two minutes.'[25]

By the time Murray had finished addressing the jury with an outline of the prosecution evidence, none of the spectators in the courtroom had any sense other than that this was going to be an open-and-shut case. As outlined by the prosecution, the eye-witness, police, and autopsy evidence—as well as Ryan's several 'confessions'—seemed entirely convincing of the defendants' guilt.

However, when the trial resumed the next day and Murray led his witnesses through their evidence, it was clear that, while the prosecution's case was strong, it was not without its points of weakness and vulnerability. Cross-examination by defence counsel duly began to reveal these points. One of the serious weaknesses in the Crown's case was that neither the bullet that killed Hodson nor its spent cartridge case had ever been found. Despite an intensive search by police, these vital pieces of evidence had never been recovered from Sydney Road or its environs. The missing bullet and spent shell were linked in the sense that a spent cartridge case from a carbine would be ejected to a distance of only five to ten feet. Since a spent shell had never been recovered in Sydney Road, the defence would argue that it was highly unlikely that Ryan had fired a shot from the rifle. This meant that whether the rifle taken by Ryan from no. 1 post had in fact been the murder weapon loomed as a major trial issue. Proving that the rifle was the weapon—an awkward and circumstantial argument in the context of the missing evidence—became the early focus of the prosecution's case as Murray took the prison-officer witnesses through their paces.

The first witness, Pentridge assistant governor Bob Duffy, gave evidence about the carbine and its handling characteristics. When the time came for his cross-examination of Duffy, Opas opened up a crucial line of argument that he would run in Ryan's defence. Opas established the possibility that, to someone inexperienced in handling the rifle and its cocking lever, it was easy to jam the carbine; and, if this happened, any attempt to clear the jam would lead to a live round being ejected. This was important in setting up the argument, upon which Opas would later elaborate, that the one missing cartridge from the carbine—the other seven live cartridges having been all accounted for—had not killed Hodson. Instead, it had been inadvertently ejected by Ryan as he wrongly cocked the rifle when confronting prison officer Lange in no. 1 post.

A related point of some significance concerned the ballistics evidence about whether the carbine had fired a shot since it had last been cleaned. This matter was open to dispute, as the rifle had been subject to dirt in the boot of the Plymouth during Ryan and Walker's trip to Sydney. It had also been inadequately stored since it had been recovered at the time of the escapees' capture; instead of being subject to careful storage and testing, it had been lying in the boot of a police officer's car, where it was subject to contamination by dirt and dust on the drive back to Melbourne. Whether the deposits in the barrel were the normal deposits left by an expended bullet (as the prosecution asserted) or whether they were simply particles of dirt from the respective car boots (as the defence submitted) was an important issue. Opas would contend that there was no conclusive evidence that the rifle commandeered by Ryan had been fired at all.[26]

As the prosecution case unfolded, prison officers gave evidence relating how Ryan and Walker had climbed into the no. 1 post, seized the officer's carbine, and escaped through the wicket gate, holding prison officers at bay at gun point. Prison officers Lange, Brown, and Bennett testified to what had happened when Ryan and Walker staged their escape, and Brigadier Hewitt gave evidence as to how he was confronted by Ryan and Walker outside the wicket-gate. On days three and four of the trial, the evidence shifted to the events in Sydney Road and the encounter that prison officers Mitchinson and Wallis had with Ryan in the Jeziorskis' car, and their attempt to arrest him as he tried to start it to make a getaway. They testified that they were close to Ryan when they saw him raise the carbine to his shoulder and fire a shot that felled Hodson. Nine other motorists and bystanders, including Frank and Pauline Jeziorski, Keith Dobson, Louis Bailey, and Margaret and John Murray, gave similar evidence.

The important strands of the defence case began to emerge through the cross-examinations of these witnesses by Opas and Lazarus. As Ryan had demonstrated in his analysis of the testimony of witnesses at the inquest, the discrepancies in the evidence were substantial and wide-ranging. While most witnesses correctly placed Ryan to the east of Hodson when the shot was heard, others said that he was to the west—which made it virtually impossible to account for the angle of entry of the bullet that killed Hodson. More significantly, while eleven of the thirteen prosecution eye-witnesses gave sworn evidence that they had seen Ryan armed with a prison carbine, waving it around, threatening motorists, and in a position to fire the fatal shot that killed Hodson, only four of them said they actually *saw* Ryan fire a shot. The rest saw Ryan aim, *heard* a shot, and saw Hodson fall. Since Ryan and prison officer Paterson were each armed with the same weapon, a .30 Mark 1 carbine, and the fatal bullet was never recovered, Opas argued that there was no acceptable evidence that the bullet which killed Hodson came from either the carbine held by Ryan or Paterson.

The defence would point to discrepancies in the prosecution's evidence, and argue the possibility, based on the trajectory of the bullet that killed Hodson, and the admission by Paterson that he aimed a shot in the general direction of Ryan and Hodson, that Ryan may not have fired the fatal shot. The defence would contend that, if an imaginary straight line were drawn from Paterson to Ryan and extended towards Hodson at the time that Paterson fired the shot, it would reveal that if Paterson had missed Ryan by a small degree, it was highly likely that the shot would have hit Hodson in exactly the way that Hodson was in fact struck. Thus, if Ryan could have shot Hodson, so could Paterson.[27] The defence were not required to prove that this occurred; but if the argument could be sustained it would undermine the prosecution's ability to prove Ryan's guilt beyond reasonable doubt.

In addition, Opas contended, the evidence of eye-witnesses was so contradictory that little store could be placed in it. Several witnesses claimed to have seen smoke coming from Ryan's rifle, although expert testimony established that the cartridges used were of a smokeless variety.[28] Nor was there agreement on the number of shots fired. With the exception of Paterson, each of the thirteen witnesses who had been in Sydney Road at the time testified that he or she had heard only one shot fired. In a similar statement made within a few hours of the incident, Paterson stated to police that, apart from the shot he fired himself, he had heard no other shot. Yet, as Opas submitted, thirteen witnesses had heard only one shot, and it was undisputed that Paterson had fired one shot; if Ryan had also fired a shot, one would expect in the nature of things that at least one witness would have heard the two shots.

With the expectation that his evidence would be crucially important, Paterson was called to the witness box on day four of the trial. A Scot with a pronounced brogue, Paterson at times was difficult to understand as Murray gently guided him through his testimony. It was not long before he became excitable and his brogue thickened perceptibly. Starke appealed him to speak more clearly: 'Try that again, Mr Paterson, and have mercy on us Anglo-Saxons,' he pleaded. Murray then asked Paterson about getting a rifle from the main gate and running out to Champ Street:

> What did you do then, once you got the rifle?
>
> –I turned on my heel and ran outside. I just got outside the door to the path when I heard the crack of a shot …

Asked about how he had come to use his rifle, Paterson replied:

> –I took aim. I took the first pressure, that is, the pressure that you take on the trigger like … And as I was beginning to squeeze, there were a woman—I dinna ken where she came from. She got in my sights, and I did that with the rifle [demonstrating by raising the rifle barrel to a vertical position]. I could not withdraw my pressure from the trigger. I had to let the shot go and it went up in the air.
>
> This woman passed across you?
>
> –Yes. She came in my sight. I dinna ken where she came from.
>
> You fired up in the air?
>
> –Yes. I had to, or the woman would have got it.[29]

When Opas cross-examined Paterson, he was able to show that, on several highly significant points of evidence, Paterson had contradicted himself in the several statements he made about what he saw, heard, and did on that day. In the first statement he made to Detective Sergeant Carton on the afternoon of 19 December 1965, the day of the escape, he said: 'I did not hear a shot fired other than the one I fired myself.'[30] Yet in his second statement, given to Senior Detective Morrison on 12 January 1966, Paterson indicated that he *had* heard a shot: 'Just as I turned into the entrance to the garden I heard a rifle shot.'[31] In his third statement, at the Hodson inquest on 3 February 1966, he repeated this version of events, saying that he had heard another shot prior to his own: 'I ran back inside and asked for a gun. I went to the Main Gate and

I received the gun and ran back again. As I was running on to the lawn I heard the crack of a shot.'[32]

Paterson changed his story, too, about who was in the line of fire when he had aimed his rifle. In his first statement on the day of the escape, he said: 'I immediately ran back through the main gate and got the rifle from the office, I then ran out again, and standing in the middle of the lawn I sighted the rifle at Ryan. I was about to fire when a woman walked into the line of fire. I then lifted the rifle … '[33] In his second statement, he said: 'I stopped and took aim at the prisoner Ryan but the two prison officers were in my line of fire so I dropped the rifle again.'[34] In his third statement, Paterson said: 'I ran onto the lawn and I could see the prisoner with a gun and he had the two officers held at gun point … I took aim and I found out I had to fire between the two officers to get him, so I lowered the gun … '[35]

Opas was also able to show, through his cross-examination of a police firearms expert, First Constable Brian Thompson, that there was no first pressure on an M1 carbine. If Paterson had taken a first pressure when he said he did, the rifle would have discharged at that point.[36]

Apart from the witness evidence relating directly to the shooting of Hodson, the prosecution relied heavily upon testimony that Ryan had, in effect, confessed to shooting Hodson on no less than four separate occasions after the escape. These related to the statements he made during the ANZ Bank hold-up in Ormond on 23 December 1965, his statements at the flat on 24 December 1965, and the two statements he made to police on 6 and 7 January 1966 after his recapture in Sydney.

Thus it was that, on the sixth day of the trial, Murray put John Fisher into the witness box to testify as to the statements Ryan had made to him. Asked by Murray whether he had a conversation with Ryan during the party at the flat in Elwood on Christmas Eve, Fisher replied that he had:

> Did you have any conversation with him which related to the shooting of the warder Hodson?
>
> –Yes, I did.
>
> Would you tell us what you said and what Ryan did?
>
> –I asked Ryan who shot the warder and he said he did.
>
> You asked Ryan who shot the warder and he said he did?
>
> –Yes.

Did he say anything more?

–He said he would have shot anyone else who got in his way.

This was damaging evidence against Ryan. In his cross-examination of Fisher, Opas immediately went on the offensive. Opas sought to characterise Fisher's evidence as the testimony of a discredited man with a criminal record, whose motivation in originally making his statement to police was to claim the £5,000 government reward offered for information leading to the recapture of the escapees:

When did you last come out of gaol?

–About two years three months ago.

Two years three months ago. You have got a long criminal record haven't you?

–Not very long.

Well, how long do you call it, ten convictions?

–No.

How many have you got?

–Might be seven at the most, it would be lucky if it is that.

When the questioning turned to the party at the flat and his conversation with Ryan, Fisher was asked by Opas how he came to ask Ryan about Hodson's shooting:

And you just, in casual conversation, said, 'Who shot the warder?' did you?

–That is correct.

And he told you he did?

–Yes.

You went straight away to the police and reported this, didn't you?

–When I got out of the flat, yes.

You went that same night to the police?

–Yes.

You knew there was a reward out?

–Yes, I knew.

And you went there to claim it, didn't you?

–No, I didn't …

And you had to make your story sound a bit good?

–No, I had no intention, I was not thinking of the reward when I went to the police.

I am putting it to you that Ryan didn't say anything of the sort to you—that he admitted that he had shot Hodson?

–He did so …

You hadn't seen him for at least two years, and you say to him out of the blue, 'Who shot the warder?' and he said he did. That is what you want us to believe?

–That is what he told me.

That is what you want the gentlemen of the jury to believe?

–Which … is true.[37]

Later the same day, Murray called the two staff from the ANZ Bank in Ormond to tell the court what Ryan had said during the course of the hold-up. Robert Sipthorpe was asked by Murray if could he see in court the man who appeared in the bank armed with a rifle. Sipthorpe identified Ryan:

Mr Sipthorpe, did that man in your hearing make any remark about the rifle?

–He did. He said he had killed a man the other day with it.

Would you just elaborate that a little? In what context did he say that?

–How do you mean?

Was that the whole of what he said in that sentence, or was it part of a longer sentence?

–I can't remember really. He said it was an M1 American carbine, and he had killed a man the other day with it.

During cross-examination by Opas, Sipthorpe was not able to be shaken from his story:

I am putting it to you all he said was, 'This is the sort of gun that killed a man a few days ago'?

–Yes.

Something like that?

–Yes.

'This is the sort of gun that killed … '?

> –No, he said, 'This is the gun that killed a man.'
>
> That is what he said, 'This is the gun that killed a man a few days ago.'?
>
> –Yes.[38]

Following Sipthorpe's evidence, bank officer George Robertson was called to the stand. After similarly identifying Ryan as the man with the rifle in the bank, Robertson was asked by Murray:

> During the time he was there with the rifle, did he make any remark about it; did he say anything about the rifle?
>
> –Yes.
>
> What did he say?
>
> –He told me that it was an American M1 rifle and that he had killed a man with it.
>
> When, when did he say that?
>
> –I am not too sure, I think he said, 'I have already killed a man with it.'[39]

Faced with the fact that two bank officers had now independently testified that Ryan had said he had killed a man with the rifle, Opas moved to establish a basis upon which he might have used such words, other than as an admission of guilt. Cross-examining Robertson, Opas sought to put a construction on events in the bank which suggested that Ryan was introducing a note of terror about the rifle in order to effect compliance from staff:

> [In] order for a hold-up of this nature to take place, obviously it has to be done quickly and it has to strike surprise in everybody?
>
> –I think so, yes ...
>
> Ryan was holding this weapon and pointing it at you and saying, 'Look, this weapon has killed a man in the last few days', or something like that?
>
> –Yes, in fact he made a few statements directly at me.
>
> At you?
>
> –Yes.
>
> What did he say to you?
>
> –When we were in the [strongroom] I was looking at him and

> he looked at me and he said, 'You look a bit green, son'. He said, 'You look like you might try something', and then he told me, 'This is a Mark 1 rifle, and the one [that killed a man]', among other things ...[40]

There were two further alleged confessions by Ryan. Over the following two days, Murray led the evidence of Detective Sergeant Bill Walters, the homicide squad officer who had interviewed Ryan in Sydney on 7 January following the escapees' recapture. This evidence was corroborated by Walters' colleague, homicide squad Senior Detective Noel Murphy. The second confession was introduced in the evidence of Senior Detective Harry Morrison, also of the homicide squad, who had accompanied the escapees back to Melbourne on the chartered aircraft later the same day.

Walters began by recounting his evidence relating to the circumstances under which Ryan made a signed statement in Sydney and made other statements, which became the unsigned record of interview. Walters said that, at the commencement of the interview, he had warned Ryan about his right to remain silent, and asked him if he understood the caution. Walters said that Ryan had then replied:

> Yes, but before you go any further I wish to make a statement. I am not making any verbal admissions. I am not trying to be smart or insult your intelligence but I would like to see counsel before I answer any questions.

Ryan then dictated his statement and had it taken down by Detective Sergeant Charlton. In the statement, Ryan commended the NSW Police and said that he had no further statements to make at this stage, either verbal or written, and that he would act under instructions after seeing his counsel in Melbourne.[41]

Coming to the unsigned record of interview, Walters told the court that Ryan had made certain admissions in relation to Hodson. The crucial admission came, Walters said, when Ryan told his side of the story, supposedly off the record:

> In the heat of the moment you sometimes do an act without thinking. I think this is what happened to Hodson. I did not know

> him personally. I know his kind ... He had no need to interfere, he was stupid. He was told to keep away. He grabbed Pete and hit him with an iron bar. He caused his own death. I didn't want to shoot him. I could have shot a lot more.[42]

Again, this was damaging to the defence case. But, during cross-examination, Opas sought to show how unlikely it was that Ryan would have made such a confession, having indicated on three separate occasions—both before and after the alleged off-the-record interview—that he would not be making any statements. At a court appearance the previous day he had specifically declared that he would not be making any statements; only minutes before the record of interview he had repeated to police that he would not make any statements; and he repeated it again later the same day at the extradition proceedings at the Sydney Central Court. Opas homed in on the obvious inconsistency, and used it to suggest that Ryan had not, in fact, made the admissions alleged against him, at all:

> Although that confession, if it is a confession, was allegedly obtained by you, you didn't put one question to [Ryan] about it, did you, when the [statement] was prepared?
>
> –That is so.
>
> And when he came into court at ... 12:30 [PM] that day, this was, as far as you know, the first occasion he was brought before the court after his arrest?
>
> –Yes.[43]
>
> He made a statement to the court then, didn't he?
>
> –Yes.
>
> He said, 'I want to protect myself against any possible allegations that the police might make.' He said something like that, didn't he?
>
> –No, I don't agree with that, sir, there is a transcript of that evidence ...
>
> In any event, he did say, didn't he, that I have made no verbal admissions, did he say that, I am not going to make them?
>
> –That is so, yes.
>
> And no contradiction was made by you at Sydney Court on that occasion to the effect that he had already made a confession?
>
> –No, sir ...

I am putting to you that this alleged verbal statement never was made?

–That is not so.

And you didn't contradict Ryan in the Court when he said he had made no statement, did you?

–First of all I was in no position to contradict any person in Court …

Who gave evidence at the extradition proceedings?

–Detective Inspector Holland …

Didn't you tell him what Ryan had told you?

–No.

I see, so that although this interview with Ryan, the whole interview we have here, was concluded by 9:30 [AM], and you didn't go into Court until 12:30 [PM], you didn't tell your own Inspector that Ryan had made admissions to you, is that so?

–I didn't tell him, no …

Yes, and of course you didn't write [the record of interview] in Ryan's presence, did you?

–No.

Or show it to him at any stage?

–No, sir.

And you sought no confirmation from him of that statement that he was supposed to have made?

–No, sir.[44]

At the following day's hearing, Murray called to the stand Senior Detective Morrison, who had travelled handcuffed to Ryan on the special flight back to Melbourne from Sydney. Murray asked Morrison to tell the court what Ryan had said during the flight:

> The accused Ryan said to me, 'We were set to go last Christmas. When we got to the wall the fellow who was with me jibbed at the wall and we had to go back. Peter and I mated up. He wanted to go also so we planned it. We had to wait until we got the right man on the wall and Sunday was the day. The warder spoilt the whole show. If he had not poked his great head into it he would not have got shot. It was either him or Peter.[45]

Like the evidence of Walters, this was a serious blow to the defence, and there was not much that could be done with it. However, tendered to the court as an exhibit was the statement that Ryan had made in his appearance before magistrate Norman Hawes in Sydney earlier on the same day:

> I wish to state that myself and Mr Walker ... have made certain non-committal verbal statements, mainly that we will act under the instructions of our counsel and I wish to state further that we will make no further statements on the trip back to Melbourne.[46]

With that pointed disavowal on the court record, Opas chose to assert a completely different version of events on the aircraft:

> Was there anybody seated on the other side of the corridor directly adjacent to [Ryan]?
>
> –No, not all the time, although Inspector Holland did on a couple of occasions sit on the opposite side of the [aircraft] to us.
>
> Before you took off from Sydney, Ryan said to you, didn't he, 'Look, Harry. I will talk about anything with you, but I'm not going to talk about the case?'
>
> –No, he did not.
>
> Did he say anything like that?
>
> –No, sir ...
>
> You would be the only one within hearing of this conversation, would you?
>
> –Yes, sir.
>
> And you would deny it, I suppose, if Ryan were to swear that no such conversation took place?
>
> –I would.[47]

Again, damning evidence against Ryan had been given by a police officer. Despite the attempt by Opas subtly to characterise these alleged confessions as inventions by police, these prosecution witnesses had not been shaken from their testimony.

At the end of Morrison's evidence, Murray told the court that this concluded the evidence for the Crown. It had been a compelling case. Eleven eye-witnesses at the scene outside Pentridge had said they had seen Ryan holding the rifle in a position to shoot the prison officer. They had all *heard* a shot fired, four of them had *seen* Ryan fire the shot, and all of them had seen Hodson fall. A former prison associate had testified that Ryan had told him that he had shot Hodson. Two bank officers had made statements that Ryan had claimed that the carbine he carried had killed a man before. And two police officers had given evidence that Ryan had admitted to them that he had shot Hodson.

At this point, Opas and Lazarus had nothing to lose by putting their clients on the witness stand in a final attempt to persuade the jury that there was a reasonable doubt. Thus, on day eight of the trial, after Opas had addressed the jury on the issue of his client's innocence, Ryan was sworn in and took the stand. Opas wasted no time in getting to the heart of the matter:

> Your name is Ronald Joseph Ryan?
> –Yes.
> You are at present a prisoner at Her Majesty's Gaol, Pentridge?
> –Yes, sir.
> Now, in November of 1964, were you sentenced to eight years' imprisonment?
> –Yes, sir.
> Did you murder Prison Officer Hodson?
> –Most emphatically not.
> Did you fire a shot at Hodson?
> –Definitely not.
> Did you fire a shot at all on the 19th of December?
> –I did not discharge that gun on the 19th of December.
> Have you ever discharged that gun … ?
> –No, I have never fired that gun …

After setting out the sequence of events during the escape, including the encounter with Lange in the tower, Ryan was asked about the incident with the lever that opened the external gate, and how he came to grab the prison rifle:

> What did you grab it for?
> –So that it couldn't be used against me … [I] saw the cocking lever on the side of the rifle. Incidentally, I had never seen one

of these M1 .30s before, I had never ever handled one, and I pulled the cocking lever back to inject the shell into the rifle or see if there was one in their first. There were none in there, so I pushed the lever forward to inject one in, to fit one, and pushed it in.

What did you do that for?

–Oh, to bluff the warder, let him know that I meant business, to impress upon him that he had better do what I told him to. However, in pushing the lever forward I noticed that the extractors, I suppose you would call them, didn't close over the head of the shell, so I pulled the lever back again to force it forward harder. In doing this it picked up another shell and forced it in behind the one which had first gone in. Consequently, my gun jammed.

What happened next?

–Well, then, I tested the gun and worked the lever and this all happened very quickly, of course, and I got the shell out, it tipped out on the floor, and I just let the lever go and this unfortunately picked up another shell, and again I was in the same predicament.

What happened to the shell that fell out on the ground?

–I don't know. I didn't pick it up, I didn't want to expose myself to attack from the warder, so I just pretended the gun was O.K.

Coming to the issue of what happened at the intersection of Sydney Road and Champ Street, Ryan described holding Mitchinson and Wallis at bay, and trying to get a car to stop as Walker was being hotly pursued by Hodson:

Were you swinging the rifle from the hip?

–I was following the car about chest high, I suppose would be a more apt description.

What were you intending to do when you were moving the gun like that?

–Well, my whole object was to get a car to pull up and in order to add to my bluff I did, while running across that intersection, pull the lever back and as I did so a shell was ejected, and then I let the lever go again …

Did you see what happened to Hodson?

–No, I didn't see what happened to Hodson. I saw Hodson who was chasing Walker—he was a pretty big fellow and very stout. He seemed to be just about at the end of his tether. He was pretty distressed—that was my impression—when he was chasing Peter. They ran from my sight behind this Plymouth. I was approaching, not exactly from the rear but from the driver's side of the rear and consequently that car did obscure my vision of Hodson and Walker. In any case, I presume they were behind a car and I just lost sight of Peter and the officer.

What happened with you? Did you hear a shot at any time?

–I couldn't swear that I heard a shot but I did hear two or three detonations, but this may have been pure auto-suggestion, because I was expecting to be fired at by the guard in No. 2 Tower at any stage, but I would not swear that I did hear shots. They could have been shots or they could have been car doors slamming because quite a few people were jumping out of cars at this stage to—well, I assume to lend [a] hand to the officers … [48]

The next day, Ryan was asked about the several confessions that witnesses said he had made:

Then what do you say about Fisher's evidence that you told him you had shot the warder? What do you say about that?

–Oh, he's a liar, sir. I am quite satisfied he was after the reward.

Well, the answer is, you didn't tell him that?

–Most emphatically not.

You deny his evidence?

–Most emphatically.[49]

Questioned about the evidence of Walters (corroborated by Murphy), Ryan was equally adamant that the words attributed to him were false. Taking Ryan through his statements to the court in which he disavowed making any statements about the shooting of Hodson, Opas asked him about the admissions that Walters said he made. Ryan denied using the words alleged by Walters:

The particular thing I am concerned with is, did you say, 'It was simply getting out, nothing planned. We got up on the wall before the screw realised we were there. He mucked us about a bit by operating the wrong lever. I think he thought I was going to shoot him when I marched him back up the tower to open the right lever.' Did you say that to him?

–No. I repeat, I made no verbal statements in between my two written statements …

Did you say, 'In the heat of the moment you sometimes do an act without thinking. I think this is what happened to Hodson. I did not know him personally. I know his kind … He had no need to interfere, he was stupid. He was told to keep away. He grabbed Pete and hit him with an iron bar. He caused his own death. I didn't want to shoot him. I could have shot a lot more'?

–I did not say those words.[50]

Opas then turned to the admission that Ryan was said to have made in the aircraft bringing the escapees back to Melbourne:

What were you talking about coming down in the plane?

–Various topics. Do you want me to relate them in detail, sir?

Well, just in broad outline, what were you talking about?

–Oh, we discussed education, the position in Vietnam, the incident of graft in the Police Force, the amount of money that was recovered when I was arrested in Sydney, and the publicity attendant upon my escape.

Well, in any event, the only thing we are concerned about is, did you say this to him, 'We were set to go last Christmas. When we got to the wall, the fellow who was with me jibbed at the wall and we had to go back. Peter and I mated up. He wanted to go also so we planned it. We had to wait until we got the right man on the wall, and Sunday was the day. The Warder spoilt the whole show. If he had not poked his great head into it he would not have got shot. It was either him or Peter.' Did you say that?

–Most definitely not. We never touched on the case at all coming down.[51]

Putting Ryan in the witness box opened him to cross-examination by the prosecution, and Murray took the opportunity to question Ryan about the escape and the shooting of Hodson. Despite close questioning, Ryan stuck to the core of his story: he had raised the rifle to his shoulder, but it had been only to cause motorists to stop so that he could commandeer a car and make a getaway.

Ryan had been in the box for several hours over two days in front of a full courtroom and a crowded public gallery. To all outward appearances, he had handled himself well: he had sounded confident, he had made no admissions, and he had offered a plausible version of events.[52] However, the impact that his testimony had is difficult to gauge. It seems possible that his appearance was unhelpful at best, and counterproductive at worst. Many years later, one member of the jury would comment that 'Ryan didn't do himself any good when he elected to go into the witness box and give evidence. He impressed as a little too sure of himself … '[53]

With Ryan's cross-examination concluded, Opas called to the stand Terry Speed, the mathematician from Monash University who had made a series of calculations concerning the trajectory of the bullet that killed Hodson. Led by Opas, Speed testified that, given the known velocity of a bullet leaving the muzzle of the carbine, and knowing the precise angle and entry point of the bullet in Hodson's shoulder and its exit point in his back, he had made mathematical projections showing the height at which the rifle would have had to be when it was fired to achieve those outcomes. The crucial element in these calculations depended upon autopsy evidence that the bullet had exited Hodson's body at a point one inch lower than it had entered. Speed drew upon diagrams he had made showing the planes of the bullet to demonstrate the height of the rifle at various distances from Hodson. Holding the diagrams before him, Opas drew Speed's evidence to a conclusion:

> So assuming that the muzzle of the rifle was a foot below his head height, to determine the height of the man firing at any given point, you would add one foot to the values you have expressed here?
>
> –Yes.
>
> And at [a distance from Hodson of] 20 feet a man would have to be 8.25 feet high in that situation and it progressively becomes a higher figure as you go back?
>
> –True, yes.
>
> Well then, the other values speak for themselves—at 150 feet … the

point of firing is 21.36 feet?

–Yes.

And at 225 feet it is 29.50?

–Yes.[54]

These calculations were important because they cast doubt on the probability of Ryan having fired the fatal shot, and potentially raised a further possibility that a prison officer on the Pentridge wall may have shot Hodson in trying to hit Ryan. But there were two fundamental problems with this defence evidence. The first problem, quickly pointed up by Murray during his cross-examination, turned on the assumption that Hodson had been running precisely vertically when he was chasing Walker. While witnesses to the shooting had testified that Hodson had been running upright, they did not necessarily mean mathematically perpendicular:

Mr. Speed, as I understand it, what you have done is to take a point as the entry of the bullet, you have allowed for the distance of travel to the point of exit, and you have allowed for the drop, and this gives you the path travelled?

–That is correct, yes …

Would you agree, that your calculations are only of any value whatsoever if you assume that figure is [precisely vertical] to the ground?

–Certainly, I would agree.

And as soon as you depart from that even by a matter of a degree or two, your calculations, you might as well forget them?

–Well, I would recalculate the whole thing …

I beg your pardon?

–One would have to recalculate the whole thing.

His Honour: What Mr. Solicitor means is you could not use them?

–Certainly.[55]

The second problem was that the introduction of the mathematical projections weakened the force of the cross-examination of prison officer Paterson. Having credibly raised the prospect that Paterson, from a point *on the ground* outside the prison's main gate, had fired a shot that may have struck Hodson, the defence had now introduced an entirely different scenario—that Hodson might have been killed by a bullet fired from another point, possibly by a prison officer *on the wall.* While the evidence may have raised a new doubt in the minds of the jury, it is possible that the effect of the mathematician's evidence was to distract and confuse them about the defence argument in relation to Paterson.[56]

With the conclusion of Speed's evidence, Opas rested his case for Ryan, and Lazarus called Walker to the witness box for what would be uneventful testimony under oath. As far as Walker was concerned, he said he was a willing party to the escape, but he had not contemplated using violence, and he had not been aware of Ryan's actions with the rifle before they had made their getaway in the Vanguard. He had not himself fired a shot, and he was unable to say who had.[57]

With the evidence completed, on day nine of the trial Opas proceeded to his final address to the jury, systematically reviewing the evidence against Ryan, summarising and criticising as he went. Opas began by setting the context for his final submission:

> Gentlemen, this charge is murder and the only penalty provided by our legislature is death. Whether it will be carried out has nothing to do with anyone taking part in this trial. But the essential first step before any such sentence can be carried out is, of course, a jury verdict recording a finding of guilty. Thus the responsibility which rests upon your shoulders and consciences is very heavy indeed, because you play the most important role in this drama …
>
> This trial is concerned with the allegation that the accused has wrongly taken the life of another. Life, we are told, is but a fleeting gleam between two eternities … Prison Officer Hodson had his life terminated by a bullet. And before you convict either accused you must be satisfied beyond reasonable doubt that the accused Ryan fired that bullet, deliberately, with the intention that the bullet should kill or seriously injure Hodson. It is not enough that you should think it more likely than not that he fired the shot. You must be sure to the degree of moral certainty. You must entertain no reasonable doubt whatever. You have three possible states of mind: You may be certain beyond reasonable doubt that he fired deliberately aiming at Hodson with intent to kill or seriously injure him. Then it is your moral duty to convict him.
>
> If you have no doubt that it was not Ryan but somebody else

who fired the shot, then equally you must do your duty and acquit him.

Then there is an intermediate stage where you cannot make up your mind. You might think to yourselves: 'He might have fired the shot, but then he might not have. The bullet was never found. There is no proof to the degree of certainty that would satisfy my conscience that the bullet which entered Hodson's body came from the rifle held by Ryan. I think it is probable that he did fire the shot, but I am not sure.' In that case, you must acquit, because the Crown would not have satisfied its burden of proving beyond reasonable doubt each element in the charge ...

[The] Crown does not win or lose criminal trials. It ensures that justice is done according to law, and that the truth should emerge whether it is in favour or against either party. This is typified in this case, where the Solicitor-General has been the very essence of impartiality and fairness. He takes no sides and has made available to me, in the interests of justice, material which greatly assists the defence but ... the existence of which I would have remained ignorant unless he told me of it.

Long before this came to trial there was most unusual publicity given to the exploits of the accused in the Press, on the radio, and over television. It would be impossible for anyone living in a capital city in Australia to approach this trial without some preconceived notions based on what he had read or heard about the case.

The evidence you have listened to so patiently and attentively for so many days must have convinced you of the inaccuracy and unreliability of many of the newspaper accounts of the shooting. The important thing is that at this stage you should put out of your minds entirely all that you may have read or heard of this case. You must act solely on what you have heard and seen in this court. You have taken oaths to return a verdict in accordance with this evidence, and that is what you must do. It is the evidence, and only the evidence, on which you must act.

It is easy to take the view of the accused that they are convicted criminals, worthless creatures on any view, therefore what does it matter if we convict them? They will never be of any use to society. Society will be better off without them. We do not like anything about them or what they stand for, and we are going to convict

> them whether we think the evidence measures up to the standard of certainty or not ...
>
> What a perfect scapegoat a convicted person would become if he became the target for a trumped-up charge ... [I]t would be most wrong to look at this case from the standpoint that Ryan and Walker are quite capable of committing any crime in the statute book. You have to be satisfied on the evidence before you that in fact they did what is alleged against them.
>
> It may be most unworthy of me to lay so much stress upon this aspect, but because of the unprecedented pre-trial publicity each of you must have known when you received your summons for the jury just what trial you were being called to. One could well imagine the parting shot from your wives as they kissed you goodbye: 'Don't come home if you let those villains off' ...[58]
>
> I do not propose to present you with the man who in fact fired the shot. I propose merely to point out to you the evidence which establishes that whoever shot warder Hodson, it was not and could not have been Ronald Ryan.[59]

Concluding his address the following day, Opas told the jury that it had to be satisfied that it was a .30 bullet from Ryan's rifle that had killed Hodson, because the fatal bullet had never been found. There was uncontradicted evidence, he said, that the rifle Ryan took from prison officer Lange contained eight shots in the magazine. Four of these had been recovered from the rifle when Ryan and Walker were recaptured in Sydney. Two others had been found on the floor of the bank that the accused had robbed in Ormond, and a further cartridge had been found on the roadway outside the gaol. This left one cartridge unaccounted for, and this could have been ejected from the rifle when Ryan was working the bolt while on the no. 1 tower with Lange. This cartridge had not been found, but prisoners often cleaned the sentry boxes and it would be most unlikely that one would have handed it in if it had been found. 'This is the key to the whole case. Did the shot go through the body of Hodson or was it left lying in the sentry box?' Opas said that Ryan had started behind the eight-ball as a convicted man, but the fact that he had convictions and the jury might not think much of his character did not make him a murderer.

With the exception of Paterson, Opas said, all of the Crown

witnesses heard only one shot. This suggested that only one shot was fired—the shot by Paterson himself. 'Whether this was the fatal shot or not is not for me to say. You should not be satisfied beyond reasonable doubt that a second shot was fired because nobody heard it.' As for the evidence of the verbal admissions—'this great unburdening by Ryan', Opas said—they could not be more unconvincing. 'I suggest you could not go home and sleep soundly in your beds if you returned a verdict of guilty against this man on the evidence you have heard in this court. The evidence is unsatisfactory. There is only one verdict and that is acquittal.'[60]

When it was Murray's turn to finally address the jury, his summing up was restrained and to the point. It was difficult to think how the Crown case against Ryan could be much stronger, he said. It was very seldom that people who were unconnected with the parties involved in a killing were able to be called as eye-witnesses. In the case against Ryan, he said, the Crown had called eleven people, all of whom had no doubt they saw the accused Ryan fire the fatal shot:

> These witnesses cannot be attacked on any of the bases on which witnesses are usually attacked. They cannot be attacked on the ground that they were being dishonest. They cannot be attacked in any way except by saying that they are human ... It would be extraordinary if a whole lot of untrained observers came along here and gave the whole story without contradicting each other in some way. In Ryan's case, what it boils down to is this: 'Did he fire the shot or did he not?' It is not a case of the gun firing accidentally or of the gun being fired in the heat of the moment. If the carbine Ryan had fired the shot, then he fired it deliberately.[61]

After Murray sat down, Lazarus gave his summing-up of the case for Walker, before Starke began his charge to the jury. Starke managed only about half an hour before the court rose for the day. The next morning, Wednesday, 30 March, would be the last of the trial. When it resumed at 10:00AM, Starke continued his summary, ranging over the evidence and giving direction to the jury on the salient points of law along the way:

> Gentlemen, the first principle of law I desire to deal with is the onus of proof and all counsel have correctly told you what it is. The

> burden of proof in a criminal trial rests on the Crown and that burden is to prove each fact and each element and each ingredient of the crime charged beyond reasonable doubt … This is not a civil case, it is a criminal case, and the civil burden of proof 'on the balance of probabilities' is not enough. It is not nearly enough. The Crown must prove each and every ingredient or element of the crime charged beyond reasonable doubt. It has been called the golden thread that runs through the criminal law. It is an insurance, insofar as one can insure in a system which is based on human frailty, that no innocent man is convicted.[62]

A crucial direction, one that would be the subject of later appeal, was Starke's direction in relation to the issue of felony-murder, whereby a killing in the course of the commission of a felony (in this case, the escape from lawful custody) is murder and not manslaughter. After giving a general definition of murder and drawing the legal distinctions between murder and manslaughter, Starke outlined the exceptional circumstances that limited the application of manslaughter:

> In certain circumstances the crime of murder may be established even though the accused had no actual intention of killing, and that is so in these circumstances. If a killing occurs by an act of violence in the course of a commission of a felony involving violence, or in the furtherance of the purpose of such felony, the accused is guilty of murder, even though there is no actual intention of killing. This is known to lawyers as felony-murder. The intention is imputed to the accused by law; it is what is called constructive intention or constructive malice.
>
> Now what has the Crown got to establish in order to establish … felony-murder? Firstly, it has got to establish that there was a felony being committed … [and] I refer you to a section of the Gaols Act which provides that, 'Every male person lawfully imprisoned for any crime who escapes shall be guilty of a felony' …
>
> The next thing is, it has got to be by an act of violence. Now, what is an act of violence in this connection? This may be said in definition, when the actor did the act … he must have contemplated, or as a reasonable man should have contemplated, that death or grievous bodily harm was likely to result … [Next], in the

> commission of a felony involving violence: commission means while he is doing it and before it is over. Once it is complete, of course, there can be no question of felony-murder. Furtherance: in the furtherance of the purpose of such felony …
>
> Now, gentlemen, in the case of an escape from gaol, it is a matter for you, of course, but it may be that the accused hoped very much that they would get away with it without anyone seeing them at all and there would not be any violence. But it is open to you to find [that] this is just the sort of crime that, if detection occurred, is very likely indeed to lead to violence of one kind or another. [If] you were satisfied of those things, satisfied beyond reasonable doubt, you would be entitled to return a verdict of murder on this basis.[63]

At 3:07PM, after Starke had taken more than four hours to sum up the case against the defendants, the jury retired to consider its verdict. As the jurors left the court, some 25 or 30 journalists, lawyers, police, and officials adjourned to the nearby Four Courts Hotel to have a drink and await the outcome. Over beer, the debate raged as to the likely outcome, with few prepared to predict a 'Not guilty' verdict.

Back in the jury room, the discussion among the jurors was running strongly against Ryan, although two jurors initially argued against a guilty verdict.[64] According to a juryman's later account of the discussion, not one member of the jury thought that Ryan would hang: '[We] were so sure that the sentence would be commuted that we didn't even discuss the manslaughter angle.'[65]

Shortly before 10:00PM, when word reached the pub that the court was resuming, drinks were hurriedly downed, and everyone rushed back to the court and took their seats. Journalists took their positions at the small press table as Ryan and Walker were led back into the courtroom from the holding cells above the court, where they had been kept since the jury retired. As the jury filed back into the courtroom, all eyes were upon the foreman in the expectation that he was about to deliver the verdict. The air of expectancy evaporated as Starke asked the jury whether, given the lateness of the hour, they wanted to continue their deliberations or resume in the morning. The foreman indicated that he thought that the jury would rather carry on.

'Very well', said Starke. 'Is there anything more you wish to say to me?'

'We have a question on a point of law,' the foreman replied. 'We seem to have stumbled on a bit. I think it might clear it up if we could have the law on "acting in concert."'[66]

To the assembled journalists, this question was ominous for Ryan. To *Truth* crime reporter, Jack Ayling, the point of this question of legal clarification could only be: 'Could the jury find Walker not guilty of murder, but Ryan guilty?' From his position at the press table, Ayling saw a tight grimace pass across Ryan's face as the question was asked. Starke's patient answer was detailed but he quickly got to the nub of it:

> If two or more persons by pre-arrangement go to some spot together and, in accordance with their pre-arranged plan do all the things necessary to constitute a criminal offence, then they are both equally responsible at law irrespective of which part of the offence was committed by one or the other.
>
> It is unnecessary for the Crown to prove an express arrangement, and usually this is impossible. You may be satisfied beyond reasonable doubt by an examination of all the circumstances. It matters not for how long or how short a time the arrangement has existed, but it must be in existence at the time of the shooting. If terminated before that, there is no common purpose.

Starke then crisply defined the limits of 'acting in concert' as it applied in this case:

> The act alleged must not go beyond the common purpose; in other words, if the common purpose is merely to escape, let us say, and one of the participants in the plan goes beyond that and uses violence, well, then, of course the other party would not be acting in concert.[67]

These questions and Starke's explanation had taken just a few minutes. After the jury again retired at 10:10PM, Ryan and Walker were led directly past the press table on their way to the cells. As Ryan passed within inches of the journalists sitting there, he caught Ayling's eye and, with the bunched right lapel of his suit jacket gripped firmly between his clenched fingers, gave a sharp downward tug. To Ayling, the meaning of the gesture was clear: 'I'm gone; they're going to hang me!'[68]

When the jury retired this time, everyone in the court knew that the verdict would not be long in coming. At 10:27PM the observers were back in court to hear the foreman give the jury's unanimous—and, by then, predictable—verdict. As the jury filed back into court, and the sombre looks on their faces was evident to all, Ryan nudged Walker as they sat in the dock. 'I think we're in *deep* shit,' he whispered.[69] Justice Starke's associate addressed the traditional questions to the foreman:

> Gentlemen of the jury, have you agreed upon your verdict?
> –We have.
> Do you find the accused Ryan guilty or not guilty of murder?
> –Guilty of murder.
> Do you find the accused Walker guilty or not guilty of murder?
> –Not guilty of murder, guilty of manslaughter.[70]

There was absolute silence in the court as the verdicts were announced. To the reporters present, Ryan seemed unmoved by his own fate, but he patted Walker on the back when the manslaughter verdict was given. He glanced in Ayling's direction and simply shrugged his shoulders, as if to say: 'That's the way it goes.'[71] Despite the tenacious defence mounted by Opas and Bourke, the jury had been convinced beyond reasonable doubt about Ryan's guilt on the charge of murder, but they had recognised a difference with respect to Walker.

Starke then asked the jury to retire to the jury room, and directed that Walker be removed from the court momentarily before he passed the mandatory sentence on Ryan. In earlier times it had been traditional that a judge pronouncing the death sentence should put on a black cap to do so—actually, a square of black silk forming part of the judicial robes—but that practice had not been followed for some time. While Starke thought that there still was a black cap floating around the court somewhere, he did not put it on before he pronounced sentence:[72]

> *Associate*: Prisoner at the bar Ryan, you have been found guilty of murder. Have you anything to say or do you know why the sentence of death should not be passed upon you according to law?
>
> *Ryan*: I still maintain my innocence. I will rely upon my counsel to appeal.[73] That is all I have to say.[74]
>
> *Justice Starke*: Ronald Joseph Ryan, you have been found guilty of the murder of George Henry Hodson. It is the sentence of this court that you be taken from here to the place from whence you

> came and, on a day and hour to be fixed by the Executive Council, you shall be hanged by the neck until you are dead. May God rest your soul.[75]

So that was it. No delay, no adjournment prior to sentencing, and no plea by the defence on sentence. After a twelve-day trial involving the evidence of 41 witnesses, the jury had found Ryan guilty of murder and Walker guilty of manslaughter, and Starke had sentenced Ryan to death as the mandatory sentence for murder. (On 29 April, after a plea by Lazarus, in which he detailed Walker's childhood and turn to crime, Starke would sentence Walker to twelve years' imprisonment for manslaughter, with no minimum term fixed.[76])

While Opas finished the trial with an uncomfortable feeling that Ryan may have been innocent, he was in no doubt that Ryan had received a fair hearing: 'Nobody had a fairer trial', he was later to write in a tribute to Starke.[77] There it might be thought that Justice Starke's involvement in the Ryan case was at an end, but at this moment Starke could have no conception of what diverse consequences would flow from the death sentence he had just been obliged to pass. Nor could he imagine the extraordinary turns his own role would take before the sentence would be brought to finality.

After the sentence was pronounced and the trial formalities concluded, Ryan and Walker were taken by prison van back to Pentridge, where they were to be returned to their cells in H Division. It was almost 11:00pm when they set off from the court building, and their conversation in the van reflected how sombre they were about the verdict. Although they were handcuffed to prison officers Bill Warner and John Fraser, they managed to shake hands across the van.

'Jesus, mate,' Walker said reassuringly, 'they'll commute it!'

'Mate, I'm in the hands of the politicians,' Ryan responded in a matter-of-fact way.[78] As they were taken from the van at Pentridge—for what neither of them then knew would be the last time they would ever see one another—Ryan's parting words to Walker were typically defiant: 'Don't lay down, fight them all the way!'[79]

In the immediate aftermath of the trial, there was a period when public awareness and interest in the Ryan and Walker case receded.

Behind the scenes, however, Ryan's defence team were preparing an appeal, and on 6 April 1966 Opas applied to the full bench of the Supreme Court sitting as a Court of Criminal Appeal for leave to appeal against Ryan's conviction.[80] On 4 May, the Full Court, comprising Chief Justice Sir Henry Winneke and Justices Hudson and McInerney, convened to hear Ryan and Walker's appeal. In an application funded by legal aid, Opas appeared for Ryan, with Brian Bourke as his junior; John Young, QC, appeared with Jack Lazarus for Walker. The Crown was again represented by Tony Murray and Geoff Byrne.

Ryan's application was on six grounds: first, that the jury's verdict in finding that Ryan fired the shot which killed Hodson was against the evidence and the weight of evidence and was unreasonable; second and third, that a ruling by the trial judge—a ruling given in the presence of the jury—in relation to a statement he had made about the evidence of a particular witness had raised a prejudice about the applicant Ryan in the minds of the jury.

Grounds four to six constituted the core of the appeal application. The fourth ground was that the trial judge was in error in ruling that at the time of the shooting the escape from lawful custody had not been completed. Opas' contention was that the felony of escaping was complete as soon as Ryan was clear of the external wall of the prison and, hence, the shot that killed Hodson was not fired in the course of committing that crime.

The contention of the fifth and sixth grounds was that, on the evidence, it was open to the jury to find a verdict of manslaughter against Ryan, and that the judge was in error in ruling that manslaughter was not a possible verdict as an alternative to murder, except in the exercise of the jury's common-law right to return such a verdict in any such case. Opas submitted that the jury could have returned a verdict of manslaughter against Ryan on the basis either that the rifle discharged accidentally or through criminal negligence on his part, and that the judge was wrong in ruling to the contrary and refusing to direct the jury accordingly.

He contended that such a finding was open on the evidence of Ryan's inexperience with the workings of the M1 carbine, and the manner in which he handled the rifle in the street prior to the shooting of Hodson. Opas also argued that a manslaughter finding was open to the jury upon the inference that might be drawn from Ryan's statement to the police after his recapture that he had no intention of firing at the police or any member of the public. Freedom was their main objective, he had claimed to police in an interview; to the best of his recollection, he did not shoot the prison officer, he would not consciously shoot a fellow human being, he had fired no shots, and shooting the prison officer would be very much out of character.

After a six-day hearing, on 8 June 1966 the full bench handed down its judgment, refusing the application on all grounds. In relation to the crucial application on manslaughter, the court ruled that Ryan's statements in their context 'afford no evidence that the rifle discharged accidentally in circumstances that would justify a finding of manslaughter'.[81]

With the Hodson murder trial and appeal concluded, there was no impediment to Walker being tried for the murder of Arthur Henderson; and so, on Monday, 18 July 1966, his trial commenced in the Supreme Court before Justice Gregory Gowans. Prosecuted by Geoff Byrne, Walker was again defended by Jack Lazarus. After a hearing lasting two weeks, the jury found him not guilty of murder but guilty of manslaughter. This was a surprising verdict to many lawyers associated with the trial, including Justice Gowans who, in sentencing Walker, made the unusual comment that he was 'unable, by speculation, to determine the basis of the verdict …'[82] Tony Murray was later to indicate in a confidential memorandum to attorney-general Arthur Rylah that he understood the jury's reluctance to convict on 'murder' had been 'actuated principally … by a dislike of capital punishment'.[83]

On 29 July, Justice Gowans sentenced Walker to twelve years' gaol with a minimum of seven years before being eligible for parole. This sentence was to be served cumulatively with the twelve years' imprisonment he had received for his part in the shooting of Hodson.[84] Combined with the unexpired portion of the sentence for the armed robbery offences he was serving at the time of the escape, the period Walker was notionally required to serve before he was eligible for parole was more than 27 years. (In the event, with remissions, Walker would spend more than nineteen years in gaol for the offences for which he had been tried and convicted, and he would not be released until 21 December 1984.)

On 18 July 1966, the same day as the start of Walker's trial for murder, the public solicitor acting for Ryan filed an application with the

High Court of Australia for leave to appeal from the decision of the Full Supreme Court against his conviction. The appeal application listed five legal grounds upon which the High Court should quash Ryan's verdict of guilty of murder, and sought an order for a new trial on the basis that the original trial had miscarried.[85] On 14 October the application was heard in the High Court before Chief Justice Sir Garfield Barwick and Justices McTiernan, Kitto, Taylor, and Menzies. The court refused the application on the sole ground that it was not persuaded that the full court's decision was erroneous, but it expressed no opinion on the matters of law found in the judgment of the Court of Appeal.[86]

Now that Ryan's legal appeals had been exhausted, a number of abolitionists began to fear that the Bolte cabinet would not commute Ryan's death sentence, and that he would be executed. In what later became known as the Tait-substitute theory, concern began to be expressed that premier Bolte was looking for an opportunity to re-assert his political authority after his defeat at the hands of abolitionist forces in the Tait case in October 1962. In December 1961, Robert Peter Tait had been convicted of the murder of an 82-year-old woman in Hawthorn. The crime provoked community outrage. On 6 August 1962, the Bolte government determined that Tait's sentence of death should proceed, but legal appeals caused the scheduled execution to be deferred. Finally, on 30 October 1962, after widespread media and public protests, lawyers acting for Tait made a successful application to the High Court to have the execution—which had been scheduled for the next morning—stayed. With the injunction, premier Bolte's wish to proceed with the hanging was effectively defeated; Tait's sentence was subsequently commuted to a term of life imprisonment without remissions.[87]

Ryan's death sentence for the murder of a prison officer, the Tait substitute theory argued, provided the opportunity that Bolte was looking for. As a report published by the Brotherhood of St Laurence advancing the theory put it: 'It is not unknown or unreasonable for men who feel they have been wrongly prevented from exerting their authority to want to assert it on another such occasion.'[88]

Fearing that Ryan's death sentence was looming, a number of churchmen, abolitionists and others approached attorney-general Rylah to make representations about capital punishment, in general, and Ryan, in particular. This approach was organised by the president of the Methodist Church of Victoria and Tasmania Conference, the Reverend John Westerman, who regarded Rylah as a friend. Westerman first met informally with Rylah at the chief secretary's office in the Old Treasury Building on Wednesday, 9 November, and requested him to receive a delegation of abolitionists about Ryan. Rylah agreed. The next day, at Parliament House, he met with more than a dozen churchmen, unionists, and committee members of the Victorian Anti-Hanging Committee, an abolitionist group originally founded in 1962 to work for a reprieve for Tait.

After the meeting, Westerman remained behind to talk privately with Rylah about Ryan. The discussion was cordial but inconclusive, and they agreed to disagree about hanging and capital punishment. Westerman was left in no doubt by Rylah, however, that—in the premier's eyes—Ryan was, indeed, a candidate for the gallows.[89] With only several weeks to go before the expected cabinet meeting to consider Ryan's fate, there was growing concern among abolitionists that the premier was preparing for an execution.

CHAPTER TWELVE

Cabinet

[W]e now know the decision of the Executive Council. For my part it was the one expected. Hence, it was no shock, and I was able to accept it with equanimity.

—Ronald Ryan

WITH ALL HIS LEGAL APPEALS seemingly exhausted, Ryan now awaited the decision of the Victorian cabinet on the possible commutation of his sentence. As the crucial cabinet meeting approached, he wrote to his mother and family from his Pentridge cell, counselling calm before his fate was known:

> Perhaps the [cabinet] will sit on my case this coming Monday. I assure you I'm O.K. so try not to worry unduly. We can only wait patiently. As usual I fill my time by reading, playing Chess and cards and otherwise I'm comfortable.[1]

It was cabinet's role to consider whether his sentence of death would be carried into effect or commuted to a term of imprisonment. Even though the Supreme Court formally determined sentence in cases of murder demanding the death penalty, death sentences had been commuted so routinely since the state's last executions in 1951 that cabinet had become the *de facto* sentencing authority for murder in Victoria. Since Sir Henry Bolte had become premier in 1955 cabinet had commuted all death sentences—with the exception of Tait in 1961—to terms of imprisonment. After Tait's sentence was ultimately commuted following a successful application for reprieve to the High Court, his papers were marked 'Never to be released'.[2]

Commutation of death sentences by cabinet had virtually become an extension of the criminal justice system. What is more, commutation had been determined in a relatively enlightened manner, given that a number of commutation cases involved quite brutal murders. Of the 35 convicted murderers whose sentences had been commuted since Bolte had come to power in June 1955, only five had been given life sentences without remissions. In some cases, with good behaviour and progress toward rehabilitation, prisoners could be released after ten years or less. Others were required to serve longer minimum periods in prison—seven of them up to 30 years or more—but in few circumstances was there no prospect of release.[3]

It had not always been so. Early Victorian and Australian history had been marked by a savagery in sentencing with few equals anywhere, and for much of the twentieth century Victoria 'possessed one of the most luxuriant collections of capital offences in the English-speaking world.'[4] Indeed, the death penalty is inextricably linked with Australian settlement. Transportation of convicts from Britain was frequently the alternative punishment to hanging and, as a punishment for crimes committed in the colony, the death penalty had been brought to Australia with the First Fleet.[5] Public executions took place in all the colonies. In the early years of colonial New South Wales and Tasmania, capital punishment was used as a sanction to a degree so frequent that it exceeded its use in England at that time, and even approached its use there in absolute terms.[6] While hanging—which was the only form of judicial execution in Australia's history—had diminished in intensity by the mid-nineteenth century, capital punishment continued in Australia for more than 100 years.[7] In the twentieth century up until Ryan's time, there were 113 executions in Australia—a statistic that indicates the discretionary nature of the use of the death penalty. In the period from 1950 to 1967, however, there were only fifteen executions.[8]

When capital punishment was first employed in Australia there were many more capital offences than the crime of murder. Historically, the death penalty in Australia was the prescribed punishment for crimes such as arson on the docks, piracy, and treason, as well as murder and rape. In the twentieth century the crimes for which the death penalty was prescribed became fewer, and in the last phase of its use in Australia the death penalty was utilised only for murder.[9] In Victoria there had been 185 judicial executions in the 125-year period from the first execution in 1842 to 1967, of which only 21 took place in the twentieth century. Of that 21, two executions were for offences other than murder—one for arson in 1902 and another for rape of a child in 1932.[10] It was not until 1949 that the death penalty was abolished in Victoria for all offences except murder and treason. Five women had been hanged in Victorian history, and several male offenders executed had been as young as eighteen or nineteen years old.[11]

Now Victoria was to consider another execution. Within days of the dismissal of Ryan's appeal to the High Court, on 14 October 1966 the chief secretary wrote to each of the government agencies concerned with the case for reports on Ryan. To fully brief them for the cabinet meeting, ministers would be presented with a substantial dossier of papers about him, some of which had not been available to the trial prosecution, the jury, or the judge. Cabinet's task would not be to decide Ryan's guilt—that had been previously determined by the jury—but to decide whether he was deserving of clemency. If cabinet determined that clemency was warranted, the premier could make a recommendation to the governor advising him to exercise the ancient royal prerogative of mercy, and to commute Ryan's death sentence to a term of imprisonment.

In considering capital cases, it was the duty of members of the cabinet to read a summary of the evidence tendered during the course of the trial. This aspect was regarded as important in order that the full details of a crime, and the subsequent trial, were thoroughly understood. Cabinet would consider the condemned man's early life and what special circumstances, if any, surrounded the murder for which he had been convicted. When all the reports from the relevant authorities were eventually gathered together by the Law Department, and hand-delivered to ministers on 24 November 1966, they formed a dossier of material on Ryan that was two inches thick.

Cabinet was scheduled to meet on 5 December 1966 to consider Ryan's case, but the meeting was postponed while ministers dealt with the Stamps Bill and other urgent end-of-year parliamentary business. In the parliament, the Bolte government faced a delicate political situation. It did not have a majority in the upper house, and a former Country

Party, now independent, member, Percy Feltham, held the balance of power. Feltham held the balance following his resignation from the Country Party after a dispute with the party leader, George Moss, over the presidency of the Legislative Council. A solicitor and farmer, Supreme Court prize-winner at the University of Melbourne in 1923, and a former associate to Justice Sir Hayden Starke of the High Court, Feltham was—unusually for a conservative politician from a rural electorate—a convinced abolitionist.[12] Elected as the Country Party member for Northern Province in 1955, Feltham left the party in 1966 and held the balance of power for over a year until his defeat at the election of April 1967. His son, John, a former member of the Victorian bar and a law tutor of Magdalen College, Oxford, later would be involved in an appeal by Ryan to the Privy Council in London.

The government was concerned not to antagonise Feltham and hence jeopardise passage of its Stamps Bill, a budget bill then before the Legislative Council. In the budget of September 1966 the Bolte government had introduced a controversial new provision under the Stamps Bill increasing duties payable on various credit arrangements. Feltham had voted with the Country Party and the Labor Party in opposing the bill at its first attempted passage. After intense and open lobbying, he subsequently switched his support to the government, and the bill was finally passed—much amended—through both houses on 7 December at the second attempt. Had Feltham held out against the bill a second time—both on the substantive grounds of his objection to the bill, and his evident desire to obviate the anticipated decision to hang Ryan—he could have defeated the bill and precipitated an early election. With the defeat of a budget bill the government may have felt entitled, or obliged, to call a double dissolution.[13]

There was another reason why the premier delayed. Bolte was concerned not to have the execution while parliament was sitting. To do so would be to provide a privileged and effective political platform for opposition attacks on the hanging. Given that the Labor opposition, the Country Party, and Feltham outnumbered the government in the Legislative Council, such a platform also might have adverse consequences for government legislation in that chamber. In seeking to avoid parliamentary scrutiny of a cabinet decision on commutation by holding an execution while parliament was in recess, Bolte was adopting a well-established political tactic. The previous eight executions in

Victoria—in 1936, 1939, 1941, and 1951—had all been held when state parliament was not sitting. With the Stamps Bill having been passed on 7 December, and parliament having risen for the summer recess, Bolte put the Ryan issue on the agenda for the cabinet meeting of 12 December 1966.

To all outward appearances, the cabinet meeting would consider the cases of Ryan and that of two other convicted murderers under sentence of death: Antonio Rosamilia, 43, and Robert David Parslow, 21. Parslow had been convicted and sentenced to death in the Supreme Court before Justice Gregory Gowans on 10 June 1966 for the shooting murder of his parents after an argument over his heavy drinking and the use of a motor car whilst his licence had been suspended. Evidence before the court was that Parslow, while extremely intoxicated, had become aggressive with his parents and had shot them in the head with a rifle.[14] On 17 June 1966, also before Justice Gowans, Rosamilia had been convicted in the Supreme Court of the stabbing murder of his estranged lover, and sentence of death had been pronounced. Evidence had been presented in court that Rosamilia had used a stiletto knife to stab his lover nine times about the body and throat, inflicting fatal injuries, before attempting suicide.[15]

Although the cases of Rosamilia and Parslow also carried the death penalty, it was cabinet's consideration of the Ryan case that was the centre of public attention and anticipation. Behind the scenes, however, Ryan's fate had already been sealed, at least as far as the premier's intentions were concerned. Although the public was unaware of the fact, Bolte had already signalled his plans for Ryan to senior Melbourne newspaper executives long before cabinet met formally on the matter. Several weeks before the cabinet meeting, Bolte had told his friend, Sir John Williams, managing director of The Herald and Weekly Times (HWT), publisher of *The Herald* and *The Sun*, that he was determined to see Ryan hanged.

Often, once a week or more, Bolte and Rylah would have a late-afternoon drink with Williams in the boardroom of HWT at its Flinders Street offices. Bolte told Williams that he supported hanging Ryan because he was concerned to protect prison officers and police from the kind of violence that Ryan had perpetrated against Hodson during the escape from Pentridge. Williams understood Bolte's concern, but on the principle of the death penalty he was unmoved. A devout Roman

Catholic and a convinced abolitionist, Williams' opposition to capital punishment was based not merely on religious conviction, but on a deep moral sense that the death penalty was wrong. Williams told Bolte that his papers would strongly oppose him on the Ryan-hanging issue.[16]

Bolte also had told executives at *The Age* that Ryan would hang. In off-the-record conversations with the managing director of David Syme & Co Limited and publisher of *The Age*, Ranald Macdonald, and the newspaper's editor, Graham Perkin, Bolte had made it plain that cabinet would not commute Ryan's sentence.[17] Supported by Macdonald, who was also at this time editor-in-chief of *The Age*, Perkin signalled his intention to editorially oppose the execution. In response, Bolte told Perkin and Macdonald that he would 'beat the press' on the issue. 'I'll take you on and I'll beat you', Bolte had said.[18]

Although there would not be any media campaign in advance of the cabinet meeting on Ryan, the lines had been drawn for a battle that would see relations between the Melbourne press and the premier—an important basis for his political success—strained to breaking point. Personal relations between Williams and Bolte would also be deeply affected; in fact, they were never fully to recover. Most importantly, it would also see the premier take the extraordinary step of involving the governor of Victoria in an attempt to stifle critical coverage of the issue by *The Age*.

As the fifteen members of cabinet entered the cabinet room on the first floor of 2 Treasury Place on Monday, 12 December, all of them were focused on the issue of Ryan and the terrible decision they would have to make. Sometimes on Sunday nights, before the weekly cabinet meeting the next morning, there would be phone calls between ministers seeking each other's views about issues on the cabinet agenda. This time there were no particular pre-cabinet discussions on Ryan.

Although all of the cabinet ministers had been involved in commutation decisions before, Ryan's case was different. The questions that normally predominated in previous cases were irrelevant in this one. Was the prisoner provoked at the time he committed the murder? Had he been submitted to a long intimidation? Had his life history been such as to create in him a tendency to act in this manner? Did he commit the offence in a fit of sudden rage? Did he attempt to commit a burglary, armed with a gun? Was he a person who had months in which to prepare plans for the murder? Did he ponder over it for a long time? These were questions for other commutation cases, but they were entirely unhelpful in considering the fate of a prisoner who had escaped from legal custody and killed a state official, a prison officer, while he was doing his duty.

In the view of ministers attending cabinet that day, what they were doing was performing the ancient duty of deciding whether to advise the head of state to exercise the royal prerogative of mercy to a condemned man because of mitigating circumstances. Cabinet was required by precedent, if not by statute, to give reason for a commutation to the governor. The formal executive authority of cabinet government was the Executive Council—the governor of Victoria acting upon the advice of ministers as his constitutional advisers. When a jury in a capital case found a defendant guilty of murder and added a recommendation for mercy—as they were entitled to do—cabinet would automatically commute the sentence.

But so long as capital punishment remained on the statute book, neither opposition to the death penalty *per se* nor public opinion about a particular case were valid reasons for commutation. To commute on these grounds would be to circumvent the legislative process and effect a temporary change in the law.[19] What ministers had to do in determining Ryan's fate, and so advising the governor, was to consider whether there were any extenuating circumstances, any mitigating factor, which might justify the commutation of his sentence. This was the sense of their obligations that ministers took with them to the cabinet room: capital punishment was the law, and they were simply following the law, except where special circumstances existed such as might justify mercy.

Prevalent though this view was among cabinet members, it had not always been followed, even by the Bolte cabinet. Indeed, sentences had been commuted without any evident extenuating circumstances. In the case of triple murderer John Desmond David, whose sentence was commuted by cabinet only ten months before Ryan's case was considered, attorney-general Rylah admitted publicly that it had been David's 'general psychiatric background' that had led cabinet to commute. He conceded that there was 'nothing specific' in that background.[20] In any event, since section 3 of the *Crimes Act 1958* quite explicitly stated: 'Whosoever is convicted of murder shall suffer death as a felon', any departure from that provision as a consequence of cabinet intervention and commutation could be argued to be 'effecting a temporary change in the law.'

Of course, to critical outsiders, there was another view about what ministers were doing at this fateful cabinet meeting and others like it. In the previous 25 years, of all the murders in respect of which sentence of death had been pronounced in Victoria, there had only been one murder that had been punished by death: the 1949 murder of Pop Kent by Jean Lee, Robert Clayton, and Norman Andrews. Capital punishment, therefore, had in fact been reserved by cabinet for quite exceptional cases. This function was sanctioned by section 496 of the *Crimes Act 1958*, which prescribed that the governor, acting upon the advice of his executive councillors, could exercise Her Majesty's prerogative of mercy and commute a sentence of death. In that event, the Executive Council had to determine a term of imprisonment and fix a minimum non-parole period. Hence, on this view, the function of the cabinet in relation to persons sentenced to death had become one of actively determining whether the case had exceptional features which made it necessary, in the interests of the community, that the death sentence be carried out.[21]

Now, as they took their places around the mahogany table in the room that had been used for Victorian cabinet meetings for 90 years, the ministers had before them the papers and reports upon which Ryan's fate would rest. There was the formal report of the trial judge, Justice Starke, notifying the attorney-general in the usual way that Ryan had been found guilty by the jury on 30 March, and that sentence of death had been pronounced.[22] There was a 56-page summary of the evidence in Ryan's trial, the summing up by Justice Starke, and the judgment of the Court of Criminal Appeal.[23] The director of the prisons division of the Social Welfare Department, Eric Shade, provided a two-page report concerning Ryan's family history and social background, his first criminal convictions, and subsequent criminal history, and gave an account of his health and prison record.

Although, as with all of these reports before ministers, it made no recommendation to cabinet, the prisons division report included all the evidence within the area of Ryan's criminal and prison record that would have been helpful to those ministers seeking to justify a commutation. In relation to the escape from Pentridge and the murder of prison officer Hodson, the report stated:

> Ryan says that when the escape was planned violence was not intended. He claims that he took the rifle from the post only because he was afraid it would be used otherwise. He still does not admit he fired the shot which killed the officer, but he says that anything that did happen was done in the heat of the moment, without pre-meditation …
>
> Ryan was 31 years old before he was first convicted, but … there is no doubt that he made a profession of crime. His early deprivations led him to value highly stable home life and material security. He says that when he was sentenced to imprisonment in 1964 he expected to have to serve 13 years imprisonment. He determined to escape, but not at any cost, and in particular he says he did not intend violence.[24]

A psychiatric report on Ryan was also provided to ministers. The three-page report of the Pentridge psychiatrist, Dr Allen Bartholomew, gave an assessment of Ryan's psychiatric condition. This was based upon eight examinations Bartholomew had made of him over a period of ten months from 8 January 1966, shortly after his re-capture in Sydney, until 10 November 1966, just six days before Bartholomew's report, when he spent two hours with him. Bartholomew concluded:

> I do not consider the prisoner suffers from any formal mental illness but that he is 'normal' unless we choose to use the label a psychopathic personality …
>
> He gives a background history (as far as he is prepared to go) that from an early childhood age (uncertain how old) he lost his father and went away to live. After his schooling he worked, rented a house and got his three younger sisters out of a convent, educated and looked after them and finally established them in society. After this, he himself got married. He therefore says, 'You see I never had a childhood or a good time as a young man—I've always been a father' …
>
> He told his whole story in a cheerful, breezy manner interwoven with some highly amusing anecdotes. By no stretch of the imagination could one say that he showed any remorse for his actions or any apparent anxiety regarding his immediate predicament …
>
> In my opinion he is a man of intelligence who shows no remorse

> and virtually no anxiety —he is 'psychopathic'. I feel that the future is basically unmeaningful to him, he enjoys 'today' and enjoys being in the spotlight. Otherwise he is psychologically 'normal'.[25]

A further submission before cabinet was an impassioned four-page letter written by Phil Opas to Arthur Rylah on 20 October 1966. Opas requested Rylah to bring the letter to the cabinet's attention in its deliberations on Ryan. Later there would be controversy about this letter, with critics of the government asserting that it had been withheld from ministers by the premier. However, this criticism was not well based, for the letter was included in the cabinet papers hand-delivered by the Law Department to ministers' private secretaries on 24 November 1966. Writing, he said, as a private citizen rather than as a lawyer, Opas urged that Ryan's life be spared. He began:

> I deplore any effort which might be made to make a political football of the issue of life or death for Ryan, and I dissociate myself entirely from any efforts, well-meant or otherwise, to use Ryan's case as a pressure point to abolish capital punishment.
>
> In fact I am not opposed to capital punishment as such, but I believe that special reasons exist for not hanging Ryan. The first of these reasons is that I am not convinced of Ryan's guilt.

Opas went on to argue that there was reasonable doubt that Ryan fired the fatal shot. In his conclusion he said:

> At the end of a long and close association with this case, I have an uncomfortable feeling that Ryan may be innocent of this killing. No amount of reconsideration of the evidence can remove this gnawing and lingering doubt that remains.[26]

Opas' letter was accompanied by a short two-page covering memorandum from Tony Murray. Rylah had asked Murray to give his views on the Opas submission.[27] In his memorandum, Murray acknowledged that Opas' letter was 'a sincere document and not … a pleading by a barrister on behalf of his client', although he concluded that 'the arguments advanced by Opas were all put to the jury and rejected by it. I am afraid I am unable to share the doubts expressed by Mr. Opas.'[28] However, knowing that his memorandum might find its way into cabinet, and fully understanding cabinet's role in considering any mitigating circumstances that might lead to a commutation, Murray added several astute and positive comments about Ryan and his crime. His comments indicated to an observant reader what had become evident to people around Murray: although he had prosecuted Ryan with all the skill and vigour at his disposal, over the course of the trial he had come to have some regard for him as a human being, and he believed that he did not deserve to hang.[29] As Murray wrote in the memorandum:

> My own impression, gained at the trial and from little bits of information from gaol officials, police, etc, is that Ryan is a fairly intelligent man and is probably not by nature violent. I believe that he was faced with the loss of his wife and children and with a long term of imprisonment. His situation led him to conceive a desperate and daring plan of escape.
>
> It is true to say that he had opportunities to act violently during the execution of the plan and did not take them. In some instances his plan would have had a better chance of success if he had been violent. For example, if he had stunned the warder whom he forced to open the gates, the alarm would not have been raised so quickly and he might have seized a car and escaped before anyone knew what had happened.
>
> My impression is that Ryan hoped to make good his escape without violence but was prepared to use violence if necessary. When he saw Walker being pursued by Hodson the necessity arose.
>
> I suppose it is also fair to say that, at the time, Ryan expected to be shot at any moment by the warder on the wall and that he, himself, fired in the heat of the moment.
>
> There is, in my opinion, no comparison between the premeditated and cold-blooded killing of Henderson by Walker (which simply amounted to an execution) and the killing of Hodson by Ryan in the circumstances in which it occurred. Walker is extremely fortunate that the jury [in Walker's trial for the murder of Henderson] (actuated principally, I am told, by a dislike of capital punishment) found him guilty of manslaughter and not murder.[30]

This was a crucially important submission. Had there been a general will among ministers to commute the death sentence, this memorandum from the man who had successfully led the prosecution team at Ryan's trial provided the basis for doing so. As the solicitor-general submitted, the murder of Hodson had been an act committed in 'the heat of the moment' and in circumstances where Ryan had hoped to avoid violence. The trial judge and jury were obliged to consider Ryan's killing of Hodson as murder because of the felony-murder rule, but cabinet could take into account—as judge and jury could not—that the murder had been committed in the heat of the moment. Of all the documents that went to cabinet on Ryan, this one offered ministers grounds for recommending to the governor a commutation of Ryan's sentence.

Also included in the dossier to ministers was a short letter from Ryan's sister, Gloria. Addressed to the director-general of social welfare, the letter was a plea for clemency:

> We find it impossible to believe our brother could kill any human being in cold blood. My brother is a man, who, at the age of 16, by sheer hard work and self-denial, made it possible for my sister and myself to leave the Good Shepherd Convent in Abbotsford where we spent almost 6 years.
>
> Even to this day I can recall how Ron returned exhausted after weeks spent in the bush cutting sleepers, so that his mother and sisters could have a decent home, food, clothing and the chance for my sister and myself to finish our education in less formidable surroundings.
>
> Our brother took upon himself this great responsibility of father, son and brother, when our invalid father could no longer support us. Surely this shows him to be a very warm and unselfish human being, not a cold-blooded killer. We can all attest to Ron's love and deep family affections, leaving it impossible to accept the fact that mother's son, and our dearest brother, might hang.
>
> In closing I can only say we live in hope, and pray the powers that be see fit to grant my brother clemency. We, his loving family and numerous friends, are still deeply distressed over the grave doubts which arose over his actual part in the unfortunate incident.[31]

While the Opas submission and Gloria's plea were positive for Ryan, there was other material that was damaging to his prospects of commutation. Perhaps the most damning report was that provided on Ryan's antecedents by Victoria Police. The purpose of a police report to cabinet was to disclose the previous convictions recorded against a prisoner, whether he had shown a tendency to assault people, whether he was a brutal type of person, and whether there were any matters that should be considered in relation to the question of clemency. Included for consideration by cabinet was a densely typed, two-page police report prepared by Detective Sergeant Walters of the homicide squad. Walters' report provided a comprehensive account of Ryan's antecedents and a summary of his adult offences going back to the arson at Noojee in 1953. Taken as a whole, it represented a substantial criminal record.[32]

In all, Ryan had been convicted of almost 30 criminal offences in the period between 1956 and 1964. More damaging, however, was Walters' listing of each of the nine offences between 4 April and 11 July 1964 for which Ryan was wanted by police in NSW. These included the armed robbery on 28 June 1964 at the Rosehill Bowling Club, to which Ryan had confessed to NSW police in a handwritten confession.[33] As the report showed, Ryan's record was one of a recidivist offender whose criminal activity had escalated from cheque forging to breaking and entering, and then to armed robbery and, finally, to murder. While there was reference to Ryan's responsible role as a father, the report concluded that Ryan 'harbours a deep seated opposition to authority in any form'.[34]

Seated around the cabinet table were the fifteen men who made up Sir Henry Bolte's ministry. Cabinet first considered the recommendations relating to the sentences of Rosamilia and Parslow, the two other murderers under sentence of death. Accepting the recommendations of the attorney-general in relation to Rosamilia, cabinet resolved to recommend to the governor that he 'extend mercy on condition that the prisoner be imprisoned for 25 years with a minimum period of twenty years during which he shall not be eligible to be released on parole'.[35] Similarly, cabinet agreed to commute Parslow's sentence to twenty years' imprisonment, with a minimum period of fifteen years to serve.[36]

Ministers next turned to the matter of Ryan. They were shortly joined in the cabinet room by an important outsider, one whose likely contribution to the discussion had troubled him for some months in advance of the meeting. Present at the request of the attorney-general was Justice John Starke. Unlike the process in other Australian states, it had been the practice in Victoria since colonial times for the governor to require a report from the trial judge when death sentences were being considered.[37] In practice, this meant that the trial judge was specially invited to attend cabinet for this purpose, and the trial judge always attended. This was to give ministers the opportunity of hearing from him first-hand about any aspects of the case that ministers might wish to raise, and to have the benefit of the judge's perspective on the trial and, particularly, the verdict.

Other Australian states, and some academic lawyers, saw this practice as an infringement upon the principle of the separation of powers—the principle that the judiciary should not be accountable to the executive for judicial decisions. However, Victorian judges historically had taken the view that, since they were invited and not required to go to cabinet for such a purpose, and since information was being imparted rather than accountability rendered, no breach of the separation-of-powers doctrine occurred.[38] The trial judge in the cases of Rosamilia and David, Justice Gregory Gowans, had earlier attended cabinet and duly indicated his views.

Like his Supreme Court brethren, Justice Starke had no problem with accepting an invitation to attend cabinet as the trial judge. Starke had not attended cabinet for such a purpose since his appointment to the Supreme Court bench in February 1964, but he knew the form such meetings took and he saw a positive value in his attendance for capital cases. Indeed, from his own experience as a criminal barrister, he knew that juries sometimes returned verdicts for 'murder' when a finding of 'manslaughter' was a more appropriate one. In those circumstances a trial judge had no alternative to pronouncing the death sentence, even though the sentence was inappropriate.

On the day that Starke attended the cabinet meeting considering the Ryan case, he knew that one of the questions he would be asked would concern his judgment about the jury's verdict. It was a question that he had dreaded and agonised about for many weeks, although his anxiety had been tempered by a lingering, irrational hope since the trial had concluded at the end of March that the government would commute Ryan's sentence after all. Starke's concern was not whether he had doubts about the validity of the verdict, for in truth he had none, but whether he should feign doubt to the cabinet. All of Starke's anti-hanging convictions told him that he had an obligation to do whatever he could to avoid an execution that offended him and which he believed to be morally repugnant. The question that had weighed heavily on the mind of John Starke, distinguished former barrister and life-long abolitionist, these several weeks and months past—and which troubled him still as he entered the cabinet room—was whether he should tell a lie to save a man's life.[39]

The core of the lie that Starke entertained in his mind was that he could cast doubt on the soundness of the verdict. Starke could think of a number of issues upon which he might base and express this fiction. Certainly, he believed that the jury had been influenced by the prosecution's evidence of Ryan's several admissions of guilt. While he felt sure that the jury had reached the right conclusion in finding Ryan guilty, Starke—casting himself in his mind momentarily as the defence advocate he had so successfully been—thought it was possible to discard as unreliable the several confessions that the prosecution said Ryan had made.

First, much had been made of the statement attributed to Ryan during the ANZ Bank hold-up, when he and Walker had menaced bank staff and customers with a rifle and exhorted: 'This is an American rifle M1, and I've already killed someone with it!' In Starke's view, the press had already widely publicised the escape and characterised the rifle as the Hodson murder weapon. That Ryan used the rifle's status to effect compliance among hold-up victims might be expected in such circumstances, but Ryan's statement did not impress 'defence advocate' Starke as an admission of guilt.

The second confession arose out of the trial testimony of John Fisher, who claimed that Ryan had confessed to the murder when he met him at the Christmas Eve party in Ormond Road, Elwood, while the escapees were hiding out. Starke knew that Fisher had a criminal history, and was keen to win the reward offered for the capture and conviction of Ryan as Hodson's killer. In Starke's view, the reliability of his evidence was questionable, to say the least.

The third confession was the unsigned, off-the-record interview taken by Detective Sergeant Walters that was produced as evidence in court, in which Ryan had said about Hodson: 'He didn't have to interfere. He was stupid. He was told to keep away. He grabbed hold of Pete and hit him with an iron bar. He caused his own death. I didn't want to shoot him. I could have shot a lot more.' Again, in Starke's mind, it was highly unlikely that Ryan would make such an admission, having moments before in a signed statement to police eschewed just such self-incrimination.

The fourth confession concerned the admission Ryan was alleged to have made to Senior Detective Morrison on the aircraft bringing him back from Sydney after his recapture. Starke believed that it was possible to argue that this had been a police verbal. Again, Ryan had gone out of his way to say, just hours before at his extradition proceedings before a magistrate, that he would not be making any admissions, and he would 'make no further statements on the trip back to Melbourne'. Now, it had been alleged, he had spilled the beans to police in a situation where there were no independent witnesses. As Starke knew from many years of experience as a criminal barrister, this was the classic setting for police verballing a suspect.

However, it was Starke's view that, even if they had discarded these confessions as unreliable, the jury had been entitled to convict Ryan. Starke was clear in his mind that the verdict of 'guilty' was sound. As he debated these issues with himself, he considered ways he could point out to the cabinet the weaknesses in the confessions, thereby conveying a doubt in his mind that the cabinet might recognise, and which they might use to decide the issue of commutation in Ryan's favour. While he held out hope that Ryan might be spared by the cabinet, Starke was convinced that Sir Henry Bolte, at least, was determined to see Ryan hanged. Knowing Bolte as he believed he did, Starke was a supporter of the Tait-substitute theory—that Bolte had been frustrated in his wish to see Tait executed, and that he had resolved to execute the next good candidate for the gallows as a way of re-asserting his political authority.

As Starke entered the cabinet room, the mood that greeted him was business-like. Taking a seat at the table next to the premier, Starke gave a summary of the evidence and his overall assessment of Ryan's crime. He was asked several questions by ministers in relation to the case. Ministers Rylah, Hamer, and Bloomfield asked questions relating to evidence at the trial, and one of them asked about the controversial evidence of prison officer Paterson. Starke indicated his view that Paterson was more erratic than untruthful. In time, after a number of questions had been asked and answered, the question that had so troubled Starke was asked by the premier:

'Do you agree with the verdict, Judge?'

The moment of truth had come for Jack Starke.

'Yes', he replied, without amplification.

For an instant after he had answered, Starke's mind raced through the terrible implications of what he had said, and he wanted to take the word back. Could he yet prevaricate successfully in some way? Was there another way he could resile from his bald affirmation and deflect ministers from the course upon which he believed they were set? There was not. Against all his instincts and beliefs about the barbarity of capital punishment, Starke's innate honesty and integrity had won out. He could not go through with his elaborately constructed barrister's demolition of the verdict. He could not tell a lie. Although ministers were unaware of his anguish, Starke's reply was an important moment in the course of the cabinet meeting, and its meaning was clear. The minister of education, John Bloomfield, later commented that he would have been very worried had Starke said he had disagreed with the verdict.[40]

It was also a significant moment in the life of Jack Starke. After the cabinet meeting, and for some time later, Starke would wonder whether, as a relatively new judge as he then was, he had been over-awed by the standing of the cabinet and the court, and his responsibilities as a member of the bench rather than to his fellow man. Should he have told a lie? Had he done the right thing? For a man who had been passionately involved for the defence in two of the most celebrated capital cases in Australian criminal history, and who now had heard the trial of a third, these were questions that would weigh heavily on his mind for the rest of his life. Not long before his death in November 1994, almost 30 years after the case, Jack Starke was still worried that, in telling the truth to cabinet, he had failed in what he saw as his simple human duty to save Ronald Ryan from the gallows.

After Starke had withdrawn from the cabinet room, the premier indicated that the attorney-general and chief secretary, Arthur Rylah, would speak to his recommendation on Ryan, and then ministers would be invited to speak on the issue. Ministers were in no doubt that Bolte was determined to have his way, but the premier was concerned to ensure that every minister around the cabinet table had an adequate opportunity to express his view. Cabinet usually operated on a consensus basis with no votes taken and, despite the gravity of the decision they were about to make, would not proceed to vote now.

As attorney-general, Rylah was the minister responsible for the administration of justice and, hence, it was his responsibility to bring forward a recommendation about how the premier might advise the governor. Rylah had been Bolte's loyal deputy for almost twelve years, and would remain so for the entirety of Bolte's premiership. Rylah had opposed the use of the death penalty generally, and—with the exception of Tait—he had recommended commutation for all cases coming before the Bolte cabinet since 1955. If Bolte had been the canny populist politician in this administration, Rylah was a tireless minister who carried a huge portfolio burden as both chief secretary and attorney-general. Rylah also pushed a reform agenda, and for many years his impressive work, particularly in the field of company law reform, had gone largely unrecognised.[41] Rylah was also more socially progressive than he was often portrayed. On Jack Galbally's private member's Trap Shooting Bill of November 1958, a bill intended to outlaw the shooting of live birds released from traps, and a bill that Bolte had vehemently opposed, Rylah with only two other Liberals, had crossed the floor and voted with the Labor Party to support it.[42] Even though Liberal members had been allowed a conscience vote on the issue, this was a bold move for Bolte's deputy.

Despite their close political partnership, Rylah and Bolte were quite different in their political styles and social outlooks. Bolte, the politically astute big-picture man with strong populist instincts, was impatient with ideas and the detail of public administration. Rylah, by contrast, relished policy development and the implementation of legislation, a passion he shared with his formidable head of department, under-secretary Jack Dillon. If it could be said about Bolte that he had the conservative outlook of a country farmer, Rylah's was that of a moderate, liberal city lawyer. On social policy issues, generally, Rylah was a pragmatic moderate; and he was, by persuasion, an opponent of the use of the death penalty in most cases. At the time of the Tait case Rylah had previously fought to commute all death sentences. But he had not supported commutation in Tait's case and, throughout the controversy that followed the decision, as attorney-general he had acted virtually as the sole government spokesman on the matter.[43]

Certainly, even longer ago, at the time of the Jean Lee case, Rylah had supported capital punishment. In December 1950, under the minority Country Party government of premier Jack McDonald—exactly sixteen years before cabinet sat on Ryan's case—Rylah had been one of a number of state politicians whose views of the decision to hang Lee,

Clayton, and Andrews had been canvassed by Melbourne newspapers. Rylah, then an opposition Liberal backbencher, had said: 'Capital punishment is a necessary deterrent in bad murder cases.'[44]

Now Rylah had brought to cabinet a recommendation that ministers advise the governor that Ryan's death sentence should go ahead. But he was worried about it for a number of reasons. Primarily, he was concerned that the Executive Council be consistent in its practice of commutation. There had been awful murder cases in the past that had not brought the death penalty: how would this one be perceived publicly when so many other murderers had had their sentences commuted? Having taken the full force of the political fall-out from the Tait case, Rylah was also worried about the damaging political consequences of a drawn-out process to bring Ryan to execution.

There was also the responsible opinion of the church leaders. Rylah then referred to a submission from the president of the Methodist Church, the Rev John Westerman. Forewarned by Rylah several days before cabinet met that no commutation was likely in Ryan's case, Westerman had prepared a number of hurried but well-expressed submissions that were given to Rylah on the morning of the cabinet meeting. The seven-page letter from Westerman contained a number of little-known facts about Ryan's background and, under six headings, gave temperate and well-argued reasons why Ryan's sentence should be commuted. Rylah said that Westerman's submission had merit.[45]

On the other hand, Rylah was concerned about Ryan's bad criminal record, and his capacity to threaten violence, particularly as it became evident in the armed robbery at Rosehill, NSW, in 1964. He drew the attention of his colleagues to the police report in their dossiers indicating that Ryan was facing extradition to NSW for the nine offences in 1964, including the Rosehill robbery in which Ryan had fired a shot. NSW police had a signed confession from Ryan regarding these offences, Rylah reminded his colleagues, even if that fact could not be disclosed publicly because Ryan had never been charged with those offences.

For all his reservations, as he put his views to his cabinet colleagues, Rylah argued that, if capital punishment was ever justified, the Ryan case fell into this category. As chief secretary, Rylah held ministerial responsibility over the social welfare department (and, hence, the department's prisons division), and the police department, and he was concerned to demonstrate loyalty to his departmental officers. Beyond those considerations there was an important responsibility on government in the Ryan case, Rylah said. The government must be seen to be 'protecting the protectors', supporting those police and prison officers who daily put their lives at risk in providing security for the community.

Rylah also referred to the two letters to *Truth* that Ryan had written during the time he was at large following the escape from Pentridge. The *Truth* letters, he emphasised, had hit out at the police force and the administration of prisons and of justice in Victoria, and announced a fantastic plan to re-distribute the wealth of the community. As we have earlier seen, the first letter, posted three days after the escape, proclaimed, *inter alia*:

> We, the Pentridge escapees, are the van of a new era in crime in Victoria—a role which we are loathe to adopt! The present state of affairs, and its explosive potential have been forced upon us by a combination of factors [:the] partial corruptness of the Victorian Police Department, injustice at their hands, ill considered harsh sentences by the judiciary: the practice of brutality and mental torture by the Gestapo-like prison warders in 'HELL' Division at Pentridge.
>
> ... [W]e refuse to accept the present social pattern and its inherent lack of fairness and chances of equality in the sense of just reward. The worker does not get a fair share of production and consequently, is condemned along with his family, to a life of glorified slavedom. I, as the last of the Ryans, on the male side, intend to put a stop to this.[46]

The second letter to *Truth* further denigrated the police, declaring:

> We feel that the offer of [an] immediate and large reward [for information leading to the escapees' capture] reflects their physical fear of <u>courageous, unjustly treated</u> men, and an acknowledgement of their incompetence.

The letter continued the theme of economic equality begun in the first letter, and announced:

> We advocate a greater share of production for all workers—a more even distribution of the country's wealth ... We implore you to support the dedicated men of the trade unions ...
>
> We, Ryan and Walker, are respected by our contemporaries, and have been unanimously elected to highlight their case for a better deal.[47]

It is doubtful that the threats contained in these letters by Ryan should be seen as other than braggadocio. Nevertheless they created a perception of Ryan at odds with the notion that he had redeeming features which might be sufficient to justify the recommendation by cabinet of the exercise of the prerogative of mercy. Certainly, if taken seriously, the *Truth* letters posed a problem for a government responsible for Ryan's secure incarceration; the prospect of him organising his fellow inmates around political issues relevant to convicted men was not one to be welcomed by the government. The more disturbing question raised by the letters was that, given that he had already escaped from legal custody, and had shot and killed a prison officer in the process, how could government ensure that Ryan would not try again to escape and commit violent acts leading to innocent lives being lost? For all these reasons, and despite his serious misgivings, Rylah's recommendation on Ryan was that the law should take its course. It was clear that, while he had reservations, Rylah was not about to desert his leader in a case where the premier was prepared to risk his political authority.

Following the attorney's recommendation, the premier opened the discussion for others to speak on the issue. Starting with the most junior ministers first—just like a court martial—the premier invited each of the ministers to indicate their views. In the event, not all ministers chose to speak on the issue. Apart from the four parliamentary leaders (Bolte and Rylah in the lower house and Gill Chandler, the leader in the upper house and his deputy, Lindsay Thompson), cabinet seniority was determined by the date at which ministers had been first appointed. In the days and weeks that followed this cabinet meeting, there would be newspaper reports that there were deep divisions on Ryan among ministers, and that four—and possibly up to seven—ministers had strongly opposed the decision that Ryan should hang. What emerged over the three-and-a-half hours of cabinet discussions, however, was subtly but importantly different. There was indeed a significant division of opinion about the principle of capital punishment and the issue of consistency in the practice of recommending commutations, with four ministers having misgivings about the use of the death penalty against Ryan. But there was no substantive difference on the merits of a commutation for Ryan.

As the newest minister, having been appointed as minister of state development just twelve months before, Jim Manson was the first to speak. A Glasgow-born Scot who had worked for several years as the public relations officer of the Liberal Party before winning the Melbourne outer-suburban seat of Ringwood, the softly spoken Manson briefly said that he was opposed to capital punishment, but conceded that Ryan's was a bad case.

Next to speak was the minister of health, Vance Dickie. Making this decision on Ryan was one that Dickie would later describe as the biggest he had ever had to make, but it was one in which he strongly supported the death penalty being invoked. Support for capital punishment had been Dickie's view for a very long time. As early as 1956, and again in 1959 and 1962, he had indicated in parliamentary debates that he was in favour of the imposition of capital punishment—arguing that, for cases of brutal murder, it was fit and proper that the punishment of hanging should be retained.[48] Invoking an analogy in all three speeches to the parliament during this period, between soldiers killing the king's enemies to safeguard the state and the state taking life to protect itself, Dickie said (rather ambiguously, but no doubt unintentionally): 'I do not believe that it is morally wrong and un-Christian-like to take the life of another human being.'[49] A strong retentionist to the end, several years later he would oppose the capital punishment abolition bill of 1975, and assert that it was a sad day when the death penalty was abolished.[50]

Dickie was followed by the minister of labour and industry, Vernon Wilcox, who was seen as a Bolte protégé. Vern Wilcox was a thoughtful and considerate man who believed that people could legitimately hold opposing views for and against capital punishment. His own views, however, were strongly in support of the death penalty. In a debate in the Legislative Assembly in September 1963 on the incidence of crime in the community, Wilcox, a barrister before his election to parliament, had expressed strong support for upholding sentences of death, and had lashed out at woolly-headed idealists who opposed them. Expressing his support for the law and his frustration with abolitionist sentiment, Wilcox had said then:

> I cannot quite see the point in allowing the death sentence to remain on the statute book unless it is carried out from time to time, as considered necessary. In the past twelve months there have been several cases in which the facts have been more than enough to justify the death penalty. If the death sentence is to remain on the statute book I believe that from time to time a criminal ... should be hanged. I do not blame the Government for the fact that the death penalty is not imposed, but I do blame a lot of woolly-headed and sentimental people for their approach to the problem of dealing with criminals. I am fed up with psychologists, psychiatrists and 'do-gooders'.[51]

Wilcox told cabinet that, for him—as he believed the premier similarly felt—the distinguishing feature of the Ryan case was that Ryan had killed someone in authority. It was not a murder committed within a domestic circle of family and others with whom the offender regularly came in contact; it involved the murder of a prison officer, 'virtually the last line of defence which law-abiding citizens have for their protection'. He told cabinet that Bolte should be supported.[52]

The minister of immigration and assistant minister of education, Jack Rossiter, was next to speak. He indicated that he opposed commuting Ryan's sentence. Although he would several years later vote for the abolition of capital punishment, in Ryan's case Rossiter did not believe that the government could do other than support the death penalty. As the discussion continued, other ministers similarly expressed the view that Ryan's was not a case where mitigating circumstances existed, and that the death penalty should go ahead. Although they did not speak, the minister of water supply, Tom Darcy, and the minister of lands, Jim Balfour, were in agreement. Their view was that commutation was not warranted.

When it was the turn of the minister for local government, Rupert (Dick) Hamer, to speak, the first serious reservations were expressed. Hamer had come into the ministry during the Tait case to fill the gap left by Sir Arthur Warner's resignation. Regarded as one of the more progressive members of the Liberal Party, Hamer was even then seen as a likely future premier. Hamer had been steadily converted towards opposition to capital punishment following his election to the Legislative Council in 1958. Each year it was Hamer's duty on behalf of the government to lead the opposition to Jack Galbally's annual presentation of a private member's bill for the abolition of capital punishment. After much study of the subject, it had become apparent to Hamer that 'execution was abhorrent, that the statistics showed that the death penalty was not a deterrent to murder, and that it was being abolished in most civilised countries without adverse effects.'[53]

In debates in the council in 1959 Hamer first voiced his concern at the prescription of the maximum penalty for all cases of murder:

> I would be the first to agree that the law and the administration of justice in connection with the matter of murder is unsatisfactory. The Royal Commission [Britain 1949-'53] thought so, too. The Commission considered that it was unsatisfactory that the death penalty should be a general penalty for the whole range of different types of murder.[54]

In November 1965, Hamer reiterated his view, stated some six years previously, that 'in the vast majority of homicide cases there are extenuating circumstances which mitigate the full severity of premeditated killing.'[55] It was Hamer's view that the extinction of a human life was such a barbarous act that it could be justified in an enlightened society only on grounds of the highest public policy. The principal support for such a policy generally emerged from the belief that for the worst of crimes—murder and treason—the death penalty had some unique deterrent effect, not shared for instance by imprisonment for life, or for a very long period. The available evidence, Hamer believed, indicated that the death penalty did not in fact act as such a 'unique deterrent'.[56]

Speaking now of Ryan, Hamer said that the government's established policy of commutation should be applied again. For Hamer, a critical issue was the nature of the capital offence. He reminded his cabinet colleagues that ministers had recommended mercy in far worse cases of murder. Indeed, he argued, there were examples in the past where cabinet had recommended commutation in murder cases of a much more repulsive kind, and there were others involving real cruelty. Ryan's murder of Hodson had been committed on the spur of the moment, and was far from being the worst case of murder that cabinet had had to consider. This had to be borne in mind in considering Ryan's case, Hamer said. Cabinet had to be consistent in the way in which it considered its recommendation to the governor for the exercise of his prerogative of mercy. Hamer conceded, however, that Ryan's record showed few redeeming features and his crime was certainly bad. As he had indicated some years before, it was difficult to commute in the circumstances of the murder of a prison officer.

After Hamer had spoken, the housing minister, Ray Meagher, indicated his view that Ryan's crime was a shocking one and that the hanging should take its course. The essence of Meagher's view was that capital punishment was warranted in extreme circumstances. Although he believed that, in the majority of cases, extenuating circumstances could be found that would justify commutation, he did not believe that Ryan's was such a case. He believed that the state should reserve the right to carry out an execution, although not doing so in the majority of cases. Where a person accidentally killed in a crime of passion, or a fit of temper, a death sentence could be commuted. No–one should hang unless the circumstances of the crime were such that no other penalty was appropriate, but people were entitled to the protection provided by the reserve power to impose the ultimate penalty. Without that reserve power the community was disarmed, he believed.[57]

After the minister of public works, Murray Porter, had spoken, indicating his opposition to commutation, George Reid, the minister for fuel and power, also spoke in support of the death penalty. This was to be Reid's only contribution to the Ryan matter. Two days later he left Australia to attend a London conference and did not return until February. A solicitor, Reid was a minister without portfolio in the first Bolte cabinet, and assisted the chief secretary and attorney-general in both these portfolios. The only Roman Catholic member of cabinet, Reid entered the ministry with a stated interest in penal reform.[58] Although Reid had joined Arthur Rylah in crossing the floor to support the Labor bill banning live-bird trap-shooting in 1958, he was no abolitionist.[59] Reid had strong feelings on the deterrent effect of capital punishment, indeed of punishment generally. He was later to advocate whipping for people convicted of bashing charges, and at the same time indicated his belief that the courts were not imposing severe enough penalties.[60]

Reid's cabinet colleague, the minister of education, John Bloomfield, a senior minister (having been a member of the first Bolte cabinet in 1955), did not share such views. Described by his friends as a man of quiet understanding, Bloomfield was a patrician QC, and a long-standing opponent of capital punishment, if not an abolitionist.[61] An accomplished artist who exhibited his work from time to time, Bloomfield had painted in oils a portrait of his friend Jack Starke, whom he had known since their time together as young men at the bar. The picture of a young Starke hung in Starke's hallway at his house in Mt Eliza. Ten years before, Bloomfield had been strongly in opposition to a move by some ministers to carry into execution the death sentence on Sandor Mede in 1957.[62] Mede, 24, had been convicted of the murder of a milk bar proprietor who had befriended him. Although the jury recommended mercy, they had not known, as cabinet had, that Mede had been convicted seven years earlier of the manslaughter of a Greek sailor.[63] In relation to Ryan, Bloomfield was concerned, with Dick Hamer, that cabinet needed to be seen to be consistent in the way it exercised the prerogative of mercy, but he conceded that it was a bad business and that extenuating circumstances were hard to find.

The minister of housing, Lindsay Thompson, was the youngest member of cabinet; in time, he would become premier of Victoria. In speeches dating back to 1959 Thompson had asserted the significant deterrent value of capital punishment, and had been consistent in his advocacy of the death penalty in those cases where there was any likelihood that a brutal murderer might escape and kill again. At other times this advocacy had assumed an emotional character—as when, in an exchange during the Tait case in 1962, Thompson interjected to accuse Labor upper house leader Jack Galbally, during debate on his private member's bill, of being a 'supporter of murderers'.[64]

During the Tait case Thompson argued that, for a number of murders, capital punishment was an inappropriate form of punishment, although for other types it was certainly appropriate. Thompson quoted approvingly from retentionist works which expressed the view that it was not the time to reduce the protection that the law afforded to warders or men, women, and children: 'In the case of a violent prisoner undergoing a life sentence, the death penalty may be the only effective deterrent against his making a murderous assault on a fellow prisoner or a member of the prison staff.'[65] Although years later he would thoughtfully revise his view of the deterrent effect of capital punishment and support its abolition in 1975, in December 1966 Thompson believed conscientiously that Ryan's murder of prison officer Hodson was not a case warranting commutation of his death sentence.

The minister of agriculture and the leader of the government in the upper house, Gill Chandler, agreed. Ryan had shown a tendency to escape, and he had killed a warder in the most recent escape. That meant that his secure incarceration could not be guaranteed. No extenuating circumstances appeared evident in the case: the law should take its course.

When he came to speak, the premier, Sir Henry Bolte, could see that while four ministers—Hamer, Bloomfield, Manson and, to some extent, Rylah—had expressed reservations about the application of the death penalty in various ways, there was no dissent to his own view that Ryan's sentence should not be commuted. That Bolte was a firm supporter of capital punishment in certain circumstances had become evident several years earlier, when he had consolidated his predominant political position in the Liberal Party by vigorously pursuing the death penalty for Tait. The early years of the Bolte government had been dominated by the Liberal leader in the upper house, Sir Arthur Warner, described as one of the 'most successful but ruthless self-made industrialists living in the State', who had been Bolte's sponsor for the leadership.[66] Although Bolte had long before asserted his independence as leader, the issue on which he put his authority to perhaps the ultimate test was the decision on a commutation for Tait in 1962. The extent of Warner's influence on cabinet had been reflected in the government's policy on capital punishment up till then. Warner was a convinced abolitionist; he had even given private assurances to that effect to Barry Jones, the leader of the Anti-Hanging Committee. Although committed to publicly supporting Liberal policy on hanging, he was firmly opposed to the use of the death penalty. Warner had insisted to Jones: 'There will be no hangings in Victoria so long as I am a member of Cabinet.'[67]

By 1962 Warner's influence was waning, and he was in poor health. While he was still a member of the ministry, cabinet decided on 6 August 1962 not to commute Tait's sentence of death. Four weeks later, on 4 September, Warner resigned from cabinet—although he continued as a member of parliament—ostensibly for health reasons.[68] The approval by cabinet of Tait's death sentence was the first such confirmation in the six-and-a-half years since Bolte had come to power. The fifteen previous commutations in this time had included those of Sandor Mede in 1957, and Marinus Gerhard Van Ast in 1961, both found guilty of brutal crimes. Van Ast, 24, had been convicted and sentenced to death for the murder of his 21-year old pregnant wife. Evidence presented at his trial revealed that Van Ast, who had suspected that his wife had been unfaithful to him, had argued violently with her before he 'stabbed her fifteen times and buried her in a shallow grave at Tyabb, after first removing the rings from her fingers'.[69]

The Tait case was for Bolte the first time under his leadership that the Liberal government was subject to bitter personal and political attack, and to an almost total defection by the normally supportive Melbourne press. The crime itself, a particularly brutal murder of an elderly woman, had occurred at a time when the number of homicides committed in Victoria had suddenly increased alarmingly. In the ten-year period from 1951 to 1960 the number of homicides in Victoria had averaged 26 per year, and had not exceeded 33 murders in any one year. In 1961 the number of homicides had jumped, unaccountably, to sixty-one.[70] Here, it seemed, was the opportunity Bolte needed to finally assert his political leadership in an unmistakable confrontation—a prototypical Boltean showdown, a crisis of authority. The Tait case was to be a personal political battle that the premier was determined to win.

At the core of Sir Henry Bolte's attitude to capital punishment was his simple belief that sufficiently bad murderers should be hanged. In the case of a prisoner who had escaped from gaol, and shot and killed a prison officer, he was especially convinced that hanging was appropriate. How else, he reasoned, could society support prison officers and police who daily put their lives at risk in protecting the community from criminals with a disposition toward violence? While, no doubt, Bolte was genuine in his belief, there were other less rational factors at work in shaping his views. The most important of these had to do with his own personal and political insecurity. Bolte was never seriously under threat as a leader, but he was defensive and insecure when he felt his authority and legitimacy were under challenge. Once the decision on Ryan was taken, Bolte's defensive instincts would come to the fore to drive him on combatively to a political victory over the sectors of the community he mistrusted and despised: academics, lawyers, churchmen, journalists, and trade unionists.

Bolte's rural upbringing was one of the experiences shaping his outlook and values. This can be seen in an exchange that took place in the Legislative Assembly in October and November 1958 during debate on the bill to ban the use of live birds in trap shooting. Frankly stating his opposition to the measure, Bolte began:

> The day I am convinced that it is cruel to the degree of, or in excess of, normal field shooting, or the ordinary way of life of the average country person, I will support its being banned … If one lives in the country one has a constant battle against the elements. Fire, flood, tempest, drought, pestilence and other things mould one's character … Unless people have experienced life in the country, particularly on a farm, they do not fully appreciate what is and what is not cruel … I am now talking about cruelty. If, during a bad year when the ewes are lambing, a lamb is left without its mother, what is the best way to handle the animal? Does one knock its brains out against a post or allow it to die from starvation? I admit that on such occasions I have killed lambs. Members of the Opposition may say that is cruel, but one has to live by the elements to understand the realities of life.

In a revealing passage Bolte concluded:

> I appreciate that the result of a recent Gallup Poll indicated that many persons favoured the banning of live-bird trap shooting, but polls or plebiscites of this nature will not exert an undue influence upon me. I am not prone to bow to public opinion and, certainly, I do not intend to seek political gain by 'grabbing something', particularly in a pre-election period.[71]

In that single parliamentary episode, the salient features of Henry Bolte's political character were clearly in evidence: his elemental simplicity, his black-and-white philosophy of nature and life, his pugnacious defensiveness, his visceral logic, and his rustic realism.[72]

Some of that defensiveness became evident at the height of the Tait case during an exchange between Bolte and two experienced journalists on 16 October 1962. Two statutory declarations made by the journalists, Ray Davie of *The Age* and Brian Hanrahan of *Truth*, swear that 'in the course of discussion, Mr. Bolte made statements or answers to questions as follows':

> *Mr. Bolte*: I believe that in the next couple of weeks Tait will be declared insane. I wouldn't be surprised if Bartholomew had a change of mind, you know what psychiatrists are. [Dr. Allen Bartholomew was the Pentridge prison psychiatrist who, as a prosecution witness, gave evidence as to Tait's sanity at the trial.] Then we would wait until he was sane again and then hang him.
>
> *Journalist*: Wouldn't you find that embarrassing, hanging a man between bursts of sanity and insanity?
>
> *Mr. Bolte*: There are no bursts of insanity?
>
> *Journalist*: There will be the appearance of it.
>
> *Mr. Bolte*: It would not embarrass us. It might embarrass somebody else, but not us.
>
> *Mr. Bolte* added: Have you thought what this insanity will mean? He will have to be taken from Pentridge to Ararat where you cannot have maximum security. You have good security, but not like Pentridge. Ararat is my area. If he gets out, imagine it. I feel so gravely about him that we would have to engage three full-time guards to watch him. That would cost the State £4,000 a year.[73]

Here, rather more blatantly than elsewhere, can be seen the perspective from which the premier viewed the question of capital punishment in general, and the hanging of Tait in particular. There seems no trace of a developed philosophy of social justice or judicial ethics. It is merely a question of power and expediency. The anticipated declaration by Dr Bartholomew that Tait was insane was a temporary inconvenience, nothing more. The premier was resolved on his course. No psychiatrist's evidence was going to be permitted to complicate the intended hanging of Tait. He would hang anyway.

As he drew together the discussion around the cabinet table on Ryan, the premier was more outspoken than was usual for him on capital cases. Bolte usually relied upon the recommendations of Arthur Rylah, and rarely entered the discussions in any forceful way. In fact, in the past Bolte had never taken the lead in capital cases.[74] Now he spoke strongly in support of the hanging, arguing that mercy was not warranted in Ryan's case. For Bolte, the key issue was that Ryan had killed a prison officer doing his duty, and the government had to safeguard the public's guardians at all costs. It was an issue the premier said he felt strongly about. The government would be failing in its responsibilities if it allowed such a crime to be met with anything less than the most severe punishment provided by the law. As well, the premier said, there were no mitigating factors that would justify commutation. On the contrary, Ryan had a bad criminal record, including armed robbery, and he had made violent threats to his former wife. Bolte then referred to Ryan's letter to Dianne Everett that he had written while on the run, a copy of which had been intercepted by police at her house in December 1965 and had been provided to the premier by the homicide squad.

The fact that Ryan's letter threatened violent retribution against anyone who might betray his whereabouts, and contained obscene and threatening references to Dorothy, was an indication that he had a violent streak and was not an appropriate candidate for mercy, Bolte said. As Ryan had written in the letter:

> I always look after my friends; and my enemies get their just reward also. If you see any of those 'bounty hunters' tell them to beware. We have the strength behind us. This is a very well organised affair; a little of which I have disclosed in this week's *Truth*. I suspect they will publish my most recent letter today—Thurs. 30—
>
> Dorothy has tried to contact me through the Missing friends column. I am dubious, as it could be a decoy and a trap. However, fool that I am, I will take a chance and see what happens. I'll cut her cunt out and strangle her with it if she is playing Judas. On the other hand you know how much I love the tunnel-cunted bitch and my lovable daughters …
>
> Darling, please don't ever think of trying to collect that £5000. All Bounty Hunters will be dead ones. If I can't then one of my many mates will 'Hit'. I relize you won't, but just caution anyone else. This is for real Kid. We are not playing 'Cops and Robbers' anymore.[75]

This letter was Bolte's trump card and, although he did not need it, he played it for all it was worth. If there were any ministers who had a mind to argue that there were qualities in Ryan that might have justified clemency, the threatening references to bounty hunters and the shocking and obscene references to Dorothy effectively silenced them.

While it is doubtful that the threats contained in this letter were seriously intended, they nevertheless created a very damaging perception of Ryan. Clearly, the image of Ryan as an armed robber with violent tendencies was at odds with the notion that he had redeeming features that might be sufficient to justify a recommendation by the premier to the governor to exercise his prerogative of mercy.

As he summed up the discussion, Bolte was gratified that while there were philosophical differences between ministers about capital punishment, and concern about consistency in the application of the prerogative of mercy, there was no fundamental disagreement that the law should be upheld in Ryan's case. Despite later accounts suggesting that ministers had voted on the issue, no vote was taken. As was usual for the Bolte cabinet, a consensus among the ministers had emerged from the discussion. Concluding on the issue, the premier said he thought ministers were agreed on their advice to the governor: the hanging should go ahead.

Cabinet government operates on a principle of cabinet solidarity. Ministers are obliged to defend cabinet decisions in public, even if they have argued against such decisions in the cabinet room. For ministers who are not prepared to do so, the alternative is clear: resignation from cabinet. This was always an unlikely course of action in the Bolte cabinet determining Ryan's case. Deserting one's cabinet colleagues over a single contentious issue about which one did not carry the day in discussion was a drastic step for any minister, and it would almost certainly end a ministerial career. As the premier observed, no minister was now contemplating that very serious course. Bolte had got his way. There were four ministers who were not entirely happy with the proposed execution, or had reservations about aspects of it, but they were in no doubt that opposing it was a lost cause. Hamer, Bloomfield, Manson, and Rylah knew that arguing for a commutation for a convicted prisoner who had escaped and killed a prison officer was always going to be difficult, especially when the boss wanted an execution and was determined on his course.

As for the premier, he knew there would be a vigorous campaign by the press, and he felt sure that the decision would not be universally popular. But this served merely as a spur to his determination to take on and beat his political opponents in the community and the media—elements he held in contempt. As far as the public presentation of the hanging decision was concerned, the way ahead was clear: there was no reason why cabinet should depart from the law. Cabinet had to do what it believed was right. Ryan would hang, cabinet had decided, and the date recommended by the chief secretary for his execution would be exactly four weeks hence: Monday, 9 January 1967.

At 2:30 in the afternoon, premier Bolte and all fourteen of his ministers met with the governor, Sir Rohan Delacombe, behind heavily soundproofed doors in the Executive Council chamber on the first floor of the Old Treasury Building in Spring Street. Only two ministers were required to form a quorum at Executive Council meetings with the governor, but in capital cases it was usual for all ministers to attend and advise the governor. The purpose of the meeting in this elegant, book-lined room was to constitute the Executive Council and give legal effect to cabinet's decisions on Ryan, Rosamilia, and Parslow. This was the sole purpose of the Executive Council on this day. Other matters requiring royal assent and orders in council would have to wait until an Executive Council meeting the following day. Bolte brought with him to the meeting a memorandum prepared by the secretary of the Premier's Department, Alex Coulthard. In the formal language of Executive Council meetings, the memorandum was addressed to His Excellency the Governor of Victoria, and read:

> Your Ministers of the Crown as Members of the Executive Council have this day given very serious consideration to the case of Ronald Joseph Ryan who was convicted of murder at the Supreme Court, Melbourne, on the thirtieth day of March, 1966, following which sentence of death was pronounced.
>
> Your Ministers as Members of the Executive Council now beg to recommend that the sentence of death be carried into execution on Monday the ninth day of January, 1967, at eight o'clock in the forenoon within the walls or enclosed yard of Pentridge gaol.[76]

Delacombe always wanted these meetings kept as brief as possible, but on this occasion—after the usual pleasantries and formalities—he departed from his usual practice. Asking the question 'Do you all agree?', Delacombe carefully went around the table before the order was formally adopted.[77] Then the governor countersigned and sealed a warrant that Rylah had already signed, directing the sheriff of the state of

Victoria to carry the sentence of death against Ryan into execution. This was Ryan's death warrant, and it meant that the process giving legal authority to his execution was complete.[78]

At 4:00PM, within minutes of the conclusion of the Executive Council meeting, Pentridge governor Ian Grindlay informed Ryan of cabinet's decision in his H Division cell. Ryan took the news quietly. 'Do you remember that play, *The Valiant*, at Bendigo?' he asked Grindlay. When Grindlay replied that he did, Ryan quoted to him the half-remembered Shakespearian lines from the play:

> The coward dies a thousand deaths,
> The Valiant dies but once.

'I won't be crying when my turn comes,' he said.[79]

Stoical as Ryan seemed, he did not yet accept that his execution was inevitable. As he wrote to his mother the next day:

> [W]e now know the decision of the Executive Council. For my part it was the one expected. Hence, it was no shock, and I was able to accept it with equanimity. My concern was for its effect on you. As a family, we are generally optimistic, conceding too much in the way of humane and generous feeling to those in power. Therefore, I can imagine your disappointment. I now advance a theory in which you may find reason for hope—even at this stage—but as I am more cynical, I am not in the least optimistic. Taking into consideration the politicians' devious ways, it is worth considering that in this case they find it expedient to refuse to commute my sentence to one of life imprisonment thus satisfying the 'Eye for an eye' element. Then, subsequent to the expected outcry from the more humane element they find it expedient to yield to the second group. Thus, in a sense, they have done their duty to both factions with no loss of face which is the politicians' way. There is ample precedent for this.[80]

In the days and weeks that followed, as the media responded to the expected decision and anti-hanging protest groups geared up for the tumultuous campaign battle to come, Ryan's novel theory—upon the success of which his life depended—would be put to the test.

CHAPTER THIRTEEN

Appeal

It seems that my [Privy Council] appeal will be heard on the 23rd ... I guess my gambling experience, etc, has conditioned my nerves for this big gamble.

—Ronald Ryan

DESPITE THE FACT that the cabinet decision had been widely speculated upon, the realisation in the Victorian community that a hanging was imminent still came as a shock. Against all reason, the Melbourne media and anti-hanging protest groups had, like Justice Starke, clung to the hope that the Bolte government would shrink from employing the ultimate penalty against Ryan. Now the hanging was to go ahead, and media and abolitionist groups reacted sharply to the decision. Supporters and opponents of the hanging were soon running a spirited battle in the court of public opinion. This political confrontation would see marches and skirmishes in the streets, extraordinary manoeuvring in the media, and passionate debate on all sides as a community confronted the prospect of executing a man in their name.

Within hours of the cabinet decision, spokesmen for a number of community organisations voiced their opposition. The Anglican Coadjutor Bishop of Melbourne, the Rt Rev Geoffrey Sambell, was the first to react when he described the cabinet decision as 'offensive', particularly in the context of the approach of Christmas.[1] The state's principal abolitionist body, the Anti-Hanging Committee, led by the well-known author, teacher, and television quiz champion Barry Jones, was also quick to enter the fray. Jones was the leading figure in the abolitionist movement, and his communication and political skills would be vitally important in the weeks ahead.[2] In his first statement on the cabinet decision, Jones took aim at the logical weaknesses in the government's approach, pointing out that in 1949 the Victorian Liberal cabinet, of which Sir Henry Bolte was a member, had reduced the number of criminal offences carrying the death penalty from twelve to two, with no apparent increase in the commission of crimes. 'It is 16 years to the day since the decision to hang Lee, Andrews and Clayton was announced', Jones said. 'Since their hanging there have been no executions in this State. If the law has fallen into disuse for so long you can hardly state the law is necessary or useful.'[3]

No sooner had the morning newspapers reported Jones' statements than the premier moved to discredit them. At 10:00AM, at the first of his twice-daily press conferences, Bolte told journalists that the people who were protesting against the hanging were, in the main, the same as those who were campaigning against the war in Vietnam. 'It will be much the same group—I don't say exactly the same—at the Universities who will protest at the decision', he said. Obviously determined to avoid a repeat occurrence of his political defeat in the Tait case, the premier also effectively crippled hopes of prospective deputations: the government simply would not receive them.[4] Critics were quick to reply. The state Labor opposition leader, Clive Stoneham, called the premier 'arrogant, dictatorial, and undemocratic' in his refusal to see deputations, and Jones described the premier as 'seriously off-key in suggesting the Anti-Hanging Committee was comprised of chronic malcontents and professional Vietniks.'[5]

A big psychological boost for opponents of the hanging came when the state parliamentary press gallery was abuzz with rumours that the cabinet decision was not unanimous. *The Herald*'s state political reporter, Barry Muir, first broke the story when, two days after the cabinet meeting, he wrote a page-one report saying that the 'vote' by ministers had been eleven to four in favour of the execution.[6] Muir, who had been leaked an outline of the cabinet-room discussion, did not name the four ministers because he believed that to have done so would have been to confirm that there had, indeed, been a leak and to thereby endanger his source. He simply said 'the decision ... was made in the face of strong opposition by a minority within the Cabinet'.[7]

Although *The Herald* and the public were unaware of it, Muir's report caused a ripple of concern in official government circles, indicating that it was accurate as to the extent of cabinet opposition to capital punishment as such. Behind the scenes it was suggested to the premier that *The Herald* or Muir should be called before the Bar of the House for a breach of parliamentary privilege. The day after Muir's story appeared, the head of the Premier's Department, Alex Coulthard, sought the views of the clerk of the Legislative Assembly on whether a breach had occurred. The clerk, John Robertson, advised Coulthard that, as Muir's report was a comment on a decision of the Executive Council and did not reflect on any minister as a member of parliament, it could not be regarded as a breach of parliamentary privilege or a contempt of parliament.[8] There the matter rested, but that it was taken up at all at the top level of the Premier's Department indicated the government's sensitivity to any perception that cabinet had been less than united on a decision that was likely to be controversial and subject to intense public and media scrutiny.

It was soon clear that anti-hanging protests would not be confined to the media and traditional political opponents of the Bolte government. Those who would come to protest the decision, and in many cases publicly campaign against it, ranged through such politically diverse organisations and individuals as the National Youth Council of Australia; the Australian Universities Liberal Federation; the Victorian branch of the Australian Labor Party; the Roman Catholic Archbishop of Sydney, Cardinal Norman Gilroy; writer and satirist Barry Humphries; federal Labor leader Arthur Calwell, MHR; left-wing federal MP Dr Jim Cairns; and right-wing political commentator Bob Santamaria. And in the margins of this opposition it was worthy of note—given Ryan's rampant shop-breaking activities some years before—that the Retail Traders' Association also would take a principled stand against the hanging.

The first flurry of angry exchanges over, the various anti-hanging groups settled down to serious consideration of moves to avert the hanging. In the past, the committee had operated variously as a pressure group, legal-aid committee, public focus of dissent, and behind-the-scenes negotiator. Even though the committee would assert itself as the most active and vigorous opposition to the planned execution, it had to regenerate itself after a period of quiescence following the successful conclusion to the Tait case. At that time, the committee had resolved to 'continue its activities until capital punishment is abolished in Victoria', but it had been lulled into believing that there would be no more hangings.[9] With speculation rife about Ryan in the lead-up to the cabinet decision of 12 December, however, executive members felt certain that the decision would go against him.

The leaders of the committee were Barry Jones, Val Doube, academics John Ryan and Rod Andrew, and Rosemary Hanbury. The committee's president, Doube was an experienced former Labor MP, who also had served for a short time as minister of health in the Cain Labor government of 1955.[10] With the prospect of Ryan being hanged, Jones and Doube quickly expanded the composition of the committee with its immediate sponsors drawn, as before, from the professional middle class. One of the two patrons of the committee was writer Arthur Koestler who, in 1937 during the Spanish Civil War, had spent three months under sentence of death as a suspected spy. Moved by his experience, Koestler subsequently wrote *Reflections on Hanging*, a brilliant abolitionist treatise that achieved literary fame after its publication in Britain in 1956 and was influential in shaping British opinion about the death penalty. Britain first limited capital punishment in 1957, had its last execution in 1964, and finally abolished the death penalty in 1965.

The second patron was the Earl of Harewood, the Queen's cousin. During World War II, Lord Harewood, then Lieutenant George Henry Hubert (the Viscount) Lascelles, was captured by the Germans in Italy in June 1944, and was a prisoner of war until May 1945. As one of a number of so-called Prominente, prisoners who had prominent family connections, Harewood was held in various POW camps, including the infamous Colditz castle near Leipzig. Only days before the end of the war in Europe, the Prominente were told by their German captors that they had orders to shoot them. Shortly after the war, it was discovered that Harewood and the others had, indeed, been the subject of a death warrant signed by Hitler.[11]

Put together by Jones and Doube, the committee boasted a number of church, academic, legal, arts, sporting, and political luminaries. It included two Anglican bishops, two queens counsel, the president of the Methodist Church in Victoria, the state Labor opposition leader, the minister of Scots Church, and ten academics including six university professors. Also included were prominent trade unionists, student leaders, teachers, lawyers, and social workers. While many of the sponsors had simply lent their well-known name to the cause and would not be active in the campaign to follow, it was an impressive line-up of the Melbourne liberal intelligentsia, and included many of the leading identities in the formation of progressive opinion in the state.[12]

On 15 December, with the newspapers daily running features and reports about community responses to the cabinet decision, the anti-hanging committee met to plan the campaign. Discussion at this first meeting centred on legal moves for Ryan, and the committee's legal members advised of the prospects of appeal. The committee agreed that moves be made for Ryan to initiate a petition for special leave to appeal to the Judicial Committee of the Privy Council on the question of the felony-murder rule, and that the government be approached to provide legal aid. If the government refused, the committee would undertake the task of raising funds. That would have to be a high priority, the treasurer, John Wilson, told the meeting. A financial report he presented showed the committee's bank balance at just four dollars.[13]

It was quickly resolved that night that the key strategy of the committee would be the public mobilisation of community opinion. Working closely with church leaders, the committee would seek to bring reason to bear on an 'unreasonable premier'. Bishop Sambell and Methodist Reverend John Westerman proposed that an immediate approach be made for a deputation to the premier comprising church leaders from various religious groups. The Anglican, Presbyterian, Methodist and Baptist Churches, the Congregational Union, Church of Christ, the Society of Friends, and the Hebrew congregation of Melbourne all stood ready to join in protesting the hanging, with only the Salvation Army, Lutherans, and the Bible Union refusing to support efforts to save Ryan.[14] Two days later, Jones wrote to the premier proposing that such a deputation 'wait upon you in order to advance reasons for executive clemency, both on the general abolitionist principle, and also on the specific difficulties which arise in the Ryan case'. Jones added:

> I hope that it is not necessary to point out that this is not a political issue to our Committee or to the 42% of abolitionists in the community at large. We approach it both as a moral issue and as a practical issue. We believe the abolition of the death penalty to be

> an important step towards the creation of a greatly reformed prison system which will have as its major aim the protection of the public and the conversion of evil into good. We hope that in this Christmas season you can find it in your heart to receive our deputation.[15]

The premier's reply was curt, but not unexpected. No useful purpose would be served, Bolte said, by him receiving the deputation suggested.[16] In the coming weeks opponents of the hanging would seek to put their views directly to the premier, but he would have none of it. No representations would be received. This was a carefully calculated political move by the premier and a continuing feature of the government's response to the protest campaign. Without the focus of deputations and representations to provide a continuing source of stories for the press, the government reasoned, protestors would be starved of media attention. Bolte's timing of the execution decision was planned to minimise parliamentary scrutiny, as well. With parliament in recess for the summer break, there was no opportunity for the opposition to effectively test the government's resolve at question time.

With the premier refusing to receive deputations, attention turned to the Victorian governor in the hope that he might be more receptive to an approach on clemency, particularly as those seeking a commutation for Ryan believed they had seen in Delacombe's manner some sympathy for their cause. On the day the cabinet took its decision, Phil Opas had presented a personal request to Delacombe seeking an interview as a private citizen. Opas said he hoped that he might persuade the governor to 'take a step which has not been taken by a sovereign for centuries, that is, to hear an appeal personally' and exercise the royal prerogative of mercy in favour of Ryan.[17] Two days later, Opas received a brief for the proposed Privy Council appeal, and he therefore wrote again to the governor asking that his earlier request for an interview be ignored. On Monday, 19 December 1966 Opas received from Delacombe the following gracious acknowledgment:

> Dear Mr. Opas,
>
> I am writing to acknowledge your letters of the 12th and 14th December on the subject of Ronald Joseph Ryan.
>
> I fully appreciate the feelings which you expressed in your letter

> of the 12th and I now note from your letter of the 14th that you do not wish to approach me in this matter.
>
> Yours sincerely,
>
> (Signed) Rohan Delacombe.[18]

When he received this response, Opas believed that the wording suggested a certain sympathetic attitude, and that 'His Excellency from the tenor of his letter would have granted me the interview sought.'[19] What Opas was not aware of, however, was that Delacombe had been advised not to see him, and would not have done so had Opas persisted with his request. After Opas' letter had arrived, the official secretary to the governor, Jack Colquhoun, had written a memorandum to Delacombe in which he indicated he had sought ministerial and departmental advice:

> Mr. Rylah, with whom I discussed the letter, feels that it may be unwise for you to receive Mr. Opas at this stage, after the [execution] decision has been made. Mr. Coulthard [Secretary of the Premier's Department] agrees with this view.[20]

The issue for Rylah—as it was with Colquhoun and later with solicitor-general Tony Murray, who was also consulted—was that the exercise of the royal prerogative of mercy was precisely the process the cabinet had adopted to consider a commutation for Ryan and advise the governor accordingly. Cabinet and the Executive Council had considered the matter, and their decision was that the prerogative would not be exercised in this case. The implication of this advice was clear: no purpose could be served by Delacombe seeing Opas.

With the scheduled hanging less than three weeks away, legal skirmishing began in earnest as Ryan's legal representatives applied to the government on his behalf for legal aid for a Privy Council appeal. The premier was having none of it. He conferred with attorney-general Rylah before announcing on 21 December that no further legal aid to Ryan would be granted. 'Over $3,600 have been paid out in fees to enable Ryan to be properly represented', the premier said, 'and it is significant that there was no suggestion of any further appeal until the government's decision not to commute the death sentence was announced.'[21]

The premier's refusal did not dent the spirits of the condemned man. In a letter to Cecilia on 22 December, Ryan wrote that he had had a visit from Opas, who told him of a new solicitor being engaged on his behalf for the planned appeal, and he had had a visit from his family. Ryan wrote that he was 'plodding along quietly and not worrying unduly', but was clearly heartened by the efforts of those seeking to avert his execution:

> George, who visited me today with Irma, informs me that in the first day of public appeal the sum of $600 has been donated toward defraying the cost of the appeal ... [A]ll possible is being done and, despite the outcome, I am pleased to find so many rallying to the cause. There have been sympathetic opinions expressed by many of the Legal profession—including Justice Starke, Mr Murray, Solicitor-General—and a few members of my jury. These, together with general public support, must be a source of hope for the family. It should, at least, allow you some peace of mind over Christmas.[22]

Ryan finished the letter with a cheery message and a half-remembered quote from Omar Khayyám:

> Well, Folks, it's Au Revoir again. Have a Happy Christmas! 'Why worry about Tomorrow if Today be sweet.'[23]

The next day was not so sweet, however, when an application for a stay of execution was made to the Supreme Court. With time running out to prepare the Privy Council appeal and lodge the necessary papers in London, Opas sought from the court a declaration that Ryan was entitled in law to seek special leave to appeal to the Privy Council, and an order to stay the execution until the appeal had been heard. Opas was worried that the government might proceed with the execution before the appeal process could be completed. It was commonly believed that this had happened once before in Victorian history, in the case of Frederick Deeming. The claim was that, in 1892, Deeming had been executed in Melbourne while his appeal was being heard by the Privy Council in London. Despite the currency of this claim it was false.[24]

Appearing before a packed courtroom with Brian Bourke, Opas applied for an injunction restraining the sheriff of the Supreme Court and the Pentridge governor from carrying out the hanging: 'We want to stay the hand of the executioner until we have time to get to London,' Opas told the court. 'I must say that I find myself appalled that there should be such haste to execute this man when we would know within a couple of months if he had a valid appeal or not.'[25]

The government was taking no chances with this application: the Crown had briefed Tony Murray, with barrister Brian Shaw as his junior, to oppose it. Murray argued that Opas was asking the court to contradict another order that had already been given. 'It appears to us that the whole basis of this application is misconceived', Murray said. After a short hearing, Justice Cliff Menhennitt dismissed the application; and in what was to be a fateful pronouncement, Menhennitt said that it was not within his power to grant such a reprieve. Based on past rulings, he said, it was doubtful if any judge could grant an injunction deferring the execution once a time and place had been fixed by the Executive Council.[26]

IN HIS PENTRIDGE CELL, Ryan was beginning to confront the seriousness of his situation. One of the issues concerning him was his religious faith, as the first signs emerged of a shift in his attitude to the Catholic Church he had left prior to his marriage more than fifteen years before. Back in early December, Ryan had been visited by the Roman Catholic chaplain of Pentridge, Father John Brosnan, and they had struck up a good relationship. Brosnan was a charismatic figure around the gaol. A knockabout priest, who had a common touch with mug punters and working-class battlers, Brosnan was as appealing a chaplain as any Hollywood Irish priest ever was. Ryan had been listed in gaol records as an Anglican at the time of his first imprisonment at the gaol in November 1964, but the constant pleadings of his mother had caused him to agree to see Father Brosnan, if only to mollify her. '[But] I won't come back to the Church for my mother, for the governor of this gaol or for you, Father', he had insisted to Brosnan. 'Nor will I stay away for what mugs in here might say. Leave me to myself.'[27]

In his own time, Ryan's faith was regained after reading and re-reading the books left for him by well-wishers, particularly Sister Madonna of the Sisters of the Good Shepherd, Abbotsford. She had come to the gaol to accompany Cecilia who, at 75, was now frail and unsteady. Sister Madonna left a book of Christ's stories, *The Eleventh Hour*, which particularly inspired him. The things that had delayed his return to the Church, Brosnan later said, 'were his desire to be consistent and his difficulty in believing in the Divinity of Christ. He felt it was inconsistent for him to live one way and die another, but finally agreed it would be foolish and stubborn of him not to, the way he felt.'[28] Two days before Christmas, Ryan asked Brosnan if he could have a Mass said for him in H Division on Christmas Day. Brosnan agreed, and Mass was said outside Ryan's cell, and he took communion with Bert Warren, a young Irish prison officer.[29]

AS THIS WAS HAPPENING, other moves from an extraordinary quarter were being made to avert the hanging. Several members of the Ryan murder-trial jury had been upset by the government's decision that the execution would go ahead, and were concerned to make a plea for a reprieve. Perhaps not surprisingly, given how long it had been since the previous executions in 1951, several of the jurors had believed at the time of the trial that capital punishment had been abolished in Victoria. Now that the hanging was certain, one of the jurors, Tom Gildea, contacted Father Brosnan to express his anxiety at the prospect. Gildea told Brosnan that there were others like him who were horrified by the thought of the approaching hanging. Gildea eventually contacted all but two members of the jury to seek their support for a plea to the government to spare Ryan.

This was a delicate matter, as jurors were sworn to confidentiality in respect of proceedings in the jury room. Brosnan sought the advice of Justice Sir John Barry, a well-known abolitionist. Barry was reluctant to offer counsel but allowed that, if the jurors felt strongly enough about the issue, they were entitled to make a public comment about their post-jury view of the matter. Barry warned Brosnan, however, that he must on no account encourage them to do so.[30] With some misgivings, Brosnan decided against public exposure of the jurymen's concerns, and instead approached anti-hanging committee member and barrister Richard McGarvie, QC, asking him to handle the matter, which he did in a purely legal way. McGarvie, who several years later would be appointed to the bench of the Victorian Supreme Court, and still later as governor of Victoria, was subsequently asked by the jurors to advise them about an appropriate course of action.[31] The essence of what they told McGarvie was devastatingly simple: a recommendation for mercy at the trial, they said, had not been considered by the jury because they had thought an execution was inconceivable.[32] McGarvie took statements from the jurors, and suggested they communicate their views to the government in the form of a petition.[33] Four jurors—Patrick John Dunn, Thomas Patrick Gildea, Lionel D Hannaford, and Kevin John Murphy—agreed to do so. Drawing upon McGarvie's advice, they prepared letters to the government.[34]

Forwarded privately and separately to the premier and the governor, the hand-written letters of petition differed slightly. But—except for the variations indicated below—they were identical to the letter sent by Tom Gildea, as follows:

> In the Matter of a Petition
> for the exercise of
> Her Majesty's Prerogative of Mercy
> in respect of Ronald Ryan by Thomas Patrick Gildea
>
> To His Excellency the Right Honorable Rohan Delacombe, K.C.M.G., Her Majesty's Governor of the State of Victoria.
>
> This Petition for the exercise of Her Majesty's mercy is humbly presented in respect of Ronald Joseph Ryan a prisoner at present under sentence of death and confined at the Metropolitan Gaol at Coburg and showeth.
>
> I, Thomas Patrick Gildea, was one of the Jury at the trial of Ronald Joseph Ryan. I was truly under the impression at that time that Capital Punishment had been abolished in the State of Victoria. Had I been aware such was not the case I would have suggested to jury that a recommendation for Mercy be added to the sentence.
>
> May it therefore please Your Excellency that Her Majesty's Prerogative of Mercy should be exercised in favor of Ronald Joseph Ryan and your petitioner will ever pray
>
> Dated this the 28th day of December 1966
> Thomas Patrick Gildea
> Petitioner[35]

The letters of jurors Murphy, Dunn, and Hannaford were similarly expressed. They varied to the extent of stating that the petitioner did not believe in capital punishment, or would have supported a plea for mercy had this been made at the time of the trial, or was under the impression, at the time of the trial, that the death penalty had been abolished in Victoria.

These letters constituted a significant appeal. In essence, one-third of the jury now declared that, had they realised that the death penalty was then in force, they would have supported a plea for mercy. It was a highly unusual occurrence that jurors were prepared to take this step and approach the government with appeals of this kind. Given the Bolte government's practice of automatically commuting death sentences where the jury had made a recommendation for mercy, there is little doubt—as Bolte much later conceded—that, had that been done at the trial, Ryan would never have been hanged.[36]

Powerful though these appeals were, the government was unmoved by them. The premier evidently took the view that, once their jury duty was complete, the jurors had no standing in respect of any of the decision-making councils then current. If the premier was unimpressed, the governor, to whom the petitions were expressly directed, was wary and suspicious. Delacombe's response suggested that his earlier letter to Opas, from which Opas had taken some encouragement, had perhaps been misinterpreted. When he received the jurors' petitions, Delacombe penned a disapproving covering note and attached it to three of the four letters which he forwarded to the chief secretary's office:

> All three arrived this morning. The wording is almost identical. The writing is very similar. Even if they come from three separate individuals who were on the jury, it smells!
>
> R.D.
>
> 30/12[37]

This would not be the last time that the governor would express forthright views on the matter of Ryan.

Meanwhile, the initiative by the anti-hanging committee to mount an appeal to the Privy Council was proceeding; but, following the refusal of the government to grant legal aid, the public solicitor was no longer able to act. Needing an instructing solicitor, Opas sought the assistance of his friend Jim Pearce at the city law firm of Ridgeway Pearce Freadman and Murray, where his daughter, Lynne, was an articled clerk. The firm agreed to do the work, and it fell to Ralph Freadman, as the only partner with substantial experience of criminal practice, to prepare an appeal.[38]

Two days before Christmas, Freadman had written to the premier to advise him that a petition on behalf of Ryan had been prepared to seek special leave to appeal to the Privy Council, and to request that a reprieve be granted to allow the appeal to proceed. The government did not initially respond to this request, but Freadman pressed on, making an application to the full court of the Supreme Court to appeal against Justice Menhennitt's ruling refusing a stay of execution pending the Privy Council appeal. Despite the Christmas vacation, the chief justice, Sir Henry Winneke, in the spirit of due legal process, agreed to convene a full court. Winneke also agreed to accept a rough photocopied version of an appeal book (a bound copy of all the relevant appeal documents) owing to the fact that, with printers closed for the holidays, the usual printed form could not be provided. 'So long as it is reasonably legible', Winneke told Freadman.[39]

A week later, on 30 December, the full court heard the application by Opas, with barrister Brian Bourke, for a stay of execution. The Crown was represented by Tony Murray and Brian Shaw. The full court, consisting of the senior puisne judge, Mr Justice Barry, and Justices Robert Monahan and George Pape, unanimously dismissed the application for the stay on the grounds that the proceeding as a civil action was misconceived and unnecessary. By a two-one majority, however, the court ruled that it was open to Opas at any time to appeal to Mr Justice Starke, as the trial judge, for a reprieve, which the judge had the power to grant until the appeal was heard. Speaking for the majority, Mr Justice Barry made it plain that he saw a reprieve for this purpose as an issue of natural justice:

> It is inconceivable ... that the Government will depart in this instance from the established practice of postponing the time of execution once it is satisfied that steps have genuinely been taken to bring a petition expeditiously before the Judicial Committee ... [T]he sentence is the judgment of this Court, not of the Executive. Under s. 485 [of the Crimes Act 1958] the duty of carrying the

> sentence into execution rests on the Sheriff, an officer of this Court, and the authority under which he does so is not a decision of the Executive, but the judgment of this Court …
>
> If it be necessary to apply to the trial judge under the common law, I consider that he has the power to grant a respite suspending the execution of the judgment of the Court and reprieving Ryan until his petition for special leave to appeal has been dealt with by the Privy Council.

In his concurring judgment, Mr Justice Monahan agreed with Barry's reasons, and set out a principle that would later assume considerable importance:

> I agree with his observations concerning the continued existence in this State of the common law power of reprieve, which resides in the trial judge, in circumstances which render the carrying out of an execution inconsistent with humanity or justice, and which can be exercised by the trial judge right up to the moment when the judgment of death pronounced by him was carried into execution.[40]

With exactly a week before the scheduled execution, on 2 January 1967 Freadman's London agents, Waterhouse & Co, lodged the application with the judicial committee of the Privy Council, and duly notified the crown solicitor in Melbourne.

With Ryan's Privy Council application on foot, it was evident that not all of his legal avenues had been exhausted. Hence the government—consistent with the expectations of the full court—moved to defer the execution until such time as the outcome of the appeal was known. Following a meeting of the Executive Council attended by Delacombe, Bolte, and Rylah at Government House at 2:30PM that same day, the executive rescinded the execution order and deferred the hanging to a day and hour to be fixed.[41] Within twenty minutes, Ryan—who was being visited by his sister Gloria at the time—was informed in his cell by governor Grindlay that his execution had been deferred.[42] Later in the afternoon Grindlay returned to Ryan's cell for a private conversation, and left him six packets of cigarettes.[43]

This respite was a welcome stay of the execution and, in the three-week period between 4 January and the hearing of the Privy Council petition on 23 January, the intensity of public attention on the Ryan issue waned. No hanging could take place until the Privy Council's decision was known, and opponents maintained a hope that an application would be allowed and the appeal succeed. As the government had refused to grant legal aid for the appeal, fund-raising efforts by the anti-hanging committee were accelerated and, within a short time, $3,000 was publicly raised to support the application. As this would cover only one fare and accommodation in London, Opas offered to appear without fee, which was accepted. Opas then wrote to Allayne Kiddle, a member of the Victorian bar, who was in London studying for a masters degree, seeking her agreement to appear as his junior, also without fee.[44] Kiddle agreed and, with the Privy Council the last remaining legal avenue left open for Ryan, Opas made ready to travel to London. On the eve of his departure, Ryan told him: 'We're in the time-on period now, Phil. You'd better kick a few goals for me.'[45]

On 12 January Opas flew to London to present the appeal. Although the Hawke Labor government would in 1986 abolish the last vestiges of Privy Council appeals on the basis that they were a colonial hangover that offended notions of Australian sovereignty and judicial independence, in 1967 appeals to the Privy Council were still the last avenue of appeal for criminal matters beyond the High Court of Australia. In essence, for those Commonwealth nations that recognised its jurisdiction, the Privy Council was the final court of appeal.[46]

Appeals to the Privy Council were heard by its judicial committee, a body created by the passage of the *Judicial Committee Act* in 1833, but the Privy Council itself went much further back in English history. The council derived its judicial powers from the ancient common-law principle recognising the right of the king's subjects to appeal for redress to the sovereign in council if they believed that they had not obtained justice in the courts. Decisions relating to the hearing of petitions by the judicial committee were therefore couched in terms of 'humbly advising Her Majesty' rather than in the form of judgments, as such. The committee consisted of the Lord Chancellor, the Lord President, ex-Lords President, nine Lords of Appeal in Ordinary, certain other privy councillors who held, or had held high judicial office, and a number of distinguished Commonwealth judges. Indeed, all judges of the High Court of Australia were members of the committee. In 1966 Chief Justice Sir

Garfield Barwick had sat for several weeks on Privy Council cases, as he would—with another of his High Court colleagues—again later in 1967. But, in the event, no Australian judge would sit on the Ryan application. This was because most of the judicial work of the committee was done by the lords of appeal, eminent British judges, who were appointed as life peers to hear appeals to the House of Lords. Criminal appeals were relatively rare before the committee, and the law lords would not hear appeals against sentence, nor would they review issues of fact. Appeals had to involve important questions of law—and then only where grave injustice may have occurred. If Ryan's petition for special leave to appeal succeeded, an appeal might be heard in several months' time.

Freadman and Opas had prepared well, and they were supported in their efforts by John Feltham, a law tutor at Magdalen College, Oxford. Feltham had been involved with law academics David Derham, Peter Brett, and Louis Waller at the Melbourne University law school in preparations for the Tait case before the High Court in 1962, and Waller had written to Feltham at Oxford, seeking his assistance. Ryan himself well understood the significance of Opas' mission and its chances of success. The tension was beginning to show, as he realised himself. As he wrote from Pentridge to his mother on 19 January:

> It seems that my appeal will be heard on the 23rd or thereabouts. It should take a couple of days. If it is successful—and mind you I am not optimistic—then time is on our side. However, should it be denied then Bolte will press ahead for an early execution …
>
> I'm O.K. I have been smoking a little more than normal and I guess this is a sign of tension. However, I don't notice any other signs. I guess my gambling experience, etc, has conditioned my nerves for this big gamble.[47]

Ryan's legal team were also well aware of the high-stakes exercise upon which they had embarked in *Ryan v. The Queen*. They knew that no appeal against a conviction for murder in Victoria had ever been upheld by the Privy Council.[48] They knew, too, that, of the 50 or so petitions for special leave to appeal that were heard each year, only about twenty succeeded and proceeded to appeal. Particularly in criminal matters, the judicial committee consistently had been reluctant to entertain applications for special leave on the grounds that it would be destructive to the administration of criminal jurisprudence in the courts from which the appeals had derived. One hundred years before, in 1867 in delivering judgment in the case of *The Attorney-General of NSW v. Bertrand*, Sir John Coleridge had observed that

> … interference by Her Majesty in Council in criminal cases is likely in so many instances to lead to mischief and inconvenience, that in them the Crown will be very slow to entertain an appeal by its Officers on behalf of itself or by individuals. The instances of such appeals being entertained are therefore very rare.[49]

Again, in 1887, in the Privy Council case of *Re Dillet*, Lord Watson observed:

> Such appeals are of rare occurrence, because the rule has been repeatedly laid down, and has been invariably followed, that Her Majesty will not review or interfere with the course of criminal proceedings, unless it is shown that, by a disregard of the forms of legal process, or by some violation of the principles of natural justice, or otherwise, substantial and grave injustice has been done.[50]

It was clear from these judgments that Opas faced a formidable barrier in presenting Ryan's application. He had to show no less than that something had gone wrong in Ryan's case that would have more general adverse consequences for the administration of criminal justice in Victoria. It was also clear from other Privy Council judgments that Opas could expect no relief from the committee if the Victorian government refused to further delay the execution: the judicial committee would not interfere. As Lord Haldane had said in delivering judgment in the case of *Balmukand and others v. The King-Emperor* in 1915:

> With regard to staying execution of the sentence of death, their Lordships are unable to interfere. As they have often said, this Board is not a Court of Criminal Appeal. The tendering of advice to His Majesty as to the exercise of his prerogative of pardon is a matter for the Executive Government and is outside their Lordships' province.[51]

It was against the weight of these decisions—but with the hope and expectations of abolitionists at home—that, at midday on 23 January, Opas appeared with Kiddle in the greystone building of the Judicial Committee of Her Majesty's Most Honourable Privy Council in Whitehall. Not numbered, this neo-classical building in Downing Street—designed by Sir John Soane and built in 1828—was next door to the British prime minister's residence at Number 10.

Appearing for the Crown as respondent was Tony Murray, with his junior, Robert Gatehouse of the English bar, instructed by Freshfields, the Victorian government's UK solicitors.[52] Unlike the usual procedure in a court, counsel, journalists, and observers were called by the court usher from an ante-room into the large oak-panelled council chamber where the law lords were already seated at a broad semi-circular oak table. In this handsome but unostentatious room, four distinguished law lords from earlier times—Macnaghten, Campbell, Loreburn, and Haldane—looked down from their gilt-framed portraits on the proceedings about to commence. The room was rather dimly lit on this bleak London winter's day, despite the three large windows on either side of the chamber and high windows above. The chamber was crowded with counsel, solicitors, and journalists as Opas and Kiddle took up their positions at the bar table. A dozen spectators sat on the chairs reserved for the public at the rear and along one side of the room.

Only three judges were required to form a quorum to hear matters of this kind but, unusually, there were five sitting on Ryan's application. The five law lords—Lords Reid, Pearce, Wilberforce, Pearson and, by a curious coincidence, Hodson—constituted the Board of the Judicial Committee on this day. These were senior judges, who brought a wealth of legal experience to the committee; their position at the table signified their relative seniority.

The presiding judge, Lord Reid, sat in the centre, flanked—to his right and then his left in turn—by the next most senior judges. Lord Reid, 76, had been a Lord of Appeal in Ordinary since 1948, and during the course of a diverse career had been an MP and later solicitor-general for Scotland from 1936 to 1941.[53] On his right sat Lord Hodson, 71, who had had a highly decorated military career before taking up the law, having served at Gallipoli in 1915 as a second lieutenant and having later won the Military Cross. Like his Privy Council colleagues in this case, Lord Hodson had been Oxbridge educated, and had risen through the ranks of the bar before accepting appointment as a judge of the High Court, Lord Justice of Appeal and, in 1960, Lord of Appeal in Ordinary.[54] On Lord Reid's left sat Lord Pearce, 65, who similarly brought a great depth of experience in the law, as first a barrister and QC, and later as a High Court judge and appeal judge. He had been appointed a Lord of Appeal in Ordinary in 1962. (Lord Pearce would go on to sit as chairman of the Press Council in Britain from 1969 to 1974, before a notable contribution to the media as chairman of the discussions on press freedom in 1976 and 1977.)[55] Lord Wilberforce, at age 59, was the youngest of the sitting law lords but, like his brother judges, had followed the career path of the bar and bench through the High Court to the Privy Council in 1964.[56] The most recent appointment to the judicial committee hearing Ryan's application was Lord Pearson, 67, a Canadian-born judge with a distinguished career in the law in Britain before his appointment as a Lord of Appeal in Ordinary in 1965.[57]

Robed in gown and wig, Opas stood at the small oak rostrum facing the judges, who were seated on red leather chairs directly opposite him on the same level. In contrast, the law lords of the highest judicial tribunal in the Commonwealth needed no raiments of office and, according to tradition, appeared unrobed in lounge suits. Opas announced his appearance to present Ryan's petition that special leave be given to appeal his conviction and sentence, at which appeal it would be argued that the conviction should be quashed and set aside and Ryan be given a new trial. In an address lasting two hours and thirty-seven minutes, Opas took the law lords through the facts of the case and submitted that, in relation to felony-murder, there had been errors of law by the trial judge and the full court, which apparently were not dissented from by the High Court. As a consequence, Opas said, 'there has been a serious miscarriage of justice in this case … [and] …unless corrected by the Judicial Committee, errors as to the application of the law relating to felony-murder will continue to be made in Australia.'[58]

Opas told the judges that his petition raised seven important points of law of general application, expressed through the following questions: Was there any room in modern law for the felony-murder rule? Was the felony-murder rule as all-embracing as legal authority suggested or was it limited in its application to felonies of violence? If the rule was so limited, was the felony of escaping from gaol a felony of violence to which the rule applied? Was the felony referred to in section 35 of the Victorian *Gaols Act 1958* an offence of a continuous nature, which continued until recapture of the prisoner? If the felony referred to in that section was not continuous, could an offence committed subsequently for the purpose solely of escaping apprehension be held to be committed in the course, or in the furtherance, of the original felony? Did intention of the felon have to be proved by the prosecution in the crime of murder irrespective of the circumstances of the killing? And, finally, was manslaughter open as a finding, which the jury might have made in this particular case?

These were all important questions, but there were two key submissions forming the core of the application. The first submission relied upon the ordinary meaning of the term 'escape', and argued that the felony relied upon by the prosecution to prove its case of felony-murder was flawed. Opas argued that this was because the felony concerned—escaping from prison—was not of a continuous nature and had been completed at the point at which Hodson was shot outside the confines of the gaol.

As Opas talked, he produced an illustrated diagram of Pentridge and its environs showing the route Ryan and Walker took in escaping from the prison and the point at which Hodson had been shot. While it was certainly a felony to escape from lawful imprisonment as laid down in the *Gaols Act 1958*, section 35, and while a gaol was defined in the act, Opas submitted 'that the felony of escaping from gaol was complete the moment the prisoners removed themselves beyond the physical confines of the gaol so defined. The shooting of the warder having taken place in the public street beyond the confines of the gaol could not amount to a killing in the course of the commission of, or in the furtherance of, a felony.'[59]

The second key submission was that the felony-murder rule was an anachronism in the modern law, that over time the once-real distinction between felonies and misdemeanours had disappeared. 'In other words', said Opas, 'it is submitted that in every case of murder, whether in the course of a commission of a felony or otherwise, it is essential before a conviction for murder can be obtained that the prosecution must prove that the killing took place intentionally.' It was the key flaw in the felony-murder principle, Opas argued, that the fundamental requirement for a murder conviction of either an 'intention to kill or cause serious bodily injury' was being over-ridden by a rule whose relevance in the modern law had been lost. If there were anything left in the principle of felony-murder, Opas added, it was limited in its application to felonies of violence. Pointing to Canadian authority, Opas argued that, for the purpose of the felony-murder rule, the felony must be one that necessarily or normally involved violence, and escaping from prison was not such a felony of violence. These were important arguments, and they had significant implications. In effect, Opas was arguing that the High Court judgment by Chief Justice Sir Adrian Knox, Justice Gavan Duffy, and Justice Hayden Starke in *Ross v. The King* (1922), which had been taken as correctly stating the law in Australia in relation to felony-murder, should be overturned.[60]

Immediately after Opas' presentation had concluded at 2:40PM, Lord Reid, the presiding judge, asked counsel, the press, and other parties to withdraw from the room so that the board might consider the matter. Their lordships took just five minutes to consult privately before a bell was rung and everyone filed back into the room to hear the decision. Lord Reid began by indicating that their lordships would not be calling the Victorian government's legal representatives. This was ominous to Ryan's legal team, as it seemed extremely unlikely that leave to appeal would be granted without first hearing from the respondent's counsel. Tony Murray had prepared a detailed rebuttal on behalf of the respondents—which had, of course, been read by their lordships in the papers submitted to the committee—but Murray would not now need to present it.[61]

It was quickly apparent that the decision not to call the respondent indeed foreshadowed the judges' intentions. Ryan's application—although well made and cogently argued by Opas on important points of law—was not such as to warrant the Privy Council interfering in the administration of criminal justice in Victoria. In 1941, the lord chancellor, Viscount Simon, had been emphatic in defining the boundaries of the judicial committee's willingness to interfere in criminal cases:

> The Judicial Committee is not a revising court of criminal appeal: that is to say, it is not prepared or required to re-try a criminal case, and does not concern itself with the weight of evidence, or the conflict of evidence or with inferences drawn from evidence, or with questions as to corroboration or contradiction of testimony, or as to whether there was sufficient evidence to satisfy the burden of

> proof. Neither is it concerned to review the exercise by the previous tribunal of its discretion as to permitting cross-examination as a hostile witness or in awarding particular punishments ... The Judicial Committee cannot be asked to review the facts of a criminal case, or set aside conclusions of fact at which the tribunal has arrived. In all such cases an appeal on such ground is useless, and is indeed an abuse of the process of the Court ...
>
> Broadly speaking, the Judicial Committee will only interfere where there has been an infringement of the essential principles of justice. An obvious example would be a conviction following a trial, where it could be seriously contended that there was a refusal to hear the case of the accused, or where the trial took place in his absence. Or where he was not allowed to call relevant witnesses. Similarly, of course, if the tribunal was shown to have been corrupt, or not properly constituted, or ... if the Court had no jurisdiction either to try the crime, or to pass the sentence ...[62]

Although the board hearing Ryan's case did not give its reasons, it had clearly resolved the issue of the application in line with the consistent reluctance of the judicial committee going back more than a century to interfere on criminal matters. Lord Reid delivered the decision: 'Their Lordships are of the opinion that notwithstanding the very clear arguments put forward by learned counsel, their Lordships are unable to grant special leave to appeal in this case, and their Lordships will therefore humbly advise Her Majesty accordingly.'[63] With that usual but all-too-brief statement that the petition had been dismissed and that the matter would not proceed to appeal, the last legal possibility of averting Ryan's execution seemed exhausted.[64]

It was 1:00AM Melbourne time on Tuesday, 24 January when the decision was announced in London; later editions of Melbourne's morning newspapers carried the page-one story that Ryan's Privy Council application had been rejected. 'We have exhausted our legal possibilities now', Opas told the Australian Associated Press journalist outside the courtroom. The only hope left, he said, was 'to appeal to someone's clemency'.[65] As it happened, his comments were carried in *The Age* on the same front page that reported that three jurors had gone beyond their petition to the governor to now publicly appeal to the Victorian government for just such clemency for Ryan. The report said that Sir Henry Bolte had refused to comment. Later the same morning the Victorian crown solicitor, Tom Mornane, was notified of the Privy Council's decision by cable from London, and minutes later Ryan was advised unofficially of the outcome by acting prison governor William Prouse as he took exercise in yard no. 1.[66]

While the news from London was being read that morning, moves to avert the hanging took on a new urgency as churchmen appealed to the Victorian governor to intervene. The new appeal was initiated behind the scenes by the Anglican Archbishop of Melbourne, Dr Frank Woods, who quickly sent a hand-delivered note to Sir Rohan Delacombe seeking an interview for himself and Bishop Arthur Fox, who was administering the Melbourne Roman Catholic archbishopric during the illness of Archbishop Justin Simonds:

> January 24th, 1967
>
> Your Excellency,
>
> I write with a very urgent request to you to grant an interview to Bishop Fox and myself if possible within the next few hours. Our intention will be to pray that you will exercise the powers of Royal prerogative specifically reserved to you in this State under Section 505 of the Crimes Act to reprieve Ronald Ryan from the gallows and, in Her Majesty's name, commute the sentence.
>
> My reason for asking Your Excellency to see us so urgently is that we feel that once the Executive Council's decision in the light of the Privy Council's rejection of Ryan's appeal is made public it would be extremely difficult for Your Excellency, even if you so desired, to exercise the powers which are given to you personally and individually as Governor under Section 505.
>
> Bishop Fox and I have no intention of allowing our request to see you, or your reply to our request, being known outside the very small circle and we are determined that it shall not be publicised in any way. We realise the great responsibility laid upon you in this clause in the constitution and we shall completely understand and respect your decision if you feel unable to see us, or, having seen us, you feel unable to comply with our request.
>
> If Your Excellency is graciously willing to receive us perhaps we might ask you to name the time and place to the bearer of this letter, the Reverend J.A. Grant, my Chaplain.

I have the honour to be,
Your Excellency's obedient servant,
(signed) Frank Woods
Archbp[67]

When he received this letter, Delacombe quickly telephoned the premier to seek advice about how to respond to the request. Bolte advised Delacombe not to see the archbishop but to reply in writing, giving his reasons.[68] Based upon that advice, Delacombe's letter was cordial but discouraging:

24th January, 1967

Your Grace,

I have received your letter of the 24th January, 1967, in which you request an interview with me, in company with Bishop Fox, to discuss the case of Ronald Joseph Ryan.

I do respect your feelings in this matter, and have given long and deep consideration to your request. I have decided that it would not be appropriate to receive Bishop Fox and yourself to discuss this subject.

Section 505 of the Crimes Act 1958, to which you refer, must be interpreted having regard to my Royal Instructions which specifically state that the Governor shall not pardon or reprieve any offender without first receiving, in capital cases, the advice of his Executive Council. As a decision has already been made in this case, on the advice of my Executive Council, it would not be competent for me to change that decision without receiving further advice from the Executive Council.

Having regard to this it is my belief that I would be exceeding my duty if I were to accept advice from other than my constitutional advisers. I regret that I cannot accede to your request, but I am sure you will know that I have not come to this decision lightly.

Yours sincerely
(Initialled)
Governor of Victoria[69]

Delacombe's response was correct in constitutional terms, but his refusal did little to dampen abolitionist activity. In an unprecedented cooperative effort, ten Christian and Jewish leaders, representing most of the major religious groups in the community, again voiced their disquiet at a number of features of the hanging.[70] One of the major reasons they advanced was that the picture of Ryan as a person was not that of a brutal, ruthless, cold-blooded killer who was beyond hope of rehabilitation. 'Without in any way excusing his criminal record or his killing of a man', the churchmen wrote, 'there is much that emerges from his story that shows him in a very different light ...'[71]

By now, the Ryan case was receiving media attention overseas, and a flood of letters arrived for the premier appealing for clemency. The anti-hanging committee had enlisted the support of the British Campaign Against Capital Punishment. Based in Bristol, the organisation was involved in activity world-wide to achieve the abolition of the death penalty. It was through the campaign that Arthur Koestler and Sidney Silverman, MP, had written to Sir Henry Bolte urging a reprieve for Ryan.[72] The letter from Silverman, who had moved the successful private member's bill abolishing capital punishment in Britain in 1964, was typical of dozens sent to the premier by members of the campaign.[73]

With pressure building, the government resolved to bring the matter to finality by announcing a new date for the hanging. The following day, 25 January, at the Executive Council chamber in the Old Treasury Building, the Executive Council, comprising Delacombe, Bolte, and Wilcox, formally determined that the sentence of death would be carried into effect at Pentridge at 8:00AM on Tuesday, 31 January.[74] Speaking to reporters after the prior cabinet meeting had decided this course, Bolte explained that he saw Ryan's murder as different from other murders. A murder against authority was different in degree from murder against society, he said. This applied to the murder of a prison officer, policeman, customs officer, or similar people who were carrying out their duty.[75]

After the high hopes held of the London appeal, opponents of the hanging decision had been brought down hard, and Ryan's prediction of a quick response by Bolte had been correct. He would be executed in less than a week. At 9:14AM on 25 January, acting governor Arthur Prouse visited Ryan in exercise yard no. 1, as he had the day before. Prouse told Ryan that governor Grindlay had just received notification officially from the sheriff that he was to be executed on 31 January. 'Very good, sir,' was Ryan's only reply.[76] Later in the afternoon he was weighed, and his fully clothed weight—twelve stone, four ounces—was recorded for the hangman.[77] Although he seemed calm, Ryan was coming to realise that his big appeal gamble had failed. He had just six days to live.

CHAPTER FOURTEEN
Protest

He's a good boy, really.
—Cecilia Ryan

FOLLOWING THE GOVERNMENT'S ANNOUNCEMENT of the new date, public feeling in Melbourne against the hanging ran high, and there was a new burst of intense protest activity as opponents realised that Ryan's execution would go ahead. With all appeals exhausted, the only hope for abolitionists now lay in the court of public opinion. What unfolded and continued intensely for the remainder of the case was a still more desperate struggle between the anti-hanging Melbourne media and the government. The media would embark upon an anti-hanging course that would surprise and anger the government and its supporters, and dismay some media proprietors and their boards of directors. In the offices of the two daily newspaper groups, the Herald & Weekly Times and David Syme & Company—traditionally supporters of conservative Victorian governments—journalists and their editors were united in their determination to thwart the government's decision. It was a political battle in which no quarter would be asked for or given. The press would campaign intensively through its columns to convince the premier that, in policy and political terms, the hanging was barbaric and indefensible.

For his part, pressed hard by a media that had hitherto been supportive on fundamental issues of state politics, the premier would seek to take every advantage, including calling up old friendships with press proprietors, to rein in journalists and newspaper management. With both sides prepared to fight out the issue, what now unfolded was a political *cause célèbre*, one that would significantly affect the political consciousness of people all over the country.

Reporting of the Ryan case had already dominated Melbourne news for the five weeks since the cabinet decision. The coverage in terms of news, features, editorials, and readers' letters, as a proportion of the total editorial space available, was vast. In the memory of newspaper journalists and executives, the hanging controversy received the most intensive and extensive treatment of any single controversy in Victorian history. The Ryan case was the page-one lead story in the three Melbourne dailies on more than a dozen occasions. After the failure of the Privy Council appeal, the issue would continue to dominate the papers' front pages and inside news pages.

As the protest pressure intensified, the premier pulled out all stops in an effort to dilute unfavourable media coverage. Bolte had some powerful friends to help politically, as he much later revealed. One supporter upon whom he could count when it mattered was Sir Frank Packer, the proprietor of *The Bulletin* and television station GTV9 in Melbourne. Packer intervened to stop the broadcast of a scheduled showing by Channel Nine of a documentary film on capital punishment. Early in January, Nine had acquired for screening 'The Penalty is Death', a 60-minute BBC documentary produced in 1961 by journalist Patrick O'Donovan. The film, which had been highly praised overseas, was an examination of the evidence for and against capital punishment. Speakers included Britain's public hangman, prominent churchmen, the ex-warden of America's San Quentin prison, and chiefs of police from the USA, England, and Norway. Murderers gave their evidence in the film, and the relatives of victims expressed their views. Although it adopted a balanced approach to the examination of capital punishment, the film reached broadly abolitionist conclusions.

The documentary was advertised for several days on Channel Nine, and its showing was published in the television listings. The program's announced viewing time was mid-evening on Wednesday, 25 January—the day after the result of the Privy Council appeal was known. However, without prior warning and a matter of only a couple of hours before it was due to be shown, the film was dropped from the evening line-up, leaving embarrassed management and staff to somehow explain the extensively promoted program's non-appearance. At

9:30PM, the scheduled time for showing, Nine newsreader Eric Pearce, making the best of an awkward situation, appeared on camera and announced on behalf of the station:

> At a time when the issue of capital punishment is being so hotly debated at all levels of the community, GTV believes that as a responsible member of that community it would be wrong to air a programme that could in any way incite the emotions of those either for or against capital punishment. GTV believes in the fair reporting of all news at all times, but feels that this question falls into a different category at this particular time.[1]

Despite this high-minded announcement, as Bolte was well aware, the program did not appear because Packer had ordered the general manager of Nine, Nigel Dick, to take it off.[2] Packer had phoned Dick from Sydney and asked whether 'that anti-hanging film' was to be shown. When Dick replied that it was, Packer said: 'Get the thing off!' Despite spirited protests from the Nine news department, the film was withdrawn and the announcement by Eric Pearce was made at the scheduled time.[3]

Protest activity also intensified at this time. The next night, Thursday 26 January, students began a silent vigil on the steps of Parliament House, vowing that it would continue 24 hours a day until the execution. In instituting the vigil, the students had the backing of the 100,000-strong national students' union. Rostered in two-hour shifts, two students robed in black academic gowns stood silently holding five-foot high torches. The diversity of students participating in the vigil was impressive. Apart from the students anti-hanging committees at Melbourne and Monash universities, there were members of the Australian Universities Liberal Federation, the Melbourne University Democratic Socialist Club, student Christian Scientists, and students from virtually every political group on the campus. (There was even a student supporter of capital punishment, who out of a sense of democratic fair play and loyalty to his anti-hanging friends when the need on the roster was great, had agreed to a regular time on the roster. He was given the less conspicuous and hard-to-fill 4:00AM to 6:00AM shift.)

The first of the relay chosen for the vigil were law students Geoff Eames, 21, and Patricia Maxwell, 21. (Twenty-five years later, Eames would be appointed a justice of the Supreme Court of Victoria.) Later that same Thursday night, Eames and Maxwell would go for a meal with their student friends and fellow protestors, Rick Campbell and Sue Murray, to Murray's home in Kintore Street, Camberwell. Murray's father, Tony Murray, was still on his way back from London following the hearing of the Privy Council application three days before, but her mother and sister were at home. As the students dined with the Murrays, the meal was interrupted by a handful of protesters outside the house chanting anti-hanging slogans and throwing stones onto the roof. As prosecutor in the trial and Victorian government representative at the Privy Council appeal, Tony Murray had become a target of anti-hanging sentiment, despite his own reservations about the execution. Struck by the irony of their situation but embarrassed by this unruly behaviour, Eames and Campbell went out to appeal to the protestors to stop.[4]

For the next ten days students would maintain the vigil, with people from all walks of life opposed to the hanging coming to the steps of Parliament House to express their support. All through the day and night they came. Signing the petition, talking to the protestors, sharing their concern—it all seemed to provide an outlet for the frustration many ordinary Melburnians felt at a decision taken in their name by a premier who was stubbornly refusing to listen. On the second night of the vigil, a well-dressed man wearing a cravat appeared at the protest to express his outrage at the hanging decision. He said he felt powerless in the face of the premier's stubborn rebuffs to responsible opinion, and wanted to show his support for the protest. His unusual expression of support was a wine basket with two glasses and a bottle of celebrated French wine from his cellar, a 1962 Côte Rôtie from the Rhone Valley, a red wine famous since the days of Rome. 'Drink this and smash the glasses on the steps', he commanded, before disappearing anonymously into the night. The wine was duly drunk, but the students could not quite bring themselves to smash the glasses.

For all the fury of opposition to the hanging, it is not possible to say that public opinion was decisively opposed to the premier on this issue. There were no newspaper polls to gauge opinion on clemency for Ryan, but it is likely that the community was evenly divided.[5] However, with an avalanche of letters to the press—the largest on any issue in living memory—running at levels of more than five to one against the hanging, the issue was hotting up and the premier was feeling the pressure.[6] When Violet, Irma, and Gloria visited Ryan in Pentridge on 27 January, there was a flurry of media attention.[7] In its evening bulletin on that day, Channel Nine in Melbourne ran a news story of the visit. Bolte rang Sir Frank Packer in Sydney to complain. 'Don't worry, Henry', Packer told Bolte, 'you leave it to me.' According to Bolte, Packer's intervention ensured that the item was pulled from the late news bulletin.[8]

Community-based protests also gathered pace. In Coburg, the location of Pentridge prison, where the intended hanging was scheduled to take place, a citizens' committee under local councillor Arthur Sanger was active in galvanising community opposition to the proposed execution. Trade unions, which had seen some fiery exchanges about the proposed hanging at meetings of the Trades Hall Council, called for industrial stoppages as a way of demonstrating their opposition. Leaders of all the Protestant churches and the Melbourne Hebrew congregation again appealed for mercy in a letter published in *The Herald*, and Cecilia made an emotional public appeal for her son's life.[9] In an immortal line, she told Channel Seven journalist Danny Webb, in a televised news interview: 'He's a good boy, really'.[10]

The next day, Parliament House was the scene of a violent display of opposition when four thousand members of the Waterside Workers' Federation and the Builders' Labourers' Federation marched up Bourke Street in the central city, and a large number of them attempted to storm Parliament House. Parliament was not sitting, and the building was largely deserted, but Parliament House had always been the symbol of Victorian government, and the preferred focus for demonstrations. This was despite the fact that the premier more usually would be found in his office in nearby Treasury Place, behind the Old Treasury Building at the top of Collins Street. When they reached Parliament House, the union marchers were greeted by a solid wall of police who tried to turn them away. Serious scuffling broke out when dozens of unionists made a wild dash up the steps for the Parliament House door and began loudly beating on it with banners and placards, and shouting 'Hang Bolte!', 'Bolte Murderer!', and 'Ryan should not hang!'[11]

After a few minutes in which police and unionists battled fiercely on the steps, organisers of the march called to the crowd to move to the gardens near Parliament House to hear speeches. Photographs of the wild scenes on the steps of Parliament House, which dominated the front page of *The Herald* later in the day, were to become an enduring image of the Ryan case. Politically, the incident was a serious blow to the anti-hanging campaign because it allowed the government to momentarily redefine the issue as one of law and order, and it dug in its heels.

Two days later, police and demonstrators clashed again at a protest rally outside Pentridge gaol. A number of arrests were made when a breakaway section of the crowd began beating on the steel door of the gaol.[12] The rally had followed a march by five thousand protestors through Sydney Road, Coburg, to the prison.[13] The premier blamed the media for the increase in public emotion over the hanging, and said they were creating an atmosphere hostile to government, as Labor had tried to do for demonstrations against the war in Vietnam. As the public clamour against the hanging intensified, the police guard on the premier was increased to five, constables being positioned both outside in Treasury Place and in the corridor outside the premier's office. At the premier's Queens Road apartment and at Kialla, his farm at Bamganie, police had been stationed for some time, never leaving the place while the premier was there.[14]

These special security measures had been stepped up following threats made to the premier's life and that of other ministers. Not long before the end of December, Bolte had received a number of telegrams expressing the wish that he should 'have a swinging New Year'. Sir Henry also received a number of threatening letters—which he threw away—as did Lady Bolte and several ministers' wives. The wives of ministers Tom Darcy, Gill Chandler, and Jim Manson had all received a duplicate threatening letter which said that because their husbands were in cabinet and responsible for the Ryan decision, they would be killed. Lady Bolte's letter was intercepted before she opened it, and she was unaware of its contents. These letters, like the telegrams, had been sent from the Fitzroy or North Fitzroy Post Office.

Police forensic examination was subsequently undertaken to establish the responsible typewriter, and fingerprint examination was made of the envelope. Senior Detective Lincoln Stanley of the special branch followed up certain leads, one of which involved interviewing a communist letter-writer otherwise the subject of special branch attention, but suspicions of communist involvement were shown to be groundless. In a memorandum which subsequently went to the premier and chief secretary, Detective Stanley concluded—in the inimitable style of a police officer making an official report—that, while it was 'thoroughly deplorable that such letters should be addressed to the wives of ministers, I would suggest that the letter's duplication as a circular somewhat mitigates the apprehension attendant on the receipt of the first missive to Lady Bolte.'[15] Further efforts to apprehend the perpetrator of the threatening letters proved fruitless.

Members of the anti-hanging groups were not immune from threatening letters, either. Crank letters were sent to the offices of the National Union of Australian University Students at 52 Storey Street, Parkville, which was serving as a coordination centre for petitions and fundraising. These letters were usually addressed by name to anyone whose profile in the media was raised by the anti-hanging campaign. Typically the letters threatened violence against 'crim lovers' and 'supporters of murderers'; some suggested that the protestors should be hanged, as well. These letters, like those received by the premier, were usually thrown away.

On 26 January, Ryan's solicitor, Ralph Freadman, tried a new tack when he sent a cable to the Queen asking her to intervene and commute or stay the execution. The telegram, on receipt at Buckingham Palace, was sent to Sandringham, where the Queen was holidaying. Within 24 hours, Buckingham Palace responded, indicating that she was not able to intervene.[16] Although the palace did not say so directly, Freadman's telegram, like Archbishop Woods' request to the governor, had been flawed in conception. The first issue, as Delacombe had suggested to Woods several days before, was that the exercise of the royal prerogative of mercy was, in fact, precisely the process that the cabinet followed in commuting sentences of death, and was the process followed when ministers considered—and declined to recommend—mercy for Ryan on 12 December. The second issue was that while the prerogative of mercy was a power notionally held by the sovereign and her vice-regal representative, in practice it was exercised only upon the advice of the premier and his ministers.

The problem was that the Victorian *Crimes Act 1958* referred to the royal prerogative of mercy in language that gave rise to the popular misconception that the prerogative was exercisable by the monarch or her vice-regal representative other than upon the advice of her constitutional advisers—that is, the premier and his cabinet. Section 505 of the *Crimes Act* said: 'Nothing in this Act shall in any manner affect Her

Majesty's royal prerogative of mercy.' Indeed, in colonial times, the Commissions, Letters Patent and Instructions to Governors from the Monarch had explicitly expressed a discretionary character to the exercise of the prerogative. In December 1855, for example, article eighteen of the commission of governor Sir Charles Hotham from Queen Victoria had instructed that, in respect of offenders sentenced to death:

> you are to decide either to extend or to withhold a pardon or reprieve according to your own deliberate judgment, whether the members of Our said Executive Council concur therein, or otherwise; entering, nevertheless, on the Minutes of the said Council, a Minute of your reasons at length, in case you should decide any such question in opposition to the judgment of the majority of the Members thereof.[17]

This provision in the royal instructions to Australian governors had persisted—albeit with some controversy—through the latter part of the nineteenth century. As late as 1863, in a robbery-under-arms case involving alleged bushranger John Bow, the governor of NSW commuted Bow's death sentence, overruling the advice of his Executive Council.[18] In the course of the public debate about the case leading up to Bow's scheduled hanging, it had been urged upon the governor, Sir John Young, that he exercise the royal prerogative independently of his constitutional advisers on the Executive Council, precisely because his royal instructions directed him to do so.[19] Despite the changes to constitutional practice consequent upon responsible government in Victoria, this provision in the royal instructions was not revised until 1892.[20]

Hence, in 1967, despite changes to constitutional practice wrought by responsible government, Federation, and the Statute of Westminster of 1931, in the minds of many people the prerogative of mercy seemed to have endured—like a pressed flower from the colonial garden—to mean that it was a special personal discretion of the Queen and her vice-regal representative to pardon criminals and reprieve offenders in capital cases. Indeed, on 25 January, Ryan's solicitors wrote to the governor of Victoria drawing his attention to the 1863 case of Sir John Young, and suggested it was a precedent he might follow in exercising his discretion.[21] This was certainly not the case. From the early 1900s the leading constitutional authorities saw the governor's prerogative powers as exercisable only with, and upon, the advice of ministers.[22] As the governor's official secretary reminded Delacombe, the royal instructions of 29 October 1900 had specifically directed that:

> The Governor shall not pardon or reprieve any offender without first receiving in capital cases the advice of the Executive Council.[23]

The palace referred to this issue in its cabled response to Freadman, which, following the protocol relevant to such matters, took a circuitous route. The private secretary to the Queen had contacted Murray Tyrrell, the official secretary to the governor-general in Canberra, requesting that the governor of Victoria inform Freadman of the following reply:

> Your telegram of the 26th January has been received by the Queen, who regrets that it is not possible for her to intervene personally on behalf of your client Ronald Joseph Ryan, since the Royal Prerogative in Victoria is exercised on Her Majesty's behalf by the Governor on the advice of his Ministers.[24]

Freadman's misconception about the governor's role was widely shared, and thousands of Victorians and people elsewhere around Australia wrote letters and sent telegrams to Delacombe urging that he exercise his powers and commute the sentence, as if he had some discretion in the matter. One such letter came from an irate member of a well-known Melbourne Liberal family. Betty Kemp was the wife of influential Liberal and the founder of the Institute of Public Affairs, CD Kemp, and the mother of David and Rod who, 30 years later, would become federal Liberal ministers. Betty Kemp was very angry about the approaching hanging, and on 27 January wrote to Delacombe to express her feelings:

> Your Excellency:
>
> As an exhausted citizen of the State of Victoria, I feel I must appeal to you to save Sir Henry Bolte and the Liberal State Government from themselves. If the execution is carried out, the Government will be classed in the minds of many responsible people as a reactionary group

> I am a Liberal voter, my family are members of the Liberal party, and I am horrified that the Premier has ignored and dismissed the distress caused by this decision as merely a press and TV furore.
>
> The injustice of the decision to hang is obvious …
>
> Could you as Governor of Victoria please suggest to the Premier, that an act of clemency would certainly be received by many of his Liberal supporters with great relief—the harm done, if this execution is carried out, will be lasting.[25]

(Certainly, Betty Kemp's disgust at premier Bolte was long-lasting and deeply felt; for years afterwards, whenever Bolte appeared on television she would get up and leave the room.[26])

That same day, Cecilia Ryan, who had come to Melbourne as the execution approached, followed up her telegram to the governor with a letter to the premier appealing for mercy and, if this could not be granted, requesting her son's body for burial:

> I plead again for the life of my son Ronald Ryan, and ask that even at [this] late hour you will reverse your decision to hang my son. If you cannot find it in your heart to grant this request then I pray [you] will grant me one last favour, that the body of my son be given into my custody immediately after his death.
>
> I pray to God for the success of this last prayer and that is that it find favour. You will understand that I must have an early answer to this so that I can make the necessary arrangements.[27]

The premier asked the crown solicitor, Tom Mornane, to give urgent advice about the matter to enable him to reply. Mornane pointed out that giving Ryan's body to his mother would be contrary to section 492 of the *Crimes Act*, which stated that 'the body of every person executed shall be buried within the precincts of the gaol in which he has been last confined …'[28] In the event, Sir Henry did not himself reply to Cecilia's letter, but a response was hand-delivered to her at the Abbotsford convent later on the same day. In the letter, the secretary of the Premier's Department, Alex Coulthard, wrote that Sir Henry was 'unable to accede to your request that the Government's recommendation in relation to your son be altered.' Citing the legal advice on the provisions of the *Crimes Act*, Coulthard wrote that 'it would be unlawful for the

Government to meet your wishes' in respect of custody of her son's body.[29] Perhaps it was just as well that the premier left it to more diplomatic officials to respond to Cecilia's request. Freed of advisers and the constraints of government formality and civility, Bolte later let loose to journalists about this mother's simple wish to give her son a Christian burial in consecrated ground: 'How ghoulish can you get?', he snapped.[30] Bolte's response produced a savage backlash among sections of the public. One irate Melbourne woman fired off a signed telegram to the premier:

> HANG HIM IF YOU MUST BUT TO REFUSE A WOMAN HER SON'S CORPSE IS MEDIEVAL BARBARISM. WHY NOT HANG IT IN SWANSTON STREET YOU EVIL CHRISTIAN.[31]

On 28 January, a new church-based appeal was made to spare Ryan when senior leaders of the Roman Catholic Church in Melbourne asked the Holy See to intervene. Bishop Fox wrote to the premier indicating that His Eminence the Cardinal Secretary of State to His Holiness had been approached, and that he had been authorised by the Apostolic Delegate in Australia, the Most Reverend Domenico Enrici, to so inform him. As Fox wrote to the premier: '... His Excellency appeals to you on humanitarian grounds not to proceed with the execution.'[32] In the event, His Holiness declined to take the matter further, with the Vatican citing a policy of papal non-intervention in the internal affairs of another country.[33]

Elsewhere in Melbourne on that day, Cecilia was visiting Sir John Williams, managing director of *The Herald*, to thank him for the paper's editorial support. It prompted Williams to ring the premier the next day to say that he would like to come up to his office and talk to him about Ryan. 'Jack, you'd be wasting your bloody time,' Bolte replied.[34] So Williams did not go to see Bolte, but he continued to direct his paper's anti-hanging editorial line, several times writing leaders himself.

In Sydney, where there was considerable interest in the case but sparse media coverage, the story was very different. At Australian Consolidated Press, the chairman, Sir Frank Packer, was doing all he could to ensure that his publications supported the Bolte government, as he had done with Channel Nine. The publication that Packer most directly controlled, the Sydney *Daily Telegraph*, was strongly in favour of the hanging. More problematic, however, was the weekly magazine *The Bulletin*, which Packer had historically allowed a greater degree of editorial independence. However, the limits of that independence were revealed when, shortly after the edition to be published on Tuesday, 31 January—the scheduled date for the hanging—was printed, some 40,000 copies were withdrawn from circulation at Packer's direction because of anti-hanging material contained in it.[35] *The Bulletin*'s general manager, Clyde Packer, told the editor, Peter Coleman, that his father would not distribute the magazine with the existing editorial material. No explanation was given, but they would have to be replaced. The material that offended Packer was a Tanner cartoon and an editorial entitled 'Day of the Quicklime', written by Coleman and Peter Samuel. The editorial bitterly attacked the hanging which, it was assumed, would have been held by the time the issue reached the newsstands. After dismissing the arguments in favour of hanging Ryan, the editorial said:

> So the white hood and rope are lowered over the head of a small time forger and thief convicted of a fatal act of violence, the hangman pulls a lever, the trap falls, and in a few moments death is seen and certified. The burial in quicklime is apparently intended as a further deterrent. The experts claim it will not have an identifiable effect on the murder rate, a large part of society is morally outraged, and Ronald Ryan, his relatives and friends are tortured, but Sir Henry Bolte and his Cabinet go about their business secure in the knowledge that Victoria and Australia are safer places to live in … The probability is still strong that Ryan killed Hodson, but there is some doubt, and there is some chance of further evidence being found which will change the balance of probabilities. If that ever happens the Ryan case will become notorious for more murders than one.[36]

Accompanying the leader was a cartoon about the hanging penned by *The Bulletin*'s art director and cartoonist, Les Tanner. It portrayed a vengeful Sir Henry Bolte dressed as the hangman, with a huge noose held furtively behind his back. The caption read: 'I do not bow to mob protests—only mob support.'

As it eventuated, withdrawing the edition was easier said than done, as distribution had already begun and trucks delivering the magazine to city newsstands had already left the press building. When the trucks returned, the drivers were told to go straight back and pick them up again. Not so easily rectified was the distribution of subscribers' copies. Six thousand of them had already been posted and were irretrievable from the mail system. It is one of the ironies of the whole incident that every library in the country that subscribed to *The Bulletin* received the offending edition and not its replacement. The 40,000 copies that had been retrieved were pulped.[37]

The nation's public broadcaster was not immune from this sort of controversy, either. As with most of the media, the Australian Broadcasting Commission's treatment of the case, both by radio and television news, was intensive. Conspicuous by its absence, however, was coverage by any of the ABC's discussion or current affairs programs. An attempt by the Victorian television current affairs program *Watch This Space* to produce a segment around the issues raised by the approaching hanging was subjected to extraordinary management interference, with the result that a considerable amount of film shot by the program was locked up and the program never shown. The ABC's only attempt at producing anything like a critical analysis of the issue was thus effectively, and finally, silenced. At precisely the moment when, with commercial media under proprietorial pressure, the ABC had an important role to play in airing the issues, decisions were taken at the most senior levels of ABC management to cause it to opt out of any coverage.[38]

WITH THEIR EDITORIAL BARRAGE obviously not producing results, the Melbourne daily papers moved to concentrate their efforts on revealing chinks in the so-far united parliamentary Liberal Party support for the hanging. Soon after the cabinet decision was taken, both *The Herald* and *The Age* had begun to canvass the views of Liberal members, hoping to draw them out on the issue. On 27 January their efforts bore fruit when the Liberal member for the marginal seat of St Kilda, Brian Dixon, disclosed that he did not believe in capital punishment, which, he said, was 'an issue of conscience beyond politics.' In a statement that revealed little of his anguish over the issue, Dixon said:

> I am disclosing my views because I regard this as an issue beyond politics and because I believe the electorate is entitled to know

> them. I believe in the sentence of life imprisonment, the security of prisons and the protection of police and other officials. But I do not believe their security is improved by hanging. The decision has been made by men who have to make it namely, the Executive Council.
>
> This is not the Parliamentary Liberal Party—it is a decision by Cabinet. These are men I have the utmost respect for. I believe they are doing what they think is right. But as a private member of Parliament and the Liberal Parliamentary Party, I disagree with their belief.[39]

The premier, furious with Dixon's statement, told journalists off-the-record at a press conference next morning that he had phoned Dixon and told him that he 'might as well look for another job because he wasn't going anywhere in politics.'[40] Dixon's public opposition to the hanging was to earn him few plaudits among his colleagues. Arriving at Parliament House the day after his comments had been published, Dixon found an anonymous note in his correspondence pigeon-hole. The abusive one-word note, written in a hand he recognised as one of his parliamentary Liberal Party colleagues, said simply: 'SCAB'.[41]

The next day saw a second Liberal MP oppose the hanging publicly. George Gibbs, the member for Portland, said he would keep Ryan in gaol rather than hang him. 'I don't like hanging', he said. 'I can't understand why Ryan has been singled out. I think hanging is un-Christian in a so-called Christian community.'[42] Gibbs, however, was in a somewhat less precarious position than Dixon, having already failed to retain pre-selection for the next election—his seat being absorbed in a re-distribution. Though Gibbs and Dixon were the only two back-benchers to make public statements opposed to the hanging, there were three other Liberal members— Alan Hunt, Ian McLaren, and Murray Byrne—who also opposed the decision, but did so privately.[43] Byrne went further by defying the premier in receiving a deputation of clergymen and members of the Ballarat Anti-Hanging Committee during the case. It was a measure of the premier's authority in the party room as well as of his determination to get his way that so few Liberals were prepared to incur his wrath by public dissent from the decision.

By now, government insiders were enraged by a media coverage that they saw as constituting a violent and unprecedented attack on the government and the premier. As a later assessment by a government official put it, the press campaign was 'vicious':

> The anti-hangers received banner headlines and the newspapers used all their tricks, wiles and everything they knew to inflame public opinion against the hanging. Mainly as a result of this vicious press propaganda, spearheaded by *The Herald* and *The Sun*, ugly incidents took place in demonstrations. The demonstrators were given every incentive to defy authority by the screaming banner headlines of the press. The Press resorted to untruths, distortions, sensationalism and hypocrisy in an endeavour to inflame public opinion against the Government ... In fact all Melbourne papers ... sank to the level of the Yellow Press.[44]

If the press was worrying the premier and cabinet, *The Age* was causing deep concern with members of the board of directors of its publisher, David Syme and Co, most of who supported capital punishment. This was not the first time that the board had been concerned at anti-hanging editorial policy. During the Tait case the then editor, Keith Sinclair, an abolitionist, took a consistent anti-hanging editorial line that, for the cautious and conservative newspaper, was unprecedented. To the seven-member Syme board, the anti-hanging attack on the government was irresponsible. *The Age* had rarely been strong on issues of social policy, and the anti-hanging campaign waged by the paper—moderate though it was—caused some board members to be apprehensive of the effect on circulation. *The Age* campaign on Ryan would be carried on with the memory of events at the newspaper during the Tait case very forcefully in mind.

Much more deliberate and condemnatory than in the Tait case, the editorial line upset some members of the board. Not only were the leaders too strong but, it was thought, the paper was editorialising through its news columns. Though rumblings of the board's discontent drifted down to the editorial offices, the issue was never raised at a board meeting, due primarily to managing director Ranald Macdonald successfully keeping it off the board's agenda—despite considerable pressure from his fellow directors. This was an achievement of some significance in view of the fact that, despite changes in board membership since the Tait case, pro-hanging opinion was still in a majority.[45]

If the Syme board was feeling the pressure of *The Age*'s editorial position on Ryan so, too, was the government. Publicly, the premier was generally angry at the coverage given by all Melbourne dailies, accusing them of inciting demonstrations; but, increasingly, his comments were directed specifically at *The Age*. The vigour of *The Age*'s stand probably surprised the government, who may have expected the paper—with a new man, Graham Perkin, as editor—to be less assertive on the issue. Perkin, who had been appointed to the job only three months before at the age of 36, was a crusading newspaperman with a strong social conscience and a commitment to fearless journalism. Deeply affected by the cabinet decision, Perkin took on the issue with a passionate conviction that the hanging was immoral and indefensible. Late in the case, Perkin had Father Brosnan sleeping on a camp stretcher in his office, as events were unfolding that required a quick editorial response and an informed source.[46]

With *The Age* campaign causing deep concern in the government, Bolte and Rylah several times phoned members of the board in an endeavour to have the editorial line toned down, although they never phoned the editor or journalists.[47] When these initiatives did not produce results, Bolte enlisted the aid of Sir Rohan Delacombe. The chairman of the Syme board, Ted Neill, and Delacombe were friends. They were both former senior military officers who had served with distinction in World War II, and they shared an outlook shaped by career army service and the exigencies of war. Born in 1906 in Malta, Delacombe had been educated at Harrow and at the Royal Military College, Sandhurst, and he had seen active service in France, Norway, Normandy, and Italy. Between 1943 and 1954, he had been Lieutenant Colonel commanding the Eighth and Second Battalions of the Royal Scots. After that, as Major General Delacombe, he had served in command of the British military sector in Berlin.

Ted Neill had been born a year earlier than Delacombe in 1905 in New Zealand and he, too, had pursued a military career, joining the Seaforth Highlanders in 1926 after taking an MA at Cambridge. Like Delacombe, in 1936 Lieutenant Colonel Neill had served in Palestine and later France, and he went on to serve in the Middle East and the Far East. Colonel Neill, as he was known to all employees of *The Age*, was a large, imposing man who wore a monocle and walked with a silver-handled cane. As chairman of *The Age* he flew his own aircraft and was chauffeured around Melbourne in an enormous, black 1965 Mercedes-Benz 600 Landaulet limousine, the only one of its type in the city, and one of a limited number in the world at the time. It was an indication of the closeness of the relationship between Neill and Delacombe that Neill had as his chauffeur Alistair Humphrey, who had been Delacombe's military driver in post-war Berlin.

Delacombe and Neill saw one another often at Government House, and there were occasions when informally Delacombe would gently chide Neill about some editorial policy of the paper with which he took issue. Neill, for his part, disavowed any influence with the editorial floor, despite the fact that his stepson, Ranald Macdonald, was the managing director and editor-in-chief: 'I am only the chairman', he would respond, plaintively. This time, Delacombe was on a mission with more serious intent. Bolte had asked Delacombe to ring Neill with the object of getting the board to instruct the editor to moderate the editorial line. Delacombe rang Neill and expressed his view that, with constant demonstrations and the threat of civil disobedience, the issue had now become one of law and order. Delacombe said that, in his position, coming into contact as he did with prominent figures in government and industry, he felt that the Victorian community was in danger of serious violence were not law and order firmly asserted. In those circumstances, *The Age* should be supporting the premier, Delacombe said.[48]

Although not widely known about at *The Age*, Delacombe's intervention caused consternation among those few senior executives, including the editor, who learned of it. As they saw it, there could be no argument that a state governor—no less than a governor-general of the Commonwealth—had a constitutional duty to warn and counsel his ministers were they to propose a legislative course that might imperil the ship of state. It was altogether another matter, however, for a governor to appear to be undertaking the political work of a premier on a contentious issue of public policy. On this view, given the apolitical nature of his office, Delacombe's call was seen as inappropriate and unwise, and his intervention was regarded by senior executives at *The Age* as a distinctly unwelcome development. Those at *The Age* who knew Delacombe knew him to be a decent and kindly man, steeped in the virtues of honesty and integrity, and as straight as an arrow. No-one ever said a bad word against him. Executives at *The Age* who knew of the

Delacombe call were in no doubt that Bolte was behind it.

Meanwhile, a last-minute legal move to reprieve Ryan was underway in the Supreme Court, where his solicitors lodged an application to allow time to gather material for a new trial, the presentation of a formal petition to the Queen, and the production of material relating to Ryan's character and background. Barrister Peter Brusey, appearing for Ryan, asked Justice Starke to intervene and grant a reprieve; but the court was unimpressed with the argument and refused the application. Starke said that, in his experience, he had never known evidence of personality and character to be given before a judge in a capital case:

> The whole argument is misconceived. The Court's function is to try the accused. His fate then remains with the Executive Council. The practice has been that the trial judge is sent for and the Ministers inquire after his views. That practice was followed in this case. I have little doubt that full information relating to Ryan's background was obtained and was before Cabinet.
>
> The argument really is that I should take on myself the responsibility of hearing evidence of what Ryan's fate should be and make a recommendation. That would be an unwarranted interference with the powers of the Executive.[49]

At Pentridge, Ryan was preparing for his execution just four days away. He received a stream of visitors, many of them concerned with his spiritual well-being. At 10:00AM Cecilia visited, as she had on most days, accompanied by Sister Madonna from the Sisters of the Good Shepherd in Abbotsford. In the afternoon, Violet, Irma, and Gloria spent 45 minutes with Ryan in his cell, and Father Brosnan had a specially sanctioned visit in the evening after the division was locked down for the night. The purpose of Brosnan's visit was to talk to Ryan about his confession the next day. Brosnan had sought special approval from the director of prisons, Eric Shade, and subsequently arranged with Father Vin Arthur of St Bernard's Church in East Coburg to hear Ryan's confession, as Brosnan believed he should not hear it.[50]

The religious visits continued through the next day. The first visitor was Keith Johanson, Ryan's old boss from his Warburton timber-cutting days, whose visit as a non-family member had to be specially approved by the director of prisons.[51] Johanson spoke with Ryan about the strength of his faith, and left with him *Steps to Christ* by Ellen White and a book of parables, *Tales Christ Told* by April Oursler Armstrong.[52] Later in the morning, special arrangements were put in place for Father Arthur to hear Ryan's confession, and it was conducted in exercise yard no. 1.[53] Ryan later described this confession, his first for many years, as very difficult. At the end of three hours with Father Arthur, he told Father Brosnan: 'Father, that took more out of me than any bust that I've ever done.'[54] In religion he appeared finally to have found something other than himself in which he could believe. For Brosnan, this was the return to the faith that he and Cecilia had prayed for.[55] With three days to go to the hanging, Ryan had made his peace with God and was ready to die.

The road outside Concord Hospital, Sydney, where Ryan and Walker were recaptured by police on 5 January 1966 after seventeen days on the run.

Walker (left) and Ryan (right) taken into custody by NSW police after their recapture outside Concord Hospital. *(The Age)*

Justice John Erskine Starke, who presided at the trial for murder of Ryan and Walker in the Supreme Court of Victoria, March 1966. *(The Age)*

Prosecutor Tony Murray, leaving the Supreme Court on the first day of the Ryan-Walker hearing, after making his first appearance in a murder trial as solicitor-general. *(The Age)*

Ryan's defence counsel, Philip Opas, QC, (left) leaves the Supreme Court with his junior, criminal barrister Brian Bourke. In time, Opas came to accept his client's claim to innocence. *(The Age)*

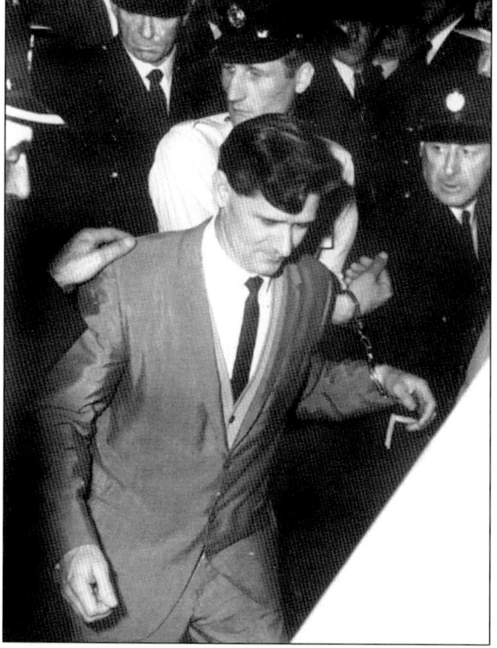

Handcuffed to a prison officer, Ryan leaves the Supreme Court at the end of the first day's hearing in his trial for murder. *(The Age)*

The premier of Victoria, Sir Henry Bolte, leaving the cabinet meeting after it had considered Ryan's fate. Bolte believed that sufficiently bad murderers should be hanged, but wanted to re-assert his political authority following his political defeat in the Tait case of 1962. *(The Age)*

The governor of Victoria, Sir Rohan Delacombe, leaves the Old Treasury Building and the Executive Council chamber after ministers had advised that the execution of Ryan should proceed. *(The Age)*

The portrait in oils of a young Jack Starke painted by his friend at the bar, John Bloomfield, who later was a minister in the Bolte cabinet that determined Ryan's fate. Invited as the trial judge to the cabinet meeting, Starke rehearsed in his mind the lie that he proposed to tell ministers in order to persuade them to commute Ryan's sentence. This portrait by Bloomfield (who, like Starke, opposed capital punishment) hung in Starke's hallway at his house in Mt Eliza. *(Reproduced with the kind permission of Thos Hodgson)*

Sir Frank Packer, proprietor of *The Bulletin*, objected to this cartoon by Les Tanner in the magazine, and directed that the edition be recalled and pulped. *(Reproduced with permission of the Picture Collection, State Library of Victoria)*

Barrister Philip Opas, QC, and his junior, Allayne Kiddle, arrive at the Privy Council chamber in London on 23 January 1967 to argue Ryan's application for special leave to appeal against his conviction for murder. *(The Herald & Weekly Times)*

On the steps of Parliament House, Melbourne, Patricia Maxwell and Geoff Eames begin the Students' Anti-Hanging Committee's silent vigil protesting against the execution. The vigil would run night and day for ten days until the execution. *(The Age)*

The secretary of the Victorian Anti-Hanging Committee, Barry Jones, shown here at a press conference on the approaching execution, ran a vigorous media campaign against the hanging. The committee worked behind the scenes to mount Ryan's legal appeal to the Privy Council in London, and later went to extraordinary lengths in an effort to secure an eleventh-hour reprieve. *(The Age)*

Community groups and unions joined forces in this protest march up Sydney Road, Coburg, to a rally at Pentridge prison on Sunday, 28 January 1967. *(The Herald & Weekly Times)*

Pentridge Roman Catholic chaplain, Father John Brosnan, escorts Cecilia Ryan into the prison for a visit to her son on 27 January 1967. With just four days to the scheduled execution, Brosnan and Cecilia were concerned to see Ryan renew his religious faith. *(The Age)*

The next day (28 January 1967), a smiling Father Brosnan talks to the media after Ryan had made his confession and returned to the faith. *(The Age)*

Driven from Mt Eliza at high speed in a police car, Justice John Starke arrives at the Supreme Court for a special sitting of the court to consider new evidence the night before the scheduled hanging.
(The Age)

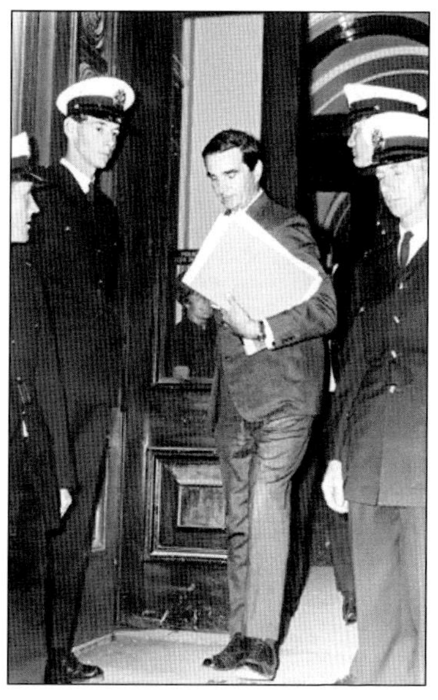

Barrister Peter Brusey leaves the packed courtroom at the Supreme Court after Justice Starke had granted his application for an injunction staying Ryan's execution scheduled for the following morning. *(The Age)*

Justice Starke strides from the Premier's Office at 2 Treasury Place on the morning of 31 January 1967 after attending cabinet and briefing ministers on his eleventh-hour stay of execution the night before.
(The Age)

Late in the day of 2 February 1967, attorney-general Arthur Rylah was served with a new petition by lawyers seeking clemency for Ryan. Rylah immediately went to premier Bolte's office, where they thrashed out the issues prior to the second Executive Council meeting on Ryan for the day. *(The Age)*

The governor, Sir Rohan Delacombe, arrives at Government House after being driven at high speed under police escort from Sorrento by his ADC, captain Anthony Fitzwilliams-Hyde. Delacombe had been recalled by the premier to preside at a special Executive Council meeting at 9:00pm—less than twelve hours before the scheduled execution. *(The Age)*

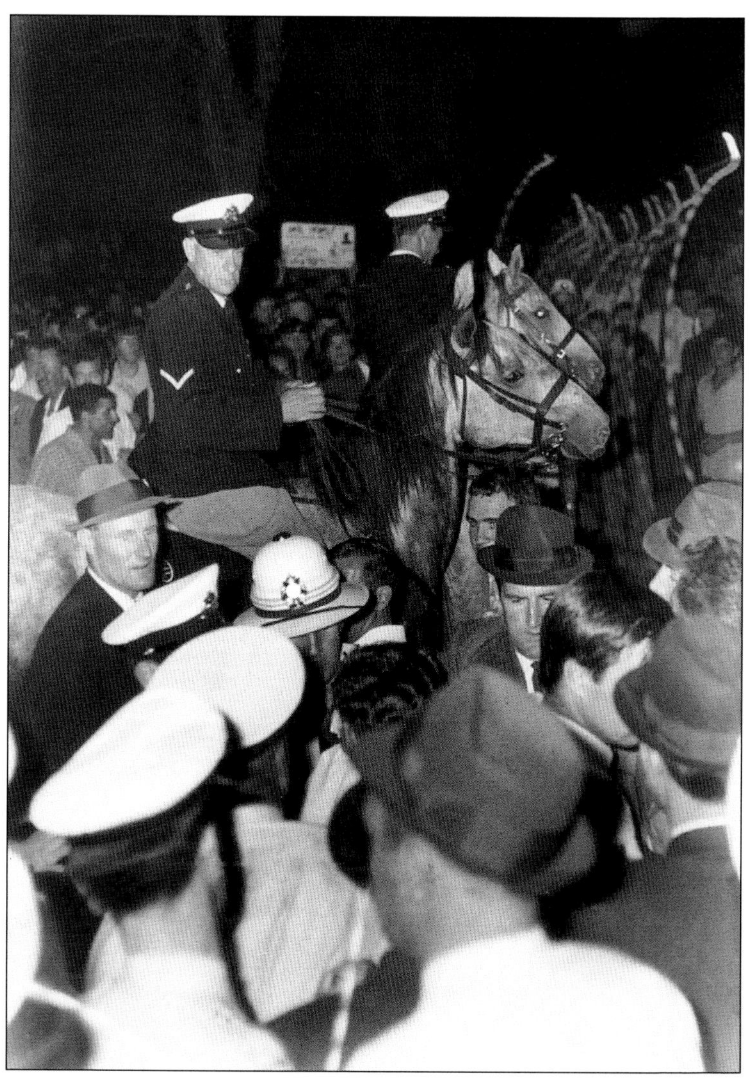

On 2 February 1967, the night before the execution, 3,000 protestors gathered outside Pentridge prison in a last great outpouring of anger and frustration. Amid emotional and, at times, wild scenes, there were 97 arrests as 200 police battled to control the demonstrators. *(The Age)*

Pentridge governor Ian Grindlay, who came to have a high regard for Ryan. After the special Executive Council meeting on the night of 2 February 1967, Grindlay went to Ryan's cell in H Division at 10:45pm to tell him that he would hang in the morning. *(The Age)*

A section of the 3,000-strong crowd outside Pentridge on the night before the hanging. Many protestors stayed throughout the night to await the execution at 8:00am the next morning. *(The Age)*

I would have you re-read this letter at a more mature age — say forty —. When in light of experience you'd be more understanding and better able to judge — Having in mind ones concern at an early age of the concern about what others may think and our self-consciousness of their views.

With regard to my guilt I say only that I am innocent of intent and have a clear conscience in the matter.

I was not content to have my loved ones committed to a life of drudgery and sought the means to establish the chance for you & your children.

For this odd thinking I must for excuse point to my childhood & history. There have been many who succeeded so that subsequent generations could point back in pride; but I must take my place of those who failed and unfortunately you share the attendant shame & disgrace. However, I'm confident you'll be equal to the task of rising above this.

As I am the last of the Ryan's — on the male side — I regret not leaving a son

A section of the letter that Ryan wrote on toilet paper in his cell the night before he was hanged—the last letter he ever wrote. The letter measures more than ten feet in length. In this section of the letter, Ryan writes: 'With regard to my guilt I say only that I am innocent of intent and have a clear conscience in the matter.'

The condemned cell, number 67, on the first level of the D Division block at Pentridge prison, adjacent to the scaffold. Ryan took five steps to reach a chalk mark on the trap. Pentridge governor Ian Grindlay stood beside him on the gallows.

The gallows in D Division at Pentridge where Ryan was hanged at 8:00am on 3 February 1967. He walked from the condemned cell at the first level at left to a point at the centre of the catwalk below the white scaffold beam. The noose was resting on the back of the railed catwalk. A green tarpaulin shielded the body from the view of witnesses as it fell through the trap.
(The Herald & Weekly Times)

Anti-hanging protestors outside Pentridge fall silent as the clock on the prison tower strikes eight.

Following execution tradition, the grave of Ronald Ryan was left unmarked in the small Pentridge burial site behind D Division. However, a plaque has now been placed in the vicinity of the burial, marking the execution of the ten criminals hanged at the prison in the period 1932 to 1967.

CHAPTER FIFTEEN

Reprieve

[T]here is no time, and in these circumstances one must not make a mistake, and consequently I propose to accede to the application and suspend the operation of the [death] sentence which I pronounced.
—Justice John Starke

As the clock continued ticking down to the 31 January date for the execution, efforts by abolitionists to avert the hanging took on a new urgency and desperation. With just 72 hours to go, the feelings in Melbourne among anti-hanging groups were at fever pitch. All of the media and protest activities had failed to budge the government, and protestors now turned more intensely to legal means to achieve a stay of execution. The focus of their efforts was on new evidence that seemed to cast doubt on Ryan's guilt. For some days after the application before the Privy Council was rejected, rumours had been circulating in Melbourne that prisoners in Pentridge at the time of the escape—prisoners never called to give evidence at the trial—had witnessed a shot being fired by a prison officer from the gaol wall.

Hearing these rumours, and being encouraged to pursue them on the basis that important new evidence might be brought to bear indicating Ryan's innocence, the executive of the anti-hanging committee resolved to make their own investigations. The members who took on the task were the president, Val Doube, and John Ryan, the vice president and co-founder. Ryan was an academic mathematician at the University of Melbourne and the chairman of the editorial committee of the left-liberal monthly *The Catholic Worker*. Working with Ralph Freadman, Doube and John Ryan would spend the next few days in a frantic search for these prisoners, particularly one whose name had been suggested to them—John Tolmie.

Tolmie's name had become a priority after 27 January when Phil Opas received a letter from a woman named Verna Dicker, living in Warragul, Victoria, who wrote saying that, some months before, Tolmie had told her that he had been in Pentridge during the escape and that he had seen prison officer Paterson fire the gun that killed Hodson. Dicker had encouraged Tolmie to come forward to tell the authorities what he knew, but Tolmie said that he had had enough of police and gaol, and she failed to persuade him.[1] Having lost contact with him, Dicker wrote to Opas at his home in Caulfield to pass on the information about Tolmie's evidence. In Opas' absence overseas at the Privy Council in London, the letter had been opened by his daughter, Lynne, an articled clerk at Ridgeway Pearce Freadman and Murray.[2] With Tolmie now the prime focus of attention by Ryan's legal counsel and the anti-hanging groups, John Ryan undertook to follow leads to his whereabouts all over country Victoria. Over several days he phoned people in Sale, Shepparton, and Murrindindi in an effort to find Tolmie and ascertain what he knew.

With a barrage of media reporting about other witnesses to the escape from Pentridge, new leads began to emerge. On Saturday, 28 January, Freadman received a telephone message at his home from a man named Ross Ponti, who said he had been an eyewitness to the escape and shooting of Hodson, but had never been called to give evidence at the trial. Freadman went to Ponti's house in Airport West and interviewed him. Ponti told him that he had been driving his car north in Sydney Road when the escape was in progress, and he had seen both Ryan and Walker running in various directions. Ponti said that he did not see Ryan lift the rifle and aim at Hodson, but he did not believe that Ryan could have fired the fatal shot because of the interval between when he saw him with the gun and Ryan's position moments after he heard the single shot and when he saw Hodson lying on the roadway.[3] Unfortunately, there was little in Ponti's statement that gave encouragement to the defence: he had not seen Ryan in the crucial few moments when Hodson was shot, and his statement was based on a supposition about positions and timing.

ELSEWHERE IN MELBOURNE on that Saturday, Ryan's ex-wife, Dorothy, was to endure a new tragedy in her life when her husband of just six weeks, David Hughan, collapsed and died at their home in Riversdale Road, Hawthorn. Hughan, 42, who had worked as a horticultural scientist in the Victorian public service, was gardening when he said he felt unwell and went into the house to lie down. A short time later, he suffered a heart attack, and died where he lay. His funeral was arranged for Tuesday, 31 January, the day scheduled for the execution.[4]

THE NEXT DAY, Sunday, 29 January, with the lawyers' investigations not producing results, John Ryan issued an appeal through the media on Freadman's behalf for Tolmie to come forward and help the defence team in their efforts to gain a reprieve for Ryan. The report appeared in *The Sun* on 30 January, quoting Freadman as saying: 'Anyone knowing the whereabouts of John Tolmie who recently left the saw-mills at Murrindindi, twenty miles north of Healesville, is asked to contact my assistant at 544 3000 urgently.' The telephone number was that of Doube at his East Oakleigh home. Freadman added: 'Someone has told me that this man, Mr. Tolmie, may have something interesting to tell me about the shooting. Time is running out, and he must be contacted.'[5]

Just before midnight that same Sunday night, Freadman and his young associate solicitor Paul Guest went to the house of another witness, Liberato Donato, who had come forward. Donato lived in Champ Street, Coburg, just outside the gaol. As a passenger in Ross Ponti's car, he had also been an eyewitness to the escape and had been on the scene during the shooting of Hodson. In an interview that lasted until one o'clock in the morning, Donato confirmed to Freadman and Guest the essence of what Ponti had said, but could not take the story further—other than to say that when he told police he was a witness on the scene, they had not followed up to interview him. Like Ponti, Donato had not been called to give evidence at the trial.[6]

In Pentridge, Ryan knew little of these legal developments. His thoughts were turned towards preparing himself for death. Those preparations involved making his peace with Dorothy and the girls. They had not visited him in these difficult last weeks, although they had sent a message through Opas, but he knew there were things he needed to say. On the usual four-page prison stationery, which he dated 29 January 1967, he set out a final goodbye in his neat, mannered hand.

'My darling', the letter began, and went on to express his condolences to Dorothy at the death of her husband, David Hughan. Referring to her as Little Lady, he told her that he had returned to the Church, and had made a very difficult confession. He had been particularly struck, he wrote, by the April Oursler Armstrong book, and by the parables they contained. He encouraged Dorothy to make her peace with God, as he said he had done. He also praised her upbringing of the children, urged her to keep her faith and strength, and spoke lovingly of his three daughters. Referring to his fate 'on Tuesday', Ryan wrote that he 'could not endure a life without love, in a loveless environment'. He concluded:

> I thank you, Janice, Wendy and Rhonda for your love and loyalty. It is not misplaced ... I wish you all the best of life and you may be sure I'll be doing my best from where I am to watch over and protect you. Remember that I love you. Just be brave and do your best and follow your heart.
>
> Love, Ron.[7]

When Ryan finished the letter, he handed it to Ian Grindlay for delivery by Father Brosnan.[8]

Meanwhile, the search for John Tolmie was the talk of Melbourne. Radio news journalists picked up the comments by Freadman about Tolmie, and his name was widely aired on Melbourne radio news bulletins on the morning of Monday, 30 January, a public holiday for Australia Day. With the city buzzing with talk about dramatic new evidence that might be about to emerge, the name Tolmie was on everyone's lips. Tolmie's brother saw Freadman's appeal in *The Sun* and went to his house at around 8:10am to tell him that Ronald Ryan's lawyers were looking for him.

As it emerged, John Tolmie was not in country Victoria at all, but in the outer-eastern Melbourne suburb of Dandenong. Urged by his brother to respond, Tolmie, who had been in bed when his brother arrived, got up and went to a nearby telephone box. When he rang the telephone number in *The Sun*'s report, Doube answered and, after a brief conversation, asked Tolmie to ring another number—that of John Ryan, which he did. Tolmie told Ryan he would not speak over the phone, but said he could come to his house. Ryan, who had not slept for three days as he had unsuccessfully pursued Tolmie through telephone calls to far-flung parts of the state, took his ten-year-old daughter, Janette, and immediately set off for Dandenong. Janette's presence, he reasoned, might help to soften Tolmie's defensive response to an urgent early-morning visit from an insistent stranger.[9]

Arriving at the modest timber house at 28 Alexander Avenue, Dandenong, with Janette in tow, Ryan knocked and was let in by Tolmie. After brief introductions, Ryan said to Tolmie: 'Are you willing to help save a man's life?' When Tolmie said he was, Ryan said: 'Well, tell me what you know.'[10] Tolmie told Ryan that he had been in Pentridge at the time of the escape, and saw a warder fire a shot from the wall. Establishing what he believed were the essential facts from Tolmie, and getting from him an undertaking that he was prepared to swear an affidavit confirming his story, Ryan left the house and, in a state of some excitement, called Freadman from the same phone-box that Tolmie had used. Freadman told Ryan that he should return to Tolmie's house and accompany him to Freadman's city office to swear the affidavit. This was done, and later in the morning at about 11:30, in an atmosphere of high drama, Tolmie met with Freadman and Barry Jones at the offices of Ridgeway Pearce Freadman & Murray in William Street.

Tolmie recounted his evidence to Freadman, who had it taken down in the form of an affidavit by Paul Guest. Tolmie's evidence was that he was sitting with some other prisoners in the yard outside the bake-house (also known as the cook-house) at Pentridge under no. 1 post at the time of the escape on 19 December 1965, and that he saw a prison officer fire a shot from the tower:

> I saw Mr. Patterson [sic] the warder on No. 1 Post aim and fire a rifle. I heard two shots and the second report seemed to come from outside and was about 10 seconds after the first. I am sure Patterson did not fire two shots. I know he fired the first shot because I saw him recoil and heard the report from it. Then I was put in the bake-house with the others and locked up.

Tolmie's affidavit continued:

> ... I had a clear view of the man on No. 1 Post and I am sure it was Mr. Patterson. He is about 5 feet 9 or 10 inches in height, of stocky build and has gingery hair, aged about 36 or 37 years. There was only one man on No. 1 Post. I know Warder Bennett by sight. I am sure that he was not on No. 1 Post at the relevant time.[11]

After the affidavit was typed up, Tolmie reviewed it and asked Freadman: 'Can this get me into trouble?' Freadman replied: 'Not if it's the truth, but if it's false, you'll go back inside.'[12] With Ryan, Jones, and Guest, Freadman took Tolmie to the Supreme Court building, a little further along William Street, to have Tolmie swear the affidavit. As it was a public holiday, the court was mostly deserted except for one judge, Mr Justice Menhennitt, who had arranged for his civil case to continue in the Thirteenth Court, and his associate, Geoffrey Mander-Jones, who was in court with the judge.[13] Through a court attendant, Jones approached Mander-Jones, who was also a commissioner for taking affidavits, to have the affidavit sworn during a break in Menhennitt's case. After Jones paid the forty cent fee, Mander-Jones invited Tolmie into his office to swear the affidavit, but—with most parts of the court building closed and locked—he could not find a Bible, so administered the oath without one.[14] Affidavits from Freadman and Guest were also sworn in relation to the statements of evidence they had taken from Ross Ponti and Liberato Donato.[15]

After securing the sworn affidavit from Tolmie, Freadman phoned barrister Peter Brusey to brief him on the application he now proposed to make to the trial judge, Justice Starke. Freadman also served the affidavit on the duty officer at the Crown Law Department, assistant crown solicitor John Downey. When Downey informally queried the veracity of the affidavit, Freadman replied that he was not then in a position to check its truth but he believed that the application should proceed in any event. Downey, in turn, telephoned Starke's associate Ron Syme to advise that Freadman was seeking to make an urgent application before Starke later that evening.

The judge could not be contacted directly, however, because he was at the Balnarring races with his wife Beth and their friends Richard and Caroline Searby.[16] Starke adored horse-racing, and he particularly enjoyed race-days at the small country track at Balnarring near Westernport Bay, where he was a committeeman—and later, president—of the Balnarring Picnic Racing Club. The Australia Day meeting was the premium fixture on the club's racing calendar, and there was a large crowd in attendance. Late in the afternoon, Starke was approached on the course by the local police inspector who said that he had a message that Starke was being asked to go to the city on urgent court business—an application was being made in the Ryan case. Misreading Starke's dismay as reluctance, the police inspector (who knew Starke well) offered to report that he could not contact the judge: 'I'll say I've looked for you and couldn't find you,' the inspector suggested helpfully. Starke quickly demurred. He said he would leave for home immediately, and would be there in half an hour.[17]

On his return to his house in Jacksons Road, Mount Eliza, Starke rang his associate, who was spending the holiday long weekend at Portsea, further down the Mornington Peninsula. Syme, who had already been advised of the application and had begun to make plans for the hearing, told Starke that a police car was later bringing him from Portsea and it would pick him up at Mount Eliza to take him to the city.[18] Leaving his wife to dine with the Searbys, Starke was duly picked up shortly after 8:00PM. The subsequent 30-mile journey to the central city from Mount Eliza—one which usually took Starke a little under an hour—took just 29 minutes, as the police car containing him and Syme was driven at high speed and with siren wailing through the traffic jam of returning holiday-makers choking the highway back to Melbourne. Press cameras flashed as the police car bringing Starke to the court arrived at the Lonsdale Street gate of the Supreme Court building.

AT PENTRIDGE, while the hangman was making ready for the execution the next morning, a daring and scarcely believable plan was being revealed. Father Brosnan was visiting Ryan after the division had been locked down for the night.[19] Following some minutes of private prayer, Ryan called Brosnan closer, out of the hearing of the death-watch prison officers on the other side of the cell bars. Ryan then told Brosnan of plans that were being hatched with his connivance outside the prison.[20]

'I hope you haven't been using the visits I've organised through Grindlay?', Brosnan chided.

'You don't need visits to get information out of this place', Ryan replied scornfully. 'There are other means.'[21]

At this moment, Grindlay was with the hangman in D Division as he tested the gallows using sandbags tied to the execution rope. The trap on the gallows crashed loudly, and the rope stretched noisily as the sandbags hurtled toward the floor below. As the trap crashed, a warder called to tell Grindlay that he was wanted on the telephone. It was Brosnan requesting Grindlay to come to Ryan's cell in H Division as quickly as possible. When Grindlay arrived, Brosnan left immediately, saying that Ryan wanted to speak to him alone. Ryan then said to Grindlay what he had earlier told Brosnan:

'I am going to trust you and tell you they are going to spring me out of here tonight.'

'Why are you telling me this?', Grindlay asked.

Ryan replied: 'I have made my peace with God and I will never be as well prepared to die as I am now. I have got nothing to lose but there has been enough bloodshed and I don't want any more. If this thing goes on it could develop into a bloodbath.'[22]

Ryan detailed to Grindlay how for the last several days and weeks a plan had been hatched between himself and three of his criminal associates to spring him from gaol. Incredulous, Grindlay listened as Ryan told him that the gang was planning to blow a hole in the Pentridge prison wall using gelignite and, with machine-guns as armament, release Ryan who, by pre-arrangement, would be waiting for the right moment.[23] Ryan said that, through a coded message from a visitor earlier that day, he had received a signal that on that night the plan to break into the gaol and release him would go ahead. Although he did not tell Grindlay, the coded message referred to several racehorses, one of them a star filly named Storm Queen, being 'ready to race'. (Storm Queen had raced earlier in the day at Moonee Valley in the William Reid Stakes, and had been nosed out in a photo finish after being sent out as a hot favourite.) The visitor was a member of Ryan's family, who at that time was acquainted with several heavy underworld figures, including the ringleader of this plan, Edward 'Jockey' Smith. Jockey Smith was a dangerous criminal who, ten years after these events, would be convicted of the attempted murder of a police officer in Sydney.[24]

Ryan told Grindlay that he had changed his mind, however, and now wanted the plan halted. He was appealing to Grindlay, he said, to get a message through to his associates to ensure that the plan was stopped. Ryan said that if he gave Grindlay a note and he and Brosnan took it to a certain address, the break-in would be called off. Concerned about the possibility of being taken hostage, Grindlay refused but, after consulting with Brosnan, agreed that they would use a trusted messenger instead. The messenger they chose on the basis of his reputation and credibility as a heavy crim was 'Jocka' Bell, a former prisoner who had been in his time a gunman and a serious criminal who had spent long stretches in gaol.[25] Jocka knew Ryan, having spent time with him in Bendigo Training Prison. Ryan wrote out the message in pencil on prison notepaper and, including the coded horses' names, addressed it to his relative: 'That matter we were talking about today. I have changed my mind and want it called off.'[26]

Brosnan subsequently went to St Bernard's Presbytery in East Coburg, where he contacted Jocka.

'Ryan's hallucinating!', Jocka exclaimed when told of the plan.[27]

But Brosnan and Grindlay persisted, and eventually secured his agreement to take the note to the address Ryan indicated, a house in Elwood. After two hours Jocka returned with his mission accomplished. He said that, in the course of delivering the message, he had seen a car 'loaded with the right sort of equipment to stage an onslaught on Pentridge. There were guns, ammunition, ropes and gelignite in the car.'[28] Jocka added: 'I doubt that I have seen more determined men in my life.'[29]

Although, in the final hours before Ryan was due to be executed, the resolve of the men involved had weakened as they realised it was a hopeless cause, the immediate reason for the plan being aborted was that Ryan himself called it off, in the belief that innocent people, prison officers and prisoners, might be injured.[30] On the basis of what he had learned, Grindlay believed that, had it gone ahead, the plan—fantastic as it seemed—would have succeeded in freeing Ryan from prison. As he later wrote in his memoirs: 'There is no doubt in my mind now that if the raid had taken place, Ryan would have got out. People would have died.'[31] (The plot was fully revealed two days later, when crime reporter Geoff Clancy wrote the story in *The Herald*. After detailing the plans to free Ryan, Clancy reported that seven police cars had circled the gaol from darkness to daylight. The police had been armed with automatic carbines.[32])

In the city, by early evening the dramatic development of Freadman's new evidence had media circles buzzing with anticipation and, with the scheduled hanging of Ryan just eleven hours away, the hearing at the Supreme Court before Justice Starke commenced at 9:00pm. The atmosphere was tense, and there was not a spare seat to be had in the First Court of the Supreme Court as lawyers, journalists, officials, and onlookers crowded into the courtroom to hear this last-ditch application.

With Ralph Freadman instructing, Peter Brusey opened for the applicant, making his submission for a stay of proceedings based upon Tolmie's evidence. Brusey was a tall, imposing Englishman whose practice was mostly in commercial, not criminal law, but he was universally regarded at the bar and among judges as an advocate of impeccable integrity and repute.[33] When Brusey stood to address the bench, the weight of that reputation was an important factor in the way his submission was received by the court and all those present. Brusey said that at the time Ryan and Walker made their escape, Tolmie, 27, a labourer, was in B Division of Pentridge serving a twelve-month sentence for forging and uttering, and larceny of a motor car. Brusey told the court that from outside the bake-house under the no. 1 post, Tolmie saw a warder, Robert Paterson, on the no. 1 post, fire a shot during the escape and that, about ten seconds later, he heard another shot from outside the gaol wall. Later, he said, Tolmie was put in the bake-house with the other prisoners and locked up.

Alerted by Freadman that Downey had raised a question about the soundness of Tolmie's affidavit, Brusey submitted to Starke that he was not in a position to vouch for its veracity, only to say that, were Tolmie's evidence well based, it might have affected the outcome of Ryan's trial. Starke agreed. Knowing the layout of Pentridge as he did, however, Starke was sceptical that Tolmie's position outside the bake-house would have offered a view of a prison officer on no. 1 post. It was conceivable from no. 2 post, Starke thought, but he doubted it was possible to see no. 1 post from the bake-house.[34]

Following the Crown's submission on the application from counsel Brian Shaw, Starke told the court he would take a short adjournment to consider his decision. Back in his chambers, Starke pondered the situation that confronted him. The application now before him represented an extraordinary twist of fate, because a little over four years before, in the Tait case, Starke had himself sought just such an order from the chief justice of the High Court of Australia, Sir Owen Dixon, to prevent the imminent execution of Tait. In that case, as Tait's counsel, Starke had argued before the High Court on 31 October 1962 to prevent Tait's execution the next morning. Starke told the Bench then: '… [P]osterity will never … get out of mind the picture that we have been bundled through this court to keep an appointment with the hangman at 8 o'clock tomorrow morning.'[35] This was now precisely the question that Starke had to consider in relation to Ryan. This time, however, he was the judge, not the applicant.

As he re-read the Tolmie affidavit in his chambers, Starke considered in his mind that, while he did not know the truth of the claims it contained, if it were well based, it would have a substantial effect on Ryan's defence. That prospect obliged him, he thought, to grant the application sought and issue an order restraining the execution scheduled for the next morning. To do otherwise, he believed, would be to deny to Ryan's counsel the same opportunity that he had successfully sought for Tait four years before. Starke was also concerned to ensure that his order to the sheriff of the Supreme Court on Ryan had the same restraining effect, and that there could be no argument about its force. To achieve that end, Starke determined to base his draft of the order on the wording contained in the injunction issued by Sir Owen Dixon in the Tait case. However, with the court closed for the public holiday, Starke did not have access to the library, nor the resources to locate Dixon's judgment. With time against him, Starke improvised. Drawing down from his shelves a copy of Creighton Burns' book, *The Tait Case*, he thumbed through to the transcript he knew the book contained and, finding it in an appendix at pages 179 to 181, copied from it the words Chief Justice Dixon had used in granting the High Court injunction:

> We shall accordingly order that the execution of the prisoner fixed for tomorrow morning be not carried out but be stayed pending the disposal of the applications to this court for special leave and of any appeal to this court in consequence of such applications.[36]

Starke would craft his own order but he would draw on the words used here to establish the principles at the core of his decision. Starke also needed to be sure that the order would have the practical consequence that he intended. In the High Court's Tait judgment, so as to put the force of the order beyond doubt, Chief Justice Dixon had added at the foot of the order: 'that we will order that the Chief Secretary and the Sheriff and his deputy or deputies be restrained accordingly.'[37] Starke's order followed this form and used these words exactly. As he completed his draft of the order, Starke recalled in his mind events associated with Dixon's injunction regarding Tait. Shortly after he had had his associate draw up the High Court restraining order, Dixon (who, like Starke, was noted for his irreverent sense of humour) had said to his associate: 'I wonder if Tait is hanged tomorrow whether Mr Rylah will be guilty of murder?'[38]

Starke returned to the packed courtroom to conclude the hearing a few moments after 11:00PM. In giving his decision, Starke told the court that a threshold question was whether he had the power to grant the injunction after the time and place of the execution had been fixed by the Governor in Council:

> The question of whether ... I have power to grant a stay of execution is a matter which has been debated in this Court before and which is the subject of a difference of opinion. I think it is clear that if any single judge has the power at this stage, it is only the trial judge. I think I would do little service to the jurisprudence relating to criminal law in this State if I were to endeavour, without the opportunity of collecting the authorities, to express my views in detail at this time ... [However] I have reached a firm conclusion as to which of the judgments is correct after having heard the helpful argument of Mr. Shaw ...
>
> I hold accordingly, that I have the power to grant a stay in proper circumstances. It is quite clear, however, that this power should only be exercised sparingly and on clear material. The trial judge has not power to decide whether or not the death penalty should be carried out. The Executive and the Executive alone is charged with this decision and this Court should not interfere with such a decision except in exceptional and rare circumstances. It can in any event only intervene as a temporary measure. However, there can be no doubt that in the long run, if the Court senses that there

> is a real possibility of a miscarriage of justice, then the Court must not hesitate to intervene.[39]

Starke quoted Lord Atkin in a decision of the Judicial Committee of the Privy Council in 1933:

> 'It would be remarkable indeed, if what may be "a scandal and perversion of justice" may be prevented during the trial, but after it has taken effect the Courts are powerless to interfere. Finality is a good thing, but justice is better.'[40]

Starke then turned to the substance of Tolmie's affidavit claim, that he had seen prison officer Paterson, the warder who Tolmie said was on no. 1 post, aim and fire a rifle:

> Assuming that is true, having presided at the trial, I believe that this evidence would necessarily have weighed heavily with the jury. Of course, one cannot in the long run, say for certain whether it would have made a decisive difference or not. The whole contest at the trial was whether Ryan fired a shot at all, or whether only one shot was fired and that by a witness ... named Paterson, who was also a warder and who admitted he fired from outside the walls of the gaol. If, and there was a great deal of evidence and a great deal of cross-examination directed to this issue, there had been introduced into the conflict of evidence which did arise during the trial, the fact that a further shot was fired at about the same time, obviously no-one can say that the verdict must have been the same, and, accordingly, I think it is not possible to say what view the Executive would have taken of this new material.
>
> In those circumstances I am put in a position in which I suppose no Judge would wish to be put. If there were time I might adjourn the proceedings and allow the Crown to file further affidavits and cross-examine Mr Tolmie if the Crown so wished so that I might form a view as to whether there was material which would or might cause the Executive to alter its view.
>
> But there is, of course, not time. The time element is one of the necessary concomitants flowing from the death penalty, and, therefore, I am in this position. Can I say, sitting in the judicial seat, that

> this affidavit must be untruthful? I can clearly see that there are criticisms to be made of the affidavit, perhaps weighty, perhaps not. The less I say about those matters probably the better. But there is the oath of an individual that he saw a man fire a rifle from No. 1 Post … [T]o disbelieve an affidavit simply because there are matters of criticisms relating to it, and perhaps of weighty criticisms, is, I think, quite beyond the judicial function. If one had an opportunity of hearing the deponent cross-examined, if one had the advantage of other affidavits, one might disbelieve it and that is the course I might normally have taken; not for the purpose of deciding what action the Executive should take, if any, and certainly not for the purpose of directing the Executive as to what course it should follow, but simply to ascertain if there were material worthy of consideration by the Executive which might affect its decision.
>
> But there is no time, and in these circumstances one must not make a mistake, and consequently I propose to accede to the application and suspend the operation of the sentence which I pronounced, solely so that the weight, if any, of this material may be considered by the Executive.[41]

Granting a stay of the execution, Starke followed the words he had written in his chambers:

> The order that I propose to make is this. Upon the undertaking of the solicitor for the prisoner to place the material which is before me, and any other material as to which he may be advised, before the Executive within 48 hours, I order that the execution of the prisoner fixed for 8 o'clock tomorrow morning, Tuesday 31st January 1967, be not carried out but be stayed until the further pleasure of His Excellency the Governor is known.[42]

Finally, Starke called before the bar the sheriff of the Supreme Court, Gerry O'Brien, who was present in court, and indicated—following Chief Justice Dixon's words from Creighton Burns' book—that he further ordered 'that the Chief Secretary and the Sheriff and his deputy or deputies be restrained accordingly'.[43] Starke sought from O'Brien an assurance that the order would be conveyed to the proper authorities and that the execution would not proceed at eight o'clock the next morning.[44] After conferring with crown counsel Brian Shaw, instructed by crown solicitor Tom Mornane, O'Brien said: 'I give that assurance.'[45]

As Starke's orders were given, journalists rushed excitedly from the court to file stories detailing these sensational late-night developments. A crowd of fifty people outside the law courts loudly broke into cheers at the decision that Ryan would not hang. Violet, Irma, and Gloria Ryan had been sitting through the hearing in court. 'Thank God for that', Violet said, 'thank God.'[46] The leader of the state Labor opposition, Clive Stoneham, MLA, who had also sat through the hearing, commented: 'The proceedings in this Court reinforce one's faith in our system of jurisprudence.'[47] News of the reprieve travelled fast but, given the lateness of the hour, most Melburnians were not aware of it. Outside Pentridge gaol, where 300 protestors were staging an all-night vigil, protest organisers used megaphones to relay the news, which was greeted by huge cheers and boisterous shouts of triumph and relief. Inside the gaol, Ryan had been told of the court development. Within minutes of the court rising, O'Brien had telephoned Pentridge, and Ryan learned from Ian Grindlay in his cell at 11:30PM that he had been given a reprieve.

Back in his chambers after the hearing of the application, Starke called in O'Brien, whom he knew as a friend, in order to ensure arrangements for him to accept service of the order, and further deliver it to Pentridge governor Ian Grindlay. At the end of the Australia Day long-weekend public holiday, however, Starke found that O'Brien had been excessively patriotic in the celebration of the national day.[48] Starke resolved to send his associate instead, and Syme duly delivered it to Grindlay at Pentridge.[49] As this was being done, the official secretary to the governor, Jack Colquhoun, was advising Sir Rohan Delacombe of the order. Similarly advised by his department, Arthur Rylah telephoned Henry Bolte at home to break the news of the eleventh-hour injunction.[50]

After this dramatic late-night sitting of the court and the relevant order had been dispatched, Starke and Syme were driven home by the same police car that had brought them to Melbourne—although this trip was to be rather more sedate. It was after midnight as the car proceeded down the Nepean Highway, and Starke listened distractedly to the intermittent radio traffic on the police car's transceiver. As he did, the radio crackled with communication between two anonymous police officers: 'Judge Starke has granted a stay of execution for Ryan,' barked one. 'Silly old bastard!', came the reply. Without a word, the police driver quickly switched off the radio.[51]

The next morning's newspapers—on a morning most Melburnians were expecting, if not dreading, an execution—carried page-one stories reporting the dramatic development of the late-night reprieve. But there was little analysis of what the restraining order meant or what next steps would occur. Religious leaders opposed to the hanging, nevertheless, saw it as a welcome development, and one that held out the hope that the hanging might be permanently stayed. Anglican Archbishop Dr Woods said he was 'very pleased and interested to hear about this. I hope that this will lead to an eventual reprieve.' Similarly, John Westerman commented: 'It is a tremendous relief to know that Ryan won't hang today. I would hope that this, regardless of any further evidence, will mean the Executive Council will commute the sentence.' The chief minister of the Melbourne Hebrew Congregation, Rabbi Dr Izaak Rapaport, shared in the sentiment: 'I am overjoyed with this development and I join personally with the thousands and thousands of loyal citizens of this State in expressing the hope that the sentence will ultimately be commuted.'[52] At Rupertswood, where the Salesian priests were celebrating the feast day of the founder of their order, Don Bosco, prayerful thanks were given for the decision.[53] At that moment, it seemed inconceivable to many Melburnians, and unlikely to most, that the hanging would not be permanently stayed.

As people were reading the papers and digesting the dramatic news, the premier called a cabinet meeting for later in the morning. At about 8:00AM Starke received a phone call at home from the chief justice of the Supreme Court, Sir Henry Winneke. The wheel of fate had turned for Winneke as well. A little over four years before, on 31 October 1962, as Victoria's solicitor general, as he then was, Winneke had appeared for attorney-general Rylah in the High Court before Chief Justice Dixon and Justices Kitto, Menzies and Owen in opposing Starke's successful eleventh-hour application for a stay of execution for Tait. Now himself chief justice, Winneke had rung Starke because Rylah had contacted him to request that Starke make himself available to brief cabinet later in the morning on the consequences attaching to his restraining order. Taken aback by his chief's request, Starke was, at first, adamant: 'Harry, I'm not going!,' he said firmly, adding that he would not put himself in the position of having to defend his action to the cabinet.[54]

There were two issues for Starke. First, the doctrine of the separation of powers meant that a justice of the Supreme Court was not accountable to the executive over a judicial decision. Unlike his role as the trial judge at the original cabinet meeting on 12 December, Starke was concerned that his presence at this new meeting of cabinet might give rise to a perception that the judicial arm of government was acquiescing in an intrusion into its jurisdiction by the executive. While a trial judge might properly accept an invitation to attend cabinet to give information on a capital case where commutation was under consideration, a summons—even if dressed up as a request—to appear and explain a judicial ruling to ministers was something else again. Starke was concerned that an important principle of the separation of powers might be breached by his attendance.[55]

Starke's second, perhaps more pressing, reason was personal. It was still in Starke's mind how enraged Bolte had been about the injunction for Tait four years before. Starke believed Bolte would see this new injunction on Ryan as a still further besting of him by Starke. Winneke gently persisted. 'That's not the purpose of the Cabinet meeting,' Winneke said. 'Ministers know only what they've read in the papers and they simply wish to have further information. You'd be helping me if you went, John.'[56] Urged in these terms by his chief, whom he both liked and respected, Starke relented and, with some misgivings about Bolte's likely attitude, agreed to meet the cabinet as requested.

If for the past few days and weeks, public attention had been focused on Ryan, now it was Starke who was uncomfortably in the spotlight. Starke's reprieve for Ryan had created legal history and provoked intense discussion among lawyers and officials about its implications. When the execution of Tait was stopped in 1962 by the High Court, that order was made by the full High Court to allow the court itself time to consider new evidence of Tait's insanity. This was necessary to determine whether, under the newly proclaimed *Mental Health Act*—which was coming into force the next day—the imminent execution was lawful. In the case of Starke's stay of Ryan's execution, by contrast, the order was made by a justice of the State Supreme Court sitting alone to allow defence counsel time to place new, untested evidence before the executive rather than the court. That significant difference prompted debate in official circles about whether Starke had the power to do what he did. Some officials took the view—after the judgment of Justice Menhennitt in the Supreme Court application by Ryan on 23 December—that once a death warrant had been approved by the Executive Council and signed by the governor and the responsible minister, no court could rescind it. In circumstances of such legal uncertainty, however, no one, least of all chief secretary Rylah, was about to defy Starke's order and test Sir Owen Dixon's wicked speculation.[57]

Out at Pentridge at 10:00AM, Ryan received the visit of Freadman and Guest, who had come to advise him of the legal implications of the reprieve.[58] In their 25 minutes with him in cell 15, he seemed relieved but cautious about whether it might mean a permanent stay.[59] A short time later, at 11:30AM, as agreed, Starke arrived outside the cabinet room on the first floor at 2 Treasury Place. After a few minutes he was greeted by Rylah, who emerged from the meeting. Starke had known Rylah well over many years, and they had a good relationship.

'How is it in there?,' Starke began.

'Pretty crook, Jack,' Rylah replied.

'Well, Arthur,' Starke said firmly, 'if Henry says one word of criticism of me in there, I'll get up and leave, and I'll tell the press what's happened. I'm not bound by any oath of secrecy; if they ask me what happened, I'll tell them.'[60]

Rylah said he would go back in and speak to Bolte. Returning several minutes later, he ushered Starke into the cabinet room. After Starke had taken his seat at the cabinet table, ministers began by asking him about the affidavit from Tolmie.

'I had no alternative to granting the application,' he began. 'I don't know whether Tolmie's claims are true or not. But if they are, Ryan's defence argument would be greatly strengthened.'

For more than 50 minutes Starke answered ministers' questions from around the cabinet table—questions about Tolmie's affidavit and the restraining order that Starke had issued the night before. Throughout this entire session with Starke in the cabinet room, the premier said not a word.[61] On his way out of the building, Starke was besieged by reporters wanting to know what had happened in cabinet. 'Come on, fellas,' Starke said to them, 'I can't tell you anything.'[62]

After Starke had left the cabinet, discussion continued among ministers about the stay and about the course that the premier might adopt in subsequently advising the governor. Under the terms of Starke's order, Ryan's defence counsel had been given 48 hours in which to place the Tolmie affidavit and any other material before the Executive Council. Ministers accepted the terms of Starke's order, so no new Executive Council decision could be taken until after eleven o'clock on Wednesday night. That meant, in effect, a cabinet meeting on Thursday morning would be the earliest opportunity for cabinet to consider the new evidence.

By now, the pressure on the government was immense. Cabinet had taken a decision to hang Ryan, and it was beginning to look like there might be a serious question about his guilt. That pressure increased significantly when—responding to the extraordinary publicity given to Tolmie—several other men came forward claiming to have been in Pentridge at the time of the escape, and asserting that they had either seen or heard a warder fire a shot. In the next 48 hours, four further prisoners or ex-prisoners—Desmond John Boone, Reginald William Brooks, Salvatori Russo, and Allan John Cane—would make statements outlining their claims. The focus of their witness statements was not the prison officer on no. 1 post, as Tolmie had claimed, but the warder on no. 2 post. Given the prisoners' position outside the Pentridge bakehouse, this was more credible as far as their line of sight was concerned.

The first was Desmond John Boone, a prisoner in Bendigo Training Prison. On the morning after Starke's stay, Tuesday, 31 January, Boone heard on the radio of Tolmie's affidavit and the court hearing before Starke. When the Bendigo stipendiary magistrate Arthur Curtain made a routine visit to the gaol as the visiting justice later that day, Boone stepped forward and stated that he was in a position to give evidence that would assist Ryan.[63] Curtain duly notified police of Boone's statement, and the next day, Wednesday, 1 February, Boone was interviewed by homicide squad Detective Sergeant Kevin Carton and, at 11:00AM, he made a statement. Shown a photograph of Tolmie by Carton, Boone said:

> … I know John Tolmie … He is definitely the man. I think he was in gaol when I got there. He was there all of the time I was there …
>
> I remember the day that Ryan and Walker escaped from gaol … I know it was December … It was about half past one or two o'clock in the afternoon. I was alongside the cook house sunbaking … From where I was lying I could see No. 2 tower and his platform. I

> saw the prison officer standing about midway on the tower. He had his rifle up to his shoulder and pointed it down on to the ground back along the wall on the outside towards B Division. That is the back of B Division. He called out 'Hold it. Drop the rifle.' He then put his rifle down and went to the phone in the tower on the corner. He went back and picked up the rifle and aimed it towards the side of the church next door. He seemed to be weaving the rifle from right to left and down towards the ground. He blew his whistle three times and he fired one shot ... He then ran up to the tower on the corner. He blew his whistle a couple of times. He had the rifle up again to his shoulder, but in the meantime I heard another shot. It was from outside and sounded close to the wall. It could have been fired by a warder outside.
>
> Ryan and Walker must have been running backwards and forwards along Sydney Road because the warder on the tower was pointing down towards Sydney Road and weaving from right to left ... He was right in the tower at the time. He was following them up and down Sydney Road with the bead of the rifle and then he fired again.
>
> We had to go inside then ... We all had to go in. Tolmie was with us ... I do not know the name of the warder who fired these two shots ... .[64]

From French Island prison farm, another prisoner, Salvatori 'Sammy' Russo, made the following statement:

> I was in front of the cookhouse on the Sunday before Christmas 18 or 19 December. The officer on the tower asked if I would bring him a cup of tea. I went inside and Mr. McGrath was off, another overseer was on, who tell the officer when he go off, he can get a cup of tea. I told the officer on the tower this. This was after 2:00PM I heard screaming. The officer said three or four times 'stop', 'stop'. Straight away he get rifle near window by enclosed part of tower. Heard a noise boom one time. Straight away he put rifle away then put head in hands and go to telephone. I ran inside.[65]

Reginald William Brooks was the third of the prisoners interviewed by police. In his statement, Brooks related:

> On 19 December 1965 I was in Pentridge working in the cook-house. I was outside between the kitchen and main west wall. I speak of the old kitchen. Albert Richard Jenkins was with me … The officer on the tower was looking out into the street, that is the street on the south side. He was on the catwalk. I could see him from waist up. I heard him call 'Drop that gun or I'll shoot.' He ran to the corner into the rotunda, then ran back with a rifle under his arm to a point on the catwalk midway between the rotunda and the kitchen roof. He had the butt under his arm and the barrel pointing down towards the ground outside the wall. He then fired one shot and put the rifle back in the rack. I don't know the name of this warder. We were then locked up in the kitchen by Mr. Carolan … I can't remember Tolmie. I remember Cane … I may know Tolmie by sight …[66]

The strongest of the new evidence was from Allen John Cane, 35, a former Pentridge prisoner who, at the time of the escape, was serving a five-year term for breaking and entering, and passing valueless cheques. On the day that Tolmie's evidence was reported, Tuesday, 31 January, Cane read about it in a newspaper in Brisbane, where he lived. Cane contacted a journalist from *The Telegraph* in Brisbane to say that he, too, had seen a prison officer fire a shot—although, initially, he said it had been fired from no. 1 tower. Cane said that he had delayed coming forward because he feared his parole might be cancelled. He said he was doing his best to live honestly in Brisbane, his wife was pregnant, and he did not want any further trouble. *The Telegraph* also reported Cane as saying that the day after the escape 'in the cookhouse a prison officer was talking to us, and some of us mentioned that we had seen the officer on the wall fire a shot, and the officer talking to us said we had better keep quiet about it.'[67]

Later that day, Cane swore an affidavit before his solicitors in Brisbane, in which he stated:

> On 19 December 1965, with six or seven other prisoners, I went out the back door of the cookhouse and was sunbaking in the prison yard. Lying with me outside the cookhouse was a prisoner by the name of Snowy Blackledge, and another prisoner, who had a goatee beard, who was nicknamed 'the goat'. I am not certain of the names

> of the other men in the group. In fact, I was not certain of the name of Snowy Blackledge and in my original statement to Brisbane *Telegraph* newspaper reporter, Patrick David Lloyd, and Sydney *Sun*/Melbourne *Herald* representative, Peter John Hall, I furnished his name as Snowy Williams.
>
> Some time after we were lying out in the sun I saw a prison warder whose name is now known to me who was stationed at one of the posts in the prison wall move hurriedly a distance of about ten yards along the catwalk and pick up a rifle put it to his shoulder calling out 'Stop or I'll shoot' and almost simultaneously fire the rifle. One of the men said 'hellow, someone has gone over the wall.' The prison wall was about twenty feet high and I was lying at a spot about twenty yards from the base of the wall where the warder was stationed. The direction of the shot was away from the position where we were lying. Almost immediately the prison hooter sounded and within a matter of minutes the overseer in charge of the cookhouse ordered the six or seven men including myself into the cookhouse, checked on our numbers and directed that we should remain in the cookhouse.[68]

Significantly, Cane's affidavit did not mention Tolmie, and Cane told his Brisbane solicitors that Tolmie was not there.[69] Although Cane was unaware of it, this was a fundamentally important feature of his evidence. For, as cabinet was meeting in Melbourne with Justice Starke, at Rylah's request officers of the social welfare department's prisons division had asked Pentridge officials to examine records relating to Tolmie's imprisonment in the gaol. It soon became apparent that Tolmie's affidavit had to be false, because the records indicated that he had not been in prison at the time of the escape on 19 December 1965. He had been in Pentridge before and after, but not during the fateful break-out. The Pentridge officers discovered that Tolmie had been discharged from prison on 26 October 1965, some two months before the escape. He had been subsequently arrested and imprisoned at Pentridge on 13 January 1966 on a number of charges, including one of stealing a motor car on 22 December 1965.[70] What Tolmie had related in his affidavit was prison lore about the escape that he had heard during his period of imprisonment at Pentridge from 13 January 1966, almost four weeks after the escape by Ryan and Walker.

Ryan's solicitors were getting suspicious, as well. After their initial visit with Ryan, Freadman and Guest had gone to look at angles of trajectory from the no. 1 post and for any evidence of bullet marks in Sydney Road. They also had had a look around the key locations in relation to the no. 1 post. It soon became obvious to them that the prison officer in the post could not be seen from outside the bake-house. At Ryan's request, they returned to cell 15 at 11:15AM for a further ten-minute visit, and told him what they had concluded.[71] Later in the morning, Freadman's office was informed by Detective Sergeant Carton that Tolmie had not been in Pentridge at the relevant time. When Tolmie later came to his office, Freadman put it to him that his statement was not true. When Tolmie persisted, Freadman suggested he clear it up with police and arranged for him to be represented by solicitor Bernie Gaynor in an appointment with police that was made for him.[72]

The Tolmie perjury was a body blow to the anti-hanging cause, but the falsity of Tolmie's claims did not explain the statements of the other prisoners, despite the premier's attempt to undermine them. Sir Henry Bolte would later pronounce what came to be termed the 'domino theory of affidavits' by saying: 'We had two other affidavits from people *claiming to be in Pentridge with Tolmie* when he wasn't there ... [W]e checked on two others *corroborating with Tolmie* when he wasn't there.'[73] The fact that Cane's affidavit did not mention Tolmie, and that Brooks' statement explicitly excluded Tolmie, evidently meant little to a premier who by then was under immense pressure and simply wanted to get the execution over with. Ryan's reprieve—and with it the last, best prospect that his execution might be permanently stayed—seemed to have foundered on false evidence.

With Tolmie's evidence discredited, police were quick to turn their attention to the offence he had committed in swearing to it, and were keen to speak to him. At around 10:00PM that night, 31 January, police interviewed him, by arrangement, at Gaynor's house in Power Street, East Hawthorn. During the course of the interview by detectives from the homicide squad, Detective Sergeant Carton, Senior Detective Phil Schmidt, and Detective First Constable John McIntyre, Tolmie admitted to the falsity of his affidavit. He told police that he had made the affidavit stating that he was in gaol at the time of Ryan's escape, 'but the truth is I was not in jail at all.' Shortly after midnight, Tolmie signed a statement, which said, in part:

> I do not know this man Ronald Ryan, I thought that I could help him some way or another that is the only reason why I did this. I am sorry for what I have done and causing a turmoil in this case.[74]

At 12:45AM, now 1 February, the detectives took Tolmie to the city watch-house where he was charged with perjury in that 'before a Commissioner of the Supreme Court for the State of Victoria for taking Affidavits, he falsely and corruptly swore an Affidavit'.[75] Later in the day he appeared in the City Court and was remanded without bail.

When news of these developments reached members of the anti-hanging committee, they were devastated and perplexed. Tolmie's evidence had been shown to be false, but what were they to make of the evidence of the other four prisoners and ex-prisoners who had come forward? But even as committee members contemplated their next move, cracks began to appear in some of that evidence, as well. The fact that Boone said he was with Tolmie, and that he saw a warder fire twice (no other claim mentioned more than one shot fired by a prison officer), effectively discredited his statement. The difficulty with Russo's statement was that while he saw a prison officer with a gun, he did not say that he saw him *fire* it. He *heard* a shot and saw the prison officer put the rifle away. Brooks' evidence was strong, in one respect, in that he claimed clearly to have seen a warder fire a shot. But this conflicted directly with the trial evidence of the warder whose position he could see—prison officer William Bennett, on no. 2 tower, who had said he had not fired a shot.

Ballistic evidence regarding Bennett's rifle had not been called at the trial, but Detective Inspector Holland and Detective Sergeant Carton had checked the rifle on the day of the escape. Their inspection showed that the rifle had not been fired, and the magazine contained the requisite number of rounds, namely eight.[76] A further weakness was that, unlike other statements, which were given in the form of sworn affidavits, Brooks' evidence was given only as an unsworn statement. Hence, his statement carried substantially less evidentiary weight. Cane's evidence was the strongest, but by then the discrediting of Tolmie's affidavit caused investigating police and officials to be highly sceptical of any new evidence.

Undaunted, the anti-hanging committee persisted in seeking to present the new evidence to ministers on the basis that an important question about Hodson's shooting remained: what if Tolmie's statement simply repeated the truthful evidence that he had heard from other prisoners? With the prospect that Cane's witness evidence was simply the source of the prison lore at the base of Tolmie's affidavit, Freadman and the committee mobilised to bring him to Melbourne and have his evidence put before cabinet. By now ministers felt under siege, with new claims being made seemingly every few hours.

At his morning press conference on Wednesday, 1 February, premier Bolte spoke about the approaching hanging to journalists, whose numbers had swelled as the date for the execution loomed. Present were a number of interstate reporters, including Ron Saw of Sydney's *Daily Mirror*. Bolte's press-conference convention was that, while he would speak candidly, his comments were for background only and not for attribution. Saw was not exempt from the convention, but he disregarded it to report in detail Bolte's off-the-record remarks:

> The campaign against me has got low in all respects. It is propaganda aimed at me personally. And it's only me. You don't see Rylah in the paper, or any other Cabinet ministers, do you?... I've got to safeguard my wife. I had to send her 100 miles away (to his farm at Meredith). The other day the police picked up two lunatics a mile from my home. They were on their way to my place. One of them was certified on the spot. Why doesn't the Press print stories like that?...
>
> Who ... are the people against hanging?
>
> A few leaders of the Church and a few leaders of the Press. And then there are a few professors at universities who think they've got to object about something. But the rest are political. The rest are thugs.[77]

At 5:00PM that day, a further cabinet meeting discussed the Ryan case in more general terms for an hour and a half, assisted by crown solicitor Tom Mornane; but, with the prospect that more statements might be forthcoming before the deadline for the submission of new evidence expired, ministers resolved to defer substantive consideration until the following day.

At 8.30AM the next morning, Thursday, 2 February—Starke's injunctive 48-hour deadline having passed—the cabinet met for final consideration of evidence that had been gathered by Ryan's solicitors and presented to the executive pursuant to Starke's court order. It was a short meeting, lasting 45 minutes. Rylah had asked the crown solicitor, Tom Mornane, to analyse the evidence of the prisoners and all the other evidence submitted in detail by Freadman. Mornane submitted a five-page memorandum plus attachments of copies of the relevant trial evidence and the police file, the latter being important in establishing the ballistic evidence that police had gathered on Bennett's rifle. This was evidence not called at the trial. In his memorandum, Mornane critically reviewed the evidence of Cane and Brooks, and set both beside the evidence of prison officer William Bennett. The memorandum presented no recommendation, but concluded with Mornane's advice:

> In my opinion there is nothing in the whole of the evidence submitted which would justify the belief that had it been submitted to the jury it would have affected the result of the trial.[78]

Ministers were also given a summary of the new evidence carefully prepared by Rylah's department. This document was a seven-page briefing note headed 'Was any Shot Fired by the Prison Officer on No. 2 Post?' This briefing note comprehensively analysed the evidence of Cane, Brooks, Boone, and Russo, and the trial evidence of Bennett, and also examined the ballistic evidence attaching to Bennett's rifle. The document drew upon Mornane's memo to similarly conclude that the evidence from the ex-prisoners would not have affected the jury's verdict had it been put at the trial.[79]

Led by premier Bolte, ministers came to the same view. There was nothing they had heard and read that persuaded them that the course they had embarked upon was wrong. To their certainty about the correctness of their course was now added a new conviction among ministers: having had the case delayed several times, cabinet now believed that it was imperative to bring the execution to finality. At this moment, the pressure on ministers seemed at its peak. For all the pressure, Bolte believed that to turn back now—whether in response to the media campaign, or the political protests, or the supposedly new evidence—would have been disastrous. Cabinet had made its decision on 12 December, and it was going to stick with it. After a brief discussion, ministers resolved that the premier would recommend to the governor that the execution be carried out without delay. The time for the execution Bolte proposed to recommend to the governor was the next day at 8:00AM.

Following the cabinet meeting, in the tradition of substantive cabinet decisions in capital cases, all the ministers (except the minister for fuel and power, George Reid, who was still overseas) left the cabinet room to drive to Government House for an Executive Council meeting. Ministers had endured astonishing political pressure, including death threats to several of them, and now they would all attend to give final legal authority to the hanging decision. After the short drive from Treasury Place to Government House, ministers reconvened at 9.30AM as the State Executive Council, at which the premier advised the governor to give constitutional effect to the cabinet decision.[80]

Shortly before 9:50AM, Sir Rohan Delacombe signed and sealed a new death warrant prepared by the chief secretary.[81] In an expression of the tortuous path of Executive Council decisions about the execution, the warrant exhaustively recited the orders and stays and rescissions of earlier warrants. In all, the execution now had been scheduled, cancelled, ordered, and re-affirmed four times from the original Executive Council meeting of 12 December. At 9:53AM the official secretary to the governor, Jack Colquhoun, telephoned the sheriff, Gerry O'Brien, to advise him of the decision, and he in turn contacted the deputy governor of Pentridge. Minutes later, Ian Grindlay, who had been waiting with Ryan in his cell since shortly after the scheduled start of the cabinet meeting, told him what he had prepared for and expected: he would be hanged in the morning.[82]

Although there would be frantic attempts in the following few hours to avert the hanging, everyone associated with the protests knew that this time there would be no last-minute stay of execution. The crowd of three thousand protestors which later gathered outside the gaol at Coburg seemed to know it, too.

A little later in the morning, Ryan received a visit from Paul Guest, the young associate from Freadman's law firm who had visited him a number of times over the previous few weeks in relation to the Privy Council and later appeals and petitions. Guest was a 26-year-old solicitor who had several times been sent from the city to pass messages to Ryan and get his instructions for the legal initiatives taken on his behalf. As the legal options dwindled in the final few days, Guest had become deeply affected by the prospect that, despite the best efforts of a large number of professionals and people in the anti-hanging campaign, Ryan was about to be executed. Now, as he sat outside Ryan's cell to say his last goodbye he learned from Ryan the news that Grindlay had brought only moments before. As they talked through the bars of the observation cell in what seemed like a conspiratorial whisper, the emotional force of the imminent hanging overwhelmed Guest, and he fought back tears. In this sterile, barren setting, so dominated by heavy bluestone walls and iron bars, Ryan's face showed not a flicker of emotion at his fate—nothing except a sympathetic expression of concern at Guest's visible distress: 'Don't be concerned about me', he said.[83] They were soon joined by Grindlay, who—amidst his own feelings of anguish and despair—added a comforting word of consolation to Guest.[84]

Although it seemed at that moment that every conceivable legal avenue had been pursued and exhausted, Ryan's defence team determined that a delay might allow the new evidence to be more fully considered and put to government. Hence, during an afternoon sitting of the Supreme Court at 3:12PM before Justice Starke—and in the absence of the Crown which was not represented—Opas sought a stay of the execution for a fortnight to allow time for Ryan's legal advisers to fully consider the new material. Opas referred to Cane's evidence, and said he had made an affidavit and also sent a sketch plan of what he had seen from the bake-house of the officer on no. 2 post. 'It is evidence which would be meaningless to anyone unfamiliar with the case', Opas said. 'We propose to call this witness and two others, whose Affidavits have not been prepared.' At this moment, Opas had reached the point of exhaustion. He had arrived from overseas just three hours before, after taking a long route home from London following the Privy Council appeal. Emotionally affected by the Privy Council decision and its meaning, he had delayed his return in order to put out of his mind the fate that he felt sure had befallen his client in his absence.[85] Drained by two sleepless nights and overcome by the seemingly inevitable outcome of this new submission, Opas recounted to Starke the issues at stake in his application:

> The whole of Ryan's case has been conducted since the end of December as a matter of great urgency. There has been none of this calm assessment of the relevant facts, which is normal when the stakes are not nearly as high as they are in this case. We want to

> bring the witness here and have him cross-examined so that Your Honour may see and assess the value of his evidence.
>
> If Your Honour felt there was a reasonable possibility for the jury to have reached a different verdict, it would be inherent for Your Honour—in fact a bounden duty—to prevent the man being executed. There is not much use in establishing Ryan's innocence after his death ...
>
> Your Honour may eventually feel that there is nothing in this evidence at all. But why is such indecent haste to dispatch this poor wretch necessary? We are not trying to stop the execution, but merely stay the hangman's hand.
>
> *His Honour*: I feel you are becoming emotionally involved, Mr Opas.
>
> *Opas*: I make no apology for that, Your Honour. I am speaking feelingly, but this is a matter in which feelings run high.[86]

As Opas spoke, his voice faltered and it was a few moments before he could continue; but his submission had run its course and Starke's decision was the expected one. Refusing the application for a reprieve, which he described as 'entirely hopeless and misconceived', Starke said that all the material placed before him had been presented to the Executive Council, which had rejected it.[87]

The matter might have seemed to have reached a final halt at this point, but for Ryan's solicitors there was still one last desperate throw of the dice. This time, Freadman petitioned the attorney-general, Arthur Rylah, to exercise his powers under section 584 of the *Crimes Act 1958* to grant clemency to Ryan. The four-page petition, drawn up by Ridgeway Pearce Freadman & Murray and signed by Freadman, said new facts and circumstances had become known which raised a doubt as to whether Ryan was rightly convicted. The fresh facts and circumstances were summarised, as follows:

> (a) The evidence of prisoners and ex-prisoners who say or as we believe, will say, that they saw the warder on No. 2 Post fire a shot. These persons are as follows:
>
> Allan John Cane
> Reginald William Brooks
> Sammy Russo (possibly)

Albert Richard Jenkins (known as 'the goat')
Tom Toogood (possibly)
Max Du Barry (possibly).

None of these witnesses was called on [at] the trial. In our submission, this body of evidence is plainly enough to warrant further enquiry.

(b) The evidence of prison officers as to inspection of firearms after the shooting. We have been informed from a reliable source that this was carried out, but no evidence was called at the trial, notwithstanding that Prison Officer Bennett was vigorously cross-examined as to whether he had fired a shot, on the basis that the 'Sun' newspaper of 20th December 1965 reported that a shot had been fired by a warder on a tower. The newspaper representative has told me that the information on which that story was based came from a highly placed public servant.[88]

There is a mark on the western footpath of Sydney Road which appears to be a bullet mark and which appears to line-up with the South-West corner of the Gaol, which is the situation of No. 2 Post.

(c) The evidence of Arthur George Dyer, who alleges that he was a prisoner at the relevant time in Pentridge and heard a shot which sounded as if it came from the direction of either No. 1 or No. 2 Post, and was very distinct as if fired from inside the walls.

(d) The evidence of the eye witnesses Ponti and Donato who were not called at the trial. This evidence, though not conclusive, tends to favour the Defence, and may have influenced the jury to acquit.

(e) The unsatisfactory nature of the evidence of Prison Officer Paterson, which left open the possibility that the shot fired by him may have killed Warder Hodson.

(f) The fact that Ryan retained the gun. The normal course of a man who has shot another is to dispose of the weapon, because it is well known the guilt can be proved by the evidence of a ballistic expert establishing the fact that the bullet was fired by a particular weapon. It could therefore be expected that Ryan, who had no reason to assume that the spent bullet would not be found, would dispose of the gun. Instead, he kept it, although he had in his possession, when arrested in Sydney, another weapon, which incidentally he did not use. He was asked why he kept it and said he did so to prove his innocence in the event of recapture, as he knew that the markings on the spent bullet would prove that it was not fired from that rifle and that he, of course, did not know that the spent bullet had not been found.

(g) The evidence of Dr. A. McQueen Thomson that he examined the body of the deceased [Hodson] immediately after the shooting. This evidence, though known to the Police, was not given at the trial. It may have tended to support the Defence, because of the argument of the Defence as to the downward path of the bullet, suggesting that it was fired from a point above ground level.[89]

At 4:40PM, Freadman personally presented the new petition at Rylah's office. With less than fifteen hours to go before the hanging, suddenly there was a serious new issue for Rylah to consider. Unlike citizens' petitions to the Queen or the governor, or legal applications to the courts, this petition was directed at the attorney-general, who was both a minister of the crown and the first law officer of the state. Section 584 was a rarely used provision in the Act—although Rylah had utilised it in another case almost ten years before—that had been introduced some 50 years before to deal with eventualities arising after all legal appeals had been exhausted.[90] One such eventuality was the situation of fresh evidence coming to light.

It was a measure of how seriously Rylah saw the new petition and the issues it raised that he immediately sought the views of the crown solicitor, Tom Mornane, and that he quickly arranged to meet with the premier. At 4:50PM, Rylah and Mornane went to Bolte's office, where for almost two hours the premier and his deputy thrashed out the issues, assisted by Mornane's advice when called upon. According to section 584, in considering whether to grant clemency, the attorney-general may, if he thinks fit, at any time, either:

(a) refer the whole case to the Full Court and the case shall then be heard and determined by that Court as in the case of an appeal by a person convicted; or

(b) if he desires the assistance of the judges of the Supreme Court on any point arising in the case with a view to the determination of the petition, refer that point to such judges for their opinion thereon, and such judges or any three of them shall

> consider the point so referred and furnish the Attorney-General with their opinion thereon accordingly.[91]

At this point, the options open to Rylah seemed two-fold. If he took the first course offered by section 584 (a), he could refer the new evidence to a Full Court of the Supreme Court, which could determine the matter as if it were a new appeal. The obvious implication of that course was that the execution could not proceed in the morning, but would have to be deferred yet again. In all likelihood, it would also mean that Ryan's sentence would have to be commuted, regardless of the outcome of the full court hearing. The likely political consequence of still another deferral was that it would be hard to resist the argument and public clamour for a permanent stay, on the grounds that it was unconscionable to put a condemned prisoner through yet another preparation for death. Ryan's execution had already been postponed twice, once for the Privy Council appeal and again for Starke's injunction. Would a third postponement be politically sustainable?

On the other hand, section 584 (b) seemed to offer an alternative. This section had been closely modelled on section 19 (b) of the English *Criminal Appeal Act 1907*.[92] Section 584 (b) was intended to allow the attorney-general to seek the opinion of a judge or judges in determining whether to refer the evidence back to court for hearing in a fresh appeal, or whether simply to exercise his discretion to recommend to the governor that mercy be granted. Clearly, if the opinion of a judge or judges was that the new evidence was sufficient to justify clemency, the attorney could simply exercise his discretion to recommend to the governor that he exercise the royal prerogative of mercy and commute Ryan's sentence.

These were weighty and troubling issues and normally, of course, one would have expected that such referral to a judge or judges, and their response, would be formal and in writing. But there was no time: speedy, informal advice would have to suffice. A man's life was poised in the balance, and Rylah was not so sure any more. Freadman's hurriedly prepared petition looked to be full of holes and hope, but what if the prisoners were telling the truth and a bullet had been fired by a warder on the wall? To proceed to execution against that possibility being proven was unthinkable. The government might fall if Ryan were hanged and the new evidence was shown to be well based when tested in a court of law. What about due process? In all likelihood, the new evidence was not persuasive, but justice also had to be seen to be done. Perhaps a further delay to properly examine the new evidence was appropriate? The attorney could not properly assess this new evidence, or its admissibility, or its effect on a jury's deliberations. Was it not the right course to refer this new evidence to a court for it to determine? On the other hand, what sort of damage to the government's credibility would follow if the hanging were called off at the eleventh hour just because there was a remote doubt? Would not the government seem weak and indecisive to call it off after all these protests and demonstrations? How could the government withstand the crowing of its detractors in the media and the opposition? Surely the government would stumble politically and find it hard to recover?

Late in the discussion it became evident to Bolte and Rylah that a special Executive Council meeting would have to be convened quickly to give legal effect to the attorney's consideration of the petition. The difficulty was that the governor, Sir Rohan Delacombe, had left Melbourne after the Executive Council meeting that morning to stay for a long weekend at the nineteenth-century cliff-top beach-house of his friend Everard Baillieu at Point King, Sorrento, on the Mornington Peninsula. With both of the governor's chauffeurs off-duty, the governor's official secretary, Jack Colquhoun, hastily had to find a replacement driver. Under some pressure, he asked the governor's young *aide-de-camp*, Captain Anthony Fitzwilliams-Hyde, to drive to Sorrento to pick up Delacombe and bring him back to Melbourne for the meeting now scheduled for 9:00PM. Told he would have a police escort at high speed, the 24-year old Fitzwilliams-Hyde jumped at the chance to open up in his car, a Mercedes 230SL sports. Armed only with the directions that Baillieu's house was named Merthon, had a high cypress hedge, and was the ninth property after the Sorrento township on the right-hand side of the Nepean Highway, Fitzwilliams-Hyde set off just before 7:00PM on what would normally be a three-hour round trip.[93]

At 7:00PM, the meeting in Treasury Place between Bolte and Rylah broke up. When the premier left his office, he was greeted by a scrum of journalists and several student protestors milling outside. As he walked toward his waiting government car, Bolte was approached by the acting secretary of the Students' Anti-Hanging Committee, who asked him to accept a new petition, bearing the signatures of 2,121 people protesting against the hanging. This took to 14,270 the number of people who had signed the petition in just four weeks. With his head down and without breaking stride, Bolte walked around the student without acknowledgment, and got into his chauffeur-driven car. Several moments later, Rylah also left the building. Alerted by a journalist to his exit, the student thought to approach him with the petition. As Rylah got into the passenger seat of his green Rover sedan, the student asked him through the wound–down window if he would accept it. For a fleeting but meaningful moment, Rylah hesitated—then, smiling gently, said 'No'. For twelve years the loyal deputy to Bolte, Rylah had been steadfast to the end, perhaps even against his inclination.[94]

Meanwhile, Fitzwilliams-Hyde was travelling fast down the Nepean Highway. As he neared Brighton, he was joined by two police motorcyclists who, with lights flashing and sirens wailing, escorted him at high speed to Baillieu's house at Point King. Delacombe was waiting at the end of the long drive at Merthon. The governor got in and, without getting out of the car, Fitzwilliams-Hyde turned around. With the police motorcycle outriders once more leading the way, he took off again for Melbourne. In the open car the wind and the sirens were so noisy that Fitzwilliams-Hyde and Delacombe exchanged not a word for the whole high-speed journey. At 9:00PM, the navy blue Mercedes carrying the governor, who was sporting a casual jacket and sunglasses, sped through the open gates of Government House, past the scrum of journalists and photographers staking out the entrance.[95]

At 9:04PM, Bolte and Rylah ran the media gauntlet at the gate and joined the governor to constitute the Executive Council for the second time that day, formally to consider Ryan's new petition. Before the Executive Council was formally convened at 9:30PM there was spirited informal discussion. This discussion took place in the main central hall near the governor's office, in front of the fireplace, amidst the splendour of the finest vice-regal house in the British Commonwealth. Afterwards, it would be thought by observers that this Executive Council meeting and its prelude had been a mere formality, that no substantive consideration of the issues had been undertaken. What journalists were not aware of, however, was that the meeting was extremely tense as, in the presence of the governor, the premier and the attorney canvassed the issues back and forth, much as they had done earlier in the evening at Bolte's office. But now there was someone else in the hall with Bolte,

Rylah, and Delacombe. Unknown to the media outside the gate, the chief justice, Sir Henry Winneke, had been called in to give his opinion.

As solicitor-general for thirteen years prior to accepting appointment as chief justice in 1964, Winneke had played a role at the highest level of government decision-making. When there had been difficult policy/legal issues for the premier and his deputy, Harry Winneke's advice had been sought, often informally. Winneke was deeply aware of the policy and executive implications of the law, and he well understood the intricacies of government. As well, he had been a crown prosecutor, he knew the criminal law intimately and, in 1950, as Henry Winneke, KC, he had prosecuted Lee, Clayton, and Andrews in their trial for the murder of Pop Kent. Both Bolte and Rylah valued Winneke's judgment highly and relied upon it, and they liked and respected him—as did Delacombe, to whom he was a close and trusted confidant. To Bolte and Rylah, Harry Winneke was one of the boys. He had a fine legal mind, the virtue of great good sense and, like them, he enjoyed a whisky and a good smoke. On occasions when Bolte and Rylah had had a difference of opinion, Winneke would be called upon to arbitrate on an informal basis, usually over a bottle of whisky at Bolte's East Melbourne apartment. After Bolte and Rylah had each said their piece, Winneke, whisky in hand and drawing on his pipe, would offer a judgment on one side or the other. 'I think Arthur's got you on this one, Henry', he might say. His 'verdict' was seldom over-ruled.[96]

Now at Government House, Chief Justice Winneke was being asked for his opinion by the attorney pursuant to section 584 (b) of the *Crimes Act 1958*, the section upon which Freadman had based his petition for clemency.[97] Certainly, Winneke's role in so advising was constitutionally proper and sanctioned by the provisions of section 584 (b). It was also consistent with the practice as it had developed in the United Kingdom, where for many years the lord chief justice's opinion under the comparable section of the UK *Criminal Appeal Act* had been both formally and informally sought and given to the home secretary.[98]

This discussion in the hallway was not yet a formal session of the Executive Council—that would happen when the way ahead was clear—but it was important to the shaping of the advice that the premier would subsequently give the governor. Back and forth the argument went over glasses of Corio whisky brought to them by the governor's *aide de camp*. With only a little over ten hours to go before the scheduled time for the hanging, the pressure on the premier and his deputy at this moment was immense. Bolte would later say that this period was the most stressful time of his life:

'You have no idea of the pressure a death sentence places on a Premier and members of his Cabinet. The pressure toward the end of the Ryan business was unreal.'[99]

After the argument had raged for some time, a consensus emerged. The new evidence was insufficient to justify recommending a fresh appeal or the exercise of the prerogative of mercy. The best advice—certainly from Mornane and almost certainly from Winneke as well—was that even if the jury had heard the evidence of the prisoners, it would not have affected the verdict. Eleven witnesses had deposed on oath that they had seen Ryan raise the carbine to his right shoulder, take aim, and had seen or heard him fire at Hodson as he closed on Walker—eleven witnesses, all sworn to tell the truth, the whole truth, and nothing but the truth. They couldn't all be wrong. Ryan's defence had argued his case before Jack Starke, who agreed with the jury's verdict, despite his strong anti-hanging convictions. They had argued before the full Supreme Court—including Winneke himself—which dismissed his appeal. The High Court did not dissent, and the Privy Council threw out his application in five minutes. How much more certainty could a government reasonably have before proceeding to uphold the law? The new evidence was not in the nature of a revelation seriously calling the verdict into question. No, there was no turning back. Rylah retained his misgivings about due process, and Delacombe was uneasy about it all, but Ryan's last petition would be rejected. At 9:30PM the decision was finally reached, and the Executive Council went into formal session to give legal effect to the premier's advice to the governor. Rylah would decline to exercise his prerogative. In due course, at the foot of the petition were typed the words:

> Having considered this petition and having conferred with the Crown Solicitor, I decline to exercise the powers given me under Section 584 of the Crimes Act 1958.
>
> Dated the 2nd day of February, 1967
> (signed) AG Rylah
> Attorney General[100]

At 9:55PM Colquhoun telephoned Tom Mornane to tell him of the decision.[101] Five minutes later, Bolte and Rylah drove out of Government House. It was left to Mornane to ring Freadman and let him know that the Executive Council had rejected Ryan's petition. At 10:25PM the announcement was made to the waiting media, who had believed that all this was mere formality. Although journalists and Ryan's legal advisers were never aware of it, with just ten hours to go there had been a serious prospect that the hanging might have been called off.

If there was a moment when it could be said that Ryan's fate was finally, legally sealed, this was it. For the Executive Council this was the end of the journey, the last in a long line of nay-sayings stretching back to 12 December, inspired by a premier determined to have an execution. It was, therefore, fitting that—unlike all the other Executive Council records of decisions—this last one should bear the imprimatur of the premier himself. Of course, all of the previous Executive Council Orders regarding Ryan's execution had been submitted to the governor by the premier. That is, after all, the role of the head of government, to advise and seek legal sanction from the head of state. But this decision—this last final, unalterable, official denial of mercy—departed from the others and disclosed the distinctive provenance of this executive act, which was fixed and enshrined and forever set down in the record. As the official secretary to the Executive Council, Jack Colquhoun, formally noted in the minutes:

> On the advice of the Executive Council, His Excellency the Governor approved an Order in Council submitted by the Honourable the Premier, recommending that a Petition requesting the exercise of Her Majesty's Prerogative of Mercy in favour of Ronald Joseph Ryan be declined.[102]

Fifteen minutes later, at 10:40PM, Allen Cane arrived at Essendon Airport, having flown to Melbourne from Brisbane in a last-ditch bid to put his evidence before ministers.[103] At Pentridge at 10:45PM, Ryan was told that his last legal application had been rejected and that he would hang in the morning. The honourable the premier, whose hand had firmly guided the course of momentous events these past few weeks and months, was going to get his way after all.

CHAPTER SIXTEEN

Execution

'You look a bit pale, Guv.'
—Ronald Ryan

EARLIER IN THE EVENING of Thursday, 2 February, even as Bolte and Rylah were still considering Freadman's petition, events at Pentridge were moving to their inexorable conclusion. Governor Grindlay had called a meeting of his senior officers to brief them about contingencies should prisoners refuse to work after the hanging the next morning. Grindlay issued an instruction that if the prisoners either refused to go to the workshops—or refused to work if they did go—they were to be ignored unless damage was done. At 7:00PM, Father Brosnan offered a special Mass outside Ryan's cell.[1] Ryan took communion with altar boy Des Purcell and prison officer Bert Warren, and said goodbye to them after the Mass.[2] Brosnan then told Ryan that the hangman had raised an objection to Brosnan being on the scaffold with him the next morning because there had been complications at a previous hanging.

The hangman, Mr Jones, was a man in his sixties who claimed he had assisted or officiated at statutory neck-breakings in Australia and elsewhere for 38 years, and he had conducted hangings at Pentridge before.[3] The complications he mentioned referred to his hanging of Lee, Clayton, and Andrews on 19 February 1951. The two vital elements in the great art, Mr Hangman Jones knew, were the position of the rope around the condemned man's neck and the precise length of the rope required for the drop. The first was simply that the 'knot' had to be under the left-hand side of the prisoner's lower jaw to ensure that the head was thrown back and the neck was broken at the end of the drop. (Precisely why the left-hand side is preferred by hangmen is a matter of conjecture. Some hangmen argue that the 'knot' is less likely to slip on the left-hand side.[4] Other authorities believe that it has less to do with technical considerations than with an ancient hangmen's tradition, a gesture to the medieval belief that malefactors were under the influence of the sinister left side.[5])

The second element was that the length of the drop had to follow a formula determined by the condemned man's weight in his clothes. Strangulation had been the result of judicial hangings through the ages; but, with elevated scaffolds and the development of the long drop in the late-nineteenth century, it was asserted by hangmen and others that more efficient execution could be achieved through fracture dislocation of the neck. In 1885, James Berry, an English hangman, had constructed a Table of Weights and Drops in which he amended and schematised the rule of thumb of his predecessor and mentor William Marwood, who had pioneered the long-drop method of execution. On the basis of the prisoner's clothed weight, Berry had calculated the length of rope required to achieve fracture dislocation from hanging, and his table had been adopted by the British Home Office.[6] Australian officials had also followed a modified Berry table. Still, if the rope were too short—if the distance he fell was not far enough—the condemned man's neck would not be broken, but he would be slowly strangled. If the distance was too long, the prisoner could be decapitated. Miscalculations involving strangulation had occurred frequently in Britain and Australia.

For much of the scarlet thread that runs through British history, hanging had been a tradition whose brutality did not much consider the relatively humane merits of various forms of hanging: executions ranged from hanging, drawing and quartering in the fifteenth century to hanging and gibbeting in the mid-eighteenth century. The Latin entry in gaoler's books, *Sus. per coll*, did not specify whether strangulation or cervical fracture was preferred. It simply meant a condemned man was to be 'hanged by the neck until his body is dead'. That was all the law required.[7] Indeed, for the first one hundred years of settlement in Australia, prior to the development of the long drop, strangulation was the norm for judicial executions.[8] Even after the long drop, it was assumed by hangmen that extra measures had to be taken to ensure certain death. When Ned Kelly was hanged in November 1880, a drop of eight feet had been used; but the hangman and his assistant still drew up Kelly's legs and dropped him a lesser distance several times more before they were sure that the long drop had done its work.[9]

On 19 February 1951, Jean Lee had been hanged at 8:00AM, and Clayton and Andrews had been hanged together at 10:00AM. The hanging of Clayton had been unaccountably botched by the hangman. He had died, not quickly from cervical displacement fracture, but slowly from strangulation—in medical terms, as the coroner found, from 'cerebral contusion, shock and asphyxia'. According to the acting government medical officer at Pentridge, Dr John Whiteside, Clayton lived at the end of the rope for five minutes after the drop.[10] There has been speculation that the positions of Andrews and Clayton were inadvertently mixed up on the gallows, and that they had been hanged with the rope lengths designated for each other. But the stronger likelihood is that the length of the drop for Clayton had been miscalculated.[11]

Ryan was unaware of all this, and his response expressed a different concern. When he was told that the hangman had objected to Brosnan being present on the scaffold, he bristled:

> 'I don't need anyone to hold my hand', Ryan told Father Brosnan with a flash of fire. 'What do they think it is, a debutante ball? Who stands where and that sort of thing?
>
> 'By a quarter-to-eight tomorrow, you'll have done all you can for me. Just you anoint me afterwards.
>
> 'We are bigger than they are.'[12]

After Brosnan left, Ryan had a visit from the chief prison officer of H Division, Bert Clark. Before the last scheduled date for execution, Clark had come to ask Ryan 'if he desired any special breakfast …' Ryan had been wary, fearing that if he ate anything it might contain a sedative.[13] 'No thanks', he had replied: 'It would only be a waste, but I would like a nip of whisky.'[14] Clark had said he would pass Ryan's request on to the proper authorities. Now Clark had called to tell Ryan that H Division governor Bob Duffy had arranged a nip of brandy in the morning.[15]

Grindlay also visited Ryan in his cell, where they talked for an hour. Ryan was calm.

He told Grindlay: 'I'll be all right, Guv. I have made my peace with God. I think I'll make it. If I do, you'll always have a friend up there.'[16]

Subdued and speaking quietly, Ryan told Grindlay that he thought the hanging was for the best. He said he could not face being confined for the rest of his life; he would always be looking for a way out.

'I couldn't face 30 years living in this loveless environment.'[17]

He said to Grindlay: 'Remember when they tried to work up a case as to whether an officer shot Hodson or I did?'

Grindlay replied: 'You never had a chance with that ... you know full well you shot him.'

Ryan looked Grindlay squarely in the face. 'Yes, that's true,' he said. 'I did shoot him. But I didn't mean to kill him ... only to stop him. I'm an expert shot. I used to be a kangaroo shooter. I aimed to hit him in the left shoulder to stop him. He almost had his hands on Peter.'

Ryan then rocked Grindlay with the comment: 'I'm going to be all right, tomorrow, but how are you going to be? You are going to be under a hell of a lot of pressure. All eyes won't be on me—they'll be on you, too. I don't know how you'll be but you'll have to show strength.'[18]

Grindlay told Ryan that he would be okay, shook hands with him, and left the cell. When he reached his residence within the prison walls, Grindlay reflected on what Ryan had said. Yes, he would fulfil his official responsibilities, but what he would have to do in the morning filled him with profound sorrow and the most gut-wrenching dread. The prisoner for whom he held such high hopes of betterment just a few short years ago at Bendigo would be killed in the morning and, but for duty, he wanted no part of it.[19]

After Grindlay left, Ryan wrote two letters. The first was a short note to Peter Walker, elsewhere in H Division. They had not seen one another for almost a year, since the last day of the murder trial back at the end of March. They had communicated through the prison grapevine, the cell toilets, with messages passed from prisoner to prisoner.[20] These were little snippets or messages of encouragement from Walker to Ryan and back again as the legal and political process unfolded: 'Beauty, you've got another stay, mate. Don't let it get you down.' Now Ryan sent Walker a handwritten note, a last message, which an obliging prison officer passed to him in his cell. 'From Ron', the officer said, as he stuck the note through the trap in Walker's cell door.

'All the best', the note read. 'You've got a lot of years ahead. Stay on top. See you again some day.'

Walker's message back was simple. 'See ya, mate,' he said, not sure if it ever got through.[21]

Next, Ryan took a long roll of thin, prison-issue toilet paper and began to write. Since the cabinet decision in December, Ryan had been freed of the prison regulation limiting him to only two letters per month, and he could have written any number of letters on the stationery issued to prisoners. But the prison stationery was issued by prison authorities and accounted for, and any letter that he wrote on it was subject to the official system of prison censorship and handling. By writing it clandestinely on toilet paper, and having it smuggled out of the gaol by a sympathetic prison officer, Ryan could be sure that he could direct it to his intended recipient securely and without prison-officer scrutiny. It was also a way of getting one up on prison authorities, a last defiant act of escaping the system. Using a blue ballpoint pen, Ryan began the letter to Dorothy and the children in which he reviewed his life and reflected on the events that had brought him to the eve of his execution.

As Ryan was writing, at around 10:40pm Allen Cane had arrived in Melbourne from Brisbane, and was immediately taken to a motel in Canterbury Road, Albert Park, where he met with several of the leading members of the anti-hanging committee, including Barry Jones and David Hirt. Hearing directly from Cane his story of the warder on the wall, Barry Jones and others were persuaded that his evidence was important enough to be put before members of the cabinet. Jones left the motel and returned home, and for the next several hours he and other committee members manned the telephones to ring ministers at their homes to try to obtain interviews at which Cane's evidence would be put to them. Their attempts were unsuccessful. Most members of the cabinet, it seemed, had left their phones off the hook. Finally, at midnight, Jones phoned Brian Dixon, MLA for St Kilda—a personal friend and a sympathiser—to ask him to place Cane's evidence before ministers. Ryan, at this stage, was due to meet the hangman in less than eight hours. Dixon immediately agreed to act as the channel of communication between Jones and Arthur Rylah.

Dixon enlisted the aid of another local Liberal MP, Edgar Tanner, who was personally close to Bolte. Several telephone conversations from committee members in Cane's motel room to Jones at home between 12:30AM and 12:45AM confirmed that Dixon and Jones would drive to Tanner's home in Elwood. In between these telephone conversations, an emotional David Hirt rang Jones and said, in effect: 'Cabinet ministers must be made to hear Cane's story. If necessary, I'll go to their homes and compel them to come—insist that they get out of bed, and meet Cane in order to save Ryan.' Jones told Hirt that this would only make matters worse, and advised him to forget it.[22]

What Jones and the others still with Cane did not know was that their calls from the motel room had been monitored—not through phone tapping, as they came to suspect, but through eavesdropping by the manager of the motel. The manager had been asked to put calls through the motel switchboard, and he had simply listened-in to the calls as he put them through. After overhearing the calls, the manager had gone to the South Melbourne police station at around 1:00AM to report that he had overheard the conversation between Jones and Hirt in which they had discussed—as he thought—a plan with Dixon to forcibly take cabinet ministers to hear what Allen Cane had to say.[23]

Within half an hour of these calls, and within fifteen minutes of the manager's tip-off to police, a squad car had pulled up outside Dixon's house at 31 Martin Street, Gardenvale. In company with two other police, Senior Constable Brian Murphy, the night-shift supervisor for the South Melbourne area, who had been directed by D24 to respond, knocked on the door demanding to see Dixon. Dixon's wife Marie told the policeman that her husband was not at home, but had gone to Edgar Tanner's house in nearby Elwood. Senior Constable Murphy went to Tanner's house at 14 Vautier Street, Elwood where, upon his arrival, he noticed Barry Jones outside in the street. Murphy spoke to Dixon, asking if he was involved in a plot to abduct cabinet ministers. The police were soon persuaded that no such plot was contemplated, but the momentum of the Cane initiative was lost, and the frantic efforts to reach Rylah were to no avail.[24]

In these early hours of Friday, 3 February, the anti-hanging committee members, exhausted and dispirited, finally had to confront the prospect that their best endeavours would not prevent the hanging. Over the previous few weeks there had been intense activity as lawyers, politicians, journalists, church leaders and members, students, trade unionists, and ordinary people protesting the decision had used every means at their disposal to prevent a man from dying. Now, with the failure of the attempt to reach cabinet ministers with Cane's evidence, Ryan's last hope that his execution might be avoided was dashed. As this was sinking in, representatives of the state of Victoria were at D Division in Pentridge, making ready for Ryan's early-morning appointment with the hangman.

IN HIS CELL, Ryan had continued to write the letter that he had begun earlier in the evening. This was the last letter Ryan would ever write. By the time he had finished, the toilet paper would form an unbroken scroll more than ten feet in length. It must have seemed that if he stopped writing, or when the roll was used up, he would die. Some observers would later see this as Ryan's speech from the gallows, but it was much too personal for that. Many of the references were fully intelligible only to his family. Quoting Shakespeare's 116th sonnet ('Let me not to the marriage of true minds ...') and speaking cryptically of emotional wounds and infidelities, Ryan was settling unfinished business with his former wife, and sending a message of love and regret and fatherly guidance to his daughters. Ryan had set the name 'Dorothy Janet Ryan (née George)' at the top of the paper, underlined these words, and addressed the letter to 'My Darling Wife & Daughters':

> It has been of the utmost concern to me that I have lost contact with you through what—to use a dramatic phrase—has been my darkest hour. It is my considered opinion that during crisis a family should be closer together in spirit and loyalty presenting a closed and united front to hostile elements and affording each other—as only a family can—comfort and support. This, despite the nature and rights or wrongs of the situation. I fully realize and am confident that this indeed would be your heartfelt desire, the spontaneous product of our shared love and intimate assessment of each other.
>
> Therefore, I have been puzzled and deeply hurt at not receiving at least a letter from one or all of you. For this—rightly or wrongly—I blame Mum; because the alternative is too unbelievably cruel and heartbreaking to accept. It has me completely baffled how

Mum can adopt such an adamant and cruel attitude as she seemingly has—I say seemingly as, optimistic fool that I am, I still seek some justifiable excuse for Mum, and, even greater sentimental fool, I am still deeply in love with Mum. This, if she could only tell you of certain actions of hers, just previous to, and during our marriage, would seem amazing. However, at this stage, I hasten to add that my own behaviour, of a similar nature, was not above reproach. As a salve to my conscience I half-heartedly blame Mum's actions for my indiscretions. She no doubt could present a similar justification which then leaves us on a par again. In a situation such as my present one, which to use a cliche is 'the moment of truth', one can see things in a truer perspective and adopt a different sense of values. Then these seemingly all important causes of friction are comparatively meaningless—collectively forming a fog which blinds one to the truly important consideration and values of life. I could ramble on at great length to bring out my point there, but for an insight I suggest you listen to the record of Al Jolson's 'Are You Lonesome Tonight' which in part says:—'I'd rather [go on hearing] your lies, than living without you', also 'If you don't come back to me they can bring the curtain down'. There is further mention—during the monalogue of Act I, etc—words to the effect of cleverly acting a part (of lover). Mum, if she chooses, could tell you how I always insisted that my love for her was the greater. This she used to vehemently deny; but I suggest that time has proved my assertion.

Oh, my Darlings, how I did and still do love your Mother. She has the capacity to stir me to the very greatest heights or plunge me to the deepest gloom. This latter was an unseen blessing in disguise as without her love and your love and the family companionship life is meaningless to me and consequently I can accept the prospect of death without [sic: presumably, the intended word was 'with'] an unusual calm and composure. Mum and I had such happy and wonderful experiences together. We both shared an exceptionally warm and passionate nature—which ironically was both our undoing in each others eyes, as through shyness, false modesty and the inhibitions caused by our upbringing we withheld too much from each other thus causing a sense of inadequacy and frustration—the contributing factors causing us to seek fulfillment elsewhere while all the time it was at hand in & for both of us. I expect that physically we could be said to much exceed the average in attentions to each other; but viewed in retrospect and in the capacity for giving and craving love we both failed to exploit our potential. What I would give for a chance to relive the past or some future years in the light of my present insight. Fool that I was to place other things before love and its demands of companionship—both physical and cerebral—and the attaining of that rapport which is of heavenly and blessed nature—a blending of the primitive and aesthetic.

This is so frustrating as my impossible task is to convey and convince both you my Darling Daughters and Mum of my love and there is a strong desire to excuse my past actions and justify them so that I may present myself as worthy of your continued love and respect. Talk about being a crazy mixed up guy—I use that term figuratively. There I go again, protectively trying to present myself in a good light or guard against your getting the slightest unfavourable impression. Hence, my Darlings to save myself a life time of writing and a task which belittles the power of mere words. I leave my guilt or otherwise to your judgment—while asking you to ignore the badly informed and sensationalism of newspaper reports; also the prejudiced reports of outsiders. In this group of prejudiced people I must include Mum's family as they were only permitted a cursory glimpse of my nature & that usually the undesirable aspects. However, I qualify the matter of prejudice as far as they are concerned. After all Mummy is their daughter and I can well imagine my own & Mum's attitude if we thought any of our Darlings was with a bounder and black sheep as I must appear to them—conformists as they are!

Seemingly, I have been writing on and on with little result except to confuse the issue. The salient points are that I very much love you, and here I point out—'That Love is not Love, which alters when it alteration finds, or bends with the remover. It is an ever fixed mark—that bears it out, even to the edge of doom.'[25]

Secondly, that my intent was honourable in all I did; but I seem fated to lose and destroy all that—family love and welfare—which I sought to foster and protect.

I must, to qualify the above, admit to being selfish to a degree and certainly thoughtless. However, I allow myself the egotistic view that your remembrance of our shared experience, and my behaviour as a father and a husband before my hectic lawlessness and its disastrous and shameful effects, will of themselves plead my case and justify your continued love.

I have only the kindest thoughts and best wishes for your future. I ask you to love wholeheartedly and be loyal to your love. Without love life is as nothing.

Mum may choose to tell you of our romantic and adventurous life—complete with elopement, separation, reunion, doubt, betrayal by each. But, to me: 'Sift the ashes and what remains is gold.'

To you my Darling—how I love you and yet feel I'd like to shake the daylights out of you—I ask you to remember that my decline started with Noojee. A song which it suits us both to lend attention to is: 'When the wheel of hurt comes wheeling round to you.' What a fool I have been and I leave you to judge yourself in that respect. But, isn't it such a pity that two people such as us—and here I have in mind our warm and generous natures and our capacity for love and understanding, the ability to be for each other all we long for—both primitively and aesthetically—and yet wasted so much time of what could have been such a heavenly existence. I think in fairness to us both it is right to say that we should each have met sooner and been each other's first and only love.

For my part I ask your forgiveness and accept you with any faults or acts of disloyalty as I would have you accept me. Given the chance, how happy I'd make you now, My Darling.

Whether you have any love left for me or not I am stuck with my love for you. Despite the jealousy and envy, I wish you all the best and can only hope that in choosing someone else to share your life, ease your loneliness and satisfy that warm, ardent nature of yours, you are fortunate. Though I secretly hope that he falls short of my better efforts.

Thank you for the better years and it is wonderful to have you as the mother of our loveable and charming daughters. How ruthless you can be when necessary. If you desired to hurt me for my hurt to you, then you were successful. Do look after our Darlings and don't let any 'mug' exploit your facile nature.

At this late hour it is only the truth that is important, so my loved ones, I ask you to accept not only my words but what you must sense I wish to convey.

I go on to whatever lies ahead counting as my greatest fortune having loved and shared so many happy hours with you.

Goodbye my Darlings and may you get the love and luck you all deserve. I am not afraid, and I think the credit is largely yours,

Lovingly yours,

Dad

Having completed the letter—written in a continuous flow with only one or two corrections—Ryan added for the girls a postscript on the back end of the toilet paper:

I would have you re-read this letter at a more mature age—say forty—. When in light of experience you'd be more understanding and better able to judge—having in mind one's concern at an early age of the concern about what others may think and our self-consciousness of their views.

With regard to my guilt I say only that I am innocent of intent and have a clear conscience in the matter.

I was not content to have my loved ones committed to a life of drudgery and sought the means to establish the chance for you and your children.

For this odd thinking I must for excuse point to my childhood and history. There have been many who have succeeded so that subsequent generations could point back in pride, but I must take my place of those who failed and unfortunately you share the attendant shame and disgrace. However, I'm confident you'll be equal to the task of rising above this.

As I am the last of the Ryans—on the male side—I regret not having a son who with the blending of Mum's qualities would have succeeded where I failed and in a more socially acceptable manner.

Well that's life I guess, and having tried and failed one must accept the bumps—or should I say the 'ups and downs'.

I suggest you each have a copy of this letter to peruse at that later date when, hopefully, you'll be less censurous.

Ron[26]

This was a remarkable letter, and it showed Ryan at his best. While there was no direct expression of remorse for his killing of Hodson, he conceded his faults, repented his wrongdoings and, despite the hurt he felt at her divorce of him, gave the credit to Dorothy and also to the girls. If there was good in him, Dorothy had been largely responsible for it. When he finished the letter, Ryan laboriously folded it back into a flat scroll and called a trusted prison officer to the cell. Giving him a £5 note, Ryan asked him to make sure it was passed to *Truth*, the newspaper to which he had turned when he was on the run and which he knew would give this private and revealing letter the exposure he craved.[27] As ever, Ryan was mindful of his place in the limelight of public attention.

Outside the gaol, three thousand protestors had gathered amid emotional and, at times, wild scenes. It was to be a last desperate outpouring of anger and frustration. Shortly before midnight more than two hundred police had been at Pentridge to control the demonstrators—90 extra police having been rushed from police headquarters as reinforcements—and there were many arrests. Earlier in the evening, police had become aware that, by prearrangement, many of Melbourne's criminal underworld had begun to gather in the Coburg Hotel on the corner of Sydney Road and O'Hea Street, directly opposite Pentridge. The pub was crowded, and the atmosphere was heavy with tension and barely contained aggression. With the prospect of violence erupting among known criminals and troublemakers as the consumption of alcohol increased, police decided to close the hotel. A phalanx of police moved up O'Hea Street, from the railway line 300 yards away where they had assembled, to sweep through the hotel. In a concerted movement, police in numbers came through each of the pub's three doors on O'Hea Street, took beers out of the hands of drinkers, and pushed them out the front door in a strong show of force.[28]

Later, outside the gaol, as mounted police and police with dogs broke up one melee after another, protestors—chanting and booing loudly—were swept forward into waiting police paddy wagons. More than 90 protestors were arrested, mostly on charges of 'offensive behaviour' and 'resisting arrest'. One of those arrested was the state Labor member for Richmond, later the state opposition leader, Clyde Holding, who was bailed up by an aggressive police dog, a German Shepherd, which seemed to take a particular dislike to him, repeatedly snarling and baring its teeth at his leg. Holding was subsequently charged with 'offensive behaviour' and 'using indecent language', and spent four hours in a police wagon and some time in the Brunswick Police Station lock-up.[29] He was later bailed by Labor Party state secretary Bill Hartley, and released at 1:00AM. By then the number of protesters at the gaol had fallen, but there was still about one thousand people determined to stay until the scheduled time for the execution.

As Holding was being released, 40 miles away the telephone rang at Justice Starke's house in Jacksons Road, Mt. Eliza. Starke had been sleeping restlessly when he picked up the phone. 'Starke', he said abruptly, wondering anxiously what new turn of events might yet await him. 'Judge Starke?', enquired the woman's voice from the other end, 'I am ringing from England to see if there is something that can be done to stop this hanging?' Somewhat taken aback at this untimely intrusion by a stranger, but sharing the caller's sentiments on the matter, Starke spoke reassuringly to the anonymous woman for several minutes, finally telling her that, alas, there was nothing more that could be done. 'How did you get my telephone number?', Starke thought to ask her before he rang off. The woman explained that she had simply placed an international call, and the subsequent Australian operator had looked him up in the Melbourne telephone book. Characteristically, he had maintained a listing under his name even after he was made a judge. Like the open door he had kept to his chambers when a barrister, Starke was accessible to the end.[30]

At Pentridge, contrary to long-established prison practice for condemned men, Ryan was spending his last night in H Division, rather than the so-called death cell in D Division. In fact, he had never spent a single night in the condemned cell following the decision of Ian Grindlay, who believed it was unduly morbid to daily expose a prisoner to the scaffold only yards away. A condemned man would have to walk past and under the scaffold each day to get to the exercise yard, Grindlay knew, and the grooves on the scaffold crossbeam above the trap caused by the scoring of the rope during a hanging would be plainly visible.[31]

ON THE MORNING of Friday, 3 February at 5:45AM, Ryan was woken. He dressed in the standard prison garb of blue-grey denim trousers, grey-white shirt, black shoes, and socks. At 6:00AM, Father Brosnan came to

Ryan's cell and vested to say a final Mass.[32] The third of February was the Feast Day of St Blaise; the Mass, Sacerdotes Dei, was for this ancient bishop who was martyred under the Roman Emperor Licinius in the early fourth century. Ironically, St Blaise's Feast Day celebrated the blessing of throats because, according to legend, a mother brought her son who was dying from choking on a fish or chicken bone, and Blaise healed him. His intercessions are therefore sought by the sick, especially those with throat problems.[33] Brosnan gave Ryan Holy Communion, and they prayed together three decades of the Rosary: 'Repent O Christian Soul in the Name of God the Father, who created you, God the Son, who redeemed you, and God the Holy Spirit, who sanctified you.'[34]

With the Mass concluded, at 6:45AM Ryan declined a sedative but accepted the nip of whisky offered by the senior attendant at the prison hospital, Arthur Alexander, and he was handed over to H Division governor Bob Duffy for his transfer to the condemned cell. Handcuffed to prison officers Bill Warner and John Fraser, Ryan was taken in a prison van by the security detail to D Division, a long bluestone building with a high lantern roof through which light poured from dusty windows.[35]

Normally, there were up to 198 prisoners in D Division, including prisoners on remand, but now there were none. At 6:00AM they had been cleared out of the D Division cells and taken to F Division dormitories. Ryan, looking pale and unshaven, was escorted to the condemned cell—a double cell, number 67—on the north side of the first floor of D Division. The division comprised two long banks of cells separated by a central open area with a steel catwalk linking the sides at the first level of three tiers of cells. The catwalk served as the gallows. Running nine feet above it, from one side of the cells to the other, was a large, white-painted timber crossbeam, with the two oak doors of the trap in the floor operated by a lever. The heavy oregon twelve-by-eight inch scaffold beam had been installed in the Melbourne Gaol in 1865, and had figured in all 51 Melbourne executions from April 1865 until the last execution at the gaol in April 1924.[36] It was later moved to Pentridge with the assistance of a condemned prisoner, David Bennett, a carpenter, who had been sentenced to death for the rape of a child. Bennett was the first person to be hanged on the relocated scaffold in September 1932. The beam had been used for all nine executions at Pentridge from 1932 up to this day.[37]

In the condemned cell, Ryan was joined by Brosnan, and they finished two decades of the Rosary: 'Into your hands, O Lord, I commit my spirit. Lord Jesus receive my soul. Holy Mary, be a mother to me. St Joseph, patron of the dying, pray for me.'[38] Brosnan then began prayers for the dying, a series of psalms and litanies said until life is extinct:[39]

> Sprinkle me with hyssop, O Lord, and
> I shall be purified; wash me and I
> shall be whiter than snow. Lord have
> mercy. Christ have mercy …
> From plague, famine and war
> deliver me O Lord …
> Let them be ashamed and con-
> founded that seek after my soul.
> Let them be turned backward
> and put to confusion that desire
> my hurt …
> May they rest in peace —Amen.

At 7:00AM, the hangman, Mr Jones, wearing a dark grey suit and a large green cloth cap and heavy dark welder's goggles, arrived at D Division, having spent the night in the prison. He was met by Grindlay, who put him in the cell opposite Ryan on the south side of the first level of cells. At 7:07AM, sheriff Gerry O'Brien and his deputy Jim Mulvey arrived at the prison's south gate, and proceeded directly to D Division.[40] By ancient law dating back to the origins of colonial settlement, and before that to English law and practice, the sheriff was empowered to enforce orders of the court, including execution orders.

Also at 7:00AM, eleven journalists and a handful of officials had been given entry to the gaol to witness the hanging.[41] The journalists included some of the most senior and respected names in the media: Tom Prior from *The Sun*; Geoff Clancy from *The Herald*; David Thorpe from *The Age*; Evan Whitton from *Truth*; Brian Morley from 3AW-Macquarie Broadcasting Network; Ron Saw from the Sydney *Daily Mirror*; Patrick Tennison from *The Australian*; Kevin Sanders from GTV9, Melbourne; Brian Joyce from HSV7, Melbourne; Keith Willey from the Sydney *Sun*; and Ross Campbell Jones from *The Sydney Morning Herald*. They had been admitted at the south gate upon presentation of the official invitation. Typed on the sheriff's letterhead, and signed and sealed by him, it read: 'Please admit the bearer ... to the execution of Ronald Joseph Ryan, on 3rd February, 1967.' This document had simply followed the historic form for executions, but it was seen as macabre by those coming to witness the hanging. And so it was, although it had at least avoided the excess of the eighteenth-century Newgate hangman-impresario, whose terse and much-sought-after invitations ran: 'We hang at eight and breakfast at nine.'[42]

In the condemned cell, Father Brosnan spent 45 minutes with Ryan, talking to him and preparing him for death. In his hands Ryan clutched Cecilia's rosary beads, which she had given him on her last visit. Before he left to take up his position below the scaffold, Brosnan and Ryan warmly shook hands. Ryan said to him: 'Goodbye and thank you very much. Never forget, no matter how long you live, you were ordained for me.'[43] After Brosnan left the cell, Grindlay, O'Brien, and the four prison officers stayed a while with Ryan. Not much was said between the men present although, as the minutes ticked by, Ryan remarked to Grindlay, 'You look a bit pale, Guv.'[44] Grindlay and O'Brien then left to attend to other aspects of the execution arrangements.

Meanwhile, the journalists and officials had been taken to the E Division reception hall where they waited, most of them smoking heavily. At 7:47AM, the journalists were given a quick briefing by a prison officer, and counselled that they were not to take photographs or make tape recordings.

'It wouldn't be cricket', the officer said, and sought an assurance that everyone would 'play the game'.[45]

He added: 'When you get there, just keep your hands in a still position, otherwise we might get suspicious. We'll just walk down quietly. Now if you'd like to come this way … '[46]

At 7:50AM, the journalists, with sixteen prison officers as well, walked the 50 yards to the D Division cell block, where they took up positions on the ground floor of the western end of the building. They stood in two lines behind a length of thin cord, much like a clothes-line, about fifteen to twenty yards from the gallows. To journalist Brian Morley, the whole cell block was pervaded with the powerful smell of carbolic. For years afterward, Morley, who had come to the execution with an open mind about the merits of capital punishment, would associate the odour of phenol disinfectant with this dreadful place and time, and feel a rush of nausea.[47] Directly in front of the witnesses and below the trap, they could see one of two heavy, green canvas sheets—the infamous green tarpaulin—forming a ten-feet-high screen at the front and back of the gallows. From rods on the undersides of the railed platform, the tarpaulins ran down to a level nine inches above the floor.

On the gallows, secured to an adjustable chain, a stout manila rope, one inch in diameter, was wound six times round the scaffold crossbeam above, with the noose end resting on the back railing. Having previously established Ryan's clothed weight of twelve stone, the hangman had carefully calculated the length of rope to equal a drop from the trap of exactly seven feet.[48] Unlike the popular representations of a hangman's knot—a Western-style slip-knot—the noose had been fashioned by running one end of a manila rope through a two-and-a-half inch brass eyelet stitched into the other end of the rope, the last 30 inches of which had been covered with sewn soft leather rubbed with wax. The noose was held in place by a leather washer. Next to the trap a chair had been placed in the event it was needed, as it was when Jean Lee was hanged in 1951.

As eight o'clock approached, there was an eerie quiet among the prisoners in Pentridge. To Peter Walker, the whole prison seemed very quiet: 'All the noises I usually heard from my cell were missing—no banging of pots as they cleaned up after breakfast. Nothing. It was as though the world had stopped temporarily.'[49] At 7:58am, Grindlay and O'Brien walked along the narrow gallery above the witness party to the condemned cell. O'Brien's task, in the presence of Grindlay and other officials, was to read to Ryan the Death Warrant. Signed and sealed by the governor of Victoria, and countersigned by chief secretary Rylah, the warrant was the legal authority for the hangman to kill a man in the name of the state of Victoria.

Straining to maintain his composure in a situation that he found deeply distressing, O'Brien began to read:

> By His Excellency Major General Sir Rohan Delacombe, Knight Commander of the Most Distinguished Order of St. Michael and St. George, Knight Commander of the Most Excellent Order of the British Empire, Companion of the Distinguished Service Order, Governor of the State of Victoria and its Dependencies in the Commonwealth of Australia, etc, etc, etc. To the Sheriff of the State

> of Victoria. WHEREAS at the Sittings of the Supreme Court of the State of Victoria for the hearing of Criminal Trials held at Melbourne in the Central Bailiwick of the said State on the first day of March, One thousand nine hundred and sixty-six, RONALD JOSEPH RYAN was duly convicted of murder and was by the said Court on the said first day of March, One thousand nine hundred and sixty-six, sentenced to death, his body to be buried within the precincts of Her Majesty's Gaol, Pentridge, in which he shall have been last confined: NOW THEREFORE I, the Governor of the State of Victoria aforesaid, having duly considered the premises, do by this writing under my hand direct that the said sentence shall be carried into execution ...[50]

As O'Brien haltingly read the warrant, it was obvious to Grindlay and O'Brien himself that he was not able to complete it. With the reading only halfway through, and with his voice trailing away, Grindlay put O'Brien out of his misery by dispensing with this formality.

As the moment to move out to the gallows approached, Ryan said to Grindlay: 'Keep up the good work, Guv, and you can quote me, "Christ showed us the way to die on the cross and Our Lord forgives sinners."'[51] A flood of emotion swept over Grindlay, and he struggled to suppress it. A moment later, the hangman emerged from the cell opposite Ryan's, paused at the railed platform and, on O'Brien's signal, came rushing, running almost, through the door of the condemned cell—'like a ferret after a rabbit', journalist Tom Prior later recalled.[52]

Assisted by Bob Duffy, he quickly put leather shackles around Ryan's ankles, although not yet clipped together, and told him to drop his arms straight down by his sides. The hangman and Duffy clasped a leather body-belt around Ryan's waist, fastening its metal buckles, and pinioned his arms securely behind his back with the wrist harness that formed part of the belt. Finally, he put on his head a round white cap of unbleached calico. According to execution ritual, the condemned man's cap was white to distinguish it from the judge's black cap traditionally worn when pronouncing the death sentence. The colour distinction was a further grim execution-tradition expressing an ancient principle: the judge mourns, the hangman rejoices.[53] The cap had a long rectangular flap at the front, which was pushed over the top and back of Ryan's head, making the cap appear to have a peak and trailing flap resembling the hoods worn by the Ku Klux Klan.

At half a minute to eight, and with the hangman in front, a prison officer on each side, and Grindlay behind in this priest-less holy procession, Ryan walked the five steps from the cell to a chalk mark on the centre division of the trap below the beam. Still holding his mother's rosary beads, he turned to face the assembled witness party of journalists and officials below and to the front of the gallows. Grindlay was two feet away to the side, so close he easily could have put his hand on Ryan's shoulder. From below, Father Brosnan could be heard reciting prayers from his position in a cell beyond the canvas screen. At this moment, standing on the brink of eternity, Ryan was quite still and looked straight ahead. His blue-grey denims and white cap made him look incredibly young. Ryan was just three weeks short of his 42nd birthday, but to journalist Ron Saw he could have been a boy of sixteen in that Ku Klux Klan hood.[54]

What followed next took less than twenty seconds as the hangman prepared the condemned man in a blur of rapid movements. In a flash he bent down and secured Ryan's legs together with the ankle shackles, which clipped together in one hit. In one swift motion he pulled the noose down over Ryan's head and under his neck, and zipped up the rope through the brass eyelet and leather washer on the left side of his jaw with three sharp tugs. As he did so, journalist Brian Morley thought to himself: 'They're going to *kill* him!'[55] His *Herald* colleague, Geoff Clancy, crossed himself.[56] With the last tug of the rope, the hangman jolted the condemned man's chin. Ryan flinched perceptibly, but kept looking straight ahead. In the moment before the hangman dropped the flap of the cap over the prisoner's face and chest, Ryan said, 'God bless you' and, recalling Jesus speaking to Judas before the kiss of betrayal, 'Whatever you do, do it quickly.'[57] As the flap dropped, Morley shut his eyes and kept them shut.[58] At that instant, in one deft movement, the hangman leapt back, hitting the lever with both hands while he was still in mid-air. As Ron Saw observed, with the hideous crash of the trapdoor the boy in the Ku Klux Klan hat shot through the trap and a wretched, tortured soul flew out of the dusty windows and out away beyond the whole dreadful business.[59]

'As he fell one heard his neck break,' the acting government medical officer, Dr Allen Bartholomew, later recorded clinically.[60] Grindlay looked down as Ryan fell. At the end of the rope Ryan gave a slight quiver. The hangman reached out and steadied the rope with the swinging body as the rope creaked and strained unevenly against its coiled strands. Through an opening in the rear canvas screen, Father Brosnan approached the body. *Truth* journalist Evan Whitton stooped to look, and saw under the green tarpaulin the black-shod feet of the priest as he ascended a step-ladder. A warder moved up to menace him. 'None of that!', he hissed.[61] Ryan's body was perfectly still as Brosnan drew back the execution hood and, with his thumb moistened with holy oil consecrated by a bishop, anointed Ryan's forehead with *oleum infirmorum*.[62] As he administered the Sacrament of Extreme Unction his voice could be heard unfalteringly through the screen reciting in Latin: '*Per istam sanctam Unctiónem, et suam piíssimam misericórdiam, indúlgeat tibi Dóminus quidquid deliquísti. Amen.*' ('Through this holy anointing and through His mercy may the Lord forgive you for whatever you have done. Amen.')[63] As he did so, Brosnan could see that the whole of the right side of Ryan's face was already black.[64]

With the ceremony completed, Dr Bartholomew joined Brosnan behind the screen and conducted an examination of the body. Bartholomew later recorded: 'After fall no movements. Heart beat for 3 to 4 minutes. No breathing.'[65] At four minutes past eight Bartholomew pronounced Ryan's life extinct.[66] With Brosnan, he emerged from behind the green tarpaulin, and they went to the chaplain's office on the western end of the ground floor. The journalists who had witnessed the execution were led from the gallows area back to the E Division reception hall. Again smoking heavily, they were silent. One of them, particularly affected by what he had seen, threw up in the toilet.[67] At 8:11AM, Gerry O'Brien arrived to formally confirm that the execution had been carried out and that Ryan had been pronounced dead. Reporters were then asked by O'Brien, who was still visibly distressed, to sign an official declaration to say they had witnessed the hanging. Eight of the eleven journalists signed the Declaration of Witness. Ron Saw, Patrick Tennison, and Kevin Sanders refused to sign, as a gesture of opposition to the execution.[68] On GTV9's television news later that night, Sanders would give a detailed eyewitness report of the hanging, but it would be severely edited by editorial management.[69] While represented by journalists at the hanging, *The Sun*, *The Herald*, and *The Age* would not publish an account of it at all.[70]

Outside the gaol, keeping vigil in a waiting radio news car, 3AW journalists Frank O'Brien and Mal Cochrane realised that the execution had taken place when they saw a flock of pigeons, startled by the loud crash of the trap, suddenly fly off the roof of the D Division cell block.[71] Nearby, the large crowd of some three thousand protestors fell silent. The great quiet was broken only by occasional sobs. At Hawthorn, in her house at 235 Riversdale Road, Dorothy sat on a sofa in the lounge room, cuddling the girls tightly as she wept. Wendy anxiously fiddled with a handkerchief. Only later did she realise she had torn it to shreds. As the minutes ticked past eight, Pip looked at a clock, thinking: 'It must be over.'[72]

Two blocks away from Pentridge, parishioners were attending a Mass at St Bernard's Roman Catholic Church at East Coburg. Worshippers were startled at eight o'clock as a gust of wind caught the heavy door to the church and slammed it shut with a loud crash. Later in the morning at St Bernard's, Cecilia and her family would attend a Requiem Mass for Ryan conducted by Father Brosnan. At Parliament House at precisely eight o'clock, students maintaining the vigil on the steps symbolically extinguished the flames on the torches that had burned night and day without interruption for more than a week. Many trams and cars in the city area pulled to a halt. Workers in many parts of the city stopped work for two minutes silence.[73] And in what, for Melbourne's staid churches was an unusual symbolic gesture, church bells across the city began to toll. For a few moments the city, it seemed, had paused as a man died.

And Ryan had died well. The pressure on everyone associated with the hanging was immense, as it was on him. Unusually for a condemned prisoner on the gallows, he had conducted himself with courage and great strength: 'He stood quite still and was cooperative with the executioner', Bartholomew recorded.[74] And his last thoughts were for others. Outwardly ever the tough guy, he had not exhibited remorse, but he had returned to the Church, confessed his crime to God, and prayed for forgiveness. He had embraced death with renewed religious faith. Well might it be said: 'Nothing in his life became him like the leaving it.'

An hour after the execution, the hangman's rope was removed and, using the same step-ladder that Brosnan had used, prison officers lowered Ryan's body to the floor. It was taken in a canvas body-bag to the prison infirmary adjoining D Division, where a room had been set up as a morgue. As the journalists left the prison, several to have a stiff drink at a nearby hotel, Brian Morley made his way to the waiting 3AW radio car, from where he broadcast live on the execution, and followed up with a live cross to BBC radio in London: 'Ronald Ryan today went to his death without flinching', he began. 'He walked firmly to the gallows and stood calmly to attention as the execution was carried out. He looked to me as prepared for death as any man could be.'[75] An hour later, back in the 3AW studio, Morley would file the report to Voice of America in the United States, which broadcast it around the world.[76]

At 8:30AM, prisoners in the gaol had staged their own protest at the hanging by sitting at their machines and refusing to work. Following Grindlay's instruction, prison officers turned an official blind eye. By noon most of them would resume work.[77] At 9:05AM, a post-mortem examination by the senior government pathologist, Dr James McNamara, was begun, with Dr Bartholomew assisting. Completed an hour later, it recorded that Ryan's death had been caused by the complete fracture dislocation of his neck between the second and third vertebrae, consistent with judicial hanging.[78] In the grisly parlance of official executioners, this had been an 'anatomically perfect' execution.[79] Dr McNamara made an examination of Ryan's vital organs, including the brain, heart, lungs, liver, kidneys, and spleen. Apart from some congestion in the liver and the brain, and a slight enlargement of the right kidney, there were no abnormalities.[80] The brain was 'macroscopically normal.'[81]

There was also a requirement for an inquest into the death, but this would be done on the papers rather than in a hearing, as such. Sitting in an office, stipendiary magistrate and coroner Harry Pascoe, assisted by Sergeant John Flynn of the Coroner's Court, examined written evidence in the form of a Report of Death from the police informant, Senior Constable Len Smith of the Coroner's Court. Sworn depositions from witnesses were presented by Dr Bartholomew, who had pronounced life extinct; Pentridge governor Ian Grindlay, who had identified the body; and sheriff Gerry O'Brien, who had presided over the execution as the representative of the Supreme Court and deposed that the hanging had been conducted according to law. O'Brien had prepared the depositions for the witnesses' signatures. Still emotionally affected by the execution, O'Brien's hand was unsteady, and when he wrote out Bartholomew's deposition the words sprawled erratically across the page.

The brief inquest was concluded when Pascoe signed the Proceedings of Inquest document for case no. 320. It was an official document redolent of monarchical symbolism:

> AN INQUISITION for our Sovereign Lady Queen Elizabeth II., taken at Her Majesty's Gaol, Pentridge, Coburg in the State of Victoria, the 3rd day of February A.D. 1967, in the 15th year of the reign of our said Lady the Queen, by me, HARRY WILLIAM PASCOE, gentleman, a Coroner of our Lady the Queen for the said State, upon the view of the body of Ronald Joseph Ryan then and there lying dead.
>
> Having inquired upon the part of our Lady the Queen when, where, and how the said Ronald Joseph Ryan came by his death, I say that on the 3rd day of February 1967, at Her Majesty's Gaol Pentridge, in the said State wherein he was a prisoner in legal Custody, the said Ronald Joseph Ryan died from fracture dislocation of the neck the result of being then and there hanged by the neck until he was dead in conformity with the sentence of the Supreme Court of Victoria for the hearing of Criminal trials held at Melbourne in Victoria on the 30th day of March, 1966 at which Court he was found guilty of Murder and in pursuance of the death warrant under the hand and seal of His Excellency the Governor of the State of Victoria dated the second day of February, 1967.[82]

With the last of the legal formalities over, Ryan's body had the brain removed by Dr McNamara for further examination, and was then roughly stitched up. Under the terms of the *Crimes Act 1958*, burial could not take place lawfully until eight hours after the execution. So it was later in the day, just after 4:00PM, that the body was taken from the hospital mortuary in a simple but respectable polished oak coffin adorned with silver handles and a large silver crucifix. On top of the casket were the rosary beads Ryan had clutched on the gallows. A burial detail of six prison officers, in shirtsleeves in the hot afternoon sun, carried the coffin along a short path to a gate leading to the prison's vegetable farm. From there, the official burial party, comprising Grindlay, Brosnan, O'Brien, Duffy, the director of prisons, Eric Shade, and the six officers swung right, and right again, to a point directly behind a high bluestone wall abutting D Division.

There, near the prison hospital, was a small burial site, marked out by an ankle-high row of raised bluestone pitchers and separated from view by a high tin fence. They stopped in front of the high bluestone wall, and rested the coffin on timber boards above an open grave dug for Robert Peter Tait in October 1962. The grave had been covered with rusted iron for years, but had been cleared of weeds and newly prepared earlier in the week by a gravedigger from the Coburg cemetery. In the vicinity of this strangely isolated place were the remains of the nine other prisoners who had been executed at Pentridge since hangings had been first carried out in the gaol in 1932. The remains of bushranger Ned Kelly—minus the skull—were also there, having been taken to Pentridge for re-burial in the late 1920s.[83]

After a moment's pause, Father Brosnan proceeded to conduct a dignified but brief service according to Roman Catholic rites, lasting less than ten minutes. When he finished his prayers, Brosnan asked Grindlay if he could have the crucifix from the coffin to give to Cecilia. Grindlay told him to go ahead and—along with the rosary beads—it was removed by the officers and given to him. With that, the boards were taken away and the coffin was gently lowered into the unconsecrated ground.[84]

Solemn and respectful though the graveside service had been, there had been no family present and no friends. There were no flowers, no music played and, apart from the prison chaplain's prayers, no-one at the grave-side spoke for him. No-one recalled the small child who had survived the brutality and neglect of a tortured, drunken father, or the eleven-year-old boy who had survived on the streets and longed for his absent mother to come home. No-one expressed a thought for Baldy Ryan and the hardship he had endured as he tried to make something of his tormented young life. No-one spoke about the teenage Ryan, who had sacrificed his youth to give his mother and sisters a home and something to look forward to; nor about the young man who had run the Balranald Athletics Club to give young kids like himself a chance at a better life; nor about the devoted father who had loved his children and tried to give them the chances in life he felt had been denied him.

Certainly, Ryan had turned bad. He had been a con man, he had committed numerous crimes, he had been violent at times, and he had terrorised people in armed hold-ups as well as those who had encountered him whilst he was on the run. Worst of all, he had taken the life of a brave and innocent man, albeit unintentionally. But against the odds of an upbringing of remorseless poverty, abuse, and neglect, he had not turned away from life, he had shown promise of better, and there was plenty of good to balance the scales.

A final reckoning did not count for much in the rush to bury a convicted murderer hanged for his crime. As the burial party turned to walk away, Grindlay looked back to see the prison officers pouring three cement bags of quicklime into the open grave before shovelling in soil. According to prison ritual, quicklime was a final symbolic indignity to an executed murderer, intended to hasten the decomposition of the evil-doer. It was an image that would torment Grindlay for years. Like all the other executed prisoners at Pentridge, Ryan's grave was left unmarked.[85]

In contrast to the obscurity of his final resting place, Ryan's execution did not pass unnoticed elsewhere. The hanging and the protests it attracted made headlines around the world. In London, the BBC broadcast Brian Morley's live report from outside Pentridge, and *The Times* ran a large picture on its front page with a Reuters wire-story headed: '97 arrests as crowd oppose hanging. Chanting and booing by 3,000 outside Melbourne gaol'. In the mass-circulation *Daily Mirror*, a six-column banner, 'Drama as Killer Dies Like a Man—97 Held as Ryan is Hanged', dominated the back page. And in New York the afternoon paper *The Post* ran an inside-page story on the late moves to reprieve Ryan.[86] Closer to home, church bells pealed in Balranald, and at Rupertswood prayers were offered for the repose of the tortured soul of a Ruppo boy who had only wanted to be with his family.

OTHER IMPORTANT FIGURES in the Ryan case had spent the morning differently. With his wife Stella, Phil Opas drove the short distance to Elwood beach where they swam. He had spent the night beside the telephone, his third consecutive night without sleep. At eight o'clock, as they were still in the water, a stranger swimming close by turned and, without recognising him, spoke to Opas: 'I suppose they've strung up that useless bastard by now. Bloody good job.'[87] Later in the morning, Justice Starke arrived at the Supreme Court to resume hearing of a part-heard case in the Causes List. Sitting in his chambers, in great distress at the execution having taken place, he was inconsolable. Approached by his associate Ron Syme, Starke said lowly: 'It was just Bolte!'[88]

Like many others whose duty caused them to be associated with the hanging, Starke and Opas would suffer badly as a consequence of their involvement. For the rest of his life, Starke would worry terribly about his role in sentencing Ryan and agonise about whether he could have done more to save him from the gallows. Opas would become so dispirited by his inability to win a reprieve for his client that he would leave the bar that he cherished. Gerry O'Brien would drink heavily to blot out the memory of what he had experienced, and his career as sheriff would be plunged into ruin. Ian Grindlay was profoundly distressed at what had occurred on the gallows, and he would say a prayer for Ryan every day of his life after the execution. Several years later he would die prematurely of a heart attack; his friends would say that he never got over the hanging. Brian Morley was so deeply affected by what he witnessed at the execution that, to this day, he cannot speak about it without weeping.

A LITTLE LATER in Treasury Place, about fifty journalists attended the premier's usual 10:00AM press conference. He was soon asked what he had been doing at eight o'clock. 'One of the three Ss, I suppose,' he replied. Asked by the journalist what he meant, Bolte said: 'A shit, a shave or a shower.'[89] It was a crass comment, and one he retreated from and thought better of some years after he had relinquished the ropes of power. But perhaps what he said disclosed something about the premier's attitude to the whole matter from the beginning. Henry Bolte never understood the concerns of people everywhere who were deeply offended by the idea of a hanging. They were Christians, Jews, humanists, Labor, Liberals, working class and middle-class people, men and women, who just thought that hanging a man by the neck until he was dead was indecent in our time. They were not woolly-headed idealists for thinking that way. Nor did they have misplaced sympathy for the perpetrator, while ignoring the innocent victim of the murder. It was just that no amount of willing it could undo Ryan's crime, or bring Hodson back to the family who loved him.

Nor was it ever enough for Bolte to simply say that 'it was the law', and that the government was simply 'upholding the law' because no mitigating factor could be found in Ryan's case. Governments can always find reasons to do things or not do them. Sir Henry Bolte did not want to turn away from a hanging because he believed that, had he done so, it would seem as if he had capitulated to his political enemies. Ryan had been executed, but neither the solicitor general who prosecuted him, nor the barristers who defended him, nor the solicitors who represented him, nor one-third of the jury who convicted him, nor the judge who sentenced him, nor the gaol governor who imprisoned him, nor one-quarter of the cabinet that condemned him, nor the sheriff who managed his execution had wanted him hanged. No, this was Henry Bolte's hanging and, but for the premier, it would never have happened. While Bolte may be remembered well for much else, he will never be forgotten as the man who hanged Ronald Ryan. Ten months and four days after he was condemned to death, Ryan had been hanged because of the singular determination of an insecure and defensive premier concerned about shoring up his own political authority.

Ronald Ryan was the 186th person to be hanged in Victoria since the first executions in Melbourne almost exactly 125 years before.[90] There would be no more hangings anywhere in the country after that. In April 1975, capital punishment would be abolished in Victoria. In August 1984, when the death penalty for murder was abolished by Western Australia, the last state government to do so, Ryan remained the last man hanged in Australia. While the extraordinary campaign to save him had not succeeded, he is remembered now as the man whose execution provoked an outcry which ensured that no person ever again in Australia would be put to death by the state. For that, and for more besides, Ronald Ryan has earned his place in our history.

He is the hanged man of our troubled and unhappy memory.

Notes

NOTE ON CITATIONS AND SOURCES

These notes should be read in conjunction with the bibliography. Here, short titles only are provided for all books and articles. The attribution of sources is complex, given that many of the official documents drawn upon for this book were accessed at a time when they resided in departmental files, and had not yet been archived (if, indeed, they ever were) in the Public Records Office. Hence the locations of these documents, and the file descriptions they bore, have been referenced as they were when they were accessed.

ABBREVIATIONS

The following abbreviations are used for frequently cited references:

ADB	*Australian Dictionary of Biography.*
CACT	Transcript of depositions in the committal proceedings involving Christina Evelyn Aitken, Patricia Meryl Puccini, Edna [O'Reilly] Hurley and Keith Desmond Hurley, Melbourne, 18 Jan. 1966.
CLD	The Crown Law Department, Melbourne.
CF	Ronald Ryan's classification file (Ryan, Ronald J, 60/540) originally held at Pentridge prison and later held in the prisons division of the Department of Social Welfare.
CHF	Ronald Ryan's case history file, held in the prisons division of the Department of Social Welfare.
IT	Transcript of evidence of the coronial inquest into the death of George Henry Hodson, Melbourne Magistrates Court, 3–4 Feb. 1966.
RBDM	Registrar of Births, Deaths & Marriages, Melbourne.
RWTT	Transcript of the trial, *The Queen v. Ryan and Walker*, Supreme Court of Victoria, 15–30 Mar. 1966.
SMH	*The Sydney Morning Herald.*
SWD	The Social Welfare Department, Melbourne.
TDT	Transcript of depositions, *The Police v. John Henry Tolmie*, Court of Petty Sessions, Melbourne, 16 Feb. 1967.
WF	Ronald Ryan's wardship file, no. 63819, held in the Department of Children's Welfare, Melbourne.
WTT	Transcript of the trial, *The Queen v. Peter John Walker*, Supreme Court of Victoria, 18–29 Jul. 1966.

PROLOGUE [pp xv–xx]

1 The letter was smuggled out of the prison by a prison officer whom Ryan had asked to take it to *Truth* newspaper. The officer duly did so, and a transcript of the letter, together with photographs of it, appeared in that newspaper in its edition of 11 Feb. 1967.
2 The prison governor, Ian Grindlay, informed the writer of this procedure, interview, 14 Jun. 1978.
3 The contents of the hangman's locker were catalogued when the locker was sent from the prisons division of the SWD to the sheriff's office in Feb. and Mar. 1976 following the abolition of capital punishment in April 1975. The catalogue appears in memoranda dated 5 Feb. 1976 and 12 Mar. 1976 held in the archives of the department. The locker, sometimes referred to as the hangman's box, forms part of the permanent National Trust exhibition on hanging at the Old Melbourne Gaol.
4 For a biographical account of the Jean Lee case, see Paul Wilson, Don Treble, and Robyn Lincoln, *Jean Lee*.
5 Ian Grindlay, interview, 14 Jun. 1978.

Chapter One: CHILDHOOD [pp 1–14]

1 Birth certificate registered at Carlton, Victoria, on 16 Mar. 1925. RBDM.
2 Ryan's birth certificate, indicating the attending physician, bears only the name 'Dr Campbell'. Dame Kate Campbell confirmed to the writer that she was in her residency at the Women's Hospital in 1925, working in the midwifery ward. (Telephone interview, 26 Apr. 1982.) For an account of Dame Kate's life, see the report of her death in *The Age*, 15 Jul. 1986; see also Kate Campbell, 'A medical life', in Patricia Grimshaw & Lynne Strahan (eds), *The Half-Open Door*, 164.
3 Ronald Ryan's birth certificate is blank under the heading designated for 'Father'.
4 Birth certificate for Eveline Young, 23 Jun. 1890, RBDM. Alhough she was born 'Eveline' and the birth certificate does not disclose another forename, she later adopted Cecilia (sometimes spelt 'Cecelia') as her middle name, and still later as her first name.
5 Marriage certificate, 20 Mar. 1915, RBDM.
6 These details are taken from the birth certificate of George Thompson, RBDM. In fact, George's birth certificate contains a notation, subsequently amended, that the name of his father and the date of his parents' marriage should not appear on the certificate. This was intended, presumably, to protect the child from later discovery that he was conceived out of wedlock.
7 Details of Harry Thompson's war service are drawn from Australian army archives and are summarised in a letter to the writer from Major DRH Harris, of the Central Army Records Office, Melbourne, 9 Nov. 1978.
8 Harry Thompson's death was the subject of a coronial inquiry on 9 Sep. 1927, and the circumstances of his fatal accident are set out in detail in the

coroner's inquiry depositions of evidence held at RBDM. (Proceedings of Inquest no. 1093, 9 Sep. 1927.) A deposition to the inquest from his mother, Mrs Ella Thompson, of Albert Street, East Brunswick, said that while Harry had been in good health prior to the accident, 'he had not been too well since he came from the War.' Harry Thompson's marital status is given on the police deposition to the inquest as 'single'. His occupation is described as 'Attendant at the Hospital for the Insane, Kew'.

9 As a child, George Thompson was told by his mother that his father had been killed in the war when he was a baby. Since his father enlisted when George was six months old, and was in Europe until he was well into his third year, it seems a fair assumption that at least the marriage never resumed after his return, and perhaps even that Cecilia and Harry had separated before his enlistment. Indeed, at his enlistment, Harry recorded his marital status as 'married', but his wife's name was not recorded. (Letter to the writer from Major DRH Harris, of the Central Army Records Office, Melbourne, 9 Nov. 1978.) On the basis of the coronial inquest documents unearthed by the writer, George learned for the first time that his father had died in a traffic accident when he was twelve years old. George then remembered that an aunt had once told him that his father had died in these circumstances, but it had never been taken up by his mother as the truth about his father's death. (George Thompson, interview, 12 Sep. 1978). [Harry Thompson is buried at Cheltenham cemetery, Melbourne. In 1982, George visited his father's grave for the first time on the occasion of the 55th anniversary of his death.] George Thompson died in Melbourne on 3 Oct. 1984. (See *The Sun,* 5 Oct. 1984.)

10 This story was told by Cecilia to one of her children, Violet, and she related it to the writer. (Violet Smith [née Ryan], interview, 20 Aug. 1978.) John Ryan's death certificate records that at the time of his death he had been resident in Victoria for 35 years, but the informant for that detail on the certificate is not known. See death certificate, 14 Jun. 1946, RBDM.

11 These details are disclosed by Jack Ryan in his marriage certificate, RBDM. Jack Ryan's birth appears not to have been registered under the name John Ronald Ryan in NSW. An exhaustive search of NSW Registry records in various years failed to locate a birth certificate for him.

12 The description of miner's phthisis is taken from Keith R Moore, medical officer, division of industrial hygiene, Commonwealth Department of Health, *Report on Investigation into the Health and Working Conditions of Employees in the Mining Industry of Victoria and Tasmania, 1928,* 11–12.

13 See birth certificate for Ronald Ryan, registered on 16 Mar. 1925, RBDM. The Sands & McDougall Municipal Directory for Victoria for this year also confirms their residency.

14 Jack Ryan's children describe him as 'illiterate'. (Violet Smith, interview, 20 Aug. 1978 and Irma Russ [née Ryan], interview, 6 Sep. 1980.) His writing on various birth certificates for his children shows a very awkward hand and the misspelling of common words. He describes his relationship to

newly born infants on two such documents as 'farther'. See, for example, birth certificate for Violet, 3 Mar. 1927 and that for Irma, 3 Sep. 1929, RBDM.

15 George Thompson related these details of Jack Ryan's employment in an interview, 12 Sep. 1978. The birth certificates for both Violet in 1927 and Irma in 1929 record Jack's occupation at that time as 'wharf labourer'.

16 Violet and Irma related these tactical manoeuvres which their parents had told them about. Violet Smith, interview, 20 Aug. 1978, and Irma Russ, interview, 6 Sep. 1980.

17 Violet's birth certificate, registered on 30 Mar. 1927, gives these details, RBDM.

18 Similarly, Irma's birth certificate provides details of residence.

19 See marriage certificate, 31 Oct. 1929, RBDM.

20 See birth certificates for Violet and Irma.

21 A short discussion of the legal implications of legitimacy and paternity in Victoria at that time can be found in *Victorian Year Book 1938–39*, 78–9. See also the Supreme Court judgment of McInerney J in *Re Peatling, deceased, Victoria Reports* (1969), 214–29.

22 See birth certificate for Gloria May Ryan, 16 Jul. 1931, RBDM.

23 The letter from Cecilia Ryan to Mr JR Henry, secretary, Children's Welfare Department, setting out the circumstances of Ronald's birth, is dated 29 Jan. 1937. The letter is in the records of the Children's Welfare Department, file 63819. (This is Ryan's wardship file, hereinafter cited as WF.)

24 Interview, George Thompson, 12 Sep. 1978.

25 *ibid.*

26 Cecilia Ryan's children eventually learned of their mother's prostitution, which in later years she confirmed to them; they related it to the writer in interviews. (George Thompson and Violet Smith, interview, 20 Aug. 1978; and Irma Russ, interview, 6 Sep. 1980.)

27 *ibid.* Commonwealth electoral rolls for some years and the Sands & McDougall directories for 1924–34 confirm residence for the Ryans in these locations. Also interviews with Violet Smith and Irma Russ, 6 Sep. 1980.

28 Violet Smith and Irma Russ, interview, 6 Sep. 1980.

29 Jack Ryan's invalid pension payments from 1 Oct. 1936 to 1 Apr. 1946 are recorded on his miners phthisis ledger card (29R/10, no. 5) held by the Victorian Treasury, which administered payments of the allowance. Recipients of the miner's phthisis allowance first had to be entitled to an invalid pension.

30 The *Victorian Year Book 1934* records the basic wage in that year as just over £3 per week.

31 Violet Smith, interview, 20 Aug. 1978; Irma Russ and Gloria Ryan, interview, 6 Sep. 1980.

32 The descriptions of Cecilia's prostitution and Jack's domestic behaviour

and attitude to Ron have been drawn from the accounts of his daughters in *ibid.*

33 George Thompson, interview, 12 Sep. 1978.

34 Violet Smith, Irma Russ, and Gloria Ryan, interview 6 Sep. 1980.

35 Irma Russ, interview, 6 Sep. 1980.

36 *ibid.*

37 Violet Smith, interview, 6 Sep. 1980.

38 Cecilia was charged in the name of 'Evelyn Ryan' although, of course, her full name was Eveline Cecilia Ryan. The details of her arrest and court hearing are recorded in the Register of the Brunswick Court of Petty Sessions, Volume: 3 Nov. 1933–7 Dec. 1935, 38.

39 Interview, Violet Smith, 6 Sep. 1980.

40 *ibid.*

41 George Thompson and Violet Smith, interview, 6 Sep. 1980.

42 *ibid.* For historical accounts of early Mitcham, see Diane Sydenham, *Windows on Nunawading*, and Niall Brennan, *The History of Nunawading.*

43 Violet Smith, interview, 6 Sep. 1980.

44 *ibid.*

45 George Thompson, interview, 12 Sep. 1978.

46 *ibid.*

47 See historical note, Joan Roczniok 'Catholics in Nunawading: Parish of St John, Mitcham' (mimeo) Nunawading Historical Society, [n.d.], 5–6.

48 The photograph was made available to the writer, and Ryan's identity confirmed, by Mrs Joyce Kotze (née Hylard), who was in Ryan's class at St John's in 1936.

49 Details of Ryan's obsessive behaviour were related by Violet Smith, Irma Russ, and Gloria Ryan, interview, 6 Sep. 1980.

50 Violet Smith, interview, 20 Aug. 1978.

51 The photograph is in the possession of Kevin Fenton, who was a pupil in Ryan's class at St John's in 1936 and who was confirmed on the same day.

52 Violet Smith, interview, 20 Aug. 1978.

53 Ryan's former wife, Dorothy, relates that he disliked the name Edmond. Later in his life, when there was trouble, Ryan told Dorothy that if he needed to communicate with her he would place an advertisement in newspaper Missing Persons columns using only the initials RER. This did, in fact, occur during the period of Ryan's escape from gaol in 1965. (Dorothy Ryan, interview, 10 Oct. 1978).

54 The history of government assistance to miners suffering from miner's phthisis was given in the Victorian parliament in September 1938, when the Dunstan government introduced amendments to the Miner's Phthisis (Treasury Allowances) Bill. (See [Victoria] *Debates 1938, 204*:618–19, 1243–4, 1298–9; and *205*:1727–36.)

Throughout the nineteenth century, gold mining had been the backbone of Victoria's economy, but it had had significant adverse effects on the health of its miners. In 1928, a study by the Commonwealth

Department of Health at a number of mines in Victoria found that 16 per cent of mine-workers had silicosis, while 11 per cent had pulmonary tuberculosis, simple or complicated by silicosis. The study found that, in one Victorian mine area, of 61 gold miners examined thirty-two had fathers who had died of miners' phthisis. It also showed that the incidence of industrial pulmonary disease was such that, after twenty years in the mines, half the total number of miners would have contracted silicosis or tuberculosis. After 40 years, the incidence of the disease among miners would have risen to 100 per cent.[55] (Keith Moore, *op. cit.*, 17–20.)

From December 1910, miners suffering from miners' phthisis might be eligible for an invalid's pension from the Commonwealth government following the passage of the *Invalid and Old Age Pensions Act 1908*. Beyond that, special compensation for this debilitating industrial disease was slow in coming. Prior to 1906, such assistance as was available came from a voluntary fund set up in Bendigo to assist goldminers there. In that year the Victorian government began subsidising this voluntary scheme, and in 1913 it took over compensation to invalid miners altogether.

55 See note 29.

56 This was related both by Sister Hildegarde (interview, 3 Aug. 1978), who taught at St John's, and by Joyce Kotze and Kevin Fenton, who were pupils in Ryan's class at St John's in 1936. (Interviews, 22 Oct. 1978.)

57 George Thompson, interview, 20 Aug. 1978; Violet Smith, interview, 20 Aug. 1978; and Irma Russ, interview, 6 Sep. 1980.

58 The charges against Ryan are recorded in the brief of evidence for a subsequent court appearance (WF). The detailed circumstances of the offence and the court appearance are not recorded.

59 This account of the theft at Mrs Noase's house and its aftermath is in the form of a statement by Ryan to police (subsequently part of the Children's Court record), and is contained in WF.

60 The tile works concerned were probably the Australian Tesselated Tile Company, which operated kilns in Mitcham. See Diane Sydenham, *op. cit.*, 104.

61 WF. The detail of the conversation with Warway and the subsequent admissions are contained in the statement which Ryan made to police, which forms part of that file.

62 These statements form part of the court record, which is contained in WF.

63 *ibid.*

64 The expiration date of his wardship is notional in the sense that, were his parents' circumstances to change for the better and they resumed guardianship of Ron, his wardship could be ended before his eighteenth birthday. But, at the point at which he entered wardship, his eighteenth birthday was the notional expiration date.

65 The statistics on neglected children in Victoria in 1936 are drawn from the *Victorian Year Book 1936–37*, 106. See also Mark Finnane, 'Larrikins, Delinquents and Cops: Police and Young People in Australian History' in

Rob White and Christine Alder (eds), *The Police and Young People in Australia*, 15–22; Mark Finnane, *Punishment in Australian Society*, 93–8; and Janet McCalman, *Struggletown*, 52.

66 The cases of juvenile offenders in England in 1836 are cited in C. Corry, 'The Headspring of that Everflowing River of Crime …'

67 Deposition to Children's Court, Ringwood, 23 Nov. 1936.

Chapter Two: WARDSHIP [pp 15–32]

1 *Victorian Year Book 1936–37*, 255.

2 See Donella Jaggs, *Neglected and Criminal: Foundations of Child Welfare Legislation in Victoria*, 25–7 and *passim*.

3 *Victorian Year Book 1973*, 568.

4 *ibid.* There was a fleet of hulks at Williamstown used for housing convicts for almost twenty years from 1852. Conditions for these convicts were extremely harsh. The biography of one of Victoria's most notorious penal administrators, John Price, documents some of these appalling conditions. See John Vincent Barry, *The Life and Death of John Price*, 73–6, 84–5, 98, 154–7.

5 *Victorian Year Book 1936–37*, 257.

6 *ibid.*, 256–7.

7 McCalman, *op. cit.*, 52.

8 Jan Kociumbas, *Australian Childhood*, 176.

9 *Victorian Year Book 1936–37*, 257–8; *1937–38*, 248–9; *1938–39*, 262–3, and 277–9.

10 *Victorian Year Book 1937–38*, 268–9.

11 WF records the recommendation by officials at the Boys' Depot that Ryan be transferred to St Augustine's at Geelong.

12 Father Joseph Dunne was Rector at the Salesian Father's Home, Sunbury, from 1936 to 1938. See Joy Munns, *Rupertswood*, 69. A later rector, Father Terry Jennings, 1976–1981—who, as a young Brother, first went to Sunbury to teach in 1940, having been a student there in 1932–1934—told the writer of Father Dunne's practice in an interview, 26 Jul. 1978. Another pupil at Rupertswood around this time, Peter O'Brien, 1938–1940, also believes the practice to have been adopted by Father Dunne and by his successor as rector, Father Joseph Ciantar (1939–1947). But O'Brien also suggests that the story of boys needing a home might have been offered to protect wards from the knowledge by other boys of their wayward backgrounds, given that there was a mix of neglected and wayward boys. (Peter O'Brien, interview, 8 Dec. 1978.)

13 The background to the Salesians' establishment in Australia, and particularly at Sunbury, is given in Joy Munns, *op. cit.*, 46.

14 Michael Clarke, *Clarke of Rupertswood 1831–1897*, a biography of his grandfather, Sir William Clarke, Bt., 78 and *passim*.

15 Joy Munns, *op. cit.*, 46.

16 This is related in E Cooper, SDB, and J Ayers, SDB '[Salesians in Australia]

The First 25 Years', 20.

17 *Victorian Year Book 1936–37*, 256. In the view of later officers of the department, the per capita grant system may simply have encouraged some institutions to cram children in, rather than improve standards. Bill Davey, family services division, SWD. (Interview, 23 Jul. 1978.)

18 Father Joseph Ciantar was rector from 1939 to 1947. Joy Munns, *op. cit.*, 69.

19 Quoted in *ibid.*, 47.

20 The minutes of the House Council of the Salesian order on 17 and 25 Nov. 1931 show that the Salesians were being urged to take on a project in which Sunnyside at Mornington was to be turned into a reformatory for Catholic boys under the order's direction. Later minutes indicate that the Salesians successfully resisted the proposal, citing 'unfavourable conditions'. Minutes, 30 Aug. 1932.

21 The minutes of the House Council of the Salesians, dated 21 Nov. 1928, record a 'Notification that the Melbourne Salesian College is registered as a charitable institution by the Charities Board'. The minutes for 9 May 1957 show that, as from 30 Jun. 1957, the college would 'officially resign from the Charities Commission' and thus would cease to be a registered charitable institution.

22 In fact, the original negotiation for the purchase of Rupertswood was only for the mansion and 105 acres, but this was extended by an extra 731 acres precisely because the Salesian Provincial, Father Mannassero, wanted to establish an agricultural school. (Joy Munns, *op. cit.*, 46.)

23 The conversation between Basil Rush and First Constable Donoghue, and the subsequent advice, is recorded in a note for file contained in WF.

24 The absconding incident related here is recorded in WF. The file has been drawn upon to establish the basic facts of the incident, which were confirmed, and elaborated upon, by Roy Wolfe, in an interview with the writer, 22 Nov. 1981. Unprompted by the writer, Wolfe's memory of the incident was quite detailed, clear, and consistent with the description given in WF. Wolfe was himself made a ward of state after his mother could not cope with him; like Ryan, after assessment at the Boy's Depot, he was sent to Rupertswood in 1936. The *Victoria Police Gazette* also carries a report about Wolfe and Ryan absconding, and includes their descriptions, including their clothing. In the *Police Gazette*, Wolfe's first name is given as Ray and the date for the absconding is given as a day later than that recorded in WF. See *Victoria Police Gazette*, 14 Jan. 1937, 24.

25 *Victoria Police Gazette*, 14 Jan. 1937, 94.

26 Roy Wolfe, interview, 22 Nov. 1981.

27 Farey Bros Bakery was a well-known landmark in the area and had been operating as a bakery since 1915; it only ceased operating as such in 1978 when it was converted to professional office suites. The large, red-brick building at 24–26 Liddiard Street, Hawthorn is still known as The Bakery.

28 As indicated above, the conversations related here are drawn from the

recollection of Roy Wolfe. Although they were being recalled almost 45 years after the event, his descriptions of sequence, locations, dates, times, and even the name of the arresting officer are consistent with the formal record as it appears in WF. (Interview, 22 Nov. 1981.)

29 WF contains details of the arrest by Detective James.

30 Like the *Victoria Police Gazette* listing, the police report in WF uses the term escapees.

31 These details are drawn from the *Victoria Police Gazette*, 1 Jan. 1939, 6, and the Commonwealth Electoral Roll for 1937.

32 Roy Wolfe, interview, 22 Nov. 1981.

33 WF records a file note by Sub-Inspector Baker on 11 Jan. 1937 that Ryan and Wolfe were to be charged with house-breaking and stealing. An earlier note dated 4 Jan. 1937 records that no charges were to be laid by Camberwell Police as a consequence of the incidents.

34 Ryan's and Wolfe's return to Rupertswood is recorded in WF.

35 Descriptions of the punishment regime at Rupertswood are drawn from Wolfe, interview, 22 Nov. 1981.

36 *ibid.*

37 The department's letter to Cecilia Ryan is contained in WF.

38 Eveline Cecilia Ryan to JR Henry, secretary, Children's Welfare Department, 29 Jan. 1937 (WF).

39 Father Terry Jennings, interview, 26 Jul. 1978.

40 A baptism certificate held at the Office of the Provincial, Salesian Order of Don Bosco, shows that he was baptised at Our Lady of Mt Carmel, Sunbury on 10 Mar. 1937 by Father John Cerutti.

41 Rupertswood school reports for Ryan and his classmates have survived and are kept at the school. A complete record of his results in Grades 6, 7 and 8 were made available to the writer by the then rector of Rupertswood, Father Terry Jennings.

42 The prefect was the second in charge after the rector; in effect, his role was that of head teacher as well as bursar.

43 Father BM Fedrigotti to secretary, Children's Welfare Department, 21 Apr. 1937 (WF).

44 *Victoria Police Gazette*, 29 Apr. 1937, 319.

45 A file note to Father Fedrigotti's letter by department officer BAR [Basil Allan Rush] on 22 Apr. 1937 records that 'Father Fedrigotti phoned to report these boys returned to Rupertswood last evening.' The circumstances of their absconding and return are not recorded.

46 The notion that head shaving was practised as a punishment at Rupertswood is contentious among former staff, pupils, and departmental officials. Father Terry Jennings believed that it was used in this punitive way, but only rarely, and was more likely adopted as a preventative measure against head lice for those boys experiencing recurring infestations. (Interview, 26 Jul. 1978.) Peter O'Brien, who was at Rupertswood from 1938 to 1940 and was two grades below Ryan in those

years, is adamant that the practice was confined to 'care and protection' children in order to facilitate identification of those who had frequently absconded. O'Brien remembers Ryan in 1938 and 1939 as having a shaved head. (Interviews, 6 Aug. and 8 Dec. 1978.) In the late 1970s, government officials in social welfare, who had some knowledge, if not experience, of practices during the 1930s believe that both reasons—head lice and punishment/identification—may have been evident, but agree that ready identification of a likely absconder was the more likely reason. Head shaving was believed to have been a common punishment at such institutions as St Augustine's, Geelong, and the likelihood is that that was so at Rupertswood, as well. It is possible, too, that the practice originated, or was carried on, at the Boys' Depot. (Bill Davey, family services division, and John Dawes, correctional services division, SWD, interviews, 23 Jul. 1978.)

47 Roy Wolfe (interview, 22 Nov. 1981) and Peter O'Brien (interview, 6 Aug. 1978) both relate that Baldy was Ryan's nickname. His siblings, Violet Smith and George Thompson, confirm that his nickname was Baldy when he was at Rupertswood. (Interview, 20 Aug. 1978). The name also lends some weight to the notion that, alone of the boys at Rupertswood, Ryan had his head kept shaved.

48 Ryan's class results were entered in an exercise book by Brother Brennan; they are held in the archives of the Salesian College, Sunbury. The book records his class position in each of the years he was at Rupertswood.

49 Violet Smith, interview, 20 Aug. 1978; George Thompson, interview, 12 Sep. 1978; Irma Russ and Gloria Ryan, interview, 6 Sep. 1980.

50 *ibid.*

51 Irma Russ, interview, 6 Sep. 1980.

52 George Thompson, interview, 12 Sep. 1978.

53 Wardship files for Violet, Irma, and Gloria were created by the then Department of Children's Welfare, from which this information was drawn.

54 These details are taken from their wardship files. Violet was committed to St Catherine's on 13 Aug. 1937; her notional date of discharge was to be 28 Mar. 1945, her eighteenth birthday. Irma was committed to St Catherine's on the same day with her notional discharge similarly on her eighteenth birthday, 29 Aug. 1947. For some reason not disclosed on the files, Gloria was not committed to St Catherine's until some five weeks later, on 20 Sep. 1937. She spent the period 28 Jun. 1937 until then at the Girls' Depot, Royal Park.

55 Violet Smith, interview, 20 Aug. 1978; George Thompson, interview, 12 Sep. 1978.

56 WF records correspondence between the Department of Children's Welfare and Cecilia Ryan in which these circumstances are disclosed.

57 Gloria confirmed to the writer that as a child she suffered badly from abscesses in her ears. Gloria Ryan, interview, 6 Sep. 1980.

58 Cecilia Ryan to J[ohn] R[ichmond] Henry, secretary, Department of Children's Welfare, 28 Oct. 1937 (WF).
59 JR Henry to Cecilia Ryan, 26 Oct. 1937 (WF). This letter by Henry had been sent in response to earlier requests from Cecilia, and crossed in the mail with her letter of 28 Oct. 1937.
60 A file note on WF records that Cecilia had called upon the department saying that, as she would not be working during the Christmas holidays, she would be at home to supervise Ronald while he was on vacation.
61 File note recorded by Basil Rush, 13 Dec. 1937.
62 *Vision & Realisation*, *1*: 375–6.
63 *Victorian Year Book 1939–40*, 117. The first outbreak of the 1937–38 epidemic of poliomyelitis was confined to certain outer-southern suburbs of Melbourne, but later spread to the inner suburbs and country districts. (*Victorian Year Book 1936–37*, 30.) The start of the 1938 school year was delayed by two weeks when the Victorian government kept the state's 2,600 schools closed to limit the spread of the disease. (*The* Age, 2 Feb. 1938.)
64 File note by M[ary] Lavelle (WF).
65 *ibid.*
66 The indemnity form is part of WF. The indemnity seems especially odd in circumstances where government policy was to keep children at home and away from other children, particularly in school.
67 File note, 20 Dec. 1937, attached to indemnity form (WF).
68 'Children's Register—History', forming part of WF (file note, dated 20 Dec. 1937, attached to indemnity form).
69 Peter O'Brien, interview, 6 Aug. 1978; Roy Wolfe, interview, 22 Nov. 1981.
70 Roy Wolfe, interview, 22 Nov. 1981.
71 Letter to the editor, *The* Age, 25 Jan. 1967.
72 George Thompson, interview, 12 Sep. 1978.
73 Letter, Ronald Ryan to Sister Josephine, 20 Dec. 1966, quoted in Ian Grindlay, *Behind Bars*, 8.
74 Class results, Rupertswood archives.
75 Violet Smith, interview, 20 Aug. 1978; George Thompson, interview, 12 Sep. 1978.
76 WF, summary of sibling wardship histories.
77 The details of visits to the girls by Jack and Cecilia, and the girls' subsequent home life, were recounted by Violet Smith, interview, 20 Aug. 1978; Irma Russ and Gloria Ryan, interview, 6 Sep. 1980.
78 These details are contained in WF.
79 Class results, Rupertswood archives.
80 Letter from secretary [Edward J Pittard], Children's Welfare Department, to Mrs Ryan, 13 Dec. 1938. This letter was based upon advice contained in a file note written by an administrative clerk, dated 12 Dec. 1938 (WF).
81 Letter, E Ryan to EJ Pittard, secretary, Children's Welfare Department, 14 Dec. 1938 (WF).

82 File note, 16 Dec. 1938 (WF).
83 Letter, secretary of Children's Welfare Department to Mrs Ryan, 17 Dec. 1938 (WF).
84 John E King wrote of these qualities in his letter to *The Age*, 25 Jan. 1967.
85 *ibid.*
86 Peter O'Brien, interview, 6 Aug. 1978; and Roy Wolfe, interview, 22 Nov. 1981.
87 Peter O'Brien, interview, 6 Aug. 1978.
88 Cooper and Ayers, *op. cit.*, 20–1 record that in 1929 the Knights held their picnic in the grounds, 'some seventy pounds being raised for the Salesians by the 528 men present.'
89 Peter O'Brien, interview, 6 Aug. 1978.
90 *ibid.*
91 *Victoria Police Gazette*, 28 Sep. 1939, at 724 contains a report of this escape and the items stolen by Ryan; and *ibid.*
92 Peter O'Brien, interview, 6 Aug. 1978. John E King also relates an account of this incident in his letter to *The Age*, 25 Jan. 1967, but there is a serious discrepancy between King's version and that of O'Brien. In King's account of it, there is no mention of anyone accompanying Ryan on the bike, nor of Ryan hitting the boy over the head with a bottle. He says Ryan set off alone telling King: 'Tell Father Ciantar he'll find the bike at the Diggers Rest station. And tell him not to worry. I'll make out!' O'Brien, (interview, 6 Aug. 1978) also describes this incident but, in his recollection, the other boy accompanied Ryan to Diggers Rest and was hit over the head by Ryan.
93 George Thompson, interview, 12 Sep. 1978.
94 *Victoria Police Gazette*, 5 Oct. 1939, 740.
95 *Victoria Police Gazette*, 12 Oct. 1939, 778.
96 George Thompson, interview, 12 Sep. 1978. (See also *Victorian Year Book 1938–39*, 261–2.)
97 *ibid.*
98 Peter O'Brien, interview, 6 Aug. 1978; and Roy Wolfe, interview, 22 Nov. 1981. Both have clear and consistent recollections of the contents of Ryan's letter.
99 *ibid.*
100 *ibid.*

Chapter Three: MANHOOD [pp 33–46]

1 George Thompson, interview, 12 Sep. 1978.
2 *ibid.* George seemed oblivious to extradition arrangements that might be effected if the Department of Children's Welfare or police had a mind to pursue this young escapee. Still, with more than 5,000 wards to worry about in 1939, Victorian authorities could not have been under great pressure to find young Ryan and return him to his wardship.
3 Tony Dingle, *The Victorians*, 189.
4 Quoted in Stephen J Pyne, *Burning Bush*, 310–11.

5 *ibid.* See also Davison, Hirst and Macintyre (eds), *The Oxford Companion to Australian History,* 73
6 George Thompson, interview, 12 Sep. 1978.
7 Arthur Feldtmann, *The Balranald Story,* 7.
8 George Thompson, interview, 12 Sep. 1978.
9 Frank Sylvester, telephone interview, 7 Aug. 1978.
10 This account of Ron's period at Balranald is drawn from George Thompson, interview, 12 Sep. 1978.
11 *ibid.*, and Violet Smith, Irma Russ, and Gloria Ryan, interview, 6 Sep. 1980; Frank Sylvester, telephone interview, 7 Aug. 1978.
12 George Thompson, interview, 6 Sep. 1980.
13 Letter, Ronald Ryan to Cecilia Ryan, 18 Dec. 1966.
14 Thompson, interview, 6 Sep. 1980, and Frank Sylvester, telephone interview, 7 Aug. 1978.
15 The Balranald weekly paper, *The Riverina Recorder*, reported the formation of the club and the election of office-bearers in its issue of 13 Jun. 1944.
16 Ryan's sporting activities and achievements in Balranald are reported in *The Riverina Recorder*, issues of 10 Jun., 24 Jun., 1 Jul., 15 Jul., 29 Jul., 2 Sep., 16 Sep., 22 Sep., 30 Sep., 7 Oct., 14 Oct., 4 Nov., and 23 Dec. 1944. Issues of *The Riverina Recorder* later than 1944 (Ryan was in Balranald from 1940 to 1948) are unavailable.
17 WF.
18 The account of the Ryan girls' experiences at the Convent of the Good Shepherd is drawn from interviews with Violet Smith, Irma Russ, and Gloria Ryan, 6 Sep. 1980
19 WF.
20 *Victorian Year Book 1936–37*, 256–7.
21 The details of the Ryan girls' wardships and Ron's letter appealing to the Department of Children's Welfare are taken from WF.
22 Violet Smith, Irma Russ, and Gloria Ryan, interview, 6 Sep. 1980.
23 *The Age*, 27 Jan. 1967.
24 Violet Smith, Irma Russ, and Gloria Ryan, interview, 6 Sep. 1980.
25 Extensive research has failed to find any documentary record of this incident; however, the woman who Ryan married six years later, Dorothy Ryan, has confirmed that, based upon admissions Ryan made to her, he was involved in this robbery attempt. (Interview, 3 Oct. 1978.) Ryan's sister, Violet Smith, interview, 6 Sep. 1980, also believes he was involved. Frank Sylvester, who was around ten years old at the time, says he grew up with the belief of his family, especially his mother, that Ryan had been responsible for the attempted bank robbery. (Frank Sylvester, telephone interview, 7 Aug. 1978.)
26 *ibid.* Each of the accounts told to the writer contains the common thread of narrative related here. In an interview with the writer, George Thompson initially was staunchly loyal to Ryan; when pressed, he did not

dispute the essential facts of the attempted robbery and Ryan's role in it. (interview, 6 Sep. 1980).

27 Mavis Sylvester's parents had suspected that Ryan was involved in the attempted bank robbery, and had sought to discourage her relationship with Ryan. She initially reacted against their discouragement by becoming even more enamoured of him. (Frank Sylvester, telephone interview, 7 Aug. 1978.) Years later Ryan admitted that he had been involved with another Balranald girl during this period. (Letter, Ryan to Cecilia, Gloria, and family, 29 Oct. 1966.)

28 Archival records of St. Joseph's Nursing Home, Northcote.

29 Death certificate, RBDM.

30 Archival records of the Springvale Cemetery.

31 Violet Smith, Irma Russ, and Gloria Ryan, interview, 6 Sep. 1980.

32 *ibid.*

33 George Thompson, interview, 6 Sep. 1978.

34 The account of the romance between Ronald Ryan and Dorothy George, and much else of their later married life together and her understanding of aspects of Ryan's earlier life, is largely drawn from a series of nine lengthy interviews the writer conducted with Dorothy in 1978, 1979, and 1980. (Interviews, 3 Oct., 10 Oct., 17 Oct. , 24 Oct., 30 Oct., and 5 Dec. 1978; 12 Feb. and 19 Feb. 1979; and 11 Aug. 1980.) For simplicity, and given that some interviews sought clarification of points made in others and, hence, produced substantial overlaps, material derived from these interviews are hereinafter cited as 'Dorothy Ryan, interviews 1978–80'.

35 Dorothy Ryan, interviews, 1978–80. Harold George was elected to the Hawthorn City Council in 1949, and was mayor in 1951–52, 1952–53, 1957–58, and 1962–63. The badge 'George Tray Body' was a relatively common sight on the trays of trucks in Melbourne from the 1940s through to the 1960s.

36 *ibid.* Dorothy's elder brother, Keith, has described his father as a 'strict disciplinarian and a strong Anglican.' He has described his mother as 'softer, tending to turn a blind eye to her only daughter's failings.' (Keith George, interview, 7 Aug. 1978.)

37 Dorothy Ryan, interviews, 1978–80. (Keith George has confirmed his parents' strong disapproval of Ryan.)

38 Ryan's obsession with cleanliness was detailed by Dorothy Ryan in interviews with the writer, 1978–80, and by Violet Smith and Irma Russ, inteview, 6 Sep. 1980.

39 The details of Dorothy's engagement and elopement were related in interviews with her, 1978–80, and with Keith George, 7 Aug. 1978.

40 Dorothy Ryan, interviews, 1978–80. Despite the seemingly token nature of his denominational conversion, it should be noted that Ryan did take Anglican communion privately with Dorothy and her family before their first two children were born. Although the marriage certificate records their address as the George family home at 64 Urquhart Street, Hawthorn

(RBDM), Ron had, in fact, moved into a rented house at 73 Kooyong Koot Road, Hawthorn, two weeks before the wedding. It was there that the couple would return after their honeymoon.

41 The details of Ryan's wedding, and the incidents and observations described here, are drawn from the writer's interviews with Dorothy, 1978–80; Keith George, 7 Aug. 1978 and Violet Smith, Irma Russ, and Gloria Ryan, 6 Sep. 1980. Keith George further relates that, while Ryan was plausible and charming to everyone at the wedding, he made him uneasy, sensing that he was something of a 'con man'.

42 See his letters to *Truth* 23 and 29 Dec. 1965 later in this book.

43 Dorothy Ryan, interviews, 1978–80. Ironically, several years later, when Ryan was in prison under sentence of death, he seems to have shifted his view. With an approaching federal election in 1966, he reflected that 'Labour has an uphill battle with small hope of success in the coming elections. Too many two-bob capitalists about.' (Letter, Ronald Ryan to Cecilia, Gloria, and family, 19 Sep. 1966.)

44 *ibid.* It is possible, of course, that Ryan's gambling on his honeymoon was an attempt to recoup some of the extravagance of his wedding expenses.

45 *ibid.*

46 Ryan's description of himself as a 'sort of executive' is contained in a social history taken from him as part of a classification assessment, Pentridge prison file no. 64/3973, 60/540, 15 Aug. 1960; and George Thompson, interview, 6 Sep. 1980.

47 The account of Ryan's dress habits and his career expectations at George Tray Bodies is drawn from Dorothy Ryan, interviews, 1978–80.

Chapter Four: DECLINE [pp 47–65]

1 Dorothy Ryan, interviews, 1978–80.

2 *ibid.*; and birth certificate for Janice Elizabeth Ryan, RBDM.

3 *ibid.* (Ryan's SEC employment history is recorded on the personnel files held in the archives of the then State Electricity Commission. They show that he was employed from 30 Apr. 1951 to 15 Aug. 1952, when he left of his own accord.)

4 *ibid.*

5 The details relating to Ryan's employment, earnings and rental accommodation, *et al*, are drawn from depositions by police informants and other witnesses in the subsequent hearing in the Melbourne Supreme Court arising from the arson at Noojee described here. See case 279/53, *The Queen v. Frederick Simpson Allan*, 16 Mar. 1953.

6 Ryan to Dorothy Janet Ryan (née George) and daughters, 2 Feb. 1967.

7 The conversation between Allan and Ryan related here forms part of Allan's statement to the court in Ryan's subsequent trial on arson charges. The trial was the subject of a lengthy report in the *Warragul Gazette*, 30 Jun. 1953.

8 Dorothy Ryan, interviews, 1978–80.

9 *Warragul Gazette,* 30 Jun. 1953.
10 *ibid.*
11 Deposition of Jack Van Damme, case 279/53, *The Queen v. Frederick Simpson Allan,* 16 Mar. 1953.
12 *Warragul Gazette,* 30 Jun. 1953.
13 The conversation between Allan and Frost is related in a deposition sworn by Frost on 6 Feb. 1953. The deposition forms part of case file 279/53, *The Queen v. Frederick Simpson Allan,* 16 Mar. 1953.
14 *ibid.*
15 Sworn statement of Detective First Constable Donald Withan, Criminal Investigation Branch, Warragul Police, 12 Feb. 1953.
16 The interview between Detective Withan and Ryan is related in Withan's statement, 12 Feb. 1953. (See also Withan's court evidence in the *Warragul Gazette,* 30 Jun. 1953.)
17 Memorandum, Detective First Constable D Withan to Superintendent, 'D' District, *Re: A request to Crown Solicitor's Office ...* , 21 Feb. 1953. Case file 279/53.
18 Case file 279/53, *The Queen v. Frederick Simpson Allan,* 16 Mar. 1953.
19 Dorothy Ryan, interviews, 1978–80.
20 *ibid.*; and Keith George, interview, 7 Aug. 1978. Harold George had paid for a car for Ron and Dorothy, and had given them money on several occasions when they were in financial difficulty.
21 Eric Hewitt, *Judges through the Years,* 72–3.
22 *Warragul Gazette,* 30 Jun. 1953.
23 Dorothy Ryan, interviews, 1978–80. Eighteen months later, in October 1954, John Bourke was appointed Queen's Counsel. In 1959 he was appointed a temporary judge of the County Court, where he served until his retirement in 1967. See Arthur Dean, *A Multitude of Counsellors,* 307 and Hewitt, *op. cit.,* 1.
24 *Warragul Gazette,* 30 Jun. 1953.
25 Dorothy Ryan, interviews, 1978–80.
26 *Warragul Gazette,* 30 Jun. 1953.
27 Birth Certificate, RBDM. Interestingly, the father's name on the birth certificate is given as Ronald *Edmond* Ryan (emphasis added).
28 Dorothy Ryan, interviews, 1978–80.
29 Keith George, interview, 7 Aug. 1978.
30 Dorothy Ryan, interviews, 1978–80.
31 Keith Johanson, telephone interview, 5 Aug. 1978.
32 *ibid.* Keith Johanson also wrote of Ryan's time in his employ in a personal memoir in 1967, 'A Condemned Man's Doubt—And a Book', 1.
33 Dorothy Ryan, interviews, 1978–80.
34 Letter, Ronald Ryan to Gloria Ryan, 13 Mar. 1966.
35 Dorothy Ryan, interviews, 1978–80.
36 Birth Certificate, RBDM.
37 Dorothy Ryan, interviews, 1978–80.

38 Details of this criminal episode are taken from the report of the subsequent court appearance in the *Dandenong Advertiser*, 23 May 1956.
39 The nature of the offence at the Myer store is recorded in the Register of the Court of Petty Sessions, Melbourne, 22 May 1956.
40 Details of the events described here are taken from statements to police and depositions of witnesses in case no. 889/56, Jul. 1956, in the files of the criminal law branch of the CLD. (The case was also reported in the *Warrnambool Standard,* 30 May 1956.)
41 *Warrnambool Standard,* 30 May 1956.
42 This plan and its detailed execution were revealed in Ryan's subsequent statement to police, Exhibit D, forming part of case no. 889/56, Jul. 1956.
43 *ibid.*
44 *Warrnambool Standard,* 30 May 1956.
45 *Warrnambool Standard,* 26 Apr. 1956 and 1 May 1956.
46 Case no. 889/56, Jul. 1956.
47 Bryan Harding, interviews, 8 May 2000 and 15 May 2000.
48 A lengthy report of Heard's court appearance appeared the next day in the *Warrnambool Standard,* 1 May 1956.
49 Bryan Harding, interviews, 8 May 2000 and 15 May 2000.
50 Ryan's statement is contained in Exhibit D, case no. 889/56, Jul. 1956.
51 *ibid.*
52 This was related by his defence counsel, Tom Doyle, appearing for Ryan, 13 Jul. 1956. (CLD) It is also confirmed by Ryan's SEC employment history, personnel archives of the then State Electricity Commission, Melbourne.
53 Case no. 889/56, Jul. 1956.
54 *Dandenong Advertiser*, 23 May 1956.
55 *Dandenong Journal*, 23 May 1956.
56 *ibid.*
57 *Dandenong Advertiser*, 23 May 1956.
58 *Dandenong Journal*, 23 May 1956.
59 Register of the Court of Petty Sessions, Melbourne, 22 May 1956.
60 *ibid.*, 25 May 1956. See also plea by defence counsel Tom Doyle appearing for Ryan, 13 Jul. 1956. CLD, 3.
61 Register of the Court of Petty Sessions, Melbourne, 25 May 1956.
62 Plea by defence counsel Tom Doyle, appearing for Ryan, 13 Jul. 1956. CLD, 3; and case no. 889/56, Jul. 1956.
63 These details are drawn from case no. 889/56, Jul. 1956; and Bryan Harding, interviews, 8 May 2000 and 15 May 2000.
64 Case file no. 889/56, Jul. 1956 records the sworn surety by Harold George, dated 22 Jun. 1956, in the sum of £200.
65 Register of the Court of Petty Sessions, Melbourne, 26 Jun. 1956
66 Transcript of hearing, Melbourne General Sessions, 13 Jul. 1956. CLD, 3.
67 *ibid.* (See also Criminal History Sheet, Ronald Joseph Ryan, Victoria Police, records section, Information Bureau, 16 Feb. 1960.)

68 Arthur Dean, *op. cit.*, 233–4.
69 Transcript of hearing, 3–4.
70 Bryan Harding, interviews, 8 May 2000 and 15 May 2000.
71 Transcript of hearing, 4–5.
72 Eric Hewitt, *op. cit.*, 83. (See also *The Sun*, 'Now He's a Judge', 16 Nov. 1955; and *The Age*, 16 Nov. 1955.) In 1973 Judge Dunn was appointed to the Supreme Court, where he served until his retirement in 1977.
73 Transcript of hearing, 5.
74 See Eric Hewitt *op. cit.*, 83.
75 Transcript of hearing, 6.

Chapter Five: CRIME [pp 67–87]

1 Criminal History Sheet, Ronald Joseph Ryan, Victoria Police, records section, Information Bureau, 16 Feb. 1960.
2 Dorothy Ryan, interviews, 1978–80.
3 Violet Smith, interview, 20 Aug. 1978; Irma Russ and Gloria Ryan, interview, 6 Sep. 1980.
4 Dorothy Ryan, interviews, 1978–80. There was one police report in 1960 that described Ryan as a 'heavy drinker' (CIB report by Detective Constable WF Bloomcamp, 1 Feb. 1960, Copy of depositions, case 724/59, CLD), but this is certainly not correct; it is contradicted by his wife (Dorothy Ryan, interviews, 1978–80) and his sisters. (Violet Smith, interviews, 20 Aug. 1978; Irma Russ and Gloria Ryan, interview, 6 Sep. 1980.) Apart from the police report cited above, in none of the many police reports about Ryan over many years was heavy drinking either observed or commented upon as a factor in his criminal activities.
5 *ibid.*
6 The greyhound was named Snowy, but it is not known if it ever raced. (Wendy Ryan, interview, 29 Jan. 1987.)
7 Violet Smith, interview, 20 Aug. 1978.
8 Ryan recalled his earnings from this business in a letter he wrote to George Thompson, Cecilia and family, 11 Jun. 1966.
9 Dorothy Ryan, interviews, 1978–80.
10 These details are drawn from interviews with Dorothy Ryan, 1978–1980. See also Birth Certificate, RBDM, for the still-born child born on 20 Dec. 1957. The child was buried at the Melbourne General Cemetery. Dorothy believes that the child was deformed at birth as a consequence of the German measles.
11 See Ryan's letter to *Truth*, dated 23 Dec. 1965 and published on 25 Dec. 1965. The letter is reproduced later in this book.
12 Dorothy Ryan, interviews, 1978–1980.
13 These details are given in a police report by Senior Detective LG Gooding, 'Ronald Joseph Gallagher', CIB report, 17 Apr. 1960, case file 729/60.
14 CIB report by Detective Constable WF Bloomcamp, 1 Feb. 1960, copy of depositions, case 724/59, CLD.

15 Ryan's height and weight are taken from the then current description in his Criminal History File, Victoria Police, Melbourne.
16 Wendy Ryan, interview, 29 Jan. 1987.
17 Senior Detective LG Gooding, 'Ronald Joseph Ryan', CIB report, 17 Apr. 1960, case file 729/60.
18 Wendy Ryan, interview, 29 Jan. 1987.
19 The details of Ryan's gambling and his response to losses, as well as the feelings he described when committing a crime, were reported by Violet Smith, Irma Russ, and Gloria Ryan, interview, 6 Sep. 1980.
20 Ryan related his failed fishing venture in subsequent statements to police when he was arrested for the offences described below. (See statement by Ryan, 7 Sep. 1959 forming part of the brief of evidence, *The Queen v. Ronald Joseph Gallagher and Ronald Ryan*, case 1698, General Sessions Court, Melbourne, 1 Oct. 1959, 4.) A CIB report by Detective Constable WF Bloomcamp (copy of depositions, case 724/59, 1 Feb. 1960, CLD) suggested that Ryan had not operated his fishing boat since about April 1959. Dorothy Ryan and his sisters confirmed some of these details. (Dorothy Ryan, interviews, 1978–1980; Violet Smith, Irma Russ, and Gloria Ryan, interview, 6 Sep. 1980.)
21 This was the phrase used by Ryan's defence counsel, Bill Lennon, in his plea on sentence for Ryan in subsequent court hearings related to these offences. See *The Age*, 18 Jun. 1960.
22 Newspaper reports of the subsequent criminal trial record differing figures; one press account reported stolen goods to the value of £28,730 (*The Sun*, 'Long Gaol Terms for Robbery', 10 Aug. 1960); another reported a value of 'more than £40,000' (*The Age*, 'Big Time Gang Got Property Worth £40,000, Court Told', 18 Jun. 1960). This latter figure appears to be a journalistic rounding-up; the exact amount involved for the offences with which Ryan was charged was £38,483.
23 This is Dorothy's estimate of the extent of Ryan's criminal wrongdoing. Dorothy Ryan, interviews, 1978–80.
24 *ibid.*
25 The detailed description of this offence is drawn from depositions in *The Queen v. Ronald Joseph Gallagher and Ronald Ryan*, case 1698, General Sessions Court, Melbourne, 1 Oct. 1959.
26 The description of this offence is drawn from depositions in *The Queen v. Ronald Ryan*, case 1723, General Sessions Court, Melbourne, 1 Oct. 1959.
27 The offences at Rampling and Hall Pty Ltd were counts 5 and 6 of the charges subsequently faced by Gallagher and Ryan when they were tried before the Melbourne Court of General Sessions on 17 Jun. 1960. For some reason not apparent to the writer, Ryan was not charged with these offences. See 'Particulars of Offences', case 1149/60, CLD.
28 Statement by Ronald Joseph Gallagher, 7 Sep. 1959, in copy of depositions, case 724/59, CLD.
29 The description of this offence is drawn from the prosecution brief in *The*

Queen v. Ronald Joseph Gallagher and Ronald Ryan, case 1678, General Sessions Court, Melbourne, 1 Oct. 1959.

30 Statement by Ryan, 7 Sep. 1959, file 225/60, in *ibid.*

31 Prosecution brief in *ibid.*

32 *ibid.*

33 *ibid.*

34 *ibid.*, 5.

35 Case files 1678, 1723, and 225/60.

36 Copy of depositions in case 44/60, *The Queen v. Ronald Joseph Gallagher and Ronald Joseph Ryan*, 18 Jan. 1960, 1.

37 *ibid.*

38 Copy of depositions, case 1149, *The Queen v. Ronald Joseph Ryan and Ronald Joseph Gallagher*, 1 Jun. 1960.

39 Dorothy Ryan, interviews, 1978–80.

40 Copy of depositions, case 729, *The Queen v. Ronald Joseph Ryan and Ronald Joseph Gallagher*, 1 Mar. 1960.

41 *ibid.* It is possible, of course, that Ryan had previously been involved in safe-blowing and that the Vacu-Lug robbery was simply the first time he was charged with an offence at which safe-blowing took place.

42 *ibid.* In his record of interview, Ron Gallagher also related that a third man had been involved in the Vacu-Lug robbery and that his role had been blowing the safe, but he did not identify him. The police depositions recorded the observation that the identity of Old Charlie had not been established.

43 *ibid.*

44 Notation on file, case 729/60, *The Queen v. Ronald Joseph Ryan and Ronald Joseph Gallagher*, 12 Feb. 1960.

45 Note by clerk of courts, Footscray, on file, case 724/59, CLD.

46 Record of interview by police, in copy of depositions, case 44/60, *The Queen v. Ronald Joseph Gallagher and Ronald Joseph Ryan*, 18 Jan. 1960, 2.

47 Record of interview by police, in copy of depositions, case 729/60, *The Queen v. Ronald Joseph Ryan and Ronald Joseph Gallagher*, 12 Feb. 1960, 3.

48 Copy of depositions, case 1149, *The Queen v. Ronald Joseph Ryan and Ronald Joseph Gallagher*, 1 Jun. 1960.

49 *ibid.*

50 *ibid.*, 3–4.

51 Record of police interview with Ryan in copy of depositions, case 1176, *The Queen v. Robert Brian Banks and Ronald Joseph Ryan*, General Sessions Court, Melbourne, 1 Jun. 1960, 3.

52 *ibid.*

53 *ibid.*

54 Record of police interview with Ryan in copy of depositions, case 1115, *The Queen v. Ronald Joseph Ryan, Robert Brian Banks and Ronald Joseph Gallagher*, 1 Jun. 1960.

55 *ibid.*

56 Record of police interview with Ryan in copy of depositions, case 1176, *The Queen v. Robert Brian Banks and Ronald Joseph Ryan*, General Sessions Court, Melbourne, 1 Jun. 1960, 3.
57 'Particulars of Offences', case 1149/60, CLD.
58 Details of the events relating to Ryan's court appearance with others on 21 Apr. 1960 and their subsequent escape from the watch-house are drawn from the copy of depositions, case 1150, General Sessions Court, Melbourne, 1 Jun. 1960. (See also the report of the committal hearing in *The Herald*, 21 Apr. 1960.)
59 Geoffrey Griffith, *Homicide*, 19.
60 *The Age*, 'Daring Escape by Five from City Cells', 22 Apr. 1960; *The Sun*, 'Five in Break-out from Watchhouse: 1 Recaptured', 22 Apr. 1960.
61 Senior Detective LG Gooding, 'Ronald Joseph Gallagher', CIB report, 17 Apr. 1960, case file 729/60.
62 Senior Detective LG Gooding, 'Ronald Joseph Ryan', in *ibid.*
63 The Charlie Robinson referred to in this report is possibly the Old Charlie mentioned earlier in relation to safe-blowing.
64 Senior Detective RE Tobin, 'Character Reports on Ronald Joseph Ryan and Ronald Joseph Gallagher awaiting trial at Melbourne General Sessions on a charge of factory breaking and stealing', CIB report, 19 Apr. 1960, case file 1698/60.
65 *ibid.*
66 Record of police interview with Burgess, copy of depositions, case 1150, General Sessions Court, Melbourne, 1 Jun. 1960, 5. (See also *The Age*, 23 Apr. 1960.) Burgess' theft of the motor car and his dexterity in starting it with silver paper suggested a certain familiarity with illegal uses of a motor car.
67 *The Age*, 23 Apr. 1960.
68 Statement of Senior Detective Ernest McKenzie Everett, copy of depositions, case 1150, General Sessions Court, Melbourne, 1 Jun. 1960, 3.
69 *The Age*, '100 Police Hunt Escaped Prisoners', 23 Apr. 1960; and *The Sun*, '100 Police Join Big Manhunt', 23 Apr. 1960.
70 Ryan's account of his whereabouts while at large are drawn from his statement to police. This statement is consistent with Banks' account, which gave more detail. Record of police interviews with Ryan and Robert Brian Banks, copy of depositions, case 1150, General Sessions Court, Melbourne, 1 Jun. 1960, 4–7.
71 Statement of Detective Bernard John Duggan, copy of depositions, case 1150, General Sessions Court, Melbourne, 1 Jun. 1960, 2. (See also *The Sun*, 'Police Swoop, Get Escapees', 25 Apr. 1960.) The tip-off came to light several years later, when police were again looking for Ryan after a prison escape. *The Herald*, 23 Dec. 1965.
72 *ibid.*, 2.
73 *The Sun*, 25 Apr. 1960.

74 *The Age*, 25 Apr. 1960. Senior Detective Tobin does not appear to have been an informant in the case; at least, his name does not appear on any of the depositions. Statements by police informants make no mention of furniture being damaged.

75 Police interview with Ronald Joseph Ryan at Russell Street on 24 Apr. 1960, Exhibit 'D', copy of depositions, case 1150, General Sessions Court, Melbourne, 1 Jun. 1960, 4.

76 Notations on files nos. 230, 225, 240, 1149, 729, 1150, 44, 1176, and 1115, CLD. (See also Ryan's Victoria Police record compiled by the breaking squad, Victoria Police, Schedule of Prior Convictions, 'Ronald Joseph Ryan', 22 Aug. 1964.)

77 *The Age*, 18 Jun. 1960, carried a lengthy report of the court hearing. (See also *The Herald*, 17 Jun. 1960.)

78 *ibid.* As is evident from earlier chapters in this book, this statement by counsel is incorrect. Newspaper reports of the statement appear, however, to be the source of the widely reported characterisation of Ryan which later was made in the press. The statement was almost certainly based upon instructions given to Lennon by Ryan.

79 *ibid.*

80 *The Age*, 10 Aug. 1960. Again, of course, defence counsel's assertions about the unapprehended mastermind may well have been based upon his client's instructions.

81 Lennon's calculation of the value of the goods stolen, £8,000 to £10,000, was probably derived from the total net value to the defendants of the £38,483 in stolen goods when they were sold on the black market.

82 *The Sun*, 10 Aug. 1960.

83 *The Age*, 10 Aug. 1960.

84 *ibid.*

85 Dorothy Ryan, interviews, 1978–80.

86 *The Sun*, 10 Aug. 1960.

87 Eric Hewitt, *op. cit.*, 1.

88 *The Sun*, 10 Aug. 1960; and *The Age*, 10 Aug. 1960.

89 The reason this charge drew a sentence of five years when the others drew sentences of lesser terms of imprisonment, presumably relates to the very much higher value of the goods stolen at Dunne Bros—£14,000; the other offences involved amounts averaging a little over £3,000.

90 Notations on files nos. 230, 225, 240, 1149, 729, 1150, 44, 1176, and 1115, CLD. Ryan's Victoria Police record compiled by the breaking squad station, Victoria Police, Schedule of Prior Convictions, 'Ronald Joseph Ryan', 22 Aug. 1964. See also *The Sun*, 'Long Gaol Terms for Robbery', 10 Aug. 1960; and *The Age*, 'Court Told Master Mind Not Caught', 10 Aug. 1960.

91 Parole Board record, Ryan's classification file (hereinafter cited as CF).

Chapter Six: PRISON [pp 89–106]

1 Copy of depositions, case 1150, General Sessions Court, Melbourne, 1 Jun. 1960.
2 *Annual Report for the Year Ending 30 Jun. 1962*, SWD, 10; Peter Lynn and George Armstrong, *op. cit.*, 26, and also *Victorian Year Book 1973*, 572.
3 Ryan's classification file records his EE—that is, the expected date of the expiration of his sentence.
4 The intricacies of the time prisoners served in sentences was explained to the writer by Darren Room, prisons division, SWD, interview, 23 Jul. 1978.
5 *Annual Report for the Year Ending 30 Jun. 1962*, SWD.
6 *Annual Report for the Year Ending 30 June. 1964*, SWD, 36.
7 The details related here are drawn from Ryan's classification file. There were one or two minor errors of detail: on his criminal record, the counts of offences states six instead of seven; and, in his social history, the date for his convictions on the false pretences charges is given as 1951 instead of 1956. A later training record file gives his name as 'Ryan, Robert Joseph'.
8 *ibid.*
9 CF. The process of classification, generally, is described in the *Annual Report for the Year Ending 30 Jun. 1962*, SWD, 40.
10 These details are drawn from the progress reports about Ryan forming part of his classification file.
11 File note, EG McMillan, 28 Nov. 1960, in CF.
12 'Classification Reviews', in CF. Ryan's transfer to H Division seems not to have been a punishment either, as his classification file is blank under the section where prison punishments were recorded.
13 See Ryan's letters to *Truth* newspaper, 23 Dec. 1965. See also the series of articles by former Pentridge governor Ian Grindlay, 'Pentridge Papers', *Truth*, 27 Mar. and 3, 10, 17 Apr. 1976.
14 'Classification Reviews', in CF. The Classifications Committee at its meeting on 22 Dec. 1960 discussed Ryan's case and resolved that he was to be returned to B Division.
15 *ibid.* The file records that, at its 26 Jun. 1961 meeting, the committee resolved to 'defer until Gov. returns'. Whether this was the governor of Pentridge who had raised the earlier objection to Ryan's transfer, or the governor of Bendigo, who had been asked about some issue to do with the proposed transfer, is not clear from the files; the likelihood is that it was the former. The date of Ryan's transfer to Bendigo is recorded on his Criminal History Record, prison's division, SWD.
16 *Annual Report for the Year Ending 30 Jun. 1961*, SWD, 10.
17 Ryan, Ronald J, progress reports, CF.
18 Ian Grindlay, *Behind Bars*, 5.
19 Training record, forming part of CF.
20 Dorothy Ryan, interviews, 1978–80.
21 Training record, in *op. cit.*
22 Summary of educational record, 'Ronald Joseph Ryan', Correspondence

School, Melbourne, written communication to the writer from Miss Ruth Potter, Principal, 22 Jun. 1978, and *ibid*.

23 Training record, in *op. cit*.

24 Summary of educational record, *op. cit*.

25 Progress reports, CF.

26 Dorothy Ryan, interviews, 1978–80.

27 *ibid*.

28 Letter, Ronald Ryan to *Truth*, 23 Dec. 1965.

29 The details of Dorothy's circumstances and the girls' activities at this time are taken from a written statement Dorothy made in support of Ryan's early release from Bendigo Prison. The statement, dated 16 May 1962, forms part of CHF. (See also NT Beggs, 'Parole Plan' in CHF.)

30 Wendy Ryan, interview, 29 Jan. 1987.

31 Dorothy's statement, CHF.

32 The administrative process referred to by Ryan, by which he could gain early release, was known as 'special authority'.

33 Ronald J Ryan to HW George, 17 Apr. 1962 (file 32.9.23, CHF).

34 Dorothy's statement, 16 May 1962 (file 32.9.23, CHF).

35 The Bendigo *Advertiser* made this claim in its report of 21 May 1962. It was repeated many years later by the governor, Ian Grindlay, in his 'Pentridge Papers' in 1976, which were reprinted and formed part of his memoirs, published as a magazine, *Behind Bars*.

36 Bendigo *Advertiser*, 21 May 1962. According to the *Advertiser* report, the drama group's participation in the eisteddfod had required the approval of the director-general of social welfare, Alec Whatmore.

37 The play is reproduced in Irwin J Zacher (ed), *Plays as Experience*, 204–33.

38 Bendigo *Advertiser*, 22 May 1962.

39 Perhaps because his was a non-speaking part, Ryan was not credited with the role in the Bendigo *Advertiser* report of the play's performance, but the then governor of the Bendigo Training Prison, Ian Grindlay, relates Ryan's role in his articles for *Truth*, and in *Behind Bars*.

40 Zacher (1962) *Plays as Experience*, 232–3. The quotation is from Shakespeare's *Julius Caesar*, Act II, scene 2; see Tragedies, 2 (London, Everyman's, 1993), 285.

41 Bendigo *Advertiser*, 'Prison Group Wins Play Competition', 21 May 1962; and Bendigo *Advertiser* 'Great Play Win', 22 May 1962.

42 Sir Ewen Cameron to Hon AG, Rylah, 2 Jun. 1962, on file 32.9.23, CHF. The nature and language of this reference is also persuasive evidence that, contrary to Barry Dickins' characterisation of Harold George as a close friend of Rylah, George was not well known to Rylah at all and, in fact, needed an introduction from Cameron. In particular, in a note to his play, Dickins (1994) writes that Harold George was a close friend of both Rylah and the premier, Sir Henry Bolte: ('… old Man George smoked five bob cigars with his friends, Arthur Rylah and Henry Bolte', *Remember Ronald Ryan*, ii.). There is no evidence for the assertion that Harold George knew

Sir Henry Bolte well. While George *was* known to Rylah, Dickins' description of the relationship appears over-stated. The nature of Harold George's relationship with Arthur Rylah has also been confirmed to the writer by George's son. (Keith George, interview, 7 Aug. 1978.)

43 *ibid.*

44 Notation on file 32.9.23, CHF.

45 AR Whatmore to JV Dillon, 28 Jun. 1962, on file 32.9.23, CHF.

46 *Victorian Year Book 1965*, 302.

47 The file referred to above does not record the outcome of official deliberations on the matter of special release, but it is evident from the timing of Ryan's eventual parole that no special authority was exercised.

48 Summary of educational record. The fact that Ryan did not sit the Intermediate examination is noteworthy because it clearly refutes a boastful claim he evidently made to Dorothy—a claim she accepted and later reported to the writer—that at the final exams for Intermediate in 1961 he 'did very well and came within the first five [students] in Victoria.' See Dorothy's statement, referred to above, dated 16 May 1962, on file 32.9.23, CHF.

49 Training record, forming part of CF.

50 Progress reports, CF.

51 Training record, forming part of CF. See also Summary of educational record.

52 As indicated above, Ryan did not, in fact, enter for the final examination in Intermediate. Summary of educational record.

53 Elsewhere on his classification file it is recorded that Ryan 'terminated Stage I Auditing and Accounting. Now doing Matriculation.' (Summary of institutional record, CF.) It seems likely that Ryan commenced but did not finish his study of Auditing and Accounting I; there is no other reference on the file to his having undertaken 'Commercial Law A.'

54 Neville F Gray to the director of prisons (EV Shade), 1 Mar. 1963. Ronald Joseph Ryan, personal file (file no. 2/18/20), prisons division, SWD.

55 Neville F Gray to the director of prisons (EV Shade), 30 Apr. 1963 in *ibid.*

56 *Annual Report for the Year Ending 30 Jun. 1964*, SWD, 38.

57 Ian Grindlay, interviews, 14 Jun. and 19 Jun. 1978.

58 Neville Drummond, officer in charge, historical section, Education Department, Victoria, and formerly teacher in the Department's Correspondence School, interview, 18 Jul. 1978.

59 Ian Grindlay, *Behind Bars*, 14.

60 Ian Grindlay, interviews, 14 Jun. and 19 Jun. 1978.

61 Summary of educational record.

62 Summary of Institutional record, CF.

63 I Grindlay, 'Governor's General Assessment', 6 May 1963, in CF.

64 NT Beggs, 'Parole Officer's Report, Ryan, Ronald Joseph', in *ibid.*

65 *ibid.*

66 *Annual Report for the Year ending 30 Jun. 1964*, SWD, 6. It had been before

Mr Justice Barry—as he then was—in the Supreme Court at Melbourne in March 1953 that Fred Allan had pleaded guilty to the charge of arson of Ryan's house at Noojee.

67 See the entry for Sir John Barry in John Ritchie (ed), *ADB, 13*:121–3; see also John Hetherington's profile of Barry in his series, 'Uncommon Men', *The Age*, 6 Jun. 1964, reprinted in Hetherington, *Uncommon Men*, 18–25.

68 The details of Ryan's imprisonment and remissions and his appearance before the Parole Board on 2 Aug. 1963 are drawn from his Parole Board Sheet, forming part of CF.

69 *Annual Report for the Year Ending 30 Jun. 1964*, SWD.

70 Ryan's role at Mobil was related to the writer by Eddie Wong, who worked alongside him in the ledger section. (Interview, 25 Jul. 1978.) Ryan's Mobil employment is also described in a homicide squad report on Ryan; police had evidently interviewed his superiors at Mobil, probably early in 1964. (Detective Sergeant KP Walters, homicide squad, to Superintendent, CIB Russell Street, 2 Aug. 1966.)

71 Keith George, interview, 7 Aug. 1978.

72 KP Walters, homicide squad report, 2 Aug. 1966.

73 Eddie Wong, interview, 25 Jul. 1978.

74 The photograph appears in the September 1963 issue of the Mobil staff magazine. It is also reproduced in Dickins, *Guts and Pity*, 18.

75 Detective Sergeant KP Walters, homicide squad, to Superintendent, CIB Russell Street, 2 Aug. 1966; and Eddie Wong, interview, 25 Jul. 1978. There has never been any suggestion that Ryan was involved in wrong-doing at Mobil. While he was involved in clerical accounting, he was not involved in handling money.

76 Dorothy Ryan, interviews, 1978–80; Keith George, interview, 7 Aug. 1978.

77 Classification Report, 3 Aug. 1964, CF.

78 K P Walters, 2 Aug. 1966.

79 *ibid.*

80 Copy of depositions, *The Queen v. Ronald Joseph Ryan*, 1 Sep. 1964. case 1707/64.

Chapter Seven: RELAPSE [pp 107–129]

1 Depositions, *The Queen v. Ronald Joseph Ryan*, case 1707/64, CLD.

2 See depositions, case 729, *The Queen v. Ronald Joseph Ryan and Ronald Joseph Gallagher*, 1 Mar. 1960.

3 Police record of interview with Ryan, 5 Jan. 1964, Exhibit N, depositions, *The Queen v. Ronald Joseph Ryan*, case 1707/64, CLD.

4 Statement of the manager, James Meats, in *ibid.*

5 Summary of evidence, 2, in *ibid.*

6 Police record of interview with Ryan, 5 Jan. 1964, Exhibit N, in *ibid.*

7 Wendy Ryan, interview, 29 Jan. 1987.

8 Dorothy Ryan, interviews, 1978-80.

9 The detail of the robbery and assault at the Mutual Finance Company are

taken from detailed reports of the offence in the press that day and the next. The robbery led the front page of *The Herald* on 18 Nov. 1963, and was the subject of prominent stories in *The Age* and *The Sun* the next day, 19 Nov. 1963. Of course, none of these reports mention Ryan. His involvement was established by linking Dorothy Ryan's description of the offence as told to her by Ryan on the day of the offence with these press reports. Ryan told Dorothy only that he had committed the offence at an upstairs finance company in the city, where he hit the elderly manager over the head before cleaning out the safe. As indicated in the text, at the time of this offence Ryan was 38 years old, his hair colour is described on his official police criminal record as 'fair' and, as is clear from earlier references in this book, Ryan was always well dressed.

10 This is the only known occasion on which Ryan used the name with which he had been born.

11 Ryan's statements to police and the details relating to his offences at East Preston, Colac, and Abbotsford are disclosed in police records of interview with Ryan, 5 Jan. 1964, Exhibits L, M, N, and O to *The Queen v. Ronald Joseph Ryan*, case 1707/64, CLD.

12 Notation on *ibid.*

13 The details of the offences committed by Ryan in NSW in 1964 are given in a letter by Detective Sergeant Noel Morey, safe squad, CIB, Sydney of the NSW Police to Detective Sergeant KP Walters, homicide squad, CIB, Victoria Police on 27 Jul. 1966. Morey's letter was in response to a request for information by Victoria Police concerning the details of Ryan's offences in NSW; at the time Ryan was in Pentridge, having been sentenced to death in Mar. 1966.

14 The police account related this incorrectly as the West Chatswood Bowling *Club,* suggesting a lawn bowls club. According to a report in Sydney's *Daily Telegraph*, the premises were, in fact, a ten-pin bowling facility. See *The Daily Telegraph*, '£250 theft', 26 Jun. 1964.

15 In subsequently quoting Morey's letter only months after the introduction of decimal currency in Australia, Walters introduces an error into the calculation of the value of the goods stolen in the theft of 11 Jul. 1964; Walters miscalculates £656-10-1 as $3,140 instead of the correct dollar value, $1,313. See KP Walters, homicide squad, Victoria Police to Superintendent CIB, *Ryan, Ronald Joseph*, 2 Aug. 1966.

16 These details are drawn from the signed hand-written confession made by Ryan whilst in custody at the Melbourne CIB in 1964 and quoted by the chief secretary, Arthur Rylah, during the controversy following the Victorian government's decision that Ryan should hang.

17 Letter, Morey to Walters, 27 Jul. 1966.

18 *The Daily Telegraph*, 29 Jun. 1964.

19 *The Sydney Morning Herald*, 30 Jun. 1964.

20 *The Daily Telegraph*, 1 Jul. 1964.

21 See, especially, the Parramatta *Advertiser*, 2 Jul. 1964.

22 *ibid.*
23 *The Daily Telegraph*, 30 Jun. 1964.
24 Letter, AG Rylah to JWR Westerman, 14 Dec. 1966.
25 Wendy Ryan, interview, 29 Jan. 1987.
26 Ryan told his parole officer, Neil Beggs, of his movements at this time, and Beggs reported them in his Breach of Parole report, 1 Mar. 1965. (File no. 64/3973, CF.)
27 Dorothy Ryan, interviews, 1978-80.
28 *ibid.*, and Wendy Ryan, interview, 29 Jan. 1987.
29 Janice Ryan, interview, 31 May 2001.
30 Wendy Ryan, interview, 29 Jan. 1987.
31 Dorothy Ryan, interviews, 1978-80. Ryan suspected that his presence in the house had been disclosed to police, but he never knew the source of the information. As he told his parole officer, he had 'unpleasant suspicions of his own family or of his in-laws, by the way in which police captured him.' He further 'hinted that someone close to him must have notified the police who arrested him …' Neil Beggs, Parole Officer, Breach of Parole report, 1 Mar. 1965. (File no. 64/3973, CF.) Two years later, Ryan told a prison source, who passed it on to a journalist at *Truth* newspaper, that he believed that Dorothy had been responsible for calling the police. Ryan said he remembered Dorothy speaking to someone on the telephone saying: 'Yes, yes, he's here,' but said he had been told that this was an aunt. (Notes taken by Evan Whitton but not published, *Truth*, newspaper library files.)
32 Dorothy Ryan, interviews, 1978-80.
33 Ryan's Criminal History Sheet, CIB Melbourne.
34 Given Ryan's propensity to confess, this confession is highly likely to have been made; however, it appears nowhere on the files.
35 The substance of Ryan's admissions to Morey is detailed in his letter to Detective Sergeant KP Walters, 27 Jul. 1966.
36 Ryan's Criminal History Sheet, CIB Melbourne.
37 'Ronald Joseph Ryan', character report, Detective First Constable John W. Stenfors, CIB St Kilda to Superintendent CIB, 28 Sep. 1964.
38 Ryan's Criminal History Sheet, CIB Melbourne.
39 Breach of Parole report, 1 Mar. 1965. (File no. 64/3973, CF.) See also Criminal History Sheet, CIB Melbourne.
40 Progress reports, CF.
41 Notes on file, case 1774/64, *The Queen v. Ronald Joseph Ryan*, CLD.
42 Notes on file, case 1707/64, *The Queen v. Ronald Joseph Ryan*, CLD.
43 An earlier 'Statement' written by Dorothy to government authorities in support of Ryan's early release from Bendigo Training Prison in 1962 describes Janice's illness as 'appendicitis' not 'peritonitis'. Ryan's reference to Dorothy on crutches is described in Dorothy's terms as a 'minor operation on her foot'. See Dorothy's letter, dated 16 May 1962, on file 32.9.23 (CHF.)

44 The letter forms part of file 1707/64, *The Queen v. Ronald Joseph Ryan*, Melbourne General Sessions, 13 Nov. 1964.
45 Eric Edgar Hewitt, *op. cit.*, 68. See also *Who's Who in Australia 1965,* 708.
46 Transcript, Court of General Sessions before Judge Read, Melbourne, 13 Nov. 1964. The case and the sentence of the judge were reported in *The Herald*, '8 Years for Big Thefts; 'Appalling record'—Judge', 13 Nov. 1964.
47 *ibid.*
48 Parole Board Sheet, CF.
49 Ryan's letter to *Truth,* 23 Dec. 1965. Ryan's comment that he was 'shocked by the severity of the ... sentences' was reported by his parole officer, Neil Beggs, in his Breach of Parole report, 1 Mar. 1965, file no. 64/3973, CF.
50 Parole Board Sheet, CF. To be precise, Ryan's expectation was that his sentence was thirteen years, three months, and 29 days' gaol. In fact, his minimum sentence was six years, seven months, and two days.
51 In part, this was because the calculations were difficult to make, even for prison authorities. On Ryan's prison file, while he was serving his sentence in Pentridge, there were three different calculations of his so-called 'Expected Expiration' of sentence date. One was 3 Mar. 1977, a second was 28 Jun. 1976, and a third was 6 Mar. 1971.
52 Ryan said this to the Pentridge Prison psychiatrist, Dr Allen A Bartholomew, in Nov. 1966, while he was in prison awaiting cabinet's decision on the possible commutation of his death sentence. Ryan referred to the eight years plus five years breach of parole that he would have had to serve. Letter from Bartholomew to secretary, Law Department, 16 Nov. 1966, forming part of Chief Secretary's File, no. 56/20, 002995. In 1966, Ryan told police that he was serving a sentence of about fifteen-and-a-half years. (Interview with Ryan by Detective Sergeant KP Walters, and Senior Detective Noel Murphy, Sydney, 7 Jan. 1966. Transcript, *The Queen v. Ryan and Walker*, 1966, 800.) The transcript of this trial is hereinafter cited as *RWTT*.
53 Rhonda Ryan and Wendy Ryan, interview, 29 Jan. 1987.
54 Violet Smith, Irma Russ, and Gloria Ryan, interview, 6 Sep. 1980.
55 Breach of Parole report, 1 Mar. 1965, file no. 64/3973, CF.
56 Notation on files 1707/64 and 1774/64, *The Queen v. Ronald Joseph Ryan*, CLD.
57 Neil Beggs, 'Ronald Joseph Ryan', Special report, 20 Apr. 1964, CF.
58 Neil Beggs, Breach of Parole report, 1 Mar. 1965, file no. 64/3973, CF.
59 Dorothy Ryan, interviews, 1978-80; and Wendy Ryan, interview, 29 Jan. 1987.
60 Notation on files 1707/64 and 1774/64, *The Queen v. Ronald Joseph Ryan*, CLD.
61 The details of the Ryan's divorce are taken from the petition and the brief of evidence in *Ryan v. Ryan*, held in the Supreme Court of Victoria. They can be documented here because, under the *Matrimonial Causes Act 1959*, then in force, divorces were not subject to the same confidentiality provi-

sions which later came to, and currently still, apply under the *Family Law Act 1975*.

62 Hewitt, *op. cit.*, 85.
63 Isabel Carter, *Woman in a Wig*, 156.
64 *Ryan v. Ryan*, Supreme Court of Victoria, 2 Jun. 1965.
65 *ibid.*
66 *ibid.* See also *Matrimonial Causes Act 1959-1973*, 633.
67 Depositions, *The Queen v. Ronald Joseph Ryan & Others*, case 1150, General Sessions Court, Melbourne. (See also *The Sun*, 10 Aug. 1960.)
68 See case 889/56, Jul. 1956.
69 *Ryan v. Ryan*, 2 Jun. 1965.
70 *ibid.* (See also a report of the granting of the decree nisi in *The Herald*, 4 Jun. 1965.)

Chapter Eight: BREAK-OUT [pp 131–155]

1 Patrick Tennison, *Defence Counsel*, 99-100; Leonard Radic, 'The Case of Ronald Ryan'.
2 Tennison, *op cit.*, 101.
3 Ryan, Ronald J 'Progress Reports' in CF.
4 Peter Walker, interview, 12 Sep. 2001.
5 Peter Walker, *Truth*, 26 Jan. 1985.
6 Leonard Radic, *op. cit.*
7 Conversation on 7 Jan. 1966 between Ryan and Detective Sergeant Harry Morrison, homicide squad, Melbourne, reproduced in the transcript of evidence of the coronial inquest before acting coroner Jim Duggan, SM, 4 Feb. 1967 (hereinafter cited as *IT*), 112.
8 Walker's Criminal History Sheet, begun 27 Jul. 1960, records section, Information Bureau, Victoria Police.
9 Birth Certificate, Peter John Walker, General Register Office, England, registered 13 May 1941.
10 The circumstances of his mother's suicide were related to the writer by Peter Walker, interview, 12 Sep. 2001.
11 Death Certificate, Alma Maud Walker, General Register Office, England, 14 Jan. 1949. The cause of death was established by a coronial inquest held on that day.
12 Peter Walker, interview, 12 Sep. 2001.
13 Peter Larson, 'Convictions: Australian shipping on the net'.
14 This account of Walker's early period in Australia draws upon several sources. The first is the interim report on the Pentridge escape by the director of prisons, Eric Shade, to the director-general of the Social Welfare Department, Alec Whatmore, 22 Dec. 1965, which, in turn, drew upon prison records. The second source is the transcript of the plea given by Walker's defence counsel, Jack Lazarus, at Walker's sentencing at the conclusion of the Hodson murder trial before Mr Justice Starke in the Supreme Court of Victoria on 29 Apr. 1966. The third is the plea by

Lazarus at the conclusion of Walker's trial for the murder of Arthur Henderson before Mr Justice Gowans in the Supreme Court on 18 Jul. 1966. The fourth source is Walker's three-part newspaper series in 1985 following his release from prison after almost twenty years in December 1984. In this series, Walker, *inter alia*, recalled his life and the events that led to his imprisonment. See 'The Life and Times of Peter Walker', *Truth*, 19 and 26 Jan. 1985 and 2 Feb. 1985. The final source is Peter Walker himself, in an interview with the writer, 12 Sep. 2001.

15 Interim report on the escape by the director of prisons [Eric Shade] to the director-general of social welfare, 22 Dec. 1965, SWD, file no. 117/12/13; and Lazarus plea, 29 Apr. 1966.

16 Peter John Walker, 'Criminal History Sheet', begun 27 Jul. 1960, records section, Information Bureau, Victoria Police; and Peter John Walker, 'Schedule of Prior Convictions', consorting squad, Victoria Police, 22 Apr. 1965.

17 *ibid.*

18 Walker's NSW offences were related by Lazarus in his plea, 18 Jul. 1966.

19 Walker, *Truth*, 19 Jan. 1985.

20 *The Age*, 13 Apr. 1965. (See also Lazarus plea, 29 Apr. 1966.)

21 *The Age*, 23 Apr. 1965. (See also Walker, *Truth*, 19 Jan. 1985.)

22 Peter John Walker, 'Criminal History Sheet', Victoria Police; and Peter John Walker, 'Schedule of Prior Convictions', Victoria Police. See also evidence presented at the coronial inquest into the death of George Henry Hodson, Melbourne Magistrates Court, 3–4 Feb. 1966, 10.

23 This account of how Ryan and Walker teamed up for their Pentridge escape bid was told by Ryan to a homicide squad detective in January 1966. The conversation is reproduced in *IT*, 112; see also Lazarus plea, 29 Apr. 1966, 5.

24 Tennison (1975) *op. cit.*, 103.

25 Walker, interview, 12 Sep. 2001.

26 Walker, *Truth*, 19 Jan. 1985.

27 Memorandum, David Hundley, director of prisons, to Alec Whatmore, director-general of social welfare, 'Questions Concerning Escape of Prisoners Ryan and Walker', 30 Dec. 1966. Prisons division, SWD, file no. 2/18/20, Prisoner: Ryan, Ronald Joseph. (personal file.)

28 *The Herald*, 14 Apr. 1952; *The Age*, 15 Apr. 1952; *The Sun*, 15 Apr. 1952. There had been a number of escapes from Pentridge prior to Joiner. Periodically, prisoners would make an attempt, as they had reportedly done in 1899, 1926, 1939, and 1940, but they were all caught within a relatively short time. The only prisoner thought to have successfully escaped from Pentridge was a man named Sparks who, on a foggy morning in 1901, got away and was never heard of again. (*The Herald*, 14 Apr. 1952.)

29 Interim report on the escape.

30 The minister responsible for prisons, chief secretary Arthur Rylah, later admitted that Pentridge was then 30 under its authorised strength of 266

prison officers. (*The Age*, 9 Feb. 1966. See also Victoria, *Parliamentary Debates*, *286*:3064.)

31 The details of the escape plans by Ryan and Walker—including the way in which the benches were taken from their mountings and the deception about an imminent escape—were told to the writer by Walker, interview, 12 Sep. 2001.

32 This account is taken from Lange's statement in *IT*, 18.

33 Walker, interview, 12 Sep. 2001.

34 'Escape of Prisoners Peter Walker and Ronald J. Ryan from Pentridge–19 Dec. 1965', supplementary report, from the director of prisons [Eric Shade] to the director-general of social welfare, [Alec Whatmore], 11 Jan. 1966. File of SWD, 'Prisoner escapes', no. 117/12/13.

35 The walls were 15 feet and 18 feet 6 inches at their highest point, but they were stepped walls and, at their lowest point, they were 13 feet 6 inches and 16 feet 6 inches respectively.

36 Interim report on the escape.

37 Until now, it has always been believed that the first wall the escapees scaled was the east-west wall of the exercise yard. Indeed, after Pentridge ceased operating as a gaol in 1997, public tours of the prison used to indicate a point on the east-west wall (which tour organisers had marked with a large painted X) where the wall was scaled. In fact, the position where Ryan and Walker went over the wall was to the left, on the north-south wall running at right angles to the one identified for tourists.

38 Peter Walker, interview, 12 Sep. 2001. Just how Ryan and Walker scaled the wall has not been fully revealed until now; although, in his unpublished series for *The Age*, Leonard Radic suggested that the prisoners created a kind of runway with the bench, which had been unscrewed and surreptitiously moved into place against the wall while the guard was absent. In his 1997 autobiography *Throw Away My Wig*, Ryan's legal counsel, Phil Opas, QC, suggested the use of two benches as a runway, as did Opas' biographer, Patrick Tennison, in his book *Defence Counsel*, 105. Interestingly, Walker himself made no mention of such an aid in his *Truth* articles, 19 and 26 Jan. 1985. The report of the official investigation by the head of the prisons division, Eric Shade, also made no mention of a bench or benches. Shade considered that Ryan and Walker might either have been assisted by other prisoners, presumably by clambering on their shoulders, or by using the grappling apparatus which they subsequently used to scale the outer wall. In his interim report, Shade cited Pentridge chief prison officer Hannan as stating that 'information from prisoners' supported the former (that is, clambering) proposition. (Interim report on the escape.)

39 *ibid.* See also Walker, *Truth*, 19 Jan. 1985.

40 Walker, *Truth*, 19 Jan. 1985.

41 Interim report on the escape.

42 Walker, interview, 12 Sep. 2001. (See also Walker, *Truth*, 19 Jan. 1985;

Tennison, *op. cit.*, 102 and Opas, *op. cit.*, 241.)
43 *ibid.*
44 Interim report on the escape.
45 Peter Walker, interview, 12 Sep. 2001.
46 Walker, *Truth*, 19 Jan. 1985.
47 The issue of the spilled round was to become a significant issue, one heavily disputed in the subsequent court proceedings arising from the escape.
48 Lange statement in *IT*, 13.
49 *ibid.*
50 Brown statement in *IT*, 26.
51 *ibid.*
52 Lange statement in *IT*, 14.
53 Brown statement in *IT*, 26.
54 This account of Lange's return to the tower at gunpoint is drawn from his statement in *IT*, 14, 17–18, 21.
55 Peter Walker, interview, 12 Sep. 2001.
56 Brown statement in *IT*, 27.
57 Peter Walker, *Truth*, 26 Jan. 1985. The arrangement for the getaway car involved an associate leaving the car in the car-park for the weekend in anticipation of the break-out. The plan simply was not implemented, which proved to be a fateful omission. Had the car been there, as arranged, Ryan and Walker may well have escaped without bloodshed.
58 Hewitt statement in *IT*, 33.
59 Statement to police by William Bennett, 19 Dec. 1965, attached to the interim report on the escape.
60 Bennett statement in *IT*, 36. (Peter Walker, interview, 12 Sep. 2001, says that Bennett had used the words 'I can't. They'll crucify me!' In Bennett's statement to the Hodson inquest, he said only that he had called out: 'I won't.' [*IT*, 36.])
61 Hewitt statement in *IT*, 34.
62 *ibid.*, 34–5. (See Grindlay, *op. cit.*, 8.)
63 Carole Barns (née Hodson), interview, 26 Mar. 2001; and *The Sun Herald*, 12 Apr. 1997.
64 Lange statement in *IT*, 14.
65 Whether Hodson knew Ryan is uncertain. It has been suggested by Father John Brosnan that Hodson did know Ryan and they were on good terms, as much as could be said about the relationship between a prison officer and a prisoner. (Father John Brosnan, interview, 14 Oct. 1968.) However, in statements to police after his re-capture, Ryan said that he did *not* know Hodson personally. (Interview between Detective Sergeant KP Walters and Ronald Ryan, Sydney, 7 Jan. 1966, forming Exhibit T in *RWTT*).
66 Peter Walker, interview, 12 Sep. 2001.
67 Franck Jeziorski statement in *IT*, 69.
68 Pauline Jeziorski statement in *IT*, 71.

69 Franck Jeziorski statement in *IT*, 69.
70 *ibid.*; and Pauline Jeziorski statement in *IT*, 71.
71 Pauline Jeziorski statement in *IT*, 71.
72 Franck Jeziorski statement in *IT*, 69; and Pauline Jeziorski statement in *IT*, 71.
73 Mitchinson statement in *IT*, 41; Wallis statement in *IT*, 50.
74 'Escape of Prisoners Peter Walker and Ronald J. Ryan from Pentridge–19 Dec. 1965', supplementary report, from the director of prisons [Eric Shade], to the director-general of social welfare [Alec Whatmore], 11 Jan. 1966. File of SWD, Prisoner escapes, no. 117/12/13.
75 Mitchinson statement in *IT*, 41.
76 Franck Jeziorski statement in *IT*, 69; Pauline Jeziorski statement in *IT*, 71.
77 Bennett statement in *IT*, 37.
78 *ibid.*
79 Statement to police by William Bennett, attached to the interim report on the escape.
80 Peter Walker, interview, 12 Sep. 2001. Walker claimed to police that Hodson had 'hit me on the head with an iron pipe'. Record of interview with Walker by Detective Sergeant Harry Morrison, homicide squad, Melbourne on 7 Jan. 1966, reproduced in *IT*, 101. The piece of pipe was subsequently recovered by police and tendered as Exhibit H at Ryan and Walker's trial for murder. (RWTT, 563–6.)
81 Whether Hodson was armed with 'an iron bar' or 'iron piping' and struck Walker with it was later controversial. None of the prison officer witnesses saw him with an iron bar or piping, and most of the civilian witnesses later gave evidence in which they said that they did not see Hodson carrying anything. However, two witnesses, Keith Dobson and Louis Bailey, who were in a car together in Sydney Road, both later gave evidence saying that Hodson had been carrying something like a baton or iron bar in his hand as he chased Walker. Dobson deposed that when he saw Hodson chasing Walker outside the front gate of the church, 'in his hand I noticed something which I took to be a baton'. (Dobson's statement in *IT*, 72.) Bailey deposed that he saw Hodson 'carrying something like an iron bar, or something of that description' as he was chasing Walker. (Bailey's statement in *ibid.*, 77.)
82 Statement to police by William Bennett, attached to the interim report on the escape; and Bennett statement in *IT*, 37.
83 Paterson statement in *IT*, 43.
84 Peter Walker, interview, 12 Sep. 2001.
85 Statement by John Anderson in *IT*, 78–9.
86 The prosecution in Ryan's subsequent trial for murder would later submit that the distance was 10 to 30 feet. (See *The Age*, 16 Mar. 1966.)
87 Paterson statement in *IT*, 43.
88 Hodson's death was the subject of a coronial inquest at which the state's senior government pathologist, Dr James McNamara, gave evidence as to

the cause of death. The description of Hodson's wounds is drawn from his evidence to that inquest. *ibid.*, 97.

89 Murray statement in *ibid.*, 83.

90 Report on the escape by acting governor Ian Grindlay, 21 Dec. 1965, forming part of SWD file no. 117/12/13; and McNamara statement in *RWTT*, 493–5.

91 Ben Lange's suicide note was tendered in evidence at the coronial inquest into his death in Jul. 1969. (*Truth*, 2 Aug. 1969.) Lange was awarded a certificate of commendation on 24 Nov. 1967.

92 Ryan said he used these words when he wrote a marginal comment on Mullins' statement in the transcript of the Hodson inquest evidence, 88.

93 Wallis statement in *IT*, 51.

94 Peter Walker, interview, 12 Sep. 2001.

95 Mitchinson statement in *IT*, 41.

96 It was later submitted by the prosecution in the subsequent trial of Ryan and Walker that—based upon witness evidence—the time between when the escapees cleared the second wall of the prison until they finally drove away in the Vanguard was 'less than two minutes'. (*The Age*, 16 Mar. 1966.)

97 Report of the acting deputy governor, Arthur Phair, 20 Dec. 1965 in SWD file no. 117/12/13. (See statement to police by Paterson, dated 19 Dec. 1965, attached to the interim report on the escape.)

98 *ibid.*

99 Carole Barns (née Hodson), interview, 26 Mar. 2001.

100 *ibid.* (See also *The Age*, 28 Oct. 1996.)

101 Walker, *Truth*, 26 Jan. 1985.

102 This account is primarily drawn from the statement to police of Hurley and O'Reilly, made on 7 Jan. 1966. There are some discrepancies between the accounts of Hurley and O'Reilly and that of Peter Walker given in interviews with the writer and in articles he wrote for *Truth* newspaper upon his release from prison in 1985. The discrepancies principally relate to what happened in the first 24 hours after the gaol break, and where Ryan and Walker slept on that first night. There is also a discrepancy about the extent of the role that Hurley and O'Reilly played in those first moments after they arrived in Kensington.

103 Dorothy Ryan, interviews 1978–80; Wendy Ryan, interview, 29 Jan. 1987.

104 The homicide squad investigations on 19 Dec. 1965 at Pentridge were recalled by Detective Inspector Frank Holland in a memorandum to Superintendent, CIB, Victoria Police, 1 Feb. 1967. Chief Secretary's Office, file no. 10788.

105 Peter Walker, interview, 12 Sep. 2001.

106 Statement to police of Edna O'Reilly, 7 Jan. 1966.

107 A barrel is a colloquial name for a working-class benefit party at which beer from a barrel is sold and consumed, the proceeds going to the benefit recipient.

108 Peter Walker, interview, 12 Sep. 2001.

109 *ibid.*

110 *The Sun*, 20 Dec. 1965.

111 Although Peter Walker, *Truth*, 26 Jan. 1985, writes that Ryan *did* know Hurley.

112 Hurley's conviction emerged in the subsequent trial for harbouring, which arose out of these incidents. See the report of the court case in *The Age*, 22 Nov. 1966.

113 Statement to police of Edna O'Reilly, 7 Jan. 1966.

114 *ibid.*

115 Peter Walker, interview, 12 Sep. 2001. In his statement to police, Hurley said that Ryan and Walker had stayed only 40 minutes. Walker wrote in his article for *Truth*, 26 Jan. 1985, that he and Ryan had spent the first night with a woman in St Kilda who was never discovered by police and that—unlike several others—she was not prosecuted for harbouring them. (See also evidence of Senior Detective Harry Morrison, homicide squad, Victoria Police in transcript, *The Queen v. Peter John Walker*, 22 Jul. 1966, 325.) This transcript is hereinafter cited as *WTT*.

116 From the ABC radio news copy file, 19 Dec. 1965. It seems likely that the addition of the word 'armed' was just a reporting mistake but, since police had provided Ryan's criminal history details to journalists, it is also possible that they wanted to communicate that—with his NSW offences for armed robbery in July 1964—Ryan was a rather more serious criminal than the one suggested by offences for 'breaking and entering'. The next day, *The Age* carried a page-one story reporting the escapees as 'Ronald James Ryan, 40', but did not repeat the reference to 'armed' robbery, describing his sentence as 'nine years for burglary'. *The Age*, 20 Dec. 1965.

117 A little over twelve months later, Whatmore set out the circumstances of his visit to Pentridge on the evening of 19 Dec. 1965, and his response to journalists' inquiries later that night, in a memorandum to the under secretary of the Chief Secretary's Office, John Dillon, dated 1 Feb. 1967. Chief Secretary's file 10788.

118 Peter Walker, interview, 12 Sep. 2001.

119 *ibid.* (See also statement to police of Edna O'Reilly, 7 Jan. 1966, forming part of the transcript of her committal hearing on harbouring charges, 18 Jan. 1966. In the statement, O'Reilly relates this incident, saying that it took place on the night of Monday, 27 Dec. 1965; but, since Walker is known to have had the revolver on 23 Dec. 1965, this is clearly incorrect. The revolver was recovered from Walker when he was recaptured in Sydney on 5 Jan. 1966.)

120 *The Sun*, 20 Dec. 1965. (Emphasis added.)

121 Memorandum, director-general of social welfare, to under secretary, Chief Secretary's Office, 1 Feb. 1967. In the memorandum, a marginal handwritten note initialled by John Dillon records that 'Mr. Whatmore has no recollection of stating that Hodson was shot three times. So advised by phone to me. J.D. 1/2[/67]'

Chapter Nine: MANHUNT [pp 157–177]

1 Peter Walker, interview, 12 Sep. 2001. In her statement to police at the Hodson inquest, Gail Farn, whom the fugitives subsequently visited in St Kilda, said that Ryan told her about this encounter, which she said involved the drunk saying: 'You're one of the escaped convicts!' Statement by Gail Farn in *IT*, 90.

2 Walker, *Truth*, 19 Jan. 1985.

3 ABC radio news copy file, 20 Dec. 1965.

4 There is some uncertainty about the events described over the next several hours and days. Indeed, some doubt remains generally about what Ryan and Walker did on that first Monday, with Walker and people subsequently charged with harbouring all giving differing accounts of that day and the following two weeks. Ryan and Walker told people assisting them to tell police that they were coerced into helping; hence these statements to police are unreliable in certain respects that primarily concern whether, or how well, these individuals knew Ryan and Walker, and how willingly they assisted them.

5 Peter Walker, interview, 12 Sep. 2001.

6 The details of Christina Aitken's prostitution convictions were led in evidence by the prosecution during testimony by Aitken as a witness in *WTT*, 185.

7 Statement of Pat Puccini in the harbouring case which eventuated before the courts from the incidents related here: *The Queen v. Christina Evelyn Aitken, Patricia Meryl Puccini, Edna [O'Reilly] Hurley and Keith Desmond Hurley*, General Sessions Court, Melbourne, 18 Jan. 1966, 75. (These statements are hereinafter cited as *CACT*.) To former inmates of Pentridge prison, which was located in Coburg, the gaol was known colloquially as the Coburg college.

8 Statement of Pat Puccini in *CACT*, 76.

9 *ibid.*, 75.

10 Statement of Gail Farn in *IT*, 90.

11 *ibid.*

12 Aitken gave evidence at her subsequent trial for harbouring Ryan and Walker in the Melbourne Court of General Sessions on 14 Jun. 1966, at which she elaborated upon these events. (*The Age*, 15 Jun. 1966.)

13 Statement by Christina Aitken in *CACT*, 64.

14 Statement by Walker taken in a record of interview by Detective Sergeant Harry Morrison, homicide squad, Melbourne, on 7 Jan. 1966, in *ibid.*, 102–3. In his statement, Walker says they went *on the first morning* of their freedom to a vacant allotment in St Kilda; but when much later he was taken to the place by police, it was shown to be Albert Street (the vacant block ran through to Vine Street) in the adjoining neighbourhood of Windsor. Later evidence by police has Walker telling them that he had gone to the allotment *in the evening*, after he had been to Pat Puccini's house. See *WTT*, 96, 298.

15 Statement by Christina Aitken in *CACT*, 70, 74.

16 Peter Walker, interview, 12 Sep. 2001.

17 Statement to police by Peter John Walker, Clarence Street Police Station, Sydney, 7 Jan. 1966.

18 Peter Walker, *Truth*, 26 Jan. 1985.

19 Statement by Christina Aitken in *CACT*, 64.

20 *The Age*, 24 Dec. 1965.

21 Walker, *Truth*, 26 Jan. 1985.

22 Statement by Christina Aitken in *CACT*, 70.

23 Despite the fact that the letters constitute a remarkable documentary record in their own right, they were ignored by the other Melbourne media at the time, presumably because they seemed so unlikely to be genuine. Sections of the letters were photographically reproduced in *Truth*, and there is no doubt from the letters' unmistakable handwriting and the language they contain that their author was Ryan. In her statement to police, Christina Aitken also says that they were written by Ryan, *ibid.*, 70.

24 Ned Kelly, *The Jerilderie Letter*, 63–4; also quoted in Frank Clune, *Ned Kelly's Last Stand*, 96–101.

25 *Truth*, 25 Dec. 1965.

26 Christmas Card, Ronald Ryan to Cecilia Ryan, undated but posted on 22 Dec. 1965. See *The Age*, 31 Dec. 1965.

27 Statement of Christina Aitken, *op. cit.* 70.

28 Peter Walker, *Truth*, 26 Jan. 1985; *The Age*, 27 Dec. 1965. *The Age* report says that the number plate had been changed from GES 880 to GES 882, but this is improbable. Walker (interview, 4 Oct. 2001) reconstructs it as GES 380 to GBS 880. That seems rather more likely.

29 Peter Walker, *Truth*, 26 Jan. 1985.

30 *The Herald*, 23 Dec. 1965; *The Sun*, 24 Dec. 1965.

31 Peter Walker, interview, 4 Oct. 2001. In a statement to police following his re-capture in Sydney, Walker said that in the bank hold-up he had used a .32 Harrington & Richardson revolver, which police had recovered. (Statement to police by Peter John Walker, Clarence Street Police Station, Sydney, 7 Jan. 1966.)

32 When he was recaptured in Sydney, Walker admitted to police that he went into the manager's office believing that guns were stored there. Detective Sergeant Frederick Krahe, New South Wales CIB, in *WTT*, 252.

33 Statement to police of Robert Sipthorpe, ANZ Bank teller, 23 Dec. 1965, 1; and statement to police of Kenneth Munro, ANZ Bank accountant, 23 Dec. 1965, 1.

34 Peter Walker, interview, 12 Sep. 2001. (See also Walker, *Truth*, 26 Jan. 1985; and *The Sun*, 24 Dec. 1965.)

35 Walker, *Truth*, 26 Jan. 1985.

36 Statement to police of Robert Sipthorpe, 23 Dec. 1965, 1.

37 Munro statement, 1.

38 Sipthorpe statement, 1.

39 These cartridges were later handed to police. Much later, they were to play an important part in Ryan's trial for murder.
40 The incident above involving June Crawford and the statements attributed to Ryan and Walker are taken from her statement to police, 20 Jan. 1966, 1–2. (See also statement to police by Peter John Walker, Clarence Street Police Station, Sydney, 7 Jan. 1966.)
41 Statement to police by Walker, 7 Jan. 1966.
42 Crawford statement, 2.
43 Giving evidence at his subsequent trial for murder, Ryan said that he thought the bank robbery had taken only three minutes. (*RWTT*, 585. See also Walker, *Truth*, 26 Jan. 1985.)
44 Munro statement, 2.
45 Melbourne daily newspapers the day after the hold-up reflected this uncertainty. *The Sun* on 24 Dec. 1965 reported that Ryan and Walker were involved, but *The Herald* on the same day was less sure, reporting only that 'Ryan was one of two men' who robbed the bank. *The Herald* also quoted an unnamed detective as saying: 'Walker could have been in the getaway car or helping somewhere else behind the scenes, but it is also likely that he has parted with Ryan.'
46 Ryan and Walker's statements and the detail of their return to the flat after the bank robbery are taken from Christina Aitken's statement in *CACT*, 65, 70.
47 Peter Walker, interview, 12 Sep. 2001; Aitken statement in *op. cit.*, 67.
48 *The Age*, 22 Dec. 1965.
49 Aitken statement in *op. cit*, 67.
50 Walker, *Truth*, 26 Jan. 1985.
51 *The Herald*, 24 Dec. 1965.
52 Walker, *Truth*, 26 Jan. 1985.
53 Aitken statement in *op. cit*, 66.
54 Statement of Arthur Carew, pawnbroker, in *CACT*, 28. (See also *The Herald*, 18 Jan. 1966.)
55 Statement of Alan Cocks, car salesman of Kevin Dennis Motors, in *CACT*, 26.
56 Aitken statement in *CACT*, 67.
57 *ibid.*
58 Evidence of Cannon's prostitution was put by Walker's defence counsel, Jack Lazarus, during Walker's trial for murder, *WTT*, 137. In Aitken's statement to police on 25 Dec. 1965, Cannon was referred to by her as Jan Howarth. In Walker's trial for murder in July 1966 she is referred to by witnesses, including Aitken, as Jan Cannon.
59 Statement of John Graham Fisher, *WTT*, 125.
60 Aitken's statement to police, 25 Dec. 1965. (Aitken went beyond her statement to police and indicated her relationship with Henderson in evidence at her subsequent trial for harbouring in the Melbourne General Sessions Court on 14 Jun. 1966. [*The Age*, 15 Jun. 1966.])

61 In evidence at his later trial, Walker described the desk and said that there was 'a pistol... a revolver, and possibly a rifle.' *WTT*, 368.
62 Fisher, in *WTT*, 141. In her statement to police, Aitken made no mention of the pointed gun, saying only that Ryan was packing as if getting ready to move. Statement of Christina Aitken in *CACT*, 68.
63 The details of the conversation above in the flat between Ryan and Aitken about Sharon and her friends Cannon, Fisher, and Henderson (as well as the overheard conversation between Ryan and Fisher) are all taken from Aitken's statement to police in *CACT*, 68–9.
64 Fisher, in his evidence at Walker's later trial for murder, *WTT*, 142; Cannon, *WTT*, 171.
65 Fisher, *WTT*, 131.
66 Jan Cannon, *WTT*, 161.
67 Fisher, statement to police, 25 Dec. 1965, 23. Fisher repeated his evidence in the Walker trial, *WTT*, 128, 149.
68 Fisher, *WTT*, 143–5.
69 Walker, *WTT*, 371.
70 Cannon, *WTT*, 163. (See also Cannon's witness evidence at the trial in the Melbourne General Sessions Court of Aitken and Puccini, reported in *The Herald*, 10 Jun. 1966.) In his evidence, Walker specifically denied that this had happened. Walker, *WTT*, 369.
71 Fisher, *WTT*, 129, 132; and Aitken in *CACT*, 69.
72 Walker, *WTT*, 372–3; and statement of Aitken in *CACT*, 69.
73 Walker's account of his trip to the sly-grog and his conversations with Henderson in the car is drawn from his evidence at his trial in *WTT*, 373–7.
74 *WTT*, 378–9.
75 Walker, *Truth*, 26 Jan. 1985.
76 Henderson's blood-alcohol level was tested by the Coroner's Court in Melbourne and evidence was given about the analysis at Walker's trial. Arnold Russell, medico-legal chemist, *WTT*, 228.
77 This statement is an amalgam of three passages of evidence given at Walker's trial: first, Walker's own evidence (*WTT*, 379–81); second, the evidence of Senior Detective Harry Morrison relating what Walker subsequently said about the incident when he was taken back to the toilet following his arrest (*WTT*, 300); and, third, the evidence of Pentridge prison officer Colin Waldron, also relating what Walker subsequently said in his presence in the toilet (*WTT*, 352).
78 Dr James McNamara, senior government pathologist, in *WTT*, 193–8. First Constable Brian Thompson, firearms identification division, Forensic Science Laboratory, Melbourne, gave expert testimony that the distance from the muzzle of the pistol to the wound in Henderson's head was one inch or less at the time the shot was fired. (Thompson in *WTT*, 236.)
79 Dr David Middleton, medical practitioner, in *WTT*, 223.

80 The medical opinion was divergent and inconclusive on this point. The crucial issue was whether Henderson had sustained a broken nose before he died, and—if he did—what had caused it. The point was important because it went to the question of whether Henderson and Walker had had a fight in the toilet block and that Henderson had been shot in that struggle (as Walker later claimed), or whether Walker had simply shot Henderson in the back of the head in an 'execution-style' killing (as the prosecution later claimed at his trial). In his post-mortem examination, Dr McNamara had not found evidence of a broken nose, but conceded that it was possible not to detect that at post-mortem. (McNamara in *WTT*, 195, 210.) He further testified that Henderson's face striking the concrete floor was the more likely cause of any break if there was one. (*WTT*, 214–15.) However, Dr Middleton, who examined Henderson upon his arrival at Prince Henry's Hospital testified that he thought Henderson did have a fractured nose (*WTT*, 223–4) and agreed, when it was put to him, that a blow to the nose by a fist was the more likely cause. (*WTT*, 227.)

81 Walker in *WTT*, 383.

82 Fisher in *WTT*, 129–30; Cannon in *WTT*, 164. According to Aitken in her statement to police, Walker told everyone that he had dropped Henderson at home 'because he didn't feel up to it'. (Aitken in *op. cit.*, 69.)

83 There is considerable uncertainty about what happened next. In his statement to police, Fisher said that Walker had given Ryan an empty cartridge case. (Fisher, statement to police, 25 Dec. 1965.) In his statement to police when he was recaptured in Sydney, Walker denied the reference to the expended cartridge case, and said that Henderson 'was going to give us up for the reward and he tried to get the gun off me so I had to shoot him.' Walker also said that he had thrown the empty cartridge case onto the beach outside the toilet block. (Record of interview between Senior Detective Harry Morrison and Peter John Walker, at Clarence Street Detectives' Office, Sydney, 7 Jan. 1966, forming part of the brief for the prosecution, *The Queen v. Ronald Joseph Ryan and Peter John Walker*, 1 Mar. 1966.) Fisher also said that Ryan had come over to him, showed him the empty cartridge case and, in front of Walker, said: 'He got rid of your mate.' (Fisher in *WTT*, 130.)

84 Walker, record of interview with police, 7 Jan. 1966. See also Walker, in *WTT*, 383.

85 Aitken statement in *CACT*, 69.

86 Cannon in *WTT*, 165.

87 Aitken statement in *CACT*, 69.

88 Peter Walker, interview, 4 Oct. 2001.

89 Cannon in *WTT*, 166–7; Fisher in *WTT*, 151.

90 Norman Haywood in *WTT*, 186.

91 *WTT, 186*. The exact time of the discovery of Henderson's body later became something of an issue. Haywood gave evidence that it was

1:40AM. Steven Prince gave evidence that it was more like 12:30AM when he logged his departure to the toilet block. In all the circumstances, Haywood's evidence seems more likely.

92 Prince in *WTT*, 190.

93 Peter Walker, interview, 12 Sep. 2001. (A slightly different version of this incident is given in Walker, *Truth*, 26 Jan. 1985 and Walker, *WTT*, 384.)

94 Statement to police of Christina Aitken, *op. cit.*, 70.

95 *The Sun*, 27 Dec. 1965.

96 Cannon in *WTT*, 167–8, 174.

97 Walker, *Truth*, 26 Jan. 1985.

98 The account of Ryan and Walker's return to McConnell Street, Kensington, and their comments to the Hurleys, is drawn from the statement to police of Keith Hurley, 7 Jan. 1966, forming part of the transcript of his committal hearing on harbouring charges, 18 Jan. 1966.

99 This was the case of Edward Leonski, a US army private stationed in Melbourne, who was subsequently convicted for the murders and hanged by US authorities at Pentridge prison on 9 Nov. 1942. See Andrew Mallon, *Leonski* and Ivan Chapman, *Leonski*.

100 Quoted in Tennison, *op. cit.*, 113.

101 Letter of assistant minister of education John Rossiter to Professor Richard Samuel, 2 Mar. 1967.

102 See *The Age*, 27 Dec. 1965; *The Herald*, 27 Dec. 1965.

Chapter Ten: RECAPTURE [pp 179–206]

1 The drive to Essendon to drop off the panel van and the subsequent hitched ride with the milkman were related by Peter Walker, interview, 4 Oct. 2001.

2 *The Sun*, 27 Dec. 1965.

3 Statement to police of Keith Hurley, 7 Jan. 1966, forming part of the transcript of his committal hearing on harbouring charges, 18 Jan. 1966. Murray's alias emerged in the subsequent court case arising from these matters. Following his conviction, Murray admitted a number of convictions dating from 1936. (See the reports of the court case in *The Age* and *The Sun*, 22 Nov. 1966.)

4 *ibid.*; and *The Herald*, 19 Jan. 1966.

5 Statement to police of Edna O'Reilly, 7 Jan. 1966, forming part of the transcript of her committal hearing on harbouring charges, 18 Jan. 1966.

6 *The Herald*, 27 Dec. 1965.

7 *ibid. The Age* next morning essentially repeated this line from Holland in a story under the headline: 'Man phones police: "I'm escapee".' (*The Age*, 28 Dec. 1965.)

8 Statement to police of Keith Hurley, 7 Jan. 1966, *op. cit.*

9 Interviews, Dorothy Ryan 1978–80; Peter Walker, interview, 12 Sep. 2001.

10 *The Sun*, 29 Dec. 1965.

11 Dorothy Ryan, interviews, 1978–80.

12 The word 'Fuck' was replaced with a dash in the version printed in *Truth*.
13 This paragraph of Ryan's letter was edited out of the version published in *Truth*.
14 Ryan had crossed out the word 'comrades' and substituted 'Friends'.
15 This letter was published in a somewhat different form and style—and with the deletions, as shown—in *Truth*, 1 Jan. 1966.
16 Statement to police of Keith Hurley, 7 Jan. 1966, *op. cit.*
17 Letter, Ronald Ryan to Dianne Everett, 30 Dec. 1965.
18 In a later court appearance in relation to this incident, Calleson was alleged to have met Walker and subsequently delivered to Davitt an envelope containing £300 to bail out Aitken and Puccini. (*The Age*, 2 Jun. 1966.) Calleson was ultimately acquitted of the charge of being an accessory after the fact to a felony. (*The Age*, 8 Jun. 1966.)
19 The text of Ryan's letter to Davitt was read into the evidence at Davitt's subsequent trial on charges of assisting the escapees. (*The Herald*, 7 Jun. 1966.)
20 *The Age*, 2 Jun. 1966.
21 Statement of evidence, Winifred Gibson, saleswoman at the New Jersey Fashion House, in *CACT*, 46.
22 Statement by Josephine Natoli, sales employee of MA Ward, newsagency, in *CACT*, 43–4.
23 Statement by Edna O'Reilly, in Exhibit V, *CACT*, 85.
24 Statement by Alfred Dewar, sales employee of Georges Ltd, in *CACT*, 47.
25 Statement by Keith Pollack, sales employee of Georges Ltd, in *CACT*, 48.
26 Statement by Detective Sergeant Kevin Carton, homicide squad, Victoria Police in *CACT*. See also evidence of George Archibald, sales employee of Ottrey's store, as reported in *The Herald*, 19 Jan. 1966.
27 Peter Walker, 4 Oct. 2001.
28 *The Sun*, 31 Dec. 1965 and 1 Jan. 1966.
29 Statement of Dianne Everett in the case of *CACT*, 45.
30 Peter Walker, interview, 12 Sep. 2001.
31 Statement by Ronald Joseph Ryan in an interview with homicide squad Detective Sergeant KP Walters, after Ryan's recapture in Sydney, 7 Jan. 1966. Exhibit N in brief for the prosecution, *The Queen v. Ryan & Walker*, 105.
32 *The Sun*, 1 Jan. 1966.
33 Peter Walker, interview, 12 Sep. 2001.
34 Walker, *Truth*, 26 Jan. 1985.
35 Peter Walker, interview, 4 Oct. 2001.
36 *ibid.* A different version of this incident figured in the evidence of Detective Sergeant KP Walters, homicide squad, Victoria Police, relating statements made by Ryan during the course of a formal interview, forming part of *IT*, 106.
37 See *The Herald*, 6 Jan. 1966.
38 Later media reports would describe the rendezvous as a double-date, but

Walker says that this was never the arrangement. Peter Walker, interview, 4 Oct. 2001.

39 *The Herald*, 5 Jan. 1966. See also *The Age*, 6 Jan. 1966, where Detective Inspector Frank Holland revealed the police deception.

40 *The Sun*, 6 Jan. 1966.

41 The detail of the Murrays' encounter with the escapees is reported in *The Age*, 7 Jan. 1966.

42 After the event, Detective Inspector Kelly provided a detailed account of the police operation to journalist Tom Prior, *The Sun*, 7 Jan. 1966, from which the account in the text is largely drawn.

43 *ibid.*, and *The Sun*, 6 Jan. 1966.

44 *The Herald*, 6 Jan. 1966.

45 Peter Walker, interview, 12 Sep. 2001.

46 *ibid.*, and Walker, *Truth*, 26 Jan. 1985.

47 *The Sun*, 7 Jan. 1966.

48 *The Herald*, 6 Jan. 1966.

49 Peter Walker, interview, 12 Sep. 2001.

50 Detective Sergeant Krahe in *WTT*, 261–2.

51 *The Sun*, 6 Jan. 1966.

52 *The Herald*, 6 Jan. 1966.

53 *ibid. The Age* (6 Jan. 1966) reported that the bag contained £300.

54 *The Sun*, 7 Jan. 1966.

55 Detective Sergeant Frederick Krahe in *WTT*, 249–51.

56 Peter Walker, interview, 12 Sep. 2001.

57 Detective Sergeant Frederick Krahe in *WTT*, 251.

58 Ryan's statement forms Exhibit S in *RWTT*, 799.

59 Evidence of Detective Sergeant KP Walters, *RWTT*, 531.

60 *RWTT*, 531A–532.

61 Interview between Detective Sergeant KP Walters and Ronald Ryan, Sydney, 7 Jan. 1966, forming Exhibit T in *RWTT*, 801.

62 *RWTT*, 802.

63 Evidence given by Detective Sergeant Frederick Krahe of the Surry Hills CIB in *WTT*, 273–4.

64 Interview between Detective Harry Morrison and Peter Walker, forming Exhibit R in *RWTT*, 797–8.

65 Deposition by Ryan at extradition proceedings, *Police v. Ronald Joseph Ryan*, Sydney, 7 Jan. 1966, forming Exhibit U in *RWTT*, 803.

66 Following his extradition to Victoria, on 18 Jan. 1966 Murray appeared in the Melbourne Court of Petty Sessions, where he was charged that he did 'receive, comfort, harbour, assist and maintain' Ryan and Walker during their period at large. (Police brief of evidence in the matter of Norman Harold Murray, 14 Jan. 1966.) Murray joined Burnie Davitt, Margaret Calleson, Pat Puccini, Christina Aitken, Keith Hurley, and Edna O'Reilly in facing charges of assisting the escapees. The seven accused were all committed for trial in the Melbourne Court of General Sessions, where

their cases were heard in three separate hearings in June and September 1966.

On 7 Jun. 1966, Margaret Calleson was acquitted on two charges of assisting the escapees. (*The Age*, 8 Jun. 1966.) Davitt was found guilty of assisting Ryan, but was acquitted of assisting Walker: he was sentenced to twelve months' imprisonment. (*The Herald*, 7 Jun. 1966.) On 16 Jun. 1966, Pat Puccini (two charges) and Christina Aitken (four charges) were each acquitted on all charges of assisting Ryan and Walker. (*The Age*, 17 Jun. 1966.) On 6 Sep. 1966, O'Reilly was acquitted on all four charges of assisting the escapees, knowing them to have escaped from lawful custody. (*The Age*, 7 Sep. 1966.) At the same trial, Hurley and Murray were acquitted of two charges of assisting, but the jury could not agree on two other charges and they were remanded to the Supreme Court of Victoria for retrial. (*ibid.*) On 21 Nov. 1966, Hurley and Murray were each convicted on two charges of having been 'an accessory after a felony', and each was sentenced to five years in prison with a minimum of four years to serve before being eligible for parole. (*The Age*, 22 Nov. 1966.)

67 Evidence of Senior Detective Harry Morrison, *RWTT*, 555.

68 Ian Grindlay, *op. cit.*, 7.

69 Peter Walker, interview, 12 Sep. 2001. The waking of Ryan and Walker would later become an issue for the Supreme Court when the trial judge became concerned that their sleep was being disturbed. A Pentridge investigation was subsequently mounted and the practice was stopped. (See Memorandum, chief prison officer HR Clark to governor, Pentridge, 'Report re the Waking of Prisoners Ryan and Walker each Half-Hour during their Trial', 9 Apr. 1966.)

70 A description of the escapees' imprisonment conditions after their recapture and return to Pentridge was given by the assistant governor of Pentridge, Bob Duffy, in evidence at Walker's trial for murder, in *WTT*, 357.

71 *Truth*, 8 Jan. 1966.

72 Tennison, *op. cit.*, 96.

Chapter Eleven: TRIAL [207–250]

1 Letter, Ronald Ryan to Cecilia Ryan, 24 Jan. 1966.

2 *The Age*, 5 Feb. 1966. (See also *IT*.)

3 (Emphasis in the original.) A transcript of evidence, with Ryan's extensive comments on it in his unmistakeable hand-writing, was sent anonymously to the writer in 1978. To this day, the identity of the sender is unknown.

4 Opas, *Throw Away My Wig*, 245.

5 *ibid.*, 240.

6 *ibid.*

7 Tennison, *op. cit.*, 117.

8 *ibid.*, 118.

9 *ibid.*, 119.

10 SEK Hulme 'Ryan judge a peerless advocate', *The Australian*, 24 Nov. 1994.

11 Starke related his period at Trinity College, including his youthful misdemeanours, in an interview with Jon Faine, *Taken on Oath*, 34–5.

12 *ibid.* In 1890, Argyle had been one of two students famously expelled from Trinity for their part in organising protests against the alleged maladministration of the warden, Dr Alexander Leeper. See AGL Shaw's entry for 'Argyle' in Bede Nairn and Geoffrey Serle (eds), *ADB*, *7*:92–4; and also JR Poynter's entry for 'Leeper' in *ADB*, *10*:54–7.

13 Hulme in his obituary of Starke, a shortened version of which was published as 'Ryan judge a peerless advocate', *The Australian*, 24 Nov. 1994.

14 See JD Merrall's entry for 'Hayden Starke' in John Ritchie (ed), *ADB*, *12*:53–4.

15 Hulme, *The Australian*, 24 Nov. 1994.

16 Hulme obituary of Starke, longer version, unpublished MS.

17 See KS Inglis, *The Stuart Case*, and Thomas Sidney Dixon, *The Wizard of Alice*, esp. 125–37.

18 See Creighton Burns, *The Tait Case.*

19 Quoted by Sir John Starke in his speech-in-reply before a gathering at his retirement from the Supreme Court, 29 Nov. 1985, Transcript of Speeches, Supreme Court of Victoria, 28. The quotation is drawn from James L High (ed), *Speeches of Lord Erskine, While at the Bar*, vol. I, 474–5. See also Lloyd Paul Stryker, *For The Defence.*

20 Sir John Starke, interview, 17 Dec. 1990.

21 *RWTT*, 1–19.

22 *The Age*, 16 Mar. 1966.

23 *RWTT*, 22; and *ibid.*

24 This story was told by the chairman of the Victorian Bar Council, Richard McGarvie, QC (later Justice McGarvie of the Supreme Court, and still later governor of Victoria) in his speech of welcome to Mr Justice Murray, as by then he had become, on his appointment to the Supreme Court of Victoria, 6 September 1974. (Transcript, Supreme Court library.)

25 *The Age*, 16 Mar. 1966.

26 *RWTT*, 467–8.

27 This argument was repeated by Opas in a letter to the chief secretary, Arthur Rylah, seeking mercy for Ryan after all appeals had failed. (PHN Opas to AG Rylah, 20 Oct. 1966.)

28 This was attested to by the prison officer who was the second in charge of the security section at Pentridge, William Kerley, *RWTT*,42; and Detective Senior Sergeant Colin Letherbarrow of the forensic ballistics section of the NSW CIB, *RWTT*, 469–70.

29 *RWTT*, 263–4.

30 Statement of witness Paterson, Exhibit R6, in *RWTT*, 816.

31 Statement of witness Paterson, Exhibit R7, in *RWTT*, 818.

32 *IT*, 43.
33 *RWTT*, 815.
34 *RWTT*, 818.
35 *IT*, 43.
36 *RWTT*, 486.
37 *RWTT*, 360–1.
38 *RWTT*, 444–6.
39 *RWTT*, 448.
40 *RWTT*, 448–9.
41 Ryan's statement forms Exhibit S in *RWTT*, 799.
42 *RWTT*, 532.
43 In fact, it was not the first time that Ryan had been before a court since his arrest. The day before, on 6 Jan. 1966, he and Walker had been brought before the Central Police Court to be charged with various weapons offences. Murray corrected the error for the record the next day. (See *RWTT*, 552–3.)
44 *RWTT*, 539.
45 Evidence of Senior Detective Harry Morrison, *RWTT*, 555.
46 Statement by Ronald Ryan at extradition proceedings, Sydney Magistrates Court, 7 Jan. 1966, (Exhibit U, *RWTT*, 803.)
47 *RWTT*, 556–7.
48 *RWTT*, 577–9.
49 *RWTT*, 585.
50 *RWTT*, 587–8.
51 *RWTT*, 588–9.
52 See Tennison, *op. cit.*, 148.
53 This comment was made by juryman Tom Gildea in August 1984 to Tom Prior, *A Knockabout Priest*, 158.
54 *RWTT*, 619.
55 *RWTT*, 619–22.
56 This is the argument advanced by criminologist Gordon Hawkins, *Beyond Reasonable Doubt*, 35–6.
57 *RWTT*, 632–4, 644–5.
58 This was, of course, almost exactly what Stella Opas had said to Phil.
59 Quoted in Tennison, *op. cit.*, 150–3.
60 *The Age*, 29 Mar. 1966.
61 *ibid.*
62 *RWTT*, 690–1.
63 *RWTT*, 694–6.
64 This was reported several years later by one of the jurymen to Tom Prior, *A Knockabout Priest*, 158.
65 *ibid.*
66 *RWTT*, 783.
67 *RWTT*, 783–4.
68 Jack Ayling, interview, 6 Jun. 1978. Ayling gives a slightly different

meaning to the gesture in his book, *Nothing But The Truth,* 196.

69 Peter Walker, interview, 14 Nov. 2001.

70 *RWTT*, 789.

71 Ayling, *op. cit.*, 196. Starke recalled Ryan patting Walker on the back—which he thought 'pretty gutsy'—in his interview with Faine, *op. cit.*, 53.

72 Sir John Starke, interview, 17 Dec. 1990.

73 *RWTT*, 789.

74 Although these words are not recorded in the transcript, they were reported by *The Age*, 31 Mar. 1966.

75 The words Justice Starke used in pronouncing the death sentence are not recorded in the transcript of the trial, merely being summarised as 'Sentence of death was then passed.' (*RWTT*, 789.) The words above were recalled by Starke in an interview with the writer on 17 Dec. 1990. Jack Ayling, *op. cit.*, 196 has a slightly different report of what Starke said.

76 Transcript of sentence hearing, *The Queen v. Peter John Walker*, 29 Apr. 1966, 9.

77 Philip Opas, QC, 'Reflections on Sir John Starke', *Victorian Bar News*, no. 92 (Autumn 1995), 21.

78 Peter Walker, interview, 14 Nov. 2001.

79 *ibid.*

80 *R. v. Ryan & Walker* (1966) *Victoria Reports*, 557.

81 *ibid.*, 569.

82 Transcript of sentence hearing, *The Queen v. Peter John Walker*, 5.

83 Memorandum, BL Murray, solicitor-general, to the attorney-general, 3 Nov. 1966. (Chief Secretary's Office, file 10788.)

84 Transcript of sentence hearing, *The Queen v. Peter John Walker*, 7.

85 Affidavit of GWA Douglas, public solicitor for Victoria, Application Book, *Ronald Joseph Ryan and The Queen*, High Court of Australia, 18 Jul. 1966, 13.

86 40 *ALJR* 326; *The Age*, 15 Oct. 1966.

87 See Burns, *op. cit.*

88 'Why is there to be a hanging?', 3. The Tait-substitute theory was first publicly advanced in this report by the Brotherhood of St Laurence in December 1966, although the theory itself had gained considerable currency by the time of the Brotherhood's publication. The special report was signed by four Brotherhood officials: the Rt Rev G Kennedy Tucker, chairman; the Rt Rev Geoffrey Sambell, Anglican co-adjutor Bishop of Melbourne, director; David Scott, associate director; and Miss Janet Paterson, director of research and social action. The report was later published in *The Herald*, 31 Dec. 1966. David Scott had figured in the Tait case as the applicant in the successful High Court injunction to stay Tait's hanging in October 1962.

89 John Westerman, interview, 12 May 1982.

Chapter Twelve: CABINET [pp 251–284]

1 Letter, Ronald Ryan to Cecilia Ryan and family, 6 December 1966.

2 Memorandum, R Glenister, secretary to the Law Department, 7 October 1966. VPS1100/P1/10.

3 *ibid.*

4 R Douglas and K Laster, 'A Matter of Life and Death: The Victorian Executive and the Decision to Execute 1842–1967', 146.

5 David Philips and Susanne Davies (eds), *A Nation of Rogues?*, 10.

6 Mark Finnane, *Punishment in Australian Society*, 128. See also Finnane, 'Capital Punishment' in Graeme Davison, John Hirst and Stuart Macintyre (eds), *The Oxford Companion to Australian History*, 109–10; and ARG Griffiths, 'Capital Punishment in South Australia, 1836–1964', 4.

7 Mark Finnane, *Punishment in Australian Society*, 129.

8 Barry Jones (ed), *The Penalty is Death*, 255–75; RN Barber and PR Wilson, '[The] Deterrent Aspect of Capital Punishment ...', 100–8. For a historical account of the discretionary nature of the use of the death penalty in one jurisdiction in the early part of this century, see Carolyn Strange 'Discretionary Justice ...' in Strange (ed), *Qualities of Mercy*.

9 Jones, *op. cit.*, 255–75; Barber and Wilson, *op. cit.*, 100–8.

10 See Peter Lynn and George Armstrong, *From Pentonville to Pentridge*, 206; and Kathy Laster 'Arbitrary Chivalry' in Philips and Davies, *op. cit.*, 168.

11 See Michael Cannon, *The Woman as Murderer*. Two young men executed had been eighteen years old and three had been nineteen years old. There may have been more but, prior to 1858, the official execution records—relating to 54 executed prisoners—did not register age.

12 See the entry for 'Percy Feltham' in Geoff Browne, *Biographical Register of the Victorian Parliament 1900–84*, 65–6. See also *Debates*, *280*:1304–5; Feltham reiterated his opposition to capital punishment after the cabinet decision on Ryan was taken. (See *The Sun*, 17 Jan. 1967).

13 For a discussion of the Stamps Bill and the balance-of-power situation in the Legislative Council, see AA Staley, 'Australian Political Chronicle, Sep.-Dec. 1966—Victoria', 112; and Peter Blazey, *Bolte*, 42.

14 Police report on Parslow by Detective First Constable BJ Ritchie to Superintendent, CIB, 20 Jul. 1966, forming part of cabinet papers for meeting of 12 Dec. 1966. The report is contained in Premier's Department file 66/2997.

15 Police report on Rosamilia by Sergeant JD Baker to Superintendent, 'A' District, 19 Aug. 1966, forming part of cabinet papers for meeting of 12 Dec. 1966. The report is contained in Premier's Department file 66/2996.

16 Sir John Williams, former chairman, managing director and editor-in-chief, The Herald & Weekly Times, interview, 22 Feb. 1979.

17 Graham Perkin, editor, *The Age*, interview, 16 Aug. 1968; Ranald Macdonald, managing director, David Syme & Co Ltd, publisher of *The Age*, interview, 28 Aug. 1968.

18 Graham Perkin (interview, 16 Aug. 1968) told the writer that Sir Henry

had told him of his intentions in these terms before the decision was taken. One of the reasons, Perkin believed, was the premier's annoyance at the editorial campaign by Melbourne newspapers during the Tait case.

19 Peter Brett, 'Conditional Pardons and the Commutation of Death Sentences', 144.

20 *The Age*, 2 Feb. 1966.

21 This view of cabinet's role was argued by the Victorian Law Reform Commissioner, and a former Supreme Court Justice, TW Smith, QC, in his report on executive commutation policy, *Law of Murder*, 21.

22 Letter, John Starke, judge of the Supreme Court to attorney-general, 31 March 1966. The letter is contained in Premier's Department file 66/2995.

23 The judge's summary and the judgment of the Court of Criminal Appeal are also in Premier's Department file 66/2995.

24 Memorandum, director of prisons, Eric Shade, to director-general of social welfare, Alec Whatmore, 15 Nov. 1966. Premier's Department file 66/2995.

25 Assessment by Pentridge prison psychiatrist Dr Allen A Bartholomew in a letter to the secretary, Law Department, 16 Nov. 1966, forming part of Premier's Department file 66/2995.

26 Letter, PHN Opas, QC to AG Rylah, 20 October 1966. There was no reply from Rylah to this letter from Opas. See file note, Chief Secretary's Office, 26 Jan. 1967, file 10788.

27 See file note, Chief Secretary's Office, 26 Jan. 1967, file 10788.

28 Memorandum, BL Murray, solicitor-general, to the attorney-general, 3 Nov. 1966. Chief Secretary's Office, file 10788.

29 Sue Campbell (née Murray) and Rick Campbell, Murray's son-in-law, personal communications, 26 Sep. 2000.

30 Memorandum, BL Murray, solicitor-general, to the attorney-general, 3 Nov. 1966. Chief Secretary's Office, file 10788.

31 Letter, Gloria Ryan to secretary (sic) general of social welfare, undated, forming part of Chief Secretary's Office file 10788.

32 Detective Sergeant KP Walters to Superintendent, CIB, 2 Aug. 1966. Premier's Department file 66/2995.

33 The police report drew upon the letter of Detective Sergeant Noel Morey, safe squad, CIB, NSW Police to Detective Sergeant KP Walters, homicide squad, CIB, Victoria Police, 27 Jul. 1966.

34 KP Walters to Superintendent, CIB, 2 Aug. 1966. Premier's Department file 66/2995.

35 Memorandum, Henry Bolte, premier, to His Excellency the Governor of Victoria, 12 Dec. 1966. Premier's Department file 66/2996.

36 Memorandum, Henry Bolte, premier, to His Excellency the Governor of Victoria, 12 Dec. 1966. Premier's Department file 66/2997.

37 From the earliest times of Victorian government, judges were summoned to attend cabinet. The practice was set in place at the time of governor Sir Charles Hotham in December 1855. Article eighteen of Hotham's

commission instructed him 'to call upon the Judge presiding at the trial of any such offender who may from time to time be condemned to suffer death, by any sentence of any Court within the said Colony, to make to you a written report of the case of such offender, and such report of the said Judge shall by you be taken into consideration at the first meeting thereafter, which may be conveniently held, of Our said Executive Council, where the said Judge shall be specially summoned to attend …' (Governor's Commission and Instructions, 20 Dec. 1855, 4.)

Some critics argued that this instruction was illegal because it was contrary to the principles of responsible government enshrined in the Victorian Constitution Act of 1855. The former Victorian liberal politician George Higinbotham was one such critic. When, in 1880, he was invited to accept appointment as a judge of the Supreme Court of Victoria, Higinbotham wrote to the premier about the royal instruction mandating attendance at Executive Council in capital cases, claiming that the Queen had no power to issue this instruction. Higinbotham indicated that, if he was appointed, he would 'officially and openly refuse to comply…' (Gwyneth M Dow, 'Higinbotham', in Douglas Pike [ed], *ADB*, 394.) Four years later, in May 1884, after sentencing a man to death for murder at Warrnambool, Justice Higinbotham refused to report to the Executive Council pursuant to the vice-regal summons, but indicated he would attend if requested to do so by 'lawful authority'—that is, by Her Majesty's ministers for Victoria. The attorney-general for Victoria duly made such a request, and Higinbotham complied. (Edward E Morris, *A Memoir of George Higinbotham*, 199–200.)

38 It is instructive to consider the British experience in this regard because, although the process there was a little different, no separation-of-powers issue arose. Until 1965, when capital punishment was abolished in the United Kingdom, consideration of commutation was not a cabinet decision but the responsibility of the home secretary alone. In coming to his decision, however, the home secretary would frequently interview the trial judge in a capital case. (Viscount Templewood [home secretary 1937–39], *The Shadow of the Gallows*, 56.)

39 In the first of my two lengthy interviews with him, which took place four years before he died in November 1994, Sir John Starke greeted me upon my arrival at his house with the anguished question: 'Do you think I did the right thing on Ryan?' Puzzled, I replied: 'Judge, what do you mean?' Starke then poured out his anxiety about the moral dilemma he had faced in going to cabinet on 12 Dec. 1966, and related in detail his thoughts as he approached the cabinet room and his responses to ministers' questions, as well as the way in which he had framed in his mind the lie he had contemplated telling when in the cabinet room. At the second interview, Starke corrected my draft of his attendance at cabinet, and elaborated upon this and other issues. As a judge invited to the cabinet room, Starke was not bound by an oath of secrecy in respect of

deliberations in his presence. (Sir John Starke, interviews, 23 Nov. 1990 and 17 Dec. 1990.)

40 Bloomfield later made the comment to Starke. (*ibid.*)
41 Blazey, *op. cit.*, 83. (See also Muir *op. cit.*, 178–87.)
42 *ibid*, 80.
43 Burns, *op. cit.*, 52.
44 *The Argus*, 12 Dec. 1950.
45 Letter, JW Westerman to AG Rylah, 12 Dec. 1966. Also John Westerman, interview, 27 Aug. 1968. Rylah later advised Westerman that he had placed his letter before his Cabinet colleagues. (Letter, AG Rylah to JW Westerman, 14 Dec. 1966.)
46 *Truth*, 25 Dec. 1965.
47 *Truth*, 1 Jan. 1966. (Emphasis in the original.)
48 *Debates*, *249*:4937.
49 *ibid.*, *258*:810.
50 *Debates*, 19 for 1975 (23 Apr. 1975), 5262.
51 *Debates*, *271*:410.
52 Vernon Wilcox, *Minister of the Crown*, 82–3, 153–4.
53 Sir Rupert Hamer indicated his conversion to an abolitionist position in a commentary he wrote upon a manuscript by Michael Cannon, subsequently published as Appendix C to Cannon, *The Woman as Murderer*, 229.
54 *Debates*, *258*:796–7.
55 *ibid. 280*:1849.
56 *Debates*, no. 13 for 1975. (4 Mar. 1975), 3820.
57 See Meagher's contribution to the parliamentary debate on the abolition bill of 1975 in *Debates*, no. 15 for 1975. (19 March 1975), 4296.
58 *The Age*, 13 Sep. 1955.
59 See Blazey, *op. cit.*, 80.
60 *The Age*, 12 Jul. 1967.
61 Barry Jones (interview, 22 May 1968) and John Westerman (interview, 27 Aug. 1968) both regarded Bloomfield as an abolitionist.
62 Barry Jones says that Bloomfield himself had told him of his strong opposition to Mede's hanging. (Barry Jones, interview, 22 May 1968.)
63 Burns, *op. cit.*, 51.
64 *Debates*, *267*:365.
65 *ibid.*, 592.
66 Burns, *op. cit.*, 42.
67 Barry Jones (ed), *op. cit.*, 263.
68 *The Age*, 5 Sep. 1962. (See also Blazey, *op. cit.*, 57, 79, 99.) Warner died in Apr. 1966. (See *The Age*, 4 Apr. 1966.)
69 Burns, *op. cit.*, 50; and Memorandum, R Glenister, secretary to the Law Department, 7 October 1966. (See also Blazey, *op. cit.*, 79–80.)
70 Figures are drawn from the Chief Secretary's Office file 10788.
71 *Debates*, *255–7*:1593–6; also quoted in Burns, *op. cit.*, 53–4.

72 This passage owes a debt to the observations of the premier by Brian Buckley, *The Bulletin*, 15 Jul. 1967.
73 Two statutory declarations sworn on the fifteenth and nineteenth of November 1962 respectively. The declarations were alluded to, and a brief passage quoted from them, in *Nation*, 2 Apr. 1967. The full text of the declarations was included in the manuscript of Creighton Burns' account of the Tait case, but—on legal advice to the publisher, Melbourne University Press—excised from the published book. (See Burns, *op. cit.*, 159.)
74 Hamer, comments in Cannon, *op. cit.*, 228.
75 Letter, Ronald Ryan to Dianne Everett, 30 Dec. 1965.
76 Memorandum, Henry Bolte, premier, to governor of Victoria, 12 Dec. 1966, Premier's Department file 66/2995.
77 Wilcox, *op. cit.*, 83.
78 Death Warrant, 12 Dec. 1966, Entered in the Register of Licences, Book No. 30, page 297, Chief Secretary's Department, file 10788.
79 Quoted by Grindlay, *op. cit.*, 5.
80 Letter, Ronald Ryan to Cecilia Ryan and Family, 13 Dec. 1966.

Chapter Thirteen: APPEAL [pp 285–310]

1 *The Herald*, 12 Dec. 1966.
2 Barry Jones would later become widely known as a state Labor MP and, even later, as a federal Labor MP, minister in the Hawke government, and national president of the Australian Labor Party.
3 *The Herald*, 13 Dec. 1966.
4 *ibid.*
5 *The Sun*, 14 Dec. 1966; *The Age*, 15 Dec. 1966.
6 *The Herald*, 14 Dec. 1966. Later press comment would wrongly claim that as many as seven ministers opposed the decision. A column in *The Bulletin*, for example, claimed that seven of the fifteen members of cabinet had 'privately dissociated themselves from the hanging decision: Chief Secretary Rylah and Ministers Thompson, Bloomfield, Rossiter, Porter, Hamer and Manson.' (See *The Bulletin*, 7 Jan. 1967). This claim gained some currency in journalistic circles and was elsewhere repeated in print.
7 Muir confirmed to the writer that the substance of the cabinet meeting was leaked to him. (Barry Muir, interview, 28 Oct. 1968.) Though Muir's story suggested that there was an actual vote, Muir has told the writer that the implication was unintended: he did not know whether or not a formal vote, as such, had been taken.
8 File note, Alex Coulthard, 15 Dec. 1966, Premier's Department file 66/2995.
9 Minutes of the Anti-Hanging Committee (Victoria), 20 Nov. 1962, 5.
10 Geoff Browne, *op. cit.*, 53.
11 See Michael Shmith, 'Revealed: the secret of the Colditz Seven', *The*

Sunday Age, 28 May 2000.

12 Members and sponsors of the anti-hanging committee included Professor Rod Andrew, dean of the faculty of medicine, Monash University; Bishop Felix Arnott, Coadjutor Bishop of Melbourne; Maurice Ashkanasy, QC; Captain Sam Benson, MHR; Harold Blair, Aboriginal singer; Professor Joe Bornstein, professor of biochemistry, Monash University; Dame Mabel Brookes; Reverend Will Clay, formerly president, Church of Christ in Victoria; Janet, Lady Clunies-Ross, senior tutor in criminology, University of Melbourne; Professor Zelman Cowen, professor of law and dean of the faculty of law, University of Melbourne; William Dargie, artist; Austin Dowling, teacher and social worker; Dr Andrew Fabinyi, publishing director of FW Cheshire; Professor Kathleen Fitzpatrick, associate professor of history, University of Melbourne; Professor Doug Gasking, professor of philosophy, University of Melbourne; Roy Grounds, architect; Rosemary Hanbury, school teacher; David Hirt, Melbourne University theology student, and former secretary, student's anti-hanging committee; Stanley Johnston, senior lecturer in criminology, University of Melbourne; Mick Jordan, secretary, Melbourne Trades Hall Council; Sir Peter MacCallum, director, Peter MacCallum Clinic; Richard McGarvie, QC; Dr Noel McLachlan, senior lecturer in history, University of Melbourne; David Martin, author; Professor Hector Monro, professor of philosophy, Monash University; Dr Stephen Murray-Smith, reader in education, University of Melbourne; Prue Myer, philanthropist; Cr Peter Norris, solicitor; Jan Paterson, director of social research and action at the Brotherhood of St Laurence; Rev Gordon Powell, Minister, Scots Church, Melbourne; John Ridley, president, National Union of Australian University Students; Myra Roper, author and lecturer; John Ryan, senior lecturer in mathematics, University of Melbourne; Geoffrey Sambell, Anglican Coadjutor Bishop of Melbourne; David Scott, associate director, Brotherhood of St. Laurence; Frank Sedgman, former Australian tennis champion and Davis Cup player; Ken Stone, assistant secretary, Melbourne Trades Hall Council; Clive Stoneham, MLA, leader of the state Labor opposition; Rev John Westerman, president, Methodist Church of Victoria and Tasmania Conference; and Rev Dr Harold Wood, principal, Methodist Ladies College.

13 Minutes of the Anti-Hanging Committee (Victoria); see also *The Age*, 15 Dec. 1966, 27.

14 It has previously been thought that the Salvation Army's reluctance to oppose the hanging reflected the organisation's sensitivity to the incident in which the Salvation Army chaplain at Pentridge had been clubbed by Ryan during the course of the escape. In fact, the reason was that the Salvation Army's territorial commander for southern Australia, commissioner Hubert Scotney, was a supporter of capital punishment. In a handwritten letter he wrote to the premier later in the case, Scotney said that 'there are some who are abusing you just now, but I am one religious

leader who would like to commend you for resolutely adhering to duty and principle rather than taking the easier road of expediency.' (Letter, Hubert Scotney to Sir Henry Bolte, 26 Jan. 1967, 'Correspondence File–Premier's Office–Ronald Joseph Ryan–Death Sentence', file 66/2995c.)

15 Letter, Barry Jones to Sir Henry Bolte, 17 Dec. 1966.

16 Letter, Sir Henry Bolte to Barry Jones, 19 Dec. 1966.

17 PHN Opas to Sir Rohan Delacombe, 12 Dec. 1966.

18 Sir Rohan Delacombe to PHN Opas, 19 Dec. 1966.

19 PHN Opas to the Archbishop of Melbourne (Dr Frank Woods), 6 Jan. 1967.

20 Memorandum, Jack Colquhoun, official secretary to the governor of Victoria, Sir Rohan Delacombe, 16 Dec. 1966. VPS 1100/P1/10.

21 Press release, 21 Dec. 1966, initialled by Alex Coulthard, secretary, Premier's Department, file 66/2995.

22 Letter, Ronald Ryan to Cecilia Ryan, 22 Dec. 1966.

23 *ibid.* The passage from Edward Fitzgerald's 1859 translation of *The Rubáiyát of Omar Khayyám* (first edn, 37) is: 'Unborn Tomorrow and dead Yesterday, Why fret about them if Today be sweet.'

24 In 1937, the English author and MP Edward Marjoribanks had wrongly asserted that Deeming was hanged while argument in his appeal before the Judicial Committee of the Privy Council was being heard. (See Edward Marjoribanks, *For The Defence*, 37–8.) In fact, Deeming's appeal had been dismissed on 19 May 1892, and he was executed on 23 May 1892. The story was put right in 1949 by PA Jacobs, *A Lawyer Tells*, 146–7, but it did not prevent the false claim being repeated by *The Herald*, 18 Jul. 1950. The story of Deeming and its falsity were referred to by Mr Justice Barry in *Ryan v. Attorney-General for Victoria*, *Victoria Reports* (1967), 518.

25 *The Age*, 24 Dec. 1966.

26 *ibid.*

27 Quoted in Prior, *A Knockabout Priest*, 150.

28 *ibid.*, 151.

29 *ibid.*

30 Brosnan, interview, 31 Mar. 2001.

31 In 1976, McGarvie was appointed a judge of the Supreme Court of Victoria. In 1992, he was appointed governor of Victoria, serving until his retirement in 1997.

32 Prior, *op. cit.*, 158. (See also *The Herald*, 23 Jan. 1967.)

33 Richard McGarvie, QC, interview, 27 Sep. 1968.

34 There is some doubt about exactly how many jurors signed a petition supporting clemency for Ryan. Tom Gildea has said that seven jurors signed a petition (Prior [1985], *op cit.*, 158). McGarvie has said he spoke only with six jurors. (Interview, 27 Sep. 1968.) However, the governor's Capital Case files disclose only four petitions having been received by

governor Sir Rohan Delacombe. Whether that reflects incomplete files, or indicates that some jurors agreed to support the petition but did not then follow through, is uncertain.

35 Petition, Thomas Patrick Gildea to Sir Rohan Delacombe, 28 Dec. 1966. (VPS 1100/P1/10.) See also petitions of Murphy, Dunn and Hannaford.

36 In the course of extensive interviews with journalist Tom Prior years later, Bolte said: 'The thing which people always seem to forget is that neither the Tait nor Ryan juries gave recommendations for mercy; if they had, it is unlikely there would have been any real chance of them being hanged.' (Prior, *Bolte by Bolte*, 166.)

37 Note from governor, Sir Rohan Delacombe, to chief secretary, 30 Dec. 1966. Chief Secretary's Office, file no. 10788.

38 Ralph Freadman's memoir of the case, 'A lawyer's work' in Anne Freadman, *The Green Tarpaulin*, 17.

39 *ibid.*

40 *Ryan v. Attorney-General for Victoria, Victoria Reports* (1967), 519–20; *The Age*, 31 Dec. 1966.

41 Minutes no. 1 of the State Executive Council, (4 Jan. 1967), 1.

42 Note for file initialled by Alex Coulthard, secretary, Premier's Department, 4 Jan. 1967, Premier's Department file 66/2995; and 'H Division Diary', Pentridge, entry for 4 Jan. 1967. The 'Diary', covering the period 1 Jan. 1967 to 31 Jul. 1971, is an official record of visits and non-routine events in H Division kept by the division's chief prison officer.

43 'H Division Diary', 4 Jan. 1967.

44 PHN Opas, *op. cit.*, 255.

45 Prior (1985), *op. cit.*, 150; Keith Willey, *Tales of the Big Country*, 50.

46 *The Australia Act 1986*, and reciprocal legislation by the United Kingdom Parliament, together called The Australia Acts 1986, abolished Privy Council appeals and other residual constitutional links with the UK. (See also David Marr, *Barwick*, 219.)

47 Letter, Ronald Ryan to Cecilia Ryan, 19 Jan. 1967.

48 See *The Herald*, 18 Jul. 1950.

49 *The Attorney-General of NSW v. Bertrand* in *Law Reports* (1867) (Privy Council Appeals), vol. 1, 530.

50 *Re Dillet, Law Reports* (Appeal Cases), vol. XII, 467.

51 *Balmukand and others v. The King-Emperor* (1915) Indian Appeals, vol. 42, 133.

52 In 1985, Gatehouse was appointed a judge of the UK High Court, Queen's Bench Division where—as Sir Robert Gatehouse—he served until his retirement in 1996.

53 *Who Was Who, 1971–1980* (Vol. VII), 660.

54 *Who Was Who, 1981–1990* (Vol. VIII), 357.

55 *ibid.*, 585.

56 *Who's Who 2001*, 2226.

57 *Who Was Who, 1971–1980* (Vol. VII), 614.

58 Petition of Ronald Joseph Ryan in *Ryan and The Queen*, Privy Council, London, 23 Jan. 1967, 4.
59 *ibid.*
60 *ibid.*, 5. (See also PHN Opas, *op. cit.*, 258.)
61 A summary of the arguments for the applicant and the respondent, together with a summary of the relevant cases, survive in the Capital Case file of the Office of Public Prosecutions at the Public Records Office, Victoria.
62 *Muhammad Nawaz v. The King-Emperor* (1941) *Indian Appeals*, vol. 68, 126.
63 *The Age,* 24 Jan. 1967; *The Times,* 24 Jan. 1967.
64 Minute of the Privy Council hearing, Privy Council Office, 23 Jan. 1967.
65 *The Age,* 24 Jan. 1967.
66 'H Division Diary', entry for 24 Jan. 1967.
67 Archbishop Dr Frank Woods to His Excellency The Governor of Victoria, 24 Jan. 1967. (Governor's Capital Case files, VPS 1100/P1/10.)
68 The premier's advice to the governor is set out in a note Delacombe penned to his official secretary, Jack Colquhoun, dated '11:20AM, 24th Jan..' Under three headings, Delacombe summarised the reasons the premier had advised him to give to Woods as to why he should not grant the interview requested. Delacombe also gave instructions to Colquhoun to liaise with Alex Coulthard, secretary of the Premier's Department, in the preparation of a letter of response for his signature. (Note, Sir Rohan Delacombe to Jack Colquhoun, 24 Jan. 1967, Governor 's Capital Case files, VPS 1100/P1/10.)
69 Letter, Sir Rohan Delacombe to Archbishop, Dr Frank Woods, 24 Jan. 1967. (Governor 's Capital Case files, VPS 1100/P1/10.)
70 The ten signatures were those of the Most Rev Dr Frank Woods, Anglican Archbishop of Melbourne; the Rev Norman Faichney, president, Victorian Council of Churches; the Rev G Bucknall, moderator, Presbyterian Assembly of Victoria; Professor R Anderson, convenor, Church and Nation Committee, Presbyterian Church; the Rev J Westerman, president, Methodist Church of Victoria and Tasmania; the Rev M Holly, chairman, Public Questions Committee, Baptist Union of Victoria; the Rev W Atkins, secretary, Church of Christ Department of Social Service; the Rev J Davies, president, Congregational Union of Victoria; Mr A Walker, Society of Friends; and Rabbi Dr I Rapaport, chief minister, Melbourne Hebrew Congregation.
71 See *The Herald,* 23 Jan. 1967.
72 Sidney Silverman, MP, to Sir Henry Bolte, 28 Dec. 1966. (See also *The Herald,* 16 Jan. 1967.)
73 Silverman's Murder (Abolition of Death Penalty) Bill was passed by the Commons at its second reading on 21 Dec. 1964, and finally enacted into law on 9 Nov. 1965. In a letter to Barry Jones after the hanging, the Secretary of the British Campaign Against Capital Punishment, Jim Little,

confirmed that dozens of letters had been sent from Britain. (Jim Little to Barry Jones, Apr. 1967.)

74 *Minutes* no. 5 of the State Executive Council (25 Jan. 1967), 127.
75 *The Sun*, 26 Jan. 1967.
76 'H Division Diary', entry for 25 Jan. 1967.
77 *ibid.*

Chapter Fourteen: PROTEST [pp 311–329]

1 Quoted in *The Age TV-Radio Guide*, 2 Feb. 1967.
2 Bolte in Prior (1990), *op. cit.*, 164.
3 Kevin Sanders, journalist/commentator, Channel Nine, interview, 5 Jul. 1968.
4 Rick Campbell, personal communication, 26 Sep. 2000.
5 The Morgan organisation would conduct a poll of public opinion within ten days showing support for the death penalty in Victoria at 44 per cent, opposition at 42 per cent, and undecideds at 14 per cent. (APOP Poll, no. 188, 4 Feb. 1967.)
6 See *The Sun*, 31 Jan. 1967.
7 See, for example, the page one story in the next day's *Sun*, 28 Jan. 1967.
8 Bolte himself tells this story and relates the words Packer used in Prior (1990) *op. cit.*, 164.
9 *The Herald*, 24 Jan. 1967.
10 *ibid.*
11 *The Herald*, 27 Jan. 1967.
12 *The Australian*, 30 Jan. 1967.
13 *The Sun*, 30 Jan. 1967.
14 Muir, *op. cit.*, 94.
15 Senior Detective LB Stanley, Special Branch, to Officer-in-Charge, CIB Special Branch, 27 Jan. 1967. Further discussion of the threatening letters and their subsequent investigation by the Special Branch is contained in a series of memos held in 'Hanging of Ronald Joseph Ryan—Confidential papers', Chief Secretary's Office, file no. 10800. Several years later, Sir Henry claimed for the first time that a bomb had been found by police in the back garden of his apartment in Queens Road, Melbourne, but that he had urged the police not to disclose the fact, fearing that the publicity might encourage other attempts. (See Blazey, *op. cit.*, 132.) No reference to such an incident appears on the above file relating to police and special branch activities associated with the Ryan case.
16 Telegram, [Murray] Tyrell, official secretary to the governor general, to official secretary to the governor of Victoria, 27 Jan. 1967 .
17 Governor's Commission and Royal Instructions, 20 Dec. 1855.
18 John Bow had been sentenced to death for his part in one of Australia's most famous gold robberies. This was the armed hold-up by a gang of eight bushrangers on 15 Jul. 1862 of a gold escort at Eugowra, in central-west NSW, and the theft of £14,000 in gold and cash. (*SMH*, 17–21 Jul.

1862.) Although shots were fired at the coach and police escort, and several of the escort sustained gunshot wounds, no one was killed. Four of the bushrangers were subsequently arrested, charged with robbery and wounding, and brought to trial. After a first trial at which the jury could not agree, they were re-tried at a Special Criminal Commission presided over by the chief justice of the Supreme Court of NSW, Sir Alfred Stephen, sitting in Sydney.

The three-day trial of the Escort Robbers, as they came to be known, in February 1863 received extraordinary coverage in *The Sydney Morning Herald*, and there was wide public interest in the case. On 26 February, the jury returned verdicts of guilty against Bow and two of his co-defendants, Henry Manns and Alexander Fordyce, and sentences of death were pronounced by the chief justice. The fourth, defendant John Macquire, was acquitted of the charge but detained on a lesser charge. (*SMH*, 24–27 Feb. 1863.) On 2 March 1863, the NSW Executive Council determined that Bow's sentence of death should be carried into effect, along with that of Manns, while Fordyce had his sentence commuted to life imprisonment at hard labour. (*SMH*, 7 Mar. 1863.) The date of the execution of Bow and Manns was set for 26 March.

In the three-week period leading up to the scheduled date for the execution, lawyers and politicians vigorously took up the cases of the condemned men. Bow's case, in particular, was the subject of spirited representation on the principal ground that he had been convicted solely upon the uncorroborated evidence of an accomplice, who had been induced to give evidence on the basis of a public promise of a free pardon—and hence had breached a standard of proof that had been adopted for many years in the English courts as the practice in relation to the evidence of accomplices. Several petitions for clemency for Bow and Manns were raised (14,071 people signed one of the petitions in Sydney in less than 48 hours), and deputations were received by the governor, Sir John Young, who was reportedly 'considerably affected' by Bow's plight. (*SMH*, 26 Mar. 1863.) Bow was just twenty years old and had no prior convictions.

Following a meeting with a deputation of members of parliament and others on 25 March 1863, the day before the scheduled hanging, Young over-ruled the 2 March decision of his Executive Council and exercised the royal prerogative of mercy to commute Bow's death sentence to a term of life imprisonment. However, he declined to extend a reprieve to Manns, arguing that the circumstances of his case distinguished it from Bow's. (*ibid.*) Manns, aged 23, was executed as scheduled the next day at Darlinghurst gaol, in a hanging that was botched. Owing to the hangman's 'miserable mistakes', Mann's 'dying agonies were needlessly prolonged.' (*SMH*, 27 Mar. 1863.) (See also the entry for 'Sir John Young' in Bede Nairn [ed], *ADB, 6*:456.)

19 See, for example, the open letter to Sir John Young by James Martin, QC,

who had defended Bow and the Escort Robbers in their first court appearance, in the *SMH*, 24 Mar. 1863.

20 The royal instructions asserting a governor's discretion in relation to the royal prerogative of mercy continued through successive appointments to the position of governor in the latter half of the nineteenth century. In 1887, the discretion was stigmatised as 'a glaring instance of … flagrant illegality' by the chief justice of the Supreme Court of Victoria, George Higinbotham, who pursued a vigorous correspondence about it with the secretary of state for the colonies, Lord Knutsford. Higinbotham argued that, with responsible government in Victoria, Executive Council decisions on all domestic matters had to be made upon, and in accordance with, the advice of ministers of the Crown. (Morris, *op. cit.*, 216.) The royal instructions were subsequently revised in 1892, omitting this provision. See also Gwyneth M Dow,'Higinbotham', in Douglas Pike (ed), *ADB*, 4:394; and Zelman Cowen, 'A Historical Survey of the Victorian Constitution, 1856 to 1956', 27.

21 Ralph Freadman to Sir Rohan Delacombe, 25 Jan. 1967. (Governor's Capital Case files, VPS 1100/P1/10.)

22 See, for example, Inglis A Clark, *Australian Constitutional Law*, 258–9; HV Evatt, *The Royal Prerogative*, 117–19.

23 Quoted in Memorandum, Jack Colquhoun, official secretary to the governor of Victoria, Sir Rohan Delacombe, 16 Dec. 1966. VPS 1100/P1/10.

24 Memorandum, Jack Colquhoun, official secretary to the governor of Victoria, to the secretary, Premier's Department, 27 Jan. 1967. Premier's Department file 66/2995.

25 Letter, Betty Kemp to Sir Rohan Delacombe, 27 Jan. 1967. Letter in the Capital Case file, Office of the Governor, Public Records Office, VPS 1100/P1/10.

26 Betty Kemp's foray into the Ryan case was consistent with her social policy outlook, generally. She was, for example, active for many years in the Aboriginal Advancement League. (Personal communication, Rod Kemp, 3 Dec. 2000.)

27 Letter, Cecilia Ryan to Sir Henry Bolte, 27 Jan. 1967. Copy in Premier's Department file 66/2995.

28 Memorandum, Thomas F Mornane, crown solicitor, to secretary, Premier's Department, 27 Jan. 1967 in Premier's Department file 66/2995.

29 Letter, AG Coulthard, secretary, Premier's Department, to Mrs C Ryan, 27 Jan. 1967 in *ibid.*

30 *The Age*, 28 Jan. 1967.

31 'Correspondence File—Premier's Office—Ronald Joseph Ryan—Death Sentence', file 66/2995c.

32 Bishop Arthur Fox to Sir Henry Bolte, 28 Jan. 1967. A copy of the letter was sent to the governor of Victoria. (Capital Case file, Office of the Governor, Public Records Office, VPS 1100/P1/10.)

33 *The Age*, 30 Jan. 1967.
34 Sir John Williams, interview, 22 Feb. 1979.
35 Les Tanner, cartoonist/art director, *The Bulletin*, interview 16 May 1968; Peter Samuel, journalist, *The Bulletin*, interview, 19 Aug. 1968.
36 *The Bulletin* (first edition) 4 Feb. 1967.
37 Les Tanner, interview, 16 May 1968; Peter Samuel, interview, 19 Aug. 1968.
38 Michael Crewdson, producer, *Watch This Space*, ABC Television, interviews, 14 October and 26 October 1968.
39 *The Age*, 28 Jan. 1967. Dixon was virtually ostracised by Liberal colleagues for many weeks after the case. (Brian Dixon, interview, 8 Aug. 1968.) Dixon was later to reiterate his views when voting to support the abolition of capital punishment in Apr. 1975. Speaking in debate on the bill, Dixon declared: 'I believe there are no circumstances in which hanging is justified.' (See *Debates*, no. 15 for 1975 [19 Mar. 1975], 4309.)
40 Tony Hill, *The Herald's* state political reporter, interview, 27 Sep. 1968. Dixon survived the wrath of the premier, but was not appointed to cabinet until after Bolte's successor, Dick Hamer, took office in 1972. Dixon subsequently held the portfolios of Youth, Sport and Recreation; Housing; and Social Welfare.
41 Brian Dixon, interview, 8 Aug. 1968.
42 *The Herald*, 28 Jan. 1967.
43 Alan Hunt later served as a minister in the Hamer and Thompson Liberal governments from 1971–82. Hunt, a solicitor, consistently spoke against capital punishment both inside and outside the house. Although he voted with the government following debate on Jack Galbally's many private member's bills to abolish capital punishment, he once began a speech with the words; 'I regard the whole concept of capital punishment ... with the most deep-rooted repugnance.' (*Debates*, vol. 267, 606.) In debate on Dick Hamer's 1975 bill to abolish capital punishment, Hunt again spoke strongly in support of abolition. (See *Debates*, no. 15 for 1975 [8 Apr. 1975], 4710, and no. 19 for 1975 [23 Apr. 1975], 5185–6, and 5275.) At the time of the Hamer Abolition Bill of 1975, Ian McLaren was deputy speaker in the Legislative Assembly and did not speak on the bill, although he ultimately voted to support it. Murray Byrne was later minister for state development and decentralisation in the Hamer government until his retirement in March 1976. At the time of the Hamer Abolition Bill in 1975, Byrne was leader of the government in the Legislative Council. Introducing the second reading speech on the bill in that chamber, Byrne paid warm tribute to Jack Galbally, who had unsuccessfully moved on 21 occasions in as many years to have the death penalty abolished. Byrne went on to support the Hamer bill in a free vote. (*Debates*, no. 18 for 1975 [15 Apr. 1975], 4885–9.)
44 This analysis is contained in an undated and unsigned document entitled 'In Re Ronald Joseph Ryan deceased'. The document forms part of the

Governor's Capital Case file VPS 1100/P1/10. From its character and style, it is likely that it was an internal document of the Premier's Department, possibly in the premier's press office, that was created several days after the execution, and forwarded as a copy to the governor.

45 Ranald Macdonald, interview, 28 Aug. 1968.
46 Graham Perkin, interview, 16 Aug. 1968
47 *ibid.*; Ranald Macdonald, interview, 28 Aug. 1968.
48 Ranald Macdonald, interview, 28 Aug. 1968.
49 *The Age*, 28 Jan. 1967.
50 The visits to Ryan at Pentridge and the special permissions required are recorded in the 'H Division Diary', entry for 27 Jan. 1967.
51 'H Divison Diary', entry for 28 Jan. 1967.
52 Keith Johanson, 'A Condemned Man's Doubt—And a Book', 1.
53 'H Divison Diary', entry for 28 Jan. 1967.
54 Prior (1985) *op. cit.*, 152.
55 *ibid.*; 'H Division Diary', entry for 29 Jan. 1967.

Chapter Fifteen: REPRIEVE [pp 331–367]

1 Statement by Verna Dicker taken from transcript of evidence in the case of *The Police v. John Henry Tolmie*, Court of Petty Sessions, Melbourne, 16 Feb. 1967, 1. This transcript is hereinafter cited as *TDT*.
2 Statement by Lynne Opas in *ibid.*, 5.
3 Statement of Ross Ponti, forming Attachment A to the affidavit sworn by Ralph Freadman at Melbourne on 30 Jan. 1967.
4 Dorothy Ryan, interviews, 1978–1980; *The Age*, 30 Jan. 1967.
5 *The Sun*, 30 Jan. 1967; *The Age*, 30 Jan. 1967.
6 Statement of Liberato Donato, forming Attachment A to the affidavit sworn by Paul Guest at Melbourne on 30 Jan. 1967.
7 Letter, Ronald Ryan to Dorothy Ryan, 29 Jan. 1967.
8 'H Division Diary', entry for 29 Jan. 1967.
9 John Ryan, interviews, 9 Aug. and 18 Oct. 1968; and Janette Ryan, interview, 3 Jul. 2000. (See also Paul Ormonde, *The Age*, 1 Feb. 1997, and his obituary of John Ryan, *The Age*, 18 May 2000.)
10 Statement by John Ryan taken from *TDT*, 6.
11 Affidavit by John Henry Tolmie in the Matter of Ronald Joseph Ryan, sworn at Melbourne, 30 Jan. 1967. According to the chief of the homicide squad, Detective Inspector Frank Holland, the Patterson referred to by Tolmie identifies a prison officer named who had worked at Pentridge in the past; he was not stationed there on 19 Dec. 1965, but at the Morwell River prison in south-eastern Victoria. The confusion between Robert Paterson at Pentridge and prison officer Patterson at Morwell River would frequently occur through this case, if only in the misspelling of Robert Paterson's name.
12 Ralph Freadman, 'A lawyer's work', in Anne Freadman, *op. cit.*, 19.
13 Statement by Geoffrey Mander-Jones taken from *TDT*, 14.

14 Statement by Barry Jones in *ibid.*, 12; Ralph Freadman in Anne Freadman, *op. cit.*, 19; and statement by Geoffrey Mander-Jones in *TDT*, 15. The affidavit later was held to be validly sworn, despite the absence of the Bible.
15 Affidavit by Ralph Freadman in the Matter of Ronald Joseph Ryan, 30 Jan. 1967; and affidavit by Paul Guest in the Matter of Ronald Joseph Ryan, 30 Jan. 1967
16 Interview, Sir John Starke, 17 Dec. 1990; Richard Searby, personal communication, 9 Aug. 2000.
17 Starke related the detail of this incident at the racecourse in interview, 17 Dec. 1990.
18 Ron Syme, personal communication, 3 Aug. 2000.
19 'H Division Diary', 30 Jan. 1967.
20 Prior (1985) *op. cit.*, 153.
21 Brosnan, interview, 31 Mar. 2001.
22 The details of this conversation between Ryan and Grindlay, and subsequent action taken by Grindlay, is narrated in his memoirs, *Behind Bars*, 10. Grindlay confirmed the incident to the writer in interviews, 14 Jul. and 19 Jul. 1978. Drawing upon the recollections of both Brosnan and Grindlay, Prior (1985), *op. cit.*, also relates the incident in similar terms, 153–7.
23 Grindlay, *op. cit.*, 10.
24 In 1977, Jockey Smith was convicted of the attempted murder of a Sydney detective, and spent fifteen years in prison for that offence. Released in 1992, he was shot and killed by police on 5 December 1992 in a shootout following a stolen-car inquiry. At the time of his death he was described by police as one of Australia's most ruthless and dangerous criminals. (See *SMH*, 7 Dec. 1992; *The Sunday Age*, 13 Dec. 1992.)
25 Prior (1985), *op. cit.*, 155. In Prior's book, Jocka Bell is disguised as 'Jogger'.
26 Gloria Ryan, interview, 6 Sep. 1980
27 Brosnan, interview, 31 March 2001.
28 Grindlay, *op. cit.*, 10.
29 Prior (1985), *op. cit.*, 156.
30 Gloria Ryan, interview, 6 Sep. 1980.
31 Grindlay, *op. cit.*, 10.
32 *The Herald*, 1 Feb. 1967; Geoff Clancy, interview, 19 Sep. 1968.
33 Three years later, Brusey, QC, would win a famous victory in his defence of Penguin Books Australia and its senior executives in the *Portnoy's Complaint* censorship case. (Hilary McPhee, *Other People's Words*, 107–9.)
34 Sir John Starke told the writer of his thoughts and responses in this hearing in two lengthy interviews with him on 23 Nov. and 17 Dec. 1990. He also gave a lengthy account of how he had framed his judgment, which is reflected in the narrative that follows in the text.
35 Burns, *op. cit.*, 168.

36 *ibid.*, 179–81.
37 *ibid.*, 181.
38 Sir John Starke, interview, 17 Dec. 1990.
39 Ex parte Ryan, *Victoria Reports* (1967), 522–3.
40 *ibid.*, quoting Atkin, LJPC, 147.
41 Ex parte Ryan, *Victoria Reports* (1967), 524.
42 *ibid.*, 525.
43 *ibid.*, and In the Matter of Ronald Joseph Ryan, Supreme Court of Victoria, Criminal Jurisdiction, 30 Jan. 1967.
44 Sir John Starke, interview, 17 Dec. 1990.
45 *The Telegraph* (Sydney), 31 Jan. 1967.
46 *The Sun*, 31 Jan. 1967.
47 *ibid.*
48 Starke gave a more colourful description of these events in his interview with Jon Faine, *Taken on Oath*, 52.
49 Ron Syme, personal communication, 3 Aug. 2000.
50 File Note, 'Ryan Case 30/1/67', AGC [Alex Coulthard, secretary of the Premier's Department], 30 Jan. 1967, Premier's Department file 66/2995.
51 Sir John Starke, interview, 17 Dec. 1990.
52 The comments of Woods, Westerman, and Rapaport were reported in *The Sun*, 31 Jan. 1967.
53 On 26 Jan. 1967, Salesian Father John Ayers of Rupertswood had written to the governor of Victoria appealing for clemency for Ryan, and expressing his particular regret that the hanging was due to take place on 31 January, Don Bosco's Feast Day. (Letter, Father John A Ayers to Sir Rohan Delacombe, 26 Jan. 1967. Governor's Capital Case files, VPS 1100/P1/10.)
54 Sir John Starke, interview, 17 Dec. 1990.
55 Controversy did erupt about Justice Starke's attendance at the cabinet meeting. In an unusually bipartisan move, the next day the New South Wales Liberal attorney-general, Ken McCaw, MLA, and one of his Labor Party predecessors as attorney, Bill Sheahan, QC, argued that the independence of the judiciary had been threatened by the Victorian cabinet calling Starke to its meeting. Telephoned by Arthur Rylah for an explanation, McCaw said his opinion depended upon whether Starke was 'invited or summoned' to attend. (*The Age*, 2 Feb. 1967; *The Herald*, 1 Feb. 1967.)
56 Sir John Starke, interview, 17 Dec. 1990.
57 Many years later, after he had retired as premier, Henry Bolte pondered what might have happened if the government had simply ignored Starke's reprieve. Interviewed in 1989, Bolte said: 'The strange thing, you know, is that we need not have taken any notice of Starke's stay of execution anyway. We did not have to get in touch with the governor of the gaol. He had his orders, the sheriff had his warrant of execution and the hangman was in attendance.' Quoted in Prior (1990), *op. cit.*, 168. Bolte's comment,

of course, overlooks the fact that, as Justice Barry pointed out in the full court decision of 30 Dec. 1966, the sheriff is an officer of the Supreme Court and not of the executive and, as the officer responsible for executions, the sheriff could not proceed if the court determined otherwise.

58 'H Division Diary', entry for 31 Jan. 1967.

59 Paul Guest, personal communication, 7 Sep. 2000.

60 This account of Justice Starke's attendance at cabinet, and the comments made by him and others above, was related to the writer by Sir John Starke, interview, 17 Dec. 1990.

61 Bolte would later boast privately about how he had grilled Starke about Tolmie: 'I beat him completely. I told him we knew all along that Tolmie was in Gippsland when he was supposed to be in Pentridge.' Quoted in Blazey, *op. cit.*, 142. Bolte's boast was repeated to Prior (1990), *op. cit.*, 168, but it was treated disdainfully by Starke, who told Jon Faine that it was 'absolutely bloody well untrue.' Faine, *op. cit.*, 52.

62 Sir John Starke, interview, 17 Dec. 1990. See also *The Herald*, 31 Jan. 1967.

63 Memorandum, Detective Sergeant KJ Carton to Superintendent, homicide squad, CIB, Victoria Police, 1 Feb. 1967. Chief Secretary's Office, file no. 10788.

64 Statement by Desmond John Boone, 1 Feb. 1967. (Copy in Chief Secretary's Office, file no. 10788.)

65 Statement of Salvatori Russo, prisoner, French Island prison, in briefing note, 'Was any Shot Fired by the Prison Officer on No. 2 Post?', Feb. 1967. (Chief Secretary's Office, file no. 10788.)

66 Statement of Reginald William Brooks in *ibid*.

67 *The Telegraph* (Brisbane) 31 Jan. 1967. See also *The Herald*, 31 Jan. 1967.

68 Affidavit by Allen John Cane in the Supreme Court of Victoria Criminal Jurisdiction in the Matter of Ronald Joseph Ryan, sworn at Brisbane, 31 Jan. 1967.

69 Jones (ed), *The Penalty is Death*, 269.

70 Statement by Lewis Northby, chief prison officer, D Division Records Office, Pentridge, in *TDT*, 17.

71 'H Division Diary', entry for 31 Jan. 1967; Paul Guest, personal communication, 20 Mar. 2001.

72 Statement by Ralph Freadman in *TDT*, 11.

73 (Emphasis added.) Quoted in Jones (ed), *op. cit.*, 269. (See also letter, Ralph Freadman to crown solicitor, 1 Feb. 1967, which accompanied these two affidavits.)

74 Statement taken by police and signed by John H Tolmie, 1 Feb. 1967.

75 *The Age*, 2 Feb. 1967. See also Memorandum, Rupert Arnold, chief commissioner of police to John Dillon, under secretary, Chief Secretary's Office, 1 Feb. 1967.

76 Memorandum, 'Ryan, Ronald Joseph—Escape from Pentridge', Detective Inspector FG Holland, homicide squad, to Superintendent, CIB, 1 Feb.

1967. Chief Secretary Office, file no. 10788.

77 Ron Saw, *The Daily Mirror*, 1 Feb. 1967. (See also Blazey, *op. cit.*, 139–40.)

78 Memorandum, 're Ronald Joseph Ryan', Thomas F Mornane, crown solicitor, to the chief secretary, undated [Feb. 1967]. Chief Secretary's Office, file no. 10788.

79 'Was any Shot Fired by the Prison Officer on No. 2 Post?', Chief Secretary's Office, Feb. 1967 in file no. 10788.

80 Minutes no. 7 of the State Executive Council (2 Feb. 1967), 163.

81 The Death Warrant was duly entered in the Register of Licences, book no. 30, at page 299, and kept in the Chief Secretary's Office, file no. 10788.

82 'H Division Diary', entry for 2 Feb. 1967. See also note for file, LJS, Chief Secretary's Office, 2 Feb. 1967, file no. 10788.

83 Paul Guest, personal communication, 20 March 2001.

84 *ibid.*, 21 Dec. 2000; 'H Division Diary', entry for 2 Feb. 1967.

85 Opas, *op. cit.*, 1–3.

86 Quoted in Tennison, *op. cit.*, 163.

87 *The Age*, 3 Feb. 1967; *The Herald*, 2 Feb. 1967.

88 This was evidently Alec Whatmore, director-general of social welfare, who was, in fact, directly quoted in the story published in *The Sun* on 20 Dec. 1965. As indicated in chapter 8, in his memorandum to the under secretary, dated 1 Feb. 1967, Whatmore denied ever making the statement or believing that the officer on the tower had fired a shot. The memorandum seems to have been prompted by media reporting of the Tolmie affidavit and the currency being given to the 'warder on the wall' theory.

89 In the Matter of The Crimes Act 1958 and In the Matter of Ronald Joseph Ryan, petition on behalf of Ronald Joseph Ryan, submitted by Ridgeway Pearce Freadman & Murray, and signed by Ralph Freadman, 2 Feb. 1967 to the attorney-general. Copy in Chief Secretary's Office, file no. 10788.

90 In 1957, Rylah had used the section 584 provision in the case of William McKay, a 27-year-old who had killed a poultry thief, shot in the act of stealing from his father's poultry farm. There was no evidence that McKay had intended to kill, but he had been given a three-year gaol term, reduced to eighteen months by the High Court on appeal. He was granted clemency and released by Rylah, exercising his discretion under section 584, after serving less than four months. (See *The Argus*, 6 Jul. 1957.) Section 584 had started its statutory life as section 19 of the Victorian *Criminal Appeals Act 1914*. (See *Victoria Parliamentary Debates* (10,17, 21 Dec. 1914) *138*:162–4, 274–9, 370–5.)

91 *Crimes Act 1958*, Victorian Statutes 1958, vol. II, 992.

92 Like many Victorian statutes, the Victorian *Criminal Appeals Act 1914* followed closely the provisions of the English law, in this case the UK *Criminal Appeals Act 1907*. The section 19 provision relating to the attorney-general's discretion became section 610 when the *Criminal Appeals Act* was consolidated in the *Crimes Act 1915*, and later became

Section 584 in the *Crimes Act 1958*.

93 The handwritten note giving Fitzwilliams-Hyde directions to Merthon in Sorrento survives in the files of the Chief Secretary's Office, file no. 10788. It was confirmed by Fitzwilliams-Hyde in a personal communication to the writer, 12 Jul. 2000.

94 *The Age*, 3 Feb. 1967.

95 Anthony Fitzwilliams-Hyde, personal communication, 12 Jul. 2000.

96 It should be noted that Sir Henry Bolte's version is that *he* was arbitrating between Harry Winneke as solicitor-general and Arthur Rylah as attorney-general. See the biography of Sir Henry Winneke by Robert Coleman, *Above Renown*, 207–8.

97 I am not here suggesting that there was any breach of the separation of powers in this matter. Victorian Supreme Court judges have given informal oral advice to the executive in other situations, always according to law. There are two clear examples of this happening.

The first is that, for more than 100 years, Victoria had departed from the other Australian states in having Supreme Court trial judges in capital cases go to cabinet and answer questions about the verdict and other trial issues when ministers were considering commutation. As evidenced in an earlier chapter on the cabinet decision, that practice had not simply developed, but had been mandated by the royal instructions to governor Sir Charles Hotham in December 1855 and followed ever since. Article eighteen of Hotham's commission instructed him 'to call upon the Judge presiding at the trial of any such offender who may from time to time be condemned to suffer death, by any sentence of any Court within the said Colony, to make to you a written report of the case of such offender, and such report of the said Judge shall by you be taken into consideration at the first meeting thereafter, which may be conveniently held, of Our said Executive Council, *where the said Judge shall be specially summoned to attend* ...' (Governor's Commission and Instructions, 20 Dec. 1855, 4. Emphasis added.)

The second example is that Justice Starke went to cabinet the morning after his late-night injunction to answer questions about his decision—that is, to give informal, oral advice as to the meaning and effect of his decision the night before. The person who encouraged him to go was Chief Justice Sir Henry Winneke. A further point to be made is that, while section 584 (a) and (b) of *The Crimes Act 1958* followed virtually word for word section 19 (a) and (b) of the UK *Criminal Appeal Act 1907*, the section had departed from it significantly in one respect. Where the UK act specified that the home secretary could, if he thought fit, refer to the *court* for its opinion, the Victorian section 584 specified that the attorney could, if he thought fit, refer to the *judges* for their opinion. In virtually all other respects the sections were identical. While the effect is precisely the same, the choice of language is interesting. It is the writer's contention that the framers of the Victorian section had it in mind precisely that the attorney might seek the opinion of a judge or judges (bearing in mind that, at the time of the framing, the Supreme Court had only five judges), very much like the process that eventuated between Rylah and Winneke.

98 A confidential memorandum issued to officials by the United Kingdom Home Office in 1970, relating to the use of the royal prerogative of mercy, discussed the procedures relating to the informal and formal advice offered by the lord chief justice pursuant to the then section 19(b) of *The Criminal Appeal Act 1907*. WH Cornish, Home Office Memorandum on the Royal Prerogative of Mercy, 105, 112–19.

99 Quoted in Prior (1990), *op. cit.*, 166–7.

100 In the Matter of The Crimes Act 1958 and In the Matter of Ronald Joseph Ryan, Copy of Petition in Chief Secretary's Office, file no. 10788.

101 Notation by Colquhoun on a covering note to the Draft Order relating to the petition for clemency considered by the Executive Council, VPS1100/P1/10.

102 Minutes no. 8 of the Executive Council (2 Feb. 1967), 164.

103 *The Age*, 3 Feb. 1967.

Chapter Sixteen: EXECUTION [pp 369–395]

1 'H Division Diary', Summary, Feb. 1967.

2 Prior (1985), *op. cit.*, 158.

3 Mr Jones made the claim in an unsigned letter to *Truth* journalist Evan Whitton, after Whitton had written an account of the hanging that included comments in passing about the hangman's performance, with which he took issue. See Evan Whitton, 'The Very Last Man To Be Hanged?', *The National Times*, 13 Jan. 1979.

4 See Pierrepoint, *Executioner*, 94.

5 Justin Atholl, *The Reluctant Hangman*, 117. See also George Ryley Scott, *The History of Capital Punishment*, 194–5.

6 See James Berry, *My Experiences as an Executioner*; Charles Duff, *A Handbook on Hanging*; and Justin Atholl, *op. cit.*

7 Colonial Victoria followed English statute and practice in enshrining legislative provisions relating to hanging in *An Act to regulate the Execution of Criminals 1855*. The two schedules to the 1855 act were intact in 1967. (See Supplement to the *Victorian Government Gazette*, 10 Oct. 1855.)

8 Instances of botched hangings abound in the extensive literature on hanging, both in Australia and Britain. For Australia, Garryowen's [Edmund Finn's] *Chronicles of Early Melbourne*, 396) documents how the first execution in Melbourne on 20 Jan. 1842—of Bob and Jack, two Van Diemonian Aborigines convicted of the murder of two sailors at Western Port—was bungled when the incompetently constructed drop failed, and 'a horrible scene of strangulation followed'. See also Ian MacFarlane, *1842*. Richard P Davis, *The Tasmanian Gallows*, includes a number of botched hangings in that state in the mid- to late-nineteenth century. Ray and

Richard Beckett, *Hangman*, provide an historical account of executions in NSW in early- to mid-nineteenth century, including some botched executions. For instances in Britain, as well as Berry, Duff, and Atholl above, see, for example, Albert Hartshorne, *Hanging in Chains*; Horace Bleackley, *The Hangmen of England*; George Ryley Scott, *The History of Capital Punishment*; Justin Atholl, *Shadow of the Gallows*; John Laurence, *A History of Capital Punishment*; John Deane Potter, *The Art of Hanging*; and VAC Gatrell, *The Hanging Tree*.

9 Ian Jones, *Ned Kelly*, 323, quoting from an eyewitness account in *The Herald*, 11 Nov. 1880.

10 'Particulars of Executions', entry for Robert David Clayton, by J Whiteside, AGMO (Sheriff's Office, Melbourne, and on loan to the National Trust permanent exhibition on hanging, Old Melbourne Gaol.)

11 See Wilson, Treble, and Lincoln, *Jean Lee*, 206–9.

12 Prior (1985), *op. cit.*, 158–9.

13 Ryan had told Father Brosnan of his fears. Brosnan, interview, 14 Oct. 1968.

14 This conversation is recorded in the 'H Division Dairy', entry for 26 Jan. 1967.

15 In his memoir for *Truth*, Ian Grindlay remembers the conversation between Ryan and Clark differently. In Grindlay's version, Ryan replies to Clark's question about what he wanted for breakfast: 'Breakfast won't do me any good, Mr Clark, but how about giving it to somebody who needs it.' (Grindlay, *op. cit.*, 10.) Grindlay also dates the conversation as 2 February, rather than 26 January. The 'H Division Diary' entry for 26 January, however, is much more likely to be accurate because it was written on that day by Clark himself. Grindlay's memoir, on the other hand, was written nine years later.

16 Grindlay, *op. cit.*, 10.

17 Brosnan related Ryan's conversation with Grindlay, interview, 14 Oct. 1968.

18 Grindlay, *op. cit.*, 10.

19 Grindlay, interviews, 14 Jul. 1978 and 19 Jul. 1978.

20 Peter Walker, interview, 12 Sep. 2001. The toilet 'telephone' was an ingenious method employed by prisoners. It involved prisoners simultaneously pumping the water out of the base of the toilet using a pillow to create an air force in the bowl and expel water from the pipes. The prisoner would then talk into the bowl, which acted like a connected sound horn.

21 The details of the messages between Ryan and Walker are recorded in Walker, *Truth*, 2 Feb. 1985.

22 Barry Jones, interview, 26 Jul. 1968.

23 The motel manager's role in overhearing the phone calls and reporting what he heard to the South Melbourne police station is documented in a confidential memo from deputy police commissioner Charles Petty to the

under-secretary of the Chief Secretary's Office, John Dillon, 9 Feb. 1967. The memo is included in a file marked 'Hanging of Ronald Joseph Ryan—Confidential Papers' held in the Chief Secretary's Office, VPRS 10800.

24 The extraordinary nature of the police visit prompted Barry Jones to suspect that the police response had been triggered by tapped telephone calls on his phone. At the time, Jones speculated—understandably but incorrectly—that, on the basis of telephone intercepts, police had been given a confused tip-off from information taken from three telephone calls made from the one phone within a 30-minute period. Jones subsequently wrote a letter to Clive Stoneham, leader of the state Labor opposition, 7 Feb. 1967, setting out his suspicions. Stoneham briefly referred to this incident publicly several days later in a speech at the opening of the Higinbotham by-election campaign. (*The Age*, 9 and 10 Feb. 1967.)

25 Shakespeare, *Sonnets*, 116. The exact lines are:

> … Love is not
> Which alters when it alteration finds,
> Or bends with the remover to remove:
> O no! it is an ever-fixed mark,
> That looks on tempests and is never shaken;
> It is the star to every wandering bark,
> Whose worth's unknown, although his height be taken.
> Love's not Time's fool, though rosy lips and cheeks
> Within his bending sickle's compass come;
> Love alters not with his brief hours and weeks,
> But bears it out even to the edge of doom …

26 Ryan to Dorothy Janet Ryan (née George) and daughters, 2 Feb. 1967.

27 The prison officer duly delivered the letter to journalist Evan Whitton at *Truth* and a transcript, together with photographs of it, appeared in *Truth*, 11 Feb. 1967. (See also Evan Whitton, 'The Very Last Man to Be Hanged?', *The National Times*, 13 Jan. 1979.)

28 The account of the police sweep through the Coburg Hotel was told to the writer by Tony Howard, QC, who, as an eighteen-year-old student, had been working as a part-time barman in the hotel's bottle-shop when it happened. (Tony Howard, personal communication, 6 Jul. 2000.)

29 *The Age*, 4 Feb. 1967. At a subsequent Magistrates Court hearing, on 7 Feb. 1967, the charges against Holding were dismissed. (See *The Age*, 8 Feb. 1967.)

30 This story was told by Sir John Starke to his friend Rob Southey, who related it to the writer. (Rob Southey, personal communication, 15 Mar. 2000.)

31 Grindlay, *op. cit.*, 4.

32 'H Division Diary', entry for 3 Feb. 1967.

33 Charles G. Herbermann *et al* [eds], *The Catholic Encyclopedia*, vol. II.

34 Brosnan, interview, 31 March 2001. (See also Father John Brosnan, 'I Was

There', *Sunday Life* magazine, *The Sunday Age*, 21 May 2000.)

35 'H Division Diary', entry for 3 Feb. 1967. The diary entry for 27 Jan. 1967 states that Ryan had asked for whisky but that the acting governor, William Prouse, had authorised brandy. However, Grindlay wrote in his memoir, and confirmed to the writer, that he was given whisky. It appears that Grindlay overruled Prouse's direction on the brandy, which had been made in his absence. The details and names above are drawn from the 'H Division Diary'.

36 On 6 Apr. 1865, *The Argus* had described the execution the day before at the Melbourne Gaol of child-murderer John Stacey, and reported that a 'new drop has been constructed at the gaol, and the general arrangements materially altered. On a level with the gallery, in front of the middle tier of cells, a small platform, part of which is composed of a trap-door, has been erected, stretching across from the gallery on one side of one of the corridors to that on the other side. Above this platform a beam has been fixed, reaching from wall to wall, and to this the rope is suspended.'

37 The 150-kilogram crossbeam was removed from Pentridge in the late-1970s. In November 2000 it was re-installed in its original location at the Old Melbourne Gaol, where it forms part of the permanent collection of National Trust exhibits on Hanging. See *The Age*, 11 Nov. 2000 and *The Weekend Australian*, 11 Nov. 2000.

38 Father Brosnan, interview, 31 Mar. 2001.

39 Evan Whitton, 'Face to Face with Death', *The Weekend Australian*, 1–2 Feb. 1997; Father Brosnan, interview, 31 Mar. 2001.

40 In several of the later journalistic accounts of the hanging, the name of the deputy sheriff, Jim Mulvey, was given as 'Murphy'. This error seems to have derived from the Declaration of Witnesses subsequently published in the *Victorian Government Gazette* on 8 Feb. 1967, which incorrectly listed 'JW Mulvey' as 'JW Murphy'.

41 The number of journalists present as witnesses to the execution is uncertain. Evan Whitton writes that there were fourteen, and adds that a fifteenth did not show. Tom Prior of *The Sun*, Keith Willey of the Sydney *Sun*, Brian Morley of Radio 3AW, Pat Tennison of *The Australian*, and Kevin Sanders of GTV9 similarly say fourteen. However, the records only disclose the presence of eleven. The discrepancy appears to arise from the fact that there were fourteen people in the witness party, but three of them were officials. Crime reporter Jack Ayling, who had covered the trial for *Truth*, was invited; but his editor, Solly Chandler, told him that through his coverage of the Ryan-Walker trial he had become too close to it all, and he did not want him to report the hanging. Evan Whitton was sent in Ayling's place. See Jack Ayling (with Tony Barnao and Norm Lipson), *Nothing But The Truth*, 198–9.

42 John Deane Potter, *op. cit.*, 107. Also quoted by Britain's former hangman, Albert Pierrepoint, in his autobiography, *op. cit.*, 70.

43 Prior (1985), *op. cit.*, 159; Brosnan, 'I Was There', *Sunday Life* magazine,

The Sunday Age, 21 May 2000.

44 Grindlay, *op. cit.*, 10.

45 Ron Saw, *Daily Mirror*, 3 Feb. 1967.

46 Evan Whitton, *The National Times*, 13 Jan. 1979.

47 Brian Morley, interview, 18 Apr. 2001. (See also Evan Whitton in *ibid.*)

48 As a guide, the hangman worked off the revised Berry table referred to above. The table was based on a long-drop formula of 1220 feet pounds divided by the condemned man's weight in his clothes, twelve stone four ounces. In Ryan's case, that would have amounted to a drop of seven feet four inches. The hangman adjusted this to exactly seven feet.

49 Walker, *Truth*, 2 Feb. 1985.

50 Death Warrant, entered on record in the Register of Licences, book no. 30, page 299. The warrant refers to Ryan having been tried and convicted on 1 March 1966 whereas, in fact, the trial did not commence until 15 March and the actual date of his sentencing was 30 March. The reference, which at times even confused ministers who thought it was a mistake, arose from the fact that, for certain purposes, the whole of the sittings of a court are in law considered as one day. (See memorandum by under secretary of the Chief Secretary's Office, John Dillon, to the crown solicitor, Tom Mornane, 13 Jan. 1967, and Mornane's reply to Dillon, 17 Jan. 1967.)

51 Grindlay, *op. cit.*, 10.

52 Prior (1985), *op. cit.*, 1.

53 Charles Duff, *A New Handbook on Hanging*, 168.

54 Ron Saw, *The Daily Mirror*, 3 Feb. 1967.

55 Brian Morley, interview, 18 Apr. 2001.

56 Geoff Clancy, chief police roundsman, *The Herald*, interview, 19 Sep. 1968.

57 John Brosnan, interview, 31 March 2001 and Paul Ormonde, *The Age*, 1 Feb. 1997. (The Bible quote is a modern version of the Book of John, chapter 13, verse 27: 'Then said Jesus unto him, "That thou doest, do quickly."') Although Brosnan was below the gallows and out of earshot of what Ryan said on the scaffold, Grindlay told him that is what he said. Nine years later in his memoirs, Grindlay remembered the words more prosaically as 'God bless you. Please make it quick.' (Grindlay, *op. cit.*, 10.) Most eyewitness accounts of the hanging by journalists do not report Ryan saying anything at all on the gallows. The reason for the discrepancy is that Grindlay was in a much better position to hear anything said, as he was just two feet away from Ryan as he stood on the trap; the journalists, on the other hand, were some fifteen to twenty yards away.

58 Brian Morley, interview, 18 Apr. 2001.

59 *The Daily Mirror*, 3 Feb. 1967.

60 AA Bartholomew, medical superintendent, 'Particulars of Executions', Sheriff's Office, Melbourne.

61 Evan Whitton, 'The Very Last Man to be Hanged?', *The National Times*, 13 Jan. 1979.

62 In normal circumstances, a priest would have anointed the places of the senses: forehead, eyes, hands and mouth. However, in extreme circumstances such as this, only the forehead would be anointed.

63 John Brosnan, interview, 14 Oct. 1968. The Sacrament of Extreme Unction in Latin is set out in *Rituale Romanum* (Romae, Tornaci, Parisiis, Desclée et Socii, 1928). The late 1960s were a time of transition in Roman Catholic liturgy; while English had been introduced into the Mass, some rituals, such as the anointing of those facing death, were still celebrated in Latin.

64 John Brosnan, interviews, 14 Oct.1968 and 31 Mar. 2001. (See also Evan Whitton, 'The Very Last Man to be Hanged?', *op. cit.*; and Larry Writer and Tony Barnao, 'I Still Love Him', *Who*, 17 Oct. 1994, 42.)

65 AA Bartholomew, medical superintendent, 'Particulars of Executions', Sheriff's Office, Melbourne. In judicial hangings, though unconsciousness is usually immediate when the neck is broken, the heart may continue to beat for some time—possibly up to twenty minutes. According to forensic pathologists, there may be 'muscular contractions of the facial muscles, twitching and convulsions of the limbs and trunk, and violent respiratory movements of the chest'. Dominick J DiMaio and Vincent JM DiMaio, *Forensic Pathology*, 231.

66 Deposition by Dr AA Bartholomew for the Coroner's Court, sworn at Melbourne, 3 Feb. 1967. (See also death certificate signed by Dr Bartholomew in *Government Gazette, Victoria* [8 Feb. 1967], 288.)

67 Tom Prior, interview, 5 Apr. 2001; Brian Morley, interview, 18 Apr. 2001.

68 Patrick Tennison, interview, 17 Sep. 1968; Kevin Sanders, interview, 5 Jul. 1968. The Declaration of Witnesses was required under the *Crimes Act 1958*; its terms were set out in schedule ten of the act. See the Declaration in Victoria, *Government Gazette* (8 Feb. 1967), 288. Published accounts of the hanging include those by Patrick Tennison in *The Australian*, 4 Feb. 1967, and by Ron Saw in *The Daily Mirror*, 3 Feb. 1967, and the unsigned article by Tom Prior in *The Australasian Post*, 16 Feb. 1967. (Since *The Sun* was not reporting the hanging except as a one-paragraph record of the execution having occurred, Prior wrote an account within hours of the hanging and sent it to *The Australasian Post*, which published it without his by-line. Prior, interview, 5 Apr. 2001.)

69 Kevin Sanders, interview, 5 Jul. 1968.

70 Attending the hanging were Tom Prior (*The Sun*), Geoff Clancy (*The Herald*), and David Thorpe, (*The Age*). These papers published only very short reports with no description.

71 Frank O'Brien, interview, 7 Oct. 1968; Brian Morley, interview, 18 Apr. 2001.

72 Wendy and Pip Ryan, interviews, 29 Jan. 1987.

73 Some twenty unions, including the large building, transport, food, and service industry unions, had called the stoppage. Union leaders estimated that some 100,000 workers had observed the ban. (*The Age*, 4 Feb. 1967.)

74 AA Bartholomew, medical superintendent, 'Particulars of Executions', Sheriff's Office, Melbourne.
75 Brian Morley's 3AW copy file, 3 Feb. 1967; Morley, interview, 18 Apr. 2001.
76 Brian Morley, interview, 18 Apr. 2001.
77 Ian Grindlay, interviews, 14 Jul. and 19 Jul. 1978.
78 Deposition by Dr JH McNamara for the Coroner's Court, sworn at Melbourne, 3 Feb. 1967, and 'Particulars of Executions' (entry for Ryan), Sheriff's Office, Melbourne.
79 See Albert Pierrepoint, *op. cit.*, 72.
80 Deposition by McNamara, *op. cit.*, 3 Feb. 1967.
81 AA Bartholomew, medical superintendent, 'Particulars of Executions', Sheriff's Office, Melbourne.
82 'Proceedings of Inquest held upon the body of Ronald Joseph Ryan', 3 Feb. 1967.
83 Kelly was buried at the Melbourne Gaol in November 1880 but re-buried at Pentridge in—it is believed—1929. The exact date of the re-burial is uncertain because the official records are incomplete. Researchers at the Old Melbourne Gaol believe the reburial occurred in the period after executions ceased at the gaol in 1929.
84 Grindlay, *op. cit.*, 10–11, and interviews, 14 Jul. and 19 Jul. 1978
85 *ibid.* Although Ryan's grave was unmarked, its position—like the others in this burial ground—was marked on a map by prison officials and given a code number.
86 *The Age*, 4 Feb. 1967 published the AAP report of the world press reaction to the hanging and the protests surrounding it.
87 Tennison, *op. cit.*, 166.
88 Ron Syme, personal communication, 3 Aug. 2000.
89 Bolte reported his comments to Tom Prior (1990), *op. cit.*, 168. When he spoke to Prior in 1989, Bolte conceded that his comment was 'a bit rough, not my usual style, but I didn't know the girl who asked the question, and she was only trying to embarrass me. Probably I did look at the clock a bit more than usual that particular morning, but no matter how often I looked, and when, it didn't alter what was happening out at Pentridge. My attitude was impersonal; it wasn't Ryan and it wasn't me, it was the law. As a matter of fact, later that day when I had the details of the execution, I said that the two people who came out of it best were Ryan and myself.' *ibid.* (See also Blazey, *op. cit.*, 144.)
90 There was a difference of opinion among journalists writing at the time about whether Ryan was the 180th or 181st person to be executed in Victoria. As the text suggests, however, neither figure is correct. Statistics on the number of persons executed in Victoria, as Creighton Burns points out (*The Tait Case*, 13), have been notoriously unreliable and have varied considerably. For example, Margaret Weidenhofer, in her 1967 edition of *Garryowen's Melbourne*, 107, incorrectly gives 1841 as the date of the first

execution. Bob and Jack, two Van Diemonian Aborigines convicted of the murder of two sailors at Western Port, were hanged in Melbourne before 'thousands of persons who felt a morbid curiosity to witness the departure of the wretches out of the world'. (Quoted from *Early Chronicles of Melbourne* in Weidenhofer, *op. cit.*, 107. See also MacFarlane, *op. cit.*)

Burns, relating this same hanging, correctly gives 20 Jan. 1842 as the date. A newspaper report of March 1936, quoting from the records of the State Executive Council, confirms this date (*The Herald*, 12 Mar. 1936), but confutes Burns' figures for the number of executions in Victoria which, he states, totalled 150 up to 1900, and 23 from 1901 to 1962—giving a total of 173. (Burns, *op. cit.*, 13.)

The Executive Council records quoted in 1936—up till then the authoritative source, it would seem—give the total number of executions then as 171 (*The Herald*, 12 Mar. 1936). Adding the nine hangings in the state from July 1936 through to the last hangings before Ryan in 1951, we arrive at a total of 180 executions—160 up to 1900 and 20 since 1901—which would have made Ryan the 181st. This figure was, in fact, repeated by *The Sun* on 22 Nov. 1966.

However, these records are also in error. The point seemed to have been finally settled in the Victorian parliament on 10 Apr. 1975 when, in answer to a question on notice, the minister for social welfare provided a complete record of all those persons hanged in Victoria from 1842 to 1975. (See *Debates*, no. 17 for 1975, 4879–83.) The list recorded that 163 persons (158 males and 5 females) were hanged in the period 1842 to 1899, and 22 persons (21 males and 1 female) were hanged in the period 1900 to 1975—a total of 185. (This total, it should be noted, excluded the execution of Private Edward Leonski of the US army, who was hanged at Pentridge in November 1942 for the murder of three Melbourne women. Leonski had not been tried within the Victorian judicial system, but had been tried and condemned by a US court martial, the sentence being confirmed by US president Franklin D. Roosevelt. Leonski was executed by US authorities.)

Michael Cannon, *op. cit.*, 221–6, reproduces a list suggesting that 186 executions took place, although he includes Leonski in that figure—hence the number of executions in the Victorian criminal justice system would be 185, consistent with the parliamentary paper. But even these figures are inaccurate, according to two former senior Victorian prisons department officers, Peter Lynn and George Armstrong, *From Pentonville to Pentridge*. Their list includes a further execution not included in the ministerial record tabled in the parliament. This was the execution of one Thomas Menard, hanged for murder at Geelong on 28 Oct. 1865. If the list is finally complete, Ronald Ryan was thus the 186th—and the last—person to be hanged in Victoria.

Bibliography

MANUSCRIPT SOURCES

Cooper, E & J Ayers, '[Salesians in Australia:] The First 25 Years, 1921-1946', (unpublished manuscript; 1977).

Corry, C, 'The Headspring of that Everflowing River of Crime: The Issue of Juvenile Delinquency in the First Half of Nineteenth Century England' (BA Hons thesis, History Department, University of Melbourne, 1979).

Hulme, SEK, 'John Erskine Starke', (Final version of obituary published as 'Ryan judge a peerless advocate', *The Australian*, 24 Nov. 1994), 10 Apr. 2001.

Jones, Barry, Correspondence, Dec. 1966 and Jan., Feb. 1967.

Radic, Len, 'The Case of Ronald Ryan' (A series of four articles commissioned by *The Age* in Mar. 1967, but not published).

Roczniok, Joan, 'Catholics in Nunawading: Parish of St John, Mitcham', (mimeo) Nunawading Historical Society, [n.d.].

Ryan, Ronald, Prison Correspondence to his mother and family, and former wife (Sep. 1965 to Feb. 1967).

Samuel, Richard H, Correspondence, Jan. and Feb., 1967.

BOOKS AND ARTICLES

Allen, John (1894), *Inquiry into the Rise and Growth of the Royal Prerogative in England* (London, Longman, Brown, Green, and Longmans).

Atholl, Justin (1954), *Shadow of the Gallows* (London, John Long).

—— (1956), *The Reluctant Hangman: The Story of James Berry, Executioner 1884-1892* (London, John Long).

Atkinson, Ann (1992), *The Dictionary of Famous Australians* (Sydney, Allen & Unwin).

Ayling, Jack (with Tony Barnao & Norm Lipson) (1993), *Nothing But The Truth: The Life and Times of Jack Ayling* (Chippendale, Pan Macmillan).

Barber, RN, & Wilson, PR (1968), '[The] Deterrent Aspect of Capital Punishment and its Effect on Conviction Rates: The Queensland Experience' *Australian and New Zealand Journal of Criminology*, no. 2.

Barry, John Vincent (1958), 'The Judgment of Death' *Sydney Law Review*, 2:3.

—— (1964), *The Life and Death of John Price* (Melbourne, Melbourne University Press).

Bates, Nicholas, Murray McAlister, Max Thomson & Jack Wacjman (1976), *Ronald Ryan: A Case Study in Criminal Proceedings* (rev ed by Marion Steele & Wilma Tabacco) (Fitzroy, VCTA Publishing).

Beckett, Ray and Richard Beckett (1980), *Hangman: The Life and Times of Alexander Green, Public Executioner to the Colony of New South Wales* (Melbourne, Nelson).

Berry, James [1892], *My Experiences as an Executioner* (London, David & Charles, 1972).

Blazey, Peter (1972), *Bolte: A Political Biography* (Melbourne, Jacaranda; 2nd edn, Mandarin, 1990).

Bleackley, Horace (1929), *The Hangmen of England* (London, Chapman and Hall).

Brennan, Niall (1972), *A History of Nunawading* (Melbourne, Hawthorn Press).

Brett, Peter (1957), 'Conditional Pardons and the Commutation of Death Sentences', *The Modern Law Review* (London), *20*.

—— (1966), *The Beamish Case* (Melbourne, Melbourne University Press).

Browne, Geoff (1985), *Biographical Register of the Victorian Parliament 1900-84* (Melbourne, VGPO).

Burns, Creighton (1962), *The Tait Case* (Melbourne, Melbourne University Press).

Cannon, Michael (1994), *The Woman as Murderer: Five Who Paid With Their Lives* (Mornington, Today's Australia Publishing).

Carter, Isabel (1970), *Woman in a Wig: Joan Rosanove, QC* (Melbourne, Lansdowne).

Chamberlain, Sir Roderic (1973), *The Stuart Affair* (Adelaide, Rigby).

Chapman, Ivan (1982), *Leonski: The Brownout Strangler* (Sydney, Hale & Iremonger).

Clark, Inglis A (1901), *Australian Constitutional Law* (Melbourne, Partridge & Co).

Clarke, Michael (1995), *Clarke of Rupertswood 1831-1897* (Melbourne, Australian Scholarly Publishing).

Clune, Frank (1962), *Ned Kelly's Last Stand* (Melbourne, Pacific).

Coleman, Robert (1988), *Above Renown: The Biography of Sir Henry Winneke* (Melbourne, Macmillan).

Cornish, WH (1970), *Home Office Memorandum on the Royal Prerogative of Mercy*, (London, HMSO).

Cowen, Zelman (1957), 'A Historical Survey of the Victorian Constitution, 1856 to 1956', *Melbourne University Law Review*, vol. 1.

Davis, Richard P (1974), *The Tasmanian Gallows* (Hobart, Cat & Fiddle Press).

Davison, Graeme, John Hirst & Stuart Macintyre (eds) (1998), *The Oxford Companion to Australian History* (Melbourne, Oxford University Press).

Dean, Arthur (1968), *A Multitude of Counsellors: A History of the Bar of Victoria*

(Melbourne, FW Cheshire).

Dickins, Barry (1994), *Remember Ronald Ryan* (Paddington, Currency Press).

—— (1996), *Guts and Pity: The Hanging that ended Capital Punishment in Australia* (Paddington, Currency Press).

DiMaio, Dominick J, and Vincent JM DiMaio (1993), *Forensic Pathology* (Boca Raton, CRC Press).

Dingle, Tony (1984), *The Victorians: Settling* (Melbourne, Fairfax, Syme & Weldon).

Dixon, Thomas Sidney (1987), *The Wizard of Alice: Father Dixon and the Stuart Case* (Morwell, Alella Books).

Douglas, R & K Laster (1991), 'A Matter of Life and Death: The Victorian Executive and the Decision to Execute, 1842-1967', *Australia and New Zealand Journal of Criminology*, 24:2.

Duff, Charles (1928), *A Handbook on Hanging* (London, The Cayme Press).

—— (1954), *A New Handbook on Hanging* (Chicago, Henry Regnery).

Education Department, Vic (1973), *Vision & Realisation*, vol. 1, (Melbourne, Education Department of Victoria).

Evatt, HV [1924], *The Royal Prerogative* (North Ryde, Law Book Co., 1987).

Faine, Jon (1992), *Taken on Oath: A Generation of Lawyers* (Sydney, Federation Press).

Feldtmann, Arthur (1976), *The Balranald Story* (Balranald, private publication).

Finnane, Mark (1997), *Punishment in Australian Society* (Melbourne, Oxford University Press).

Freadman, Anne (1999), 'The Green Tarpaulin: Another Story of the Ryan Hanging' *The UTS Review* 5:2.

Garryowen [Edmund Finn] (1888), *Chronicles of Early Melbourne* (Melbourne, Fergusson and Mitchell).

Gatrell, VAC (1994), *The Hanging Tree: Execution and the English People 1770-1868* (Oxford, Oxford University Press).

Griffith, Geoffrey (1967), *Homicide* (Sydney, Farleigh Books).

Griffiths, ARG (1970), 'Capital Punishment in South Australia, 1836-1964', *Australia and New Zealand Journal of Criminology*, 3.

Grimshaw, Patricia & Lynne Strahan (eds) (1982), *The Half-Open Door: Sixteen Modern Australian Women look at Professional Life and Achievement* (Sydney, Hale & Iremonger).

Grindlay, Ian (1976), *Behind Bars: Memoirs of Jail Governor, Ian Grindlay* (Melbourne, Southdown).

Hartshorne, Albert (1891), *Hanging in Chains* (London, T Fisher Unwin).

Hawkins, Gordon (1977), *Beyond Reasonable Doubt* (Sydney, ABC Books).

Herbermann, Charles G, *et al* (eds) (1907), *The Catholic Encyclopedia* (New York, Robert Appleton).

Hetherington, John (1965), *Uncommon Men* (Melbourne, FW Cheshire).

Hewitt, Eric Edgar (1984), *Judges Through the Years* (Melbourne, Hyland House).

High, James L (ed) (1876), *Speeches of Lord Erskine While at the Bar*, 4 vols. (Chicago, Callaghan & Co).

Jacobs, PA (1949), *A Lawyer Tells* (Melbourne, FW Cheshire).

Inglis, KS (1961), *The Stuart Case* (Melbourne, Melbourne University Press).

Jaggs, Donella (1986), *Neglected and Criminal: Foundations of Child Welfare Legislation in Victoria* (Melbourne, Philip Institute of Technology).

Johanson, Keith (1967), 'A Condemned Man's Doubt—And a Book' (private; mimeo).

Jones, Barry (ed) (1968), *The Penalty is Death: Capital Punishment in the Twentieth Century* (Melbourne, Sun Books).

Jones, Ian (1995), *Ned Kelly: A Short Life* (Melbourne, Thomas C Lothian).

Kelly, Ned [1879], *The Jerilderie Letter* (Melbourne, Text, 2001).

Kociumbas, Jan (1997), *Australian Childhood: A History* (Sydney, Allen & Unwin).

Koestler, Arthur (1956), *Reflections on Hanging* (London, Gollancz).

Larson, Peter, 'Convictions: Australian shipping on the net' (http://www.blaxland.com/ozships/plist.htm).

Laster, Kathy & Mary-Anne Robinson (1992), 'Capitalising on Stories: Ronald Ryan Twenty-five Years On', *Journal of Australian Studies*, 33.

Laurence, John (1960), *A History of Capital Punishment* (New York, Citadel).

Lynn, Peter & George Armstrong (1996), *From Pentonville to Pentridge: A History of Prisons in Victoria* (Melbourne, State Library of Victoria).

McCalman, Janet (1984), *Struggletown: Public and Private Life in Richmond, 1900-1965* (Melbourne, Melbourne University Press).

MacFarlane, Ian (1984), *1842: The Public Executions at Melbourne* (Melbourne, Public Record Office).

McPhee, Hilary (2001), *Other People's Words* (Sydney, Pan Macmillan).

Mallon, Andrew (1979), *Leonski: The Brown-out Murders* (Collingwood, Outback Press).

Marjoribanks, Edward (1929), *For The Defence: The Life Of Sir Edward Marshall Hall* (New York, Macmillan).

Marr, David (1980), *Barwick* (North Sydney, Allen & Unwin).

Moore, Keith R. [1929?], *Report on Investigation into the Health and Working Conditions of Employees in the Mining Industry of Victoria and Tasmania, 1928* (Canberra, Department of Health).

Morris, Edward E (1895), *A Memoir of George Higinbotham* (London, Macmillan).

Muir, Barry (1973), *Bolte from Bamganie* (Melbourne, Hill of Content).

Munns, Joy (1987), *Rupertswood: A Living History* (Sunbury, published by the author).

Nairn, Bede (ed) (1976), *Australian Dictionary of Biography*, vol. 6 (Melbourne, Melbourne University Press).

—— & Geoffrey Serle (eds) (1979) *Australian Dictionary of Biography*, vol. 7 (Melbourne, Melbourne University Press).

—— (eds) (1986) *Australian Dictionary of Biography*, vol. 10 (Melbourne,

Melbourne University Press).
Opas, Philip (1997), *Throw Away My Wig: An Autobiography* (Melbourne, published by the author).
Philips, David & Susanne Davies (eds) (1994), *A Nation of Rogues? Crime, Law and Punishment in Colonial Australia* (Melbourne, Melbourne University Press).
Pierrepoint, Albert (1974), *Executioner: Pierrepoint* (London, Harrap).
Pike, Douglas (ed) (1972), *Australian Dictionary of Biography* vol. 4 (Melbourne, Melbourne University Press).
Potter, John Deane (1969), *The Art of Hanging: The Fatal Gallows Tree in English History* (New York, AS Barnes).
Prior, Tom (1985), *A Knockabout Priest: The Story of Father John Brosnan* (North Melbourne, Hargreen).
—— (1990), *Bolte by Bolte* (Melbourne, Craftsman Publishing).
Pyne, Stephen J (1998), *Burning Bush: A Fire History of Australia* (Seattle, University of Washington Press).
Ritchie, John (ed) (1990), *Australian Dictionary of Biography* vol. 12 (Melbourne, Melbourne University Press).
—— (1993), *Australian Dictionary of Biography* vol. 13 (Melbourne, Melbourne University Press).
Royal Commission on Capital Punishment 1949-1953 (1953), *Report* (London, HMSO).
Scott, George Ryley (1950), *The History of Capital Punishment* (London, Torchstream Books).
Slattery, Bernard & Deirdre Slattery (1994), *The Hanging of Ronald Ryan: Capital Punishment and the Victorian Community* (Melbourne, State Library of Victoria).
Smith, TW (1974), *Law of Murder* (Melbourne, Victorian Law Reform Commission).
Staley, AA (1967), 'Australian Political Chronicle, Sept.-Dec. 1966–Victoria', *Australian Journal of Politics and History, 13*:1.
Strange, Carolyn (ed) (1996), *Qualities of Mercy: Justice, Punishment, and Discretion* (Vancouver, University of British Columbia Press).
Stryker, Lloyd Paul (1947), *For the Defense: Thomas Erskine, The Most Enlightened Liberal of His Times, 1750-1823* (New York, Doubleday).
Sydenham, Diane (1990), *Windows on Nunawading* (North Melbourne, Hargreen).
Templewood, Viscount (1951), *The Shadow of the Gallows: The Case Against Capital Punishment* (London, Gollancz).
Tennison, Patrick (1975), *Defence Counsel* (Melbourne, Hill of Content).
Victorian Year Book (1936-39), (Melbourne, Victorian Government Publisher).
Walker, Peter (1985), 'The Life and Times of Peter Walker', *Truth*, 19, 26 Jan., 2 Feb. 1985.
Weidenhofer, Margaret (ed) (1967), *Garryowen's Melbourne* (Melbourne, Thomas Nelson).

White, Rob and Christine Alder (eds) (1994), *The Police and Young People in Australia* (Cambridge, Cambridge University Press).
Wilcox, Vernon (2001), *Minister of the Crown* (Collingwood, published by the author).
Willey, Keith (1972), *Tales of the Big Country* (Adelaide, Rigby).
Wilson, Paul, Don Treble & Robyn Lincoln (1997), *Jean Lee: The Last Woman Hanged in Australia* (Milsons Point, Random House).
Zacher, Irwin J (ed) (1962), *Plays as Experience* (New York, Odyssey Press).

Index